Lecture Notes in Computer Science   12716

More information about this subseries at http://www.springer.com/series/7410

Shlomi Dolev · Oded Margalit · Benny Pinkas ·
Alexander Schwarzmann (Eds.)

Cyber Security Cryptography and Machine Learning

5th International Symposium, CSCML 2021
Be'er Sheva, Israel, July 8–9, 2021
Proceedings

Springer

Editors
Shlomi Dolev
Ben-Gurion University of the Negev
Be'er Sheva, Israel

Oded Margalit
Ben-Gurion University of the Negev
Be'er Sheva, Israel

Benny Pinkas
Bar-Ilan University
Tel Aviv, Israel

Alexander Schwarzmann
Augusta University
Augusta, GA, USA

ISSN 0302-9743   ISSN 1611-3349 (electronic)
Lecture Notes in Computer Science
ISBN 978-3-030-78085-2   ISBN 978-3-030-78086-9 (eBook)
https://doi.org/10.1007/978-3-030-78086-9

LNCS Sublibrary: SL4 – Security and Cryptology

This Springer imprint is published by the registered company Springer Nature Switzerland AG
The registered company address is: Gewerbestrasse 11, 6330 Cham, Switzerland

Preface

CSCML, the International Symposium on Cyber Security Cryptography and Machine Learning, is an international forum for researchers, entrepreneurs, and practitioners in the theory, design, analysis, implementation, or application of cyber security, cryptography, and machine learning systems and networks, and, in particular, of conceptually innovative topics in these research areas.

Information technology has become crucial to our everyday lives, an indispensable infrastructure of our society and therefore a target for attacks by malicious parties. Cyber security is one of the most important fields of research these days because of these developments. Two of the (sometimes competing) fields of research, cryptology and machine learning, are the most important building blocks of cyber security.

Topics of interest for CSCML include cyber security design; secure software development methodologies; formal methods, semantics and verification of secure systems; fault tolerance, reliability, and availability of distributed secure systems; game-theoretic approaches to secure computing; automatic recovery self-stabilizing and self-organizing systems; communication, authentication, and identification security; cyber security for mobile systems and the Internet of Things; cyber security of corporations; security and privacy for cloud, Edge and Fog computing; cryptocurrency; blockchain; cryptography; cryptographic implementation analysis and construction; secure multi-party computation; privacy-enhancing technologies and anonymity; post-quantum cryptology and security; machine learning and big data; anomaly detection and malware identification; business intelligence and security; digital forensics, digital rights management; trust management and reputation systems; and information retrieval, risk analysis, and DoS.

The 5th CSCML took place during July 8–9, 2021, in Beer-Sheva, Israel. The keynote speakers were Steve Blank, serial entrepreneur and one of the founding fathers of Silicon Valley; Bruce Schneier, Fellow of the Harvard Kennedy School of Government and internationally renowned security technologist; and Nir Zuk, founder and CTO of Palo Alto Networks. This year the conference was organized in cooperation with the International Association for Cryptologic Research (IACR) and selected papers will appear in a dedicated special issue of the Information and Computation Journal. This volume contains 22 contributions selected by the Program Committee from 48 submissions, and also includes 13 short papers (of at most 8 pages). All submitted papers were read and evaluated by Program Committee members, assisted by external reviewers. We are grateful to the EasyChair system in assisting the reviewing process. The support of Ben-Gurion University of the Negev (BGU), in particular BGU-NHSA, the BGU Lynne and William

Frankel Center for Computer Science, the BGU Cyber Security Research Center, and the Department of Computer Science, and IBM is also gratefully acknowledged.

March 2021

Shlomi Dolev
Oded Margalit
Benny Pinkas
Alexander Schwarzmann

Organization

CSCML, the International Symposium on Cyber Security Cryptography and Machine Learning, is an international forum for researchers, entrepreneurs and practitioners in the theory, design, analysis, implementation, or application of cyber security, cryptology, and machine learning systems and networks, and, in particular, of conceptually innovative topics in the scope.

Founding Steering Committee

Orna Berry	DELLEMC, Israel
Shlomi Dolev (Chair)	Ben-Gurion University, Israel
Yuval Elovici	Ben-Gurion University, Israel
Bezalel Gavish	Southern Methodist University, USA
Ehud Gudes	Ben-Gurion University, Israel
Jonathan Katz	University of Maryland, USA
Rafail Ostrovsky	UCLA, USA
Jeffrey D. Ullman	Stanford University, USA
Kalyan Veeramachaneni	MIT, USA
Yaron Wolfsthal	IBM, Israel
Moti Yung	Columbia University and Google, USA

Organizing Committee

General Chair

Shlomi Dolev	Ben-Gurion University, Israel

Program Chairs

Oded Margalit	Ben-Gurion University, Israel
Benny Pinkas	Bar-Ilan University, Israel
Alexander Schwarzmann	Augusta University, USA

Organizing Chair

Amanda Lapidot	Ben-Gurion University, Israel

Program Committee

Adi Akavia	University of Haifa, Israel
Don Beaver	FOR.ai, USA
Carlo Blundo	Università degli Studi di Salerno, Italy
Christina Boura	University of Versailles, France
Lucas Davi	University of Duisburg-Essen, Germany
Camil Demetrescu	Sapienza University of Rome, Italy
Itai Dinur	Ben-Gurion University, Israel
Orr Dunkelman	University of Haifa, Israel
Eman El-Sheikh	University of West Florida, USA
Chen Feng	University of British Columbia Okanagan, Canada
Rosario Gennaro	City University of New York, USA
Shay Gueron	University of Haifa and Intel Corporation, Israel
David Hay	The Hebrew University, Israel
Amir Herzberg	University of Connecticut, USA
Çetin Kaya Koç	University of California, Santa Barbara, USA
Vladimir Kolesnikov	Georgia Institute of Technology, USA
Łukasz Krzywiecki	Wrocław University of Science and Technology, Poland
Ana Milanova	Rensselaer Polytechnic Institute, USA
Tal Moran	IDC Herzliya, Israel
David Naccache	ENS, France
Ariel Nof	Technion, Israel
Nisha Panwar	Augusta University, USA
Giuseppe Persiano	Università degli Studi di Salerno, Italy
Leo Reyzin	Boston University, USA
Eyal Ronen	Tel Aviv University, Israel
Tirza Routtenberg	Ben-Gurion University, Israel
Alexander Russell	University of Connecticut, USA
Baruch Schieber	New Jersey Institute of Technology, USA
Sandeep Shukla	IIT Kanpur, India
Moshe Sipper	Ben-Gurion University, Israel
Yannis Stamatiou	University of Patras, Greece
Uri Stemmer	Ben-Gurion University, Israel
Daniel Takabi	Georgia State University, USA
Qiang Tang	New Jersey Institute of Technology, USA
Nikos Triandopoulos	Stevens Institute of Technology, USA
Eran Tromer	Tel Aviv University, Israel
Qianhong Wu	Beihang University, China
Marten van Dijk	CWI, Netherlands
Thijs Veugen	TNO and CWI, Netherlands

External Reviewers

Alexander Binun
Nishanth Chandran
Long Chen
Jins de Jong
Philip Derbeko
Hanwen Feng
Guillermo Francia Iii
Fangyu Gai
Kaiwen Guo
Maanak Gupta
Sheng Hu
Jin Jin
Walter Krawec
Ximing Li
Yin Li

Vikas Maurya
Christian Niesler
Jianyu Niu
Primal Pappachan
Rami Puzis
Tian Qiu
Menachem Sadigurschi
Ramprasad Saptharishi
Shantanu Sharma
Moshe Shechner
Sebastian Surminski
Guoxi Wang
Kun Wang
Masaya Yasuda
Yan Zhu

Sponsors

אוניברסיטת בן-גוריון בנגב
Ben-Gurion University of the Negev

In cooperation with

Contents

Programmable Bootstrapping Enables Efficient Homomorphic Inference of Deep Neural Networks

Ilaria Chillotti, Marc Joye[(✉)], and Pascal Paillier

Zama, Paris, France

Abstract. In many cases, machine learning and privacy are perceived to be at odds. Privacy concerns are especially relevant when the involved data are sensitive. This paper deals with the privacy-preserving inference of deep neural networks.

We report on first experiments with a new library implementing a variant of the TFHE fully homomorphic encryption scheme. The underlying key technology is the programmable bootstrapping. It enables the homomorphic evaluation of any function of a ciphertext, with a controlled level of noise. Our results indicate for the first time that deep neural networks are now within the reach of fully homomorphic encryption. Importantly, in contrast to prior works, our framework does not necessitate re-training the model.

Keywords: Fully homomorphic encryption · Programmable bootstrapping · Data privacy · Machine learning · Deep neural networks

1 Introduction

Machine learning algorithms are extremely useful in many areas but the type of data that they deal with is often sensitive. Typical examples include algorithms for the detection of certain genetic diseases from DNA samples or the ones used for face recognition or email classification, to name a few. The processed data contain private information about users and could be used in many ways, from target advertising to blackmail or even threat in some cases. This is why it is essential to protect the data being used in machine learning applications. Privacy requirements are also pushed by recent regulations companies dealing with user's data must comply with, like the GDPR (General Data Protection Regulation) [14] in Europe or the CCPA (California Consumer Privacy Act) [8] in the US.

Fully Homomorphic Encryption. Cryptographic techniques are methods of choice when it comes to the protection of data. But traditional encryption algorithms merely protect data while it is in transit or at rest. Indeed, one limitation and structural property of traditional encryption schemes is that data first needs to be decrypted prior to being processed. As discussed earlier, this is not suited for

© Springer Nature Switzerland AG 2021
S. Dolev et al. (Eds.): CSCML 2021, LNCS 12716, pp. 1–19, 2021.
https://doi.org/10.1007/978-3-030-78086-9_1

machine learning applications. With traditional encryption schemes, the privacy control lies in the hands of the recipient of the encrypted data. A fundamentally different approach is to rely on *fully homomorphic encryption* (FHE), first posed as a challenge in 1978 [26] and only solved in 2009 in a breakthrough result by Gentry [15]. In contrast to traditional encryption schemes, fully homomorphic encryption schemes allow the recipient to directly operate on encrypted data.

Controlling the Noise. At the core of Gentry's result resides the technique of *bootstrapping*. All known instantiations of fully homomorphic encryption schemes produce noisy ciphertexts. Running homomorphic operations on these ciphertexts in turn increases the noise level in the resulting ciphertext. At some point, the noise present in a ciphertext may become too large and the ciphertext is no longer decryptable. A homomorphic encryption scheme supporting a predetermined noise threshold is termed *leveled*. Bootstrapping is a generic technique that allows refreshing ciphertexts. It therefore enables one to turn leveled homomorphic encryption schemes into *fully* homomorphic encryption schemes, and so to make them evaluate any possible function on ciphertexts. The key idea behind bootstrapping is to homomorphically evaluate the decryption circuit.

The works that followed Gentry's publication were aimed at proposing new schemes or at improving the bootstrapping in order to make FHE more efficient in practice. The most famous constructions are DGHV [11], BGV [5], GSW [16], and their variants. While the constructions that were successively proposed made the bootstrapping more practical, it still constituted the bottleneck (each bootstrapping taking a few minutes). A much faster bootstrapping, based on a GSW-type scheme, was later devised by Ducas and Micciancio [13], reducing the bootstrapping time to a sub second. Their technique was further improved and refined, which led to the development of the TFHE scheme [10].

Our Techniques and Contributions. This paper builds on the state-of-the-art TFHE scheme and extends the TFHE techniques to homomorphically evaluate deep neural networks. TFHE can operate in two modes: leveled and bootstrapped. The *leveled mode* supports linear combinations and a predetermined number of (external) products. The operations evaluated in this mode make the noise always grow. The leveled mode can be used to evaluate small-depth circuits. As for the *bootstrapped mode*, it enables a fine control of the noise by reducing it to a given level whenever it exceeds a certain threshold. Further, as will be shown, the bootstrapped mode is programmable and therefore enables the evaluation of more complex functions. For problems involving circuits of large depth, only the bootstrapped mode is applicable. Deep neural networks belong to that case.

Earlier works attempted to evaluate neural networks using fully homomorphic encryption. Cryptonets [12] was the first initiative towards this goal. They were able to perform a homomorphic inference over 5 layers against the MNIST dataset [21]. In order to limit the noise growth, the standard activation function was replaced with the square function. A number of subsequent works have adopted a similar approach and improved it in various directions. Among them, it is worth mentioning the results of the iDASH competition [17]. The winning solutions of the homomorphic encryption track of the last editions (namely, [2, 19] for 2018 and [18] for 2019) have all in common to rely on *leveled* homomorphic encryption.

Leveled solutions are however inherently limited in the type of tasks they can perform. In particular, in the case of neural networks, they can only accommodate networks with a moderate number of layers. In this paper, we want to emphasize that depth is *not* necessarily an issue and that deep neural networks can actually be evaluated homomorphically. For a specialized type of networks, this was already pointed out in a paper by Bourse *et al.* [4]; specifically, for discretized neural networks whose signals are restricted to the set $\{-1, 1\}$ and where the activation function is the sign function. Central to their scalable construction is an adaptation of the TFHE scheme so as to enable the evaluation of the sign function during a bootstrapping step. In a recent work, Boura *et al.* [3] investigated the applicability of fully homomorphic encryption for *classical* deep neural networks. They simulated the effect of noise propagation by adding a noise value drawn from a normal distribution to intermediate values, while evaluating the model *in the clear*. These experiments were carried out with models making use of the standard ReLU activation function but also with models making use of FHE-friendly variants thereof. Similar experiments were run by replacing max-pooling layers with FHE-friendly average-pooling layers. As a conclusion of their study, the authors of [3] recommend to favor FHE-friendly operations as they appear to be usually more resilient to noise perturbations.

This paper departs from previous works. We do not seek to design new operations or to modify the topology in order to make a given neural network more amenable to an FHE-based implementation. On the contrary, we stick to the original neural network model. This presents the tremendous advantage of not requiring to re-train a new model. As the operations and topology are unchanged, the already trained model can be used as is. The efforts to train a neural network should not be overlooked. This is a costly and time-consuming operation. Furthermore, in many cases, producing a new model is not even possible as this implies having access to the training dataset, which may demand the prior approval of the data owners or of some regulatory authorities.

In our approach, the evaluation of complex functions is achieved thanks to a combination of programmable bootstrapping techniques and leveled operations. Being *programmable* means that any function (including non-linear functions) of an input ciphertext can be obtained as the output of the bootstrapping. Interestingly, the resulting ciphertext features a controlled level of noise. The process can therefore be iterated over and over. So, in the case of machine learning applications, the depth of neural networks can be arbitrarily large. Our techniques are efficient and directly operate on words of a chosen size.

2   Preliminaries

2.1   Torus and Torus Polynomials

The letter 'T' in TFHE refers to the real torus $\mathbb{T} = \mathbb{R}/\mathbb{Z}$, that is, the set of real numbers modulo 1. Any two elements of $\mathbb{T}$ can be added modulo 1: $(\mathbb{T}, +)$ forms an abelian group. But $\mathbb{T}$ is not a ring as the internal product $\times$ of torus elements is not defined. The *external* product $\cdot$ between integers and torus elements is however well defined. Given $k \in \mathbb{Z}$ and $t \in \mathbb{T}$, the element $k \cdot t \in \mathbb{T}$ is defined as $k \cdot t = t + \cdots + t$ (k times) if $k \geq 0$ and $k \cdot t = (-k) \cdot (-t)$ if $k < 0$. Mathematically, $\mathbb{T}$ is endowed with a $\mathbb{Z}$-*module* structure.

Polynomials can as well be defined over the torus. As will become apparent, they allow for cryptographic operations otherwise not feasible. Let $\varPhi := \varPhi(X)$ denote the M-th cyclotomic polynomial and let N denote its degree. For performance reasons, M is chosen as a power of 2, in which case it turns out that $N = M/2$ and $\varPhi(X) = X^N + 1$. Consider the polynomial rings $\mathbb{R}_N[X] := \mathbb{R}[X]/(X^N + 1)$ and $\mathbb{Z}_N[X] := \mathbb{Z}[X]/(X^N + 1)$. This defines the $\mathbb{Z}_N[X]$-module $\mathbb{T}_N[X] := \mathbb{R}_N[X]/\mathbb{Z}_N[X] = \mathbb{T}[X]/(X^N + 1)$. Elements of $\mathbb{T}_N[X]$ can therefore be seen as polynomials modulo $X^N + 1$ with coefficients in $\mathbb{T}$. Being a $\mathbb{Z}_N[X]$-module, elements in $\mathbb{T}_N[X]$ can be added together and (externally) multiplied by polynomials of $\mathbb{Z}_N[X]$.

Vectors are viewed as row matrices and are denoted with bold letters. Elements in $\mathbb{Z}$ or $\mathbb{T}$ are denoted with roman letters while polynomials are denoted with calligraphic letters. $\mathbb{B}$ is the integer subset $\{0, 1\}$ and, for N a power of 2, $\mathbb{B}_N[X]$ is the subset of polynomials in $\mathbb{Z}_N[X]$ with coefficients in $\mathbb{B}$. For a vector $\boldsymbol{z} \in (\mathbb{Z}/q\mathbb{Z})^n$, its norm $\|\boldsymbol{z}\|$ is defined as the shortest norm among the equivalent classes of $\boldsymbol{z} \in (\mathbb{Z}/q\mathbb{Z})^n$ in $\mathbb{Z}^n$. A polynomial in $\mathbb{Z}_N[X]$ can be identified with a vector in $\mathbb{Z}^N$: to a polynomial $\mathfrak{p} = p_0 + p_1 X + \cdots + p_{N-1} X^{N-1}$ is associated the vector $(p_0, p_1, \ldots, p_{N-1})$. The norm of a polynomial is defined as the norm of its associated vector.

2.2   Probability Distributions

Two probability distributions will be used: the uniform distribution and the normal (a.k.a. Gaussian) distribution. They are respectively denoted by $\mathcal{U}$ and $\mathcal{N}$.

When the uniform distribution $\mathcal{U}$ is defined over an interval $[a, b]$, it is written $\mathcal{U}([a, b])$. Discrete intervals are indicated by double brackets; e.g., $[\![a, b]\!]$. The normal distribution is parametrized by its mean μ and its variance σ^2 and is written as $\mathcal{N}(\mu, \sigma^2)$. A normal distribution over the real numbers induces a discretized normal distribution over $\mathbb{Z}$: to a real value $X \in \mathbb{R}$ corresponds an integer value $Z = \lfloor X q \rceil$.

If $\mathcal{D}$ is a distribution over a space S then $s \leftarrow \mathcal{D}(S)$ indicates that s is chosen at random in S according to $\mathcal{D}$; $s \xleftarrow{\$} S$ is a shorthand for $s \leftarrow \mathcal{U}(S)$.

3   Discretized TFHE

The LWE assumption over the torus (cf. Definition 1, Appendix A) essentially says that a torus element $r \in \mathbb{T}$ constructed as $r = \sum_{j=1}^{n} s_j \cdot a_j + e$ cannot be distinguished from a *random* torus element $r \in \mathbb{T}$, even if the torus vector $(a_1, \ldots, a_n)$ is given. Torus element $r = \sum_{j=1}^{n} s_j \cdot a_j + e$ can therefore be used as a random mask to conceal a "plaintext message" $\mu \in \mathbb{T}$ so as to form a ciphertext $\boldsymbol{c} = (a_1, \ldots, a_n, r + \mu) \in \mathbb{T}^{n+1}$, where $s = (s_1, \ldots, s_n) \in \mathbb{B}^n$ plays the role of the private encryption key. The noise e is sampled from a normal error distribution $\chi = \mathcal{N}(0, \sigma^2)$. In the same way, the GLWE assumption (cf. Definition 2, Appendix A) gives rise to an encryption mechanism for polynomials of $\mathbb{T}_N[X]$: the encryption of $\mu \in \mathbb{T}_N[X]$ under key $\mathfrak{s} = (\mathfrak{s}_1, \ldots, \mathfrak{s}_k) \in \mathbb{B}_N[X]^k$ being given by $\mathbf{c} = (a_1, \ldots, a_k, r + \mu) \in \mathbb{T}_N[X]^{k+1}$ with $r = \sum_{j=1}^{k} \mathfrak{s}_j \cdot a_j + e$. The noise e is sampled from a normal error distribution $\chi = \mathcal{N}(0, \sigma^2)$ over $\mathbb{R}_N[X]$; namely, over polynomials of $\mathbb{R}_N[X]$ with coefficients drawn in $\mathcal{N}(0, \sigma^2)$.

As already pointed out in [10], LWE-based ciphertexts can be viewed as a special instance of GLWE-based ciphertexts for $(k, N) = (n, 1)$. Indeed, when $N = 1$, it turns out that $\mathbb{R}_N[X] = \mathbb{R}$, $\mathbb{Z}_N[X] = \mathbb{Z}$, and $\mathbb{T}_N[X] = \mathbb{T}$. Hence, to keep the presentation as general as possible, we will stick to the GLWE setting; LWE-based encryption being a particular case.

In the most generic setting, ciphertexts $\mathbf{c} = (a_1, \ldots, a_k, r + \mu)$ are vectors of polynomials over $\mathbb{T}_N[X]$. These polynomials can in turn be regarded as vectors over $\mathbb{T}$. In a practical implementation, torus elements are represented with a finite precision (typically, 32 or 64 bits). Let Ω denote the bit-precision—for example, $\Omega = 32$ if the ciphertext components are represented with a precision of 32 bits. In this case, torus elements are restricted to elements of the form $\sum_{i=1}^{\Omega} t_i \cdot 2^{-i} \pmod 1$ with $t_i \in \{0, 1\}$. Essentially, the effect of working with a finite precision boils down to replacing $\mathbb{T}$ with the submodule

$$\hat{\mathbb{T}} := q^{-1}\mathbb{Z}/\mathbb{Z} \subset \mathbb{T} \quad \text{where } q = 2^{\Omega}$$

and doing computations in $\hat{\mathbb{T}}_N[X] := \hat{\mathbb{T}}[X]/(X^N + 1)$. Viewing $\frac{1}{q}$ as an element in $\hat{\mathbb{T}}_N[X]$, any polynomial $\mu \in \hat{\mathbb{T}}_N[X]$ can be written as

$$\mu = \bar{\mu} \cdot \frac{1}{q} \quad \text{for some } \bar{\mu} \in \hat{\mathbb{Z}}_N[X]$$

where $\hat{\mathbb{Z}}_N[X] := (\mathbb{Z}/q\mathbb{Z})[X]/(X^N + 1)$.

3.1 Encoding/Decoding Messages

The input messages, prior to encryption, can be in any format. The role of the encoding/decoding process is to make them compatible with the encryption scheme.

It is useful to introduce some terminology and notation. An element $\bar{\mu} \in \hat{\mathbb{Z}}_N[X]$ entering the encryption algorithm is referred to as the *plaintext*. It matches a *cleartext* m in a certain finite message space $\mathcal{M}$. The correspondence between cleartexts and plaintexts is given by a message encoding function Encode; the reverse operation is the decoding function Decode. It is required that, for any cleartext $m \in \mathcal{M}$, the relation $\text{Decode}(\text{Encode}(m)) = m$ holds.

Let $\bar{\mu} = \bar{\mu}_0 + \bar{\mu}_1 X + \cdots + \bar{\mu}_{N-1} X^{N-1} \in \hat{\mathbb{Z}}_N[X]$ be a plaintext. Because ciphertexts are noisy and the noise is added to the right (i.e., less significant position), only the upper bits of $\bar{\mu}_i$ are used to encode cleartext messages. In order to successfully complete, certain homomorphic operations demand some of the leading bits of $\bar{\mu}_i$ to be provisioned and set to 0. In the most general case, we let $\varpi \geq 0$

denote the number of these bits (called padding bits) and $\varpi \geq 1$ the number of bits that are actually used to represent input cleartexts so that $\varpi + \omega \leq \Omega$. We define $p = 2^{\varpi+\omega}$. Parameter ω is referred to as the message bit-precision and parameter p as the message modulus. The coefficients $\bar{\mu}_i$ of plaintext polynomial $\bar{\mu} \in \hat{\mathbb{Z}}_N[X]$ are therefore of the form $\bar{\mu}_i = 2^{\Omega-(\varpi+\omega)}(\bar{\nu}_i \bmod 2^\omega)$ for some $\bar{\nu}_i$, as shown in Fig. 1.

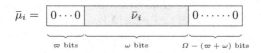

Fig. 1. Plaintext representation.

For an arbitrary element $\bar{x} = \bar{x}_H \frac{q}{p} \pm \bar{x}_L \in \mathbb{Z}/q\mathbb{Z}$ with $0 \leq \bar{x}_L \leq \frac{q}{2p}$, we define the function Upper that returns the value of $\bar{x}_H \frac{q}{p}$. It is specified as Upper: $\mathbb{Z}/q\mathbb{Z} \to \mathbb{Z}/q\mathbb{Z}$, $\bar{x} \mapsto \mathrm{Upper}(\bar{x})$ with

$$\mathrm{Upper}_{q,p}(\bar{x}) = \frac{q}{p}\left\lfloor \frac{p\,\mathrm{lift}(\bar{x})}{q} \right\rceil \quad (\bmod\ q)$$

where the function lift lifts elements of $\mathbb{Z}/q\mathbb{Z}$ to $\mathbb{Z}$. The function Upper naturally extends to polynomials of $\hat{\mathbb{Z}}_N[X]$ by applying it coefficient-wise.

In particular, for $q = 2^\Omega$ and $p = 2^{\varpi+\omega}$, the function reads as $\mathrm{Upper}_{q,p}(\bar{x}) = 2^{\Omega-(\varpi+\omega)}\left\lfloor \frac{2^{\varpi+\omega}\,\mathrm{lift}(\bar{x})}{2^\Omega} \right\rceil$ $(\bmod\ q)$. Note that if $\bar{x} = \bar{x}_H 2^{\Omega-(\varpi+\omega)} \pm \bar{x}_L \in \mathbb{Z}/q\mathbb{Z}$ with $0 \leq \bar{x}_L \leq 2^{\Omega-(\varpi+\omega)-1}$ then $\mathrm{Upper}_{q,p}(\bar{x}) = \bar{x}_H 2^{\Omega-(\varpi+\omega)}$.

3.2   Description

We are now ready to present the implementation of TFHE encryption with a finite representation precision. We write $\overline{\mathrm{GLWE}}$ the corresponding encryption algorithm in the general case. The $\overline{\mathrm{LWE}}$ encryption algorithm coincides with the particular case $(k, N) = (n, 1)$.

KeyGen(1^λ) On input security parameter λ, define a pair of integers (k, N) with $k \geq 1$ and N a power of 2. Define also a normal error distribution $\chi = \mathcal{N}(0, \sigma^2)$ over $\mathbb{R}_N[X]$. Sample uniformly at random a vector $\mathfrak{s} = (\mathfrak{s}_1, \ldots, \mathfrak{s}_k) \xleftarrow{\$} \mathbb{B}_N[X]^k$. The plaintext space is $\mathscr{P}_N[X] = (\frac{q}{p}\mathbb{Z}/q\mathbb{Z})[X]/(X^N+1) \subset \hat{\mathbb{Z}}_N[X] = (\mathbb{Z}/q\mathbb{Z})[X]/(X^N+1)$ where $q = 2^\Omega$ and the message modulus is $p = 2^{\varpi+\omega}$, with $\Omega \geq \varpi + \omega$.

The public parameters are $\mathsf{pp} = \{k, N, \sigma, p, q\}$ and the private key is $\mathsf{sk} = \mathfrak{s}$.

Encrypt$_{sk}(\bar{\mu})$ The encryption of a plaintext $\bar{\mu} \in \mathscr{P}_N[X]$ is given by

$$\bar{c} \leftarrow \overline{\mathrm{GLWE}}_{\mathfrak{s}}(\bar{\mu}) := (\bar{a}_1, \ldots, \bar{a}_k, \bar{b}) \in \hat{\mathbb{Z}}_N[X]^{k+1}$$

with

$$\begin{cases} \bar{\mu}^* = \bar{\mu} + \bar{e} \quad (\mathrm{mod}\ (q, X^N + 1)) \\ \bar{b} = \sum_{j=1}^{k} \mathfrak{s}_j\, \bar{a}_j + \bar{\mu}^* \quad (\mathrm{mod}\ (q, X^N + 1)) \end{cases}$$

for a random polynomial vector $(\bar{a}_1, \ldots, \bar{a}_k) \xleftarrow{\$} \hat{\mathbb{Z}}_N[X]^k$ and a discrete noise $\bar{e} = \lfloor e\, q \rceil$ for some $e \leftarrow \mathbb{R}_N[X]$ whose coefficients are sampled in $\mathcal{N}(0, \sigma^2)$. Decrypt$_{sk}(\bar{c})$ To decrypt $\bar{c} = (\bar{a}_1, \ldots, \bar{a}_k, \bar{b})$, use private key $\mathfrak{s} = (\mathfrak{s}_1, \ldots, \mathfrak{s}_k)$, compute in $\hat{\mathbb{Z}}_N[X]$

$$\bar{\mu}^* = \bar{b} - \sum_{j=1}^{k} \mathfrak{s}_j\, \bar{a}_j \quad (\mathrm{mod}\ (q, X^N + 1)),$$

and output Upper$_{q,p}(\bar{\mu}^*)$.

Correctness. Let $p = 2^{\varpi+\omega}$, $q = 2^{\Omega}$ and $\bar{\mu} = \bar{\mu}_0 + \cdots + \bar{\mu}_{N-1} X^{N-1}$ with $\bar{\mu}_i = \frac{q}{p}(\bar{\nu}_i \bmod 2^\omega)$ for some $\bar{\nu}_i$; see Sect. 3.1. It can be verified that if $\bar{c} \leftarrow \mathrm{Encrypt}_{\mathfrak{s}}(\bar{\mu})$ then $\mathrm{Decrypt}_{\mathfrak{s}}(\bar{c}) = \bar{\mu}$, provided that $\|\bar{e}\|_\infty < \frac{q}{2p} = 2^{\Omega-(-\varpi+\omega)-1}$. Note that the same holds true even if some of the ϖ leading bits of the $\bar{\mu}_i$'s are non-zero.

In certain applications, it is acceptable that the decryption algorithm does not recover the *exact* initial plaintext but a close approximation thereof. In this case, the requirement becomes $\mathrm{Decrypt}_{\mathfrak{s}}(\bar{c}) \approx \bar{\mu}$ and the condition on the bound of $\|\bar{e}\|_\infty$ can be relaxed.

3.3 Leveled Operations

FHE enables directly performing operations on ciphertexts. Depending on the type of operation, the resulting noise level increases more or less.

Addition. Clearly, $\overline{\mathrm{GLWE}}$ ciphertexts are homomorphic with respect to the addition. Let $\bar{c}_1 \leftarrow \overline{\mathrm{GLWE}}_{\mathfrak{s}}(\bar{\mu}_1)$ and $\bar{c}_2 \leftarrow \overline{\mathrm{GLWE}}_{\mathfrak{s}}(\bar{\mu}_2)$ with $\bar{c}_1, \bar{c}_2 \in \hat{\mathbb{Z}}_N[X]^{k+1}$ be the respective encryptions of plaintexts $\bar{\mu}_1, \bar{\mu}_2 \in \mathscr{P}_N[X]$; i.e.,

$$\bar{c}_i = (\bar{a}_1^{(i)}, \ldots, \bar{a}_k^{(i)}, \bar{b}_i) \qquad (i \in \{1, 2\})$$

with $\bar{b}_i = \sum_{j=1}^{k} \mathfrak{s}_j\, \bar{a}_j^{(i)} + \bar{\mu}_i + \bar{e}_i$. Then $\bar{c}_3 = \bar{c}_1 + \bar{c}_2 = (\bar{a}_1^{(1)} + \bar{a}_1^{(2)}, \ldots, \bar{a}_k^{(1)} + \bar{a}_k^{(2)}, \bar{b}_1 + \bar{b}_2)$ is a $\overline{\mathrm{GLWE}}$ encryption of $(\bar{\mu}_1 + \bar{\mu}_2) \in \mathscr{P}_N[X]$, provided that the resulting noise $\bar{e}_3 = \bar{e}_1 + \bar{e}_2$ keeps small.

Scalar Multiplication. By extension, $\overline{\mathrm{GLWE}}$ ciphertexts are homomorphic with respect to the multiplication by a constant. Let $K \in \mathbb{Z}_{\geq 0}$ and $\bar{c} \leftarrow \overline{\mathrm{GLWE}}_{\mathfrak{s}}(\bar{\mu}) = (\bar{a}_1, \ldots, \bar{a}_k, \bar{b})$ with $\bar{b} = \sum_{j=1}^{k} \mathfrak{s}_j\, \bar{a}_j + \bar{\mu} + \bar{e}$. Then, for $K \geq 0$, $K \cdot \bar{c} = \bar{c} + \cdots + \bar{c}$ (K times) is an encryption of $K \cdot \bar{\mu} \in \mathscr{P}_N[X]$, provided that $K \cdot \bar{e}$ keeps small. If $K < 0$ then $K \cdot \bar{c} = (-K) \cdot (-\bar{c})$. More generally, if $\mathscr{K} \in \mathbb{Z}_N[X]$ then $\mathscr{K} \cdot \bar{c}$ is an encryption of $\mathscr{K} \cdot \bar{\mu} \in \mathscr{P}_N[X]$, provided that $\mathscr{K} \cdot \bar{e}$ keeps small.

External Product. $\overline{\text{GLWE}}$ ciphertexts do not support a native internal multiplication which, in practice, means that two $\overline{\text{GLWE}}$ ciphertexts cannot be directly multiplied. In order to perform a multiplication, a clever matrix-based approach put forward in the GSW construction [16] can be used. By analogy, we write $\overline{\text{GGSW}}$ the corresponding encryption algorithm in the general case; the particular case $(k, N) = (n, 1)$ is denoted by $\overline{\text{GSW}}$.

With the previous $\overline{\text{GLWE}}$ notation, let parameters $B = 2^\beta$ and ℓ with $\beta, \ell \geq 1$ and such that $\ell\beta \leq \Omega$. Define also the vector $\boldsymbol{g} = (2^{\Omega-\beta}, 2^{\Omega-2\beta}, \ldots, 2^{\Omega-\ell\beta})$. The $\overline{\text{GGSW}}$ encryption of a plaintext $m \in \mathbb{Z}_N[X]$ with respect to a $\overline{\text{GLWE}}$ encryption key $\mathfrak{s} \in \mathbb{B}_N[X]^k$ is defined as

$$\overline{\mathscr{C}} \leftarrow \overline{\text{GGSW}}_{\mathfrak{s}}(m) := \overline{\overline{\mathfrak{X}}} + m \cdot \mathbf{G}^\mathsf{T} \in \hat{\mathbb{Z}}_N[X]^{(k+1)\ell \times (k+1)}$$

where

$$\overline{\overline{\mathfrak{X}}} \leftarrow \left. \begin{pmatrix} \overline{\text{GLWE}}_{\mathfrak{s}}(0) \\ \vdots \\ \overline{\text{GLWE}}_{\mathfrak{s}}(0) \end{pmatrix} \right\} (k+1)\ell \text{ rows}$$

is a matrix containing on each row a fresh $\overline{\text{GLWE}}$ encryption of 0 and where

$$\mathbf{G}^\mathsf{T} = \mathbf{I}_{k+1} \otimes \boldsymbol{g}^\mathsf{T} = \text{diag}(\underbrace{\boldsymbol{g}^\mathsf{T}, \ldots, \boldsymbol{g}^\mathsf{T}}_{k+1}) \in \mathbb{Z}_N[X]^{(k+1)\ell \times (k+1)}$$

is the so-called *gadget matrix* [23], with $\mathbf{I}_{k+1}$ the identity matrix of size $k + 1$. It is worth noting that any element d in $\mathbb{Z}/q\mathbb{Z}$, viewed as an integer in $[\![-\frac{q}{2}, \frac{q}{2}[\![$, can always be approximated by a signed-digit radix-B expansion of size ℓ as

$$d \approx q \sum_{i=1}^{\ell} d_i B^{-i} = \sum_{i=1}^{\ell} d_i 2^{\Omega-i\beta} = \boldsymbol{g}^{-1}(d)\,\boldsymbol{g}^\mathsf{T}$$

where $\boldsymbol{g}^{-1}(d) := (d_1, \ldots, d_\ell) \in \mathbb{Z}^\ell$ with digits $d_i \in [\![-\frac{B}{2}, \frac{B}{2}[\![$ and with an approximation error that is bounded by $\left| \boldsymbol{g}^{-1}(d)\,\boldsymbol{g}^\mathsf{T} - d \right| \leq q/(2B^\ell) = 2^{\Omega-\beta\ell-1}$.

By extension, for a polynomial $p = p_0 + \cdots + p_{N-1} X^{N-1} \in \hat{\mathbb{Z}}_N[X]$ whose coefficients are viewed as integers in $[\![-\frac{q}{2}, \frac{q}{2}[\![$, the decomposition $\boldsymbol{g}^{-1}(p) \in \mathbb{Z}_N[X]^\ell$ is defined as $\boldsymbol{g}^{-1}(p) = \sum_{j=0}^{N-1} \boldsymbol{g}^{-1}(p_j) X^j$. Clearly, it holds that $\left\| \boldsymbol{g}^{-1}(p)\,\boldsymbol{g}^\mathsf{T} - p \right\|_\infty \leq 2^{\Omega-\beta\ell-1}$. Finally, for a vector of $k + 1$ polynomials, $\boldsymbol{p} = (p_1, \ldots, p_{k+1}) \in \hat{\mathbb{Z}}_N[X]^{k+1}$, the decomposition $\mathbf{G}^{-1}(\boldsymbol{p}) \in \mathbb{Z}_N[X]^{(k+1)\ell}$ is defined as $\mathbf{G}^{-1}(\boldsymbol{p}) = (\boldsymbol{g}^{-1}(p_1), \ldots, \boldsymbol{g}^{-1}(p_{k+1}))$ and $\left\| \mathbf{G}^{-1}(\boldsymbol{p})\,\mathbf{G}^\mathsf{T} - \boldsymbol{p} \right\|_\infty \leq 2^{\Omega-\beta\ell-1}$.

Interestingly, the gadget decomposition of $\overline{\text{GLWE}}$ ciphertexts gives rise to an *external product* [10] with $\overline{\text{GGSW}}$ ciphertexts. Specifically, for plaintexts $m_1 \in \mathbb{Z}_N[X]$ and $\mu_2 \in \mathscr{P}_N[X]$, if $\overline{\mathscr{C}}_1 \leftarrow \overline{\text{GGSW}}_{\mathfrak{s}}(m_1)$ and $\bar{\mathfrak{c}}_2 \leftarrow \overline{\text{GLWE}}(\mu_2)$ then their external product, denoted by $\boxdot$, is given by

$$\bar{\mathfrak{c}}_3 = \overline{\mathscr{C}}_1 \boxdot \bar{\mathfrak{c}}_2 := \mathbf{G}^{-1}(\bar{\mathfrak{c}}_2)\,\overline{\mathscr{C}}_1 \ .$$

A little algebra shows that

$$\bar{\mathfrak{c}}_3 = \mathbf{G}^{-1}(\bar{\mathfrak{c}}_2)\,(\overline{\mathfrak{X}} + m_1 \cdot \mathbf{G}^\mathsf{T}) = \underbrace{\mathbf{G}^{-1}(\bar{\mathfrak{c}}_2)\,\overline{\mathfrak{X}}}_{=\overline{\mathrm{GLWE}}_\mathfrak{s}(0)} + \underbrace{m_1 \cdot \mathbf{G}^{-1}(\bar{\mathfrak{c}}_2)\,\mathbf{G}^\mathsf{T}}_{\approx m_1\,\bar{\mathfrak{c}}_2}$$

is a $\overline{\mathrm{GLWE}}$ encryption of $m_1\,\mu_2 \in \mathscr{P}_N[X]$, provided that the resulting noise (including the approximation error) keeps small.

The CMux Gate. Starting from the external product, a new leveled operation can be defined: the 'controlled' multiplexer or CMux [10, § 3.4]. A CMux acts as a selector according to a bit—but over encrypted data. It takes as input two $\overline{\mathrm{GLWE}}$ ciphertexts $\bar{\mathfrak{c}}_0$ and $\bar{\mathfrak{c}}_1$, respectively encrypting plaintexts u_0 and $u_1 \in \mathscr{P}_N[X]$, and a $\overline{\mathrm{GGSW}}$ ciphertext $\overline{\mathscr{C}}$ encrypting a bit b. The result is a $\overline{\mathrm{GLWE}}$ ciphertext $\bar{\mathfrak{c}}'$ encrypting u_b, provided that the resulting noise keeps small. The CMux gate is given by:

$$\bar{\mathfrak{c}}' \leftarrow \mathrm{CMux}(\overline{\mathscr{C}}, \bar{\mathfrak{c}}_0, \bar{\mathfrak{c}}_1) := \overline{\mathscr{C}} \boxdot (\bar{\mathfrak{c}}_1 - \bar{\mathfrak{c}}_0) + \bar{\mathfrak{c}}_0 \ .$$

It plays a central role in the performance of homomorphic computations and, especially, inside the bootstrapping.

4   Programmable Bootstrapping

The *programmable bootstrapping* is an extension of the bootstrapping technique that allows resetting the noise to a fixed level while—at the same time—evaluating a function on the input ciphertext.

In this section, we first explain in detail how to perform the regular bootstrapping. We then proceed with the programmable bootstrapping and show how to evaluate any function expressed as a look-up table. When f is the identity function, that coincides with a regular bootstrapping.

4.1   Blind Rotation

As aforementioned, Gentry's bootstrapping boils down to homomorphically decrypt a ciphertext using a homomorphic encryption of its own decryption key, with the goal of reducing the noise the ciphertext contains.

Intuition. Consider an $\overline{\mathrm{LWE}}$ ciphertext $\bar{c} \leftarrow \overline{\mathrm{LWE}}_s(\bar{\mu}) = (\bar{a}_1, \ldots, \bar{a}_n, \bar{b}) \in (\mathbb{Z}/q\mathbb{Z})^{n+1}$ where $\bar{a}_j \xleftarrow{\$} \mathbb{Z}/q\mathbb{Z}$ and $\bar{b} = \sum_{j=1}^n s_j\,\bar{a}_j + \bar{\mu}^*$ with $\bar{\mu}^* = \bar{\mu} + \bar{e}$ for some discrete noise $\bar{e} = \lfloor e\,q \rceil$ with $e \leftarrow \mathcal{N}(0, \sigma^2)$. Ciphertext $\bar{c}$ is an encryption of plaintext $\bar{\mu} \in \mathscr{P} = \frac{q}{p}\mathbb{Z}/q\mathbb{Z}$ under the secret key $s = (s_1, \ldots, s_n) \in \mathbb{B}^n$. It can be decrypted using s in two steps as $\bar{\mu}^* \leftarrow \bar{b} - \sum_{j=1}^n s_j\,\bar{a}_j$ and $\bar{\mu} \leftarrow \mathrm{Upper}_{q,p}(\bar{\mu}^*)$.

In order to bootstrap, one way to look at the decryption (without the rounding) is to see that

$$-\bar{\mu}^* = -\bar{b} + \textstyle\sum_{j=1}^n s_j\,\bar{a}_j \pmod{q}$$

and to put this value at the exponent of X to get the monomial $X^{-\bar{\mu}^*}$. Note that there are q possible values for $\bar{\mu}^*$. The rough idea (more technical details are given later) is then to build a polynomial—that we call *test polynomial*—such that each one of its coefficients encodes the noise-free value corresponding to $\bar{\mu}^*$ (namely, $\bar{\mu} = \mathrm{Upper}_{q,p}(\bar{\mu}^*)$), for all the possible $\bar{\mu}^*$'s. Specifically, if we suppose for a moment that the test polynomial is the degree-q polynomial $\bar{v} = \bar{v}_0 + \bar{v}_1 X + \cdots + \bar{v}_{q-1} X^{q-1}$ then its ith coefficient is set to $\bar{v}_i = \mathrm{Upper}_{q,p}(i \bmod q)$. By rotating the test polynomial of $\bar{\mu}^*$ positions, the value of $\bar{\mu}$ moves to the constant coefficient position. This is illustrated in Fig. 2. It then remains to extract it.

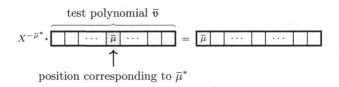

Fig. 2. Rotating the test polynomial.

Of course, this rotation is done homomorphically (hence the name blind rotation) and since $X^{-\bar{\mu}^*} \cdot \bar{v}$ is a polynomial, this is where $\overline{\mathrm{GLWE}}$ encryption comes into play.

Polynomials used in $\overline{\mathrm{GLWE}}$ are defined modulo $X^N + 1$. This means that X as a multiplicative element of $\mathbb{Z}_N[X]$ is of order $2N$. However, as appearing in the $\overline{\mathrm{LWE}}$ encryption, $\bar{\mu}^*$ is defined modulo q. It therefore needs to be rescaled modulo $2N$. As a consequence, instead of using the relation $-\bar{\mu}^* = -\bar{b} + \sum_{j=1}^n s_j \bar{a}_j \pmod{q}$, we have to rely on the approximation

$$-\tilde{\mu}^* = -\tilde{b} + \sum_{j=1}^n s_j \tilde{a}_j \pmod{2N},$$

where $\tilde{b} = \left\lfloor \frac{2N(\bar{b} \bmod q)}{q} \right\rceil$ and $\tilde{a}_j = \left\lfloor \frac{2N(\bar{a}_j \bmod q)}{q} \right\rceil$. This approximation may generate a small additional error that adds to the noise. We call this additional error *drift*. It depends on both the size n of the input $\overline{\mathrm{LWE}}$ and the ring size N used in $\overline{\mathrm{GLWE}}$ during the rotation. The impact of the drift on the result can be dealt with by a careful choice of the parameters. In particular, a smaller value for n or a larger value for N is expected to decrease the resulting drift.

Also, because the test polynomial $\bar{v}$ lies in $\hat{\mathbb{Z}}_N[X]$ and thus has N coefficients, at most N values for $\tilde{\mu}^*$ can be encoded. This is addressed by ensuring that the most significant bit of $\tilde{\mu}^*$ is set to 0; that is, parameter $\varpi \geq 1$ (see Sect. 3.1). In this case, $\tilde{\mu}^*$ can take at most N possible values and the test polynomial is formed as $\bar{v} = \bar{v}_0 + \cdots + \bar{v}_{N-1} X^{N-1}$ with

$$\bar{v}_i = \mathrm{Upper}_{q,p}\left(\tfrac{q}{2N} i \bmod q\right) .$$

Implementation. It remains to explain how to compute the product between $X^{-\tilde{\mu}^*}$ and the test polynomial $\bar{v}$ under $\overline{\text{GLWE}}$ encryption. It turns out that such a computation can be computed as a succession of CMux gates [10, § 4.3].

An accumulator ACC is initialized with a $\overline{\text{GLWE}}$ encryption of $X^{-\tilde{b}} \cdot \bar{v}$. It is then updated in a for-loop where, at iteration i (for $1 \leq i \leq n$) it is multiplied by $X^{s_i \tilde{a}_i}$. The multiplication is performed thanks to the CMux operation, ACC $\leftarrow$ CMux(bsk[i], ACC, $X^{\tilde{a}_i} \cdot$ ACC). Here, bsk[i] $\leftarrow$ $\overline{\text{GGSW}}_{\mathfrak{s}'}(s_i)$ (for $i = 1, \ldots, n$), are the *bootstrapping keys*; i.e., a list of $\overline{\text{GGSW}}$ encryptions of the elements of the secret key $\mathfrak{s}$ under some encryption key $\mathfrak{s}' \in \mathbb{B}_N[X]^k$. The output of the blind rotation is ACC $\leftarrow$ $\overline{\text{GLWE}}_{\mathfrak{s}'}(X^{-\tilde{\mu}^*} \cdot \bar{v})$. More details about this procedure are provided in Appendix B.1.

Sample Extraction. The remaining step of the bootstrapping consists in extracting the constant coefficient of $\bar{u} := X^{-\tilde{\mu}^*} \cdot \bar{v}$ as a $\overline{\text{LWE}}$ ciphertext of $\bar{\mu}$. This is an easy operation—called *sample extraction*—which is performed by simply extracting some of the coefficients of the $\overline{\text{GLWE}}$ ciphertext. See Appendix B.2.

Key Switching. The loop is almost closed. With the above procedure, input ciphertext $\bar{c} \leftarrow \overline{\text{LWE}}_{\mathfrak{s}}(\bar{\mu}) \in (\mathbb{Z}/q\mathbb{Z})^{n+1}$ and resulting output ciphertext $\bar{c}' \leftarrow \overline{\text{LWE}}_{\mathfrak{s}'}(\bar{\mu}) \in (\mathbb{Z}/q\mathbb{Z})^{kN+1}$ both encrypt plaintext $\bar{\mu}$ but make use of different keys and have a different format.

In order to convert $\bar{c}'$ back to the original setting, an operation called *key switching* can be performed. The key-switching technique is classical in FHE. See Appendix B.3 for a detailed description.

4.2   Look-Up Table Evaluation

In the previous section, the blind rotation is used to perform a bootstrapping. Surprisingly, the same technique can be adapted so as to evaluate a function at the same time. The function is evaluated as a look-up table that is encoded in the test polynomial.

Specifically, suppose we intend to evaluate—over encrypted data—an arbitrary function f with domain $\mathscr{D}$ and image $\mathscr{I}$, $f \colon \mathscr{D} \rightarrow \mathscr{I}, x \mapsto y = f(x)$. We assume we are given the encoding functions Encode$\colon \mathscr{D} \rightarrow \mathbb{Z}/q\mathbb{Z}$ and Encode$'\colon \mathscr{I} \rightarrow \mathbb{Z}/q\mathbb{Z}$, and the matching decoding functions Decode and Decode$'$, as specified in Sect. 3.1.

We showed in the previous section that selecting for the test polynomial $\bar{v} = \bar{v}_0 + \cdots + \bar{v}_{N-1} X^{N-1}$ with $\bar{v}_i = \text{Upper}_{q,p}\left(\frac{q}{2N} i \bmod q\right)$ transforms a ciphertext of $\bar{\mu}$ into another ciphertext of $\bar{\mu}$ with a lesser noise.

Consider now the following diagram

$$
\begin{array}{ccc}
\mathbb{Z}/q\mathbb{Z} & \longrightarrow & \mathbb{Z}/q\mathbb{Z} \\
\text{Decode} \downarrow & & \uparrow \text{Encode}' \\
\mathscr{D} & \xrightarrow{ f } & \mathscr{I}
\end{array}
$$

and suppose we define a look-up table as pairs $(i, T[i])$ for $0 \le i \le N - 1$ with

$$T[i] = \text{Encode}' \circ f \circ \text{Decode} \circ \text{Upper}_{q,p}\left(\tfrac{q}{2N}\, i \bmod q\right) \ .$$

As the diagram suggests, we program the test polynomial as

$$\bar{\mathfrak{v}} = \bar{v}_0 + \cdots + \bar{v}_{N-1}\, X^{N-1} \quad \text{with } \bar{v}_i = T[i]\,,$$

the rest of the process described in Sect. 4.1 remains unchanged. Doing so, up to the drift, an input ciphertext of $\bar{\mu}$ (encoding some value $x \in \mathcal{D}$) will be transformed into a ciphertext of a value encoding $f(x)$. Furthermore, being the output of a bootstrapping, the resulting ciphertext enjoys a low level of noise. The whole process is what we call *programmable bootstrapping*.

Remark 1. As explained, the regular bootstrapping requires an encoding parameter $\varpi \ge 1$ (cf. Sect. 4.1). This condition can be lifted in the programmable bootstrapping when the entries of the look-up table are negacyclic; i.e., when $T[i + N] \equiv -T[i] \pmod{2N}$. In that case, $2N$ values are actually programmed.

5 Application to Neural Networks

All the tools that we need are now on the table. In this section, we apply them in order to evaluate homomorphically neural networks.

Neural networks (NN) were originally built in computer science by analogy to the human brain in order to solve complex problems that machines were not able to solve before. The neural networks can be trained and then used to classify objects, detect diseases, do face recognition, and so on.

The different layers in a neural network are typically aimed at successively extracting discriminating features or patterns from the input data. The number of layers and the type of operations that is performed in each layer depend on the task the neural network is trying to achieve.

We review below a number of layers that are commonly used to build neural networks. The list is non-exhaustive. Our techniques are generic and support all known types of layers. Each layer receives inputs from the previous layer, performs some computations, and produces outputs. The outputs then flow to the next layer as inputs. Two types of layers are distinguished when working over encrypted data:

– layers that can be evaluated homomorphically using leveled operations; and
– layers involving non-linear or more complex operations, in which case one or several programmable bootstrappings (PBS) are required.

We note that the first type of layers may also resort to bootstrap operations on some intermediate values whenever the noise exceeds a certain threshold.

5.1 Layers Without PBS

Dense/Linear Layer. A (fully connected) dense layer computes the dot product between the inputs and a matrix of weights. A bias vector can be added. An activation function is then applied component-wise to produce the outputs. When there is no activation function, a dense layer is also called linear layer.

When evaluated homomorphically, the weights and the bias vector are provided in the clear. The evaluation of a dense layer (the activation excepted) thus consists of a series of multiplications by constants and additions, which are all leveled operations.

The activation functions are treated in the next section (see *activation layer*).

Convolution Layer. A convolution layer convolves the input layer with a convolution kernel (a.k.a. filter) that is composed of a tensor of weights so as to produce a tensor of outputs. Biases can be added to the outputs. Moreover, an activation function can be applied to the outputs.

The filters are provided in the clear. Hence, as for the dense layer, the homomorphic evaluation of a convolution layer (without activation) consists of a series of multiplications by constants and additions.

Addition Layer. An addition layer performs component-wise additions. Over encrypted data, those are leveled operations.

Flatten Layer. A flatten layer reshapes its input into a lower-dimensional array so that it can for example be fed into a subsequent dense layer.

Over encrypted data, the flattening function simply consists in rearranging the input ciphertexts. No homomorphic operation is required.

Global Average Pooling Layer. A global average pooling layer computes the average of the components of its inputs. Specifically, if n denotes the number of components and a_i denotes the value of component i, the global average pooling function computes $\left(\sum_{i=1}^{n} a_i\right)/n$.

In a homomorphic evaluation, the global average pooling can be reduced to the computation of the sum $\sum_{i=1}^{n} a_i$. The division by n is then performed in the next programmable bootstrapping—e.g., in a dense layer or a convolution layer—by dividing the weights by the same quantity. Hence, the sole homomorphic operation required to evaluate a global average pooling layer is the addition of ciphertexts, which is a leveled operation.

5.2 Layers with PBS

Activation Layer: ReLU. An activation layer is used to inject non-linearity in the neural networks. It is crucial in the learning. There are many activation functions that can be used in an activation layer. One of the most popular activation functions is the Rectified Linear Unit (ReLU) function. Other commonly used activations include the sigmoid function or the hyperbolic tangent function.

As detailed in Sect. 4, the homomorphic evaluation of an activation function (as any function) can be performed via a programmable bootstrapping (PBS), with the outputs of the function encoded inside the test polynomial.

Max-Pooling Layer. A max-pooling layer extracts a fixed-size subset of components from the inputs and computes their maximum.

At first sight, as the max function is multivariate (i.e., it takes multiple arguments on input), it is unclear how it can be evaluated homomorphically. With two arguments, the max function can however be expressed using the [univariate] ReLU function, $\max(x, y) = y + \text{ReLU}(x - y)$. Hence, from $\text{Encrypt}(x)$ and $\text{Encrypt}(y)$, their maximum can be evaluated as $\text{Encrypt}(\max(x, y)) = \text{Encrypt}(y) + \text{Encrypt}(\text{ReLU}(z))$ with $\text{Encrypt}(z) = \text{Encrypt}(x) - \text{Encrypt}(y)$. This requires a couple of addition/subtraction of ciphertexts plus the homomorphic evaluation of a ReLU function, the cost of which is one PBS. When there are more than two arguments, the basic relation $\max(x_1, \ldots, x_{k-1}, x_k) = \max(y_k, x_k)$ with $y_k = \max(x_1, \ldots, x_{k-1})$ can be used. For a series of k components $(x_1, \ldots, x_k)$, the homomorphic evaluation of the max-pooling function thus amounts to $(k - 1)$ PBS.

6   Experimental Results and Benchmarks

We conducted a series of numerical experiments to assess the performance. We report below results against the MNIST dataset [21], which contains 28×28 images of handwritten digits. For testing purposes, we designed depth-20, 50, 100 neural networks, respectively noted NN-20, NN-50 and NN-100. These networks all include dense and convolution layers with activation functions; every hidden layer possesses at least 92 active neurons.

Parameter Sets. The overall targeted security levels are 80 bits and 128 bits. The selected cryptographic parameters are defined by (k, N, σ) for $\overline{\text{GLWE}}$ encryption and (n, σ) for $\overline{\text{LWE}}$ encryption. The word-size is $\Omega = 64$ bits.

Table 1. Cryptographic parameters.

Security level		GLWE			LWE	
		k	N	σ	n	σ
80 bits	I	1	1024	2^{-40}	542	2^{-21}
	II	1	2048	2^{-60}	592	2^{-23}
128 bits	III	1	4096	2^{-62}	938	2^{-23}

The different parameter sets I, II & III in Table 1 meet at least the claimed security level and were validated using the `lwe-estimator` (https://bitbucket.org/malb/lwe-estimator/) [1]. They can be used for the homomorphic inference of networks requiring a maximal precision of 8 bits up to 12 bits.

Performance Analysis. Experiments were performed on three different types of machines, respectively referred to as PC, AWS, and AWS2:

- a personal computer with 2.6 GHz 6-Core Intel® Core™ i7 processor,
- a 3.00 GHz Intel® Xeon® Platinum 8275CL processor with 96 vCPUs hosted on AWS, and
- as above but with 8 NVIDIA® A100 Tensor Core GPUs.

Table 2. Performance comparison (computed from 1000 runs).

(a) Results in the clear.

	Run-time		Accuracy
	PC	AWS	
NN-20	0.17 ms	0.19 ms	97.5 %
NN-50	0.20 ms	0.30 ms	95.4 %
NN-100	0.33 ms	0.46 ms	95.2 %

(b) Results over encrypted data.

		Run-time			Accuracy
		PC	AWS	AWS2	
80-bit security:					
NN-20	(I)	12.49 s	2.85 s	0.69 s	97.2 %
	(II)	30.04 s	6.19 s	2.10 s	**97.5 %**
NN-50	(I)	26.71 s	5.90 s	1.73 s	93.4 %
	(II)	71.71 s	13.00 s	5.27 s	**95.1 %**
NN-100	(I)	46.61 s	11.18 s	3.46 s	87.3 %
	(II)	108.73 s	24.13 s	10.24 s	**91.1 %**
128-bit security:					
NN-20	(III)	115.52 s	21.17 s	7.53 s	97.1 %
NN-50	(III)	233.55 s	43.91 s	18.89 s	**94.7 %**
NN-100	(III)	481.61 s	81.47 s	37.65 s	**83.0 %**

For reference, Table 2a lists the run-time and accuracy for an unencrypted inference. They were measured using ONNX Runtime [24]. The run-time and accuracy over encrypted data for different settings are presented in Table 2b. These clearly indicate the importance of the parameter choice and the different trade-offs that can be obtained. In particular, for a given security level, a larger value for parameter N increases the accuracy (at the expense of more processing). It is important to note that the given times correspond to the evaluation of a single inference run independently; in particular, the times are not amortized over a batch of inferences.

7   Conclusion

We presented a general framework for the evaluation of deep neural networks using fully homomorphic encryption. Our approach scales efficiently with the number of layers while providing good accuracy results. To do so we employ a versatile combination of encoding methods and of programmable bootstrapping techniques. To the best of our knowledge, our results set new records in the homomorphic inference of deep neural networks.

The practicality of our framework invites further works. First, it would be interesting to know the impact of the use of specialized hardware in our framework. We believe that several orders of magnitude in the processing times could be gained in that way. Another interesting work would be to investigate how to extend our techniques to the homomorphic training of neural networks or, more generally, to other intensive machine-learning tasks.

Acknowledgments. We are grateful to our colleagues at Zama for their help and support in running the experiments.

Availability. The library implementing our extended version of TFHE has been developed in Rust. It is available as an open-source project on GitHub at URL https://github.com/zama-ai/concrete.

A   Complexity Assumptions Over the Real Torus

In 2005, Regev [25] introduced the *learning with errors (LWE) problem*. Generalizations and extensions to ring structures were subsequently proposed in [22,27]. The security of TFHE relies on the hardness of torus-based problems [6,9]: the LWE assumption and the GLWE assumption [5,20] over the torus.

Definition 1 (LWE problem over the torus). *Let $n \in \mathbb{N}$ and let $s = (s_1, \ldots, s_n) \xleftarrow{\$} \mathbb{B}^n$. Let also χ be an error distribution over $\mathbb{R}$. The* learning with errors *(LWE) over the torus problem is to distinguish the following distributions:*

- $\mathscr{D}_0 = \{(a, r) \mid a \xleftarrow{\$} \mathbb{T}^n, r \xleftarrow{\$} \mathbb{T}\}$;
- $\mathscr{D}_1 = \{(a, r) \mid a = (a_1, \ldots, a_n) \xleftarrow{\$} \mathbb{T}^n, r = \sum_{j=1}^n s_j \cdot a_j + e, e \leftarrow \chi\}$.

Definition 2 (GLWE problem over the torus). *Let $N, k \in \mathbb{N}$ with N a power of 2 and let $\mathfrak{s} = (\mathfrak{s}_1, \ldots, \mathfrak{s}_k) \xleftarrow{\$} \mathbb{B}_N[X]^k$. Let also χ be an error distribution over $\mathbb{R}_N[X]$. The* general learning with errors *(GLWE) over the torus problem is to distinguish the following distributions:*

- $\mathcal{D}_0 = \{(\boldsymbol{a}, r) \mid \boldsymbol{a} \xleftarrow{\$} \mathbb{T}_N[X]^k, r \xleftarrow{\$} \mathbb{T}_N[X]\};$
- $\mathcal{D}_1 = \{(\boldsymbol{a}, r) \mid \boldsymbol{a} = (a_1, \ldots, a_k) \xleftarrow{\$} \mathbb{T}_N[X]^k, r = \sum_{j=1}^{k} \mathfrak{s}_j \cdot a_j + e, e \leftarrow \chi\}.$

The *decisional LWE assumption* (resp. the *decisional GLWE assumption*) asserts that solving the LWE problem (resp. GLWE problem) is infeasible for some security parameter λ, where $n := n(\lambda)$ and $\chi := \chi(\lambda)$ (resp. $N := N(\lambda)$, $k = k(\lambda)$, and $\chi := \chi(\lambda)$).

B   Algorithms

We use the notations of Sect. 4. The input of the (programmable) bootstrapping is an $\overline{\text{LWE}}$ ciphertext $\bar{c} \leftarrow \overline{\text{LWE}}_{\boldsymbol{s}}(\bar{\mu}) = (\bar{a}_1, \ldots, \bar{a}_n, \bar{b}) \in (\mathbb{Z}/q\mathbb{Z})^{n+1}$ that encrypts a plaintext $\bar{\mu} \in \mathbb{Z}/q\mathbb{Z}$ under the secret key $\boldsymbol{s} = (s_1, \ldots, s_n) \in \mathbb{B}^n$.

B.1   Blind Rotation

The secret key bits s_j used to encrypt the input $\overline{\text{LWE}}$ ciphertext cannot be revealed. They are instead provided as *bootstrapping keys*; i.e., encrypted under some encryption key $\mathfrak{s}' \in \mathbb{B}_N[X]^k$: $\mathsf{bsk}[j] \leftarrow \overline{\text{GGSW}}_{\mathfrak{s}'}(s_j)$ for all $j = 1, \ldots, n$.
    We then have:

Algorithm 1: Blind rotation.

$\text{ACC} \leftarrow (0, \ldots, 0, X^{-\bar{b}} \cdot \bar{v})$
for $i = 1$ **to** n **do**
 | $\text{ACC} \leftarrow \text{CMux}(\mathsf{bsk}[i], \text{ACC}, X^{\bar{a}_i} \cdot \text{ACC})$
end for

return ACC

At the end of the loop, ACC contains a $\overline{\text{GLWE}}$ encryption of $X^{-\bar{\mu}^*} \cdot \bar{v}$ under key $\mathfrak{s}'$.

B.2   Sample Extraction

The sample extraction algorithm extracts the constant coefficient $\bar{\mu}$ of polynomial $\bar{u} \in \hat{\mathbb{Z}}_N[X]$ in $\overline{\text{GLWE}}$ ciphertext $\bar{c}'$ as a $\overline{\text{LWE}}$ ciphertext of $\bar{\mu}$. In more detail, let $\mathfrak{s}' = (\mathfrak{s}'_1, \ldots, \mathfrak{s}'_k) \in \mathbb{B}_N[X]^k$ with $\mathfrak{s}'_j = s'_{j,0} + \cdots + s'_{j,N-1} X^{N-1}$ for $1 \leq j \leq k$. Parsing $\bar{c}' \leftarrow \overline{\text{GLWE}}_{\mathfrak{s}'}(\bar{u}) \in \hat{\mathbb{Z}}_N[X]^k$ as $(\bar{a}'_1, \ldots, \bar{a}'_k, \bar{b}')$ with $\bar{a}'_j = \bar{a}'_{j,0} + \cdots + \bar{a}'_{j,N-1} X^{N-1}$ for $1 \leq j \leq k$ and $\bar{b}' = \bar{b}'_0 + \cdots + \bar{b}'_{N-1} X^{N-1}$, it can be verified that $\bar{c}' := (\bar{a}'_{1,0}, -\bar{a}'_{1,N-1}, \ldots, -\bar{a}'_{1,1}, \ldots, \bar{a}'_{k,0}, -\bar{a}'_{k,N-1}, \ldots, -\bar{a}'_{k,1}, \bar{b}'_0) \in (\mathbb{Z}/q\mathbb{Z})^{kN+1}$ is a $\overline{\text{LWE}}$ encryption of $\bar{\mu}$ under the key $\boldsymbol{s}' = (s'_1, \ldots, s'_{kN}) \in \mathbb{B}^{kN}$ where $s'_{l+1+(j-1)N} := s'_{j,l}$ for $1 \leq j \leq k$ and $0 \leq l \leq N-1$.

B.3   Key Switching

The key switching technique can be used to switch encryption keys in different parameter sets [7, §1.2]. Its implementation requires *key-switching keys*, i.e., $\overline{\text{LWE}}$ encryptions of the key bits of s' with respect to the original key s. Assume we are given the key-switching keys $\mathsf{ksk}[i,j] \leftarrow \overline{\text{LWE}}_s\left(s'_i \cdot \frac{q}{B_{\mathsf{KS}}^j}\right)$ for all $1 \leq i \leq kN$ and $1 \leq j \leq \ell_{\mathsf{KS}}$, for some parameters $B := B_{\mathsf{KS}}$ and $\ell := \ell_{\mathsf{KS}}$ defining a gadget decomposition (see Sect. 3.3). Adapting [10, §4.1] teaches that, on input $\overline{\text{LWE}}$ ciphertext $c' \leftarrow \overline{\text{LWE}}_{s'}(\bar{\mu}) = (\bar{a}'_1, \ldots, \bar{a}'_{kN}, \bar{b}') \in (\mathbb{Z}/q\mathbb{Z})^{kN+1}$ under the key $s' = (s_1, \ldots, s_{kN}) \in \mathbb{B}^{kN}$,

$$\bar{c}'' := (0, \ldots, 0, \bar{b}') - \sum_{i=1}^{kN} \sum_{j=1}^{\ell_{\mathsf{KS}}} \bar{a}'_{i,j}\, \mathsf{ksk}[i,j] \in (\mathbb{Z}/q\mathbb{Z})^{n+1}$$

where $(\bar{a}'_{i,1}, \ldots, \bar{a}'_{i,\ell_{\mathsf{KS}}}) = g^{-1}(\bar{a}'_i)$ is an $\overline{\text{LWE}}$ encryption of $\bar{\mu}$ under key s, provided that the resulting noise keeps small.

References

1. Albrecht, M.R., Player, R., Scott, S.: On the concrete hardness of learning with errors. J. Math. Cryptol. **9**(3), 169–203 (2015)
2. Blatt, M., Gusev, A., Polyakov, Y., Goldwasser, S.: Secure large-scale genome-wide association studies using homomorphic encryption. Cryptology ePrint Archive, Report 2020/563 (2020)
3. Boura, C., Gama, N., Georgieva, M., Jetchev, D.: Simulating homomorphic evaluation of deep learning predictions. In: Dolev, S., Hendler, D., Lodha, S., Yung, M. (eds.) CSCML 2019. LNCS, vol. 11527, pp. 212–230. Springer, Cham (2019). https://doi.org/10.1007/978-3-030-20951-3_20
4. Bourse, F., Minelli, M., Minihold, M., Paillier, P.: Fast homomorphic evaluation of deep discretized neural networks. In: Shacham, H., Boldyreva, A. (eds.) CRYPTO 2018. LNCS, vol. 10993, pp. 483–512. Springer, Cham (2018). https://doi.org/10.1007/978-3-319-96878-0_17
5. Brakerski, Z., Gentry, C., Vaikuntanathan, V.: (Leveled) fully homomorphic encryption without bootstrapping. ACM Trans. Comput. Theory **6**(3), 13:1–13:36 (2014). Earlier version in ITCS 2012
6. Brakerski, Z., Langlois, A., Peikert, C., Regev, O., Stehlé, D.: Classical hardness of learning with errors. In: 45th Annual ACM Symposium on Theory of Computing, pp. 575–584. ACM Press (2013)
7. Brakerski, Z., Vaikuntanathan, V.: Efficient fully homomorphic encryption from (standard) LWE. SIAM J. Comput. **43**(2), 831–871 (2014). Earlier version in FOCS 2011
8. California Consumer Privacy Act (CCPA). https://www.oag.ca.gov/privacy/ccpa
9. Cheon, J.H., Stehlé, D.: Fully homomophic encryption over the integers revisited. In: Oswald, E., Fischlin, M. (eds.) EUROCRYPT 2015. LNCS, vol. 9056, pp. 513–536. Springer, Heidelberg (2015). https://doi.org/10.1007/978-3-662-46800-5_20
10. Chillotti, I., Gama, N., Georgieva, M., Izabachène, M.: TFHE: fast fully homomorphic encryption over the torus. J. Cryptol. **33**(1), 34–91 (2020). Earlier versions in ASIACRYPT 2016 and 2017

11. van Dijk, M., Gentry, C., Halevi, S., Vaikuntanathan, V.: Fully homomorphic encryption over the integers. In: Gilbert, H. (ed.) EUROCRYPT 2010. LNCS, vol. 6110, pp. 24–43. Springer, Heidelberg (2010). https://doi.org/10.1007/978-3-642-13190-5_2

12. Dowlin, N., Gilad-Bachrach, R., Laine, K., Lauter, K., Naehrig, M., Wernsing, J.: CryptoNets: applying neural networks to encrypted data with high throughput and accuracy. In: 33rd International Conference on Machine Learning (ICML 2016). Proceedings of Machine Learning Research, vol. 48, pp. 201–210. PMLR (2016)

13. Ducas, L., Micciancio, D.: FHEW: bootstrapping homomorphic encryption in less than a second. In: Oswald, E., Fischlin, M. (eds.) EUROCRYPT 2015. LNCS, vol. 9056, pp. 617–640. Springer, Heidelberg (2015). https://doi.org/10.1007/978-3-662-46800-5_24

14. The EU General Data Protection Regulation (GDPR). https://eur-lex.europa.eu/legal-content/EN/TXT/HTML/?uri=CELEX:32016R0679&from=EN

15. Gentry, C.: Computing arbitrary functions of encrypted data. Commun. ACM **53**(3), 97–105 (2010). Earlier version in STOC 2009

16. Gentry, C., Sahai, A., Waters, B.: Homomorphic encryption from learning with errors: conceptually-simpler, asymptotically-faster, attribute-based. In: Canetti, R., Garay, J.A. (eds.) CRYPTO 2013. LNCS, vol. 8042, pp. 75–92. Springer, Heidelberg (2013). https://doi.org/10.1007/978-3-642-40041-4_5

17. iDASH secure genome analysis competition. http://www.humangenomeprivacy.org

18. Kim, M., et al.: Ultra-fast homomorphic encryption models enable secure outsourcing of genotype imputation. bioXxiv (2020)

19. Kim, M., Song, Y., Li, B., Micciancio, D.: Semi-parallel logistic regression for GWAS on encrypted data. Cryptology ePrint Archive, Report 2019/294 (2019)

20. Langlois, A., Stehlé, D.: Worst-case to average-case reductions for module lattices. Des. Codes Crypt. **75**(3), 565–599 (2014). https://doi.org/10.1007/s10623-014-9938-4

21. LeCun, Y., Cortez, C., Burges, C.C.J.: The MNIST database of handwritten digits. http://yann.lecun.com/exdb/mnist/

22. Lyubashevsky, V., Peikert, C., Regev, O.: On ideal lattices and learning with errors over rings. J. ACM **60**(6), 43:1–43:35 (2013). Earlier version in EUROCRYPT 2010

23. Micciancio, D., Peikert, C.: Trapdoors for lattices: simpler, tighter, faster, smaller. In: Pointcheval, D., Johansson, T. (eds.) EUROCRYPT 2012. LNCS, vol. 7237, pp. 700–718. Springer, Heidelberg (2012). https://doi.org/10.1007/978-3-642-29011-4_41

24. ONNX Runtime: Optimize and accelerate machine learning inferencing and training. https://microsoft.github.io/onnxruntime/index.html

25. Regev, O.: On lattices, learning with errors, random linear codes, and cryptography. J. ACM **56**(6), 34:1–34:40 (2009). Earlier version in STOC 2005

26. Rivest, R.L., Adleman, L., Detouzos, M.L.: On data banks and privacy homomorphisms. In: Foundations of Secure Computation, pp. 165–179. Academic Press (1978)

27. Stehlé, D., Steinfeld, R., Tanaka, K., Xagawa, K.: Efficient public key encryption based on ideal lattices. In: Matsui, M. (ed.) ASIACRYPT 2009. LNCS, vol. 5912, pp. 617–635. Springer, Heidelberg (2009). https://doi.org/10.1007/978-3-642-10366-7_36

Adversaries Strike Hard: Adversarial Attacks Against Malware Classifiers Using Dynamic API Calls as Features

Hariom, Anand Handa$^{(\boxtimes)}$, Nitesh Kumar, and Sandeep Kumar Shukla

C3i Center, Department of CSE, Indian Institute of Technology Kanpur,
Kanpur, India
{hariom,ahanda,niteshkr,sandeeps}@cse.iitk.ac.in

Abstract. Malware designers have become increasingly sophisticated over time, crafting polymorphic and metamorphic malware employing obfuscation tricks such as packing and encryption to evade signature-based malware detection systems. Therefore, security professionals use machine learning-based systems to toughen their defenses – based on malware's dynamic behavioral features. However, these systems are susceptible to adversarial inputs. Some malware designers exploit this vulnerability to bypass detection. In this work, we develop two approaches to evade machine learning-based classifiers. First, we create a Generative Adversarial Networks (GAN) based method, which we call 'Malware Evasion using GAN' (MEGAN) and the extended version 'Malware Evasion using GAN with Reduced Perturbation (MEGAN-RP).' Second, we develop a novel reinforcement learning-based approach called 'Malware Evasion using Reinforcement Agent (MERA).' We generate adversarial malware that simultaneously minimizes the recall of a target classifier and the amount of perturbation needed in the actual malware to evade detection. We evaluate our work against 13 different BlackBox detection models – all of which use dynamic presence-absence of API calls as features. We observe that our approaches reduce the recall of almost all BlackBox models to zero. Further, MERA outperforms all the other models and reduces True Positive Rate (TPR) to zero against all target models except the Decision Tree (DT) – with minimum perturbation in 6 out of 13 target models. We also present experimental results on adversarial retraining defense and its evasion for GAN based strategies.

Keywords: Adversarial machine learning · Evasion attacks · API call sequence · Dynamic analysis

1 Introduction

The AV-TEST [2] report shows that over $350K$ new malicious programs (malware) and Potentially Unwanted Applications (PUAs) are registered every day.

Partially Supported by SERB, Government of India.

S. Dolev et al. (Eds.): CSCML 2021, LNCS 12716, pp. 20–37, 2021.
https://doi.org/10.1007/978-3-030-78086-9_2

As the malware are evolving every day, signature-based threat detection and mitigation are no longer fully effective. Signatures detect known threats, but with more than 100K new unknown variants striking every day, using signatures is no longer sufficient. Modern malware employs many techniques to evade detection. Malware creators use packers and smart coding methods like metamorphism and polymorphism, making it even harder for anti-virus programs to match the signatures and quarantine the file.

Zeus [24] is an example of automated mutation engines that changed malware features such as filenames or hashes and modified their code after each execution to evade detection by signature-based methods. In 2017, 97% of new malware samples used polymorphic techniques [34] thereby evading detection by signature-based tools.

Security professionals are now developing machine learning-based intrusion or malware detection systems to circumvent the problems faced by signature-based tools. They train models to learn static features extracted from executable or dynamic features obtained by observing behavior while executing malware within a sandbox. Static features are obtained without executing the binary and include API import list, different section names, the SUID bit, etc. Static feature-based classifiers do not always perform well against polymorphic and metamorphic viruses, as most of the binary is densely packed and encrypted. Dynamic features of a binary file include API call sequences, network capture, memory footprint, etc. Dynamic features based classifiers overcome the limitations of the static analysis based classifiers. However, machine learning classifiers' susceptibility to adversarial attacks is a well-known issue in which an adversary trains a machine learning model to modify a malware so that the classifier misclassifies the malware as benign.

In this paper, we present an extension of our previous work [12] where we showed how to generate adversarial malware from an existing one – without changing the functionality while evading any classifier that uses API call sequences as features. However, in [12], we did not impose any constraint on the number of perturbations made to the original binary keeping the functionality intact. The main goal was to evade the machine learning classifiers. However, more perturbations lead to an enlarged size of the binary, limiting its use as payload in many scenarios. In this work, we take a different approach and also minimize the perturbations while generating adversarial malware. The main contributions of this work are as follows:

– **Using GAN and Reinforcement learning to generate adversarial PE malware automatically** - We demonstrate using GAN (Generative Adversarial Network) and a novel approach using RL (Reinforcement Learning) to systematically and automatically craft PE32 malware capable of evading detection by API call presence-absence based classifiers with minimal modification.

- **Develop methods for minimizing the perturbation in the original malware while generating adversarial malware** - Modifying a malware is a complicated and tricky task as there is generally a constraint on the amount of perturbation possible in any malware file to keep its malicious behavior intact. Our method improves against previous work by minimizing the amount of perturbation required to generate the adversarial malware.
- **Demonstration of technique to limit modifications only to modifiable features** – In reality, every malware, whether PE32 or not, is associated with a list of modifiable and non-modifiable features. Our RL method limits the modifications to a particular set of modifiable features.
- **Evaluation of our techniques against previous work** – We compare and contrast the results of previous work MALGAN [17]. We propose improved evasion techniques MEGAN-RP and RL based approach MERA.
- A test framework to evaluate the performance of malware classifiers in the presence of adversarial samples.

The rest of the paper is organized as follows: In Sect. 2, we describe our problem statement. We explain adversarial learning background with defenses against adversarial attacks in Sect. 3. Section 4 describes related work. In Sect. 5, we discuss the proposed method's design and implementation. Section 6 consists of our evaluation results and observations. Section 7 concludes the paper with ideas about possible future work and the scope of improvements.

2   Problem Statement

Let $\vec{M}$ be a set of feature vectors for a collection of malware and C be a trained malware classifier on dynamic API call presence or absence as binary features. Let each $\vec{m} \in \vec{M}$ be correctly classified by C. We have to propose a systematic approach to generate a set of adversarial malware features given by

$$\vec{M}' = \{\vec{m}' = \vec{m} + \vec{\delta} \mid C(\vec{m}') \neq C(\vec{m}) \ \forall \ \vec{m} \in \vec{M}\} \tag{1}$$

with minimal perturbation $|\vec{\delta}|_{l1}$ such that $\vec{\delta}$ corresponds to a feasible change in actual malware feature vector without changing the functionality of the original malware. The adversary can query C with input $\vec{x}$ for the label $C(\vec{x})$. The adversary has the list of API calls whose presence or absence are used as features in C.

3   Adversarial Learning Background

Researchers have shown that many machine learning models for data classification can be misled by crafting adversarial inputs in recent years. Adversarial inputs are specially crafted feature vectors by introducing a small change to a real input vector. The change does not affect the intrinsic nature of the information – but enough to misdirect the machine learning model towards misclassification.

Suppose the target is a binary classifier C. Adversary is capable of querying C for the label $C(\vec{x})$ for any input $\vec{x}$. Since labels do not contain any information about the underlying probability distribution of C, the adversary is weak. The output label $C(\vec{x})$ is the class index with the highest posterior probability. Let $C_i(\vec{x})$ be the ith component of the probability vector then the output is expressed as:

$$C(\vec{x}) = \underset{i \in \{0,1\}}{argmax} \; C_i(\vec{x}) \tag{2}$$

The goal of adversary is to produce a minimally modified vector $\vec{x}^*$ for input $\vec{x}$ such that:

$$\vec{x}^* = \vec{x} + arg \; min_{|\vec{z}|_{l_1}} \{\vec{z} : C(\vec{x} + \vec{z}) \neq C(\vec{x})\} = \vec{x} + \delta_{\vec{x}} \tag{3}$$

Studies [20, 25] show that adversarial examples are used to fool the classifiers. Papernot et al. [28] consider an attacker who has access only to the output of the target model. The adversary has no information about the target model's internal parameters or architecture, such as the number of layers, type of layers, number of neurons in layers, and the training data used to train the target model. The attack is performed in a full BlackBox setting. The adversary generates a synthetic dataset and labels it by querying the labels from the target model. Due to adversarial examples' transferable characteristics, if the adversary crafts an adversarial example for a substitute model, the same adversarial sample may also be misclassified by the target model. They successfully craft adversarial examples for 84.24% samples. On further calibration, they achieve misclassification rates up to 97%.

Researchers also have been working on defenses to adversarial attacks. The most successful defenses are adversarial training and defensive distillation.

- **Adversarial training:** The intuition is if a model is misclassifying examples of particular distribution, add samples from that distribution to the model's training set. Suppose we generate many adversarial examples and train the target model on a combination of adversarial examples and original examples. In that case, the target model becomes robust to adversarial examples to some extent. However, this defense only works well against white-box attacks due to gradient masking [31]. Our work tests the robustness of this defense strategy in the field of malware classification.
- **Defensive distillation:** Papernot et al. [27] propose a knowledge distillation strategy as a defense against adversarial examples for image data sets. In this method, they train one model with the softmax layer as the output layer. The temperature of the softmax layer is kept high so that the distribution is smooth. The first model's probabilities are given as input to the second model and the same data set used to train the first model. The second model uses the value of temperature hyper-parameter for softmax layer as 1 for producing hard labels. This defense strategy is not used in this work.

4   Related Work

There is a lot of work in the field of adversarial learning for image [19], audio [33], text [10] and malware [1,13,17] data sets. However, generating adversarial examples for malware classifiers is different than image, speech, or text classifiers. Szegedy et al. [15] present an adversarial attack on GoogLeNet, which is trained on ImageNet. To generate an adversarial image, the authors add a small vector to an image input prepared using Fast Gradient Sign Method (FGSM). But even a small change in any PE binary file can make the file corrupt or non-functional or change its malicious functions. When generating adversarial malware, there is an additional constraint on the amount and type of perturbation added to the existing malware file. In addition to generating adversarial samples, we also need to preserve the malicious functionality in generated samples. Hence for the API call presence-absence-based feature set, we only consider changes that add additional API calls. These additions must be made so that they neither change the programs' original internal states nor do the additional API calls have any real effect on the program state.

Goodfellow et al. [14] first propose generative adversarial networks (GAN) in 2014. This framework is used to generate artificial training samples. They iteratively train a generative model G, which tries to learn real training data distribution. They iteratively train a discriminative model D, which estimates the probability that a sample is not fake, which G generates. The objective of training G is to mislead D into classifying fake as a real sample. The aim of training D is to resist getting misled. Initially, D properly distinguishes real from counterfeit, but after every iteration of training G, it gets worse at discerning real from fake. After each iteration, G gets better in generating samples to mislead the discriminator. This framework corresponds to a mini-max adversarial game. They show that a unique solution exists for arbitrary G and D. G eventually learns the distribution for real training data, and D can no longer distinguish real data from fake by more than the probability of a head in a coin toss, i.e., $\frac{1}{2}$. This entire system is trained with back-propagation if neural networks are used as generators and discriminators.

Hu et al. [17] propose a GAN based method to generate adversarial malware examples in a BlackBox setting called MALGAN. They use PE files in the data set consisting of a 160-dimensional binary vector based on system-level API calls. The target model is a trained BlackBox classifier oracle O. The adversary queries O for any sample input $\vec{x}$ to get the label $O(\vec{x})$. The discriminator is trained to mimic the characteristics of the target model O. A generative network is trained to minimize the substitute detector's malicious probabilities for generated adversarial examples. The authors reduce the TPR of machine learning models for adversarial examples to 0.16%, while the original BlackBox had a TPR of 93% for initial samples. They also show that the adversarial training defense performs inadequately against their attack. Even after MALGAN is retrained, it again reduces TPR to almost zero for BlackBox models used in their work. Perturbation using MALGAN is restricted to adding new API calls only. This work successfully creates adversarial malware but does not quantify the amount of perturbation added to the binaries. Since there is no constraint on the amount of perturbation; as a result, a malware with 40 API calls can end up with extra 150 API calls in its adversarial form. Our work overcomes this limitation by putting a penalty on the amount of perturbation. Our work ensures that a generated adversarial malware functionality preserving and as little different in size and features from the original.

Mnih et al. [23] introduce the first deep Q-learning model to learn control policies directly from high-dimensional sensory input using reinforcement learning.

Fang et al. [13] propose a reinforcement learning framework named DQEAF (Deep Q-network to Evade Antimalware engines Framework). Binary features extracted from raw bytes of PE files are fed as input to the target classifier. The agent's list of valid actions includes appending random bytes to the end of the PE file, appending a random library with random functions to the IAT, appending a random section to the section table, and removing a signature from the certificate table of the Data Directory. They achieve an evasion rate ranging from 17.5% to 75% for different malware families. Other studies using RL like Anderson et al. [1] work also use a similar approach; raw sequences of bytes are converted to input vector using hashing trick. Their method also fails to preserve the functionality of malware files in some cases. Mnih et al. [23] introduce the first deep Q-learning model to learn control policies directly from high-dimensional sensory input using reinforcement learning.

Among these previous work, we observe that Hu et al. [17] approach MAL-GAN has a hidden assumption that the adversary also knows the list of features used in the target BlackBox classifier. In our work, make this assumption explicit. In the past RL-based studies [1,13] use static features such as raw bytes of PE as input to the target classifier. Polymorphic and metamorphic programs with obfuscation can easily evade such classifiers. Modifying raw bytes of binary often fails to preserve functionality [1]. Also, these RL-based works lack promising results. Our DQN-based work MERA uses dynamic API calls as features for target models. None of the previous work in this field put any constraint on the amount of perturbation that is to be added to malware features. Our work MEGAN-RP and MERA minimizes the probability of detection by the target model while reducing the size of perturbation required to generate adversarial malware. Our work is the first study to use dynamic API call presence as features and generate adversarial malware using Reinforcement Learning to the best of our knowledge.

5   Design and Implementation

In this work, we implement adversarial attack strategies against 13 different malware classifiers as target models that use a list of dynamic system-level API calls extracted during samples' execution as features. We present two different GAN and RL-based approaches – MEGAN, MEGAN-RP, and MERA to achieve the same objective. We assume a target model as a BlackBox. The only knowledge about the target model that the adversary has is a list of API calls used by the models. However, the adversary does not know the learning algorithms and the internal parameters of the target model. We train a substitute detector that tries to mimic the target model. Suppose the ground truth labels of the substitute detector's training set input are the assigned labels queried from the target model. In that case, the substitute detector will try to mimic the target model. The substitute detector will encapsulate partial characteristics of the target model after sufficient training data is fed. Also, we get the probability of a sample being malware using a substitute detector. Figure 1 shows the key highlights of our previous and extended work. This section is subcategorized as follows.

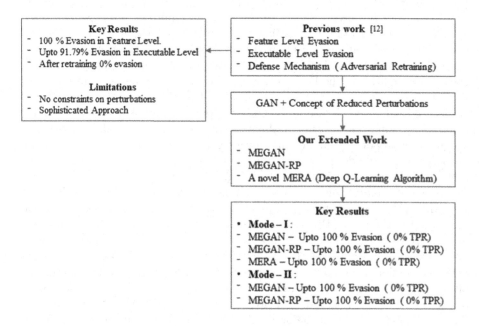

Fig. 1. Overview of our work

5.1 Data Set Collection and Features Extraction

We collect 43,902 PE files consisting of 27,655 malicious PE executable and 16,247 benign PE executable files from public sources like VirusShare [32] and Malwr [21]. Cuckoo sandbox [11] is set up on a system with 3.4 GHz Intel Core i7 processor, 32 GB RAM and 3 TB hard drive. We configure cuckoo to submit the sample for execution in a controlled environment. We extract the JSON file, which is generated after the sample's execution in the cuckoo sandbox. The JSON report contains information about the behavior of the analysed executable. Three parallel instances of Cuckoo Virtualized Windows 7 32-bit Environment are run to analyse execution for a duration of a maximum of 180 s each. The User

Account Control (UAC) and firewall are disabled in the snapshot to leave the machine susceptible to malware exploitation to the full extent. Each cuckoo VM is assigned 1 core and 4 GB RAM to evade sandbox environment checks by malware. All the generated JSON reports for malware and benign are put together in a folder. Then we parse each JSON report file using a python script and create a summarised custom JSON report file which looks like:

```
1  HANDLE  CreateFileA (
2  LPCSTR                 FileName,
3  DWORD                  DesiredAccess,
4  DWORD                  ShareMode,
5  LPSECURITY_ATTRIBUTES  SecurityAttributes,
6  DWORD                  CreationDisposition,
7  DWORD                  FlagsAndAttributes,
8  HANDLE                 TemplateFile
9  );
```

We traverse all custom JSON report files and extract the list of all invoked API calls **A**. The total number of invoked API calls is 327 in our data set. We randomly split the dataset into two equal parts, namely the BlackBox dataset ($BB_{dataset}$) and the GAN/RL dataset ($RL_{dataset}$) such that the ratio of malware to benign files remains the same in both parts. We further do a label-based $70\% - 30\%$ stratified split of $BB_{dataset}$ into BlackBox train dataset BB_{train} and BlackBox test dataset BB_{test}. We take a zero vector of length $len(A)$ and set the ith index of API denoted by $A[i]$ present in the report file. We fit a Random Forest [3] model on the entire BlackBox dataset to extract all API calls of importance. The adversary uses the same API calls irrespective of their importance in the GAN/RL training data set. We sort the features in non-increasing order of their importance and select the top 200 API calls for use as features throughout this study. The average number of API calls present per binary is approximately 64 API calls in our final data set.

5.2   Target BlackBox Models

We train 13 different classifiers namely Decision Tree (DT) [29], Logistic Regression (LR) [16], Gaussian Naive Bayes (GNB) [5], Linear Support Vector Classifier (LSVC) [8], RBF Support Vector Classifier (RBF-SVC) [9], Multilayer Perceptron (MLP) [30], Keras Neural Network (Keras) [18], Random Forest (RF), Bagging using DT (BAG) [4], Adaptive Boosting using DT (AdaB) [22], Gradient Boosting (GB) [6], eXtreme Gradient Boosting (XGB) [26] and Voting Classifier (Vote) [7]. The inputs for all the target models are 200 − dimensional binary vectors based on the most crucial system-level API calls present in the Black-Box dataset. The ratio of malware to benign PE files in the dataset is approx 3:2. Malware samples come from a variety of families including Backdoor, Virus, Trojan, PWS, Worm and Rootkit etc.

5.3   Malware Evasion Using GAN (MEGAN) and MEGAN with Reduced Perturbation (MEGAN-RP)

Our implementation MEGAN is similar to the existing approach MALGAN [17] with some modification, as we have already discussed in Sect. 4. MEGAN uses 200 API calls as features, but MALGAN uses only 160 API calls. MALGAN uses a small 20-dimensional noise vector that restricts the generator to generate adversarial examples of different types, so MEGAN overcomes this by using a 50-dimensional uniform noise vector. MALGAN uses no activation in hidden layers, which allows it to learn linear mappings only. Still, MEGAN uses Leaky Rectified Linear Unit (Leaky RELU) as an activation function with tuned hyper-parameter α to introduce non-linearity. Our study finds that MALGAN and MEGAN do not reduce the perturbation required to generate adversarial samples. We claim that MEGAN with Reduced Perturbation (MEGAN-RP) overcomes this shortcoming using a custom loss for training GAN given by the Eq. 4.

$$Loss_{GAN} = \sum_{i=1}^{B} BCE(y_{i_{true}}, y_{i_{pred}}) \times \frac{\sum_{i=1}^{B}\sum_{j=1}^{200} o_{ij}}{\sum_{i=1}^{B}\sum_{j=1}^{200} x_{ij}} \tag{4}$$

where, **BCE** is Binary Cross Entropy, **B** is Batch Size *(Default 128)*, $\mathbf{y_{i_{true}}}$ is ground truth label for sample $\vec{x}_i$, $\mathbf{y_{i_{pred}}}$ is predicted label for sample $\vec{x}_i$, $\mathbf{x_{ij}}$ is value of jth feature of sample $\vec{x}_i$, and $\mathbf{o_{ij}}$ is value of jth feature of generator output $\vec{o}_i$.

MEGAN-RP is an extension of MEGAN, which minimizes the required perturbation for malware to get an adversarial sample. We do not add any extra custom loss layer, so there are no changes in the GAN's trainable parameters. We keep almost the same neural network architecture for both MALGAN and MEGAN-RP, except the activation functions in the hidden layer. In the case of MALGAN, the activation function used by the last layer is sigmoid, whereas, in our work, we use ReLu as an activation function. So we properly compare both approaches and validate our claim that MEGAN-RP is better at simultaneously minimizing both TPR and the required perturbation for adversarial examples than MALGAN.

As mentioned in our problem statement, we need to ensure any change in the feature vector to generate an adversarial feature vector, which must correspond to a possible change in the actual PE binary file, which also preserves the PE file's malicious functionality. Towards that objective, we know that the highest layer in Keras does an element-wise max operation between two tensors. Also, it does not cause any issues with gradient backpropagation. The use of the Sigmoid layer and malware sample batch $\vec{X}$ as input to the last maximum layer of generator ensures that the output batch of generator $\vec{O}$ contains real-valued vectors with values ranging from [0,1]. Furthermore, all the features which are present in malware input $\vec{x}_i \in \vec{X}$ will be present in the adversarial output $\vec{o}_i \in \vec{O}$. Thus we adhere to the restriction of additive modification only. The generated output batch and a fresh batch of benign samples are fed to the discriminator with labels obtained by queries from the target model. This helps the discriminator to mimic the behavior of the target model. The generated output batch is still a collection of real-valued vectors. To extract the final binary adversarial output, we round off the values of features in the vector. We use Adam optimizer with a learning rate of 0.001 in all neural network models. Binary cross entropy is the loss function used in the generator and discriminator of MALGAN and MEGAN-RP. For MEGAN-RP, binary cross-entropy is used as the discriminator loss function, and a custom loss function defined by Eq. 4 is used for the generator. The idea behind this loss function is that the number of present APIs in the input batch $\vec{X}$ should be close to the number of present APIs in the output batch $\vec{O}$. We know that the ratio of the sum of the values of the generated real-valued adversarial output batch $\vec{O}$ to the sum of the values of input batch $\vec{X}$ denoted by Ω will always be greater than or equal to 1. If *perturbation* $\longrightarrow 0$ then $\Omega \longrightarrow 1$ i.e. *Custom Loss* $\longrightarrow BCE$. We scale the Binary cross-entropy loss for an entire batch by Ω. To minimize the total loss, GAN will try to minimize BCE and Ω simultaneously. The Algorithm 1 describes the whole process of MEGAN and MEGAN-RP training. This algorithm is based upon MALGAN work.

Algorithm 1: Training MEGAN and MEGAN-RP

---

1 **while** *not converged* **do**
2   Sample two batches of malware $\mathbf{M_1}$ and $\mathbf{M_2}$ from $GAN_{dataset}$;
3   Generate two batches of noise $\mathbf{Z_1} \sim uniform_{[0,1)}$ and
      $\mathbf{Z_2} \sim uniform_{[0,1)}$;
4   Generate adversarial examples $\mathbf{M'_1}$ from the generator for $[\mathbf{M_1}, \mathbf{Z_1}]$;
5   Sample a minibatch of benignware $\mathbf{B}$ from $GAN_{dataset}$;
6   Label $\mathbf{M'_1}$ and $\mathbf{B}$ using the target BlackBox detector and feed this to
      discriminator;
7   Update the discriminator's weights $\theta_{\mathbf{d}}$ by descending along the
      gradient $\nabla_{\theta_d} L_D$;
8   Label $[\mathbf{M_2}, \mathbf{Z_2}]$ as BENIGN and feed this into generator input to train
      GAN;
9   Update the generator's weights $\theta_{\mathbf{g}}$ by descending along the gradient
      $\nabla_{\theta_g} L_G$;
10 **end**

5.4 Malware Evasion Using Reinforcement Agents

We propose a novel framework named Malware Evasion using Reinforcement Agents (MERA), which uses deep Q-Learning to generate adversarial malware. The target BlackBox classifiers are the same classifiers we used for MALGAN, MEGAN, and MEGAN-RP. The threat model is the same for GAN based models and MERA. The dataset division is also the same except we now refer to $GAN_{dataset}$ as $RL_{dataset}$. RL involves making random as well as informed decisions using a trained agent. We generate adversarial examples using a trained agent and an untrained agent to compare MERA-Trained effectiveness with MERA-Random. Reinforcement learning (RL) is an area of machine learning that focuses on training software agents to take actions in an interactive environment to maximize a cumulative reward conception. The agents learn by trial and error. Rewards and penalties control the behavior of learning in response to an action.

Adversarial Malware Generation as Deep Q-Learning Problem. Formally a reinforcement learning problem is expressed by a 5-tuple given by

RL Problem : (*State, Action, Reward, Transition Dynamics, Discount Factor*)

We formulate the task of adversarial malware generation as a Deep Q-Learning problem in the following way:

- **Assumption:** We have a substitute classifier C, which uses binary feature vector of system-level API calls and can give the probability of a sample $\vec{x}$ being malware.
- **$C(\vec{x})$** : Probability of sample $\vec{x}$ being malware.
- **Agent:** Agents are functions that take the next action after interpreting the reward for reaching the current state. The model we train is the agent.
- **State(S_t):** The state of a malware sample $\vec{x}$ is the current binary feature vector of API calls $\vec{x'}$ obtained after modifications to original malware $\vec{x}$ by taking actions. The indices of S_t, which are equal to 1, correspond to API calls present in malware's current state. We keep taking action until the current state of malware is classified as benign by the target BlackBox model.
- **Action(A_t):** An integer denoting the best possible API call to include in current state. All possible actions include API calls indices that can be set in the current malware state feature vector S_t. Our work uses 200 API calls as features, so $A_t \in [0, 200)$.
- **Next state(S_{t+1}):** State obtained by setting index A_t in S_t to 1 i.e. Do $S_t[A_t] = 1$. Clearly each step adds one API call to the current state of malware in hopes of making it benign.
- **Reward(R_{t+1}):** A reward is a feedback from the environment to an agent as interpretation for quality of action A_t in current state S_t. A high positive reward means the action was good, and a high negative reward means the action was bad. Suppose a vital component of the reward function is the difference in the probability of a current state being malware and the probability of the next state being malware. In that case, the agent will favor actions that lead to states and actions that minimize the current state's probability of fetching positive rewards. As the probabilities are very small, we scale this by a large number $\alpha = 100$. We also put a penalty on the number of actions taken to reach the goal state. This ensures the generation of adversarial samples with reduced perturbation. The final reward function can be expressed as:

$$R_{t+1} = \alpha(C(S_t) - C(S_{t+1})) - \frac{\sum\limits_{i=1}^{200} S_{t_i}}{\sum\limits_{i=1}^{200} x_i} \tag{5}$$

- **Transition Dynamics:** The transition function constitute a mapping between action taken in a particular state to the resulting state i.e. $\delta(S_t, A_t) \longrightarrow S_{t+1}$
- **Discount Factor**(γ)**:** Discount factor $\gamma \in [0,1)$ is a value that specifies the importance of the future rewards. A discount factor of 1 means the future rewards at any state is just as important as immediate rewards. After all, future rewards are just an estimation, so there is always an element of uncertainty. Hence we always keep $\gamma < 1$.
- **Q-value**$(Q_\pi(S_t, A_t))$**:** It is defined as maximum expected achievable reward if the agent takes an action A_t in current state S_t under a policy π. It is expressed as a combination of immediate reward and discounted future reward for the next state.

$$Q_\pi(S_t, A_t) = R_{t+1} + \gamma \max_{A_{t+1}} Q(S_{t+1}, A_{t+1}) \tag{6}$$

Training Substitute Detectors. We know that the adversary can only query a particular malware sample's label but not the probabilities assigned to each class to come up with the label. We need a substitute detector C such that $C(\vec{x})$ gives the probability of a sample $\vec{x}$ being malware as per our assumption in Sect. 5. We engineered the reward function given by Eq. 5 on top of this assumption. We separate the malware and benign portion of our $RL_{dataset}$ as $RL_{malware}$ and RL_{benign} respectively. We do a 60%–40% split of $RL_{malware}$ into $RL_{Substitute}$ and $RL_{Training}$ where $RL_{Training}$ is used to train RL agent for generating adversarial malware samples. We combine the $RL_{Substitute}$ and RL_{benign} samples and name it $C_{dataset}$. We again do a 85%–15% split of $C_{dataset}$ into C_{train} and $C_{validation}$ respectively. The training of substitute detector C should be such that the classification boundary learned by C should mimic the target model's behavior. For this purpose, we do not use the ground truth labels from dataset C_{train} and $C_{validation}$. Instead, we use the labels obtained from the target model. Since there are 13 target models, we train different substitute detectors for each of them. The substitute detector is a soft voting classifier using 3 base classifiers, which produce the highest validation TPR, namely Multilayer Perceptron (MLP), eXtreme Gradient Boosting (XGB), and Random Forest (RF).

Environment Preparation. We prepare a stochastic environment. The environment is responsible for laying the path for the agent. Our environment has many equally likely initial states. The set of possible initial states is the set of all the malware feature vectors from any dataset. For training the agent $S_{initial} \in RL_{malware}$ and during evaluation $S_{initial} \in BB_{test_{malware}}$. When the environment receives an action A_t in the current state S_t, it updates its current state by performing $S_t[A_t] = 1$, equivalent to adding one more API call to the current state. Internally, the environment fetches current and previous states' probabilities as malware from a substitute detector and calculates the reward function given by Eq. 5. According to the target model, the label for the current state decides the termination flag's value. The next state, reward, and termination flag are sent to the agent. After the end of an episode, the environment resets and returns to one of its initial states, i.e., a new random real malware is selected to learn. The observation dimension and the action dimension is equal to the number of API calls used as features. The termination flag is set if the current state is classified as benign by the target model, or no API call is left to add. Since we can set all the 200 indices in a feature vector if there is an adversarial sample for a malware input.

6   Evaluation Results

In this work, we use the BlackBox training and testing dataset for evaluation using the two metrics TPR (True Positive Rate) and Perturbation Percentage (Δ). TPR is also called the *recall* or *probability of detection*. A good target model should have a high true positive rate indicating it can detect most malware. Throughout this section, we denote the true positive rate percent using TPR. *Original TPR* refers to the TPR of the target model on real malware. *Adversarial TPR* refers to the TPR of the target model in the presence of adversarial examples and real samples. Perturbation Percentage (Δ) is the ratio of the number of extra API calls in the adversarial dataset to a total number of API calls in a real dataset as shown in Eq. 7.

$$\Delta = \frac{\sum_{i=1}^{n}\sum_{j=1}^{d} o_{ij} - \sum_{i=1}^{n}\sum_{j=1}^{d} x_{ij}}{\sum_{i=1}^{n}\sum_{j=1}^{d} x_{ij}} \times 100\% \tag{7}$$

The lower its value, the better the adversarial dataset. For an input malware feature matrix $\vec{X}_{n \times d}$ and the corresponding adversarial malware feature matrix $\vec{O}_{n \times d}$.

We first train our target models on the original BlackBox dataset and calculate original TPR for all the 13 target models. Table 1 shows the original train and test the TPR score for all the target BlackBox models.

Table 1. Original TPR for BlackBox target model

Model	Keras	MLP	LR	GNB	DT	RF	AdaBoost
Train TPR	100	94.73	89.93	87.08	100	100	89.44
Test TPR	93.62	92.39	90.32	87.85	89.66	93.93	90.27
Model	Grad Boost	XGrad Boost	Bagging	Linear SVC	RBF-SVC	Vote	-
Train TPR	91.8	97.73	99.04	89.74	92.95	95.81	-
Test TPR	92.12	93.27	91.95	90.18	91.99	93.31	-

where *MLP = Multilayer Perceptron, LR = Logistic Regression, GNB = Gaussian Naive Bayes,*
RF = Random Forest, AdaBoost = Adaptive Boosted, Grad Boost = Gradient Boosted,
XGrad Boost = eXtreme Gradient Boosted, Linear SVC = Linear Support Vector Classifier,
RBF-SVC = Radial Basis Function SVC, DT = Decision Tree, Vote = Hard Voting

For evaluating our approach MEGAN and MEGAN-RP, we perform experiments in two modes – mode-I and mode-II. In the first step, mode-I, we train GAN to generate adversarial examples and evade the target model trained using the original BlackBox dataset. In our previous work [12], we have proven adversarial retraining as a defense mechanism to protect the machine learning classifiers against such evasion. Hence, in mode-II, we retrain our target model on the combination of the original dataset and the corresponding adversarial dataset generated by GAN in mode-I. Also, in mode-II, we evade detection against adversarial retraining defense mechanism using the same GAN to generate adversarial examples putting a constraint on the number of perturbations for MEGAN and MEGAN-RP. To evaluate our novel approach MERA, we perform experiments only in mode -I. Though we perform experiments for mode-II, MERA fails to evade the defense mechanism. Hence, we didn't present the results and taken as a future directive.

Table 2. Experimental results for Mode-I

Target models	Train TPR, Test TPR				
	MALGAN	MEGAN	MEGAN-RP	MERA-Trained	MERA-Random
Keras DNN	0.02, 0.04	0.00, 0.00	0.00, 0.00	0.00, 0.00	0.00, 0.00
MLP	0.00, 0.00	0.00, 0.00	0.00, 0.00	0.00, 0.00	0.00, 0.00
LR	0.00, 0.00	0.00, 0.00	0.00, 0.04	0.00, 0.00	0.00, 0.00
GNB	0.00, 0.00	0.00, 0.00	0.00, 0.00	0.00, 0.00	0.00, 0.00
DT	51.10, 50.22	24.03, 20.64	46.77, 45.64	16.28, 15.58	21.72, 21.04
RF	0.00, 0.00	0.04, 0.04	3.38, 2.60	0.00, 0.00	0.00, 0.00
AdaBoost	0.00, 0.00	0.00, 0.00	0.02, 0.04	0.00, 0.00	0.00, 0.00
GradBoost	0.00, 0.00	0.30, 0.35	0.00, 0.00	0.00, 0.00	0.00, 0.00
XGB	0.02, 0.00	0.04, 0.00	0.00, 0.00	0.00, 0.00	0.00, 0.00
Bagging	1.06, 1.23	2.32, 2.11	2.55, 2.29	0.00, 0.00	0.00, 0.00
Linear SVC	0.00, 0.00	0.00, 0.00	0.00, 0.00	0.00, 0.00	0.00, 0.00
RBF SVC	0.00, 0.00	0.06, 0.04	0.02, 0.04	0.00, 0.00	0.00, 0.00
Vote	0.00, 0.00	0.06, 0.00	0.00, 0.00	0.00, 0.00	0.00, 0.00
Target models	Train Δ, Test Δ				
	MALGAN	MEGAN	MEGAN-RP	MERA-Trained	MERA-Random
Keras DNN	102.75, 106.38	101.62, 105.14	30.96, 31.75	48.00, 47.84	98.60, 99.81
MLP	76.11, 79.13	85.05, 88.24	41.40, 42.72	42.60, 44.55	84.73, 86.94
LR	101.07, 104.69	87.86, 91.09	25.32, 25.79	35.34, 36.80	78.26, 89.95
GNB	148.26, 153.12	132.15, 136.65	44.40, 45.66	9.27, 9.67	27.69, 28.72
DT	130.59, 134.81	71.95, 74.94	98.46, 101.90	51.28, 45.91	68.64, 62.77
RF	138.61, 143.14	125.58, 129.65	64.87, 67.39	90.14, 87.42	105.86, 103.19
AdaBoost	96.41, 99.88	92.05, 95.36	19.18, 19.80	32.92, 35.29	70.26, 76.67
GradBoost	80.70, 83.78	112.35, 116.34	73.62, 76.12	49.71, 50.68	85.90, 89.52
XGB	110.68, 114.43	116.13, 120.04	96.39, 99.77	75.17, 74.30	100.71, 100.85
Bagging	128.76, 133.00	96.75, 100.18	51.92, 53.62	35.40, 32.40	53.32, 51.25
Linear SVC	90.55, 93.98	90.97, 94.08	29.28, 29.94	37.42, 39.07	61.53, 62.43
RBF SVC	89.33, 92.66	81.38, 84.37	52.71, 54.70	86.61, 87.86	114.61, 117.97
Vote	94.23, 97.79	83.18, 86.22	61.52, 63.51	53.23, 53.11	88.48, 89.77

Table 2 shows the experimental results for mode-I. From Table 2, we observe that in the mode-I experiment, when the target model is trained using the original dataset for Keras, MLP, LR, RF, AdaBoost, Linear SVC, RBF SVC, and hard voting classifiers, MEGAN-RP outperforms MERA-Trained and MALGAN in perturbation percentage on BlackBox training and testing set. MEGAN-RP and MERA-Trained produce comparable results for these eight classifiers. For GNB, GradBoost, XGB, and Bagging classifiers MERA-Trained outperforms MEGAN-RP and MALGAN in perturbation percentage on BlackBox training and testing set. None of the models can reduce TPR to zero in the DT classifier, i.e., DT Black-Box is harder to fool. However, MERA-Trained and MERA-Random are implemented so that TPR must reduce to zero even with high perturbation because they can add all possible API calls to make the malware benign if needed. Non-zero TPR for MERA models implies that some malware remains malware in any modified state. According to DT, certain API calls indices, which, if set, make the sample malware regardless of other features' presence or absence.

Table 3. New adversarial TPR after retraining BlackBox target model

Model	Train TPR			Test TPR		
	MALGAN	MEGAN	MEGAN-RP	MALGAN	MEGAN	MEGAN-RP
Keras	100	99.98	100	100	100	100
MLP	100	100	100	99.96	99.91	100
LR	99.92	99.77	99.97	99.96	99.69	99.97
DT	100	100	100	100	100	100
RF	100	100	100	100	100	100
Adaboost	99.98	99.96	99.94	99.91	99.96	99.87
XGB	100	100	100	100	100	100
Bagging	100	100	100	100	100	100
Linear SVC	99.77	99.87	99.79	99.87	99.78	99.69
GNB	100	100	100	100	100	100
GradBoost	100	100	100	100	100	100
RBF SVC	100	100	100	99.87	100	100
Vote	100	100	100	100	100	100

The target BlackBox applies adversarial training defense against trained GAN. So we retrain target classifiers with the help of combining the original BlackBox dataset and adversarial examples dataset generated during the mode-I experiment. Table 3 shows the adversarial TPR for the retrained target models. We experiment with mode-II by retraining the GAN to bypass the Adversarial defense strategy of BlackBox.

Table 4 shows the experimental results for the mode-II phase. From Table 4, we observe that in Keras, MLP, LR, GNB, AdaBoost, Bagging, Linear SVC,

RBF SVC, and hard voting classifiers, all three GANs can defeat adversarial training defense with MEGAN outperforming the other two. For the DT classifier, none of the three GANs can defeat adversarial training defense with much success. In the RF classifier, MEGAN trades off TPR with perturbation and beats adversarial training defense to a great extent. For GradBoost classifier MalGAN and MEGAN defeat adversarial training defense, whereas MEGAN-RP reduces the TPR to approximately 50% in adversarial defense mode. In XGB classifier MALGAN and MEGAN defeat adversarial training defense.

Table 4. Experimental results for Mode-II

Target models	Train TPR, Test TPR			Train Δ, Test Δ		
	MALGAN	MEGAN	MEGAN-RP	MALGAN	MEGAN	MEGAN-RP
Keras DNN	1.06, 1.54	3.25, 2.82	0.00, 0.00	74.56, 76.77	50.62, 52.52	69.53, 71.55
MLP	0.00, 0.00	0.00, 0.00	0.00, 0.00	119.57, 123.47	73.95, 76.30	91.77, 94.74
LR	0.85, 0.66	0.21, 0.09	0.02, 0.00	90.17, 93.32	40.75, 42.02	55.76, 57.58
GNB	19.36, 17.08	18.68, 16.77	5.35, 5.37	54.56, 56.65	87.35, 90.45	1.54, 1.58
DT	95.11, 95.47	50.51, 48.64	71.84, 70.33	72.42, 75.05	99.44, 102.69	71.92, 74.34
RF	0.00, 0.00	15.02, 14.61	57.41, 54.45	119.37, 123.63	105.08, 108.96	76.94, 79.47
AdaBoost	0.00, 0.04	0.04, 0.00	0.04, 0.00	95.71, 98.77	94.09, 97.26	22.23, 22.79
GradBoost	0.02, 0.00	8.63, 7.00	50.47, 49.52	110.64, 114.44	51.42, 53.48	22.85, 23.53
XGB	0.70, 0.84	16.06, 13.60	84.11, 80.55	126.82, 131.02	75.67, 78.07	9.52, 9.75
Bagging	3.00, 3.30	25.58, 23.72	2.17, 2.64	80.68, 83.54	88.73, 91.89	49.76, 51.41
Linear SVC	0.00, 0.00	0.04, 0.00	0.00, 0.00	98.65, 101.99	93.43, 96.71	53.15, 54.16
RBF SVC	0.24, 0.31	0.04, 0.04	0.04, 0.04	90.82, 93.85	56.11, 57.88	27.99, 28.41
Vote	0.02, 0.00	0.02, 0.00	1.55, 1.54	102.93, 106.14	75.72, 78.12	20.10, 20.32

The overall observations from the evaluation of mode-I and mode-II experiments are that all strategies reduce the TPR of the target model to almost zero except for the Decision Tree. MEGAN outperforms MALGAN in 8 out of 13 and produces comparable results in 3 out of 13 target BlackBox classifiers. MERA-Random never beats MERA-Trained on any metric, which implies that the RL agent is successfully exploiting the collected experiences. MEGAN-RP outperforms all other strategies for 6 out of 13 target BlackBox classifiers, so MEGAN-RP is the best among GAN-based strategy. MERA-Trained beats all other strategies for 6 and comparable to MEGAN-RP in 1 (MLP) out of the 13 target BlackBox model, so MERA-Trained is the best strategy. All the strategies applied in mode-II experiments successfully defeat adversarial training defense by BlackBox for 9 out of 13 target BlackBox classifiers, so we infer that adversarial training defense is not foolproof.

7 Conclusion and Future Work

This work investigates five (MALGAN, MEGAN, MEGAN-RP, MERA-Trained, and MERA-Random) different attack strategies against 13 BlackBox classifiers.

All methods successfully generate adversarial malware, and we propose changes in MALGAN to include the idea of minimal perturbation works. Our MEGAN-RP approach with proposed changes works best among all GAN models. Also, we suggest a novel deep Q-Learning based approach MERA performs as good as existing state-of-the-art MEGAN-RP. Our work starts with malware analysis and ends at adversarial malware feature generation. Our future work includes converting these features back to malware using the idea of IAT hooking. Using a partially overlapping set of features between BlackBox and GAN/RL training, Reinforcement Learning-based approach to fool API sequence-based BlackBox classifiers. This work demonstrates that a large class of machine learning malware classifiers based on API call sequences are not effective against adversarial attacks.

References

1. Anderson, H.S., Kharkar, A., Filar, B., Evans, D., Roth, P.: Learning to evade static PE machine learning malware models via reinforcement learning. CoRR abs/1801.08917 (2018). http://arxiv.org/abs/1801.08917
2. AVTest: AV-Test Institute Statistics of Malware (2020). https://www.av-test.org/en/statistics/malware/. Accessed 21 May
3. Breiman, L.: Random forests. Mach. Learn. **45**(1), 5–32 (2001)
4. scikit-learn developers (BSD License): Bootstrap Aggregating Decision Tree (2019). https://scikit-learn.org/stable/modules/generated/sklearn.ensemble.BaggingClassifier.html#sklearn.ensemble.BaggingClassifier
5. scikit-learn developers (BSD License): Gaussian Naive Bayes (2019). https://scikit-learn.org/stable/modules/generated/sklearn.naive_bayes.GaussianNB.html
6. scikit-learn developers (BSD License): Gradient Boosting Classifier (2019). https://scikit-learn.org/stable/modules/generated/sklearn.ensemble.GradientBoostingClassifier.html
7. scikit-learn developers (BSD License): Hard Voting (2019). https://scikit-learn.org/stable/modules/generated/sklearn.ensemble.VotingClassifier.html
8. scikit-learn developers (BSD License): Linear SVC (2019). https://scikit-learn.org/stable/modules/generated/sklearn.svm.LinearSVC.html
9. scikit-learn developers (BSD License): RBF SVC (2019). https://scikit-learn.org/stable/auto_examples/svm/plot_rbf_parameters.html
10. Cheng, M., Yi, J., Chen, P.Y., Zhang, H., Hsieh, C.J.: Seq2Sick: Evaluating the Robustness of Sequence-to-Sequence Models with Adversarial Examples (2018)
11. Cuckoo: Cuckoo Sandbox Architecture (2020). https://cuckoo.sh/docs. Accessed 10 June
12. Fadadu, F., Handa, A., Kumar, N., Shukla, S.K.: Evading API call sequence based malware classifiers. In: Zhou, J., Luo, X., Shen, Q., Xu, Z. (eds.) ICICS 2019. LNCS, vol. 11999, pp. 18–33. Springer, Cham (2020). https://doi.org/10.1007/978-3-030-41579-2_2
13. Fang, Z., Wang, J., Li, B., Wu, S., Zhou, Y., Huang, H.: Evading anti-malware engines with deep reinforcement learning. IEEE Access **7**, 48867–48879 (2019)
14. Goodfellow, I., et al.: Generative adversarial nets. In: Advances in Neural Information Processing Systems, pp. 2672–2680 (2014)
15. Goodfellow, I.J., Shlens, J., Szegedy, C.: Explaining and Harnessing Adversarial Examples. arXiv stat.ML eprint 1412.6572 (2014)

16. Hosmer Jr., D.W., Lemeshow, S., Sturdivant, R.X.: Applied Logistic Regression, vol. 398. Wiley, Hoboken (2013)
17. Hu, W., Tan, Y.: Generating Adversarial Malware Examples for Black-Box Attacks Based on GAN. arXiv preprint arXiv:1702.05983 (2017)
18. Keras: Keras Library (2020). https://www.keras.io. Accessed 10 June
19. Kurakin, A., Goodfellow, I., Bengio, S.: Adversarial Machine Learning at Scale. arXiv cs.CV eprint 1611.01236 (2016)
20. Liu, Y., Chen, X., Liu, C., Song, D.: Delving into Transferable Adversarial Examples and Black-box Attacks. arXiv cs.LG eprint 1611.02770 (2016)
21. Malwr: Malware Dataset Repository (2019). https://www.malwr.ee. Accessed 27 Dec
22. Margineantu, D.D., Dietterich, T.G.: Pruning adaptive boosting. In: ICML, vol. 97, pp. 211–218. Citeseer (1997)
23. Mnih, V., et al.: Playing Atari with Deep Reinforcement Learning. arXiv cs.LG eprint 1312.5602 (2013)
24. Mohaisen, A., Alrawi, O.: Unveiling zeus: automated classification of malware samples. In: Proceedings of the 22nd International Conference on World Wide Web, pp. 829–832 (2013)
25. Moosavi-Dezfooli, S.M., Fawzi, A., Fawzi, O., Frossard, P.: Universal Adversarial Perturbations. arXiv cs.CV eprint 1610.08401 (2016)
26. Nishida, K.: Extreme Gradient Boosting Classifier (2019). https://blog. exploratory.io/introduction-to-extreme-gradient-boosting-in-exploratory-7bbec55 4ac7
27. Papernot, N., McDaniel, P., Wu, X., Jha, S., Swami, A.: Distillation as a defense to adversarial perturbations against deep neural networks. In: 2016 IEEE Symposium on Security and Privacy (SP), pp. 582–597 (2016)
28. Papernot, N., McDaniel, P., Goodfellow, I., Jha, S., Celik, Z.B., Swami, A.: Practical black-box attacks against machine learning. In: Proceedings of the 2017 ACM on Asia Conference on Computer and Communications Security (2017). https:// doi.org/10.1145/3052973.3053009
29. Quinlan, R.: C4.5: Programs for Machine Learning. Morgan Kaufmann Publishers, San Mateo (1993)
30. Ruck, D.W., Rogers, S.K., Kabrisky, M., Oxley, M.E., Suter, B.W.: The multilayer perceptron as an approximation to a Bayes optimal discriminant function. IEEE Trans. Neural Netw. 1(4), 296–298 (1990)
31. Tramèr, F., Kurakin, A., Papernot, N., Goodfellow, I., Boneh, D., McDaniel, P.: Ensemble Adversarial Training: Attacks and Defenses. arXiv stat.ML eprint 1705.07204 (2017)
32. Virusshare: Malware Dataset Repository (2020). https://www.virusshare.com. Accessed 5 Jan
33. Wang, R., et al.: DeepSonar: Towards Effective and Robust Detection of AI-Synthesized Fake Voices (2020)
34. Webroot: Webroot Threat Brief (2016). https://webroot-cms-cdn.s3.amazonaws. com/7814/5617/2382/Webroot-2016-Threat-Brief.pdf. Accessed 21 May

Privacy-Preserving Coupling of Vertically-Partitioned Databases and Subsequent Training with Gradient Descent

Thijs Veugen[1,2]([⊠]), Bart Kamphorst[1], Natasja van de L'Isle[3], and Marie Beth van Egmond[1]

[1] TNO, The Hague, The Netherlands
thijs.veugen@tno.nl
[2] Centrum Wiskunde & Informatica, Amsterdam, The Netherlands
[3] TMC Data Science, Eindhoven, The Netherlands

Abstract. We show how multiple data-owning parties can collaboratively train several machine learning algorithms without jeopardizing the privacy of their sensitive data. In particular, we assume that every party knows specific features of an overlapping set of people. Using a secure implementation of an advanced hidden set intersection protocol and a privacy-preserving Gradient Descent algorithm, we are able to train a Ridge, LASSO or SVM model over the intersection of people in their data sets. Both the hidden set intersection protocol and privacy-preserving LASSO implementation are unprecedented in literature.

Keywords: Secure multi-party computation · Secure set intersection · Gradient descent · Privacy-preserving LASSO regression

1 Introduction

Over the last two decades, the data mining community has seen a rapid growth in the use of privacy-preserving approaches to a wide range of machine learning problems including association rule mining [19,40], clustering [18,22,37], classification [10,38,39,42] and regression [20,29] problems. In this article, we concentrate on the training phase of classification and regression models and investigate the setting where sensitive data is partitioned over multiple parties.

In particular, we implemented the Gradient Descent approach with a secure multi-party computation (MPC) platform, yielding a secure and flexible solution, suitable for various machine learning algorithms. Federated machine learning has proven successful for certain machine learning methods in case of

© Springer Nature Switzerland AG 2021
S. Dolev et al. (Eds.): CSCML 2021, LNCS 12716, pp. 38–51, 2021.
https://doi.org/10.1007/978-3-030-78086-9_3

horizontally-partitioned data[1], but a secure method like MPC is especially needed in case the data is vertically partitioned.

Although most known privacy-preserving solutions assume horizontally- partitioned data, in several domains it is very common for the data to be vertically partitioned. For example in the health domain, where many different organisations collect data on patients during their patient life cycle. Think of hospitals, pharmacies, general practitioners, health care providers, and many different medical specialists. Analysing these vertically-distributed medical data is important for improving health care, estimating the effect of medication, etc.

We propose a two-step approach. In the first step, which we call hidden set intersection, a secret-shared table is constructed that contains the attributes of all samples that occur in the data set of every party. In the second step, the Gradient Descent algorithm is performed on the secret-shared table, using MPC. In this way, parties are able to securely link partitioned data for training a machine learning model, without ever leaking sensitive attribute information, e.g. identities of people or bank account numbers.

After an overview of related work, we describe the two steps in more detail, and illustrate the broad usage of the Gradient Descent algorithm. Then, we explain the chosen MPC platform, the way we securely implemented the Gradient Descent algorithm and the way we used this algorithm to implement several regression and classification algorithms. Finally, we share some performance results.

1.1 Related Work

Various work has been done on secure set intersection, starting with [12], and more recently [26]. Although these works find the intersection of two sets of identifiers, and the circuit-based private set intersection [27] even enables secure computations on the intersection, the presented protocols do not involve obtaining attribute information from overlapping items. Labeled private set intersection [5] does incorporate attribute information, but only from one party, and more importantly the set intersection needs to be revealed. We contribute to existing literature by presenting a secure inner join protocol; in particular, the protocol takes multiple identifier-attributes arrays as input and returns an array with, for every identifier in the overlap, a row that contains the corresponding attributes from both input arrays. However, we would like to mention a recent development known as "private-ID and streaming private secret shared set intersection" [4], giving a similar solution for two parties, which could possibly be extended to multiple parties, like our solution.

After securely computing the set intersection, including all attributes, the next challenge is to train a classification or regression model on this hidden data. Gradient descent approaches are widely applicable to optimization problems. In

---

[1] Data is said to be horizontally partitioned, if every partition contains all features (columns) of a non-overlapping selection of samples (rows). Alternatively, every partition of a vertically-partitioned data set contains a non-overlapping selection of features for all samples.

this work, we specifically target their application to Ridge and LASSO regression problems and to the support-vector machine (SVM) classifier problem. Ridge and LASSO regression both generalize the ordinary least squares linear regression problem, where the best solution to a (noisy) linear system of equations is found. Both methods introduce a specific regularization function to this objective in order to make certain solutions more favourable (e.g. give zero weight to some attributes). An SVM looks for the hyperplane that best separates the records in the data with respect to their (binary) labels. The formal definitions are provided later in this paper.

Both in the classical and privacy-preserving setting, Ridge regression is typically solved in either of two ways: by solving the normal equations or by minimizing the objective function in a more general fashion, e.g. by application of Gradient Descent algorithm. The privacy-preserving implementations [2,3,6–8,15,17,24] all train a Ridge regression model by solving the normal equations, which boils down to matrix inversion. The matrix inversion can be implemented more efficiently by first performing a Cholesky [6,24], LDLT [6] or LU decomposition [3]. Privacy is often preserved by using homomorphic encryption (HE) techniques [7,8,15], optionally enhanced with packing [1,17], yet there are also implementations with secret-sharing [2,3] and garbled circuits (GC) [24].

The works of [6,13,14,17,23] all present privacy-preserving Gradient Descent solutions for training Ridge regression models. In [13], the authors extent the pioneering two-phase approach of [24] to vertically-partitioned data and improve the running time of the second phase by using a conjugate Gradient Descent algorithm instead of a Cholesky decomposition. Sequentially, [14] improve over [13] by designing an ad-hoc second phase that computes the ridge regression model over encrypted coefficients, thereby reducing the communication complexity. Finally, the authors of [6] train a linear regression model via a variation of the standard Gradient Descent method, namely conjugate Gradient Descent. Privacy is preserved via HE [6,14,17] and GC [13].

Considering the body of research on Ridge regression with secure multi-party computation techniques, surprisingly little attention has been given to privacy-preserving implementations of LASSO. To the best of the authors' knowledge, no researchers have looked into MPC-implementations of LASSO. In this respect, our work presents the first MPC-implementation for training the LASSO regression model.

Support-vector machines (SVM) received an increasing amount of attention [21,28,33,34,41,43,44]. Several works [21,33,41,43,44] focus on secure computation of the Gram matrix. This approach often allows application of the kernel trick, so that not only the linear SVM but also non-linear SVM can be trained [21,33]. Instead, [34] describe a privacy-preserving proximal support vector machine. Proximal SVM solves an approximation of the SVM dual problem, resulting in a much faster algorithm.

1.2 Outline

This paper is structured as follows. In Sect. 2, we present our hidden set intersection protocol. In Sect. 3 we present a secure protocol for the gradient descent algorithm, allowing to securely train several classification and regression models. The experimental results are described in Sect. 4. Finally, we address the implications of our work and possibilities for follow-up in Sect. 5.

2   Hidden Set Intersection

In case of vertically-partitioned data, we first need to construct a secret table of the intersection with the proper attributes. We assume that the parties are not willing to share the identifiers in their databases, making it much harder to securely construct a hidden, shared table that contains all information of the intersection of their identifiers. See Fig. 1 for an illustration of the envisioned hidden table. After the secret table has been constructed, any machine learning method can be executed on this table securely.

ID	Attribute X	Attribute Y	...
17	2	1	...
25	3	12	...
91	6	5	...

ID	Attribute Z
25	50
91	17
101	50

ID	Attribute X	Attribute Y	Attribute Z	...
[25]	[3]	[12]	[50]	...
[91]	[6]	[5]	[17]	...

Fig. 1. Illustration of hidden set intersection. Two parties that both have a database (top left and right table), wish to securely construct a hidden table that contains all attributes of the identifiers that occur in both their databases (bottom table).

There are several variations for generating a hidden table. We present one such variation that is most suitable for the MPC platform and setting that we consider. For simplicity assume that we have only two parties, each having only one attribute. At first sight, the second party will obtain an encrypted table of size $|\mathcal{B}|$, with zeros at the overlapping identifiers. As the machine learning algorithm should touch all table elements, one would like to minimise the table size. Therefore, we first need to securely eliminate the rows that belong to non-overlapping items, such that the number of rows of the table will equal the cardinality of the intersection (and not the size of one of the original databases).

We use an additively homomorphic encryption system [.], where the first party holds the decryption key. Let $\mathcal{A}$ be the set of identities known to the first party, an let α_i denote the attributes of identity $i \in \mathcal{A}$ that are known to the first party. Similarly, let $\mathcal{B}$ be the set of identities known to the second party and let β_j denote the attributes of identity $j \in \mathcal{B}$ that are known to the second party.

To deal with $\mathcal{A}$'s attribute α, we introduce a second polynomial q, such that $q(i) = \alpha_i$, $i \in \mathcal{A}$, just as in labeled PSI [5]. In this way, the second party can construct the encrypted table $(p(j), q(j), \beta_j)$, $j \in \mathcal{B}$. The rows with $p(j) = 0$ form the encrypted table that we are looking for. The protocol below describes a secure way of eliminating the rows with $p(j) \neq 0$, such that the second party obtains an encrypted table of size $|\mathcal{A} \cap \mathcal{B}|$.

1. The $[p(j)]$, which are the (additively homomorphic) encrypted p-evaluations, are multiplicatively blinded by the second party (to avoid learning elements outside the intersection), and the $[q(j)]$ are additively blinded with large random numbers r_j to $[q(j)+r_j]$. The $|\mathcal{B}|$ encrypted blinded pairs are returned to the first party, in random order.
2. The first party decrypts the p-evaluations, and learns $|\mathcal{A} \cap \mathcal{B}| = |\{j \in \mathcal{B} \mid p(j) = 0\}|$, but not the elements because of the random permutation.
3. The first party returns the re-randomised (because the second party might recognize them) encryptions of $[q(k) + r_k]$, $k \in \mathcal{A} \cap \mathcal{B}$, and an encrypted binary matrix Δ of size $|\mathcal{A} \cap \mathcal{B}| \times |\mathcal{B}|$ that denotes the intersecting positions ($\Delta_{kj} = 1$, if and only if, the k-th overlapping identifier equals second party's identifier j).
4. Using the encrypted matrix (and its own random permutation), the second party can compute $[r_k] = \prod_{j=1}^{|\mathcal{B}|} [\Delta_{kj}]^{r_j}$ and $[\beta_k] = \prod_{j=1}^{|\mathcal{B}|} [\Delta_{kj}]^{\beta_j}$, for $k \in \mathcal{A} \cap \mathcal{B}$. The second party uses the encrypted blinding number $[r_k]$ to unblind the previous obtained $[q(k) + r_k]$, and obtain the encrypted $[\alpha_k]$.

We use standard techniques to achieve security in the semi-honest model: the second party only receives encrypted values, and all values towards the first party are either additively, or multiplicatively, blinded by sufficiently large random numbers.

Although the protocol is presented in a two-party setting, it could be extended to multiple parties, by using threshold decryption. E.g., with three parties, the third party could construct an encrypted table, given two oblivious polynomial evaluations $[p^1(j)]$ and $[p^2(j)]$, and combining it to $[p^1(j) + p^2(j)]$, which is an encrypted zero, only when the identifier is in all three data sets (with very large probability), and constructing two indicator matrices Δ^1 and Δ^2 next.

Given the encrypted table, held by one party, one can construct an additively secret-shared version, using fresh random numbers and the additively homomorphic encryption scheme (with threshold decryption). By resharing these additive shares as Shamir secret-sharings, one then obtains a Shamir secret-shared table. In the next section we show how a gradient descent algorithm can be trained on the Shamir secret-shared table using the MPyC framework (see Sect. 3.4).

3   Secure Gradient Descent

In this section, we introduce regression and classification problems and explain how the Gradient Descent algorithm can solve these problems.

3.1   Regression

A basic linear regression problem boils down to the following question: for a known matrix $X \in \mathbb{R}^{n \times m}$, where n is the number of samples and m is the number of features, and vector $y \in \mathbb{R}^{n \times 1}$ (output data), can we find a *weight vector* $\mathbf{w}$ such that the equality $X\mathbf{w} = \mathbf{y}$ is satisfied? In general the system is over-determined and there exists no solution. Instead, one aims to find $\mathbf{w}$ such that some function of the approximation error vector $X\mathbf{w} - \mathbf{y}$ (and possibly some other arguments) is minimized.

Traditionally, researches focused on minimizing the ℓ^2-norm $\|X\mathbf{w} - \mathbf{y}\|_2^2$; this is known as (ordinary) least squares linear regression (OLS). Alternatively to OLS, we implemented Ridge and LASSO, that favor solutions with zero-valued entries because of a regularization term. Both methods have different regularization terms in the minimization objective

$$F(w) = \frac{1}{n}\|X\mathbf{w} - y\|_2^2 + f(\mathbf{w}). \tag{1}$$

- If $f(\mathbf{w}) = \lambda\|\mathbf{w}\|_2^2 = \sum_{i=1}^n w_i^2$, $\lambda > 0$, then this is known as Ridge regression [16]. This model is well-suited for mathematical analysis by the (almost everywhere) differentiability of the ℓ^2-norm.
- If $f(\mathbf{w}) = \lambda\|\mathbf{w}\|_1 = \sum_{i=1}^n |w_i|$, $\lambda > 0$, then this is known as the "least absolute shrinkage and selection operator" (LASSO regression) [36]. LASSO aims to perform better variable selection then Ridge regression, yet it is harder to analyze.

The parameter λ is used to balance the approximation error versus the penalty incurred by the regularization function. Note that both methods reduce to OLS if λ is set to zero.

3.2   Classification

Support-vector machine (SVM) is a linear classification method [35]. The problem is similar as for regression, only now our output data is divided into two categories, i.e. $y \in \{-1, 1\}$. To classify, one wants to find a weight vector $\mathbf{w}$ such that the hyper-plane $\mathbf{w} \cdot \mathbf{x} = 0$ divides the samples into the two categories. The *hard margin* method aims to minimize the weight vector such that every sample $\mathbf{x}_i$ above the line $\mathbf{w} \cdot \mathbf{x} = 1$ is classified as 1, and every sample under the line $\mathbf{w} \cdot \mathbf{x} = -1$ is classified as -1. In other words, it minimizes $\|\mathbf{w}\|_2$ with the constraint that $y_i(\mathbf{w} \cdot \mathbf{x}_i) \geq 1$ for $i = 1, \ldots, n$. Unfortunately, no feasible solution to this problem exists if the two categories are not linearly separable. As such, the *soft margin* method tries to minimize the hinge loss function

$h(\mathbf{x}, y, \mathbf{w}) = \max(0, 1 - y(\mathbf{w} \cdot \mathbf{x}))$ for every sample. Now, if a sample $\mathbf{x}_i$ lies on the correct side of the margin, the hinge loss for that sample equals zero and no penalty is incurred. If the sample lies on the wrong side of the margin, the hinge loss is proportional to the distance from the margin. We want to minimize

$$F(\mathbf{w}) = \frac{1}{n} \sum_{i=1}^{n} h(\mathbf{x}_i, y_i, \mathbf{w}) + \lambda ||\mathbf{w}||_2^2, \tag{2}$$

where λ is the hyper-parameter that controls the trade-off between a large margin and a small hinge loss.

3.3 Gradient Descent Approach

Gradient Descent (GD) is a general optimization algorithm that finds a local minimum of an objective function. The algorithm computes updates of the gradient function determined by a specific model. As such, GD is a secure building block for many different models, the models discussed here, but also Logistic Regression for example. GD comes in different forms. We have implemented GD such that it can be used for Batch, Mini-Batch and Stochastic GD. For these algorithms, the difference lies in the number of samples used in each update, the so-called batch size B. Let n be the total number of samples, then the number of iterations (nr_iters) equals $\frac{B}{n}$, where $B = 1$ for Stochastic, $B = b$ for mini-batch and $B = n$ for batch. Let θ be the learning rate, initialize $\theta_0 = 1/\max(X^T X)$ and let $l(\theta)$ be the update function for the learning rate. The algorithm for GD that we used in our implementation is described in Algorithm 1. In addition to the normal GD, we have also implemented the SAG [30] algorithm that incorporates the average of past gradients in the update. For our regression methods we have the following gradient functions (CALC_GRADIENT):

Algorithm 1. Gradient Descent Algorithm

1: **procedure** GD(X, y, B, nr_epoch, $model$, $*params$)
2:    **for** epoch in 1:nr_epoch **do**
3:        $X', y' =$ PERMUTE_DATA(X, y)
4:        $\theta = l(\theta_0)$
5:        **for** iter in $1 : nr\_iters$ **do**
6:            $X'_s = X'[nr\_iters * B : (nr\_iters + 1) * B,]$ ▷ Subset X' and y'
7:            $y'_s = y'[nr\_iters * B : (nr\_iters + 1) * B]$
8:            $g =$ CALC_GRADIENT($X'_s, y'_s, w, n, model, *params$)
9:            $w = w - \theta g$
      return w

- For Ridge Regression, we find as a gradient for (1)

$$\nabla(F(\mathbf{w})) = \frac{2}{n} X^T (X\mathbf{w} - y) + \frac{2\lambda}{n} \mathbf{w}.$$

– Because of the ℓ^1-norm in (1), the objective function for LASSO is non-differentiable. We therefore apply a proximal gradient method known as Iterative Soft Thresholding Algorithm (ISTA) [9]; meaning that we compute $g(\mathbf{w}) := \frac{2}{n}X^T(X\mathbf{w}-y)$ then apply the following update to $\mathbf{w}_t$: $\mathbf{w}_{t+1} := S_\lambda(\mathbf{g})$, where the i-th component $(S_\lambda(\mathbf{g}))_i$ of $S_\lambda(\mathbf{g})$ is given by

$$
S_\lambda(g_i) := \begin{cases} g_i - \lambda, & \text{if } g_i > \lambda, \\ 0, & \text{if } |g_i| \leq \lambda, \text{ and} \\ g_i + \lambda, & \text{if } g_i < -\lambda. \end{cases} \tag{3}
$$

The function $S(\cdot)$ is the soft-threshold function.
– For SVM, one may see that the hinge loss in (2) is not differentiable. We therefore compute the subgradient

$$
\nabla F(\mathbf{w}) = -\frac{1}{n}\sum_{i=1}^{n}[h(x_i, y_i, \mathbf{w}) = 0] \cdot y_i \cdot x_i + 2\lambda\mathbf{w}, \tag{4}
$$

that incurs an additional penalty for samples that have non-zero hinge loss.

3.4 MPyC

For the implementation of our algorithms, the MPyC framework [31] is used within a semi-honest security model. This framework is based on threshold Shamir secret sharing [32] and built in Python. For an m-party computation, the framework tolerates a dishonest minority of up to t passively corrupt parties, $m \geq 1$ and $0 \leq t \leq (m-1)/2$. Note that this provides security only if $m \geq 3$.

MPyC provides secure (secret-shared) number types that can be used for computation. Some mathematical operations such as addition and multiplication can be done with basic Python operators through operator overloading. Moreover, the framework provides functions to efficiently compute other (more complex) operations, such as calculating the in-product and secure comparisons. Matrix and vector operations are used to effectively implement the Gradient Descent algorithms.

Although most operations of the Gradient Descent algorithm are additions and multiplications, it is worthwhile to consider secure implementation of the soft-thresholding function S_λ from Eq. (3). The value of $S_\lambda(g_i)$ is computed from one of three functions, depending on the value of g_i. Disclosing g_i would reveal the gradient and therefore reveal some information about the input data, which is clearly undesirable. Therefore, we compute $S_\lambda(g_i)$ as in Algorithm 2, leveraging the MPyC implementation of a secure comparison to securely cover all cases without explicitly indicating which branch was taken. A similar approach allows one to securely compute the SVM hinge loss in Eq. (4).

4 Performance

In this section, we give a brief account on the accuracy and speed of our privacy-preserving Gradient Descent implementation for training a Ridge and LASSO

Algorithm 2. Secure soft thresholding

1: **procedure** SOFTTHRESHOLDING(λ, g)
2:    **for** i in $0 : len(g)$ **do**
3:        $ge\_g = mpyc.ge(g[i], 0)$ ▷ secret-shared bit indicating $(g[i] >= 0)$
4:        $sign\_g = 2 * ge\_g - 1$ ▷ sign of $g[i]$, assumes value 1 if $g[i] == 0$
5:        $abs\_g = sign\_g * g[i]$
6:        $gtrLambda = mpyc.ge(abs\_g, \lambda)$ ▷ secret-shared bit indicating $(|g[i]| >= \lambda)$
7:        $S[i] = gtrLambda * (g[i] - sgn\_g * \lambda)$
      return S

---

regression model, and a SVM classification model. Here, we define the accuracy of a model as the ratio of the objective values of (1) the privacy-preserving implementation using fixed-point arithmetic, and (2) the equivalent plain-text implementation of the model, using floating-point arithmetic.

4.1 Run-Time

For every test, three parties are simulated by running the script in three independent processes on a single Linux server. As such, the communication costs are negligible and the speed test mainly captures the computational effort for each party.

The data set for every test was loaded, or generated by the Python package scikit-learn [25]. Every model was iteratively trained with our privacy-preserving Gradient Descent implementation until the ℓ^2-norm of the difference between the old and the new weight vector became less than 0.01.

For a numerical evaluation of the computational effort, we used scikit-learn's `make_regression` module to generate artificial data sets that are specifically designed for training and testing regression models. By generating data sets of various sizes and subsequently training a Ridge model on this data, we were able to assess the impact of the number of samples, and the number of features, see Fig. 2. Our tests show that the time needed to train the model scales linearly in the number of samples and sub-linearly in the number of features. This conclusion also holds for LASSO regression and SVM classification. We omitted the plain-text running times, which were only a few seconds.

The hidden set intersection protocol scales linearly in the number of parties, and in the number of features (attributes). However, as the hidden set intersection protocol takes $\mathcal{O}(|\mathcal{A}| \cdot |\mathcal{B}|)$ exponentiations of homomorphically encrypted values, it doesn't scale linearly, but quadratically in the number of samples. Preliminary results show that the execution time of hidden set intersection is still low, compared to secure LASSO regression for databases up to $10,000$ records [11].

4.2 Accuracy

Ridge Regression. The accuracy of the trained Ridge regression model was tested with the scikit-learn `diabetes` data set. This data set contains 442 samples

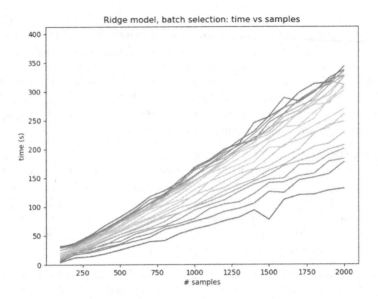

(a) Computational effort for fixed number of features (bottom=1, top=20) as function of the number of samples.

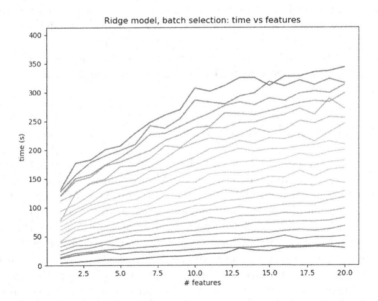

(b) Computational effort for fixed number of samples (bottom=100, top=2000) as function of the number of features.

Fig. 2. Computational effort (in seconds) for training a Ridge regression model on artificial data sets of various sizes. The computational effort increases linearly in the number of samples and sub-linearly in the number of features.

with 10 features each. The features assume real values in the interval $(-0.2, 0.2)$, whereas the targets y assume integer values in the interval $[25, 346]$. Of this set, a random selection of 398 samples was used to train the models and the other samples were used for testing. With $\lambda = 10^{-2}$, our privacy-preserving trained model scored an objective value of 4777.064 on the test data, equal to the plain-text trained model that also scored 4777.064. Additionally, the R^2 scores for the training set, $R^2_{plain} = 0.2879$ and $R^2_{MPC} = 0.2879$ were equal. Hence, the accuracy of the two implementations is very similar.

LASSO Regression. LASSO regression was tested with the same data set as Ridge, the scikit-learn `diabetes` data set. Outcomes were found to equal the plain-text variant. Important to note is that the weight vector was also similar, with the same coefficients set to zero. The R^2 scores are similar for both training and test set. In addition to the `diabetes` data set, we have also tested a data set with Gaussian Noise, created with a generator function from scikit-learn for regression. Again outcomes are equal in plain-text.

SVM Classification. The accuracy of the trained SVM model was tested with the scikit-learn `breast_cancer` data set. This data set contains 569 samples with 30 features each, divided into two categories (212 vs. 357 samples). We scaled the data set such that the features are in the interval $(-3.1, 12.1)$ and the targets are in the set $\{-1, 1\}$. Of this data set, a random selection of 512 samples was used to train the models, and the other samples were used for testing. With $\lambda = 10^{-3}$, using batch GD, our privacy-preserving trained model scored an objective value of 14554.2 on the test data, whereas the plain-text trained model scored 14502.0. The ratio of 1.0035 shows that the two implementations are very similar in accuracy. Furthermore, 96.4% of the test data was predicted correctly by the trained model.

5   Conclusions and Future Work

We presented a two-phase solution that allows multiple collaborating parties to train various regression and classification models without disclosing their data. In the first phase, using a novel MPC implementation, the parties construct a hidden table that contains data of all people that occur in the intersection of all their databases. In the second phase, the hidden table facilitates the training of several regression and classification models. Particularly, we presented the first privacy-preserving training of a LASSO regression model. All these implementations are build on a modular, privacy-preserving implementation of the Gradient Descent algorithm, which allows for easy extension to many more optimization problems, including but not limited to: non-linear SVM, Logistic Regression and Neural Networks.

References

1. Akavia, A., Shaul, H., Weiss, M., Yakhini, Z.: Linear-regression on packed encrypted data in the two-server model. In: Proceedings of the 7th ACM Workshop on Encrypted Computing & Applied Homomorphic Cryptography, WAHC 2019, pp. 21–32. Association for Computing Machinery, New York (2019). https://doi.org/10.1145/3338469.3358942

2. Blom, F., Bouman, N., Schoenmakers, B., Vreede, N.: Efficient Secure Ridge Regression from Randomized Gaussian Elimination. IACR Cryptology ePrint Archive (2019)

3. Bogdanov, D., Kamm, L., Laur, S., Sokk, V.: Rmind: a tool for cryptographically secure statistical analysis. IEEE Trans. Dependable Secure Comput. **15**(3), 481–495 (2018)

4. Buddhavarapu, P., Knox, A., Mohassel, P., Sengupta, S., Taubeneck, E., Vlaskin, V.: Private matching for compute. Cryptology ePrint Archive, Report 2020/599 (2020). https://eprint.iacr.org/2020/599

5. Chen, H., Huang, Z., Laine, K., Rindal, P.: Labeled PSI from fully homomorphic encryption with malicious security. In: Proceedings of the 2018 ACM SIGSAC Conference on Computer and Communications Security, CCS 2018, pp. 1223–1237. Association for Computing Machinery, New York (2018). https://doi.org/10.1145/3243734.3243836

6. Chen, Y.R., Rezapour, A., Tzeng, W.G.: Privacy-preserving ridge regression on distributed data. Inf. Sci. **451–452**, 34–49 (2018). https://doi.org/10.1016/j.ins.2018.03.061. http://www.sciencedirect.com/science/article/pii/S0020025518302500

7. de Cock, M., Dowsley, R., Nascimento, A.C., Newman, S.C.: Fast, privacy preserving linear regression over distributed datasets based on pre-distributed data. In: Proceedings of the 8th ACM Workshop on Artificial Intelligence and Security, pp. 3–14. ACM (2015)

8. Dankar, F.K., Brien, R., Adams, C., Matwin, S.: Secure multi-party linear regression. In: EDBT/ICDT Workshops, pp. 406–414. Citeseer (2014)

9. Daubechies, I., Defrise, M., De Mol, C.: An iterative thresholding algorithm for linear inverse problems with a sparsity constraint. arXiv:math/0307152, November 2003

10. Du, W., Zhan, Z.: Building decision tree classifier on private data. In: Proceedings of the IEEE International Conference on Privacy, Security and Data Mining, vol. 14, pp. 1–8. Australian Computer Society, Inc. (2002)

11. van Egmond, M.B., et al.: Predicting heart-failure risk using privacy-preserving dataset combination and lasso regression. Submitted to BMC Medical Informatics and Decision Making (2021)

12. Freedman, M.J., Nissim, K., Pinkas, B.: Efficient private matching and set intersection. In: Cachin, C., Camenisch, J.L. (eds.) EUROCRYPT 2004. LNCS, vol. 3027, pp. 1–19. Springer, Heidelberg (2004). https://doi.org/10.1007/978-3-540-24676-3_1

13. Gascón, A., et al.: Privacy-preserving distributed linear regression on high-dimensional data. Proc. Privacy Enhancing Technol. **2017**(4), 345–364 (2017)

14. Giacomelli, I., Jha, S., Page, C.D., Yoon, K.: Privacy-preserving ridge regression on distributed data. IACR Cryptology ePrint Archive 2017/707 (2017)

15. Hall, R., Fienberg, S.E., Nardi, Y.: Secure multiple linear regression based on homomorphic encryption. J. Off. Stat. **27**(4), 669 (2011)

16. Hoerl, A.E., Kennard, R.W.: Ridge regression: biased estimation for nonorthogonal problems. Technometrics **12**(1), 55–67 (1970). https://doi.org/10.1080/00401706.1970.10488634

17. Hu, S., Wang, Q., Wang, J., Chow, S.S.M., Zou, Q.: Securing fast learning! ridge regression over encrypted big data. In: 2016 IEEE Trustcom/BigDataSE/ISPA, pp. 19–26 (2016). https://doi.org/10.1109/TrustCom.2016.0041

18. Jagannathan, G., Wright, R.N.: Privacy-preserving distributed k-means clustering over arbitrarily partitioned data. In: Proceedings of the Eleventh ACM SIGKDD International Conference on Knowledge Discovery in Data Mining, pp. 593–599. ACM (2005)

19. Kantarcioglu, M., Clifton, C.: Privacy-preserving distributed mining of association rules on horizontally partitioned data. IEEE Trans. Knowl. Data Eng. **16**(9), 1026–1037 (2004). https://doi.org/10.1109/TKDE.2004.45

20. Karr, A.F., Lin, X., Sanil, A.P., Reiter, J.P.: Regression on distributed databases via secure multi-party computation. In: Proceedings of the 2004 Annual National Conference on Digital Government Research, dg.o 2004, pp. 1–2. Digital Government Society of North America (2004). http://dl.acm.org/citation.cfm?id=1124191.1124299

21. Lin, K., Chen, M.: On the design and analysis of the privacy-preserving SVM classifier. IEEE Trans. Knowl. Data Eng. **23**(11), 1704–1717 (2011). https://doi.org/10.1109/TKDE.2010.193

22. Lin, X., Clifton, C., Zhu, M.: Privacy-preserving clustering with distributed EM mixture modeling. Knowl. Inf. Syst. **8**(1), 68–81 (2005)

23. Mohassel, P., Zhang, Y.: Secureml: a system for scalable privacy-preserving machine learning. In: 2017 IEEE Symposium on Security and Privacy (SP), pp. 19–38 (2017). https://doi.org/10.1109/SP.2017.12

24. Nikolaenko, V., Weinsberg, U., Ioannidis, S., Joye, M., Boneh, D., Taft, N.: Privacy-preserving ridge regression on hundreds of millions of records. In: 2013 IEEE Symposium on Security and Privacy, pp. 334–348. IEEE (2013)

25. Pedregosa, F., et al.: Scikit-learn: machine learning in python. J. Mach. Learn. Res. **12**(Oct), 2825–2830 (2011)

26. Pinkas, B., Rosulek, M., Trieu, N., Yanai, A.: Spot-light: lightweight private set intersection from sparse OT extension. Cryptology ePrint Archive (2019)

27. Pinkas, B., Schneider, T., Tkachenko, O., Yanai, A.: Efficient circuit-based PSI with linear communication. In: Ishai, Y., Rijmen, V. (eds.) EUROCRYPT 2019. LNCS, vol. 11478, pp. 122–153. Springer, Cham (2019). https://doi.org/10.1007/978-3-030-17659-4_5

28. Que, J., Jiang, X., Ohno-Machado, L.: A collaborative framework for distributed privacy-preserving support vector machine learning. In: AMIA Annual Symposium Proceedings, vol. 2012, pp. 1350–1359. American Medical Informatics Association (2012)

29. Sanil, A.P., Karr, A.F., Lin, X., Reiter, J.P.: Privacy preserving regression modelling via distributed computation. In: Proceedings of the Tenth ACM SIGKDD International Conference on Knowledge Discovery and Data Mining, KDD 2004, pp. 677–682. ACM, New York (2004). https://doi.org/10.1145/1014052.1014139

30. Schmidt, M., Le Roux, N., Bach, F.: Minimizing finite sums with the stochastic average gradient. Math. Program. **162**(1–2), 83–112 (2017). https://doi.org/10.1007/s10107-016-1030-6

31. Schoenmakers, B.: MPyC - secure multiparty computation in python. https://github.com/lschoe/mpyc

32. Shamir, A.: How to share a secret. Commun. ACM **22**(11), 612–613 (1979)

33. Sumana, M., Hareesha, K.: Modelling a secure support vector machine classifier for private data. Int. J. Inf. Comput. Secur. **10**(1), 25–40 (2018)

34. Sun, L., Mu, W.S., Qi, B., Zhou, Z.J.: A new privacy-preserving proximal support vector machine for classification of vertically partitioned data. Int. J. Mach. Learn. Cybern. **6**(1), 109–118 (2015). https://doi.org/10.1007/s13042-014-0245-1

35. Suykens, J., Vandewalle, J.: Least squares support vector machine classifiers. Neural Process. Lett. **9**(3), 293–300 (1999). https://doi.org/10.1023/A:1018628609742

36. Tibshirani, R.: Regression shrinkage and selection via the lasso. J. R. Stat. Soc. Ser. B (Methodol.) **58**(1), 267–288 (1996). https://doi.org/10.1111/j.2517-6161. 1996.tb02080.x

37. Vaidya, J., Clifton, C.: Privacy-preserving k-means clustering over vertically partitioned data. In: Proceedings of the Ninth ACM SIGKDD International Conference on Knowledge Discovery and Data Mining, pp. 206–215. ACM (2003)

38. Vaidya, J., Clifton, C.: Privacy preserving Naive Bayes classifier for vertically partitioned data. In: Proceedings of the 2004 SIAM International Conference on Data Mining, pp. 522–526. SIAM (2004)

39. Vaidya, J., Clifton, C.: Privacy-preserving decision trees over vertically partitioned data. In: Jajodia, S., Wijesekera, D. (eds.) DBSec 2005. LNCS, vol. 3654, pp. 139–152. Springer, Heidelberg (2005). https://doi.org/10.1007/11535706_11

40. Vaidya, J., Clifton, C.: Secure set intersection cardinality with application to association rule mining. J. Comput. Secur. **13**(4), 593–622 (2005)

41. Vaidya, J., Yu, H., Jiang, X.: Privacy-preserving SVM classification. Knowl. Inf. Syst. **14**(2), 161–178 (2008). https://doi.org/10.1007/s10115-007-0073-7

42. Wright, R., Yang, Z.: Privacy-preserving Bayesian network structure computation on distributed heterogeneous data. In: Proceedings of the Tenth ACM SIGKDD International Conference on Knowledge Discovery and Data Mining, pp. 713–718. ACM (2004)

43. Yu, H., Jiang, X., Vaidya, J.: Privacy-preserving SVM using nonlinear kernels on horizontally partitioned data. In: Proceedings of the 2006 ACM Symposium on Applied Computing, SAC 2006, pp. 603–610. ACM, New York (2006). https://doi. org/10.1145/1141277.1141415

44. Yu, H., Vaidya, J., Jiang, X.: Privacy-preserving SVM classification on vertically partitioned data. In: Ng, W.-K., Kitsuregawa, M., Li, J., Chang, K. (eds.) PAKDD 2006. LNCS (LNAI), vol. 3918, pp. 647–656. Springer, Heidelberg (2006). https:// doi.org/10.1007/11731139_74

Principal Component Analysis Using CKKS Homomorphic Scheme

Samanvaya Panda[✉]

International Institute of Information Technology, Hyderabad, Hyderabad, India
samanvaya.panda@research.iiit.ac.in

Abstract. Principal component analysis (PCA) is one of the most popular linear dimensionality reduction techniques in machine learning. In this paper, we try to present a method for performing PCA on encrypted data using a homomorphic encryption scheme. In a client-server model where the server performs computations on the encrypted data, it (server) does not require to perform any matrix operations like multiplication, inversion, etc. on the encrypted data. This reduces the number of computations significantly since matrix operations on encrypted data are very computationally expensive. For our purpose, we used the CKKS homomorphic encryption scheme since it is most suitable for machine learning tasks allowing approximate computations on real numbers. We also present the experimental results of our proposed Homomorphic PCA (HPCA) algorithm on a few datasets. We measure the R2 score on the reconstructed data and use it as an evaluation metric for our HPCA algorithm.

Keywords: Homomorphic encryption · Principal Component Analysis (PCA) · CKKS scheme · Goldschmidt's Algorithm

1 Introduction

With the rise of outsourcing of computational tasks through cloud computing and services, quintillion bytes of data are produced every day. Data analytics performed on these data provide several insights to the clients at the same to the cloud servers. This has raised several privacy issues and concerns among individuals, organizations, and government officials. With ever-increasing privacy issues, performing machine learning tasks on encrypted data has become the need of the hour. Several privacy-preserving machine learning tasks have been accomplished using fully homomorphic encryption (FHE) schemes and secure multiparty computations (MPC) based schemes, demonstrating their potential. Due to the interactive nature of MPC-based schemes, people started looking for FHE-based schemes as an alternative.

Gentry in [12,13] provided the construction of a leveled-HE scheme. Then the construction was converted to a FHE scheme using bootstrapping that allowed an arbitrary number of computations on the ciphertext. However, the scheme was not efficient to be used in practice. Various improvements have been made since then, and FHE schemes have become efficient and practical. One such

© Springer Nature Switzerland AG 2021
S. Dolev et al. (Eds.): CSCML 2021, LNCS 12716, pp. 52–70, 2021.
https://doi.org/10.1007/978-3-030-78086-9_4

scheme that was introduced recently is the CKKS [7] homomorphic encryption scheme. CKKS scheme supports approximate arithmetic over encrypted data. It supports computations on real and complex values, which makes it most suitable for machine learning tasks. Application of CKKS scheme in various machine learning techniques have been already demonstrated in [2, 3, 8, 10, 14–16].

This paper focuses on using the CKKS homomorphic encryption scheme to perform principal component analysis (PCA) - a popular linear dimensionality reduction technique. Dimensionality reduction techniques transform higher dimensional data into a representation with a few intrinsic dimensions while retaining the original data's properties. When used as input to a machine learning model, such a low dimensional representation reduces the model's complexity and makes it simpler. For this reason, dimensionality reduction has numerous applications in fields such as data visualization, data compression, noise removal, pre-processing technique. Few attempts have been made in the past to perform PCA on encrypted data. Lu et al. in [19] and Rathee et al. in [22] performed PCA using the BGV scheme. However, both of them performed PCA on categorical datasets with relatively fewer attributes (≤ 20). Also, they provided experimentation results for the first principal component only. In [19] and [22] computing subsequent principal components requires communication between the client and the server because the client computes the eigenvalue. This makes their algorithm interactive.

Contributions

In this paper, we propose a technique to perform PCA using the CKKS homomorphic encryption scheme. Unlike in [19, 22] where they converted the real dataset to an integer dataset through appropriate scaling, we take advantage of using the CKKS scheme that can handle real numbers. We also propose a sub-ciphertext packing technique in which every vector is packed as a sub-ciphertext within a ciphertext. The length of the sub-ciphertext is almost equal to the size of the vector. The primary advantage of using such a packing technique is that most of the operations become polynomial in the sub-ciphertext length rather than polynomial in ciphertext's length. Since the sub-ciphertext length is almost the same as that of the original vector, computations become polynomial in the initial vector's length.

We compute the norm of vectors homomorphically, which makes our algorithm non-interactive for computing subsequent principal components. Our proposed Homomorphic PCA (HPCA) algorithm does not require performing any matrix operations like matrix-vector multiplication and matrix-matrix multiplication on encrypted data, significantly reducing computations.

We provide an implementation of our HPCA algorithm in SEAL-Python [24] (A python binding for SEAL [23] library). Other than just categorical datasets with a few dimensions, we provide experimentation results on higher-dimensional datasets. Also, we perform computations to find more than just one principal component as opposed to in [19, 22] which only considered the computation of the first principal component. We also measure the R2 score of the reconstructed data as an evaluation metric for our HPCA algorithm. We do not use bootstrapping in our HPCA algorithm implementation because it is not provided as an API in the SEAL library. Instead, we re-encrypt some of the encrypted parameters to eliminate noise in them. The re-encryption procedure could be ideally replaced by bootstrapping without making any changes in other parts. However, the algorithm's runtime may increase since bootstrapping in the CKKS scheme is a costlier operation than re-encryption.

2   Preliminaries

2.1   CKKS Homomorphic Encryption Scheme

The CKKS (Cheon-Kim-Kim-Song) scheme [7] is a leveled homomorphic encryption scheme that relies on the hardness of RLWE (Ring Learning With Errors) problem for its security. Unlike other HE schemes, CKKS supports approximate arithmetic on real and complex numbers with predefined precision. The main idea behind the CKKS scheme is that it treats noise generated upon decryption as an error in computation for real numbers. This makes it an ideal candidate for performing machine learning tasks where most of the computations are approximate. With the use of bootstrapping technique as mentioned in [6] and [5], the CKKS scheme becomes a FHE (fully homomorphic encryption) scheme.

Let $N = \phi(M)$ be the degree of the M-th cyclotomic polynomial $\Phi_M(X)$. If N is chosen as a power of 2 then $M = 2N$ and the M-th cyclotomic polynomial $\Phi_M(X) = X^N + 1$. Let $\mathcal{R} = \mathbb{Z}[X]/\Phi_M(X) = \mathbb{Z}[X]/(X^N + 1)$ be the ring of polynomials defined for the plaintext space. Let $\mathcal{R}_q = \mathcal{R}/q\mathcal{R} = \mathbb{Z}_q[X]/(X^N + 1)$ be the residue ring defined for the ciphertext space. Let $\mathbb{H}$ be a subspace of $\mathbb{C}^N$ which is isomorphic to $\mathbb{C}^{N/2}$. Let $\sigma : \mathcal{R} \to \sigma(\mathcal{R}) \subseteq \mathbb{H}$ be a canonical embedding. Let $\pi : \mathbb{H} \to \mathbb{C}^{N/2}$ be a map that projects a vector from a subspace of $\mathbb{C}^N$ to $\mathbb{C}^{N/2}$.

The CKKS scheme provides the following operations:

KeyGen(N). Let $s(X) \in \mathbb{Z}_q[X]/(X^N + 1)$ be the secret polynomial and $p(X) = (-a(X) \cdot s(X) + e(X), a(X))$ be the public polynomial where $a(X) \in \mathbb{Z}_q[X]/(X^N + 1)$ is a polynomial chosen uniformly random and $e(X) \in \mathbb{Z}_q[X]/(X^N + 1)$ is a small noisy polynomial. Let $r(x) = (-a(X) \cdot s(X) + b \cdot s(X)^2 + e(X), a(X))$ be the relinearisation key where $b \in \mathbb{Z}_q$ is a large integer.

Encode(z). To encode a message vector $z \in \mathbb{C}^{N/2}$ to a message polynomial $m(X) \in \mathcal{R}$, we first expand the message vector z from $\mathbb{C}^{N/2}$ to $\mathbb{H}$ by applying $\pi^{-1}(z)$. Then we appropriately scale the vector by multiplying a scaling factor Δ followed by random rounding to $\lfloor \Delta \cdot \pi^{-1}(z) \rceil$. Scaling is done to achieve predefined precision since precision bits may be lost due to rounding. To obtain the message polynomial we apply the inverse of canonical embedding σ^{-1} and get $m(X) = \sigma^{-1}(\lfloor \Delta \cdot \pi^{-1}(z) \rceil) \in \mathcal{R}$.

Decode($m(X)$). To decode a message polynomial $m(X) \in \mathcal{R}$ to a message vector $z \in \mathbb{C}^{N/2}$, we first apply the canonical embedding σ to get $z = \lfloor \Delta \cdot \pi^{-1}(z) \rceil \in \mathbb{H}$. Then we divide it by the scaling factor Δ to obtain $\Delta^{-1} \lfloor \Delta \cdot \pi^{-1}(z) \rceil \approx \pi^{-1}(z)$. To obtain the message vector, we project the vector using π and get $\pi(\pi^{-1}(z)) = z \in \mathbb{C}^{N/2}$.

Encrypt($m(X), p(X)$). To obtain the ciphertext polynomial $c(X)$ corresponding to the message polynomial $m(X) \in \mathcal{R}$, we apply the RLWE encryption and get $c(X) = (c_0(X), c_1(X)) = (m(X), 0) + p(X) = (m(X) - a(X) \cdot s(X) + e(X), a(X)) \in (\mathbb{Z}_q[X]/(X^N + 1))^2$.

Decrypt($c(X), s(X)$). To obtain the message polynomial corresponding to the ciphertext polynomial $c(X) \in (\mathbb{Z}_q[X]/(X^N+1))$, we apply the RLWE decryption using the secret polynomial $s(X)$ and get $m(X) \approx c_0(X) + c_1(X) \cdot s = m(X) + e(X)$

Apart from the above operations, it also provides specialised ciphertext operations which include:

Multiply($c(X), c'(X)$). Multiplication of two ciphertexts $c(X)$ and $c'(X)$ generates a ciphertext $c_m(X) = (c_0 c'_0, c'_0 c_1 + c_0 c'_1, c'_0 c'_1) = (c_0(X), c_1(X), c_2(X))$. Then ciphertext is relinearised and modulus is switched subsequently.

Relinearise($c_m(X), r(X)$). Relinearisation reduces the size of the ciphertext after multiplication of two ciphertexts. Let $c_m(X) = (c_0(X), c_1(X), c_2(X))$ be the resultant ciphertext after multiplication of two ciphertexts. After relinearisation, we obtain the ciphertext $c_r(X) = (c_0(X), c_1(X)) + \lfloor b^{-1} \cdot c_2(X) \cdot r(X) \rceil mod(q)$

Modulus Switching (c(X)). Modulus switching is rescaling of the ciphertext after multiplication in the RNS system. In addition to rescaling (dividing by scale and rounding), we the take ciphertext modulus of the next prime in the chain (lower level). The ciphertext obtained after modulus switching $c_s(X) = \lfloor \Delta^{-1} \cdot c(X) \rceil mod(q_{l-1}) = \lfloor \frac{q_{l-1}}{q_l} \cdot c(X) \rceil mod(q_{l-1})$.

Some other operations that are also supported by CKKS scheme are:

- add($c(X), c'(X)$) - to add 2 ciphertext polynomials.
- rotate_left($c(X), i$) - to rotate the ciphertext polynomial by i positions left.
- rotate_right($c(X), i$) - to rotate the ciphertext polynomial by i positions right.

2.2   Principal Component Analysis (PCA)

Principal component analysis (PCA) is an unsupervised dimensionality linear reduction technique. The PCA method searches for dimensions along which variance is maximized and from which one can reconstruct the original data with minimal reconstruction error. Let u be the dimension that maximizes the variance of a vector x after projection in that direction. So, PCA could be formulated as maximization of variance problem:

$$\max_{u} \quad \frac{1}{n} \sum_{i=1}^{n} (u^T x_i - u^T \mu)^2$$

$$\max_{u} \quad \frac{1}{n} u^T \Sigma u \tag{1}$$

$$\text{subject to} \quad \|u\| = 1$$

where $\Sigma = \sum_{i=1}^{n} (x_i - \mu)(x_i - \mu)^T$ is the covariance matrix and $\mu = \sum_{i=1}^{n} u_i$ is the mean vector.

From the above formulation, it is evident that the solution to the maximization problem would be the largest eigenvector of the covariance matrix Σ. To find the largest eigenvector, we use an iterative technique called the Power method. The power method finds the dominant eigenvector of a given matrix A by repeatedly multiplying a random vector u. As the number of iterations i increases, the product $A^i u$ converges to the largest eigenvector.

Algorithm 1. First principal component (Power Method)

Input: X : Data Matrix of row vectors.
Output: λ, w: Largest eigenvalue and corresponding eigenvector of X.

$w \xleftarrow{\$} \mathbb{R}^d$
for $i = 1$ to t **do**
$\quad s = \sum_{x \in X} x^T (x \cdot w)$
$\quad \lambda = \|s\|$
$\quad w = \frac{s}{\|s\|}$
end for
return λ, w

In Algorithm 1, instead of using covariance matrix Σ, we use the sum of the outer product of x_i's. In this approach, we do not require to store the covariance matrix Σ and only store a vector. Also, we are not required to perform any matrix operations, which could be useful for us in the homomorphic setting.

If we desire to find subsequent ($2^{nd}, 3^{rd}, \cdots l^{th}$ largest) eigenvectors then we need to use the Eigen shift procedure. The Eigen shift procedure would remove the largest eigenvalue and corresponding eigenvector from A.

By combining the Eigen shift procedure with the power method, we would be able to find out l largest eigenvectors of covariance matrix Σ, which would be the top l principal components of the given data matrix X.

Algorithm 2. Eigen Shift Procedure

Input: Σ : Covariance Matrix, λ: Largest eigen value of Σ, w: Eigen vector corresponding to λ.
Output: Σ': Shifted covariance Matrix
  $\Sigma' \leftarrow \Sigma - \lambda \cdot w^T w$
  return Σ'

2.3   Goldschmidt's Algorithm

Goldschmidt's algorithm [4, 20] is an iterative algorithm that finds the value of a fraction. To find the value of the fraction a_0/b_0, it multiplies a series of variables $r_0, r_1, \cdots$ to both numerator (a_0) and denominator (b_0) such that the value of the resultant denominator converges to 1 and the value of the resultant numerator tends to the desired result.

$$\frac{a_0}{b_0} = \frac{a_0}{b_0} \cdot \frac{r_0}{r_0} \cdot \frac{r_1}{r_2} \cdots \frac{r_\alpha}{r_\alpha}, \quad b_0 \cdot r_0 \cdot r_1 \cdots r_\alpha \to 1$$

An initial guess of value the $r_0 \approx 1/b_0$ is required. An good approximation of r_0 is considered to be when $3/4 \leq r_0 b_0 \leq 3/2$. The successive values of the fraction after each iteration are estimated as:

$$\frac{a_i}{b_i} = \frac{a_{i-1}}{b_{i-1}} \cdot \frac{r_{i-1}}{r_{i-1}}, \quad \text{and } r_i = 2 - b_i \ \forall i = 1, 2, \cdots, \alpha$$

Algorithm 3. Top l principal component (Power Method)

Input: X : Data Matrix of row vectors.
Output: Λ, W: Largest l-eigenvalues and corresponding eigenvectors of X.
  $W \leftarrow \{\}$
  $\Lambda \leftarrow \{\}$
  for components $= 1$ to l **do**
    $r \xleftarrow{\$} \mathbb{R}^d$
    for $i = 1$ to t **do**
      $s1 = \sum\limits_{x \in X} x^T (x \cdot r)$
      $s2 = \sum\limits_{w \in W, \lambda \in \Lambda} \lambda w^T (w \cdot r)$
      $s = s1 - s2$
      $\lambda = \|s\|$
      $r = \frac{s}{\|s\|}$
    end for
    $W \leftarrow W \cup r$
    $\Lambda \leftarrow \Lambda \cup \lambda$
  end for
  return Λ, W

Using Goldschmidt's algorithm, we can find the square root and its inverse simultaneously. The fused multiply-add version of Goldschmidt's algorithm [27] is mentioned in Algorithm 4.

Algorithm 4. Goldschmidt's Algorithm

Input: val
Output: x: The square root of val, h: The inverse square root of val.
$\quad y \approx 1/\sqrt{val}$
$\quad x \leftarrow val \cdot y$
$\quad h \leftarrow y/2$
$\quad$**for** $i = 1$ to l **do**
$\quad\quad r \leftarrow 0.5 - xh$
$\quad\quad x \leftarrow x + xr$
$\quad\quad h \leftarrow h + hr$
$\quad$**end for**
$\quad$**return** $x, 2h$

2.4 R2 Score

R2, also known as the coefficient of determination measures the goodness of fit of a model. It computes the amount of variance captured by the dependent variables in a model. Let y_i be a true output value and y_i' be the corresponding output predicted by the model. Then the coefficient of determination (R2 score) is defined as:

$$R2 = 1 - \frac{SS_{res}}{SS_{total}} \tag{2}$$

where $SS_{res} = \sum_{i}(y_i - y_i')^2$ is the sum of squares of residuals and $SS_{total} = \sum_{i}(y_i - \bar{y})^2$ is the total variance.

3 Vector Operations

3.1 Norm and Inversion by Norm

Computing the norm of a vector requires a square root operation to be performed. Since we can not perform square root directly on ciphertext, we use Goldschmidt's algorithm to find the square root of a number as mentioned in [4]. The advantage of using Goldschmidt's algorithm is that along with the square root, it also finds the inverse of the square root, which is precisely what we need. But the Goldschmidt's algorithm requires a good initial approximation of $\frac{1}{\sqrt{x}}$ for faster convergence.

We could use a good initial guess for $\frac{1}{\sqrt{x}}$ using the fast inverse square root algorithm [18,26]. But such approximations are difficult to realize in the homomorphic setting because it requires conversion from IEEE representation (single and double precision floating point) to integer and vice-versa. Instead, we use a linear approximation of $\frac{1}{\sqrt{x}}$ in a given interval and use it as an initial guess for Newton's method. Then we perform few iterations of Newton's method to improve our guess.

For computing Newton's method on $\frac{1}{\sqrt{x}}$ we have $f(x) = x^{-2} - b$. The derivative would be $f'(x) = -2x^{-3}$. In each iteration, the update would be:

$$x_{i+1} = x_i - \frac{f(x_i)}{f'(x_i)}$$

$$\implies x_{i+1} = \frac{x_i}{2}(-bx_i^2 + 3) \tag{3}$$

For linear approximation of $\frac{1}{\sqrt{x}}$, we use constrained linear regression which is formulated as the following minimization problem:

$$\min_{w} \quad \frac{1}{n}\sum_{i=1}^{n}(y_i - w^T x_i)^2 \tag{4}$$
$$\text{subject to} \quad y_i - w^T x_i \geq 0 \quad \forall\, i = \{1, 2, \cdots n\}$$

The additional constraints $y_i - w^T x_i \geq 0 \,\forall i$ are necessary because $\frac{1}{\sqrt{x}}$ would have a positive and a negative value. The constraint ensures that the initial guess is a positive value and Newton's method doesn't diverge towards the negative value. The minimization problem in Eq. 4 is solved using SLSQP (Sequential Least Squares Quadratic Programming) solver.

3.2   Ciphertext Packing

We consider all vectors as row vectors and thus consider only row-wise packing of vectors in a ciphertext. We partition the number of ciphertext slots equally among all the vectors such that the number of zeros present in each partition is the same. Let d be the dimension of each vector and N be the total number of ciphertext slots. Then the number of partitions in the ciphertext would be N/k where k is a factor of N larger than d. In this paper, we consider N to be a power of 2. So finding k would be equivalent to calculating the closet power of 2 greater than d. This can be done very efficiently using binary search in $O(\log\log(N))$ steps.

Suppose $u_1, u_2, \cdots u_j$ are the vectors to be packed in a ciphertext where $j = N/k$. Let $z = k - d$ be the number of trailing zeros for each vector. Then the vectors $u_1, u_2, \cdots u_j$ would packed in a ciphertext as:

$$c = [u'_1, u'_2, \cdots, u'_j] \tag{5}$$

where $u'_i = \text{Ciphertext}\,(u_i || \underbrace{0, 0, \cdots, 0}_{z\ times}), \forall\, i = \{1, 2, \cdots, j\}$.

Each vector, along with trailing zeros, could be thought of as a sub-ciphertext of size k. Instead of partitioning the number of ciphertext slots into $\lceil N/d \rceil$ partitions, we instead preferred N/k partitions because the former doesn't guarantee equipartition of ciphertext slots among all vectors. If there are many vectors, then the last vector would spill over to the next ciphertext leaving behind trailing zeros at the end of each ciphertext which is not ideal for our operations. Hence, we distribute the zeros equally among all the vectors packed in a ciphertext.

If a particular row vector needs to be packed in an entire ciphertext, then the row vector is appended with $z = k - d$ trailing zeros to form a sub-ciphertext. This sub-ciphertext would be then be repeated in each partition. For example, let v be a vector that has to be packed into an entire ciphertext. Then the sub-ciphertext $v' = \text{Ciphertext } (v || \underbrace{0, 0, \cdots, 0}_{z\ times})$. Then the ciphertext would be:

$$c = [v', v', \cdots, v']$$

In [19], each vector was packed into a separate ciphertext, whereas in [22] the entire dataset was packed into a single ciphertext. Our sub-ciphertext packing technique is somewhat in between those two packing techniques. Partitioning the ciphertext into sub-ciphertext helps to achieve an overall reduction in operations. The operations that were earlier polynomial in the length of ciphertext (both in [19] and [22]) now would become polynomial in the length of sub-ciphertext, which is almost equal to the vector's length. Another advantage of using sub-ciphertext packing is that it provides much parallelism as operations are performed independently on each ciphertext.

3.3   Vector Operations on Ciphertext and Sub-ciphertexts

Sum of Elements. Since we consider the size of ciphertext to be a power of 2, to add all the elements in a ciphertext homomorphically, we need to rotate the ciphertext by increasing power of 2 and add it to itself.

Algorithm 5. Sum(c)

Input: c : Ciphertext.
Output: c': Sum of all the elements in ciphertext c.
   temp $\leftarrow$ Ciphertext()
   $c' \leftarrow c$
   for $i = 0$ to $\log(N) - 1$ **do**
      temp $\leftarrow$ rotate_left$(c', 2^i)$
      $c' \leftarrow c' +$ temp
   end for
   return c'

Partial Sum of Ciphertext. Partial sum of a ciphertext is the sum of all the elements within a sub-ciphertext for every sub-ciphertext in any given ciphertext. Suppose $c = [u'_1, u'_2, \cdots, u'_j]$ is a ciphertext and $u'_i = (u_i || 0, 0, \cdots, 0)$ be a sub-ciphertext. Then partial sum of c would result in a ciphertext $c' = [Su_1, Su_2, \cdots, Su_j]$ where $Su_i = \left(\sum_{q=1}^{k} u_{iq}, \sum_{q=1}^{k} u_{iq}, \cdots, \sum_{q=1}^{k} u_{iq} \right)$.

Algorithm 6. Partial_Sum(c)

Input: c : Ciphertext.
Output: c': Co-ordinate wise sum of all sub-ciphertexts in c.
   init $\leftarrow$ Ciphertext$(1, 1, \cdots || 0, 0, \cdots)$ {1^{st} half is all 1's and 2nd half is all 0's}
   $c' \leftarrow$ Ciphertext(c)
   for $i = \log(k) - 1$ to 0 **do**
      temp $\leftarrow$ rotate_right(init, 2^i)
      s1 $\leftarrow$ multiply(init, c')
      s2 $\leftarrow$ multiply(temp, c')
      s2 $\leftarrow$ rotate_left(s2, 2^i)
      $c' \leftarrow$ add(s1, s2)
      if $i > 0$ **then**
         temp $\leftarrow$ rotate_left(temp, $2^i + 2^{i-1}$)
         init $\leftarrow$ multiply(temp, init)
      end if
   end for
   for $i = 0$ to $\log(k)$ **do**
      temp $\leftarrow$ rotate_right(c', 2^i)
      $c' \leftarrow$ add(c', temp)
   end for
   return c'

Let $c = [(1, 2, 3, 4), (2, 3, 4, 5)]$ be a ciphertext with $j = 2$ sub-ciphertexts. Then the partial sum of ciphertext would be $c' = [(10, 10, 10, 10), (14, 14, 14, 14)]$.

Lemma 1. *Let k be the size of sub-ciphertext. Then the multiplicative depth required by the Algorithm 6 is $\log(k)$.*

Sum of Sub-ciphertexts. Addition of all the sub-ciphertexts is the coordinate-wise sum of all sub-ciphertexts in a ciphertext. Suppose $c = [u'_1, u'_2, \cdots, u'_j]$ is a ciphertext with j sub-ciphertexts. Then the sum of all sub-ciphertexts in ciphertext c would result in a ciphertext $c' = [\sum_{i=1}^{j} u'_{i1}, \sum_{i=1}^{k} u'_{i2}, \cdots, \sum_{i=1}^{k} u'_{ij}]$

Let $c = [(1, 2, 3, 4), (2, 3, 4, 5)]$ be a ciphertext with $j = 2$ sub-ciphertexts. Then the sum of sub-ciphertexts would be $c' = [(1 + 2, 2 + 3, 3 + 4, 4 + 5), (1 + 2, 2 + 3, 3 + 4, 4 + 5)] = [(3, 5, 7, 9), (3, 5, 7, 9)]$.

Algorithm 7. Sub_Sum(c)

Input: c : Ciphertext.
Output: c': Coordinate-wise sum of all sub-ciphertexts in c.
  temp ← Ciphertext()
  $c' ← c$
  for $i = 0$ to $\log(j) - 1$ **do**
    temp ← rotate_left($c', 2^i \cdot k$)
    $c' ← c' +$ temp
  end for
  return c'

Inner Product. Let v be ciphertext packed with a vector in all its sub-ciphertexts. The inner product of v and a ciphertext c packed with j sub-ciphertexts can be found by multiplying each element co-ordinate wise and then performing a partial sum on the resultant ciphertext.

Algorithm 8. InnerProduct (c, v)

Input: c : Ciphertext, v : Vector packed in an entire Ciphertext.
Output: c': Inner product of j vectors with v.
  $c' ←$ multiply(c, v)
  $c' ←$ Partial_Sum(c')
  return c'

Lemma 2. *Let k be the size of each sub-ciphertext. Then the multiplicative depth of Algorithm 8 is $\log k + 1$.*

4 Homomorphic Evaluations

After defining all the vector operations and ciphertext packing technique, we will now move forward and describe the methods for performing PCA using CKKS homomorphic scheme. This section would first define the homomorphic version of Goldschmidt's algorithm and the power iteration method essential for performing PCA. Finally, we bundle together all the methods to produce a single method for performing PCA homomorphically.

4.1 Homomorhpic Goldschmidt's Algorithm

Goldschmidt's algorithm [27] is an iterative algorithm that computes the square root and its inverse simultaneously. It converges faster than Newton's method. Similar to newton's method, Goldschmidt's algorithm also requires a good initial approximation (of $\frac{1}{\sqrt{x}}$) for faster convergence. We use Algorithm 9 to obtain a good initial approximation of $\frac{1}{\sqrt{x}}$.

Approximation of $\frac{1}{\sqrt{x}}$. Algorithm 9 provides us with an initial approximation of $\frac{1}{\sqrt{x}}$. It is a homomorphic adaptation of the fast square root inverse algorithm [18]. The approach is similar to the one in [18] where we first find a linear approximation of $\frac{1}{\sqrt{x}}$ and then use that as an initial guess for newton's method and improve upon our approximation in a few iterations.

Algorithm 9. InvNormApprox($norm$)

Input: $norm$: Ciphertext with sum of squares.
Output: $guess$: Approximate inverse of norm of c.
   neg_half ← Ciphertext(-0.5) {A ciphertext with all its entries as -0.5}
   three_half ← Ciphertext(1.5) {A ciphertext with all its entries as 1.5}
   guess ← linear_approx(norm)
   for $i = 1$ to $iterations$ **do**
      sq ← multiply(sq, square(guess))
      sq ← multiply(multiply(guess, neg_half), sq)
      temp ← multiply(three_half, guess)
      guess ← add(temp, sq)
   end for
   return guess

Lemma 3. *Let l_1 be the number of iterations in Algorithm 9. Then the multiplicative depth of Algorithm 9 is $3l_1 + 1$*

Lemma 4. *Let l_1, l_2 be the number of iterations in Algorithms 9 and 10 respectively. Let k be the size of the sub-ciphertext. Then the multiplicative depth of Algorithm 10 is $\log k + 3(l_1 + l_2) + 2$.*

4.2   Homomorphic Power Method

The homomorphic power method computes the top l principal components of the data matrix X homomorphically. It finds the largest eigenvector of the covariance matrix and uses the Eigen shift procedure to find the subsequent eigenvectors. It uses Algorithm 10 to compute the norm and its inverse.

Lemma 5. *Let l_1, l_2, l_3 be the number of iterations in Algorithms 9, 10, 11 respectively. Let k be the size of the sub-ciphertext and l be the number principal components. Then the multiplicative depth of the Algorithm 11 is $ll_3(2\log(k) + 3(l_1 + l_2) + 7)$*

4.3   Homomorphic PCA

We perform PCA (principal component analysis) homomorphically using Algorithm 12. In Algorithm 12, the client first computes the mean vector and subtracts the mean vector from all other vectors to center the data matrix about

---

Algorithm 10. Goldschmidt(c)

Input: c : Ciphertext,
Output: x: Norm of c, h: Inverse of norm of c
  half $\leftarrow$ Ciphertext(0.5) {A ciphertext with all its entries as 0.5}
  neg_one $\leftarrow$ Ciphertext(-1.0) {A ciphertext with all its entries as -1.0}
  norm $\leftarrow$ Re_encrypt(Partial_sum(square(c)))
  $y \leftarrow$ Re_encrypt(InvNormApprox(norm))
  $x \leftarrow$ multiply(norm, y)
  $h \leftarrow$ multiply(norm, half)
  for $i = 1$ to *iterations* **do**
    temp_r $\leftarrow$ multiply(multiply(x, h), neg_one)
    $r \leftarrow$ add(temp_r, half)
    $x \leftarrow$ add(x, multiply(x, r))
    $h \leftarrow$ add(h, multiply(h, r))
    if depth(x) ≤ 2 **then**
      $x \leftarrow$ Re_encrypt(x)
      $h \leftarrow$ Re_encrypt(h)
    end if
  end for
  two $\leftarrow$ Ciphertext(2.0) {A ciphertext with all its entries as 2.0}
  $h \leftarrow$ multiply(h, two)
  return x, h

Algorithm 11. PowerMethod(X)

Input: X: Ciphertext packing of the original data matrix
Output: W: Top l principal components of X
  $W \leftarrow \{\}$
  $\Lambda \leftarrow \{\}$
  neg_one $\leftarrow$ Ciphertext(-1.0) {A ciphertext with all its entries as -1.0}
  for components $= 1$ to l **do**
    $r \xleftarrow{\$} \mathbb{R}^d$
    for $i = 1$ to *iterations* **do**
      $s1 \leftarrow \sum_{x \in X}$ multiply(x, InnerProduct(x, r))
      $s1 \leftarrow$ SubSum($s1$)
      $s1 \leftarrow$ Re_encrypt($s1$)
      $s2 \leftarrow \sum_{\lambda \in \Lambda; w \in W}$ multiply(λ, multiply(w, InnerProduct(w, r)))
      $s2 \leftarrow$ Re_encrypt($s2$)
      $s2 \leftarrow$ multiply($s2$, neg_one)
      $s \leftarrow$ add(s1, s2)
      eig_val, eig_inv $\leftarrow$ Goldschmidt(s)
      $r \leftarrow$ Re_encrypt(multiply(eig_inv, s))
    end for
    $W \leftarrow W \cup r$
    $\Lambda \leftarrow \Lambda \cup$ eig_val
  end for
  return W

its mean. Then, the original data's principal components are obtained from the server using Algorithm 11 by performing computations on encrypted data. Finally, the principal components are multiplied by the client to get the lower dimensional representation of the original data.

Algorithm 12. HPCA(X)

Input: X : Data Matrix with row vectors
Output: X_red: Reduced data matrix with k principal components of X
  Server:
  Recieve X' from Client.
  $W \leftarrow$ PowerMethod(X')
  Send W to Client.
  Client:
  $X\_tmp \leftarrow X -$ mean(X)
  $X' \leftarrow$ Encrypt(X_tmp)
  Send X' to Server.
  Receive W from Server.
  $W \leftarrow$ Decrypt(W)
  $X\_red \leftarrow X\_tmp \cdot W$
  return X_red

---

5 Implementation Details and Results

We implemented all the procedures described in this paper using Python. We used SEAL-Python [24] (A python binding for Microsoft SEAL library [23]) for the implementation of the CKKS scheme. All the experiments were run on a machine with Intel® Core™ i5-7200U CPU @ 2.50 GHz having 4 cores. The machine ran on 64-bit Ubuntu 20.04.2 LTS with a memory of 7.6 GiB and a disk capacity of 1 TB. We conducted experiments on seven datasets. Four of them were categorical datasets - air quality [11], Parkinsons telemonitoring [25], winequailty-red [9] and winequality-white [9]. The other three were image datasets - MNIST handwritten digits [17], Fashion-MNIST [28] and Yale face database [1]. We computed each dataset's first few principal components and verified our HPCA algorithm's efficiency by computing the R2 score on the reconstructed data. R2 score gives a measure of the variance captured in the reconstructed data and provides the goodness of fit.

Datasets were scaled appropriately so that eigenvalues are small enough to be handled properly. The Yale database was converted from three channels to a single channel and then resized from 195×231 pixels to 16×16 pixels using bicubic interpolation. Similarly, the MNIST handwritten and Fashion-MNIST datasets were resized from 28×28 pixels to 16×16 by trimming the images' outer boundaries as they contain 0's only. We also conducted few experiments by eliminating the last five features of the Parkinsons telemonitoring dataset to make the number of features exact power of 2 (from 21 to 16). For linear approximation of $\frac{1}{\sqrt{x}}$, we considered the interval $[0.001, 750]$ and obtained the coefficients for the line $y = ax + b$ as $a = -0.00019703$ and $b = 0.14777278$ using SLSQP solver. The negative slope illustrates the decreasing trend of $\frac{1}{\sqrt{x}}$ function. The values for number of iterations l_1, l_2 and l_3 for Algorithms 9, 10 and 11 were fixed to be 2, 4, 4 respectively.

5.1 Parameter Selection

We did not use bootstrapping in our implementation as it is not provided as an inbuilt API in the SEAL library. Instead, we re-encrypted some of the parameters to get rid of the noise in them. Re-encryptions are used to be ideally replaced by bootstrapping without making changes to any other part of the algorithm. We ensured that we do not have to re-encrypt any ciphertext from the input, making the number of re-encryptions independent of the dataset. For this, we observe that the maximum depth required by each ciphertext is $\log(k) + 2$ in Algorithm 11. To further reduce the number of re-encryptions, we also restricted the re-encryption of eigenvectors. For this, we require a maximum depth of $\log(k) + 3$ in Algorithm 11. So, the maximum depth used was $\log(k) + 3$.

Re-encryption could be thought of as a server sending a ciphertext back to the client in public-key setting. The client re-encrypts the ciphertext and sends it back to the server. This would require some bytes of communication between the server and the client. For $N = 16384$, we communicate about 128 KB and for $N = 32768$, we communicate about 256 KB of information in a single round trip. Using Lemma 6, we compute the total communication cost between the client and server as shown in Table 1.

Lemma 6. *Let l_2, l_3 be the number of iterations of Algorithms 10, 11 respectively. Let l be the number of principal components and z be the maximum depth used. Then the number of re-encryptions required by Algorithm 12 is $l(l_3(5 + \lceil \frac{3l_2}{z} \rceil))$*

Table 1. Communication cost for re-encryption

N	z	l	Re-encryptions	Bits communicated (in MB)
16384	7	2	72	9.009
16384	8	2	56	7.007
32768	11	4	112	14.014
32768	11	5	140	17.517
32768	11	6	168	21.021

In all of our experiments, we used the polynomial modulus degree (N) of 16384 and 32768. This gave us a total of 438, 881 bits respectively for coefficient modulus to achieve 128-bit security. The scale was chosen to be 2^{40} to achieve 20 bits of precision after the decimal point.

5.2   Results

We computed the first few principal components for each dataset. Then we measured the R2 score of the reconstructed data to use it as an evaluation metric. We also compared the results obtained by performing PCA on un-encrypted data to verify the efficiency of our HPCA algorithm. An R2 score between 0.3–0.7 is considered a good fit for the original data. We also measured the total time taken by all the procedures on different datasets. Table 2 summarizes all the results obtained after experimentation on different datasets[1].

Table 2. Performance of HPCA (Homomorphic PCA) algorithm on different datasets

Dataset	d	k	N	$j = \frac{N}{2k}$	n	l	Depth	R2 Score (Encrypted)	R2 Score (Un-encrypted)	Time Taken (in mins)
MNIST	256	256	32768	64	100	4	11	0.15667	0.3320	9.2965
	256	256	32768	64	200	4	11	0.1410	0.4124	12.9907
Fashion-MNIST	256	256	32768	64	100	4	11	0.4199	0.5013	9.2878
	256	256	32768	64	200	4	11	0.4111	0.4762	12.9968
Yale	256	256	32768	64	165	4	11	0.5292	0.5191	11.0622
	256	256	32768	64	165	5	11	0.5729	0.6012	15.3264
	256	256	32768	64	165	6	11	0.5790	0.6758	19.8646
Winequailty-white	11	16	16384	512	4898	2	7	0.2517	0.25502	2.4066
	11	16	32768	1024	4898	2	11	0.2544	0.25502	5.2634
Winequailty-red	11	16	16384	512	1599	2	7	0.1487	0.20001	1.4447
	11	16	32768	1024	1599	2	11	0.1463	0.20001	2.8728
Air Quality	13	16	16384	512	9357	2	7	0.6012	0.6062	3.3823
	13	16	32768	1024	9357	2	11	0.6054	0.6062	8.6394
Parkinsons	16	16	16384	512	9357	2	7	0.1509	0.1604	2.2068
	21	32	16384	256	9357	2	8	0.14488	0.1604	5.4160
	16	16	32768	1024	9357	2	11	0.1506	0.1604	5.8734

From Table 2 we observe that our HPCA algorithm can capture variance to a considerable amount in different datasets. It does not perform well on the MNIST dataset, with a significant difference between the R2 score on encrypted and unencrypted data. It performs moderately well on Fashion-MNIST and winequality-red datasets. But it performs pretty well on the Yale face database, air quality, winequality-white and Parkinson's telemonitoring datasets. The datasets on which our HPCA algorithm's performance on encrypted data are similar to that of PCA on un-encrypted data are the datasets that either have a considerable difference between their successive eigenvalues of the variance is captured by the first few principal components. Figure 1 shows the first 4 eigenfaces obtained by the HPCA algorithm. Figure 2 shows how an image looks after reconstruction using a few principal components.

---

[1] Time taken mentioned in Table 2 doesn't take into account the communication time required for re-encryption.

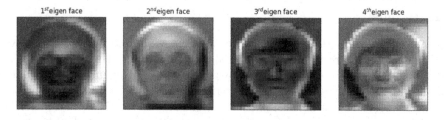

Fig. 1. First four eigenfaces for Yale face Database obtained using HPCA algorithm

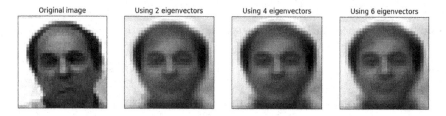

Fig. 2. Reconstruction of a image from Yale face database using principal components obtained from HPCA algorithm

6   Conclusion and Future Work

This paper presents the HPCA algorithm that performs PCA on encrypted data using CKKS homomorphic encryption scheme. Our HPCA algorithm does not require any matrix operations and doesn't require us to store the original data's covariance matrix. This reduces the memory and computational requirements significantly. Calculation of the norm and its inverse are the most computationally heavy operations in the HPCA algorithm. Most of the previous works, including [22] and [19] do not compute norm or its inverse homomorphically. Instead, the client is required to calculate the norm after decryption. This makes their algorithm interactive in nature for computing subsequent principal components. We tried to overcome this problem and tried to reduce the client's computational burden by evaluating the norm and its inverse homomorphically on the client-side. With the use of bootstrapping, our algorithm would become totally non-interactive.

Numerical stability of various algorithms could be studied as appropriate scaling of data is required for obtaining the first few principal components. Iterative algorithms like the power method accumulate noise after each iteration. This seems to be the major drawback of our HPCA algorithm, which restricts us from computing only the first few principal components. It would be interesting to learn how noise grows for each component of the HPCA algorithm with each iteration and how it affects the maximum number of principal components found in a given setting. Other alternatives of power method like gradient descent could also be used instead. Finally, we measure the R2 score of the reconstructed data for different datasets to demonstrate our algorithm's efficiency.

The R2 score obtained from our HPCA algorithm is almost comparable to the R2 score obtained on most of the datasets without encryption. The implementation of all the algorithms can be found in [21]. A parallelized version of HPCA could also be developed to achieve faster runtime.

Acknowledgement. We would like to sincerely thank all the anonymous reviewers for their valuable feedback and Dr. Kannan Srinathan for providing the necessary motivation.

References

1. Belhumeur, P.N., Hespanha, J.P., Kriegman, D.J.: Eigenfaces vs. fisherfaces: recognition using class specific linear projection. IEEE Trans. Pattern Anal. Mach. Intell. **19**(7), 711–720 (1997). https://doi.org/10.1109/34.598228

2. Boura, C., Gama, N., Georgieva, M., Jetchev, D.: Chimera: combining ring-LWE-based fully homomorphic encryption schemes. Cryptology ePrint Archive, Report 2018/758 (2018). https://eprint.iacr.org/2018/758

3. Boura, C., Gama, N., Georgieva, M., Jetchev, D.: Simulating homomorphic evaluation of deep learning predictions. Cryptology ePrint Archive, Report 2019/591 (2019). https://eprint.iacr.org/2019/591

4. Cetin, G.S., Doroz, Y., Sunar, B., Martin, W.J.: Arithmetic using word-wise homomorphic encryption. Cryptology ePrint Archive, Report 2015/1195 (2015). https://eprint.iacr.org/2015/1195

5. Chen, H., Chillotti, I., Song, Y.: Improved bootstrapping for approximate homomorphic encryption. Cryptology ePrint Archive, Report 2018/1043 (2018). https://eprint.iacr.org/2018/1043

6. Cheon, J.H., Han, K., Kim, A., Kim, M., Song, Y.: Bootstrapping for approximate homomorphic encryption. Cryptology ePrint Archive, Report 2018/153 (2018). https://eprint.iacr.org/2018/153

7. Cheon, J.H., Kim, A., Kim, M., Song, Y.: Homomorphic encryption for arithmetic of approximate numbers. Cryptology ePrint Archive, Report 2016/421 (2016). https://eprint.iacr.org/2016/421

8. Cheon, J.H., Kim, A., Yhee, D.: Multi-dimensional packing for heaan for approximate matrix arithmetics. Cryptology ePrint Archive, Report 2018/1245 (2018). https://eprint.iacr.org/2018/1245

9. Cortez, P., Cerdeira, A., Almeida, F., Matos, T., Reis, J.: Modeling wine preferences by data mining from physicochemical properties. Decis. Support Syst. **47**(4), 547–553 (2009). https://doi.org/10.1016/j.dss.2009.05.016. https://www.sciencedirect.com/science/article/pii/S0167923609001377. Smart Business Networks: Concepts and Empirical Evidence

10. Crockett, E.: A low-depth homomorphic circuit for logistic regression model training. Cryptology ePrint Archive, Report 2020/1483 (2020). https://eprint.iacr.org/2020/1483

11. De Vito, S., Massera, E., Piga, M., Martinotto, L., Di Francia, G.: On field calibration of an electronic nose for benzene estimation in an urban pollution monitoring scenario. Sens. Actuators B Chem. **129**(2), 750–757 (2008). https://doi.org/10.1016/j.snb.2007.09.060. https://www.sciencedirect.com/science/article/pii/S0925400507007691

12. Gentry, C.: A fully homomorphic encryption scheme. Ph.D. thesis, Stanford University (2009). https://crypto.stanford.edu/craig
13. Gentry, C.: Fully homomorphic encryption using ideal lattices. In: Proceedings of STOC, pp. 169–178 (2009)
14. Han, K., Hong, S., Cheon, J.H., Park, D.: Efficient logistic regression on large encrypted data. Cryptology ePrint Archive, Report 2018/662 (2018). https://eprint.iacr.org/2018/662
15. Kim, A., Song, Y., Kim, M., Lee, K., Cheon, J.H.: Logistic regression model training based on the approximate homomorphic encryption. Cryptology ePrint Archive, Report 2018/254 (2018). https://eprint.iacr.org/2018/254
16. Kim, M., Song, Y., Wang, S., Xia, Y., Jiang, X.: Secure logistic regression based on homomorphic encryption: design and evaluation. Cryptology ePrint Archive, Report 2018/074 (2018). https://eprint.iacr.org/2018/074
17. LeCun, Y., Cortes, C., Burges, C.: Mnist handwritten digit database. ATT Labs, vol. 2 (2010). http://yann.lecun.com/exdb/mnist
18. Lomont, C.: Fast inverse square root. Purdue University, Technical report (2003). http://www.matrix67.com/data/InvSqrt.pdf
19. Lu, W., Kawasaki, S., Sakuma, J.: Using fully homomorphic encryption for statistical analysis of categorical, ordinal and numerical data. Cryptology ePrint Archive, Report 2016/1163 (2016). https://eprint.iacr.org/2016/1163
20. Markstein, P.: Software division and square root using Goldschmidt's algorithms (2004)
21. Panda, S.: Homomorphic PCA (2021). https://github.com/pandasamanvaya/Homomorphic_PCA
22. Rathee, D., Mishra, P.K., Yasuda, M.: Faster PCA and linear regression through hypercubes in helib. Cryptology ePrint Archive, Report 2018/801 (2018). https://eprint.iacr.org/2018/801
23. Microsoft SEAL (release 3.6), Microsoft Research, Redmond, November 2020. https://github.com/Microsoft/SEAL
24. Python binding for the Microsoft SEAL library. https://github.com/Huelse/SEAL-Python
25. Tsanas, A., Little, M., Mcsharry, P., Ramig, L.: Accurate telemonitoring of Parkinson's disease progression by noninvasive speech tests. IEEE Trans. Biomed. Eng. **57**, 884–93 (2009). https://doi.org/10.1109/TBME.2009.2036000
26. Wikipedia contributors: Fast inverse square root (2021). https://en.wikipedia.org/wiki/Fast_inverse_square_root
27. Wikipedia contributors: Goldschmidt's algorithm – Wikipedia, the free encyclopedia (2021). https://en.wikipedia.org/wiki/Methods_of_computing_square_roots
28. Xiao, H., Rasul, K., Vollgraf, R.: Fashion-mnist: a novel image dataset for benchmarking machine learning algorithms (2017)

DepthStAr: Deep Strange Arguments Detection

Michael Berlin[1]([✉]) [ID], Oded Margalit[1,2] [ID], and Gera Weiss[1] [ID]

[1] Ben-Gurion University of the Negev, Beersheba, Israel
{berlinm,odedm}@post.bgu.ac.il
[2] Computer Science, Citi, Tel Aviv, Israel

Abstract. We present a tool for detecting a new type of bad smell in software code and describe how it was used to find critical security bugs, some of which exist in Linux code for many years and are still present in current distributions. Our tool applies state-of-the-art formal methods and static analysis techniques to scan the execution paths of programs. In this scan, the tool detects conditions that may lead to calling certain functions with strange combinations of arguments, called Abnormal Argument Case (AAC) in this paper. These conditions are presented to the developers as they often point at potential bugs and security vulnerabilities. The paper explains how the tool works and describes an empirical evaluation of its performance.

1 Introduction

In light of several cases of (intentional?) software bugs with serious security implications that has been recently discovered [11], we show a way to preemptively find a new type of code smells that can point developers to possible software vulnerabilities.

The term "code smells" was coined by Kent Beck in the late 90s to describe certain patterns in computer programs that indicate a potential for problems [2]. In this paper, we focus on a specific type of smell that we call Abnormal Argument Case (AAC) or, more commonly, "Strange Arguments". An AAC occurs when the arguments to a function are such that the function behaves in a qualitatively different way than usual. This is potentially harmful because the caller may not have considered the specific conditions that may drive the software to the AAC and therefore, may not have considered the abnormal behaviour of the function. Think, for example, of a program that calls the method realloc with a data-dependent argument. It may happen that the programmers have not considered the fact that, under some conditions, the data may be such that realloc is called with argument zero. In this case, the programmer may have wrongly treated the case where realloc returns NULL as an indication that there is a memory allocation error and did not consider that realloc actually **frees** the space when the new allocation size is zero.

Note that bad smells are usually reported to the programmers for manual analysis. Then, the programmer, when shown the AAC conditions, may notice

© Springer Nature Switzerland AG 2021
S. Dolev et al. (Eds.): CSCML 2021, LNCS 12716, pp. 71–85, 2021.
https://doi.org/10.1007/978-3-030-78086-9_5

that the problem may occur not only when the allocation size is zero, but also when it has overflowed to be small.

In this paper we describe a tool, called DepthStAr, that we have developed for identifying AACs. Our tool is based on the *angr* open-source python framework for analyzing binaries [13]. We use *angr*'s support of state-of-the-art symbolic and concolic execution techniques and other static analysis tools to search for conditions that lead to strange combinations of arguments. Specifically, our tool takes a binary and analyzes conditions that may lead to suspicious invocation of certain functions, as described above. When such conditions are found, the tool generates a report to the programmers that points them to the suspected vulnerability.

We report on two success stories:

1. DepthStAr found known and new bugs in the *libcurl* client-side URL transfer library;
2. DepthStAr pointed at a potential for buffer overrun in a program bundled in most, if not all, Linux distributions, potentially allowing unintended access to privileged operation.

All but one of the AACs we found in *libcurl* where previously found and fixed by others. One was listed as a CWE. This indicates that the AACs that we find are considered harmful by the programmers and by the community. The fact that we found two new AACs shows that our tool is capable of identifying risks that were not discovered by other tools. We obfuscated the details of the second AAC and have informed the developers of our findings as a responsible disclosure (to prevent malicious misuse of our work). We will publish all the details once the vulnerability is mitigated.

The structure of our paper is: In Sect. 2 we describe the goals of our work; in Sect. 3 we explain the *bad code smells* idea; in Sect. 4 we show the methodology we are using; in Sect. 5 we describe the implementation of our approach; in Sect. 6 we evaluate the results of DepthStAr; in Sect. 7 we give a high-level arguments on why our approach is a powerful to get practical results; and in Sect. 8 we summarize the work and suggest directions for future research.

2 Goals

The following list is the set of goals that we designated for our work:

- Identification of common simple and indicative patterns (bad code smells) in software which in many cases are directly associated with potential security weakness.
- Design and build a practical method to help developers easily detect those bad smells and fix them without much effort.
- Make the solution as generic and flexible as possible: we want it to be amenable for further heuristics and improvements, and propose flexible interfaces to developers.

A tool like DepthStAr that involves a human's review to examine weaknesses has to be committed to two evaluation goals in order to be effective:

1. A low percentage of false positives. For practical reasons, the "bad smell" needs to be indicative enough so that the tool will not waste much human time on false positive alerts, that is, cases where an AAC occurs but no actual problem or vulnerability in the code exists.
2. Have improvement over manual human review. It is a seemingly possible claim that if we introduce a human-in-the-loop, then the same human can manually go over all the calls to the functions in the AACs and check if there is a weakness or vulnerability around them.

We achieve both these goals using the *angr* [13] framework to filter out irrelevant cases. Specifically, before pointing users' attention to a code, we run an advanced analysis that filters out a significant portion of the false alarms. In Sect. 6 we relate to these two goals using the statistics of the evaluation. We bring statistics on how many of the reported AACs by our tool were actually weaknesses or vulnerabilities and how many of the calls to key functions in the code were reported as an AAC.

3   Pattern Description

We identify some specific key functions that when called with certain combinations of arguments, behave qualitatively different than usual. Alternatively, the behavior can be expected, but the call itself does not make sense and, in most cases, is part of an execution path that the developer has not considered. An example of the latter is the call to the library function malloc with zero as a size argument. The function behaves just as expected, allocates no memory and returns a NULL pointer. Nevertheless, the programmer could have missed such an odd case and treated the returned value as an indication of a regular allocation error. We denote such key functions and vulnerable arguments as an Abnormal Argument Case (AAC). The vulnerable value of an AAC is often an edge value for the parameter domain. A typical example is a zero argument to an unsigned int parameter caused by an integer overflow.

For comparison, the static code analysis tool *lint* points the programmer to things that are legal C code but do things that might be different than what the programmer meant (if (x=0) instead of if x==0 for example, or even suggest changing to if 0==x). In a similar way, our tool focuses developer' attention the critical places. These places often coincide with other, much more complex, security weaknesses. Thus pointing programmers at AACs often open the gate for locating other types of vulnerabilities and bugs. For example, in *glibcrypt*, a heap overflow vulnerability was recently found [14]. This issue occurred because of an integer wrapped, which is of the type of bugs found when examining AACs. This shows that detailed examination of AACs is a practical way to find all kind of vulnerabilities rooted in the bug that lead to the strange call.

4   Methodology

Symbolic execution is a technique that introduces symbolic, non-concrete values to the program's input. The symbolic values then propagate to other parts of the program. Upon reaching conditional branches, symbolic execution uses Satisfiability Modulo Theories (SMT) solvers to solve the conditions (i.e., path constraints) and continue execution only on satisfiable paths. One of the key advantages of this method is the ease of data flow analysis it provides. For example, consider a case where sensitive data reaches non-authorized regions in memory. Symbolic execution is a useful tool to detect such an issue because it can analyze the dependency of the data in the non-authorized regions. In our case, given some function vfunc and some vulnerable value varg, if the function call vfunc(varg) is considered a security weakness, then the general use of symbolic execution to detect this weakness is as follows: during symbolic execution, for each symbolic state s from which the program is about to make a function call func(arg), we check the satisfiability of the following constraint:

$$\pi_s \wedge func = vfunc \wedge arg = varg$$

where π_s is the path constraint corresponds to the state s (see Sect. 4.1). An example of such work is [1].

Although symbolic execution might help find abnormal values in key function arguments with the method described above, there are many different approaches to how we make practical use of the technique to find full exploitable vulnerabilities without it becoming computationally too hard. Much research has been done to automate such processes. We propose to involve a human review in the process rather than trying to automate the whole process, which might be impractical. Empirically speaking, a simple glance from the original programmer on our tool's output often makes the difference when trying to understand the security weakness's root cause. The involvement of the human review might be in the end or at the middle of the analysis pipeline. This approach seeks to take advantage of symbolic execution's ability to formalize data flow correctly and the programmer's semantic understanding of his or her application.

```
1  void do_task_with_rest(int rest_time) {
2    time_t start_iter, begin_task, end_task;
3    int work_rest_ratio;
4    while (1) {
5      start_iter = time(NULL);
6      sleep(rest_time);
7      start_task = time(NULL);
8      /* long task */
9      end_task = time(NULL);
10     work_rest_ratio = (end_task - start_task) /
11         (start_task - start_iter);
12     if (work_rest_ratio < 5) { return; }
13 }}
```

In the example above, if the function will be called with argument rest_time 0, the time difference between the tasks will also be zero, and a division by zero error will occur. A full report detecting the divide-by-zero bug generated by a fully-automated symbolic execution tool would require an in-depth analysis of the data flow between the sleep and time functions, correct characterization of the environment, and much more complex analysis than is actually needed. A much simpler to obtain output, looking for possible call to sleep(0) and alerting the programmer of the detected AAC, would have the same effect. Note that in the example above, the computational complexity of the analysis is sourced in the need to model physical processes, such as passage of time, in order to correctly identify the problem. The complexity of the analysis could also be rooted in cryptography functions, or even in a complex data structure.

4.1 A Formal Outline of the Algorithm

Below, we define some terms in order to formalize the potential security weaknesses and the algorithm for their detection.

A symbolic state s is defined by the instruction pointer IP_s and by a mix of symbolic and concrete values of memory regions and registers.

For a symbolic state s, the path constraints π_s is defined as the conjunction of all the conditions that must be met along the symbolic execution path in order for a state s to be reached.

A single-value AAC instance is defined by:

1. Target function: The key function we identify.
2. Vulnerable parameter: The index of the critical parameter.
3. Vulnerable value: The value which is considered a potential weakness, when passed as the vulnerable parameter to the target function.

More generally, AACs can also be defined for any target function with parameters $p_1, p_2, \ldots, p_n$ and any predicate of the form:

$$pred \colon \mathrm{Dom}(p_1) \times \cdots \times \mathrm{Dom}(p_n) \to \mathrm{Boolean}$$

This definition allows us to detect more general scenarios. Imagine, for example, that a memory allocation function realloc_from(new_size, orig_size) is being used. In this function, a case where value passed as the new_size argument, and the value passed as the orig_size argument are equal, is an apparent AAC. This case cannot be described with a single-value AAC, but it can be easily described with the predicate based generalization. Another example is the call fopen("", "w+"). Meaning, opening a file with an empty name and creating it if it does not exist. This call is, of course, not legal and returns a NULL pointer, as expected. The error code is then set to the value ENOENT which means "No such file or directory" which may lead to misinterpreting the error and eventually to incorrect behavior.

We focused on single-valued AACs in our tool and in the paper because they are more common and because they are easier to explain and to be used by programmers. Practically speaking, in order to implement a test on a new, general AAC, even given our tool, one needs a firm grasp of the *angr* framework. As we set a goal to build a simple method for developers to use our approach, we bring only the simple-to-create AACs. Creating a single-value AAC requires the user to supply our tool with the three primitive parameters specified in the definition. A symbolic state s where the next instruction to be executed is a function call $F(a_1, \ldots, a_n)$ will be considered a detection of an $AAC = (TF, pred)$ if the conjunction of the following is satisfiable:

– $F = TF$, meaning that the called function is the target function of the AAC.
– $pred(a_1, \ldots, a_n) =$ true.
– π_s.

Given an AAC instance, a verification function VF_{AAC} on a state s will be a predicate which returns true if and only if s is a detection of the instance. A report about an AAC includes The source function from which the symbolic execution began, the call and jump trace of history of the reached state, the path constraint π_s, and the symbolic or concrete values of the passed critical arguments.

The general algorithm we propose:

Algorithm 1: AAC Detection

---

initialization;
for *function f in the binary* **do**
    for *AAC* **do**
        | set a break-point at the target function (TF) of the AAC[1];
    end
    symbolic_execute(start_from=f)
end

---

[1]When at break-point on s a detection report is generated if $VF_{AAC}(s)$ is true.

4.2 Suggested Workflow to Find Exploitable Security Weaknesses

As stated in Sect. 2, we aimed at building a flexible solution. This means keeping the general API simple: a user only needs to specify an AAC as described in Sect. 4.1, and (optionally) a point to start execution from (otherwise, all functions will be considered as starting points). Because of this flexibility, our approach can be effectively applied several times in order to detect real exploitable security weaknesses after the detection of a bad smell: The first time will detect an AAC. Thus, The same API can help one find a possible input to the program such that the AAC detection state will be reached. The entry point should be modified to an actual entry point of the binary (main function or some exported function in case of shared libraries), and a new AAC should be added: this will usually be the source function, from which the execution began, with arguments that are case dependent and are up to the developer - this is the part where the human review can be used within the analysis pipeline. As stated in Sect. 4, from our experience, this part takes, for a skilled programmer, around 15 min, even in large-scale systems even when the human reviewer is not the original developer. The second run's goal is to reduce the AAC location's depth relative to the entry point. If the case is detected when the execution begins from the entry point, we can be sure that it is reachable and, if it points to some vulnerability, it is also exploitable.

5   Implementation

5.1   The *angr* Framework

The *angr* [13] package is an open-source, binary analysis, Python library and software framework. It was initially designed to solve CTF (Capture The Flag) puzzles. It was later extended with functionalities that implement the state-of-the-art symbolic execution and concolic execution techniques, as well as other static analysis features such as control flow graph (CFG) and data flow graph (DFG) generation. Those capabilities make *angr* a very useful tool for research and development in the area of binary analysis techniques, as it can help implement novel approaches and techniques without spending time and efforts on implementing infrastructure and known algorithms.

5.2   Implementation Details

The main functions of *angr* that we used are:

- The CLE loader: Can load different binary types, resolve and load their imported libraries and provide process' memory abstraction to imitate real OS's loader.
- CFG generation: This allows to generate a Control Flow Graph (CFG), including indirect jump resolution. Moreover, this allows function identification by their source object, construction of an object for each function and building and sorting them into a comfortable data structure. This is done by applying heuristics and reasonable assumptions to keep the process short.
- Identification of regions in the binary that belong to the main object and are not loaded from libraries. This helps us to only start the analysis from the functions of the software we are testing, rather than wasting time on verifying library functions.
- Event based break points: *angr* has a state plugin called inspect. It allows setting breakpoints on the symbolic execution, based on various events (memory read/write, register read/write, call/return from functions etc.). We leverage this ability for intercepting symbolic execution at function calls and test the satisfiability of a detection.
- Solver engine: *angr* is using the Z3 SMT solver [10] to solve constraints, and Z3 has an API which *angr* can use to send specific queries within some symbolic state context.

During the implementation of our tool, several bugs of *angr* were discovered, reported and quickly patched by the *angr* team.

In addition, we implemented an exploration technique, i.e., an *angr* extension, which is responsible for bounding the time and space consumed by the execution. This is done by two configurable parameters:

1. Timeout: Maximum time in seconds that each execution is allowed to run. Every source function from which execution begins, we consider a new execution for the timeout. Execution is terminated upon timeout.
2. States Limit: Maximum number of active states. Execution is terminated upon this limit reach.

Solving SAT problems is NP-Hard problem, so expecting to have an efficient algorithm is not realistic. On the other hand, our work showed that we do get practical solutions to our needs. The two parameters above are just an initial demonstration of how heuristics be used to make practical progress. We believe that there is much more to it and leave this for future research.

For example, we changed the above parameters according to logical considerations. When a function called "main" was executed, we turned on aggressive mode. This means that we increased the parameters specified above by a factor of ten. The idea behind this mode is that we want to go deeper in the execution tree when we start from the "main" function because it is more likely that normal execution will go deeper when starting from this function. For this reason, we are willing to spend more time and space once on every binary we test.

6   Evaluation

We set three empirically-measurable requirements to our work:

1. Low percentage of false positives. That is, cases where an AAC is reported but no actual problem was present in the code should be avoided.
2. Have improvement over manual human review. We test this by showing the ratio between the detections reported and the verifications made by DepthStAr.
3. The ability to detect security weaknesses or vulnerabilities in common open-source software, that have not been detected before.

In this section, we show the evaluation of DepthStAr and use it to explain how it was able to meet the requirements set above. In Table 1, are the parameters that measure the first two requirements. The table shows that the number of verifications had to be made by our tool is significantly larger than the amount of detections. Thus, it would be very impractical to imitate these results with manual review of all the key functions. Moreover, we see that the number of total detections sums up to a few on each binary that is tested. Detections, out of which, a none negligible amount turns out to be real problems in the code. The AAC reports, produced by DepthStAr, are detailed and have much information about the case. This gives the programmer the ability to review an AAC quickly, and it turns the classification of one as a false positive into a matter of minutes. For this reason, even a ratio of one true positive on six detections, as it is in the *libcurl*-7.75.0 test case, is acceptable.

Table 1. Top-level data on the analysis

Binary	Number of verifications	Number of detections	Number of true positives
libcurl v7.50.1	2742	9	8
libcurl-7.75.0	764	6	1
–	29	1	1

6.1 Rediscovery of Known Weaknesses in *libcurl*

We tested our tool on a previous version of the cURL tool library, called *libcurl*, version 7.50.1. This, to test if it finds some weaknesses we already knew were there, and maybe others that were already patched but we were not aware of. In Table 2 are some of the memory-related security weaknesses and bad smells our tool detected.

Table 2. AACs detected in *libcurl v7.50.1*

Function	AAC	Time (Sec.)[a]	Constraint size	Jump depth[b]
curl_easy_escape	realloc with size 0	1.5	4	4
curl_easy_escape	malloc with size 0	<0.5	1	1
AddFormData	memcpy with size 0	2	7	4
Curl_ssl_init_certinfo	calloc with size 0	0.5	2	2
alloc_addbyter[c]	realloc with size 0	0.5	3	3
Curl_ftp_parselist[d]	realloc with size 0	2	3	4

[a]Executed on a computer cluster with an allocation of 100 GB of memory and 16 CPU cores. Time from the beginning of the function execution.
[b]Number of jumps (calls and returns) along the path.
[c]This AAC led to a listed CWE-415 [7].
[d]This AAC is present in the current version of libcurl and discussed in Sect. 6.2.

Except for the last one, all of the cases we detected were fixed in the code and are no longer present in the current version of *libcurl*. Some of the cases were denoted as weaknesses and patched. The rest were refactored without special documentation as exploitable security weaknesses. This addresses the first requirement presented in the beginning of this section. It shows that the AACs almost always point towards a piece of code that should ideally be patched or refactored. Another takeaway from Table 2 is that all of the detected cases were detected in a relatively low-depth in the execution tree. This supports the claim

in Sect. 5.2 that introducing an improvement in the path selection algorithm
can lead to better results, reaching deeper states of execution. Section 6.3 discusses the current scaling capabilities and limitations from the perspective of
the dimensions of the states tree.

6.2   Newly Detected Weaknesses

We achieved our major success story using DepthStAr while testing one of the
most common programs, bundled in most, if not all, Linux distributions for many
years. This program frequently interacts with the kernel and sensitive data, and
thus its compromise might constitute some severe risks to the vulnerable systems. We will not reveal the name of the program out of responsible disclosure
considerations. A call to malloc was detected, with a size argument that can
potentially have an integer overflow and wrap to a small integer, thus allocating
a too-small buffer and then copying user-controlled data into it, potentially over-
flowing from its boundaries and forming severe security exposure. The function
below is a paraphrased[2] version of the original function present in the program
we tested. It is called upon almost every execution of the main program. The
argument to this function is passed directly from user input.

```
ret_type func( char *arg) ) {
    ...
    var = malloc (CONST*strlen(arg));
    ...
    copy(var, user_data);
    ...
}
```

We also tested DepthStAr on the most recent *libcurl* version - *libcurl*-7.75.0.
We wanted to test and compare the old version to the previous one in terms of
the number of detected AACs. The tool's results on the latest version confirm
that few detections are left and that good, actively maintained software should
strive to reduce the number of such cases.

```
char *tmp = realloc(finfo ->b_data,
finfo ->b_size + FTP_BUFFER_ALLOCSIZE);
if (tmp) { /* ... */ }
else { /* ... */ goto fail; }
/* ... */
fail: /* Clean up any allocated memory */
if (parser ->file_data) {
    Curl_fileinfo_cleanup (parser ->file_data);
    parser ->file_data = NULL;
}
```

Above are the relevant parts of the code from the recent *libcurl* version. We
see a standard-issue when a call to realloc with size argument 0 is possible. If

---

[2] To make it harder to find the program.

such a call happens in the code shown above, the call to the realloc function will free the block passed in the first argument and return NULL. The return value will lead the calling code to fail and to eventually freeing the block once again.

6.3   Synthetic Evaluation

To show how our method scales, we tailored a code where the complexity of looking for AAC increases. The idea behind these test cases is to gradually increase the level of difficulty and test the code's properties the time-to-detection depends on. The difficulty is measured by the dimensions of the states tree; depth and total number of states. We show and discuss the performance of DepthStAr as a function of these two parameters.

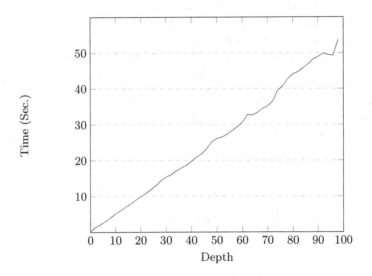

Fig. 1. Time to detection as a function of state's depth

```
1  int main(int argc, char* argv[]){
2      int number, depth = atoi(argv[1]);
3      for (int i = 0; i < depth; i++){
4          number = rand() % 100;
5          if (number > 50){ exit(0); }
6      }
7      malloc(number);
8  }
```

In Fig. 1 are the results of DepthStAr, tested on a code where the states tree goes increasingly deeper, but not wider. This is achieved with the code above. We use the random function as a method of introducing a fresh symbolic integer on each iteration. This could also be user input or anything that is unknown at static time. The graph's linearity shows that in our implementation, detecting AACs that reside at deep states can be done without increasing the run-time (by more than the time it takes to reach the deep state). This supports the claim that applying heuristics and improving the path selection algorithm will be beneficial to our method. Such algorithms will artificially turn tested programs to be more alike to the above code, meaning a branch will be cut off when it is not likely or impossible to lead to an AAC.

```
int func(int depth){
    if (depth == 3){ return 1; }
    if (depth == 1){ return 0; }
    int number = rand() % 100;
    return number > 50 ? func(depth / 2) : func(depth - 1);
}
```

In Fig. 2 are the results of DepthStAr, tested on a code where the states tree goes increasingly deeper and wider. This is achieved using the code above. The graph shows the performance when the states tree grows exponentially to the normal execution length (depth). We see that the time it takes to detect all the AACs, unsurprisingly, grows together with the number of states. Nevertheless, detecting some low-depth AACs is still practical and is not damaged by the growing number of states. This indicates that our method can scale for even large programs. In such, it will manage to detect not all, but some, of the AACs in them.

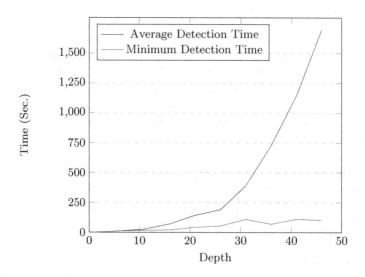

Fig. 2. Time to detection as a function of state's depth

7   A More General Take Away

In this paper we discussed a specific type of bad smells and its detection. Many other studies have been made in the field of symbolic execution improvement [6] and their practical application to automate the process of vulnerability detection [3,5,8]. Attempts also has been made to automate the exploit generation process on some vulnerabilities [9]. This is often achieved by applying sophisticated heuristics in the path selection algorithm of symbolic execution. The goal of this heuristics is to explore states that are deeper and more likely to be vulnerable [4]. An interesting debate regarding the scientific efforts in this field is whether it should focus on these automation techniques rather than on finding bad smells. We give some high-level arguments on why we believe our approach, of detecting bad smells in code and pointing the developer in the right direction, is the right way to get practical results. As discussed in Sect. 4, there are numerous challenges for fully-automatic tools to get practical results. Among them are the use of cryptographic functions, physical properties like time and sensory information, complex data structures, obfuscation, packers, and many others. We argue that it is more practical to identify the points of complexity and correctly delegate them to a human-in-the-loop. The reason being that many of those difficulties are relatively simple for a human being to overcome. Many times, human look at problem with abstractions that allow them to put aside details that are not relevant for solving the problem. As said above, these details may significantly complicate things for solvers.

An example of this phenomenon can be observed in an unrelated topic: chess engines. In Fig. 3, we see an odd chess situation. All of the black pieces are locked-up on the board's left side and cannot move unless the white player moves the pawn on c6. In addition, there are three black bishops outside the locked zone. Even beginner chess players would recognize immediately that the black bishops cannot checkmate the white king because they cannot "see" the light squares. Thus, this position is completely drawn. On the contrary, chess engines give black 18 points (equivalent to being up two queens) of advantage in this position. This is because in order to realize black could never use his material advantage to wtn the game if white plays the optimal moves (only with the king), the engine needs to go very deep into the game tree.

That is not to say that an attempt to automate processes is by any way a mistake, only that we should not underestimate the human mind's potential contribution to this automation. The best way, to our approach, is the correct co-operation between the automating techniques and a human-in-the-loop—each one, solving the challenges that are best suited to it.

Fig. 3. Chess example. Taken from [12]

8   Conclusion

In this study, we have shown that using symbolic execution techniques and identifying simple, but critical bad smells in code, it is possible to detect vulnerabilities. We give multiple examples of such bad smells throughout this paper and explain how they can be harmful. We propose a practical method, using symbolic execution, to quickly detect those bad smells. DepthStAr is a tool we implemented on top of the *angr* binary analysis framework. Thanks to *angr*'s state-of-the-art symbolic execution techniques, together with robust support for loading binaries and analyzing them, we were able to implement our approach simply and practically. We report a success story achieved by DepthStAr while testing our tool on one of the most common Linux programs bundled in almost every Linux distribution in the world. Our tool detected a bad smell, which led us to learn and report a potential buffer overflow vulnerability in the software, leading to almost unlimited writing of user-controlled data to the program's heap. We also report another detection of previously unknown potential weakness in the library of the commonly used Linux cURL program and compare the results to detections of our tool on some older versions of the library.

Acknowledgement. We wish to thank the anonymous reviewers for their valuable comments and suggestions. Specifically, we wish to thank the reviewer that pointed us to the acute need to avoid false positive alarms when a human is involved in the loop.

References

1. Abadi, A., Ettinger, R., Feldman, Y.A., Shomrat, M.: Automatically fixing security vulnerabilities in java code. In: Proceedings of the ACM International Conference Companion on Object Oriented Programming Systems Languages and Applications Companion, pp. 3–4 (2011)
2. Beck, K.: Code smell (1999). https://wiki.c2.com/?CodeSmell. Accessed 20 Feb 2021

3. Boudjema, E.H., Verlan, S., Mokdad, L., Faure, C.: VYPER: vulnerability detection in binary code. Secur. Priv. **3**(2), e100 (2020)

4. Cadar, C., Dunbar, D., Engler, D.R., et al.: Klee: unassisted and automatic generation of high-coverage tests for complex systems programs. In: OSDI, vol. 8, pp. 209–224 (2008)

5. Chen, B., Yang, Z., Lei, L., Cong, K., Xie, F.: Automated bug detection and replay for cots Linux kernel modules with concolic execution. In: 2020 IEEE 27th International Conference on Software Analysis, Evolution and Reengineering (SANER), pp. 172–183 (2020). https://doi.org/10.1109/SANER48275.2020.9054797

6. Chipounov, V., Kuznetsov, V., Candea, G.: S2E: a platform for in-vivo multi-path analysis of software systems. ACM SIGPLAN Not. **46**(3), 265–278 (2011)

7. Cure53: double-free in curl_maprintf (2016). https://curl.se/docs/CVE-2016-8618.html. Accessed 19 Feb 2021

8. Li, H., Kim, T., Bat-Erdene, M., Lee, H.: Software vulnerability detection using backward trace analysis and symbolic execution. In: 2013 International Conference on Availability, Reliability and Security, pp. 446–454. IEEE (2013). https://doi.org/10.1109/ARES.2013.59

9. Lu, K., Walter, M.T., Pfaff, D., Nümberger, S., Lee, W., Backes, M.: Unleashing use-before-initialization vulnerabilities in the Linux kernel using targeted stack spraying. In: NDSS (2017)

10. de Moura, L., Bjørner, N.: Z3: an efficient SMT solver. In: Ramakrishnan, C.R., Rehof, J. (eds.) TACAS 2008. LNCS, vol. 4963, pp. 337–340. Springer, Heidelberg (2008). https://doi.org/10.1007/978-3-540-78800-3_24

11. Novet, J.: Solar winds hack has shaved 23 percent from software company's stock this week (2020). https://www.cnbc.com/2020/12/16/solarwinds-hack-triggers-23percent-stock-haircut-this-week-so-far.html

12. Penrose, R.: Chess problem computers can't solve? (2017). https://www.consciousentities.com/2017/03/chess-problem-computers-cant-solve/

13. Shoshitaishvili, Y., et al.: Sok:(state of) the art of war: Offensive techniques in binary analysis. In: 2016 IEEE Symposium on Security and Privacy (SP), pp. 138–157. IEEE (2016)

14. taviso@google.com: gpg: heap buffer overflow in libgcrypt (2021). https://bugs.chromium.org/p/project-zero/issues/detail?id=2145. Accessed 19 Feb 2021

Robust Multivariate Anomaly-Based Intrusion Detection System for Cyber-Physical Systems

Aneet Kumar Dutta[✉], Rohit Negi, and Sandeep Kumar Shukla

C3i Center, Department of Computer Science and Engineering,
Indian Institute of Technology Kanpur, Kanpur, India
{aneet,rohit,sandeeps}@cse.iitk.ac.in

Abstract. Cyber-physical critical infrastructures such as power plants are no longer air-gapped. Due to IP-Convergence, the control systems and sensor/actuator communication networks are often directly or indirectly connected to the Internet. While network intrusion detection can provide certain cyber defense capabilities, that is not sufficient due to covert attacks or insider attacks. Therefore, in recent years, a lot of research is being carried out to detect intrusion by observing anomalies in the plants' physical dynamics. In this work, we propose a robust anomaly detection mechanism based on a semi-supervised machine learning technique allowing us near real-time localization of attacks. Deep neural network architecture is used to detect anomaly – based on reconstruction error. We demonstrate our method's efficacy on the SWaT dataset. Our method outperforms other existing anomaly detection techniques with an AUC score of 0.9275.

Keywords: SWàT dataset · Neural networks · Robustness · Localization · Autoencoder · Denoising autoencoder · Vulnerabilty · Cyber-physical system · Industrial control system · SCADA · MODBUS · Intrusion detection system

1 Introduction

According to the NIST Cyber Security Framework (CSF) [11], a critical industrial control system (ICS) must implement five functions for cybersecurity – *identify, protect, detect, respond, and recover*. One of the basic assumptions for *security-in-depth* is that while protective security controls must be implemented, one cannot exclude the possibility of attackers circumventing protection such as strong authentication, firewall, network intrusion detection systems (NIDS), host intrusion detection systems (HIDS) etc., as none of these are infallible. Therefore, detecting an ongoing cyber attack must be the next line of defense. While NIDS, HIDS, etc., also are meant to detect intrusion, there are other indicators of an attack in an ICS – in the form of anomalies in the plant's physical dynamics under control. Suppose that the NIDS or HIDS cannot detect the attack due

© Springer Nature Switzerland AG 2021
S. Dolev et al. (Eds.): CSCML 2021, LNCS 12716, pp. 86–93, 2021.
https://doi.org/10.1007/978-3-030-78086-9_6

to evasive techniques used by an attacker. In that case, changes in the physical dynamics will be unavoidable if that is an attacker's goal. Standard bad data detection techniques such as χ^2-test might also fail to detect slowly encroaching changes if the attacker plans the attack to hide the changes in the dynamics within the noise margins.

Other than changes in the plant's actual dynamics, an attacker may manipulate the sensors or inject false data into the industrial protocols carrying sensor data to the controllers for the controllers to make erroneous state estimation and control. Therefore, it is essential to detect anomalies in the sensor measurements at the controllers or at the SCADA in real-time and localize which sensor measurements are anomalous to swiftly alert the security engineers for immediate response actions.

Traditional intrusion detection systems (IDS) consist of rules [1–3] designed to check whether the system dynamics' safety properties are violated. The IDS in Industrial Control System (ICS) generally models the system's behavior because the system follows the proper laws of physics. These systems are large and complex, consisting of many physical parameters measured by devices called sensors and manipulated by actuators. Therefore, manually identifying rules to model the behavior of these complex systems is not scalable. The data-driven approach [4–6,9,10,13,14] helps us in sketching the behavior of ICS and understanding the underlying dynamics of the system. In real-time, when the system's functioning deviates from the modeled behavior beyond a predetermined threshold, it is considered an anomaly. The proposed models are both univariate and multivariate. However, the assumptions of outlier-free training data and entire training data belonging to a normal class persists. Therefore, these IDS cannot guarantee robustness essential for a practical scenario.

The main contributions of this paper are:

1. We propose a multivariate model to detect anomalies in the behavior such that our detection models can be implemented in resource constrained devices.
2. The proposed intrusion detection model is robust and is not affected by the presence of outliers in the training data.
3. Our method retrofits to the existing infrastructure of an ICS.
4. Our method allows real-time localization of the attack points enabling isolation of the victim sections of the infrastructure and enabling containment of damages.

2   Threat Model

This paper considers the communication link between the PLC and SCADA to be the threat vector due to vulnerable industrial communication protocols like MODBUS. Since command injection, false data injection, replay, and MITM attacks are possible in such systems, it will enable an attacker to change their state. The attack scenarios generated are by manipulating the sensor and actuator values in the data packets communicated between the PLC and SCADA (false data injection attacks). So, any number of sensors or actuators or combinations of sensors or actuators can be modified, which implies that the number of classes of attack scenarios that can be constructed is $2^d - 1$ where d is the dimension of the state vector.

3   Proposed Methodology

Considering the behavioral characteristics of the cyber-physical systems, it has a stochastic behavior abiding by laws of physics. The problem of intrusion detection in a stochastic system is about detecting or observing unusual or undesired behavior. So, intrusion detection in a cyber-physical system can be generalized as an anomaly detection problem. Rather than treating our anomaly detection mechanism as a classification problem, our paper finds the reason for the anomaly, which helps us to pinpoint the targeted variables and isolating the compromised section of the system enabling minimization of the damages to the system.

3.1   Anomaly Detection Algorithm-Denoising Autoencoder (DAE)

The reason for choosing the neural network architecture called Autoencoder can be summarized as follows:

- The Autoencoder is trained in an unsupervised setting that does not require any output label y. Since there is a scarcity of labeled data in the cyber-physical system, the Autoencoder satisfies this constraint.
- The Autoencoder enables us to learn the stochastic behavior of the cyber-physical system because the latent features determined by the Autoencoder can model the functioning of the cyber-physical system accurately.
- Autoencoder can transform non-linear dimensionality reduction with its non-linear activation function, which performs better than linear dimensionality technique like Principal Component Ananlysis (PCA) [8].

For robustifying the Autoencoder, we added Gaussian noise or randomly set several individual data entries to 0, thus corrupting the data. This method of adding noise to the training data before training the Autoencoder is known as Denoising Autoencoder [12]. The advantages of performing the denoising task are:

- It makes the algorithm robust to outlier/noise in the training data.
- Prevent identity mapping, i.e., merely copying the input to the output.
- Corrupting the input data results in better learning of the latent representation of the data in lower-dimensional space, resulting in better reconstruction.

The loss function which is optimized during training the denoising autoencoder is:

$$\Phi, \Psi = argmin_{\Phi, \Psi}||X - Z||^2.$$

where Φ and Ψ are the encoding and decoding function respectively.

The reconstruction error between the original input X and the reconstructed input Z is minimized in Denoising autoencoder like an autoencoder, but the reconstruction is done from the latent representation of the corrupted input X' and not original the input X, which prevents the neural network from identity mapping.

The geometric interpretation behind the Denoising Autoencoder's robustness is that the latent representation is the function of X' and not of X. The low dimensional space in which the latent representation of X' lies needs to be closer to the latent representation of X because better encoding of the latent representation is necessary for better reconstruction. Ultimately, the loss function optimized is the difference between the reconstructed input Z and the original input X and not the corrupted input X'. Learning the reconstruction from the corrupted input guarantees robustness of the denoising autoencoder.

Anomaly Score Calculation and Threshold Determination. The anomaly score (d) is calculated by

$$d = ||X - Z||^2$$

where X is the test input data and Z is the reconstructed input $(\Phi o \Psi)X$.

In the threshold (Θ) determination phase, the Anomaly score (d) is calculated for a set of normal data and the maximum anomaly score in this phase is the threshold.

$$\Theta = max\{d_i\}$$

where $i \in [n + 1, m]$ where d_i is the anomaly score corresponding to each data point, n is the number of data points used during learning the parameter of the denoising autoencoder and m is the total number of data points used in the training and threshold determination phase.

3.2   Localization of the Attack Points

The localization of the targeted sensor or actuator is necessary to understand which set of sensors and actuators of the cyber-physical system is malfunctioning. The affected zone or variables can be restored with a backup of the desired state, making the cyber-physical system resilient.

Let Z be the reconstructed data point of the test data, and $\tilde{x}$ be the mean of the reconstructed data points of the normal data points, which is a vector. The targeted variable is identified by the following equation:

$$f = \sqrt{\frac{\sum_{i=1}^{N} Z_i - \tilde{x}}{N - 1}}$$

$$k = argmax_m\{f_m\}$$

where f is a $m * 1$ vector where m is the number of features. f contains the standard deviation of each feature in the reconstructed test data point, and N is the number of data points in the particular time window. k is the index of the targeted variable.

4   Experiments and Results

4.1   Dataset

The SWaT dataset [7] $\{\mathbf{x}_i, y_i\}_{i=1}^m$, $\mathbf{x}_i \in \mathbb{R}^d$, has $m = 449919$ and $d = 51$. The vector $\mathbf{x}_i$ consists of reading of actuators and sensors at ith timestamp. It is a labeled dataset where y_i is the label representing the state of the system either under normal condition or under attack. Since our IDS is designed to work even with unlabelled data, it does not require the labels. However, as a statistical information of the dataset, the label identify that 88% of training data points are normal and rest 12% are under attack. There are total 36 attack scenarios in this dataset.

4.2   Training Phase

In the training phase of the denoising autoencoder, only data representing normal behavior is included. There are a total of 395298 data points belonging to the normal class in the dataset. 70% of these data points, i.e., on 276710, are utilized for training the denoising autoencoder. On another 15%, the denoising autoencoder is validated. The rest 15%, i.e., 59000 data points, are used in the evaluation phase to determine the false-positive rate of our IDS.

Fig. 1 and Fig. 2 is the 2-dimensional plot of the original data point and the reconstructed data point by the denoising autoencoder after training. The root mean squared error is 3.455.

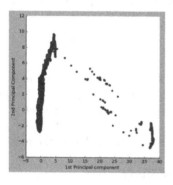

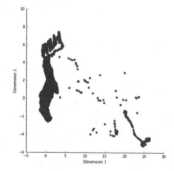

Fig. 1. Original Data points after applying PCA for visualization purpose

Fig. 2. Reconstructed Data points after applying PCA for visualization purpose

4.3   Performance Evaluation Phase

To evaluate our Intrusion Detection model's performance, we used the attack scenarios included in the SWaT dataset and the normal data points in the dataset which are not included in the training phase of the model. The dataset contains a total of 36 attack scenarios.

Attack Scenario 1

In attack scenario 1, the attacker's intent is to overflow tank 1. The attacker targeted the actuator MV-101 to remain OPEN and even after the water level rises above the highest permitted level (800 mm). The level of the tank is indicated by the sensor LIT-101. Figure 3 shows that the LIT101 value increases even after reaching its maximum value.

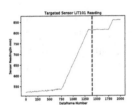
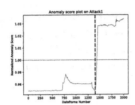
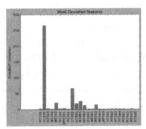

Fig. 3. Sensor reading of LIT101 when under attack

Fig. 4. Normalized anomaly score at each time step

Fig. 5. Standard deviation of all the variables during attack

The attack started from 1400 time step, and it is seen in Fig. 4 that there was a sudden peak in the anomaly score above the threshold when the attack started, from which it can be stated that our IDS is successful in detecting the attack.

Figure 5 shows that the targeted variable (LIT101) shows the maximum deviation among all the variables, enabling us to localize the attack points in real-time.

For brevity we are not demonstrating all the 34 attack scenarios detected successfully.

False Positive Rate

It is observed that there are 287 instances of false positives on 59000 test data points. Therefore, the **false positive rate** is **0.4%**.

Following Table 1 is the evaluation of denoising autoencoder based IDS (DAE) on SWaT dataset.

Table 2 shows the AUC score of different anomaly detection techniques when evaluated over SWaT dataset.

Table 1. Performance metric of denoising autoencoder based IDS on SWaT dataset

Sensitivity	Specificity	Precision	Accuracy	F1-Score	AUC Score
0.8847	0.9939	0.9951	0.9301	0.9367	0.9275

Table 2. AUC score of different anomaly detection methods on SWaT dataset in normal setting

Method	DAE (This paper)	APAE [13]	AE [9]	PCA	OC-SVM [14]	MAD-GAN [4]
AUC	**0.9275**	0.9136	0.896	0.788	0.801	0.532

4.4 Robustness in the Presence of Adversary During Training

Outliers are introduced in the training data in the form of burst outliers at random time points.

However, introducing outliers in the training data does not correspond to a significant drop in the performance of denoising autoencoder based IDS (DAE). In contrast, it is observed that the presence of outliers in the training data significantly diminishes the performance of Autoencoder based IDS without denoising (Table 3).

Table 3. Performance metric comparison between Denoising Autoencoder and Autoencoder in the presence of outliers in the training data

Method	Sensitivity	Specificity	Precision	Accuracy	F1-Score	AUC score
DAE (This paper)	0.8359	0.9931	0.9947	0.8975	0.9085	0.908
AE	0.5930	0.6655	0.8163	0.6137	0.6870	0.605

5 Deployment of DAE in Real Time

The proposed IDS is deployed within the host, which runs the SCADA software where the IDS can read the sensors and actuators reading in real-time at each timestamp from the historian server. The memory size needed to store the denoising autoencoder model developed for the SWaT dataset is 68.6 kB. The time taken to reconstruct data and compare it with the pre-defined threshold is 0.4 ms. The general-purpose machines in which the SCADA software operates have a RAM of 256 MB. Therefore, the proposed IDS is feasible to be deployed in real infrastructure within the SCADA host to detect attacks in real-time.

6 Conclusion

In this paper we proposed a multivariate robust anomaly-based intrusion detection system (IDS) that is resistant to outliers, accurate in detecting attacks, has low false-positive rates, and can identify the targeted sensor/actuator so that the targeted variables can be amputated and restored thus making the critical infrastructure resilient. Compared with other existing anomaly detection techniques developed in normal settings, i.e., no outlier is present in the training data, our proposed denoising-based IDS achieved the highest AUC score of 0.9275.

References

1. Bernabeu, E.E., Thorp, J.S., Centeno, V.: Methodology for a security/dependability adaptive protection scheme based on data mining. IEEE Trans. Power Deliv. **27**(1), 104–111 (2011)
2. Goldenberg, N., Wool, A.: Accurate modeling of Modbus/TCP for intrusion detection in SCADA systems. Int. J. Crit. Infrastruct. Prot. **6**, 63–75 (2013)
3. Adepu, S., Mathur, A.: Distributed Attack Detection in a Water Treatment Plant: Method and Case Study (2018)
4. Li, D., Chen, D., Jin, B., Shi, L., Goh, J., Ng, S.-K.: MAD-GAN: Multivariate Anomaly Detection for Time Series Data with Generative Adversarial Networks, arXiv:1901.04997v1 [cs.LG], 15 January 2019
5. Goh, J., Adepu, S., Tan, M., Lee, Z.S.: Anomaly detection in cyber-physical systems using recurrent neural networks. In: Proceedings of HASE, pp. 140–145. IEEE (2017)
6. Malhotra, P., Vig, L., Shroff, G., Agarwal, P.: Long short term memory networks for anomaly detection in time series. In: Proceedings of ESANN, p. 89 (2015)
7. Goh, J., Adepu, S., Junejo, K.N., Mathur, A.: A dataset to support research in the design of secure water treatment systems. In: Havarneanu, G., Setola, R., Nassopoulos, H., Wolthusen, S. (eds.) CRITIS 2016. LNCS, vol. 10242, pp. 88–99. Springer, Cham (2017). https://doi.org/10.1007/978-3-319-71368-7_8
8. Morita, T., et al.: Detection of cyber-attacks with zone dividing and PCA. In: The Proceedings of the 17th International Conference on Knowledge Based and Intelligent Information and Engineering Systems (2013)
9. Malhotra, P., Ramakrishnan, A., Anand, G., Vig, L., Agarwal, P., Shroff, G.: LSTM-based encoder-decoder for multi-sensor anomaly detection. In: ICML 2016 Anomaly Detection Workshop, New York, NY, USA (2016)
10. Filonov, P., Lavrentyev, A., Vorontsov, A.: Multivariate Industrial Time Series with Cyber-Attack Simulation: Fault Detection Using an LSTM-based Predictive Data Model, arXiv:1612.06676v2cs.LG], 26 December 2016
11. US National Institute of Standards and Technology. NIST cyber security framework, USA (2018)
12. Vincent, P., Larochelle, H., Lajoie, I., Bengio, Y., Manzagol, P.-A.: Stacked denoising autoencoders: learning useful representations in a deep network with a local denoising criterion. J. Mach. Learn. Res. **11**, 3371–3408 (2010)
13. Adam, G., Bryan, H., See Kiong, N., Wee Siong, N.: Robustness of autoencoders for anomaly detection under adversarial impact. In: Proceedings of the Twenty-Ninth International Joint Conference on Artificial Intelligence, (IJCAI 2020) (2020). https://doi.org/10.24963/ijcai.2020/173
14. Chen, Y., Zhou, X.S., Huang, T.S.: One-class SVM for learning in image retrieval. In: International Conference on Image Processing, pp. 34–37. Citeseer (2001)

Privacy-Preserving Password Strength Meters with FHE

Nitesh Emmadi$^{(\boxtimes)}$, Imtiyazuddin Shaik, Harshal Tupsamudre,
Harika Narumanchi, Rajan Mindigal Alasingara Bhattachar,
and Sachin Premsukh Lodha

Cyber Security and Privacy Research Group TCS Research and Innovation, Tata
Consultancy Services, Hyderabad, India
{nitesh.emmadi1,imtiyazuddin.shaik,
h.narumanch,rajan.ma,sachin.lodha}@tcs.com

Abstract. Password strength meter service enables users to assess
strength of the passwords and assist users in setting stronger passwords
for their accounts. However, passwords are private to the users and
may contain sensitive information about them. Hence, it is important
to query password strength meter service in a privacy preserving manner. To address this, we propose fully homomorphic encryption (FHE)
based privacy preserving password strength meters constructed using
widely studied Markov model and Probabilistic Context Free Grammar
(PCFG) model. These privacy preserving strength meters allow clients
to securely evaluate strength of password by providing end-to-end query
privacy to the users. The primitive operation in these constructions comprises of search operation. However, search over large datasets in FHE
domain is expensive and induces worst case complexity. Therefore, our
constructions focus on optimizing search space to suit FHE domain that
improves the efficiency of privacy preserving password strength meter.
Our construction achieves practical performance with accurate guessing
probabilities.

Keywords: Markov model · PCFG model · Privacy · Fully
homomorphic encryption · Password strength.

1 Introduction

Passwords are most widely used means of authentication and are considered to
be most convenient form of authentication for near future [1]. Since end-users
use many passwords on a daily basis, they tend to keep easier passwords with
minor changes across different accounts so that they can remember them easily.
However, keeping passwords with meaningful words or names etc. can make
it easy for an attacker to guess/crack the password [2]. Usually, this kind of
guessing techniques [3–5] rely on probabilistic data distribution models derived
from breached password databases [6]. Retrospectively, these guessing models
can also be used to analyze strengths of passwords too i.e., higher the guessing

© Springer Nature Switzerland AG 2021
S. Dolev et al. (Eds.): CSCML 2021, LNCS 12716, pp. 94–103, 2021.
https://doi.org/10.1007/978-3-030-78086-9_7

probability, lesser the strength of a password. These models can be leveraged to develop password strength meters that can be used by users to assess the strength of the passwords they create.

Passwords are sensitive for users and should be kept private, even from password strength meters. One leaked password might give away the pattern which users use to create many other passwords. Hence, a password strength meter has to be queried in a privacy preserving manner to make sure server doesn't learn anything about user's password. We choose fully homomorphic encryption (FHE) [7] to develop privacy preserving password strength meters. FHE enables computations on encrypted data wherein the encrypted password can be sent to the password strength meter and enable operations on the encrypted password.

Our Contribution: Most notable probabilistic password strength meters in literature are based on Markov model [8,9] and Context free grammar (CFG) [10]. In this paper, we aim to provide end-to-end query privacy for Markov and CFG based strength meters using FHE. This enables clients to send encrypted password to the server for strength analysis and obtain encrypted password strength scores back. Most important operation in these strength meters is search over a dictionary of key-value pairs (a sub-string and corresponding guessing probability). However, a major limitation of FHE is inefficiency to search over large datasets [11]. To address this, we present modified optimized models with reduced search space. We provide an empirical analysis of how this optimization introduce trade-offs in terms of privacy and provide an alternative mechanism of including honey passwords to mitigate this. Furthermore, we also present a privacy preserving index search approach that significantly improves the search functionality.

Related Work: Most recently, [12] explores use of FHE to build privacy preserving strength meters based on NIST standard password strength metering. Authors study performance of primitive operations involved in password strength analysis. Search is the primitive component of any password strength meter and is significant to making password strength meters practical. [12] describes "Dictionary Checker", a hash-based search primitive to search for entries in tables stored on the server. This involves sending the plain hashes to server along with ciphertexts. Additionally, the search method might result in false positives in search, which can be avoided by using appropriately secure hash function with larger output. These becomes a significant overhead on the server side.

These password strength meters are not suitable for encrypted domain due to the computational complexity involved with encrypted search. Complexity of the search operation in encrypted domain is always worst-case, $O(n)$. Therefore, search space optimization i.e., reducing "n", is crucial in making the encrypted password strength meters practical. We propose search space optimizations to these existing password strength meters, making them practical to use in FHE domain. Also, we leverage a much simpler and efficient privacy preserving index search that is error-free and uses packed ciphertexts when compared to Dictionary checker [12]. All parameters related to FHE are set to give 120-bit security whereas [12] considers 80-bit security.

2   Fully Homomorphic Encryption

Fully Homomorphic Encryption (FHE) [7], considered as holy grail of cryptography, enables computations on encrypted data without the need for decryption, thereby preserving privacy of the data. For a set of FHE ciphertexts corresponding to a set of plaintexts, any arbitrary function can be evaluated without revealing the plaintexts. FHE supports addition and multiplication as primitive operations and any arbitrary computation can be realized using these operations.

$$\text{Enc(a+b)=Enc(a) + Enc(b)} \quad (1) \qquad \text{Enc(a*b)=Enc(a) * Enc(b)} \quad (2)$$

To improve the efficiency of homomorphic operations and to reduce space complexity, one can leverage homomorphic batching technique [13] where multiple plaintexts are batched into a single ciphertext, enabling operations to be performed on component wise plaintexts in Single Instruction Multiple Data (SIMD) manner.

Of several FHE schemes known in literature, we choose CKKS [14] scheme implementation from HEAAN [15] library because of its support for floating point arithmetic over encrypted packed ciphertexts [16].

2.1   Privacy Preserving Search

Privacy preserving search function exhaustively searches for a given encrypted key string $\text{Enc}(\sigma)$ in unencrypted look up table ϕ (with key-value pairs $\{\sigma, p_\sigma\}$) and outputs corresponding encrypted score value $\text{Enc}(p_\sigma)$. Each key x in look up table ϕ, is encoded using binary encoding as a bit l-bit string $\{x_1 \ldots x_l\}$. The input $\text{Enc}(\sigma)$ is encoded as an encrypted bit string $\{\text{Enc}(y_1) \ldots \text{Enc}(y_l)\}$. Note that, in FHE domain, binary encoding of plaintext is efficient for comparison dependent applications such as sorting and searching [17].

For each key x in table ϕ, comparison with encoded encrypted bit string $\{\text{Enc}(y_1) \ldots \text{Enc}(y_l)\}$, is given by

$$\text{Enc(comp)}_i = \prod_{k \in [l]} (\text{Enc}(y_k) \oplus x_k \oplus 1) \tag{3}$$

Similarly, the encrypted probability of matched key is given by:

$$\text{Enc}(p_\sigma) = \sum_{i=1}^{|\phi|} (\text{Enc(comp)} * p_i) \tag{4}$$

As we need to iterate exhaustively through the entire table, the complexity of privacy preserving search is worst case, $O(n)$, where n is size of the list.

2.2 Privacy Preserving Index Search

Privacy preserving index search [18] retrieves value at index i in the table of key-value pairs ϕ (`string`, `score`), without actually comparing the target key with keys in the table. The order of keys in the table is assumed to be public (or shared to the client) and values are private to the server. On client side, for alphabet of size Σ, we generate all possible combination strings of length $\Sigma!$. We then generate a vector of same size $(\Sigma!)$ and set value in the target index to 1 and remaining to 0. We encrypt this vector into a batched ciphertext and send it to the server. On server side, we multiply this batched ciphertext with scores vector in the table. The resultant vector will have the required score at the target position and the other position will have encryptions of zero. The target score can be retrieved by rotating the packed ciphertext. .

1. Consider n-grams, score table for alphabet $\Sigma = \{a, b, c\}$:

2. Packed ciphertext to retrive probability of n-gram acb

3. Multiplied packed ciphertext with packed score:

abc	Enc(p_1)
acb	Enc(p_2)
bca	Enc(p_3)
bac	Enc(p_4)
cab	Enc(p_5)
cba	Enc(p_6)

$$\begin{bmatrix} \text{Enc}(0) \\ \text{Enc}(1) \\ \text{Enc}(0) \\ \text{Enc}(0) \\ \text{Enc}(0) \\ \text{Enc}(0) \end{bmatrix}$$

$$\begin{bmatrix} \text{Enc}(p_1) \\ \text{Enc}(p_2) \\ \text{Enc}(p_3) \\ \text{Enc}(p_4) \\ \text{Enc}(p_5) \\ \text{Enc}(p_6) \end{bmatrix} \times \begin{bmatrix} \text{Enc}(0) \\ \text{Enc}(1) \\ \text{Enc}(0) \\ \text{Enc}(0) \\ \text{Enc}(0) \\ \text{Enc}(0) \end{bmatrix} = \begin{bmatrix} \text{Enc}(0) \\ \text{Enc}(p_2) \\ \text{Enc}(0) \\ \text{Enc}(0) \\ \text{Enc}(0) \\ \text{Enc}(0) \end{bmatrix}$$

Enc(p_2) can be fetched into first slot of the packed ciphertext by performing rotations.

3 Privacy Preserving Password Strength Meters

In this paper, we consider Markov model and PCFG model for computing password strength in encrypted domain. The alphabet set we considered for our models consists of 68 elements (26 lowercase letters, 10 digits and 32 special characters), in contrast to original dataset which has 95 elements (26 uppercase letters, 26 lowercase letters, 10 digits, 32 special characters and 1 space). Markov and PCFG models rely mostly on search operation. As the search operation in encrypted domain is an exhaustive worst-case search, larger alphabet size will increase the number of potential passwords, associated n-grams, etc., thus, increasing the search space. Hence, to enable efficient password strength meter in encrypted domain, we consider smaller alphabet size, with 68 alphabets by replacing uppercase characters with lowercase letters [9,10]. Note that this makes probability calculation to be conservative by assigning higher guessing probability for a password enabling users to be more cautious while selecting passwords.

For experiments, we trained password strength meters on RockYou dataset (with count) [6] which contains more than 14 Million entries. All experiments were run on a standard desktop with Intel Xeon Gold CPU clocked at 3.1 Ghz, 16 GB RAM and run on 4 cores. Training Markov and PCFG models have taken 30 mins and 7 h respectively and is done on plain data.

3.1   Privacy Preserving Markov Model

For any string, the probability of a particular character depends on the previous characters in that string. The Markov Model utilizes these conditional probabilities to compute the guessing probability of the whole string. Given a string represented as a sequence of characters $s_1 \ldots s_m$, the guessing probability of the string is given by:

$$P(s_1 \ldots s_m) = \prod_{i=1}^{m} P(s_i | s_{i-n+1} \ldots s_{i-1}) \tag{5}$$

In this paper, we compute information scores from probabilities to score strength of a password as [9,10].

$$H = -\log(p) \tag{6}$$

In FHE, multiplication of ciphertexts is expensive and usually complexity of a computation is determined by the multiplicative depth. Using probabilities for scoring will increase multiplication depth since all probabilities have to be multiplied to get the final score of the password. Hence, using information scores is efficient as it requires adding (instead of multiplication) all the information scores for n-grams or variables to compute overall score of a password. Moreover, the probabilities can be very small values and can incur additional scaling overheads for processing in FHE. Also, floating-point arithmetic in FHE can only serve efficiently up to a certain precision [19]. Beyond a threshold, error increases significantly resulting in inaccurate guessing probabilities for passwords.

We assume a client-server model in which client delegates a password strength computation to a server and obtains password score as result. On the server, using the breached password dataset, we build a Markov model where each n-gram has an associated score generated based on the frequency of that n-gram in the passwords. The server generates n-grams for each of the entry, upto some suitable value of n. For any queried password x, the scores of the corresponding sub-strings (n-gram, a sub-string of length n) are fetched from corresponding n-gram tables and added to result in the guessing score of the password x.

As the n value increases, size of tables becomes huge (for example, for an alphabet size 68, size of 3-g table is 68^3), hence the search space also increases. As search in encrypted domain induces worst case complexity, hence, it is important to reduce search space.

To reduce the search space, for n-gram tables where $n \geq 3$, we sub-divide them into 3-g tables based on the structure of $n\text{-}gram$ to get a set of independent tables. This reduces the search space, thereby improving algorithm efficiency. Though the n-grams of the password that are sent to the server are encrypted, the corresponding structures are sent in plain to enable server to search in the corresponding structure tables. Considering the case of $n = 3$, the original Markov model will have three tables namely 1-g, 2-g and 3-g, where in each table will have the n-grams along with scores associated with them. The query for 1-g and 2-g are manageable in encrypted setting, since table size is 68 and $68^2 (= 4624)$ for 1-g and 2-g respectively and hence they are not

Table 1. Passwords distribution for RockYou dataset using Markov model

Password-type	Threshold	% in dataset
Very-weak	≤20	0.90
Weak	20–30	27.66
Medium	30–40	44.42
Strong	40–50	17.97
Very-strong	≥50	9.03

Table 2. Passwords distribution for RockYou dataset using PCFG and proposed model

Password-type	Original PCFG		Proposed method	
	Threshold	Percentage	Threshold	Percentage
Very-weak	≤20	1.21	≤25	6.93
Weak	20–30	65.34	25–40	59.24
Medium	30–40	23.05	40–55	24.86
Strong	40–50	6.99	55–70	6.586
Very-strong	≥50	3.4018	≥70	2.35

modified. The 3-g table however is partitioned based on the structure of 3-g. This gives us $27(3^3)$ tables, one each for a permutation of structures L,D,S, from $L3$ to $S3$. Table 1 gives distribution of passwords in RockYou dataset as per Markov model using threshold based on scores. We divide passwords into 5 classes $\{Very - weak, Weak, Medium, Strong, Very - Strong\}$. The scoring remains same as the original Markov model, only search space is reduced by dividing 3-g tables into smaller tables using structure information.

The operational flow of the client server model of new Markov strength meter is described as follows:

- Client extracts n-grams $\{\sigma_1, \ldots \sigma_k\}$ from input password x where k is the number of n-grams for a given string. All the uppercase letters and converted to lowercase letters.
- Using his publickey, pk, client forms a batched ciphertexts for each of the n-grams using the privacy preserving indexing search described in Sect. 2.2 and send them to server. For n-grams with $n \geq 3$, the client also sends their corresponding plain structures.
- For 1-g and 2-g ciphertexts, the server performs index search on 1-g and 2-g table and results in packed ciphertexts that consist of encrypted scores. For $n \geq 3$, the server performs index search for n-grams with corresponding n-gram tables based on their structures. The server then rotates and adds slots of these resultant packed ciphertexts to obtain score to the first slot of the ciphertexts.
- These packed ciphertexts with scores in the first slot are homomorphically added to obtain final encrypted score of the password.
- The final encrypted score is sent back to the client.

As we are sending structures of n-grams in plaintext to the server, there is some leakage of password information to the server. To mitigate this, we obfuscate n-grams of the actual password by combining them with dummy passwords (honey passwords). The honey structures obfuscate the actual structures present in the original password. The computation on server homomorphically evaluates only the score of the actual password while nullifying the scores of honey passwords, without server being able to differentiate between honey or actual pass-

words. For our experiments, we have selected honey passwords randomly from
RockYou dataset. Table 4 shows performance of query with honey passwords.

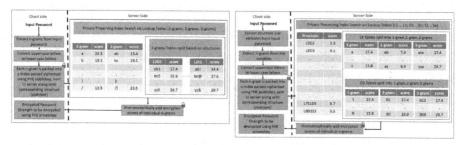

(a) Optimized Markov Model   (b) Optimized PCFG model

Fig. 1. Optimized Markov and PCFG models

3.2   Privacy Preserving PCFG Model

A Probabilistic Context-Free Grammar (PCFG) consists of probabilities
assigned to the production rules. The probability of an input generation is the
product of the probabilities of the production rules contained in that input.
These probabilities can be viewed as parameters of the model. The soundness of
probabilistic grammar is constrained by context of its training dataset.

To build a PCFG model for a password strength analysis model, consider an
example password, "password123" . Here structure will be L8D3. L8 is a non-
terminal indicating lowercase alphabets followed by its count I.e. 8. Similarly,
next non-terminal is D3 which represents digits followed by its count which is
3. This structure of the password is now assigned to a start symbol as "$S->$
$L8D3$" and this is added as rule to the grammar with count as 1. Then a new rule
is added to grammar to define the non-terminal L8 as "$L8-> password$" and a
rule for non-terminal D3 as "$D3-> 123$" with count as 1 for both. Now server
processes all the passwords in similar way and if the structure is already there in
the grammar then the count is simply incremented, otherwise a new rule is added
in the grammar. Once the server completes building the model, the rules with the
same non-terminal are bucketed as one table. The probability for each entry in
the table is calculated as its respective count divided by total of counts of all the
entries in the table. As in the case of Markov model, we calculate corresponding
scores using $-\log(p)$. Thus, server obtains the final grammar which acts as a
model for calculating strength of the password.

For any queried password, its structure is first extracted and it is then split
into variables based on this structure. These variables and structures are queried
in corresponding tables stored on the server to retrieve their scores. These individual scores are aggregated to obtain the final score of the password.

Table 3. Query performance for PCFG model with Honey password

Query	Client side		Server side	
	Time (s)	Memory (MB)	Time (s)	Memory (MB)
1-password + no Honey	0.2	30	4.2	35
1-password + 4-Honey	1.87	287.7	25.2	390
1-password + 9-Honey	2.46	383.1	36.13	499.9
1-password + 14-Honey	3.6	522	54.9	656.7
1-password + 19-Honey	4.78	658.6	72.2	810.7

Table 4. Query performance for Markov model with Honey password

Query	Client side		Server side	
	Time (s)	Memory (MB)	Time (s)	Memory (MB)
1-password + no-Honey	0.37	49	6.4	52
1-password + 4-Honey	3.7	579.8	55.3	819.7
1-password + 9-Honey	5.6	855.6	85.5	1095.7
1-password + 14-Honey	7.5	1104.3	113.6	1344.3
1-password + 19-Honey	9.1	1283.7	135.7	1523.7

In case of encrypted domain, since the search is exhaustive, it becomes expensive to search over huge variable tables. For example, an L8 table could potentially have at-most 26^8 entries and an exhaustive search can be tedious. We can improve the efficiency of search operation by reducing the size of these variable tables. In order to decrease the size of variable tables, we generate intermediate 3-g tables (as in n-gram model 3.1) for each variable table along with the scores. For usual PCFG case, the size of variable table is at-most 32^k (for a structure with k special characters) where k is the size variable length of that table (For example, S8 table will have at-most 32^8 entries). By generating n-gram tables with n = 3, the size of table is reduced at-most 32^3 (for a structure k special characters). To get the probability of a string corresponding to a variable, we generate 3-g for the string, look up the scores in intermediate 3-g tables and add scores of each 3-g to obtain score of the whole variable. It is important to note that in this approach, the scores of the 3-g generated from variable table are higher, which results in higher overall guessing probability of the password. This will result in conservative scoring for a given password which is an advantage to the user.

The operational flow of the client and server (Fig. 1b) is as follows:

- Client extracts structure of the input password and splits the password into variables and corresponding strings based on the structure. All the uppercase letters and converted to lowercase letters.
- For each of the strings, if the length is greater than 3, then 3-g are extracted from the string.
- Using publickey, pk, client forms a batched ciphertext for each of the n-grams using the privacy preserving indexing search described in Sect. 2.2 and send them to server along with their plain structures.
- For each of the n-grams, the server computes privacy preserving index search of the packed ciphertext with server's n-gram table of corresponding structure. The server then rotates and adds slots of these resultant packed ciphertexts to obtain score to the first slot of the ciphertexts.
- These packed ciphertexts with scores in the first slot are homomorphically added to obtain final encrypted score of the password.
- The final encrypted score is sent back to the client.

Original PCFG model is first trained on RockYou dataset to get two types of tables (*i*) structure table (*ii*) variable tables. Since we provide structure information along with variables query ciphertexts, no separate query ciphertext is needed for structure table. Variable tables can be very large, hence in our proposed method we divide each variable table into smaller tables of 1-g, 2-g and 3-g using the Markov model on top of the variable table (here we are using n = 3). Table 2 depicts password distribution using the original PCFG and proposed method. In Table 2, threshold values are different for original PCFG and proposed method because of the following reasons:(1) Minimum score for a password using PCFG method is 6.9 and proposed method is 8.3. (2) Median of scores for passwords using PCFG method is 25.68 and proposed method is 35.7. We infer that this is because of additional 1-g and 2-g generated for each variable table, hence the rise in threshold values. We note that our scoring mechanism is conservative and helps users to choose stronger passwords. Table 3 shows performance of query with honey passwords. As mentioned in Sect. 3.1, we obfuscate variables of the actual password by combining them with dummy passwords (honey passwords). The honey structures conceal the actual structures present in the original password.

4   Conclusion and Future Work

In this paper, we constructed privacy preserving password strength meters by optimizing widely studied n-grams based Markov model and PCFG model. We modelled our solution to provide end-to-end query privacy for the users using fully homomorphic encryption. As deploying existing password strength meters as is in FHE domain exerts computational overhead, we optimize these models to suit the operational model of FHE and improve efficiency. Since search is the primitive operation of both these models. To improve the search efficiency, we also leverage privacy preserving index search that significantly improves the performance. Moreover, to improve efficiency of search in encrypted domain, we perform optimizations to reduce search space by revealing certain information (structures) to the server. We mitigate this by using honey passwords to conceal structure information. As part of future work, we plan to explore privacy preserving computation of machine learning based password strength meters [20].

References

1. Bonneau, J., Herley, C., Oorschot, P.C.V., Stajano, F.: The quest to replace passwords: a framework for comparative evaluation of web authentication schemes. In: 2012 IEEE Symposium on Security and Privacy, pp. 553–567 (2012)
2. John the ripper password cracker (2017). http://www.openwall.com/john/
3. Narayanan, A., Shmatikov, V.: Fast dictionary attacks on passwords using time-space tradeoff. In: Proceedings of the 12th ACM Conference on Computer and Communications Security, CCS '05, pp. 364–372. Association for Computing Machinery, New York, NY, USA (2005)

4. Morris, R., Thompson, K.: Password security: a case history. Commun. ACM **22**(11), 594–597 (1979)
5. Bonneau, J.: The science of guessing: analyzing an anonymized corpus of 70 million passwords. In: 2012 IEEE Symposium on Security and Privacy, pp. 538–552 (2012)
6. Rockyou dataset (2017). https://wiki.skullsecurity.org/Passwords
7. Gentry, C., Boneh, D.: A Fully Homomorphic Encryption Scheme, vol. 20. Stanford University Stanford (2009)
8. Tupsamudre, H., Banahatti, V., Lodha, S.: Poster: improved markov strength meters for passwords. In: Proceedings of the 2016 ACM SIGSAC Conference on Computer and Communications Security, CCS '16, pp. 1775–1777. Association for Computing Machinery, New York, NY, USA (2016)
9. Castelluccia, C., Dürmuth, M., Perito, D.: Adaptive password-strength meters from markov models. In: NDSS (2012)
10. Weir, M., Aggarwal, S., de Medeiros, B., Glodek, B.: Password cracking using probabilistic context-free grammars. In: Proceedings of the 2009 30th IEEE Symposium on Security and Privacy, SP '09, pp. 391–405. IEEE Computer Society, USA (2009)
11. Rivest, R.L., Adleman, L., Dertouzos, M.L., et al.: On data banks and privacy homomorphisms. Found. Secure Comput. **4**(11), 169–180 (1978)
12. Pyung, K., Younho, L., Youn-Sik, H., Taekyoung, K.: A password meter without password exposure. Sensors **21**(2) (2021)
13. Brakerski, Z., Gentry, C., Halevi, S.: Packed ciphertexts in LWE-based homomorphic encryption. In: Kurosawa, K., Hanaoka, G. (eds.) Public-Key Cryptography - PKC 2013. PKC 2013. Lecture Notes in Computer Science, vol. 7778. Springer, Berlin, Heidelberg (2013). https://doi.org/10.1007/978-3-642-36362-7_1
14. Cheon, J.H., Kim, A., Kim, M., Song, Y.: Homomorphic encryption for arithmetic of approximate numbers. In: Takagi, T., Peyrin, T. (eds.) ASIACRYPT 2017. LNCS, vol. 10624, pp. 409–437. Springer, Cham (2017). https://doi.org/10.1007/978-3-319-70694-8_15
15. HEEAN library (2017). https://github.com/kimandrik/HEAAN
16. Shaik, I., Singh, A.K., Narumanchi, H., Emmadi, N., Bhattachar, R.M.A.: A recommender system for efficient implementation of privacy preserving machine learning primitives based on FHE. In: Dolev, S., Kolesnikov, V., Lodha, S., Weiss G. (eds.) Cyber Security Cryptography and Machine Learning. CSCML 2020. Lecture Notes in Computer Science, vol. 12161, pp. 193–218. Springer, Cham (2020). https://doi.org/10.1007/978-3-030-49785-9_13
17. Narumanchi, H., Goyal, D., Emmadi, N., Gauravaram, P.: Performance analysis of sorting of fhe data: integer-wise comparison vs bit-wise comparison. In: 2017 IEEE 31st International Conference on Advanced Information Networking and Applications (AINA), pp. 902–908 (2017)
18. Du, M., Wang, Q., He, M., Weng, J.: Privacy-preserving indexing and query processing for secure dynamic cloud storage. IEEE Trans. Inf. Forensics Secur. **13**(9), 2320–2332 (2018)
19. Arita, S., Nakasato, S.: Fully homomorphic encryption for point numbers. IACR Cryptol. ePrint Arch **2016**, 402 (2016)
20. Melicher, W., Ur, B., Segreti, S.M., Komanduri, S., Bauer, L., Christin, N., Cranor, L.F.: Fast, lean, and accurate: modeling password guessability using neural networks. In: 25th {USENIX} Security Symposium ({USENIX} Security 16), pp. 175–191 (2016)

Automatic Detection of Water Stress in Corn Using Image Processing and Deep Learning

Mor Soffer[1]([✉]), Ofer Hadar[1], and Naftali Lazarovitch[2]

[1] School of Electrical and Computer Engineering,
Ben-Gurion University of the Negev, 8410501 Beer Sheva, Israel
morelm@post.bgu.ac.il, hadar@bgu.ac.il
[2] Wyler Department of Dryland Agriculture, French Associates Institute for
Agriculture and Biotechnology of Drylands, Ben-Gurion University of the Negev,
Sede Boqer Campus, 84990 Beer Sheva, Israel

Abstract. Water stress is one of the main environmental constraints that directly disrupts agriculture and global food supply, thus early and accurate detection of water stress is necessary in order to maintain high agricultural productivity. Using an image dataset collected during a dedicated experiment, we propose a new method for water stress level classification using deep learning and digital images only. Classification is performed in two stages, using a Convolutional Neural Network for spatial feature extraction and a Long Short-Term Memory for temporal features extraction. Outperforming all other methods examined, our model is able to classify five different levels of water stress with 91.7% accuracy and Mean Absolute Error of 0.1, and to detect changes in water stress levels during the day.

Keywords: Water stress · Convolutional Neural Network · Long short Term Memory · Hierarchical classification

1 Introduction

Water limitation is one of the main environmental constraints that adversely affects agricultural crop production around the world. Precise and rapid detection of plant water stress is critical for increasing agricultural productivity and water use efficiency. Numerous studies conducted over the years have attempted to find effective ways to correctly recognize situations of water stress in order to determine irrigation regimes [1,5,10,11,14,16]. Water stress detection is currently done by various methods that are not ideal, as these methods are often very expensive, destructive and cumbersome. Image processing is an alternative way to visually recognize water stress levels. Such analysis is non-destructive, inexpensive and allows examining in an automatic way the spatial variability of stress level under field conditions.

© Springer Nature Switzerland AG 2021
S. Dolev et al. (Eds.): CSCML 2021, LNCS 12716, pp. 104–113, 2021.
https://doi.org/10.1007/978-3-030-78086-9_8

In recent years, there has been significant progress in the field of Deep Neural Networks (DNN), a sub-field of Machine Learning (ML) which has shown excellent performance in many areas, including computer vision. Convolutional Neural Network (CNN), a specialized type of DNN designed for images, became the de facto leading framework for analysis of visual data thanks to its great performance and its ability to learn relevant features automatically, compared to classic ML methods where features are hand-engineered. As a result, many DNN models for agricultural applications have been developed, including models for water stress detection. Some of them [2–4,8,17,20] use State-of-the-Art CNN frameworks, such as ResNet [6] and AlexNet [12], for spatial feature extraction and classification of different water stress levels of various plants photographed continuously. Few of them [9,13,18,19] combine tools for temporal analysis of plants images, such as Long Short-Term Memory (LSTM) [7] and Optical Flow, which consider the plants status over time.

While most of these studies have reported excellent results, some of them have describe a common dataset splitting, in which images are randomly divided into train and test sets although plants images taken every few minutes, thus resulting in information leakage as both train and test sets consist of similar images. In addition, some studies have used images of plants taken from different distances, or whose unique background has not been removed. Using these images for water stress prediction can cause biased results, as the non-uniform distance or non-uniform background is a unique identifier of each treatment group.

In this paper we propose a new method for water stress level classification in corn plants using deep learning and digital images only, while utilizing spatial and temporal features of the plants' images. The classification is performed in two stages to maintain the hierarchical structure of water stress levels, and to simplify the classification task. Several countermeasures were applied to prevent any information leakage, as reported earlier, and the proposed model was evaluated using two datasets.

To the best of our knowledge, this work is the first to take advantage of the ordinal structure of water stress levels, and the first to use a hierarchical structured DNN model for water stress level classification.

2   Proposed Approach

2.1   Dataset

For this study, images were collected during a three-month experiment that have been conducted in a research greenhouse at the Sede Boqer campus of Ben-Gurion University of the Negev, between October to December 2019. In this experiment, five groups of corn that were differently irrigated to induce five different levels of water stress, were examined. In this document we refer to these groups as groups A-E, where group A has the poorest irrigation treatment and group E has the best irrigation treatment. Each group was photographed continuously by a web camera located two meters from the center of each group, such that in each image four clusters of corn plants were observed (see Fig. 3).

As an exploratory data analysis, the average image of each treatment group was calculated by averaging the value of each pixel across all relevant observations, as presented in Fig. 1. Several visual differences between the groups can be observed (especially between groups A and B compared to the other groups), and general group characteristics can be learned from this statistic feature. As detailed in Sect. 3, this analysis can explain some of the model results.

To maintain uniformity and avoid information leakage as introduced earlier, segmentation was applied to all images in order to remove any characteristic that is not related to the plant itself. Segmentation was done using Otsu's method [15], which is commonly used to perform automatic image thresholding.

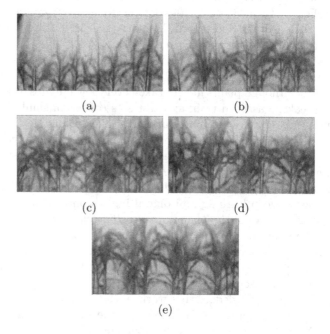

Fig. 1. Average images of groups A-E, represented by (a)-(e) respectively. Calculated by averaging the pixel values across all observations of each group.

2.2 Proposed Method

Unlike previous methods, the proposed model is based on two distinctions: 1) Water stress level classification should not be considered as a standard classification task, as water stress levels hold an *ordinal relationship*, thus form an *ordered set* (the error of classifying a plant from group A to group B is less severe than the error of classifying it to group D). 2) Differences between well irrigated groups to ill irrigated groups might eclipse the subtle differences between similar irrigation treatments, and should be treated with a "divide and conquer" approach to increase attention to details.

Utilizing the above two distinctions, the proposed model consists of two classification stages. In the **first stage**, given an image of a plant and its history (represented by a sequence of images, as detailed below), the model performs a general classification into one of two options - "good irrigation treatment" or "poor irrigation treatment", each represents about half of the groups in the dataset.

In the **second stage**, the model performs a specific classification into treatment groups, given the classification results of the first stage. For example, a plant classified in the first stage as a plant with poor irrigation treatment, will be classified in the second stage into one of the groups A, B or C. The hierarchical architecture allows gradual image classification, thus narrows the model's sample space at each stage to facilitate the final classification. Figure 2 summarizes the model structure.

Assuming that water stress cannot be optimally detected by considering a plant's current state only, the proposed model predicts the water stress level of a plant given its history. Formally put, the model predicts $y(x_t|x_{t-\tau}, x_{t-2\tau}, ..., x_{t-S*\tau})$ instead of $y(x_t)$, where y is the label (group) of image x at time t, given a sequence of images of length S taken at different days.

Both classification stages are performed using a classifier ("CLS" in Fig. 2) consisting of two main modules – a CNN module and an LSTM module. The base network of the CNN module, ResNet50 [6], was retrained with ImageNet weights as initial weights to extract spatial features and create various feature maps. Then, these feature maps are processed by the LSTM module to extract latent temporal features of the sequence. The LSTM's output is then processed by two fully-connected layers, where the latter is used for final prediction. All three classifiers (one in the first stage, two in the second stage) have the same structure, but each is completely independent and learns different features relevant to its task.

3   Results

For model evaluation and to avoid biased conclusions, we have used a cross-validation technique and averaged the results; each image in the dataset was split into 4 separate images, where in every round, a different set consisting of three of the four split images was selected for training, and the remaining set was used for validation (see Fig. 3). This division ensured robustness to bias, as there were no images of the same plant across sets, thus prevented information leakage, in contrast to previous studies.

The proposed hierarchical model resulted in **91.7%** accuracy and a Mean Absolute Error (MAE) of 0.1 on average, with 96.3% success in the first stage, and 95.1% success in the second stage. Figure 4 shows the average accuracy of each group in both stages. In total, groups A and B yielded the highest classification score due to the striking visual differences between them and the other groups (see Fig. 1). Group C, an intermediate group which is more visually

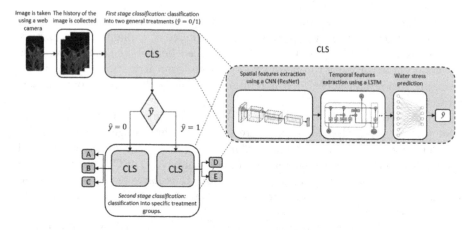

Fig. 2. Proposed two-stage model. "CLS" is the CNN-LSTM classifier. All three classifiers have the same structure, but each is completely independent.

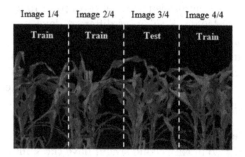

Fig. 3. Example of image splitting to train and test sets. This division ensured robustness to bias, as there were no images of the same plant across sets.

similar to groups D and E (see Fig. 1), had the lowest accuracy in the first stage, but the highest accuracy in the second stage. Group D, on the other hand, has the lowest overall accuracy resulting from a low success rate in the second classification stage. The low accuracy is mainly due to misclassification of samples of the rightmost plant in the group (which visually differs from the rest of the group, see Fig. 1d).

Figure 5 shows the average error rate of each group for each of the experimental days tested, indicating a general trend of error reduction as the experiment progresses. The error values are not uniform for all test sets, thus some fluctuations can be observed. (in Fig. 1, for example, one can see that the rightmost plant in group A is visually different from the rest of the group. Therefore, when this plant is used as a test set, the average error increases slightly on some days). "Exceptional" values are due to extreme lighting changes resulting from winter weather.

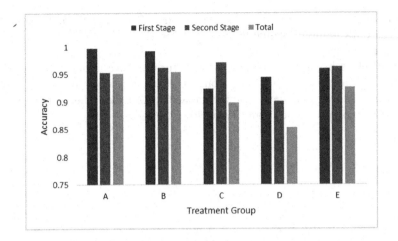

Fig. 4. Classification results of each stage of the model, per group.

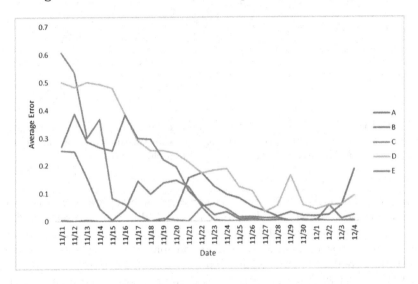

Fig. 5. Average error rate $(1 - accuracy)$ for each of the experimental days tested.

Figure 6 shows a comparison between the classification results of different methods reviewed at the beginning of this work, in terms of accuracy and MAE. As Fig. 6 presents, the proposed model outperformed all other mentioned methods, including ML-based methods (using the Light Gradient Boosting Machine algorithm and the features described in [21], with and without time-dependent features), CNN-only-based methods (using the ResNet50 architecture as base network) and CNN-LSTM-based methods, and managed to accurately classify groups that other models failed to classify. Notice that this improvement is due to a *combination* of the pre-mentioned classifier together with the hierarchical structure of the proposed model. As mentioned in Sect. 2.2, the natural hierarchy of the data is highly valuable, and ignoring those class relationships could reduce performance.

Conversely, a hierarchical classification naturally has a larger capacity (three CNN-LSTM classifiers, in our case, compared to one), while flat classification methods are simple and have a lower capacity. As usual, there is a trade-off between the model's capacity and its accuracy.

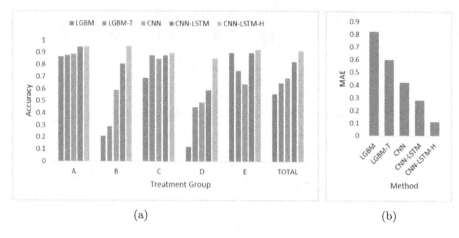

(a)   (b)

Fig. 6. (a) Average accuracy of all tested methods per group. (b) Average MAE. LGBM-T refers to LGBM algorithm (ML-based method) with time-dependent characteristics, CNN-LSTM-H refers to the proposed hierarchical model.

The trained model's ability to detect changes in plant water status during the day was also examined, and validated using a different dataset containing images of corn plants taken at May-June. The average plants' status predicted by the model is presented in Fig. 7. As clearly visible, several changes in the plant water status were detected by the model during the day, when the irrigation levels predicted at noon were significantly lower than those predicted in the morning and evening. The changes in plants' water status predicted by the model are consistent with known biological changes – at noon the weather is significantly warmer than morning and evening hours, thus the transpiration rate increases and the amount of water available to the plant decreases, causing a temporary water stress situation. The model was able to predict these changes from images of an entirely different experiment, confirming its reliability and ability to detect changes in water stress levels. Note that it is very unlikely that the above results are due to lighting changes only, since in summer the lighting is relatively uniform throughout the day, and a number of augmentation methods have been adopted to neutralize the effect of lighting on the model results.

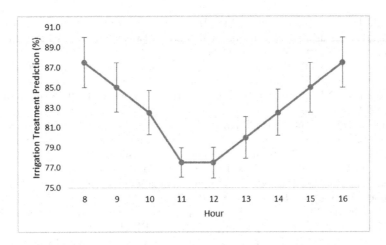

Fig. 7. Average predicted irrigation treatment of corn images taken from another experiment, during the day hours. All images were taken from the same treatment group during the mentioned experiment.

4   Conclusions

This study constitutes a proof of concept for the possibility of detecting water stress in plants using digital images only, as this study aims to automate the process of water stress identification, while keeping low equipment costs. Outperforming all other methods examined throughout this work, the proposed hierarchical model consisted of a CNN-LSTM classifier, was able to classify five different levels of water stress with 91.7% accuracy and MAE = 0.1, in exchange for larger model capacity. Using the trained model to detect changes in a plant's water stress levels during the day using images from another experiment showed remarkable performance, consistent with known biological changes. These findings indicate the ability of the proposed method to successfully detect changes and classify water stress levels of corn plants. Since it does not require special architecture beyond splitting the problem into smaller parts, a hierarchical model may also be useful for other plants and other types of stress and diseases.

For future work, we suggest examining additional photography angles, specifically photographing the canopy of the plant from above, since studies indicate that this angle is more indicative of water stress. In addition, plants can be examined under real field conditions, and additional crops could be investigated.

References

1. Amatya, S., Karkee, M., Kumar, A., Larbi, P., Adhikari, B.: Hyperspectral imaging for detecting water stress in potatoes, vol. 7 (2012). https://doi.org/10.13031/2013.42218

2. An, J., Li, W., Li, M., Cui, S., Yue, H.: Identification and classification of maize drought stress using deep convolutional neural network. Symmetry **11**, 256 (2019). https://doi.org/10.3390/sym11020256

3. Azimi, S., Kaur, T., Gandhi, T.K.: Water stress identification in chickpea plant shoot images using deep learning. In: 2020 IEEE 17th India Council International Conference (INDICON), pp. 1–7 (2020). https://doi.org/10.1109/INDICON49873.2020.9342388

4. Chandel, N.S., Chakraborty, S.K., Rajwade, Y.A., Dubey, K., Tiwari, M.K., Jat, D.: Identifying crop water stress using deep learning models. Neural Comput. Appl. **33**(10), 5353–5367 (2020). https://doi.org/10.1007/s00521-020-05325-4

5. Grant, O.M., Tronina, Ł, Jones, H.G., Chaves, M.M.: Exploring thermal imaging variables for the detection of stress responses in grapevine under different irrigation regimes. J. Exp. Bot. **58**(4), 815–825 (2007)

6. He, K., Zhang, X., Ren, S., Sun, J.: Deep residual learning for image recognition, pp. 770–778 (2016). https://doi.org/10.1109/CVPR.2016.90

7. Hochreiter, S., Schmidhuber, J.: Long short-term memory. Neural Comput. **9**(8), 1735–1780 (1997)

8. Jiang, B., Wang, P., Zhuang, S., Li, M., Gong, Z.: Drought stress detection in the middle growth stage of maize based on gabor filter and deep learning, pp. 7751–7756 (2019). https://doi.org/10.23919/ChiCC.2019.8866057

9. Kaneda, Y., Shibata, S., Mineno, H.: Multi-modal sliding window-based support vector regression for predicting plant water stress. Knowl.-Based Syst. **134** (2017). https://doi.org/10.1016/j.knosys.2017.07.028

10. Kim, D., et al.: Highly sensitive image-derived indices of water-stressed plants using hyperspectral imaging in swir and histogram analysis. Sci. Rep. **5**, 15919 (2015). https://doi.org/10.1038/srep15919

11. Kim, Y., Glenn, D., Park, J., Ngugi, H., Lehman, B.: Hyperspectral image analysis for water stress detection of apple trees. Comput. Electr. Agric. **77**, 155–160 (2011). https://doi.org/10.1016/j.compag.2011.04.008

12. Krizhevsky, A., Sutskever, I., Hinton, G.: Imagenet classification with deep convolutional neural networks. Neural Inf. Process. Syst. **25** (2012). https://doi.org/10.1145/3065386

13. Li, H., Yin, Z., Manley, II, P., Burken, J., Fahlgren, N., Mockler, T.: Early drought plant stress detection with bi-directional long-term memory networks. Photogram. Eng. Remote Sens. **84**, 459–468 (2018). https://doi.org/10.14358/PERS.84.7.459

14. MN, I., Nachit, M.: Visual monitoring of water deficit stress using infra-red thermography in wheat (2008)

15. Otsu, N.: A threshold selection method from gray-level histograms. IEEE Trans. Syst. Man Cybern. **9**(1), 62–66 (1979)

16. Padhi, J., Misra, R., Payero, J.: Use of infrared thermography to detect water deficit response in an irrigated cotton crop (2009)

17. Ramos, P., Reberg-Horton, C., Locke, A., Mirsky, S., Lobaton, E.: Drought stress detection using low-cost computer vision systems and machine learning techniques. IT Prof. **22**, 27–29 (2020). https://doi.org/10.1109/MITP.2020.2986103

18. Shibata, S., Kaneda, Y., Mineno, H.: Motion-specialized deep convolutional descriptor for plant water stress estimation, pp. 3–14 (2017). https://doi.org/10.1007/978-3-319-65172-9_1

19. Wakamori, K., Mizuno, R., Nakanishi, G., Mineno, H.: Multimodal neural network with clustering-based drop for estimating plant water stress. Comput. Electr. Agric. **168** (2020)

20. Zhuang, S., Wang, P., Jiang, B., Li, M.: Learned features of leaf phenotype to monitor maize water status in the fields. Comput. Electr. Agric. **172**, 105347 (2020). https://doi.org/10.1016/j.compag.2020.105347
21. Zhuang, S., Wang, P., Jiang, B., Li, M., Gong, Z.: Early detection of water stress in maize based on digital images. Comput. Electr. Agric. **140**, 461–468 (2017). https://doi.org/10.1016/j.compag.2017.06.022

Tortoise and Hares Consensus:
The Meshcash Framework
for Incentive-Compatible, Scalable
Cryptocurrencies

Iddo Bentov[1], Pavel Hubáček[2], Tal Moran[3], and Asaf Nadler[4(✉)]

[1] Cornell Tech, New York, NY 10044, USA
iddobentov@cornell.edu
[2] Charles University, Malostranské nám. 25, 118 00 Prague, Czech Republic
hubacek@iuuk.mff.cuni.cz
[3] IDC Herzliya, 8 HaUniversita Street, 4610101 Herzliya, Israel
talm@idc.ac.il
[4] Ben-Gurion University of The Negev, 8410501 Beer-Sheva, Israel
asafnadl@post.bgu.ac.il

Abstract. We propose Meshcash, a protocol for implementing a permissionless ledger (blockchain) via proofs of work, suitable for use as the underlying consensus mechanism of a cryptocurrency. Unlike most existing proof-of-work based consensus protocols, Meshcash does not rely on leader-election (e.g., the single miner who managed to extend the longest chain). Rather, we use ideas from traditional (permissioned) Byzantine agreement protocols in a novel way to guarantee convergence to a consensus from any starting state. Our construction combines a local "hare" protocol that guarantees fast consensus on recent blocks (but doesn't, by itself, imply irreversibility) with a global "tortoise" protocol that guarantees irreversibility. Our global protocol also allows the ledger to "self-heal" from arbitrary violations of the security assumptions, reconverging to consensus after the assumptions hold again.

Meshcash is designed to be *race-free*: there is no "race" to generate the next block and honestly-generated blocks are always rewarded. This property, which we define formally as a game-theoretic notion, turns out to be useful in analyzing rational miners' behavior: we prove (using a generalization of the blockchain mining games of Kiayias et al.) that race-free blockchain protocols are incentive-compatible and satisfy linearity of rewards (i.e., a party receives rewards proportional to its computational power). Because Meshcash can tolerate a high block rate regardless of network propagation delays (which will only affect latency), it allows us to lower both the variance and the expected time between blocks for

A full version of this paper is available as [4]

P. Hubáček—This work was performed while at the Foundations and Applications of Cryptographic Theory (FACT) center, IDC Herzliya, Israel

T. Moran—This work was supported in part by the Bar-Ilan Cyber Center

© Springer Nature Switzerland AG 2021
S. Dolev et al. (Eds.): CSCML 2021, LNCS 12716, pp. 114–127, 2021.
https://doi.org/10.1007/978-3-030-78086-9_9

honest miners; together with linearity of rewards, this makes pooled mining far less attractive. Moreover, race-free protocols scale more easily (in terms of transaction rate). This is because the race-free property implies that the network propagation delays are not a factor in terms of rewards, which removes the main impediment to accommodating a larger volume of transactions.

We formally prove that all of our guarantees hold in the bounded-delay communication model of Pass, Seeman and shelat, and against a constant fraction of Byzantine (malicious) miners; not just rational ones.

Keywords: Blockchain · Byzantine agreement · Consensus · Scalablility

1   Introduction

The problem of how to achieve a distributed consensus is one that has been widely studied, both as a theoretic question and as a practical matter. In the classical formulation of the problem (and the one most studied), the set of participating parties are fixed in advance and known to each other. This is a good model for the problems that motivated Lamport, Shostak and Peace in their seminal paper [14]—how a small number of servers, some of whom may be faulty, can still provably reach agreement.

Several decades later, with the advent of cryptocurrencies, we have a new motivation achieving distributed consensus. All currencies, and cryptocurrencies among them, inherently require consensus—if Charlie believes that Alice paid Bob, then Dana and Eve should not believe a contradicting claim.

The cryptocurrency setting doesn't fit neatly into the classical Byzantine agreement model. First, requiring every participating party to know every other party in advance is not feasible at "Internet Scale". In addition, without a trusted third party, the problem of identity verification on the Internet is notoriously hard. Together with the impossibility of Byzantine agreement without an honest majority, it seems that achieving provable consensus is impossible in this setting. Surprisingly, there is a way to sidestep these barriers—by changing the model to let participants prove that they possess scarce resources. Indeed, this is precisely what Nakamoto did with the invention of Bitcoin [20].

1.1   Consensus, Money, and Contracts

The technical descriptions of cryptocurrencies usually specify one intricate protocol that "solves" multiple problems at once: how to agree on history, what the currency can do (what is a transaction/smart contract) and the currency's monetary policy (e.g., how the coin supply is controlled). However, the solutions to these problems are, in many ways, independent.

We can separate the building blocks of a cryptocurrency intro three layers:

1. **Ledger**: The ledger layer is responsible for generating a consensus on an "append-only ledger". The ledger maintains a list of *transactions*: the protocol specifies how someone who attaches to the network can retrieve this list. Although different parties might get slightly different lists, the ledger protocol should guarantee several properties to be useful for a cryptocurrency:
   - *Safety (consensus on transaction order)*: all honest parties must agree on the set of transactions that appear in the ledger *and their order*. There may be disagreement about recent entries in the ledger, but as we look further back in history the probability of disagreement should go down exponentially.
   - *Irreversibility*: the ledger cannot be modified—only extended with additional entries (as with safety, irreversibility is only required to hold for "sufficiently old" transactions).
   - *Liveness*: the ledger grows over time (i.e., an adversary can't prevent *some* new transactions from eventually being added to the ledger).
   - *Fairness*: the fraction of honest transactions in the ledger is proportional to the accumulated resources of the honest users. In particular, attackers cannot force the ledger to include only their own transactions.

   This notion of ledger is equivalent to what Pass, Seeman and shelat formally define as a *blockchain* [21].
2. **Consensus Computer**: The consensus computer [17] is a state machine responsible for transforming an ordered list of transactions into a useful "state". At this layer we can define coins, accounts and contracts, and specify how transactions can manipulate them.
3. **Economy**: The economy layer describes how coins are created and destroyed and how monetary policy is determined and implemented. Examples of questions addressed in this layer are "is the supply of coins is capped?", "do old coins expire?" and "how do we allocate the initial distribution of funds?".

This work focuses on the design of the *ledger* layer. For the purposes of this layer, transactions are opaque strings—there is no need to interpret them in any way. This is an important property, since it allows us to "modularize" cryptocurrencies—the underlying ledger can replaced without changing the layers above it.[1]

1.2 Permissionless Consensus via PoW

In a *permissionless* distributed consensus protocol (cf. [3]), parties do not have to ask permission from others in order to join the protocol execution. The challenge in constructing a permissionless protocol is handling malicious adversaries that can create an unbounded number of "fake" identities.

---

[1] For optimization purposes, a cryptocurrency built on top of the ledger can add additional restrictions to prevent clearly invalid transactions from entering the ledger in the first place, but we ignore that here.

To solve this problem in Bitcoin, Nakamoto added a new assumption to the model: the adversary controls less than half of the total computing power invested in the protocol. At a high level, one can think of the participants in the Bitcoin protocol (called *miners*) as "voting" on the consensus value, but instead of having one vote per miner, each vote must be accompanied by a Proof of Work (PoW): a proof that computational power was "wasted" in order to generate that vote. Since we assume honestly-behaved users control a majority of the computational power, they can cast more votes than the adversary.

The details are, of course, a little more complex. In an Internet-scale protocol, it's infeasible to have every user constantly send "votes" to the entire network (this would require all users to have extremely high communication bandwidth and make verification very costly). Instead, Bitcoin employs a "lottery": one can think of the PoW as composed of many purchases of lottery tickets. Each purchase costs little in terms of computational power, but the probability of winning is very low, so many attempts (and hence, many CPU cycles) are required to find a winning ticket. The big advantage of this scheme is that only the lottery winner needs to publish a ticket. Since the cost of verifying a winning ticket is tiny compared to finding one, both communication and computation costs can be made very low.

1.3   Importance of Incentive-Compatibility

How reasonable is Nakamoto's assumption? Since cryptocurrencies have become a widespread phenomenon backed by "real" money, it seems unlikely that a majority of the computational power is controlled by *unconditionally honest* parties—at the sums involved, if parties can gain a significant financial advantage by deviating from the honest protocol is very likely that most will do so. That is, it seems more reasonable to model a majority of the parties as *rational* rather than honest. Thus, for security to hold—i.e., for honestly-*behaving* parties to control a majority of the computational power—we need to ensure that rational parties prefer to behave honestly. Protocols that satisfy this property are called *incentive-compatible*.

1.4   Drawbacks of Leader Election

The Bitcoin PoW "lottery" is a special case of what we call a *leader-election*-based consensus protocol. In leader-election-based protocols, a single party is (perhaps implicitly) selected as a "leader" at every time period (in the case of Bitcoin, the leader is the latest miner to "win" the lottery). Almost all existing cryptocurrency protocols are based on leader-election (most take an approach similar to Bitcoin's). Although it appears to be a mere technical distinction, it turns out that basing a protocol on leader-election can have negative consequences. In protocols based on leader-election, by definition, only one miner can "win" at any given time. On the other hand, in the real world the underlying communication network will have propagation delays (possibly under adversarial control), so multiple honest parties may believe they have won at the same time. This kind of collision creates a "race"; if the incentive structure for the protocol is tied to winning (e.g., in Bitcoin only the winning parties are rewarded), this can create incentives to behave maliciously. For example, adversaries can increase their own probability of winning by using denial-of-service attacks against other users. Indeed, Bitcoin is known to be vulnerable to several types of "rational" attacks (such as "selfish mining" [9,10,13,21,23] and "undercutting" [5] attacks).

The risk of rational deviations can severely limit a cryptocurrency in other ways as well. For example, Bitcoin suffers from centralization of the mining power in the hands of few large data centers [7,19] as well as scalability barriers w.r.t. high volume of commerce [6,15,25]. Intuitively, these arise since to increasing the throughput of transactions (or rewards, in the case of the centralization problem) we must either increase the frequency of "winning", in which case we have more races, or increase communication per win, which in Bitcoin increases the network propagation delay—again causing more races (see the full version for additional details).

1.5 Our Contributions

In this work, we present a new permissionless ledger protocol that aims to either solve or mitigate the aforementioned risks.

Leaderless Protocol, Provable Security. The fundamental idea behind Meshcash is a novel permissionless consensus protocol that is not based on leader-election. Unlike most alternative permissionless consensus protocols, we prove our security guarantees with regards to *malicious* adversaries and in a semi-synchronous communication model (with bounded delay, cf. [21]). This is to say, our protocol is robust even against non-rational adversaries, as long as they do not have too large a fraction of the computation power.

Self-healing Consensus. A long-term protocol that is intended to be used for decades must take into account even very low-probability events, if the probability that they occur over the lifetime of the protocol is still significant. For example, the probability of a massive space-storm that disrupts global communication, or of widespread blackouts, is minuscule for any given day—but something that is entirely non-negligible over a century.

Violations of common security assumptions fall into this category; e.g., the bounded delay assumption would fail if communication was sufficiently disrupted, and widespread blackouts might cause a large fraction of honest miners to drop out of the network until power is restored. Thus, robust cryptocurrency ledger protocols must be resilient in the face of temporary violations of their assumptions.

In essence, we gives "two tiers" of security guarantees:

1. As long as the standard security assumptions hold, Meshcash achieves fast consensus against adversaries controlling up to 1/3 of the hash power, and consensus about sufficiently old blocks is irreversible against an adversary controlling up to 1/2 of the hash power. Note that since Meshcash disincentivizes pool mining, a broader distribution of hashpower is more likely (cf. Sect. 1.5). Thus, when compared to a ledger protocol that tends towards centralized pools, Meshcash's security assumption is more conservative even with an identical hashpower threshold.

2. Even if the security assumptions are temporarily violated (e.g., the adversary controls the hash power of the *entire* network for some period of time), once the attack is over the protocol can "self-heal"; after a period of "healing time" that depends on the severity and duration of the violation, all honest users will converge again to consensus (during the "healing time" we require slightly stricter security assumptions—the adversary must control less than 1/15 of the network hashpower). Note that irreversibility of consensus on old blocks continues to hold as long as the total computation power expended by the adversary after the block publication is less than the total computational power expended by honest users.

We note that Bitcoin self-heals in a similar manner, but its formal proofs [10,21] do not offer this analysis, whereas we give a rigorous proof of Meshcash's self-healing guarantee.

Ideas from Permissioned Distributed Consensus. One of our main technical contributions is using ideas from the permissioned Byzantine agreement literature in order to achieve a consensus on multiple generated blocks in each time period, rather than having a race to choose the "leader" of the next round. An example is the use of a "weak coin protocol" to give fast, probabilistic consensus even when honest parties are initially split in their opinions. Weak coins have been used as black boxes in traditional consensus protocols too. Possibly of independent interest, we construct a weak-coin protocol with provable guarantees based only on PoWs.

Our techniques give a **qualitatively different type of permissionless consensus protocol**, and may prove useful to improve scalability and incentive-compatibility in other ledger designs as well (including those not based on PoWs).

Semi-permissioned Committee Selection. Another novel contribution, that may be of independent interest, is a subprotocol used by miners to reach consensus on a "committee" that includes all honest miners who generated valid blocks in a given time period. This protocol is "semi-permissioned" in that the number of participants is bounded, but honest parties may not agree on *who* is participating. We construct an SPCS protocol in the synchronous model that is resilient to *any* fraction of corrupted adversaries. The protocol is based on the Dolev-Strong synchronous broadcast; a more detailed description appears in the full version. The goal and underlying ideas are similar to that of Andrychowicz and Dziembowski [1], but our protocol is simpler.

Race-Freeness. We prove that in the Meshcash protocol, one miner's success does not prevent the success of another. This "race-free" property is highly desirable; we show that it is a sufficient condition for a protocol to be incentive-compatible (under some simplifying assumptions). Thus, we can show that even if *none* of the parties are honest, and the non-malicious participants are merely rational, honest behavior is an equilibrium for the protocol. This makes the "honest majority" assumption far more believable in practice.

Improvements over Bitcoin. Our protocol replaces the single chain of blocks (in which only one block can be next) with a *mesh*—a layered directed acyclic graph (DAG) which allows multiple blocks to coexist in parallel, while the rewards are still shared proportionally to the work performed. This offers mitigating factors for the risks that Bitcoin faces:

- **Greatly reduced incentives for pool mining.** This risk stems from the simple fact that the expected time and variance of solving blocks is too high for a hobbyist miner. For example, if there are 100,000 miners with equal hashrate, and the Bitcoin difficulty dictates it takes 10 min on average to solve a block, then each miner will need to wait for 1 million minutes (slightly less than 2 years) on average before solving a block. This would obviously be unacceptable from the point of view of the individual miners, as they have running expenses and their mining equipment may fail before they are ever rewarded. Therefore, Bitcoin miners have a strong incentive to combine their resources into centralized pools. This is unhealthy for decentralization, because pools tend to increase in size over time. As a remedy against the centralization pressure, many more blocks would get created per unit of time in Meshcash (e.g., we can easily support 200 blocks in every 10-minute period), and hence solo-mining or participating in small pools is more feasible compared to Bitcoin.

- **Improved scalability.** One of the main barriers to scalability is the effect of larger block sizes on the network propagation delay. By removing the "race" aspect of mining, the propagation delay becomes much less relevant, allowing the system to support larger block sizes (see the full version for more details).

- **Incentive-compatible verification.** When a Bitcoin miner verifies and includes certain transactions in a block that she creates, she collects the transaction fees as her reward. Other miners should also verify those transactions and thereby ensure that the chain that they try to extend is valid, even though they do not collect any rewards for those transactions. Thus, rational miners can do a cost-benefit analysis, and may decide to skip the verification of transactions in prior blocks [17]. Indeed, this behavior appears to be widespread among Bitcoin miners, as some miners lost a significant amount of funds due to the BIP66 softfork [18]. In Meshcash this risk is mitigated because miners do not engage in tight races against one another, therefore they have plenty of time to verify the transactions that reside in the blocks that they endorse. Thus, it is less risky to have transactions with complex scripts in Meshcash relative to blockchain protocols.

- **Incentive-compatible propagation.** A rational Bitcoin miner may decline to re-transmit transactions that were sent to her, thereby increasing the likelihood that she will collect more fees when she eventually solves a block [2]. Such a behavior damages the performance of the Bitcoin system from the point of view of its users, as transactions would become confirmed at a slower pace overall. Since Meshcash divides the transaction fees among all miners who created blocks in the recent layers, an individual miner does not gain by keeping transactions secret.

- **Resistance to bribe attacks.** In Bitcoin, rational and malicious parties may benefit from offering bribes to other miners, by sending in-band messages in an anonymous fashion [16]. A rational miner may fork a high-value block by collecting only some of its transactions, to incentivize the next miners to extend her forked block and earn extra fees by picking up the rest of the transactions. A malicious adversary may even put a "poisonous" transaction tx_1 in the honest chain and then offer high fees for blocks that include another transaction that conflicts with tx_1, thus bribing rational miners to work on a fork. In Meshcash, the fees are shared and conflicting transactions in a layer do not invalidate blocks that reference them, hence these kinds of bribe strategies are ineffective.
- **Resistance to forking.** An important property of our protocol (and one that, to the best of our knowledge, is not satisfied by any previous cryptocurrency) is that forking the mesh is hard even for an attacker with a constant fraction of the computational power. This makes it much easier to argue about rational behavior—honest miners know that with high probability their work will not go to waste. In particular, it makes the standard selfish-mining attacks moot.

Informally, Meshcash achieves the following guarantees.

Theorem 1 (Security—informal). *If the adversary controls less than a $q < 1/3$ fraction of the computational power then the Meshcash protocol satisfies the safety, irreversibility, liveness and fairness properties of a permissionless ledger.*

Theorem 2 (Self-healing—informal). *Regardless of the initial state of the honest parties, after a sufficiently long period in which the adversary controls a $q < \frac{1}{15}$ fraction of the computational power, the Meshcash protocol will satisfy the safety, irreversibility, liveness and fairness properties.*

For the formal statements see the full version. Note that we expect the security of the protocol in practice to be much better than our worst-case analysis shows—our analysis is optimized for readability and asymptotic results rather than reducing the constants.

1.6   Related Works

The idea of replacing the blockchain with a DAG is not new; to the best of our knowledge the earliest consideration of it was in [22]. However, many previous discussions of DAG-based cryptocurrencies lack formal analysis (most even lack a full specification). Unsurprisingly, the "devil is in the details"—constructing protocols that can withstand attack by a malicious adversary that can affect network messages is highly non-trivial. This is evidenced by the fact that even for Bitcoin, which is relatively simple and well studied, followup analysis showed vulnerabilities due to network delays [9,10,21]. It should be noted that many cryptocurrencies retain the chain topology but replace the PoW element with other kinds of

Sybil-resistant mechanisms, such as *Proof of Stake*. Examples of stake-based protocols include Algorand [11] and Ouroboros [12]. Indeed, [11, Sect. 2] raises the idea of improving the scalability of Algorand via a DAG topology.

In protocols based on leader election (e.g., GHOST [25], Bitcoin-NG [8]), consensus is achieved by selecting some "special" party (the leader) in each round of the protocol. Since only one party can be special in a round, these protocols all imply some sort of "race". We note that this is a property of the consensus protocol, not the reward mechanism; thus, in theory, a leader-election-based protocol can still be completely race-free according to our definition.

There are far fewer examples of protocols that do not require a leader election. The best-known protocols (with formal analysis) are SPECTRE [24] and PHANTOM [26].

See the full version for a more detailed comparison of related works.

2   Informal Protocol Overview

In this section we provide an overview of Meshcash. The complete protocol is appears on the full version.

Meshcash is a permissionless ledger protocol; participants in the protocol can join and leave the protocol at any time.

System Stakeholders. Every participant may play one or more of the following roles:

- *miners* are responsible for the security of the system, and participate by running the Meshcash mining protocol. At a high level, this is very similar to Bitcoin's mining—it consists of listening for new blocks on the network while performing computations to generate blocks (which they then publish).
- *validators*, receive blocks published by the miners and are responsible for determining which blocks are valid (i.e., are contained in the ledger) and their order.
- *users* publish transactions that they would like to add to the ledger.

Communication Model. In terms of execution, miners and validators in the Meshcash protocol behave similarly to Bitcoin—the parties are connected via a "gossip network". Our assumption is that every two honest parties are connected via the gossip network with some bounded delay.

Block DAG. In Bitcoin, each block points to one previous block, forming a chain. In Meshcash, the structure is instead a layered DAG; each block belongs to a layer (it contains a field that explicitly declares the layer number) and points to blocks in previous layers.

Types of Block Validity. We classify validity rules into two types: *syntactic* and *contextual*. Syntactic validity is what can be determined entirely by the contents of the block (and the block's *view*—the blocks reachable from it in the DAG). This includes things like whether the PoW is valid, and whether the blocks it points to have valid PoWs.

We call any validity rule that isn't syntactic a contextual validity rule. This includes rules that depend on other blocks received later (e.g., the Bitcoin "longest-chain" rule is contextual, since a block can be invalidated if another, longer, chain is received by the miner).

Syntactic Validity Rules. The syntactic validity rules are very simple. Like Bitcoin, we require the PoW to be valid for the block and match the block's difficulty level (optionally, as an efficiency optimization, we can also require all included transactions to be syntactically valid—but in any case we don't check conflicts with transactions in other blocks). In addition, we require every block to point to at least T_{min} blocks in the previous layer (where T_{min} is a tunable parameter). This is one of the innovations in our protocol; it makes it much harder for the adversary to pre-generate blocks in future layers—since to do so it would have to pre-generate T_{min} blocks in *every* layer; we rely on this heavily in our proof that the protocol can "self-heal" from an arbitrary adversarial state (in which the adversary may have pre-computed many blocks).

Contextual Validity Rules. The contextual validity rules are a little more complex, and the technical heart of the protocol. At a high level, the idea is that we let every block "vote" about all previous blocks in its view. For exposition purposes, think of these votes as being explicitly encoded in each block (in the actual protocol, we will do the encoding implicitly). To decide whether a block is valid, the validator counts the votes from all (syntactically-valid) blocks in its view, and takes the majority.

For very recently published blocks, the miners can't use this strategy (since not enough subsequent blocks have voted yet). Instead the miners who published blocks in the previous layer use local timing information to decide on validity of the blocks in that layer, and then run a "semi-permissioned" byzantine agreement protocol to reach consensus on their validity. The output of this local protocol (i.e., the validity of each block in the target layer) is signed by each miner and published. Validators decide on the validity of recent blocks by taking a majority of the signed outputs.

If we don't care about self-healing, the protocol as described above would suffice. However, if security assumptions fail—even temporarily—the local protocol is no longer guaranteed to reach consensus (since it requires a majority of the blocks to be honestly generated in each layer). In this case, by timing the publication of a block, the adversary could cause honest parties to disagree about its contextual validity, and then use a "balancing attack" to keep the honest parties evenly split. Balancing requires only a small fraction of the honest party's resources, so the split could continue indefinitely even after the security assumptions hold again.

To overcome this type of attack, we add another condition to the contextual validity rule: if the "vote margin" is small (i.e., the number of blocks voting for and against is similar), the miner will "flip a coin" instead of relying on the vote. The trick is that we will use a weak *common* coin—that is, with some known, constant probability all honest parties will agree on the result of the coin flip. Intuitively, when the adversary guesses the coin's value incorrectly, it will support the "wrong" side and the balancing will fail.

Mining Algorithm. A Meshcash miner uses only syntactic validity in order to decide which blocks to point to—the miner will point to *every* syntactically-valid "head" block it sees (i.e., blocks with in-degree 0). Thus, although the contextual validity rules are more complex than Bitcoin's, the mining algorithm is almost as simple; indeed, we implemented the mining algorithm in just over 100 lines of python code (the count includes only the top-level algorithm, without e.g., the local protocol or PoW implementation).[2]

3   Meshcash Security

Our basic security properties are as defined in [21]:

- *consistency*: with overwhelming probability (in T), at any point, the valid DAGs of two honest players can differ only in the last T blocks;
- *future self-consistence*: with overwhelming probability (in T), at any two points in time $r < s$ the valid DAGs of any honest user at r and s differ only in the last T blocks (as they appear at time r);
- *g-chain-growth*: with overwhelming probability (in T), at any point in the execution, the valid DAG of honest players grew by at least T blocks in the last T/g rounds, where g is called the chain-growth of the protocol;
- *μ-chain quality*: with overwhelming probability (in T), for any T consecutive blocks in any valid DAG held by some honest player, the fraction of blocks that were "contributed by honest players" is at least μ.

3.1   Security Proof Overview

In this section we give an informal overview of our security proof and intuitions.

Consistency (Safety). When security assumptions are satisfied, the set of blocks in every consecutive range of *ldist* layers will have an honest majority except with negligible probability. This follows from the fact that the adversary cannot pre-generate too many blocks (e.g., as shown in the full version, when $q < 1/3$ the adversary can't have much more than $\frac{1}{2}T_{\min}$ blocks of layer i at start_i), hence with high probability the fraction of adversarial blocks in a given time period cannot be much more than q (e.g., when *ldist* $= 2$ and $q = 1/3$, the adversary would have less than half of the blocks w.h.p.).

At layer t, the local protocol uses a consensus algorithm between miners who generated blocks in the past *ldist* layers to agree on the validity of blocks in layer $t - ldist$; this is guaranteed to achieve consensus when the majority of the blocks are honest.

---

[2] The code can be found on https://github.com/anon444/meshcash.git.

Future Self-consistency (Irreversibility). At a high level, we can view the global protocol as a voting process: every new block "votes" for or against each previous block. The irreversibility of the protocol stems from the fact that once consensus is reached, all honest users will vote in the same direction; this causes the margin of votes (the difference between positive and negative votes) to increase linearly with time. Similarly to the Bitcoin race analysis, an adversary can only reverse history by generating enough votes to overturn the current consensus. However, since the adversary generates blocks at a lower rate than the honest parties, the probability that this can be done decreases exponentially with time. We formalize this race analysis in the full version and show that the vote margin will grow linearly with the number of layers.

Self-healing Irreversibility. The main challenge here is that the adversary might keep a "reserve" of unpublished blocks and then publish them at a later date to reverse what seems like a consensus with large margin. However, in order to reverse the honest users' consensus about a block A, the adversary's reserve must contain "future" blocks (whose layer id is greater than that of block A)— since only future blocks have a "vote" regarding A.

We show this cannot happen by bounding the adversary's ability to keep a large reserve of "future" blocks. In the full version, we show that, irrespective of the initial conditions, there will be a layer in which the adversary's future reserve reaches a steady-state. Additionally, we use the fact that with overwhelming probability no layer is "too long" to prove that once in a steady state, the probability that the adversary leaves it is negligible; since in order to generate enough "future" blocks, the adversary needs a long layer-interval (see the full version).

When the adversary is in its future reserve steady state, consistency and future self-consistency are guaranteed (see explanation in the full version). The idea here is straightforward—once we have achieved consensus in the local protocol, the honest parties all vote in the same direction, hence the margin will grow until it reaches the threshold for irreversibility to apply.

Self-healing Consistency. The harder part of the proof is to show that consensus will always (eventually) be achieved, even under active attack. Intuitively, the difficulty of guaranteeing consensus is due to the adversary's ability to "play" with network latency. By sending blocks near the "edge" of a layer, some honest parties would consider the block valid, while others would not. The voting scheme does not help in this instance, since the honest parties now disagree on the votes themselves (each vote is a block). Further complicating the analysis is that the adversary can generate and maintain a "reserve" of valid blocks (for the current or future layers) that can be used strategically to cause disagreements among the honest miners on the contents of the layers.

Our main technical theorem that appears in the full version, shows that for any initial reserve of blocks (here we do not care about whether they are in the future or the past), the global protocol will eventually arrive at consensus. We do this by a case analysis on the adversary's strategy, showing that the adversary has to "spend" her reserve in order to keep honest parties from agreement. Since the adversary's ability to generate new blocks is limited, either the honest parties will reach consensus, or the adversary will exhaust her reserve (in which case the honest parties will also reach consensus).

At a lower level, to show that the adversary must spend blocks from its reserve, we consider basically the following cases:

Case 1: There is already a large vote margin. In this case, the adversary has to spend at least that much blocks from her reserve to prevent consensus.
Case 2: The vote margin is small. In this case, some honest parties will use a coin-flip to choose how they vote, while others might see a large enough margin that they vote disregarding the coin. If the adversary spends too few blocks, we show that all parties that disregard the coin will vote in the same direction, so if the adversary does not guess the outcome of the coin correctly, all honest parties will agree.

Chain Quality (Fairness), Chain Growth (Liveness) and Race-Freeness.
To show that honestly-generated blocks are always in the consensus (i.e., ensuring optimal $(1 - q)$ chain quality), we need to lower-bound the number of honest blocks in every layer (since honest blocks are "guaranteed" by the local protocol to vote for other honest blocks). We can do this when the adversary is in a future reserve steady-state, by showing that no layer is too short (since the adversary can only shorten a layer by "dumping" blocks from its future reserve), which implies that the honest parties have enough time to generate blocks in every layer. Chain growth also follows from the property that every honestly generated block will be considered valid, i.e., Meshcash achieves g-chain growth where g is the expected number of honest blocks in a network round. See the full version for further details.

References

1. Andrychowicz, M., Dziembowski, S.: Pow-based distributed cryptography with no trusted setup. In: Gennaro, R., Robshaw, M. (eds.) Advances in Cryptology - CRYPTO 2015-35th Annual Cryptology Conference, Santa Barbara, CA, USA, August 16–20, 2015, Proceedings, Part II, volume 9216 of Lecture Notes in Computer Science, pp. 379–399. Springer (2015). https://doi.org/10.1007/978-3-662-48000-7_19
2. Babaioff, M., Dobzinski, S., Oren, S., Zohar, A.: On Bitcoin and red balloons. In: ACM Conference on Electronic Commerce, pp. 56–73 (2012)
3. Barak, B., Canetti, R., Lindell, Y., Pass, R., Rabin, T.: Secure computation without authentication. In: CRYPTO, Yehuda Lindell (2005)
4. Bentov, I., Hubáček, P., Moran, T., Nadler, A.: Tortoise and hares consensus: the meshcash framework for incentive-compatible, scalable cryptocurrencies. Cryptology ePrint Archive, Report 2017/300 (2017). https://eprint.iacr.org/2017/300
5. Carlsten, M., Kalodner, H., Weinberg, S.M., Narayanan, A.: On the instability of bitcoin without the block reward. In: ACM CCS, pp. 154–167 (2016)

6. Croman, K.: On scaling decentralized blockchains. In: Financial Cryptography 3rd Bitcoin Workshop (2016)
7. Eyal, I.: The miner's dilemma. In: IEEE S&P (2015)
8. Eyal, I.: Gencer, A.E., Sirer, E.G., van Renesse, R.: A scalable blockchain protocol. In: NSDI, Bitcoin-NG (2016)
9. Eyal, I., Sirer, E.: Majority is not enough: Bitcoin mining is vulnerable. In: Financial Cryptography (2014)
10. Garay, J., Kiayias, A., Leonardos, N.: The Bitcoin backbone protocol: analysis and applications. In: Eurocrypt (2015). http://eprint.iacr.org/2014/765
11. Gilad, Y., Hemo, R., Micali, S., Vlachos, G., Zeldovich, N.: Algorand: scaling byzantine agreements for cryptocurrencies. In: SOSP, pp. 51–68. ACM (2017). https://eprint.iacr.org/2017/454
12. Kiayias, A., Russell, A., David, B., Oliynykov, R.: Ouroboros: a provably secure proof-of-stake blockchain protocol. In: Katz, J., Shacham, H. (eds.) Advances in Cryptology - CRYPTO 2017–37th Annual International Cryptology Conference, Santa Barbara, CA, USA, August 20–24, 2017, Proceedings, Part I, volume 10401 of Lecture Notes in Computer Science, pp. 357–388. Springer (2017)
13. Kiffer, L., Rajaraman, R., Shelat, A.: A better method to analyze blockchain consistency. In: ACM CCS 2018 (2018)
14. Lamport, L., Shostak, R., Pease, M.: The byzantine generals problem. ACM Trans. Prog. Lang. Syst. 4(3), 382–401 (1982)
15. Lewenberg, Y., Sompolinsky, Y., Zohar, A.: Inclusive block chain protocols. In: Financial Cryptography and Data Security, pp. 528–547 (2015)
16. Liao, K., Katz, J.: Incentivizing double-spend collusion in Bitcoin. In: Financial Cryptography Bitcoin Workshop (2017)
17. Luu, L., Teutsch, J., Kulkarni, R., Saxena, P.: Demystifying incentives in the consensus computer. In: 22nd ACM CCS (2015)
18. Maxwell, G.: (2015). https://bitcointalk.org/index.php?topic=1108304.msg117860 46#msg11786046
19. Miller, A., Kosba, A.E., Katz, J., Shi, E.: Nonoutsourceable scratch-off puzzles to discourage Bitcoin mining coalitions. In: 22nd ACM CCS (2015)
20. Nakamoto, S.: Bitcoin: a peer-to-peer electronic cash system. Bitcoin.org (2008). http://www.bitcoin.org/bitcoin.pdf
21. Pass, R., Seeman, L., Shelat, A.: Analysis of the blockchain protocol in asynchronous networks. In: Eurocrypt 2017 (2017). http://eprint.iacr.org/2016/454
22. "Maged" (pseudonym). Re: Unfreezable blockchain (2012). URL: https://bitcointalk.org/index.php?topic=57647.msg686497#msg686497
23. Sapirshtein, A., Sompolinsky, Y., Zohar, A.: Optimal selfish mining strategies in Bitcoin. In: Financial Cryptography (2016)
24. Sompolinsky, Y., Lewenberg, Y., Zohar, Spectre, A.: A fast and scalable cryptocurrency protocol (2016). https://eprint.iacr.org/2016/1159
25. Sompolinsky, Y., Zohar, A.: Secure high-rate transaction processing in Bitcoin. In: 19th Financial Cryptography and Data Security (2015)
26. Sompolinsky, Y., Zohar, A.: PHANTOM: a scalable blockdag protocol. IACR Cryptology ePrint Archive, 2018:104 (2018). http://eprint.iacr.org/2018/104

Game of Drones - Detecting Spying Drones Using Time Domain Analysis

Ben Nassi[1]([⊠]), Raz Ben-Netanel[1], Adi Shamir[2], and Yuval Elovici[1]

[1] Department of Software and Information Systems Engineering, B.G.U.,
Be'er-Sheva, Israel
{nassib,razx,elovici}@post.bgu.ac.il
[2] Computer Science Department, Weizmann Institute of Science, Rehovot, Israel
adi.shamir@weizmann.ac.il

Abstract. Drones have created a new threat to people's privacy. We are now in an era in which anyone with a drone equipped with a video camera can use it to invade a subject privacy by filming the subject in his/her private space using encrypted First Person View (FPV) channel. Although many methods have been suggested to detect a nearby drone, they all suffer from the same shortcoming: they cannot detect what specifically is being captured and therefore they fail to distinguish between the legitimate use of a drone that does not invade a subject's privacy (for example, neighbor's drone flying and shoot his garden) and illegitimate use (same drone shooting the subject's property), where in many cases depends on the orientation of the drone's video camera rather than on the drone's location. In this paper we present a method that utilizes a flicker in order to detect whether the drone's camera is directed towards the private space by analyzing the encrypted video stream sent from the drone in real time. We investigate the influence of changing pixels on the transmitted traffic (in a lab setup). We leverage our conclusions and demonstrate how an interceptor can apply a side-channel attack to detect that a subject is video streamed by DJI Mavic drone from its encrypted FPV channel when the subject is located inside a private house.

Keywords: Drones · Cryptanalysis · Side channels

1 Introduction

The proliferation of consumer drones over the last few years [12] has created a new privacy threat [18]. We are living in an era in which anyone with a drone equipped with a video camera can invade another individual's privacy by maneuvering the drone to the individual's house and directing the drone's camera to the window of the house in order to film or record the subject in his/her private space. Many privacy invasion incidents have been reported in the media, and laws are being updated to deal with this new threat [2, 16, 21, 22, 26, 34, 37].

Video - https://youtu.be/3wEsbafsUxg.

© Springer Nature Switzerland AG 2021
S. Dolev et al. (Eds.): CSCML 2021, LNCS 12716, pp. 128–144, 2021.
https://doi.org/10.1007/978-3-030-78086-9_10

State of the art drones provide video piloting capabilities, a.k.a. first person view (FPV), a communication channel designed to (1) stream the video captured by the drone's video camera to the operator's controller in order to present the video stream to the operator in real-time, and (2) maneuver the drone by transmitting commands from the controller. FPV provides excellent infrastructure for a malicious operator to invade someone's privacy without being detected because: (1) it eliminates the need for a malicious operator to be close to the drone or to the target by allowing the operator to maneuver the drone to a target that is located far away from his/her location, (2) its traffic can be encrypted, and (3) it supports HD resolutions that enable the attacker to obtain high resolution images and close ups (by using video camera's zooming capabilities) that captured by the drone far from target point of interest (POI).

Many studies suggested methods for detecting whether a drone is nearby (e.g., using RADAR, video camera, LiDAR, microphones arrays [18]), however they all fail to detect what specifically is being captured and therefore they fail to distinguish between the legitimate use of the drone (e.g., to film a selfie from the air) and illegitimate use (e.g., to stream the view into the window of someone's apartment) that in some cases depends on the orientation of drone's video camera rather than on the drone's location.

In this research we present a method that can be used by an interceptor to detect whether a particular POI (e.g., his/her house, a subject) is being tracked by a drone even if the FPV channel is encrypted; in order to accomplish this our proposed method triggers a physical stimulus that influence the encrypted FPV channel, sent from the drone to its controller, and can use an interceptor to apply a side-channel attack to the encrypted video stream in order to detect if a specific POI is being tracked. We investigate the influence of changing pixels on the transmitted traffic in a lab setup. We leverage our conclusions and demonstrate how an interceptor can apply a side-channel attack to detect that a subject is video streamed by DJI Mavic drone from its encrypted FPV channel when the subject is located inside a private house We evaluate the required time of physical stimulus to achieve zero FPR.

This study makes the following contributions: (1) We demonstrate a method that extracts a targeted POI from encrypted FPV channel and can be used to distinguish between the legitimate use of a drone that does not invade a subject's privacy and illegitimate use the difference between each of the uses depends on the angle of the video camera and not on the location of the drone as demonstrated in Fig. 2. (2) We present an external interception model that utilizes a radio frequency (RF) scanner that was empirically evaluated outside a lab setup. (3) We present an effective method that analyzes encrypted traffic without any prior knowledge regarding the cryptography algorithm that is being used. We only use the length of the cryptogram that can be extracted from the second layer of the OSI model instead of higher levels of the OSI model that was used by other studies [15,30] to classify video streams.

The rest of this paper is structured as follow: in Sect. 2 we discuss about protocols and coding algorithms of video streams. In Sect. 3 we review related works in two main areas: information leakage from video streams and known methods to detect a nearby drone. In Sect. 4 we present adversarial model of an attacker that performs privacy invasion attack and present an external interception model for detection of captured POI. In Sect. 5 we investigate the influence of changing pixels on the transmitted traffic (in a lab setup). In Sect. 6 we evaluate the performance of our method, and in Sect. 7 we suggest about future work.

2   Background

Modern drones provide video piloting capabilities (FPV channel) based on Wi-Fi signals, allowing an operator to control a drone using a smartphone [3]. Wi-Fi signals between the controller and the drone are sent over a secured access point that is opened by either the drone or the controller (both parties are connected to the access point). Using dedicated hardware (e.g., a controller with a Wi-Fi signal range extender) current drone models provide operators the ability to control a drone using FPV from a distance of 5–7 km over Wi-Fi channels [9,24].

2.1   Video Coding Algorithms

Video encoding [14,23,36] begins with a raw image captured from a camera. The camera converts analog signals generated from striking photons into a digital image format. Video is simply a series of such images generally captured five to 120 times per second (referred to as frames per second or FPS). The stream of raw digital data is then processed by a video encoder in order to decrease the amount of traffic that is required to transmit a video stream. Video encoders use two techniques to compress a video: intra-frame coding (spatial compression) and inter-frame coding (temporal compression).

Intra-frame coding creates an **I-Frame**, a time periodic reference frame that is strictly intra-coded. The receiver decodes an I-frame without additional information. Intra-frame prediction exploits spatial redundancy, i.e., correlation among pixels within one frame, by calculating prediction values through extrapolation from already coded pixels for effective delta coding. The intra-coding process contains the following stages [14,17]:

1. Color conversion and chroma sub-sampling - The human eye has a lower sensitivity to color information than to dark-bright contrasts. First a conversion from RGB color space into YUV color components (e.g., YCbCr) is applied, and then some of the chrominance information of the image is removed. This is a lossy stage.
2. Partition - The actual frame is divided into non overlapping macroblocks.
3. Transform - A block is represented in the frequency domain.
4. Quantization - This process is applied to the block to remove the insignificant part (high frequencies) and results in a compressed block with a smaller amount of information. This is a lossy stage.
5. Entropy coding - Compression algorithms are used to represent the data by mapping frequently occurring patterns with a few bits and rarely occurring patterns with many bits (e.g., using Huffman coding).

Over the years various optimizations have been introduced for each of the stages, including: (1) dynamic partitioning techniques, (2) novel prediction algorithms and varying the amount of reference frames, (3) different domain transforms, and (4) quantization methods. These optimizations boost the transmission rate from 1.5 Mbps (MPEG-1) to 150 Mbps (MPEG-4).

Inter-frame coding exploits temporal redundancy by using a buffer of neighboring frames that contains the last M number of frames, and creates a delta frame. A delta frame is a description of a frame as a delta of another frame in the buffer. The receiver decodes a delta frame using a received reference frame. There are two major types of delta frames: P-Frame and B-Frame. **P-Frames** can use data from previous frames to decompress and are more compressible than I-Frames. **B-Frames** can use both previous and upcoming frames for data reference to get the greatest amount of data compression. The process of generating a delta frame consists of applying the following stages to a frame:

1. Partition - dividing the actual frame into non overlapping macroblocks.
2. Reference block matching - finding a similar block in another frame.
3. Motion vector extraction - extracting the difference between the two blocks by calculating the prediction error.

The order in which I, B, and P-Frames are arranged is specified by a GOP (group of pictures) structure. A GOP is a collection of successive pictures within a coded video stream. It usually consists of two I-Frames, one at the beginning and one at the end. In the middle of the GOP structure, P and B-Frames are ordered periodically. An example of a GOP structure, with I, P, and B-Frames, can be seen in Fig. 1. Occasionally B-Frames are not used in real-time streaming due to delays.

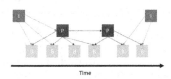

Fig. 1. GOP structure - I,B, and P-Frames

Intra-framing and Inter-framing techniques were integrated into the MPEG-1 standard in the 1990s. Naturally, integrating these techniques into the protocol creates a variable bitrate (VBR) in the transmission of a video which is influenced by changes between frames and the content of the frame itself. A frame that can be represented as a set of prediction blocks of a similar neighboring frame (that has already been captured and transmitted) requires a smaller amount of data to be represented. The same thing is also true for video streams with a lot of redundancy in their frames. On the other hand, a frame with less similarity to other neighboring frames (e.g., as a result of the movement of several objects) requires a larger amount of data to be represented as a set of prediction blocks of other frames. The same thing is also true for a frame with less redundancy. Even if the video stream is encrypted at the transport layer (e.g., using TLS), the sizes of the packets and times of arrival are visible to anyone watching the network. In terms of cyber security such a coupling between the captured stream and its cryptogram series can be used to extract meaningful information as described in Sect. 3.

3   Related Work

Fig. 2. From left to right: (a) a drone boxed in red, two people boxed in blue, and a window of an organization boxed in yellow, (b) illegitimate use of the drone camera - filming the organization, (c) a legitimate use for selfie purposes. (Color figure online)

In this section we describe: (1) methods that exploit information leakage of encrypted video stream to extract insights about the stream, and (2) methods for nearby drone detection. In the area of **video hosting services**, several studies exploited video stream information leakage to classify a video stream sent from a video hosting service (e.g., YouTube, Netflix, etc.) over Dynamic Adaptive Streaming over HTTP (DASH) protocols (a.k.a. MPEG-DASH). This attack model relies on two steps: (A) building a database of reference traces of video streams, and (B) classifying a query trace of an intercepted video stream by matching it to the database. Saponas et al. [30] analyzed Slingbox's encrypted streams sent over wired and wireless connections to a client installed on a computer, and managed to achieve a 89% accuracy in classifying 26 different movies by analyzing 40 min of the stream's bitrate. Schuster et al. [31] classified video streams sent from Netflix, Amazon, YouTube, and Vimeo by analyzing burst patterns using convolutional neural networks. Reed et al. [27,28] classified Netflix's video streams and reached accuracy over 90% by analyzing only eight minutes of the stream. In a similar area to video hosting services, Liu et al. [15] constructed robust video signatures using wavelet-based analysis by analyzing traffic sent over the RTP of a **IPTV**. In the area of **VoIP**, Wright et al. showed that VBR leakage in encrypted VoIP communication can be used for the detection of the speaker's language [39] and phrases [38]. White et al. [35] extended this approach to extract conversation transcripts. Wampler et al. [33] analyzed packets' average inter-arrival time, packets' average size, average bandwidth, and the number of received packets in a window, in order to extract hand movement and ambient light changes from **IP camera** traffic sent over RTP.

In terms of the attack model, they did not conduct their experiments using an external RF scanner (NIC in monitor mode), so their attack model requires a malware installed on the targeted network/computer in order to detect the video streams.

In the area of **drone detection**, various methods were introduced over the last few years to detect a nearby drone [18]. Radar is a traditional method of detecting drones. However, the case of small consumer drones requires expensive high-frequency radar systems [10]. Several studies suggested computer vision techniques to detect a drone by using a camera to analyze motion cues [6,29]. However, these methods suffer from false positive detections due to: (1) the increasing number of drone models, and (2) the similarities between the movements of drones and birds [6]. In order to distinguish between birds and drones, several approaches analyzed the noise of the rotors captured by microphones [6,7]. However, in order to address the challenges arising from the ambient noise and the distance between the drone to the microphone, very expensive equipment is required [7]. A hybrid method that combines all of the methods discussed in this section was suggested by [32] in order to improve the accuracy of detection. However, such a method is very expensive to deploy. Two other studies proposed a method to detect a consumer/civilian drone controlled using Wi-Fi signals. The first method [25] analyzes the protocols' signatures of the Wi-Fi connection between the drone and its controller. The second method [5] analyzes the received signal strength (RSS) using a RF scanner (e.g., Wi-Fi receiver).

All of the described methods for drone detection lack the ability to determine whether the drone was used to invade privacy (by video recording the subject/target). More specifically, they are unable to understand what exactly is being recorded by the drone. In crowded areas, the difference between legitimate and illegitimate use is based on the angle of the drone's camera. Figure 2 presents a legitimate use and illegitimate use of a drone. All of the described methods [5–7,10,25,29,32] fail to distinguish between the act of taking a selfie and a privacy invasion attack. Our method does not suffer from the described problem. In this research we show methods for: (1) determining exactly what is being recorded, and (2) providing a subject with a proof that they were under surveillance.

4 Adversary Model and Proposed Detection Scheme

We consider an adversary operator that uses a drone to shot a target (subject or organization) for:

1. Self entertainment - the attacker considers a privacy invasion attack as an entertainment and use it to fulfill his/her curiosity. Besides of fulfilling his/her curiosity, no future damage is being applied to the target.

2. Malicious Purpose - the attacker uses the drone's video camera to collect
   information about the target for malicious purpose. For example in cases in
   which the target is an organization, the malicious purpose can be to break
   into an organization (and the drone can be used to count the number of
   subjects that leave the building). Another malicious purpose can be to disable
   a confidential facility (in which the captured video from the drone is used to
   map the organizational assets). In cases of which the target is a subject, the
   purpose can be to understand whether the subject is cheating in his wife or
   husband by using the drone's video camera to spy after the subject (as was
   shown in [26]).

The interceptor's goal is to determine whether a target is being captured by a
drone's video camera. We assume that an interceptor has detected the presence
of a drone nearby (using one of the known methods for drone detection [5–
7,10,25,29,32]) or by analyzing suspicious access points. In addition we assume
that the interceptor owns an RF scanner (e.g., an NIC) that is connected to a
computer with an adequate antenna that captures the traffic being sent from
the drone to the controller. The interceptor triggers a physical stimulus to the
target in a random pattern and analyzes the intercepted traffic in a detection
model. Figure 3 presents proposed detection scheme and the involved parties.

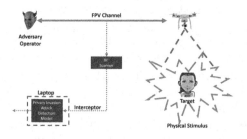

Fig. 3. Adversary model and proposed system

4.1   Detection Model

Algorithm 1 presents target's detection model. It receives: (1) the intercepted Wi-
Fi stream (that was captured by the NIC); (2) a watermarking pattern (binary
sequence) that was modulated by the physical stimulus, (3) a window for each
bit that was modulated. In addition the algorithm receives (4) begin and (5)
end time of the watermarked pattern (in Epoch representation). First, the intercepted Wi-Fi traffic converted to a bitrate array (line 3). A *stableInterval* is
being extracted from 4 s before the first physical stimulus begins until the beginning time of the physical stimulus (line 5). A *stimulusInterval* is being extracted
from the time in which the first physical stimulus begins and 4 s ahead (line 6).

A *stableBitrate* and a *stimulusBitrate* are being calculated by averaging intervals *stableInterval* and *stimulusInterval* (lines 8–9). A *cutoff* is been calculated as the middle between the *stableInterval* and *stimulusBitrate* (line 10). Each of the pattern bits are extracted from *bitrateArray*, calculated, and classified as 0/1 bits using a loop for (lines 11–17). A threshold (cutoff) is calculated by averaging the bitrate of the Wi-Fi traffic (PCAP file) until the modulation begins. The algorithm iterates over the bitrate array and appends 1 if the value is beyond the threshold and 0 if otherwise. Finally, a confidence value between 0–1 is returned by comparing the result to the received pattern (line 18).

Algorithm 1. Privacy Invasion Attack Detection

Input:
1) intercepted-WiFI-Stream // Intercepted by the NIC
2) watermarkingPattern // binary sequence (e.g., 101..01)
3) window // milliseconds for single bit modulating
4) beginPatternTime // begin time of pattern (Epoch)
5) endPatternTime // end time of pattern (Epoch)
Output: Boolean result

1: **procedure underDetection?**
2:     *extractedPattern* ← *""*
3:     *bitrateArray = extractBitrateArray(intercepted-WiFI-Stream)*
4:     *stableBeginTime = beginPatternTime - 4000*
5:     *stableInterval = bitrateArray.subarray(stableBeginTime, beginPatternTime)*
6:     *endStimulusTime = beginPatternTime + 4000*
7:     *stimulusInterval = bitrateArray.subarray(beginStimulusTime, endStimulusTime)*
8:     *stableBitrate = average(stableInterval)*
9:     *stimulusBitrate =* average(stimulusInterval)
10:    *cutoff = (stumulusBitrate + stableBitrate)/2*
11:    **for** *(i = beginPatternTime; i ¡ endPatternTime; i = i+window)* **do**
12:        *interval = bitrateArray.subArray(i,i+window)*
13:        *avg = average(interval)*
14:        **if** avg ¿ cutoff **then**
15:            *result = result + "1"*
16:        **else**
17:            *result = result + "0"*
18:        return (watermarkingPattern == extractedPattern)

4.2 Detecting FPV Channels

Many commercial drones provide FPV capabilities over Wi-Fi channels. The drone/controller exposes a secured access point in which both parties are connect to using authentication. The FPV channel is sent over Wi-Fi communication and can be intercepted using a NIC (in monitoring mode). An antenna can be used by an interceptor in order to extend interception range. DJI Mavic, DJI Spark, and Parrot Bebop 2 use Wi-Fi Protected Access II (WPA2) protocols to secure their networks. Detecting access points of FPV channels can be done by changing a NIC mode of a laptop to monitoring mode (or using a software defined radio instead) and using dedicated tools (such as airmon, inSSIDer. etc.), that can even detect hidden networks, in order to find suspicious access points. After finding suspicious access points, a specific access point can be found by searching for known BSSIDs or known MAC IDs of drones. In order to overcome changes of BSSIDs and MAC IDs, the interceptor can use a method to detect the type of the drone using forensic analysis applied to the access point communication as was suggested by Peacock et al. [25]. Another option is to analyze each of the access points within the range of the target in the detection model without any filters applied to find a FPV channel.

5   Influence of Physical Stimulus

In this section we investigate the influence of changing pixels on the transmitted traffic (in a lab setup). All of the methods described in this section make use of a simple principle that changes in the number of pixels from a frame to a consecutive frame requires data to encode, therefore changing a large number of pixels results in more data to encode and causes the bitrate to increase (intra-frame coding). We show how actions like flickering and changing the locations of objects can be used by an interceptor to influence the traffic by triggering a side-channel attack in the real world outside a lab.

5.1   Lab Experiments

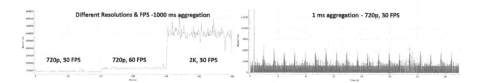

Fig. 4. Bitrate of captured Wi-Fi signals of white wall in different resolution

In the preliminary lab experiments described below we assess the influence of various changes to the pixels on the traffic using a Mavic Pro [8] consumer drone. The drone was configured to transmit video at a rate of 24 frames per second (FPS), its default configuration. We took a laptop (Dell Latitude 7480) that runs Kali Linux with a standard NIC (Intel Dual-Band Wireless-AC 8265 Wi-Fi [13]) that was used for interception. We enabled the monitor mode on the NIC using airmon-ng [1] and intercepted the encrypted video traffic of the

Mavic's AP. The Mavic's AP uses 802.11n to transfer the data between the connected parties. From the external interception perspective, we were able to extract only the second layer (data link layer) meta-data which includes the following: BSSID, source MAC address, destination MAC address, and packet length. The payload of the packet is encrypted.

We started by analyzing the Mavic's traffic when the captured video is steady. We placed the Mavic in front of a white wall. Figure 4a shows the bitrate of the traffic that was transmitted from the drone during a period of 240 s and captured using an NIC using external interception at 1000 ms aggregation at three different resolutions and rates (720p 30 FPS, 720p 60 FPS, and 2K 30 FPS). As can be seen from the results in Fig. 4, the bitrate is almost fixed for every resolution over time, however higher resolutions generated higher bitrates.

In the rest of the experiments in this section, we placed the Mavic in front of a laptop in order to expose the drone to specific images/objects on the monitor. The experimental setup is presented in Fig. 5.

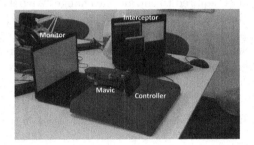

Fig. 5. Lab Setup - The DJI Mavic was placed in front of a laptop monitor. A second laptop is being used to intercept the traffic (using its NIC in monitoring mode)

First, we investigated the effect of changing X percent of the captured pixels on the traffic. We programmed a Python code to present a flickering rectangle on the screen in the middle of the monitor. We tested the effect of various rectangle sizes on the traffic that was sent from the drone to the controller using external interception (the interception laptop was not connected to AP; its NIC was on monitor mode). The rectangle flickered from white to black, and vice versa, over a white background for 40 s.

Table 1. Influence of changing the amount of pixels on the traffic

Percentage of changing pixels	0%	1.2%	2.50%	5%	10%	25%	50%	75%	100%
Bitrate (KB)	120	130	135	161	170	230	260	290	320
Delta Bitrate (KB)	0	10	15	41	50	110	140	170	200
Delta Bitrate (%)	0%	8%	13%	34%	42%	92%	117%	142%	167%

As can be seen from the results presented in Table 1, there is a strong connection between the number of pixels changed and the amount of traffic that was sent from the drone. This phenomena occurs because a larger amount of changing pixels results in a larger amount of changing macroblocks. A larger amount of changing macroblocks means that the encoder must use more data to encode the delta-frames that increase the amount of traffic. In addition, as the results show, very small changes (<2.5%) are effectively absorbed and merged with the background noise.

Next, we aimed to determine the effect of separating the pixels and dividing them across several objects (rather than centralizing them on one object) on the amount of traffic generated (given a fixed number of changed pixels). In this series of experiments we fixed the amount of changing pixels but presented a different number of rectangles, dividing the fixed number of pixels to form smaller equal sized rectangles (2, 4, 8, 16, 32), and positioned them in different places on the monitor. As can be seen from the results presented in Table 2, there is a strong connection between increasing the number of rectangles and an increase in the amount of traffic that is required to encode the change. We believe that this phenomena can be explained as follows: dividing a single rectangle (which centralized the fixed number of pixels) into smaller pieces (thereby dividing the fixed number of pixels) and separating them from each other on the monitor results in the intersection with more macroblocks that change compared to the centralized object. Therefore, this requires more data to encode and increases the amount of traffic.

Table 2. Influence of dividing an area into pieces on the traffic

Pieces	1	2	4	8	16	32
Bitrate (KB)	250	260	275	300	325	340
Bitrate Delta (KB)	0	10	25	50	75	90
Bitrate Delta (%)	0.00%	4.00%	10.0%	20.0%	30.0%	36.00%

Finally, we assessed whether the objects' position on the monitor affects the traffic. In order to do this, we conducted an experiment in which we flickered a rectangle that is one fourth the size of the screen in four different places on the monitor: top right, top left, bottom left, and bottom right. As can be seen from the results presented in Table 3, each of the flickering rectangles had the same effect on the traffic. Therefore, we believe that when the objects' size remains fixed, the location on the monitor has no effect, since the same number of changing macroblocks are involved.

From this set of experiment we were able to conclude that (1) the larger the number of pixels changed, the greater the influence on traffic (larger number of changing macroblocks), and (2) the influence is even greater if the pixels are not clustered together (intersection with a larger number of macroblocks).

After investigating the effect of the number of pixels changed, the objects' location on the monitor, and the difference between keeping the pixels centralized

Table 3. Influence of locating an object on the traffic

	White screen	Top left	Top right	Bottom left	Bottom left
Bitrate (KB)	120	195	195	195	195
Bitrate Delta (KB)	0	75	75	75	75
Bitrate Delta (%)	0.00%	62.500%	62.500%	62.500%	62.500%

vs. dividing them, we moved on to assess the effect of the object's color on the amount of traffic. We conducted an experiment in which we flickered different colored rectangles (black, green, blue, red, orange, yellow, pink, purple, and white) in the size on the monitor.

Table 4. Influence of changing colors of an object on the traffic

	No flicker	Black	Red	Green	Orange	Yellow	Gray	Purple	Blue	Pink
RGB value										
Bitrate (KB)	100	325	325	325	325	325	325	325	325	325
Delta Bitrate (KB)	0	225	225	225	225	225	225	225	225	225
Delta Bitrate (%)	0%	225%	225%	225%	225%	225%	225%	225%	225%	225%

As can be seen from results presented in Table 4, each color caused the same effect on the amount of traffic that was sent from the drone. From this experiment we can conclude that no color significantly outperforms another.

Rather than using the RGB color space, video encoders use different color spaces to represent a picture including: YCbCr, YCoCg, etc. Video encoders transform a captured picture from an RGB color space to a luma value (denoted as Y) and two chroma values. The Y component can be stored with a high resolution or transmitted at a high bandwidth, and the two chroma components can be bandwidth-reduced, subsampled, compressed, or otherwise treated separately for improved system efficiency. Considering this information, we then tested the effect of different brightness levels of the same color on the traffic. To do so, we conducted an experiment in which we flickered two colors (green and blue) at five different brightness levels.

Table 5. Influence of brightness level of an object on the traffic

Brightness	No flicker	0%	20%	40%	60%	80%
Bitrate (KB)	100	300	300	310	320	350
Bitrate Delta (KB)	0	200	200	210	220	250
Bitrate Delta (%)	0%	200%	200%	210%	220%	250%

As can be seen from the results presented in Table 5 increasing the level of brightness of the object increases the amount of traffic sent from the drone to the controller. The results obtained from the captured traffic was identical for blue and green colors. From these results, we concluded that brighter shades outperform darker shades of the same color.

In the next section we leverage our findings to detect privacy invasion attack against a subject located in a private house.

6   Evaluation

In this section we present the evaluation for target detection in two cases: when the target is located inside a private house.

We now demonstrate a method to secure a building from privacy invasion attack using physical stimulus. As was shown in the lab experiments, flickering objects influence the amount of traffic that is required to encode the flickering objects over time. Taking this into consideration, we show how a smart-film (a.k.a. smart glass) can be used as a means of triggering a physical stimulus in order to detect whether a building is being tracked by a drone. We purchased a smart film with an RF controller and attached it to a window of a private house of which we wanted to secure. The smart film switches between two modes: transparent and white given a radio command sent from its controller.

We wrote a simple Python program that uses a software defined radio (HackRF) to modulate a given signal using OOK modulation. Each bit of the signal was modulated using a window of 2 s. For 1 bits we flickered the smart film, and for 0 bits we switched the smart film to be transparent for the entire time. We randomly draw the sequence 1,1,1,1,0,0,0,0,1,1,1,1,1,1,1,1,0,0,0,0,0,0 as a signal to be modulated using the physical stimulus.

In order to demonstrate an illegitimate use of the drone, we asked an operator to fly the DJI Mavic and film his neighbor's garden and private house from the operator's property. The default resolution and FPS were picked: 720p and 24 FPS. We connected a parabolic antenna, TP-Link TL-ANT2424B 2.4GHz 24dBi Grid Parabolic, that we purchased to a laptop and intercepted the outgoing traffic from the DJI Mavic sent over the access point. We run our Python code to create a visual stimulus using the smart-film. Figure 6 presents two snapshots that were taken from the streamed video and the results of applying Algorithm 1 to the intercepted traffic. The peaks in the bitrate correlate to the time at which the smart-film was flickered. The flicker that was used to modulate the 1 bits increased the bitrate up to 1.5–2 times, from an average of 300–350 KB up to 450–570 KB. As can be seen from intercepted traffic, the flicker that was produced using the smart-film influenced the bitrate in a way that watermarked the bitrate to the given pattern that was programmed in the Python code.

In order to prove that the physical stimulus is the reason that effects the traffic, we conducted one more experiment in which we streamed the same house for 20 min without any physical stimulus conducted. In addition in order to prove that this effect cannot be reproduced by another house (that is not the target) we

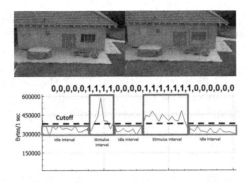

Fig. 6. A smart film controlled via a HackRF connected to a laptop

streamed another house (the neighbor's house) for 20 min. In both cases we intercepted the traffic using the same experimental setup. We applied Algorithm 1 to the intercepted traffic and calculated the false positive rate as a function of required physical stimulus time of the original signal 111100001111111000000. As can be seen from the results that presented in Fig. 7, a pattern of 10 s is sufficient to exclude detection mistakes of filming another target (with a FPR of 0.032). In addition, as can be seen from the result, a pattern of 10 s is sufficient to exclude mistakes of the same generated pattern without any physical stimulus made by a coincidence as a result of wind or another physical movement (with a FPR of 0.027). Figure 7 presents a FPR graph as a function of the required seconds of physical stimulus.

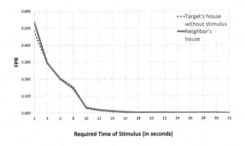

Fig. 7. FPR as a function physical stimulus time (in seconds)

7   Conclusions and Future Work

In this research we showed methods that use physical stimulus that can be used to detect whether an object has been captured and is being streamed from a drone camera to its controller. While many methods were suggested over the last years to detect the presence of a nearby drone, this research is the first to introduce methods that distinguish between the legitimate use of a nearby drone that does not invade a subject's privacy and illegitimate use. As Future Work we suggest to: (1) compare the performance of the suggested method to detect spying drones in the time domain with the performance of other methods that suggested the use of frequency domain analysis [4,19] and (2) to examine whether the method can be applied using infrared flicker, exploiting the fact that a narrow spectrum of frequencies, the near infrared, is also captured by some CMOS sensors (this fact was exploited to establish an optical covert channel [11,20]).

References

1. Airmon-ng: https://www.aircrack-ng.org/doku.php?id=airmon-ng
2. 360, L.: An update on drone privacy concerns. https://www.law360.com/articles/848165/an-update-on-drone-privacy-concerns
3. Androidauthority: 8 fun drones you can control with your smartphone
4. Ben-Netanel, R., Nassi, B., Shamir, A., Elovici, Y.: Detecting spying drones. IEEE Secur. Priv. (2020). https://doi.org/10.1109/msec.2020.3034171
5. Birnbach, S., Baker, R., Martinovic, I.: Wi-fly?: detecting privacy invasion attacks by consumer drones. NDSS (2017)
6. Busset, J.: Detection and tracking of drones using advanced acoustic cameras. In: Unmanned/Unattended Sensors and Sensor Networks XI; and Advanced Free-Space Optical Communication Techniques and Applications, vol. 9647, p. 96470F. International Society for Optics and Photonics (2015)
7. Case, E.E., Zelnio, A.M., Rigling, B.D.: Low-cost acoustic array for small uav detection and tracking. In: Aerospace and Electronics Conference, 2008. NAECON 2008. IEEE National, pp. 110–113. IEEE (2008)
8. DJI: Mavic pro. https://www.dji.com/mavic
9. DJI: Spark remote controller. https://store.dji.com/product/spark-remote-controller
10. Eshel, T.: Mobile radar optimized to detect UAVS, precision guided weapons. Defense Update (2013)
11. Guri, M., Bykhovsky, D.: Air-jumper: covert air-gap exfiltration/infiltration via security cameras and infrared (IR). Comput. Secur. **82**, 15–29 (2019)
12. Insider, B.: Commercial unmanned aerial vehicle (UAV) market analysis. http://www.businessinsider.com/commercial-uav-market-analysis-2017-8
13. Intel: Intel dual band wireless ac 8265. http://ark.intel.com/products/94150/Intel-Dual-Band-Wireless-AC-8265
14. Jack, K.: Video Demystified: A Handbook for the Digital Engineer. Elsevier (2011)
15. Liu, Y., Sadeghi, A.R., Ghosal, D., Mukherjee, B.: Video streaming forensic-content identification with traffic snooping. In: Burmester, M., Tsudik, G., Magliveras, S., Ilic, I. (eds.) ISC 2010. LNCS, vol. 6531, pp. 129–135. Springer, Heidelberg (2011). https://doi.org/10.1007/978-3-642-18178-8_11
16. Mail, D.: Woman grabs gun shoots nosy neighbour's drone. http://www.dailymail.co.uk/news/article-4283486/Woman-grabs-gun-shoots-nosy-neighbour-s-drone.html
17. Mitrovic, D.: Video Compression. University of Edinburgh
18. Nassi, B., Bitton, R., Masuoka, R., Shabtai, A., Elovici, Y.: Sok: security and privacy in the age of commercial drones. In: 2021 IEEE Symposium on Security and Privacy (SP), pp. 73–90. IEEE Computer Society, Los Alamitos, CA, USA (2021). https://doi.org/10.1109/SP40001.2021.00005, https://doi.ieeecomputersociety.org/10.1109/SP40001.2021.00005

19. Nassi, B., Ben-Netanel, R., Shamir, A., Elovici, Y.: Drones' cryptanalysis-smashing cryptography with a flicker. In: 2019 IEEE Symposium on Security and Privacy (SP), pp. 1397–1414. IEEE (2019)

20. Nassi, B., Shamir, A., Elovici, Y.: Xerox day vulnerability. IEEE Trans. Inf. Forensics Secur. **14**(2), 415–430 (2018)

21. News, N.: Case dismissed against William H. merideth, kentucky man arrested for shooting down drone. http://www.nbcnews.com/news/us-news/case-dismissed-against-william-h-merideth-kentucky-man-arrested-shooting-n452281

22. News, N.: Kentucky man arrested after shooting down neighbor's drone. http://www.nbcnews.com/news/us-news/not-my-backyard-man-arrested-after-shooting-drone-down-n402271

23. Ostermann, J.: Video coding with h. 264/avc: tools, performance, and complexity. IEEE Circ. Syst. Mag. **4**(1), 7–28 (2004)

24. Parrot: Parrot skycontroller. https://www.parrot.com/global/accessories/drones/parrot-skycontroller#parrot-skycontroller

25. Peacock, M., Johnstone, M.N.: Towards detection and control of civilian unmanned aerial vehicles (2013)

26. Post, N.Y.: Husband uses drone to catch cheating wife (2016). https://nypost.com/2016/11/16/husband-uses-drone-to-catch-cheating-wife/

27. Reed, A., Klimkowski, B.: Leaky streams: identifying variable bitrate dash videos streamed over encrypted 802.11 n connections. In: 2016 13th IEEE Annual Consumer Communications and Networking Conference (CCNC), pp. 1107–1112. IEEE (2016)

28. Reed, A., Kranch, M.: Identifying https-protected netflix videos in real-time. In: Proceedings of the Seventh ACM on Conference on Data and Application Security and Privacy, pp. 361–368. ACM (2017)

29. Rozantsev, A., Lepetit, V., Fua, P.: Flying objects detection from a single moving camera. In: Proceedings of the IEEE Conference on Computer Vision and Pattern Recognition, pp. 4128–4136 (2015)

30. Saponas, T.S., Lester, J., Hartung, C., Agarwal, S., Kohno, T., et al.: Devices that tell on you: privacy trends in consumer ubiquitous computing. In: USENIX Security Symposium, pp. 55–70 (2007)

31. Schuster, R., Shmatikov, V., Tromer, E.: Beauty and the burst: remote identification of encrypted video streams. In: 26th USENIX Security Symposium (USENIX Security 17), pp. 1357–1374. USENIX Association, Vancouver, BC (2017). https://www.usenix.org/conference/usenixsecurity17/technical-sessions/presentation/schuster

32. Vasquez, J.R., Tarplee, K.M., Case, E.E., Zelnio, A.M., Rigling, B.D.: Multisensor 3d tracking for counter small unmanned air vehicles (CSUAV). In: Proceedings of the SPIE, vol. 6971, p. 697107 (2008)

33. Wampler, C., Uluagac, S., Beyah, R.: Information leakage in encrypted IP video traffic. In: 2015 IEEE Global Communications Conference (GLOBECOM), pp. 1–7 (2015). https://doi.org/10.1109/GLOCOM.2015.7417767

34. Washington, N.: Virginia woman shoots down drone near actor robert duvalls home. http://www.nbcwashington.com/news/local/Virginia-Woman-Shoots-Down-Drone-Near-Actor-Robert-Duvalls-Home-391423411.html

35. White, A.M., Matthews, A.R., Snow, K.Z., Monrose, F.: Phonotactic reconstruction of encrypted VOIP conversations: hookt on fon-iks. In: 2011 IEEE Symposium on Security and Privacy (SP), pp. 3–18. IEEE (2011)

36. Wiegand, T., Sullivan, G.J., Bjontegaard, G., Luthra, A.: Overview of the h. 264/avc video coding standard. IEEE Trans. Circ. Syst. Video Technol. **13**(7), 560–576 (2003)
37. World, N.: You cant shoot a drone so what can you do if it invades your privacy. http://www.networkworld.com/article/2941952/opensource-subnet/you-cant-shoot-a-drone-so-what-can-you-do-if-it-invades-your-privacy.html
38. Wright, C.V., Ballard, L., Coull, S.E., Monrose, F., Masson, G.M.: Spot me if you can: uncovering spoken phrases in encrypted VOIP conversations. In: IEEE Symposium on Security and Privacy, 2008. SP 2008, pp. 35–49. IEEE (2008)
39. Wright, C.V., Ballard, L., Monrose, F., Masson, G.M.: Language identification of encrypted voip traffic: Alejandra y roberto or alice and bob? USENIX Secur. Symp. **3**, 43–54 (2007)

Privacy Vulnerability of NeNDS Collaborative Filtering

Eyal Nussbaum[(✉)] and Michael Segal

School of Electrical and Computer Engineering,
Communication Systems Engineering Department,
Ben-Gurion University, 84105 Beer-Sheva, Israel

Abstract. Many of the data we collect today can easily be linked to an individual, household or entity. Unfortunately, using data without protecting the identity of the data owner can lead to data leaks and potential lawsuits. To maintain user privacy when a publication of data occurs many databases employ anonymization techniques, either on the query results or the data itself. In this paper we examine variant of such technique, "data perturbation" and discuss its vulnerability. The data perturbation method deals with changing the values of records in the dataset while maintaining a level of accuracy over the resulting queries. We focus on a relatively new data perturbation method called NeNDS [1] and show a possible partial knowledge privacy attack on this method.

Keywords: Collaborative filtering · Privacy · NeNDS

1 Introduction

Collaborative filtering (CF) is a technique commonly used to build personalized recommendations on the Web. In collaborative filtering, algorithms are used to make automatic predictions about a user's interests by compiling preferences from several users. Su et al. [2] survey these techniques in depth. In order to provide personalized information to a user, the CF system needs to be provided with sufficient information regarding his or her preferences, behavioral characteristics, as well as demographic information of the individual. The accuracy of the recommendations is dependent largely on how much of this information is known to the CF system. However, this information can prove to be extremely dangerous if it falls in the wrong hands. Several methods aimed at hiding and anonymizing user data have been proposed and studied in an attempt to reduce the privacy issues of collaborative filtering. These methods include data obfuscation, random perturbation, data suppression and others [3–6]. Most of these methods rely on experimental results alone to show effectiveness, and some have already been shown to have weaknesses that can be exploited in order to recover the original user data [7,8].

© Springer Nature Switzerland AG 2021
S. Dolev et al. (Eds.): CSCML 2021, LNCS 12716, pp. 145–152, 2021.
https://doi.org/10.1007/978-3-030-78086-9_11

Parameswaran and Blough [1,3] propose a new data obfuscation technique dubbed "Nearest Neighbor Data Substitution" (NeNDS). Using this approach, items in each column of the database are clustered into groups by closeness of their values, and a substitution algorithm is applied to each group. The algorithm gives each item a new location within the group such that each item's value now corresponds to a different row in the original database. The relative closeness in values of the substituted items allows for the recommendation system to maintain a good degree of approximation when the CF algorithm is applied to obtain recommendations, while the substitution itself offers a level of privacy by hiding the original values associated with each individual user. Implementations of NeNDS today can be seen in US patent number 10102398 [9] and in "BronzeGate", an obfuscated solution for Oracle's "GoldenGate" system [10]. The former is based on the same mechanism as NeNDS, while the latter uses a "furthest neighbor" substitution variation with similar behavior. We detail a partial knowledge de-anonymization attack on NeNDS, as well as address some of the shortcomings of this method.

In this paper, we demonstrate the possibility of a privacy attack on the substituted database by an attacker with partial knowledge of the original data. Additionally, we highlight a complexity issue with the NeNDS algorithm, and offer a simpler method for certain data types.

This paper is organized as follows. In the next section we explain the NeNDS techniques. Section 3 contains the explanations of privacy attack we perform. We explain how to improve the run time of the original solution in Sect. 4. Finally, we conclude in Sect. 5.

2   The NeNDS Algorithm

The Nearest Neighbor Data Substitution (NeNDS) technique is a lossless data obfuscation technique that preserves the privacy of individual data elements by substituting them with one of their Euclidean space neighbors. NeNDS uses a permutation-based approach in which groups of similar items undergo permutation. The permutation approach hides the original value of a data item by substituting it with another data item that is similar to it but not the same. NeNDs treats each column in the database as a separate dataset. The first step in NeNDS is the creation of similar sets of items called neighborhoods. These items contained in each neighborhood are selected in a manner that maintains Euclidean closeness between neighbors using some distance measuring function suited to the data. Each data set is divided into a pre-specified number of neighborhoods based on a minimal neighborhood size. The items in each neighborhood are then permuted in such a way that each item is displaced from its original position, no two items undergo swapping, and the difference between the values of the original and the obfuscated items is minimal. The number of neighbors in each neighborhood is denoted NH_{size}, with $3 \leq NH_{size} \leq N$ where N is the number of items in the dataset (this is due to the fact that $NH_{size} = 1$ does not allow any permutation and $NH_{size} = 2$ is the trivial case of swapping between 2 items and easily reversible).

The substitution process is performed by determining the optimal permutation set subject to the following conditions:

- No two elements in the neighborhood undergo swapping.
- The elements are displaced from their original position.
- Substitution is not performed between duplicate elements.

The permutation mapping is done by creating a tree depicting all possible permutation paths and selecting the path with the minimal maximum distance between any 2 substitutions. For example, we look at the case of the neighborhood $[75, 77, 82, 70]$. The optimal path for substitution would be $75 \rightarrow 70 \rightarrow 77 \rightarrow 82 \rightarrow 75$ with the new neighborhood order being $[82, 70, 77, 75]$ and the maximal difference between any 2 substituted items being ($70 \rightarrow 77$ and $82 \rightarrow 75$). Once the substitutions in each neighborhood is complete, the column of the original database is replaced with column containing the new item positions. The detailed algorithm can be found in [3]. Note that this algorithm is deterministic for any given value of NH_{size}, and will yield the same permutations given any original order of the original dataset. However, the root node of the tree is dependant on the original dataset order, and therefore the original tree cannot be recreated given the perturbed data order. The first item in the neighborhood is selected to be the root node, and its child nodes are ordered left to right by distance from the parent. Each sub-tree for a child node is then created from the remaining items in the neighborhood in the same manner as shown in Fig. 1. Selecting a different item as the root node may change the resulting perturbation, and without this information the reconstruction of the substitution path is not trivial.

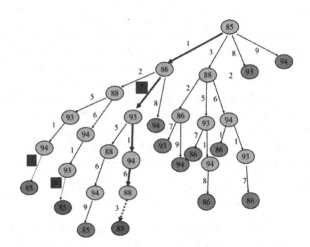

Fig. 1. NeNDS tree algorithm for neighborhood [85, 88, 93, 94, 86]

3   Privacy Attack on NeNDS

In this section we will show an attack on a NeNDS permutated database by an
attacker with partial knowledge of the original database, specifically the attacker
knows the original position of at least $NH_{size} - 2$ items in each neighborhood.
The attack is performed under the following assumptions:

- The attacker has complete knowledge of the NeNDS algorithm.
- The attacker knows the neighborhood size, NH_{size} used by the algorithm.
- The attacker can measure the Euclidean distance between the items in the
  database.
- The attacker has access to the output permutated database (i.e. the new
  positions of all items).

We will show the attack for a single dataset (column), however since the algorithm is performed independently for each dataset, this can be extended to the
entire database. For a given dataset of size n, we define the following notations:

- Let X be the original dataset $[x_1, x_2, \ldots, x_n]$.
- Let Y be the NeNDS obfuscated dataset $[y_1, y_2, \ldots, y_n]$.
- Let X_p be the original data items in the pth neighborhood, $[x_{p1}, x_{p2}, \ldots, x_{pn}]$.
- Let Y_p be the obfuscated data items in the pth neighborhood,
  $[y_{p1}, y_{p2}, \ldots, y_{pn}]$.
- Let u_{p1}, u_{p2} be the 2 items in X_p whose original position is unknown to the
  attacker.

The attack is successful if the attacker can determine the original position in X
of u_{p1} and u_{p2} for all values of $p, 1 \le p \le \frac{n}{NH_{size}}$.

The Case of $NH_{size} = 3$

We look at the simple case of the minimal neighborhood size, $NH_{size} = 3$. In this
case, we have for each value of p the neighborhood $[x_{p1}, x_{p2}, x_{p3}]$. The attacker
can only know the location of 1 of these items. Assume, without loss of generality,
that the attacker knows the position of x_{p1}, and as such the original dataset to
be $[x_{p1}, u_{p1}, u_{p2}]$ where both u_{p1} and u_{p2} could be the original positions of x_{p2}
and x_{p3}. We now look at the output neighborhood after the NeNDS algorithm.
Due to the restrictions of the NeNDS algorithm which require each item to be
relocated and do not allow swapping between 2 items, the resulting neighborhood
Y_p can only be one of the following permutations:

1. $[y_{p1}, y_{p2}, y_{p3}] = [x_{p2}, x_{p3}, x_{p1}]$.
2. $[y_{p1}, y_{p2}, y_{p3}] = [x_{p3}, x_{p1}, x_{p2}]$.

Any other permutation would entail leaving an item in its original position.
Assume permutation (1). The attacker can determine that the value y_{p1} could
not have originally been in position u_{p2} since this is the current position of x_{p1}
and the algorithm does not allow swapping between 2 items. Therefore, $u_{p2} = x_{p3}$
and $u_{p1} = x_{p2}$. Assume permutation (2). The attacker can determine that the
value y_{p1} could not have originally been in position u_{p1} for the same reason,

and reaches the same conclusion - the original order for the neighborhood p is $[x_{p1}, x_{p2}, x_{p3}]$.

The General Case of any NH_{size}

In this section we will show that the knowledge of $NH_{size} - 2$ original value positions is enough for an attacker to learn the original positions of all NH_{size} values in a neighborhood. We define $L_o(x)$ and $L_n(x)$ for any value $x \in X$ to be the original and new location (row) of that value respectively. Taking some neighborhood X_p in X, the attacker knows the position $L_o(x_{pi})$ for $NH_{size} - 2$ values in X_p. For 2 values, u_{p1}, u_{p2}, positions $L_o(u_{p1}), L_o(u_{p2})$ remain unknown. After obfuscation, all new positions $L_n(y_{pi})$ are known to the attacker. With this knowledge, since the values in the neighborhood X_p are chosen by their Euclidean closeness, the attacker learns the 2 values $[u_{p1}, u_{p2}]$ and their new positions $[L_n(u_{p1}), L_n(u_{p2})]$. There remain 2 possible original positions $L_o(u_{p1}), L_o(u_{p2})$ between which the attacker cannot distinguish (i.e. each one of the values could have been at each one of the possible positions originally).

We now examine the new values in $L_o(u_{p1}), L_o(u_{p2})$. There are 2 cases: either 1 of the values is u_{p1} or u_{p2}, or both values are from the other values in X_p whose original position is known to the attacker. Note that the case $L_o(u_{p1}) = L_n(u_{p2}), L_o(u_{p2}) = L_n(u_{p1})$ cannot exist since by definition of the algorithm, no 2 items undergo swapping. We now show the attack for both cases, resulting in the discovery of the original positions for u_{p1}, u_{p2}.

Case 1

Assume, without loss of generality, that u_{p1} resides in a position whose original value is unknown, meaning was either u_{p1} or u_{p2}. It is easy to see that $L_n(u_{p1}) = L_o(u_{p2})$ since no item remains in the same position after obfuscation. In addition, the remaining unknown position is $L_o(u_{p1})$. The attacker now knows the original position of both previously unknown values.

Case 1

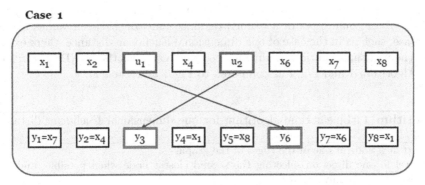

Case 2

In this case, both $L_o(u_{p1})$ and $L_o(u_{p2})$ now contain values whose original position were known to the attacker. We arbitrarily define those positions to be L_1 and L_2 and their original values u_1 and u_2 respectively. The attacker can know use the following method to backtrack the obfuscation path and find the original positions of u_{p1} and u_{p2}. We look at the value currently in L_1 and denote this value y_{p1}. This was the item in the obfuscation path immediately before u_1. $L_o(y_{p1})$ is known to the attacker and contains the value that was in the obfuscation path before y_{p1}. Denote this value y_{p2}. We now continue this backtracking of the path by examining the value in $L_o(y_{p2})$ and so on until we reach on of the values u_{p1}, u_{p2}. Since the path is created using a tree structure which contains no cycles, the first unknown value we will find must correspond to u_2 (as u_1 will be that last item found in our backtracking and complete the path). Assume, without loss of generality, that $u_2 = u_{p1}$. The attacker now knows that $L_2 = L_o(u_{p1})$ and vice versa.

Case 2

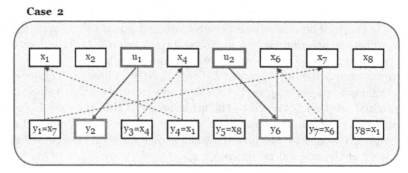

4   NeNDS Shortcomings

In addition to being susceptible to partial knowledge reconstruction, the NeNDS algorithm has an exponential run time which is not suitable for real world applications. It can be shown the NeNDS algorithm solves the Bottleneck Traveling Salesman problem (BTSP), which is known to be NP-Complete in the general case. For some cases of a defined distance function between values in the database, such as in the case of one dimensional Euclidean distance, there exists a polynomial time solution producing the same results as the NeNDS algorithm (see Algorithm 1 and Fig. 2 as compared to Fig. 1 and Table 1).

Algorithm 1. Linear time algorithm for one dimensional Euclidean distance BTSP

---

1. Start at a node at one of the edges of the graph.

2. Travel in one direction selecting the second closest node when possible, and the closest node when only one remains.

3. Then, travel in the other direction via each node that has not been added to the path until the originating node has been reached.

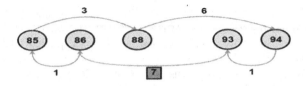

Fig. 2. Bottleneck TSP on linear graph (linear run time) based on same neighborhood as Fig. 1

In the general case, there are approximation algorithms for BTSP, such as given by Kao and Sanghi [11] that can be adapted for the case of NeNDS-like perturbation, giving the same level of privacy while achieving an approximate level of accuracy.

Table 1. NeNDS transformation result table - same for both algorithms.

Row	Original value	Transformed value
1	86	93
2	88	85
3	93	94
4	85	86
5	94	88

5 Conclusions

In this paper we have presented a privacy attack on the substituted NeNDS database by an attacker with partial knowledge of the original data. While this method claims to maintain privacy unless all but 1 of the values in a neighborhood are known to the attacker, we show that an attacker missing only 2 values in a neighborhood may also reconstruct the original data before obfuscation. Additionally as we point out, the NeNDS algorithm can be shown to be NP-complete for the general distance function between values. While this renders the method problematic for large neighborhood sizes, we show that a simpler perturbation algorithm can be used when the data adheres to the one dimensional Euclidean distance function. This allows for larger neighborhoods, which will require more side knowledge by the attacker.

It would be interesting to continue research into whether our approach can be generalized for the special case where the attacker knows the position of less than $NH_{size} - 2$ original items in each neighborhood.

References

1. Parameswaran, R., Blough, D.M.: Privacy preserving data obfuscation for inherently clustered data. Int. J. Inf. Comput. Secur. **2**(1), 4–26 (2008)
2. Su, X., Khoshgoftaar, T.M.: A survey of collaborative filtering techniques. Adv. in Artif. Intell. **2009**, 421425:1–421425:19 (2009)

3. Parameswaran, R., Blough, D.M.: Privacy preserving collaborative filtering using data obfuscation. In: Proceedings of the 2007 IEEE International Conference on Granular Computing, GRC 2007, Washington, DC, USA, pp. 380–386. IEEE Computer Society (2007)

4. Polat, H., Du, W.: Privacy-preserving collaborative filtering using randomized perturbation techniques. In: Proceedings of the Third IEEE International Conference on Data Mining, ICDM 2003, Washington, DC, USA, pp. 625–628. IEEE Computer Society (2003)

5. Parra-Arnau, J., Rebollo-Monedero, D., Forné, J.: A privacy-protecting architecture for collaborative filtering via forgery and suppression of ratings. In: Garcia-Alfaro, J., Navarro-Arribas, G., Cuppens-Boulahia, N., de Capitani di Vimercati, S. (eds.) DPM/SETOP - 2011. LNCS, vol. 7122, pp. 42–57. Springer, Heidelberg (2012). https://doi.org/10.1007/978-3-642-28879-1_4

6. Canny, J.: Collaborative filtering with privacy via factor analysis. In: Proceedings of the 25th Annual International ACM SIGIR Conference on Research and Development in Information Retrieval, SIGIR 2002, New York, NY, USA, pp. 238–245. ACM (2002)

7. Huang, Z., Du, W., Chen, B.: Deriving private information from randomized data. In: Proceedings of the 2005 ACM SIGMOD International Conference on Management of Data, SIGMOD 2005, New York, NY, USA, pp. 37–48. ACM (2005)

8. Kargupta, H., Datta, S., Wang, Q., Sivakumar, K.: On the privacy preserving properties of random data perturbation techniques. In: Proceedings of the Third IEEE International Conference on Data Mining, ICDM 2003, Washington, DC, USA, pp. 99–106. IEEE Computer Society (2003)

9. Naargaard, P.: Generating obfuscated data. US Patent, October 2018

10. Guirguis, S., Pareek, A.: Real-time transactional data obfuscation for Goldengate. In: Proceedings of the 13th International Conference on Extending Database Technology, EDBT 2010, New York, NY, USA, pp. 645–650. ACM (2010)

11. Kao, M.-Y., Sanghi, M.: An approximation algorithm for a bottleneck traveling salesman problem. In: Calamoneri, T., Finocchi, I., Italiano, G.F. (eds.) CIAC 2006. LNCS, vol. 3998, pp. 223–235. Springer, Heidelberg (2006). https://doi.org/10.1007/11758471_23

Lawful Interception in WebRTC Peer-To-Peer Communication

Assaf Wagner and Rami Puzis[(✉)] [iD]

Telekom Innovation Laboratories,
Ben-Gurion University of the Negev, Beer-Sheva, Israel
puzis@bgu.ac.il

Abstract. Lawful interception is the act of giving law enforcement officials access to communication between private individuals or organizations. According to the European Telecommunications Standards Institute (ETSI), *service providers are expected to ensure that the entire contents of communication associated with the target identity being intercepted can be intercepted during the entire period of the lawful authorization,* and that *the delivery of the interception related information is reliable.*

In traditional telephone networks, authorized surveillance takes place by duplicating the conversation data at the service provider premises and forwarding it to law enforcement agencies (LEA). The same approach is suitable for VoIP communication, as long as the data is transferred via a mediator located on the service provider's premises. Today, direct VoIP communication between clients is the preferred approach due to better call quality and reduced network footprint. Although, VoIP service providers are obliged to provide lawful interception according to ETSI, the traditional model for lawful interception is no longer applicable for direct VoIP communication.

In this article, we present a technique to intercept direct VoIP communication between two clients using the state of the art WebRTC technology. This paper addresses an important unmet need of service providers to enable lawful interception in P2P VoIP calls. The new approach maintains high performance without degrading the user experience.

Keywords: Lawful interception · VoIP · WebRTC P2P communication

1 Introduction

Over the years, telecommunication between clients has progressed from a public switched telephone network (PSTN) within a centralized model to voice over IP (VoIP) telecommunication within a distributed model. Extensive research has been conducted in order to improve the efficiency of data transportation between VoIP clients and protect user's privacy. This, together with efforts to develop an easy way to share real time media on the Web, contributed to the development of new alternatives to the traditional telecommunication service providers.

© Springer Nature Switzerland AG 2021
S. Dolev et al. (Eds.): CSCML 2021, LNCS 12716, pp. 153–170, 2021.
https://doi.org/10.1007/978-3-030-78086-9_12

WebRTC (Web Real-Time Communication) is a standard, which includes a set of simple APIs, to provide secured and high quality communication between browsers. The APIs enable to establish a direct connection between browsers and to transfer streams of data through peer connections. The first public draft of the WebRTC standard was published in 2011, and a few months later, Chrome[1] and other leading browser manufacturers began to integrate the standard in their products.

In 2011, Google released a WebRTC open source software package, which permits sharing data between browsers in a secure manner [3,4]. The main components of the software are aimed at providing access to the user's resources and easily establishing a secure peer-to-peer connection. In the future, such software will permit the transfer of structured data as well.

According to law enforcement agency (LEA) requirements [2], as described in a technical specification document of the European Telecommunications Standards Institute (ETSI) [1], service providers are expected to ensure that 1) the entire Content of Communication (CC) of a target identity can be intercepted, and 2) the meta data of the intercepted communication, a.k.a. Interception Related Information (IRI) is reliable and accurate. Intercepting of PSTN calls is fully addressed using standard controls, implemented and supervised by service providers on their equipment. Similarly, interception of VoIP calls when media streams are transferred via a mediator is performed by the service provider who manages the mediator.

However, interception of VoIP calls when media streams are transferred directly between the clients is largely unresolved. The difference between direct communication and communication using a mediator is shown in Fig. 1. In this paper we present an elegant interception scheme of peer-to-peer (P2P) VoIP calls where media streams are transferred directly between clients. According to our solution the LEA joins the intercepted conversation as a hidden third party without the need to wire-tap the service provider's gateway or control the end devices at customer premises. We present a practical approach for intercepting P2P VoIP conversations executed using standard WebRTC technology. A loophole in the original WebRTC specification allows the proposed approach to integrate well within the existing WebRTC implementations without any amendments to the WebRTC APIs. Lawful Interception of P2P VoIP calls presented in this paper relies on unsolicited multi-party communication established via standard browsers supporting WebRTC.

2   Background and Related Work

2.1   Browsers' Support and Open Source WebRTC Libraries

In this research we focus on VoIP communication supplied by service providers, which is subject to the regulatory requirements of law authorities. The purpose

---

[1] http://lists.w3.org/Archives/Public/public-webrtc/2011May/0022.html.

of our research is developing a systemic approach for intercepting VoIP calls, in which call signaling infrastructure is provided by the service providers, and the content of the conversation is transferred between the clients' trusted applications using a direct communication channel.

The use of public browsers and an open source technology to establish secure communication poses a challenge for service providers who need to supply interception for regulatory purposes. This is complicated by the fact that browser manufacturers are anxious to preserve users' privacy and obstruct attempts to hijack network traffic. In this paper we present an application level control for intercepting the conversation using a public browser and WebRTC, in presence of the extensive browser security systems and the high security standards of WebRTC.

In order to avoid arousing the suspicions of the target identity, it is extremely important that the browser's typical behavior is maintained during surveillance. With our proposed interception model, we remain undetectable to users, as long as they don't make special efforts to detect network traffic anomalies. For example, with network debugging tools, users may be able to determine that a connection has been made with another peer. However, in normal network conditions, numerous connections are made during Web browsing. The ability to remain undetectable, depends on the users expertise to differentiate between the normal network traffic and the network traffic during the surveillance. This should be considered by the law enforcement agencies in each case.

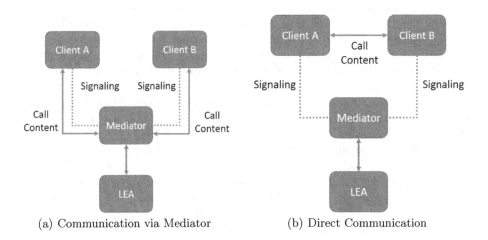

(a) Communication via Mediator   (b) Direct Communication

Fig. 1. Communication via a mediator vs direct communication

WebRTC technology was used because it eliminates the need for developers to handle media transfer issues and enables direct media streaming between clients with ease.

Our research expands the current standards for the act of lawful interception for telecommunication over the Internet.

2.2 ETSI Reference Model for Lawful Interception

Lawful interception is the act of giving law enforcement officials access to the communication between private individuals or organizations. The process is legally authorized, and communication includes phone calls, email messages, text messages (SMS), photo messages (MMS), and other types of data interchange. In 2000, the Internet Engineering Task Force (IETF) decided not to consider the requirements for wiretapping over the Internet [5]. On the other hand, the IETF mentioned that *mechanisms designed to facilitate or enable wiretapping facilities for [legal] purposes, should be openly described.* Although such standards and protocols had not been described, in 2001, the technical committee of the European Telecommunications Standards Institute (ETSI) described the lawful interception procedure in detail and published a reference model, which was adopted by the majority of EU countries.

The technical committee of the ETSI organization (TC LI) has published three standards to define interception for traditional communication and communication over the Internet [6]: handover specification for IP delivery interception (TS-102-232 [7,8]), service specific details for email services interception (TS-102-233), and service specific details for Internet access services interception (TS-102-234).

In a separate document (TS-101-671 [9]), the technical committee describes a generic handover interface (HI) for the provision of lawful interception for network operators, access providers, and service providers. The handover specifications describe three interfaces (see Fig. 2): HI1 describes the administrative functionality (Handover Manager), which enforces integrity and applies an encryption mechanism if required. HI2 and HI3 describe the interception data: the Interception Related Information (IRI) and the Content of Communication (CC), respectively. Mediation Functions (MF) are responsible for receiving the IRI and CC information within the service provider network.

The MFs are responsible for correlating and formatting the relevant information in real-time before delivering it to the LEA over the HI2 and HI3 handover interfaces. All data is transferred to law enforcement agencies via the Law Enforcement Monitoring Facility (LEMF). According to the LEA requirements, any service coding or encryption which has been applied to the content of the communication or to the interception related information, should be removed at the request of the LEA [1].

2.3 Current Solutions for Intercepting VoIP Calls

Intercepting PSTN calls has been addressed and massive standardization was provided by the regulatory authorities. In this case, interception is handled by management controls, implemented and supervised by service providers. Mediation functions are responsible for transferring the intercepted data.

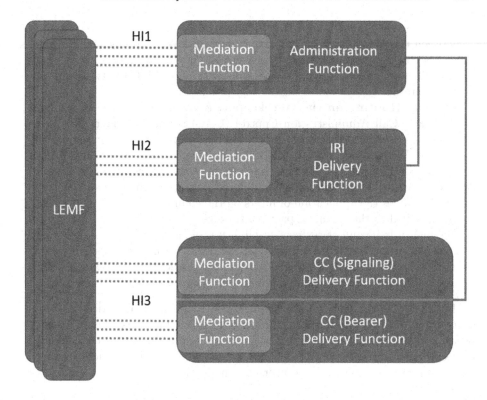

Fig. 2. Reference model for LI system by ETSI

As the development of the Internet infrastructure progressed, telecommunications service providers began to investigate the potential of VoIP calls and develop communication products accordingly. However, the interception of VoIP calls posed a significant challenge to the LEAs. In traditional telecommunication systems, service providers are obligated to provide an entry point for authorities, and the call data that is transferred via gateways is duplicated. Hence, the interception of VoIP calls while media streams are transferred via a mediator has also been resolved, while the interception of VoIP calls as media streams that are transferred directly between the clients remains an open problem.

The obligation of service providers to adhere to regulations and the lack of effective solutions for lawful interception, have delayed advancements in the development of peer-to-peer VoIP calls as an alternative to PSTN. As a consequence to the refusal of the main standards body of the Internet (IETF) to be involved in LI [5], and following the ETSI's publication of a reference model in 2001, efforts were made to outline a model to intercept telecommunication conversations over the Internet.

In 2003, Milanović et al. [10] described four basic methods for intercepting a call in an IP telephone network, based on the H.323 standard, and described their advantages and disadvantages:

1. **Wiretap on Gateway:** In the H.323 standard, a gateway is an adapter between the H.323 network and other networks. Wiretapping via this gateway is suitable for calls between a client in the H.323 system and a client in a different network. In this case, calls within the H.323 network are not interceptable.
2. **Wiretap Routing on the Gatekeeper:** A gatekeeper, in the H.323 standard, is a Call Administration Control (CAC) service provider. In routing mode, the Gatekeeper acts as a proxy for both signaling and communication services. Wiretapping via Gatekeeper interception is applied for all calls, but it degrades the quality of the call and can be detected by an expert user.
3. **Fixed Route Wiretap:** This is a different version of the previous method, which enables the application of filters on the communication properties that are attached to the signaling packets. However, this method does not resolve the quality issue and raises new scalability problems.
4. **Promiscuous Wiretap:** In this method, a device in a promiscuous mode monitors all of the network traffic. In this case, the device should be connected to the local area network and configured to forward all of the traffic data.

In other research, also published in 2003, Milanović et al. [11] outlined an abstract model to support the interception methods for a distributed IP telephony network based on the H.323 standard. The assumption in this model is that call data is transferred via a gateway and not in a direct mode between clients. In case of direct peer-to-peer communication, the call data cannot be intercepted.

In 2004, Cisco published an RFC [12] that described a reference model to support LI in an IP network, without any limitations for a specific architecture (centralized versus distributed) or protocol. Device manufacturers essentially provide the ability to integrate interception in VoIP telecommunication systems. The architecture model of the Cisco Service Independent Intercept (SII) device is shown in Fig. 3. According to Cisco, all the devices must be part of the service provider's domain. Essentially, this model fails when service provider has no control over the end devices.

In 2007, Balamurugan et al. [13] discussed the challenges of the interception of VoIP calls. The authors propose an additional solution to LI which relies on interception at the gateway. They proposed monitoring architecture for VoIP networks which based on Session Initiation Protocol (SIP). In their research, they defined signaling and data delivery functions to transfer SIP and RTP (Real-time Transport Protocol) packets to the LEA from a gateway in the Communications Service Provider (CSP) domain.

All LI solutions for VoIP proposed so far rely on a centralized device (gateway, mediator, etc.) which controls the media stream between clients. Meanwhile, due to network traffic efficiency and conversation quality, direct P2P communication has become the preferred approach for VoIP calls. In this case, the call data does not pass through a mediator, but is routed directly between the clients and the service providers are unable to intercept it and deliver to LEA using standard methods.

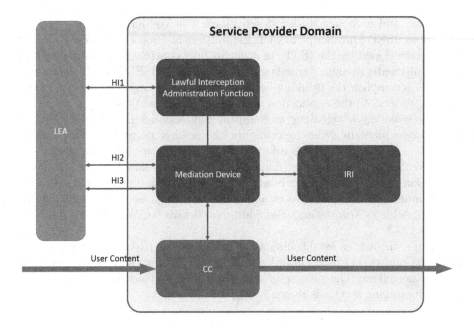

Fig. 3. Cisco SII model

3 WebRTC

WebRTC (Web Real-Time Communication) is a standard of the World Wide Web Consortium (W3C) that provides rich and high quality communication between browsers via simple APIs. The advantage of WebRTC over other technologies is its ability to transfer data between standard browsers, with no need of additional plug-ins. In the rest of this section we discuss the essential details of WebRTC, putting special focus on P2P voice/video communication and the relevant security controls.

In 2011, Google released WebRTC 1.0[2], an open source JavaScript package. WebRTC's main components provide web developers access to user's resources (camera and microphone) and peer connection infrastructure. The browser has access to the user resources, and during session initiation, the browser requests the user's permission to use his/her resources. If the request is declined, the session handshake is cancelled; otherwise, the session continues. For example, user permission is required when the a Web application requests access to either one of the client media devices using the getUserMedia API call. However, as the following analysis reveals, the peer connection does not require any user permission.

3.1 Connection Initiation

Signaling is used to coordinate communication and send control messages between clients. In WebRTC, signaling is used to detect peers, initiate the session

---

[2] https://webrtc.org.

handshake, and exchange session descriptions. The WebRTC signaling process is based on JSEP (JavaScript Session Establishment Protocol), a new standard that was developed by the IETF, in order to fully control the signaling process of the multimedia session. According to the authors of JSEP [14], the new standard will accomplish the thinking behind WebRTC, leaving the selection of the signaling process to the application developer as much as possible.

After selecting a signaling mechanism, bidirectional negotiation between clients takes place in order to configure the session properties. The Session Description Protocol[3] (SDP) is a format to lay out the session parameters.

In WebRTC, all connection management is encapsulated in an RTCPeerConnection object. This object is associated with the Interactive Connectivity Establishment (ICE) service to establish end-to-end connectivity behind NAT (Network Address Translation). See additional details on WebRTC NAT traversal in Sect. 3.3.

When a client tries establishing a call with another party, he/she creates an RTCPeerConnection object, in order to deliver SDP offers and media metadata to the other client. The process of creating a data connection between clients using a messaging service is shown in Fig. 4.

3.2   Encryption

Encryption is a mandatory feature in WebRTC and is enforced on all components, including signaling mechanisms. The encryption protocol used depends on the channel type. Data streams are encrypted using Datagram Transport Layer Security (DTLS), which is based on TLS with an asymmetric encryption methodology, and media streams are encrypted using Secure Real-time Transport Protocol (SRTP). The key exchange process is encrypted with DTLS-SRTP.

3.3   P2P Communication

Peer discovery is the way clients signal their friends. Although, client address books are not implemented in WebRTC, open source projects such as AppRTC[4], WebRTC.io[5], easyRTC[6] and other projects are available for this purpose. It is also possible to implement a local host server using Node.js [15].

The ICE (Interactive Connectivity Establishment) mechanism overcomes the complexity of initiating peer connections in presence of NAT. First it attempts using the host's operating system address. The fallback scenario is to use Session Traversal Utilities for NAT (STUN) [16] to determine the public IP addresses of both sides and assist in establishing a P2P connection.

When a direct communication path cannot be found, it is necessary to use a TURN server (Traversal Using Relays around NAT [17]) which acts as a relay

---

[3] https://tools.ietf.org/html/rfc4566.
[4] https://apprtc.appspot.com.
[5] https://github.com/webRTC-io/webRTC.io.
[6] https://github.com/priologic/easyrtc.

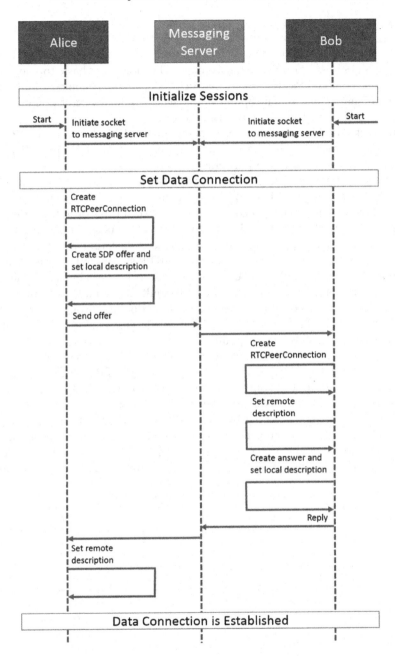

Fig. 4. WebRTC data connection initiation process

for the packets. The client can control some aspects of the relay. Note that even in case that a TURN server is used as a relay, it may not be under the control of the service provider and thus, interception at the relay may not be possible.

3.4   Multi-party Conversations

There are several different architectures suitable for a conference call with multiple endpoints in an RTP based environment. The following basic topologies for multiple endpoint RTPs were described in RFC 7667 [18]: point to multipoint using multicast, point to multipoint using mesh, point to multipoint using a translator, and point to multipoint using a mixer.

Multicast (see Fig. 5(a)) is a technique supported by device in an IP layer that enables participants in a group to send a packet with the expectation that the packet will reach all group participants.

In a mesh topology (see Fig. 5(c)), all nodes are connected to each other. Although this architecture is theoretically inefficient, it is very easy to use and has been found to be efficient in conversations between three or four participants [19]. In this case, all of the data is sent to all of the users simultaneously.

A translator (transport translator or media translator) receives an RTP stream on one side and generates an individual RTP stream in the other domain. Transport translators do not modify the RTP stream itself but are concerned with transport parameters, such as unicast to multicast. In a very simple transport translator, the translator connects multiple endpoints through unicast. This scenario is called a relay translation (see Fig. 5(b)). The relay forwards all of the traffic it receives to all other endpoints.

The mixer (see Fig. 5(b)) is a middlebox that aggregates multiple RTP streams which are part of a session and generates new RTP streams by manipulating the media data. The content that the mixer provides is the mixed aggregate of the data that the mixer received.

The mixer is a sender and receiver of RTP streams. In addition to the regular connectivity handling, the mixer responds an RTP reports to the incoming and outgoing stream. For incoming streams, the mixer responds an RTP receiver reports and for outgoing streams, the mixer generates an RTP sender reports.

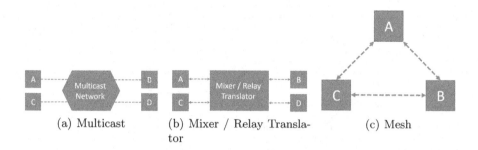

(a) Multicast   (b) Mixer / Relay Translator   (c) Mesh

Fig. 5. Multiparty topologies

Multiparty Conversation Session Initiation. In 2006, the IETF published a specification for creating a conference session between multiple user agents [20].

The process of initiating a conference call between Alice, Bob, and Carol starts with an INVITE request sent from Alice to a focus server to create a conference session.

A focus server is a conference application server, which hosts the SIP conference and maintains the SIP signaling relationship with each participant in the conference.

After the conference session has been created, Alice sends a REFER request in order to join Carol and Bob in the conference.

In WebRTC, a conference session for a small group of users is implemented in a mesh architecture; for a large group of users, a multipoint conferencing unit device (MCU) performs the media mixing.

In some cases, the MCU device supports SIP and H.323 protocols as well. Otherwise, a different server is required for the signaling process.

4   The Interception Model

The interception process begins after the LEA management application sets up a clean session with the SIP service. The clients' conversation depends on their session with the same SIP service.

When Alice wants to initiate a media connection with Bob, the web application will ask for her permission to use her local media resources. This is done using the getUserMedia method. This method is integrated in the browser's API, and as a consequence, the browser will display a message dialog box to request Alice's permission to use her media resources.

When Alice confirms the media request, the web application can continue on to send an invitation to Bob.

At this point in the process, the application would ordinarily send a single invitation to Bob. Instead, our web application will send two invitations. The first is to Bob and the second is to the LEA.

Both invitations will be sent directly. It is highly recommended to ensure that the both invitations (to Bob and to the LEA) arrives, before we continue in the invitations process. This is required in order to prevent from the conversation to begin, before the LEA has the ability to start the interception process.

When Bob's web application receives the offer, his web application asks for permission to use his local media resources.

After Bob confirms the use of the media resources, his web application creates a response, and designates Alice's offer. At the same time, Bob's web application creates another invitation, and sends it to the LEA.

Bob's web application then sends the response to Alice, and the VoIP conversation begins.

When the LEA receives Alice and Bob's offers, it can send a confirmation as a response and continue with the session initiation. The LEA can decide to confirm both of the offers, to confirm only one of the offers, or to decline both offers.

The interception model includes the following components:

4.1   Signaling Services

In practical terms, a signaling service is designed to exchange small messages between clients. In telecommunication, signaling messages are valuable during the conversation life cycle for preserving the client's availability.

There are several alternatives for implementing signaling services:

1. **Polling:** The user initiates a request to the signaling server, in order to obtain his/her pending messages. The act of making the request is carried out by the user, or periodically by the application, according to a predefined business logic.

   This approach is relevant for systems that need to receive the messages at regular intervals. Polling is thought of as inefficient. When there are a few messages waiting for a client, most of the requests will be returned with an empty response.

   In terms of telecommunication, this approach means that the caller sends his/her request to the signaling server and will only get an answer after the second client pulls the caller's request and answers it.

2. **Push:** The user initiates a request to the signaling server and waits until a message is ready to be flushed. The connection does not have a time-out limitation, and the client can wait as long as needed. When a message arrives, the server flushes the data, and the connection remains open and ready to receive new data.

   This approach is efficient in terms of system resources and provides a solution for real-time systems.

   In terms of telecommunication, this approach means that the caller sends his/her request to the signaling server, and the second client will get the request in real-time.

3. **Long Polling:** This approach is a combination of the previous alternatives. The user initiates a request to the signaling server and waits until a message is ready to be pulled. If no messages are available, the server holds the response as long as it can (until a time-out exception occurs, according to the binding configurations).

   When a message arrives, the client pulls the message and closes the connection. When the connection has been closed (after a message was pulled or after a time-out exception occurs), the user initiates a new request to the server and waits.

   This approach is relevant for real-time response, but it is inefficient compared to the push alternative.

In telecommunication systems, only push and long-polling methods are applicable.

4.2   Web Applications

The core of the interception model is the trusted client application. This application is a web application, based on WebRTC components.

Both invitations are sent using RTCPeerConnection WebRTC objects. These objects generate a local SDP offer and are responsible for sending the invitation requests to their destination.

When Bob's web application receives the offer, his web application use the 'getUserMedia' method in order to receive a permission to use his local media resources.

After Bob confirms the use of the media resources, his web application creates an RTCPeerConnection, which generates an SDP response and designates Alice's SDP offer as the remote SDP. At the same time, Bob's web application creates another invitation using RTCPeerConnection, and sends it to the LEA.

Bob's web application then sends the response to Alice, and the VoIP conversation begins.

When the LEA receives Alice and Bob's offers, it can send a confirmation as a response and continue with the session initiation. The LEA can decide to confirm both of the offers, to confirm only one of the offers, or to decline both offers.

The interception model is based on the fact that the client's conversation data is sent to the LEA, in addition to the obvious tunnel between the clients. Our interception approach is based on the secondary invitaions to the LEA.

5 Showcase

5.1 Signaling Services

According to the LEA requirement, a list of the current users connected and the metadata, in addition to the call content, must be supplied. For this reason, the use of a flexible signaling server, which can handle the requests of the clients and the LEA's regulations, is recommended. For commercial use, Asterisk releases[7] are an adequate choice, while for smaller entities Node.js[8] with the PeerJS server extension[9] is sufficient.

To fulfill the LEA request regarding the connected users, interception device manufacturers supply an API. In Asterisk, the *'show peers'* command is used, and Node.js with the PeerJS server uses the *'allow discovery'* option.

Due to the extensive use of signaling messages, signaling services must be very efficient. In mobile communication systems, signaling services also remain active while the system is in an idle state, in order to supply a current snapshot of the devices, including their location and ability to establish a media connection, at all times.

Both server options described (Asterisk and PeerJS), implement an SDP that meets the WebRTC requirements. For Asterisk, an additional set of modules (SRTP, WebSocket, pjproject and others) is required. In addition, a set of

---

[7] http://www.asterisk.org.

[8] https://nodejs.org.

[9] https://github.com/peers/peerjs-server.

configuration setups is required before use[10]. The PeerJS server exposes the SDP interface originally, and no extra setup is required.

For security reasons, WebRTC requires full encryption of every interaction during the signaling process. Both servers are capable of securing the hand-shake and conversation data. The configuration process includes the setup of the encryption keys and certifications.

5.2 Web Applications

Various packages, that have been created by the developers community and third parties, can be used to establish WebRTC conversation with a correlation to SIP servers. The packages include both WebRTC and SIP communication components and simplify the coding process.

The relevant JavaScript packages are the open source projects, JsSIP[11] and SIP.js[12] and the free commercial package, Dubango SIPML5[13]. These packages use WebSockets to communicate with the SIP server and contain WebRTC com-ponents to establish VoIP calls using the browser.

Cloning a branch from the SIP.js open source project[14] and customizing the code to meet specific needs is recommended for commercial use. However, for small and medium sized entities, the PeerJS client with the Peer Server combination is recommended.

5.3 LEA Management Console

According to the ETSI HI1, a management tool for the LEA is required.

In order to obtain a list of the currently logged in clients, the web application will consume the SIP service API. Both Asterisk and PeerJS supply an interface for external clients.

The open source project, CEF (Chromium Embedded Framework[15]), can be used in order to accept and manage many sessions with the target identities. This CEF component is written in C++ and is suitable for use within desktop appli-cations or service modules. Due to the large volume of connection requests, the filter application can be allocated in multiple servers and handle many requests in parallel.

As shown in Fig. 3, the service provider does not serve as a gateway between the clients for call content in P2P VoIP calls for Cisco's RFC. However, according to our model, it is the service provider's responsibility to host the LEA virtual

---

[10] The detailed tutorial can be found in https://wiki.asterisk.org/wiki/display/AST/Asterisk+WebRTC+Support.

[11] http://jssip.net.

[12] http://sipjs.com.

[13] https://www.doubango.org/sipml5.

[14] https://github.com/onsip/sip.js.

[15] https://bitbucket.org/chromiumembedded/cef.

clients and ensure their availability. This issue should be considered by the regulatory agencies. The proposed component architecture in reference to the Cisco model is shown in Fig. 6.

According to the Lawful Interception Administration Function, the mediation device should orchestrate the availability of virtual clients and their connections to the target identities. The LEA is responsible for the management console and handling the intercepted identities, and this shall remain in their local domain.

This model describes an interception that has been initiated before the conversation begins, during the clients' handshake. This approach is static and is not applicable for the request of the LEA to join the conversation when needed. In the real world, the interception begins after the signaling messages of the target identity have arrived at the LEA systems and the act of interception has been approved by the relevant authorities.

As mentioned at the beginning of this section, the SIP is a messaging service. Opening a secondary connection to the LEA is also possible during the conversation. This can be achieved using the SIP mechanism, but it depends on the development business logic. When a known message arrives at the client, the web application can trigger the interception process.

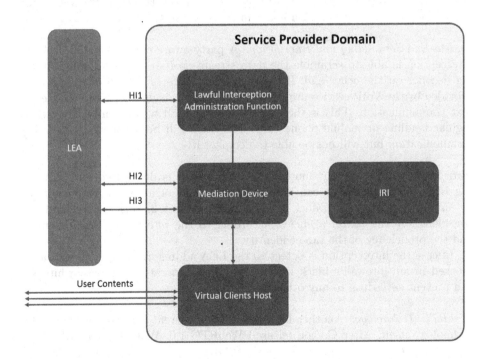

Fig. 6. Proposed interception model

6   Limitation of the Current Work

The Browser. The trusted client application is a crucial characteristic of the interception model. The model is based on the fact that the user confirmed the use of his/her media resources for his/her personal use to initiate a hidden session with the LEA. However, the main idea behind WebRTC, and the technology's primary benefit, is the ability to use the browser in order to establish a real-time media connection. This fact strengthens the hypothesis of the trusted client application.

We did not discuss the option of hijacking the browser for interception purposes, without obtaining permission to use the media resources, or even without initiation of the session between the LEA and the target identity.

Trusted Web Application. We assumed a trusted application as a basis to the interception model. The client application duplicate the data transportaion. Hence, one of the options to disable the lawful interception is to sabotage the dupllication code. This could be done by making a local copy of the web aplpication, and disable the relevant code lines. Signing the application code is one of the available options to verify a trusted application. However, the ability to create a trusted web application is not in the scope of this paper.

End-to-End Scrambling and Encryption. A party aware of the possibility of an interception is able to scramble the data stream on its end provided a matching decoder on the other end. If the scrambler operates on top of the service provided by the VoIP service provider then the latter, is unable to tap the cleartext communication. This is the exact same situation we currently have with regular landline or mobile phone calls. The LEA will be acknowledged of the communication but will not be able to decipher it.

Network Detection. In our model, the interception is duplicated and sent to the LEA. An expert user can detect the existance of a running interception by sniffing the network traffic. As mentioned in Sect. 2, this issue should be considered by the lawful agencies, according to the interception commonness and the proficiency of the target identity.

In case the interception is detected, the LEA addresses can be detected and blocked in any firewall's black list. For hardened operating systems, whitelist can prevent eavesdrop to any other destinations.

WebRTC Technology. Another limitation of the current work is the WebRTC technology itself. After Google released WebRTC 1.0, W3C announced[16] that its groups were working on a new project: ORTC (Object Real-Time Communication), the next generation of RTC. Although it is aimed primarily at APIs and exposing features from the lower level of WebRTC's main components, it remains unclear whether further security restrictions will be imposed on the

---

[16] https://www.w3.org/community/ortc.

browser. Furthermore, the implementation described in Sect. 5.2 was evaluated on a standard browser. It is expected that service providers will consume the WebRTC technology in a customizable application.

7   Conclusion

Although there are extensive regulations for lawful interception in telecommunication systems and network traffic, existing regulations for VoIP calls are inadequate and have not kept pace with today's phenomenon of P2P calls.

In this research we introduced a practical model to tackle the obstacle of lawful interception for P2P VoIP communications. This paper demonstrates the ability to intercept WebRTC communication, a protocol established by the W3C, and provides the basis for further discussion by the ETSI organization's technical committee and a means of addressing the current lack of regulations for P2P VoIP calls. We introduce a prototype of an interception model for P2P VoIP calls, along with a preliminary schematic architectural design. The research shows that it is possible to intercept WebRTC VoIP calls without being detected by the user in normal conditions, when no network monitoring is being done. Moreover, this paper demonstrates the ability to establish a hidden media connection, in the guise of another legitimate WebRTC media connection. This fact should be considered by the W3C Privacy Interest Group.

While being an important law-enforcement tool, lawful interception technology may be misused to gain unsolicited illegal access to third party communication infringing basic human rights. This raises significant ethical issues. The ethics of lawful interception as a whole are not within the scope of this article. However, service provider applications are trusted and they are the only entities capable of executing the critical parts of the interception. It is therefore the obligation of service providers to acknowledge their cooperation with law enforcement in front of their users. The users, in turn, should not trust spurious VoIP service providers who may eavesdrop their communication without a court order.

The need to provide users a high level of security and privacy protection, along with the regulatory requirements associated with lawful interception, motivated us to develop a balanced solution that considers the interests of all of the parties involved: the clients, service providers, law enforcement agencies, and the regulatory organizations. The proposed model accomplishes this, using state of the art WebRTC technology to enable lawful interception while protecting the user and ensuring that service providers meet the legal and regulatory requirements.

We believe that the rapid development of VoIP technologies, will continue to provide additional challenges to service providers and regulatory authorities in the years to come.

References

1. ETSI TC-STAG: Security techniques advisory group (stag); definition of user requirements for lawful interception of telecommunications: requirements of the law enforcement agencies (1996)
2. The Council of the European Union: Council resolution of 17 January 1995 on the lawful interception of telecommunications. Off. J. C **329**, 0001–0006 (1996)
3. Rescorla, E.: WebRTC security architecture draft-ietf-rtcweb-securityarch-07. Technical report, Internet-Draft, Internet Engineering Task Force, July 2013. http://tools.ietf.org/id/draft-ietf-rtcweb-security-arch-07.txt. Accessed Jan 2014
4. Rescorla, E.: WebRTC security architecture (2016)
5. Network Working Group et al.: IETF policy on wiretapping. Technical report, RFC 2804, May 2000
6. TR ETSI: 101 943 v2. 1.1 (10/2004) lawful interception (li). Concepts of Interception in a Generic Network Architecture
7. TS ETSI: 102 232-1: Lawful Interception (LI). Handover Interface and Service-Specific Details (SSD) for IP delivery, pp. 2016–03 (2008)
8. Lawful Interception: Handover interface and service-specific details (SSD) for IP delivery; part 5: service-specific details for IP multimedia services; ETSI TS 102 232-5 ETSI standards, Lis, Sophia Antipolis Cedex, France, vol. 2008 (2008)
9. Interception, L.: Handover interface for the lawful interception of telecommunications traffic. ETSI ES **201**, 671 (2004)
10. Milanovic, A., Srbljic, S., Ražnjević, I., Sladden, D., Matošević, I., Skrobo, D.: Methods for lawful interception in IP telephony networks based on h. 323. In: EUROCON 2003. Computer as a Tool. The IEEE Region 8, vol. 1, pp. 198–202. IEEE (2003)
11. Milanović, A., Srbljić, S., Ražnjević, I., Sladden, D., Skrobo, D., Matošević, I.: Distributed system for lawful interception in VoUnetworks. In EUROCON: 2003. Computer as a Tool. The IEEE Region 8, vol. 1, pp. 203–207. IEEE (2003)
12. Baker, F., Foster, B., Sharp, C.: Cisco architecture for lawful intercept in IP networks. Technical report (2004)
13. Karpagavinayagam, B., State, R., Festor, O.: Monitoring architecture for lawful interception in VoIP networks. In: Second International Conference on Internet Monitoring and Protection, ICIMP 2007, pp. 5–5. IEEE (2007)
14. Jennings, C., Uberti, J., Rescorla, E.: Javascript session establishment protocol (2016)
15. Werner, M.J., Vogt, C., Schmidt, T.C.: Let our browsers socialize: building user-centric content communities on WebRTC. In: 2014 IEEE 34th International Conference on Distributed Computing Systems Workshops (ICDCSW), pp. 37–44. IEEE (2014)
16. Rosenberg, J., Mahy, R., Huitema, C., Weinberger, J.: Stun-simple traversal of UDP through network address translators (2003)
17. Matthews, P., Mahy, R., Rosenberg, J.: Traversal using relays around nat (turn): relay extensions to session traversal utilities for nat (stun) (2010)
18. RTP Topologies: Internet engineering task force (IETF) M. Westerlund request for comments: 7667 Ericsson obsoletes: 5117 S. Wenger category: Informational vidyo (2015)
19. Singh, K., Nair, G., Schulzrinne, H.: Centralized conferencing using sip. In: Internet Telephony Workshop, vol. 7, pp. 57–63 (2001)
20. Johnston, A., Levin, O.: Session initiation protocol (SIP) call control-conferencing for user agents (2006)

Hierarchical Ring Signatures Immune to Randomness Injection Attacks

Łukasz Krzywiecki$^{(\boxtimes)}$, Mirosław Kutyłowski$^{(\boxtimes)}$, Rafał Rothenberger, and Bartosz Drzazga

Department of Computer Science, Faculty of Fundamental Problems of Technology, Wrocław University of Science and Technology, Wrocław, Poland
{lukasz.krzywiecki,miroslaw.kutylowski}@pwr.edu.pl

Abstract. We propose a modification of the hierarchical-ring-signature scheme, which may be regarded as an extension to a regular ring signature scheme. The scheme is defined over a structure of nodes, where each node is a root of its own tree, and its *anonymity-set* spans over all its leaf nodes. Our modified construction is resistant to an exposure of randomness from a signing device, on any level of the hierarchy. The proposed scheme is provably secure in a stronger security model, in which we allow a forger to inject the randomness into the signing device. We define the scheme to be secure if such an injection, will not give any advantage to the adversary and does not lead to a fresh forgery. The proposed scheme can be applied in scenarios with untrusted hardware, or weak pseudo-random number generators.

Keywords: Ring signature · Hierarchical signature
Schnorr signature · Ephemeral secret setting · Randomness leakage

1 Introduction

A hierarchical-signature scheme (HRS), firstly discussed in [1], and later elaborated in [2], enables a user to sign anonymously a message in a manner similar to ring-signing. In a regular ring signature scheme, the actual signer is hidden in a set of other potential signers (ring members), whose public keys were used during signature creation. First ring signature constructions proposed results with signature tuples of the length proportional to the cardinality of the set of public keys (*linear constructions*). In those schemes, the computational complexity of signing procedure is linear in the number of ring members. Hierarchical scheme, recalled here [1,2] allows for smaller signature lengths and smaller computational complexity, providing better anonymity at the same time. It has modular construction, and is based on regular signatures and ring signatures. Reusing existing, well known and analyzed schemes, make subsequent commercial deployment

The research was partially financed from the Fundamental Research Fund nr 8201003902 of the Wrocław University of Science and Technology.

S. Dolev et al. (Eds.): CSCML 2021, LNCS 12716, pp. 171–186, 2021.
https://doi.org/10.1007/978-3-030-78086-9_13

easier, as implementors may utilize already tested and verified libraries. Hierarchical signature system is build on top of a public repository of signatures. The users create and upload nodes, each consisting of: a message, a ring-like signature over that message, a ring, and new public key of that node, updating in this way a public structure. Members of the ring (potential signers in the node) are signers of the predecessors of that node, i.e. the set of public keys in the ring consists of public keys from predecessor nodes. This relation goes recursively to the leaf level nodes, which are based on public keys certified to particular users registered in the system. As each ring signature provides anonymity, the set of potential signers of a given node spans across all of leaves of sub-trees rooted in this node. Additionally, the structure provides a kind of a time-stamping functionality, as subsequent nodes are created on top of the previous ones.

Problem Statement. Many signature schemes use linear combination of random values and long-term secret keys, mutually masking each other, to provide keys secrecy and produce a non-deterministic output. Such a solution is efficient if the ephemeral values created for signatures are not predictable to a potential adversary. As randomness is manageable on a hardware and operating system level, malicious manufactures or OS implementors can mount successful attacks on such schemes. These seems to be primarily relevant for schemes deployed on popular portable devices, smartphones or wearables. The problem of bits leakage from computation was initially analyzed by Chari *et al.* [3], and independently by Goubin and Patarin [4], follwed by e.g. Alwen *et al.* in [5]. Leaking bits from cryptographic keys was analyzed by Canetti *et al.* [6], and continued in later works on memory leakage [7–9]. Memory resets were studied by Canetti *et al.* in [10]. We refer to [11] for the survey on leakage-resilient cryptography. The problem for potential ephemeral leakage and setup in untrusted devices was later analyzed for many fundamental cryptographic schemes, e.g. identification [12–14], key exchange [15–20], signatures [21–23], or credential systems [24]. However, the similar problem was not yet addressed for the hierarchical ring constructions.

Contribution. The contribution of the paper is the following:

- We propose a new strong security model for a hierarchical-signature scheme, introduced in [2], in which we allow the *forger* to inject ephemeral keys (random values used in signing) into the signer device. We define the scheme to be secure if this will not allow the attacker to forge any new signature in the hierarchy afterwards.
- We propose a modification to the scheme from [2], which is provably secure in our stronger model. The proposed scheme provides unconditional anonymity, as the knowledge of all secret keys of ring members and predecessor nodes, does not allow to distinguish the actual node signer.
- We test the feasibility of the proposed construction and evaluate its computational overhead via our *proof-of-concept* implementation.

Like the original scheme, our modified HRS, can be used to create a secure bulletin board that can be used for example in e-voting scenarios. The scheme can be also applied in public tenders, to allow anonymous submissions thus preventing discrimination, e.g. based on the company's country of origin, or time of market presence. Thanks to the hierarchy, the winner can reveal himself by signing the disclosure message using the previous offer as the only member of the ring. If the tender would operate as an auction, the original offer and the previous bids can be used to send new bids, creating a linear hierarchy that also acts as a history for all bids of a given user.

Related Work. Ring signatures were introduced by Rivest et al. in [25]. Identity-based ring signatures schemes for different domains were analyzed in [26–31]. Schemes for linking together ring signatures signed with the same secret key, were presented in [32] and [33]. Confessable threshold ring signature scheme, in which the signer can prove its authorship were proposed in [34]. A stronger notion of unforgeability and anonymity for ring signatures were analysed in [35]. In [36] and [37] ring signatures of sub-linear sizes, provably secure without random oracle model were presented. In [38] authors propose ring signatures which do not rely on a trusted setup or the random oracle, with logarithmic size in the number of ring members. The scheme can be extended into linkable ring signatures. The first hierarchical scheme from [1], based on non interactive zero knowledge proof of equality of discrete logarithm, does not provide perfect anonymity - users can deny authorship if they expose their private keys. Subsequent version of hierarchical scheme from [2], based on Schnorr ring signatures [39], proven to be unconditionally anonymous and unforgeable under the Forking Lemma in ROM, is vulnerable to the ephemeral leakage attacks. Our modification proposed in this paper address this issue.

Organization of the Paper. In Sect. 2 we recall the original HRS scheme and describe used notation. In Sect. 3 we define our stronger model with active malicious forger setting ephemeral values in signing queries. In Sect. 4 we propose the modified version of HRS and prove its security in our model. Finally, we present the benchmarks collected from our proof-of-concept implementation of the scheme.

2   Hierarchical Signature Scheme

2.1   Preliminaries and Notation

Let $\{x_i\}_1^n \leftarrow_\$ X$ denotes that each x_i is sampled uniformly at random from the set X. Let $\mathcal{H} : \{0,1\}^* \rightarrow A$ be a hash function modeled as the *Random Oracle* (ROM), which outputs the results from the set A. Let $\mathcal{G}(1^\lambda)$ be a group generation algorithm that takes as an input 1^λ, and outputs a tuple $\mathbb{G} = (q, g, G)$, where g denotes a generator of a group $\langle g \rangle = G$ of order q. We assume that computations are done in elliptic curve groups. Public keys and signatures are elements of a chosen elliptic curve group. The proposed scheme uses a bilinear pairing for verification. The security of the original and the proposed HRS schemes relies the existence of random oracles, and the intractability of CDH, GDH in the chosen groups of computation. We recall the required assumptions below.

Definition 1 (The discrete logarithm problem (DLP) assumption). *For any probabilistic polynomial time (PPT) algorithm $\mathcal{A}_{\mathsf{DLP}}$ it holds that:*

$$\Pr[\mathcal{A}_{\mathsf{DLP}}(\mathbb{G}, g^x) = x \mid \mathbb{G} \leftarrow_\$ \mathcal{G}(1^\lambda), x \leftarrow_\$ \mathbb{Z}_q^*] \leq \epsilon_{\mathsf{DLP}}(\lambda),$$

where $\epsilon_{\mathsf{DLP}}(\lambda)$ is negligible.

Definition 2 (Bilinear Map). *Let G_T be another group of a prime order q. We assume that $\hat{e} : G \times G \to G_T$ is a bilinear map s.t. following condition holds:*
1) Bilinearity: $\forall a, b \in \mathbb{Z}_q^*, \forall g, g \in G$: $\hat{e}(g^a, g^b) = \hat{e}(g, g)^{ab}$.
2) Non-degeneracy: $\hat{e}(g, g) \neq 1$.
3) Computability: $\hat{e}$ is efficiently computable.

Definition 3 (The computational Diffie-Hellman (CDH) assumption). *For any probabilistic polynomial time (PPT) algorithm $\mathcal{A}_{\mathsf{CDH}}$ it holds that:*

$$\Pr[\mathcal{A}_{\mathsf{CDH}}(\mathbb{G}, g^x, g^y) = g^{xy} \mid \mathbb{G} \leftarrow_\$ \mathcal{G}(1^\lambda), x \leftarrow_\$ \mathbb{Z}_q^*, y \leftarrow_\$ \mathbb{Z}_q^*] \leq \epsilon_{\mathsf{CDH}}(\lambda),$$

where $\epsilon_{\mathsf{CDH}}(\lambda)$ is negligible.

Definition 4 (The decisional Diffie-Hellman oracle). *Let decisional Diffie-Hellman oracle $\mathcal{O}_{\mathsf{DDH}}$ be (PPT) algorithm, which for $\mathbb{G} \leftarrow_\$ \mathcal{G}(1^\lambda), x \in \mathbb{Z}_q^*, y \in \mathbb{Z}_q^*, z \in \mathbb{Z}_q^*$ evaluates like follows:*

$$\mathcal{O}_{\mathsf{DDH}}(\mathbb{G}, g^x, g^y, g^z) = \begin{cases} 1 & \text{if } z = xy \mod q, \\ 0 & \text{if } z \neq xy \mod q. \end{cases}$$

Definition 5 (The gap computational Diffie-Hellman (GDH) assumption). *For any probabilistic polynomial time (PPT) algorithm $\mathcal{A}_{\mathsf{GDH}}^{\mathcal{O}_{\mathsf{DDH}}}$ that has access to decisional Diffie-Hellman oracle $\mathcal{O}_{\mathsf{DDH}}$ it holds that:*

$$\Pr[\mathcal{A}_{\mathsf{GDH}}^{\mathcal{O}_{\mathsf{DDH}}}(\mathbb{G}, g^x, g^y) = g^{xy} \mid \mathbb{G} \leftarrow_\$ \mathcal{G}(1^\lambda), x \leftarrow_\$ \mathbb{Z}_q^*, y \leftarrow_\$ \mathbb{Z}_q^*] \leq \epsilon_{\mathsf{GDH}}(\lambda),$$

where $\epsilon_{\mathsf{GDH}}(\lambda)$ is negligible.

2.2   Definition of Hierarchical-Signature Scheme

A hierarchical-signature scheme is a system build for a group of signers, having a set of certified public keys $\mathsf{L} = \{\mathsf{pk}\}$, each linked to the corresponding secret key sk. We assume that the certified public keys identify the users registered in the system. Let $\mathsf{S} = \{(m, \sigma, \mathsf{pkn}, \mathsf{Y})\}$ denotes a set of nodes in the system. A node is defined by a tuple $(m, \sigma, \mathsf{pkn}, \mathsf{Y})$, which binds: a message m, a *ring*-like signature σ over m, a unique public key pkn, and a set of public keys Y of the direct predecessor nodes (children). Each node $(m, \sigma, \mathsf{pkn}, \mathsf{Y})$ is a root of its own tree. Let $\mathsf{N} = \{\mathsf{pkn}\}$ denote a set of public keys of all nodes, each corresponding to its secret key skn. Initially, the set of node key-pairs $\{(\mathsf{skn}, \mathsf{pkn})\}$ is empty, and it grows steadily with the construction of new signatures. A signer can create a new *ring*-like signature σ over a message m, using a subset $Y \subset L \cup N$, s.t. all nodes whose public keys belong to Y, are not mutual predecessors of each other in S. We call that a *non-predecessor-condition* for Y, and denote by $T(Y)$. We say that Y is *correct* in this case. Each *node*-signature σ is linked with a new key pair (skn, pkn) constructed altogether with σ, and with the set Y. Immediately, after creation, the tuple $(m, \sigma, \text{pkn}, Y)$ is added to the set S, i.e. $S = S \cup \{(m, \sigma, \text{pkn}, Y)\}$, the public key pkn is added to the set N, i.e. $N = N \cup \{\text{pkn}\}$, and the corresponding skn is kept secret by the node signer. We denote $H = \{L, N, S\}$ as a structure of the scheme. Let H_0 denote the initial state of the system only with the registered public keys $L = \{\text{pk}\}$, but without signatures. By H_1 we denote the system with one node, i.e. one signature added, H_2 with two nodes (signatures), etc. The structure H_{i+i} is constructed from H_i by adding just one valid node. Let $\{H_i\}_0^\ell$ denote a sequence of structures obtained from H_0 after ℓ subsequent node creations. In Fig. 1 we demonstrate the structure in which the nodes were added in the order indicated by the message indexes. Thus H_0 has only public keys L, H_1 consists of node $(m_1, \sigma_1, \text{pkn}_1, Y_1)$, H_2 has two nodes: $(m_1, \sigma_1, \text{pkn}_1, Y_1)$ and $(m_2, \sigma_2, \text{pkn}_2, Y_2)$, etc. Formally we define the following:

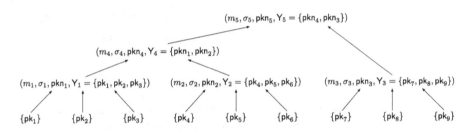

Fig. 1. HRS example.

Definition 6 (Hierarchical-Ring-Signature Scheme (HRS)). *A hiera rchical-ring-signature scheme is a tuple* (ParGen, KeyGen, NRSign, NRVerify), *where:*

params $\leftarrow$ ParGen(1^λ): *inputs a security parameter λ, and outputs public parameters' available to all users of the system (we omit them from the rest of the description).*

$\{(\text{sk}, \text{pk})\} \leftarrow$ KeyGen(): *outputs the set of key-pairs: a secret key sk and the corresponding public key pk. $L = L \cup \{\text{pk}\}$.*

$(\sigma, (\text{skn}, \text{pkn})) \leftarrow$ NRSign(m, x_j, Y, H): *denotes the signing procedure which take on input: a message m, a secret key x_j corresponding to one public key $y_j \in Y$ from the structure H, s.t. $T(Y)$. It outputs a signature σ with a pair (skn, pkn) which define a new node $(m, \sigma, \text{pkn}, Y)$ in H. $H = \{L, N \cup \{\text{pkn}\}, S \cup \{(m, \sigma, \text{pkn}, Y)\}\}$*

1 / 0 ← NRVerify$((m, \sigma, \mathsf{pkn}, Y), H)$: *denotes the verification procedure, which takes on input: a node* $(m, \sigma, \mathsf{pkn}, Y)$, *s.t.* $T(Y)$ *in* H. *It outputs 1 if the verification is successful, i.e.:* y_j *corresponds to* x_j *used in* NRSign(m, x_j, Y, H) *for* σ, *and* $y_j \in Y \subset L \cup N$, *s.t.* $T(Y)$ *in* H. *It outputs 0 otherwise.*

Let $H_{i+1} \leftarrow_{\mathsf{NRSign}} H_i$ denote that H_{i+1} is obtained via NRSign for some message m and a correct set Y:

$$(\sigma, (\mathsf{skn}, \mathsf{pkn})) \leftarrow \mathsf{NRSign}(m, x_j, Y, H_i), H_i = \{L, N_i, S_i\}.$$

Let $1 \leftarrow_{\mathsf{NRVerify}} \{H_i, H_{i+1}\}$ denote that a node $(m, \sigma, \mathsf{pkn}, Y)$ in structure

$$H_{i+1} = \{L, N_i \cup \{\mathsf{pkn}\}, S_i \cup \{(m, \sigma, \mathsf{pkn}, Y)\}\},$$

that was added by $H_{i+1} \leftarrow_{\mathsf{NRSign}} H_i$, is verified positively:

$$1 \leftarrow \mathsf{NRVerify}(m, (\sigma, \mathsf{pkn}), Y, H_{i+1}).$$

Definition 7 (HRS Correctness). HRS *is correct if any structure created via* NRSign *is recursively verifiable to 1 via* NRVerify(), *i.e.:*

$$\Pr[\mathsf{params} \leftarrow \mathsf{ParGen}(1^\lambda); \{(\mathsf{sk}, \mathsf{pk})\} \leftarrow \mathsf{KeyGen}(); L = \{\mathsf{pk}\}; H_0 = \{L, \emptyset, \emptyset\}$$
$$\{H_i\}_0^\ell : \forall_{i \in \{0, \dots, \ell-1\}} 1 \leftarrow_{\mathsf{NRVerify}} \{H_i, H_{i+1}\}; H_{i+1} \leftarrow_{\mathsf{NRSign}} H_i] = 1 .$$

2.2.1   Original HRS Scheme The original HRS scheme from [2], recalled in the left column of Fig. 2, is based on a ring signatures construction introduced in [39]. Its security is based on *Forking Lemma* for ring signatures of the form $(R_1, \dots, R_{|Y|}, h_1, \dots, h_{|Y|}, s)$, where $R_1, \dots, R_{|Y|}$ $(R_i \neq R_j)$ are the random values, h_i is a hash over m and R_i, while s depends on $m, R_1, \dots, R_{|Y|}$, $h_1, \dots, h_{|Y|}$, and the private key of the signer corresponding to one of public keys from Y. If an effective forger exists, it can be used to obtain, with non negligible probability, two different valid signatures with the same randomness: $(R_1, \dots, R_{|Y|}, h_1, \dots, h_{|Y|}, s)$ and $(R_1, \dots, R_{|Y|}, h'_1, \dots, h'_{|Y|}, s')$ s.t. $h_j \neq h'_j$ for some j, and $h_i = h'_i$ for all $i \neq j$. These tuples can be used to break the underlying assumption (DLP), which contradicts the initial forger existence. The original HRS construction from [2] uses the regular Schnorr Sign as subprocedure in NRSign, which itself is a modified ring signing procedure from [39]. The NRSign creates a tuple $R = \{(R_i, \sigma_i)\}_1^{|Y|}$ in the following way: a new pair of private/public keys $(\mathsf{skn}, \mathsf{pkn})$ is created; the private key skn is used to produce a set of a Schnorr signatures $\sigma_1 = \mathsf{Sign}(R_1, \mathsf{skn}), \dots, \sigma_{|Y|} = \mathsf{Sign}(R_{|Y|}, \mathsf{skn})$ over the nonces $R_1, \dots, R_{|Y|}$; each pair (R_i, σ_i) is hashed with the message m, to produce the vector: $h_1, \dots, h_{|Y|}$. The public key pkn is included in the resulting node $(m, (\{(R_i, \sigma_i)\}_1^{|Y|}, s), \mathsf{pkn}, Y)$. The node can be regarded as a self-certificate, in

HRS scheme	Modified HRS scheme
ParGen(1^λ): $\quad \mathbb{G} = (q, g, G) \leftarrow \mathcal{G}(1^\lambda)$, $\quad \mathcal{H} : \{0,1\}^* \to \mathbb{Z}_q^*$, $\quad$ params $= (q, g, \mathbb{G}, \mathcal{H})$.	ParGen(1^λ): $\quad \mathbb{G} = (q, g, G, G_T, \hat{e}) \leftarrow \mathcal{G}(1^\lambda)$, $\quad \mathcal{H} : \{0,1\}^* \to \mathbb{Z}_q^*$, $\mathcal{H}_g : \{0,1\}^* \to G$ $\quad$ params $= (q, g, \mathbb{G}, \mathcal{H}, \mathcal{H}_g)$.
KeyGen(): Generate random sk $\leftarrow_\$ \mathbb{Z}_q^*$, $\quad$ compute pk $= g^{\mathsf{sk}}$ and output (sk, pk).	KeyGen is the same.
Sign(m, skn): $\quad$ 1. $r =\leftarrow_\$ \mathbb{Z}_q^*$, $R = g^r$. $\quad$ 3. $h = \mathcal{H}(m, R)$. $\quad$ 4. $s = r + h\mathsf{skn}$. $\quad$ 5. return $\sigma = (R, s)$.	modSign(m, skn): $\quad$ 1. $r =\leftarrow_\$ \mathbb{Z}_q^*$, $R = g^r$. $\quad$ 3. $h = \mathcal{H}(m, R)$. $\quad$ 4. $s = r + h\mathsf{skn}$. $\quad\quad \hat{g} = \mathcal{H}_g(R, m)$. $\quad\quad \hat{S} = \hat{g}^s$. $\quad$ 5. return $\sigma = (R, \hat{S})$.
Verify$(m, \sigma, \mathsf{pkn})$: $\quad$ 1. $h = \mathcal{H}(m, R)$. $\quad$ 2. Output: $\quad\quad$ 1 if $g^s = R\mathsf{pkn}^h$, $\quad\quad$ 0 otherwise	modVerify$(m, \sigma, \mathsf{pkn})$: $\quad$ 1. $h = \mathcal{H}(m, R)$. $\quad\quad \hat{g} = \mathcal{H}_g(R, m)$, $\quad$ 2. Output: $\quad\quad$ 1 if $\hat{e}(\hat{S}, g) = \hat{e}(\hat{g}, R\mathsf{pkn}^h)$, $\quad\quad$ 0 otherwise.
NRSign$(m, x_j, \mathsf{Y}, \mathsf{H})$: $\quad$ 1. $(\mathsf{skn}, \mathsf{pkn}) \leftarrow$ KeyGen(). $\quad$ 2. For each $y_i \in \mathsf{Y}, i \neq j$ do $\quad\quad r_i \leftarrow_\$ \mathbb{Z}_q^*, R_i = g^{r_i}$. $\quad\quad \sigma_i = \mathsf{Sign}(R_i, \mathsf{skn})$. $\quad\quad h_i = \mathcal{H}(m, R_i, \sigma_i)$. $\quad$ 3. $r_j \leftarrow_\$ \mathbb{Z}_q^*$. $\quad$ 4. $R_j = g^{r_j} \prod_{i \neq j} y_i^{-h_i}$. $\quad$ 5. $\sigma_j = \mathsf{Sign}(R_j, \mathsf{skn})$. $\quad$ 6. $R = \{(R_i, \sigma_i)\}_1^{|\mathsf{Y}|}$. $\quad$ 7. $h_j = \mathcal{H}(m, R_j, \sigma_j)$. $\quad$ 8. $s = \sum_{i \neq j} r_i + r_j + x_j h_j$. $\quad$ 9. $\sigma = (R, s)$. $\quad$ Return $(m, \sigma, \mathsf{pkn}, \mathsf{Y})$.	modNRSign$(m, x_j, \mathsf{Y}, \mathsf{H})$: $\quad$ 1. $(\mathsf{skn}, \mathsf{pkn}) \leftarrow$ KeyGen(). $\quad$ 2. For each $y_i \in \mathsf{Y}, i \neq j$ do $\quad\quad r_i \leftarrow_\$ \mathbb{Z}_q^*, R_i = g^{r_i}$. $\quad\quad \sigma_i = \mathsf{modSign}(R_i, \mathsf{skn})$. $\quad\quad h_i = \mathcal{H}(m, R_i, \sigma_i)$. $\quad$ 3. $r_j \leftarrow_\$ \mathbb{Z}_q^*$. $\quad$ 4. $R_j = g^{r_j} \prod_{i \neq j} y_i^{-h_i}$. $\quad$ 5. $\sigma_j = \mathsf{modSign}(R_j, \mathsf{skn})$. $\quad$ 6. $R = \{(R_i, \sigma_i)\}_1^{|\mathsf{Y}|}$. $\quad$ 7. $h_j = \mathcal{H}(m, R_j, \sigma_j)$. $\quad$ 8. $s = \sum_{i \neq j} r_i + r_j + x_j h_j$. $\quad\quad \hat{g} = \mathcal{H}_g(R, m)$. $\quad\quad \hat{S} = \hat{g}^s$. $\quad$ 9. $\hat{\sigma} = (R, \hat{S})$. $\quad$ Return $(m, \hat{\sigma}, \mathsf{pkn}, \mathsf{Y})$.
NRVerify$((m, \hat{\sigma}, \mathsf{pkn}, \mathsf{Y}), \mathsf{H})$: $\quad$ 1. For each $y_i \in \mathsf{Y}$ do $\quad\quad w_i = \mathsf{Verify}(R_i, \sigma_i, \mathsf{pkn})$. $\quad\quad h_i = \mathcal{H}(m, R_i, \sigma_i)$. $\quad$ 2. Output: $\quad\quad$ 1 if $(g^s = \prod_{y_i \in \mathsf{Y}} R_i y_i^{h_i})$ $\quad\quad$ and $(1 == \prod_i w_i)$, $\quad\quad$ 0 otherwise.	modNRVerify$((m, \hat{\sigma}, \mathsf{pkn}, \mathsf{Y}), \mathsf{H})$: $\quad$ 1. For each $y_i \in \mathsf{Y}$ do $\quad\quad w_i = \mathsf{modVerify}(R_i, \sigma_i, \mathsf{pkn})$. $\quad\quad h_i = \mathcal{H}(m, R_i, \sigma_i)$. $\quad$ 2 $\hat{g} = \mathcal{H}_g(R, m)$. $\quad$ 3. Output: $\quad\quad$ 1 if $\hat{e}(\hat{S}, g) = \hat{e}(\hat{g}, \prod_{y_i \in \mathsf{Y}} R_i y_i^{h_i})$ $\quad\quad$ and $(1 == \prod_i w_i)$, $\quad\quad$ 0 otherwise.

Fig. 2. Modified scheme.

which the regular signatures σ_i and the ring value s mutually certify themselves. The verification procedure NRVerify verifies all signatures σ_i from the node via regular Schnorr Verify(R_i, σ_i, pkn), and subsequently verifies the ring value s according to [39]. If all the verifications hold, the node is accepted. The verifier concludes: the node creator is the holder of a one private key corresponding to one of the public keys from the ring Y, and at the same time it is the holder of the new pair (skn, pkn). In other words: the ring signature certifies the new public key pkn of the node. The pair (skn, pkn) becomes a new private/public key for the creator of the node, and is used to identify that creator later on. Thus, in Fig. 1, the actual signer of $(m_5, \sigma_5, \mathsf{pkn}_5, \mathsf{Y}_5)$ could be any holder of the public key from $\mathsf{L} = \{\mathsf{pk}_1, \ldots, \mathsf{pk}_9\}$.

3   New Security Model

3.1   Anonymity Model

The anonymity of the node is the uncertainty about the secret keys used by the node signer. Intuitively, if the set of the secret keys in L is of the cardinality n, and the node is a root of a tree with leafs in L of cardinality n, then the probability of distinguishing which particular user from L did create the node, should be $1/n$. We analyze the model in which the secret keys are known to the distinguisher.

Definition 8 (Anonymity). *Let* HRS=(ParGen, KeyGen, NRSign, NRVerify) *is a scheme from Definition 6. We define anonymity experiment* $\mathrm{Exp}_{\mathsf{HRS}}^{\mathrm{Ano}, \lambda, \ell}$:

Init stage : *Let* params $\leftarrow$ ParGen(1^λ) $\{(\mathsf{sk}_i, \mathsf{pk}_i)\}_1^n \leftarrow$ KeyGen();
  $\mathsf{L} = \{\mathsf{pk}_i\}_1^n$; $\mathsf{H}_0 = \{\mathsf{L}, \emptyset, \emptyset\}$. *Let the adversary* $\mathcal{A}$, *be the malicious algorithm given the set of all keys* $\{(\mathsf{sk}_i, \mathsf{pk}_i)\}_1^n$.
Challenge stage : *A challenger* $\mathcal{C}$ *draws random indexes* $d \in \{1, \ldots, n\}$, *and produces* $\{\mathsf{H}_i\}_0^\ell$, *s.t the last node in* H_ℓ *was added by user holding* $(\mathsf{sk}_d, \mathsf{pk}_d)$. *Each time* H_i *is created, the corresponding* $(\mathsf{skn}_i, \mathsf{pkn}_i)$ *of its last node are given to* $\mathcal{A}$. *After that adversary outputs its own index* $\hat{d} \leftarrow \mathcal{A}$. *The adversary wins the experiment if* $\hat{d} = d$.

We define the advantage of $\mathcal{A}$ *in the experiment* $\mathrm{Exp}_{\mathsf{HRS}}^{\mathrm{Ano}, \lambda, \ell}$ *as:*

$$\mathbf{Adv}(\mathcal{A}, \mathrm{Exp}_{\mathsf{HRS}}^{\mathrm{Ano}, \lambda, \ell}) = |\Pr[\hat{d} = d] - 1/n|.$$

We say that the HRS *is anonymous if* $\mathbf{Adv}(\mathcal{A}, \mathrm{Exp}_{\mathsf{HRS}}^{\mathrm{Ano}, \lambda, \ell})$ *is negligible in* λ, ℓ.

3.2   Strong Unforgeability Model

In this section we propose the new stronger security model for HRS. In this model we assume that during sign queries, the forger $\mathcal{F}$ can inject its own random values into the signing device. We model it by a specific sign query definition $\mathcal{O}_{\mathsf{Sign}}^{\bar{r}}$, where $\bar{r}$ denotes the randomness chosen and adjusted adaptively by $\mathcal{F}$ according to responses from all oracles.

Definition 9 (Chosen Ephemeral Forgery (CEF)).
Let HRS=(ParGen, KeyGen, NRSign, NRVerify) *is a scheme from Definition 6.*
We define security experiment $\text{Exp}_{\text{HRS}}^{\text{CEF},\lambda,\ell_1,\ell_2}$:

Init stage : *Let* params $\leftarrow$ ParGen(1^λ) $\{(\text{sk}_i,\text{pk}_i)\}_1^n \leftarrow$ KeyGen(); L $= \{\text{pk}_i\}_1^n$;
$\quad$ $H_0 = \{L, \emptyset, \emptyset\}$.
Hash Oracles : *Hash oracles* $\{\mathcal{O}_\mathcal{H}\}$ *is a set of oracles to serve queries issued in*
$\quad$ *the experiment during signature creation and verification. Let* ℓ_1 *denotes the*
$\quad$ *maximum number of queries to those oracles.*
Sign Oracle : *Sign oracle* $\mathcal{O}_{\text{Sign}}^{\bar{r}}$ *answers a polynomial number* ℓ_2 *of sign queries*
$\quad$ *using injected ephemerals* $\bar{r}$. *These result with a sequence of structures* $\{H_i\}_0^{\ell_2}$
$\quad$ *over corresponding queried messages* $M = \{m_i\}_1^{\ell_2}$.
Forger : *Let the forger* $\mathcal{F}^{\{\mathcal{O}_\mathcal{H}\},\mathcal{O}_{\text{Sign}}^{\bar{r}}}$ *be the malicious algorithm given access to*
$\quad$ *the hash and the sign oracles, and the initial structure* $H_0 = \{L, \emptyset, \emptyset\}$. $\mathcal{F}$
$\quad$ *can interact with* $\mathcal{O}_{\text{Sign}}^{\bar{r}}$ *in a polynomial number* (ℓ_2 *at maximum*) *of signing*
$\quad$ *procedures, injecting the ephemerals* $\bar{r}$ *each time.*
Forgery : $\mathcal{F}^{\{\mathcal{O}_\mathcal{H}\},\mathcal{O}_{\text{Sign}}^{\bar{r}}}$ *produces a new node containing a signature* σ^* *over a*
$\quad$ *message* m^* *with group of public keys* Y, *s.t. the node was not a result from*
$\quad$ *previous queries to* $\mathcal{O}_{\text{Sign}}^{\bar{r}}$ *for* m^* *and* Y:

$$(m^*,\sigma^*,\text{pkn}^*,Y) \leftarrow \mathcal{F}^{\{\mathcal{O}_\mathcal{H}\},\mathcal{O}_{\text{Sign}}^{\bar{r}}}, (m^*,\sigma^*,\text{pkn}^*,Y) \notin \{H_i\}_0^{\ell_2}.$$

We define the advantage of $\mathcal{F}^{\{\mathcal{O}_\mathcal{H}\},\mathcal{O}_{\text{Sign}}^{\bar{r}}}$ *in the experiment* $\text{Exp}_{\text{HRS}}^{\text{CEF},\lambda,\ell_1,\ell_2}$ *as the*
probability of acceptance of forged node in the NRVerify *procedure for any struc-*
ture $H \in \{H_i\}_0^{\ell_2}$:

$$\mathbf{Adv}(\mathcal{F}^{\{\mathcal{O}_\mathcal{H}\},\mathcal{O}_{\text{Sign}}^{\bar{r}}}, \text{Exp}_{\text{HRS}}^{\text{CEF},\lambda,\ell_1,\ell_2})$$
$$= \Pr[\text{NRVerify}((m^*,\sigma^*,\text{pkn}^*,Y),H) = 1, H \in \{H_i\}_0^{\ell_2}].$$

We say that the scheme HRS *is secure if* $\mathbf{Adv}(\mathcal{F}^{\{\mathcal{O}_\mathcal{H}\},\mathcal{O}_{\text{Sign}}^{\bar{r}}}, \text{Exp}_{\text{HRS}}^{\text{CEF},\lambda,\ell_1,\ell_2})$ *is neg-*
ligible for parameters λ, ℓ_1, ℓ_2.

Theorem 1. *The original* HRS *scheme depicted in the left column of Fig. 2 is*
not secure in the proposed CEF *model (as of Definition 9).*

Proof. Once the forger which has possibility to inject $\bar{r}$, $\{\bar{r}_i\}_1^{|Y|}$ used in Sign
and NRSign procedures, it can compute the secret keys: $\text{skn} = \frac{s-\bar{r}}{h}$, and $x_j =$
$\frac{s-\sum_1^{|Y|}\bar{r}_i}{h_j}$. These allows impersonation and signing on behalf of the key holder. $\square$

4 Modified Specific HRS Scheme

The proposed modified modHRS scheme is presented in the right column of
Fig. 2. Our goal is to disable the adversary from solving linear equations: $s =$
$r + \text{skn}h$ (step 4 of Sign), and $s = \sum_{i\neq j} r_i + r_j + x_j h_j$ (step 8 of NRSign) for the

secret skn, x_j, and known (leaked or set) values $r, \{r_i\}_0^{|Y|}$. In our modification we use the technique introduced in [12]. Namely, we replace the explicit values of s in original procedures, with the corresponding values $\hat{S} = \hat{g}^s$ (step 4b of modSign, step 8c of modNRSign) for a new generator $\hat{g} = \mathcal{H}_g(R, m)$, unique in every signature. The corresponding verification is done with pairing function $\hat{e}$ to check equality in the exponents: $\hat{e}(\hat{S}, g) = \hat{e}(\hat{g}, R\mathsf{pkn}^h)$ in modVerify, and $\hat{e}(\hat{S}, g) = \hat{e}(\hat{g}, \prod_{y_i \in Y} R_i y_i^{h_i})$ in modNRVerify respectively.

4.1   Unforgeability Analysis

The proof of unforgeability of the proposed scheme is done by contradiction. Assuming that the advantage of the forger $\mathcal{F}^{\{\mathcal{O}_\mathcal{H}\}, \mathcal{O}_{\mathsf{Sign}}^{\hat{r}}}$ in $\mathsf{Exp}_{\mathsf{HRS}}^{\mathsf{CEF}, \lambda, \ell_1, \ell_2}$ is non-negligible, we fork the execution of a forgery attempt on a query to the hash oracle $\mathcal{H}$ with the same randomness $\{R_i\}_1^{|Y|}$. Thus we obtain, with non negligible probability, two different valid signatures: $(\{R_i\}_1^{|Y|}, h_1, \ldots, h_{|Y|}, s)$ and $(\{R_i\}_1^{|Y|}, h_1', \ldots, h_{|Y|}', s')$, s.t. $h_j \neq h_j'$ for some j. Those will help us to break the underlying GDH problem, with non-negligible probability.

Theorem 2. *The modified HRS scheme (shown in the right column of Fig. 2) is unforgeable (as of Definition 9), i.e.* $\mathbf{Adv}(\mathcal{F}^{\{\mathcal{O}_\mathcal{H}\}, \mathcal{O}_{\mathsf{Sign}}^{\hat{r}}}, \mathsf{Exp}_{\mathsf{HRS}}^{\mathsf{CESF}, \lambda, \ell_1, \ell_2})$ *is negligible in* λ, ℓ_1, ℓ_2, *for any PPT algorithm* $\mathcal{F}^{\{\mathcal{O}_\mathcal{H}\}, \mathcal{O}_{\mathsf{Sign}}^{\hat{r}}}$ *accessing hash and sign oracles:* $\mathcal{O}_\mathcal{H}, \mathcal{O}_{\mathcal{H}_g}, \mathcal{O}_{\mathsf{Sign}}^{\hat{r}}$.

Proof (Sketch). Suppose there is a forger $\mathcal{F}^{\{\mathcal{O}_\mathcal{H}\}, \mathcal{O}_{\mathsf{Sign}}^{\hat{r}}}$ for which the advantage in the experiment $\mathsf{Exp}_{\mathsf{HRS}}^{\mathsf{CESF}, \lambda, \ell_1, \ell_2}$ is non-negligible. Then it can be used to create algorithm $\mathcal{A}_{\mathsf{GDH}}$ that breaks the GDH for a given instance g^α, g^β, computing $g^{\alpha\beta}$ with non-negligible probability.

Init stage : Let params $\leftarrow \mathbb{G} = (q, g, G, G_T, \hat{e})$. Let (g^α, g^β) is GDH instance in $\mathbb{G}$. Set and record random masks $\{w_i\}_1^{|Y|} \leftarrow_\$ \mathbb{Z}_q^*$. Set the leaf keys $\mathsf{L} = \{\mathsf{pkn}_i = (g^\alpha)^{w_i}\}_1^{|Y|}$.

Serving $\mathcal{O}_\mathcal{H}$ Oracles : The $\mathcal{O}_\mathcal{H}$ hash query table is set up with two columns: I and H, for inputs and outputs respectively. If there is a new query with an input I_i to oracle, an output H_i is coined at random from $\mathbb{Z}_q^*$, saved in table and returned. If the input I_i exists already in the table, the corresponding H_i is returned.

Serving $\mathcal{O}_{\mathcal{H}_g}$ Oracle : The table for $\mathcal{H}_g$ has three columns: I, H, d, for the input, the output, and the masked exponent respectively. $\mathcal{O}_{\mathcal{H}_g}$ is queried a polynomial number ℓ_2 times at maximum, and the queries are indexed. At the beginning we choose a random index $j \leftarrow_\$ \{1 \ldots, \ell_2\}$. The current query is denoted by an index $i \in \{1, \ldots, \ell_2\}$.

  Case : $i \neq j$ When I_i is a new query to $\mathcal{H}_g$, a random mask $d_i \leftarrow_\$ \mathbb{Z}_q^*$ is generated, the output $H_i = g^{d_i}$ is computed, the new row (I_i, H_i, d_i) is placed into the table, and H_i is returned. If I_i is already registered in table, the corresponding H_i is returned.

Case : i = j When I_j is a new query to $\mathcal{H}_g$ we output $H_j = g^\beta$, the new row (I_j, H_j) is placed into the table, and H_j is returned. If I_i is already registered in table, the corresponding H_i is returned.

Serving Sign Oracle : When the sign oracle $\mathcal{O}^{\bar{r}}_{\mathsf{Sign}}$ is invoked, the injected randomness is used to compute: $R = g^{\bar{r}}$, $\{R_i = g^{\bar{r}_i}\}_1^{|\mathsf{Y}|}$ in modSign, modNRSign. Subsequently $\mathcal{O}_{\mathcal{H}_g}$ is invoked to obtain new generators $\hat{g}$ for those procedures. We have the following cases:

Case : (R, m) is not j fresh query to $\mathcal{O}_{\mathcal{H}_g}$:

For modSign we set $(\mathsf{skn}, \mathsf{pkn}) = (\perp, (g^\alpha)^w)$, for a random w we record. We update $\mathsf{N} = \mathsf{N} \cup \{\mathsf{pkn}\}$ and output it to the adversary. We compute $\hat{S} = \hat{g}^s = \hat{g}^{\bar{r}}\hat{g}^{h\mathsf{skn}} = g^{d\bar{r}}g^{dh\mathsf{skn}} = R\ ^d\mathsf{pkn}^{dh}$ for some value d registered in ROM table. This computation does not require the knowledge of the secret key skn. The verification in modVerify holds: $\hat{e}(\hat{S}, g) = \hat{e}(g^{d\bar{r}}g^{dh\mathsf{skn}}, g) = \hat{e}(\hat{g}, R\mathsf{pkn}^h)$.

For modNRSign we set $\hat{S} = \hat{g}^s = \hat{g}^{\sum_{i \neq j} \bar{r}_i + \bar{r}_j + x_j h_j} = g^{d\sum_i \bar{r}_i}g^{dh_j x_j} = g^{d\sum_i \bar{r}_i} \cdot y_j^{dh_j}$ for a value d registered in ROM table. This computation does not require the knowledge of the secret key x_j. The verification in modNRVerify holds: $\hat{e}(\hat{S}, g) = \hat{e}(g^{d\sum_i \bar{r}_i} \cdot y_j^{dh_j}, g) = \hat{e}(\hat{g}, \prod_{y_i \in \mathsf{Y}} R_i y_i^{h_i})$.

Case : (R, m) is j fresh query to $\mathcal{O}_{\mathcal{H}_g}$: In this case the oracle outputs $\perp$ and stop.

Forgery : The forger $\mathcal{F}^{\{\mathcal{O}_\mathcal{H}\}, \mathcal{O}^{\bar{r}}_{\mathsf{Sign}}}$ queries the above defined oracles, and with non-negligible probability, we successfully answer his all hash and sign queries, without outputting $\perp$. Moreover, to get the generator for the forgery, it accesses $\mathcal{O}_{\mathcal{H}_g}$, and is given $\hat{g} = g^\beta$ with non-negligible probability $1/\ell_2$. where d is a random mask. According to *forking lemma* [39], we obtain two valid signatures: $(\{R_i\}_1^{|\mathsf{Y}|}, h_1, \ldots, h_{|\mathsf{Y}|}, \hat{S})$ and $(\{R_i\}_1^{|\mathsf{Y}|}, h'_1, \ldots, h'_{|\mathsf{Y}|}, \hat{S}')$, s.t. $h_k \neq h'_k$ for some k. Thus we compute:

$$\hat{S}/\hat{S}' = (\hat{g}^{r_k + x_k h_k} \prod_{i \neq k} \hat{g}^{r_i + x_i h_i})/(\hat{g}^{r_k + x_k h'_k} \prod_{i \neq k} \hat{g}^{r_i + x_i h_i}).$$

So $\hat{S}/\hat{S}' = \hat{g}^{x_k(h_k - h'_k)} = (g^\beta)^{\alpha w_k(h_k - h'_k)}$, where w_k is a known random mask we recorded previously. Therefore we are able to compute $g^{\beta\alpha} = (\hat{S}/\hat{S}')^{w_k(h'_k - h_k)}$ which contradicts the GDH assumption. $\qquad\square$

4.2   Anonymity Analysis

Theorem 3. *The modified* HRS *scheme (shown in the right column of Fig. 2) is anonymous (as of Definition 8), i.e. the advantage* $\mathbf{Adv}(\mathcal{A}, \mathrm{Exp}^{\mathsf{Ano},\lambda,\ell}_{\mathsf{HRS}})$ *of any PPT algorithm* $\mathcal{A}$ *is negligible in* λ, ℓ.

Proof. First we analyze the anonymity of a node $(m, \sigma, \mathsf{pkn}, \mathsf{Y})$ created for the set of public keys Y via modNRSign. This is a modified ring signature procedure. Here we paraphrase the original proof from [2], which itself is based on the anonymity proof from [39]. The key observation here is that the probability choices of the real signer in modNRSign are independent from the signer index. Let $(m, \sigma, \mathsf{pkn}, \mathsf{Y})$ be a valid node created via modNRSign. Let j denotes a potential node signer, i.e. a holder of one public key from Y. The probability that j computes the pkn of the questioned node does not depend on j. The probability that j computes the R_i's of the questioned node does not depend on j. The probability that j computes the correct $\sigma_i = \mathsf{modSign}(R_i, \mathsf{skn})$ for a given R_i and skn corresponding to pkn, does not depend on j. The probability that j chooses exactly the only value $r_j \in \mathbb{Z}_q$ that leads to the value R_j of σ_j, does not depend on j. The probability that j computes the correct $\sigma_j = \mathsf{modSign}(R_j, \mathsf{skn})$ for a given R_j and skn corresponding to pkn does not depend on j. Summing up, the probability that j generates the exact values in the given node does not depend on j, so it is the same for each member of the ring. Now the above reasoning can be done for all nodes in a tree rooted in the $(m, \sigma, \mathsf{pkn}, \mathsf{Y})$. Therefore the set of potential signers has the same cardinality as the set of all paths from $(m, \sigma, \mathsf{pkn}, \mathsf{Y})$ to the leafs in L for that tree.   □

5   Implementation

For a *proof-of-concept* implementation, the original and the modified HRS were programmed in Python Charm-Crypto library [40] using SS512 symmetric curve with a 512-bit base field. Benchmarks were collected on Intel Core i7 7700K 4.4 GHz, running Ubuntu 18.04.3 LTS operating system. Benchmarks in Table 1 are averages from 1000 executions.

Table 1. Operation and time complexity comparison.

		NRSign	modNRSign	NRVerify	modNRVerify*
Operations (n denotes ring size)	G:mul	$n-1$	$n-1$	$3n-1$	$3n-1$
	G:pow	$3n$	$4n+1$	$3n+1$	$2n$
	G:hash	-	$n+1$	-	$n+1$
	Zr:add	$2n$	$2n$	-	-
	Zr:mul	$n+1$	$n+1$	-	-
	Zr:hash	$2n$	$2n$	$2n$	$2n$
	pairing	-	-	-	$2(n+1)$
Total time [ms]	$n=2$	6.9056	10.0233	6.8193	9.2008
	$n=3$	9.8538	13.0087	9.7360	12.1092
	$n=4$	12.8420	15.9743	12.6089	15.0134
	$n=8$	24.5782	27.7796	24.3665	26.7950
	$n=16$	48.2854	51.5113	47.6071	50.0007
	$n=32$	95.3582	98.9072	94.0676	96.8479

In Table 2 we collect timings from the verification of an entire tree of the same topology for both scheme versions. Note, that the verification process can be improved: each fresh node entering the system can be automatically verified by a trusted managing third party. Only valid nodes would be certified and subsequently added to the system structure. Therefore users, creating new nodes, would not need to recursively verify the tree themselves, and the structure would maintain the permanent valid state.

Table 2. Tree verification timings. d denotes depth of the tree and n denotes ring size.

			HRS ver.	modHRS ver.
Total time [ms]	$d = 2$	$n = 2$	57.1829	76.4051
		$n = 3$	126.6224	157.6635
		$n = 4$	152.9543	184.2096
		$n = 8$	257.6268	26.7950
		$n = 16$	467.5049	501.1358
	$d = 5$	$n = 2$	1429.6564	1869.4216
		$n = 3$	3548.5692	4408.6378
		$n = 4$	4259.1884	5150.1035
		$n = 8$	7112.9722	8002.3510
		$n = 16$	12835.1486	13740.8850

Simultaneously to the current proof-of-concept, we are working on the implementation using WebAssembly (WASM) version of MCL library [41]. That proof-of-concept will be available on-line, as a fully functional bulletin board system.

6   Conclusion

In this paper we modified the HRS scheme from [2] in such a way, that it becomes immune to the adversarial randomness setting. The benchmarks collected out of our proof-of-concept implementations are very promising, showing that the complexity overhead of the construction is acceptable.

References

1. Krzywiecki, Ł., Kutyłowski, M., Lauks, A.: Hierarchical ring signatures. In: Slides Presented at 'Western European Workshop on Research in Cryptology 2009' (2009)
2. Krzywiecki, Ł, Sulkowska, M., Zagórski, F.: Hierarchical ring signatures revisited – unconditionally and perfectly anonymous Schnorr version. In: Chakraborty, R.S., Schwabe, P., Solworth, J. (eds.) SPACE 2015. LNCS, vol. 9354, pp. 329–346. Springer, Cham (2015). https://doi.org/10.1007/978-3-319-24126-5_19
3. Chari, S., Jutla, C.S., Rao, J.R., Rohatgi, P.: Towards sound approaches to counteract power-analysis attacks. In: Wiener, M. (ed.) CRYPTO 1999. LNCS, vol. 1666, pp. 398–412. Springer, Heidelberg (1999). https://doi.org/10.1007/3-540-48405-1_26

4. Goubin, L., Patarin, J.: DES and differential power analysis the "Duplication" method. In: Koç, Ç.K., Paar, C. (eds.) CHES 1999. LNCS, vol. 1717, pp. 158–172. Springer, Heidelberg (1999). https://doi.org/10.1007/3-540-48059-5_15

5. Alwen, J., Dodis, Y., Wichs, D.: Leakage-resilient public-key cryptography in the bounded-retrieval model. IACR Cryptology ePrint Archive **2009**, 160 (2009)

6. Canetti, R., Dodis, Y., Halevi, S., Kushilevitz, E., Sahai, A.: Exposure-resilient functions and all-or-nothing transforms. In: Preneel, B. (ed.) EUROCRYPT 2000. LNCS, vol. 1807, pp. 453–469. Springer, Heidelberg (2000). https://doi.org/10.1007/3-540-45539-6_33

7. Dziembowski, S.: Intrusion-resilience via the bounded-storage model. In: Halevi, S., Rabin, T. (eds.) TCC 2006. LNCS, vol. 3876, pp. 207–224. Springer, Heidelberg (2006). https://doi.org/10.1007/11681878_11

8. Di Crescenzo, G., Lipton, R., Walfish, S.: Perfectly secure password protocols in the bounded retrieval model. In: Halevi, S., Rabin, T. (eds.) TCC 2006. LNCS, vol. 3876, pp. 225–244. Springer, Heidelberg (2006). https://doi.org/10.1007/11681878_12

9. Akavia, A., Goldwasser, S., Vaikuntanathan, V.: Simultaneous hardcore bits and cryptography against memory attacks. In: Reingold, O. (ed.) TCC 2009. LNCS, vol. 5444, pp. 474–495. Springer, Heidelberg (2009). https://doi.org/10.1007/978-3-642-00457-5_28

10. Canetti, R., Goldreich, O., Goldwasser, S., Micali, S.: Resettable zero-knowledge (extended abstract). In: Proceedings of the Thirty-Second Annual ACM Symposium on Theory of Computing, 21–23 May 2000, Portland, OR, USA, pp. 235–244 (2000)

11. Kalai, Y.T., Reyzin, L.: A survey of leakage-resilient cryptography. IACR Cryptology ePrint Archive **2019**, 302 (2019)

12. Krzywiecki, Ł: Schnorr-like identification scheme resistant to malicious subliminal setting of ephemeral secret. In: Bica, I., Reyhanitabar, R. (eds.) SECITC 2016. LNCS, vol. 10006, pp. 137–148. Springer, Cham (2016). https://doi.org/10.1007/978-3-319-47238-6_10

13. Krzywiecki, L., Kutylowski, M.: Security of Okamoto identification scheme: a defense against ephemeral key leakage and setup. In: SCC@AsiaCCS, pp. 43–50. ACM (2017)

14. Krzywiecki, Ł, Słowik, M.: Strongly deniable identification schemes immune to Prover's and verifier's ephemeral leakage. In: Farshim, P., Simion, E. (eds.) SecITC 2017. LNCS, vol. 10543, pp. 115–128. Springer, Cham (2017). https://doi.org/10.1007/978-3-319-69284-5_9

15. LaMacchia, B., Lauter, K., Mityagin, A.: Stronger security of authenticated key exchange. In: Susilo, W., Liu, J.K., Mu, Y. (eds.) ProvSec 2007. LNCS, vol. 4784, pp. 1–16. Springer, Heidelberg (2007). https://doi.org/10.1007/978-3-540-75670-5_1

16. Lee, J., Park, J.H.: Authenticated key exchange secure under the computational Diffie-Hellman assumption. Cryptology ePrint Archive, Report 2008/344 (2008)

17. Ustaoglu, B.: Obtaining a secure and efficient key agreement protocol from (H)MQV and NAXOS. Cryptology ePrint Archive, Report 2007/123 (2007)

18. Kim, M., Fujioka, A., Ustaoglu, B.: Strongly secure authenticated key exchange without Naxos' approach under computational Diffie-Hellman assumption. IEICE Trans. **95-A**(1), 29–39 (2012)

19. Krzywiecki, L., Wlislocki, T.: Deniable key establishment resistance against eKCI attacks. Secur. Commun. Netw. **2017**, 7810352:1–7810352:13 (2017)

20. Krzywiecki, L., Kluczniak, K., Koziel, P., Panwar, N.: Privacy-oriented dependency via deniable SIGMA protocol. Comput. Secur. **79**, 53–67 (2018)
21. Koziel, P., Krzywiecki, L., Stygar, D.: Identity-based conditional privacy-preserving authentication scheme resistant to malicious subliminal setting of ephemeral secret. In: Obaidat, M.S., Samarati, P. (eds.) Proceedings of the 16th International Joint Conference on e-Business and Telecommunications, ICETE 2019 - SECRYPT, Prague, Czech Republic, 26–28 July 2019, vol. 2, pp. 492–497. SciTePress (2019)
22. Krzywiecki, L, Słowik, M., Szala, M.: Identity-based signature scheme secure in ephemeral setup and leakage scenarios. In: Heng, S.-H., Lopez, J. (eds.) ISPEC 2019. LNCS, vol. 11879, pp. 310–324. Springer, Cham (2019). https://doi.org/10.1007/978-3-030-34339-2_17
23. Krzywiecki, L., Koziel, P., Panwar, N.: Signature based authentication for ephemeral setup attacks in vehicular sensor networks. In: Gkoulalas-Divanis, A., Marchetti, M., Avresky, D.R. (eds.) 18th IEEE International Symposium on Network Computing and Applications, NCA 2019, Cambridge, MA, USA, 26–28 September 2019, pp. 1–4. IEEE (2019)
24. Krzywiecki, Ł, Wszoła, M., Kutyłowski, M.: Brief announcement: anonymous credentials secure to ephemeral leakage. In: Dolev, S., Lodha, S. (eds.) CSCML 2017. LNCS, vol. 10332, pp. 96–98. Springer, Cham (2017). https://doi.org/10.1007/978-3-319-60080-2_7
25. Rivest, R.L., Shamir, A., Tauman, Y.: How to leak a secret. In: Boyd, C. (ed.) ASIACRYPT 2001. LNCS, vol. 2248, pp. 552–565. Springer, Heidelberg (2001). https://doi.org/10.1007/3-540-45682-1_32
26. Zhang, F., Kim, K.: ID-based blind signature and ring signature from pairings. In: Zheng, Y. (ed.) ASIACRYPT 2002. LNCS, vol. 2501, pp. 533–547. Springer, Heidelberg (2002). https://doi.org/10.1007/3-540-36178-2_33
27. Herranz, J., Sáez, G.: A provably secure ID-based ring signature scheme. Cryptology ePrint Archive, Report 2003/261 (2003). http://eprint.iacr.org/
28. Lin, C.Y., Wu, T.C.: An identity-based ring signature scheme from bilinear pairings. Cryptology ePrint Archive, Report 2003/117 (2003). http://eprint.iacr.org/
29. Chow, S.S.M., Yiu, S.-M., Hui, L.C.K.: Efficient identity based ring signature. In: Ioannidis, J., Keromytis, A., Yung, M. (eds.) ACNS 2005. LNCS, vol. 3531, pp. 499–512. Springer, Heidelberg (2005). https://doi.org/10.1007/11496137_34
30. Awasthi, A.K., Lal, S.: Id-based ring signature and proxy ring signature schemes from bilinear pairings. arXiv Computer Science e-prints, April 2005
31. Au, M.H., Liu, J.K., Yuen, T.H., Wong, D.S.: ID-based ring signature scheme secure in the standard model. In: Yoshiura, H., Sakurai, K., Rannenberg, K., Murayama, Y., Kawamura, S. (eds.) IWSEC 2006. LNCS, vol. 4266, pp. 1–16. Springer, Heidelberg (2006). https://doi.org/10.1007/11908739_1
32. Au, M.H., Chow, S.S.M., Susilo, W., Tsang, P.P.: Short linkable ring signatures revisited. In: Atzeni, A.S., Lioy, A. (eds.) EuroPKI 2006. LNCS, vol. 4043, pp. 101–115. Springer, Heidelberg (2006). https://doi.org/10.1007/11774716_9
33. Tsang, P.P., Wei, V.K.: Short linkable ring signatures for e-voting, e-cash and attestation. In: Deng, R.H., Bao, F., Pang, H.H., Zhou, J. (eds.) ISPEC 2005. LNCS, vol. 3439, pp. 48–60. Springer, Heidelberg (2005). https://doi.org/10.1007/978-3-540-31979-5_5
34. Chen, Y.S., Lei, C.L., Chiu, Y.P., Huang, C.Y.: Confessible threshold ring signatures. In: ICSNC, vol. 25. IEEE Computer Society (2006)

35. Bender, A., Katz, J., Morselli, R.: Ring signatures: stronger definitions, and constructions without random oracles. In: Halevi, S., Rabin, T. (eds.) TCC 2006. LNCS, vol. 3876, pp. 60–79. Springer, Heidelberg (2006). https://doi.org/10.1007/11681878_4

36. Dodis, Y., Kiayias, A., Nicolosi, A., Shoup, V.: Anonymous identification in *ad hoc* groups. In: Cachin, C., Camenisch, J.L. (eds.) EUROCRYPT 2004. LNCS, vol. 3027, pp. 609–626. Springer, Heidelberg (2004). https://doi.org/10.1007/978-3-540-24676-3_36

37. Chandran, N., Groth, J., Sahai, A.: Ring signatures of sub-linear size without random oracles. In: Arge, L., Cachin, C., Jurdziński, T., Tarlecki, A. (eds.) ICALP 2007. LNCS, vol. 4596, pp. 423–434. Springer, Heidelberg (2007). https://doi.org/10.1007/978-3-540-73420-8_38

38. Backes, M., Döttling, N., Hanzlik, L., Kluczniak, K., Schneider, J.: Ring signatures: logarithmic-size, no setup—from standard assumptions. In: Ishai, Y., Rijmen, V. (eds.) EUROCRYPT 2019. LNCS, vol. 11478, pp. 281–311. Springer, Cham (2019). https://doi.org/10.1007/978-3-030-17659-4_10

39. Herranz, J., Sáez, G.: Forking lemmas for ring signature schemes. In: Johansson, T., Maitra, S. (eds.) INDOCRYPT 2003. LNCS, vol. 2904, pp. 266–279. Springer, Heidelberg (2003). https://doi.org/10.1007/978-3-540-24582-7_20

40. Akinyele, J.A., et al.: Charm: a framework for rapidly prototyping cryptosystems. J. Cryptogr. Eng. **3**(2), 111–128 (2013)

41. Mitsunari, S.: MCL cryptolibrary (2019). https://github.com/herumi/mcl

Theoretical Aspects of a Priori On-Line Assessment of Data Predictability in Applied Tasks

Sergey Frenkel[✉]

Federal Research Center "Computer Science and Control", Russian Academy of Science, Moscow, Russia

Abstract. We will call a set of programs a Prediction Tool (PT) that can be used to solve a particular applied prediction problem, for example, predicting the volumes of traffic under consideration at certain points in the future. The goal may be a forecast for the network administrator. We analyze what kind of information about the predicted data and the predictors should be used to develop (design) PT. The paper analyzes some principal questions, the solution of which is essential for specified procedures of choosing a predictor in the prediction online scheme. This is primarily a question about the properties of predictability of random sequences, and the required and achievable accuracy of the estimate of the conditional probability of prediction obtained from past results. Although some of these issues have been considered in sufficient detail in the literature, for example, such as the analysis of predictability measures, accuracy metrics, however, as will be shown, they are more focused on the problems of constructing specific prediction algorithms than on the choice of ready-made predictors.

It is shown how the specified properties of sequences and probability estimates affect the quality of the choice of predictors. Based on this analysis, a rule for choosing a predictor based on the results of previous predictions is formulated.

Keywords: Predictability · Random sequences

1 Introduction

The designer of a forecasting subsystem, for example, a traffic management and/or network security system, should provide for the possibility of assessing the expected quality and possible costs of forecasting at every required moment when the forecasting subsystem is running. This requires a tool for assessing the effectiveness of forecasting in a given time interval.

We will call a set of programs that implement prediction algorithms as Prediction Tool (PT) which can be used to solve a particular applied prediction problem, for example, predicting the volumes of the traffic at certain points in the future or possible malicious attacks. The quality of the forecast at some point in time depends on how well the algorithm used by the predictor based on the data in the past reflects the situation in the future. In general, these issues are considered as "predictability" ones, by both

© Springer Nature Switzerland AG 2021
S. Dolev et al. (Eds.): CSCML 2021, LNCS 12716, pp. 187–195, 2021.
https://doi.org/10.1007/978-3-030-78086-9_14

probabilistic-statistical and logical-semantic viewpoint. PT user must perform a forecast at a given time (e.g., a certain communication session) according to the information available at the moment, that is online. In general, the users do not know the details of the prediction algorithm by this predictor, and only information (statistical, in particular) about the results of its use on certain arrays of the data under consideration (for example, the volume of network traffic), and they should make a decision on the choice of a predictor from a suit of available predictors based on this information.

The paper analyzes a number of fundamental issues, the solution of which is essential for the specified procedure for choosing a predictor in the described online scheme.

This is primarily a question about the properties of the predictability of random sequences. Although the issues of predictability measures, prediction accuracy metrics, etc. have been considered in the literature [1–3, 7], they were more focused on the problem of constructing specific prediction algorithms than on the choice of ready-made predictors. In [1–3] criteria for the selection of predictors based on comparison with the so-called "universal" predictor were theoretically substantiated. However, as the analysis performed has shown, it does not always agree well with the cost criteria used in practice, especially for binary sequences that naturally arise in the problems of predicting the direction of changes in values of numerical time series. In Sects. 2 and 3, a rule for choosing a predictor based on the results of previous predictions from a suit of predictors is formulated. Then it is shown how certain properties (not necessarily statistical and probabilistic) of sequences can be used (Sects. 4 and 5).

2 Description and Problem Definitions

We will consider data and related to them events as ordered (e.g. on terms "earlier" or "later") sequences of their representations (for example, symbolic objects). Let x_1, x_2, ..., x_t... is the specified ordered set. The observer consistently observes the values x_1, x_2, ..., x_t of known types, for example, symbols in some alphabet A. At time t, having received the values x_1, x_2,..., x_t, the observer calculates according to some rule or algorithm the value b_{t+1} (in A), which will be received by the element of the sequence x_{t+1}. To make a decision about the value of x_{t+1}, an observer (PT user) can use some prediction algorithm (rule) from a set of known and available PT. The task is to determine the sequence of actions of the observer (with supporting the PT), that provides an effective solution to the prediction problem.

Currently for solving this problem, there are two kinds of models for predicting data values from previously known data: probabilistic models and "ontological models" [9, 10]. In the paper we will consider a probabilistic prediction model with an assessment of the possibility of using certain non-probabilistic characteristics of the predicted data.

Prediction in modern literature [1–3] is understood as the computation of the conditional probability $\gamma(x_{t+1}|x_1, x_2, ..., x_t)$, defined on all elements of the sequence for which the natural condition is satisfied $\sum_{a \in A} \gamma(x_{t+1} = a \mid x_1, x_2, ..., x_t) = 1$. The function $\gamma()$ is also called a predictor.

Formally, a statistical hypothesis is equivalent to a prediction strategy, which is also a function of the finite sequences and their distributions on A [2]. Note, that the predictor is also called software products (for example, some modules of cloud MS AWS Azure ML, Google Cloud ML, etc.), which are used for prediction.

The subject of research in the field of predictions is both the algorithms used in software tools and the issues of choosing ready-made prediction software. From the above, the following two questions arise: (i) how to use the estimated values of $\gamma()$ for making a decision, and (ii) what is the required accuracy of the estimate? These questions can relate to both the estimation algorithm and the application of the estimation results by a specific predictor (fully or partially known, for example, knowing that the predictor belongs to a neural network. An example of using of such partial knowledge see in Sect. 4). In our scheme, we evaluate several predictors at time t, and think about which one to use for time $t + 1$. By online prediction we mean that for consecutive units of time t, our predictor p makes a prediction based on past observations [6].

3   Metrics of Predictability: Related Work

Questions related to the ability of certain datasets to be predicted by predictors of certain classes will be called *Predictability* issues. It follows from the above that the main issue of predictability is the possibility of accurate approximating conditional distributions. We can talk either about a parametric estimate, when the general form of the parametric probability distribution is known to which the segment of the sequence belongs, or a nonparametric estimate of the conditional probability distribution, for example, according to the Kolmogorov-Smirnov test. However, the approximation of probability distributions for discrete random sequences is rather difficult [5], which stimulate to deal with a prediction that is not associated with the explicit probabilistic models of the data. Therefore, so-called. "Universal schemes" [1, 2, 11], in which predictions are performed without explicit probabilistic models of sequences, although with certain assumptions about the probabilistic measures of hypothetical sources generating these sequences, say about their ergodicity (in our methods, these assumptions are not always necessary - see below).

The well-known Lempel-Ziv (LZ) compression algorithm [12] is an example of the universal method. In fact, LZ can act as a predictor by defining x_{t+1} as the corresponding leaf in the partial matches tree [1, 11] with the conditional probability induced by the incremental parsing algorithm. But it is important, that for any method of prediction there exists such a stationary ergodic process that with probability 1:

$\lim_{t\to\infty}\sup |P'(x_{t+2}|x_1 \ldots x_{t+1}) - P(x_{t+2}|x_1 \ldots x_{t+1})|>0$, where $P'()$ is an estimation (by universal prediction scheme), and there is no method whose error goes to 0 for every stationary ergodic time series (when t goes to infinity) [3]. But it also depends on the definition of the error, which may differ from the trivial probability of a wrong prediction. In particular, it was proven [2] that there exists a prediction for which the convergence to 0 of the following Cesaro average is true: $\lim_{t\to\infty}t^{-1}\Sigma_{m=0,t-1}|P'(x_{t+2}|x_1, \ldots x_{t+1})-P(x_{t+2}|x_1 \ldots x_{t+1})$. So, there are no consistent estimates if the consistency is considered in a wide one of the sense, but there are consistent estimates in the Cesaro average sense.

One of the measures of distributions closeness is the Kullback-Leible (KL) discrepancy. There are sequences for which the error in terms of KL according to Cesaro (similar to the above) tends to zero as t increases infinitely (for example, the Laplace predictor for the Bernoulli sequence (see Sect. 4)). Unfortunately, there is no predictor with this property for any stationary ergodic source. However, for such sources, there are predictors for which a weaker property holds: the Cesaro means of errors tends to zero. That is [1–3, 11]) the predictor $\gamma()$ is universal for the set of sources Ω (generated corresponding sequences) if the Cesaro average-like error convergence to 0 with $t \to \infty$ for any $\omega \in \Omega$. Thus, when choosing a predictor, in order to achieve at least asymptotic prediction accuracy on it for a specific data set, a preliminary analysis is required, which can be associated with instrumental errors analysis. At the same time, the average in the Cesaro sense, as dependent on past estimates, may not correspond to the user's situation at the moment $t + 1$ of making a new decision, for example, if the cost and time of choosing a specific predictor, say, in a cloud resource, changes dramatically [13]. One of the ways to overcome these difficulties is to use models of minimization of "losses" from erroneous prediction.

3.1 Selection of a Predictor Based on the Model of Losses from Erroneous Predictions

So, let's look at what we need to know about the consequences of mispredictions by predictors in order to assess the effect of predictor property on prediction quality.

We consider predictors (as the program tools) as a set of functions belonging to some family of one or more classes (for example, neural networks, Gradient-based, etc. [9]) $f = (f_1, f_2,...): \{0,1\}^t \to \{0,1\}$. That is the predictor f_p, $i = 1, 2, ..$, is any function.

$b_{t+1} = f_p(x_{t-m}, ..., x_t)$, which calculates the value of the random sequence predicted by the predictor f_i for the moment $t + 1$, m is the number of terms in the sequence preceding t that this predictor uses (p) to obtain prediction b_{t+1}, which is an estimate of the true value of x_{t+1}. (Note that, for prediction at time $t + 1$, not only the previous results for a given predictor, but also the results of predictions obtained by other predictors before this time may be used. In this case the problem is close to prediction with experts [6]). Based on the obtained b_t value, the user (or some software solver built into PT) makes a decision, the error of which may have a certain price.

The loss function $l(p, x)$ for the predictor p for the sequence x is the loss that we associate with the forecast result (deciding on the value of b_t) if it turns out that b_t does not coincide with x_t. For example, if the purpose of prediction is to prevent DDoS attacks, and as a result of an incorrect prediction, the attack was missed, then the losses are maximum and the value of the loss function should be $l(x_t, b_t) = 1$. Otherwise, $l(x_t, b_t)$ should be equal to 0. Obviously, this requirement is satisfied by the Hamming distance $H(x, b)$.

Since the accuracy of the prediction depends on both the characteristics of the predictor and the probabilistic properties of the sequence, and the characteristics of the predictor also usually depend on these probabilistic distributions, the estimation of which, as noted, can be difficult, as a criterion for the quality of the choice of the predictor in [3] the so-called "regret" is proposed, which is the difference between some loss function when using the universal predictor U and, in a sense, the best of the set of predictors. However, as the performed analysis shows (we do not present it here due to lack of space), there are many difficulties for its practical implementation, (online, in particular) due to the asymptotic nature of the accuracy of universal predictors. Thus, for choosing a predictor by assessing the magnitude of regret it is important to integrate some characteristics of the predictor algorithm into the procedure choice, considering the predictor as a "black box". Such a possibility exists, for example, in [4], where it is assumed that the predictor algorithm is described as a finite state machine, and asymptotic dependences of the regret value on the number of states are obtained. Our analysis showed, however, the complexity of such an assessment, which can be partially overcome by using an online procedure that uses not only data, which should be predicted by their past values, but also past results of attempts to apply predictors for this dataset.

4 Model and Procedure for Choosing a Predictor

The stated theoretical results concerning the properties of predictability of random sequences can be used to somewhat increase the efficiency of working with prediction tools on-line.

Suppose we use a predictor p, to predict the value of a binary time series at time $t + 1$, knowing the predicted values at times $\{t - M, \ldots t\}$, where M is the window size, used for prediction at the moments within $(t - M, t)$. Let the success rate of the predictor be $SR_p = N_p\backslash M$ in the window $\{t - M, \ldots t\}$, where N_p is the number of correct predictions by the predictor in the window of size M. Since the predictor (for probabilistic prediction models) is described by the conditional probability $\gamma\,(x_{t+1}/x_t, \ldots x_{t-m})$, then we will consider the possibility of its representation (expression) in terms of the specified data segments and measurements.

It is clear that $N_p = \Sigma_{i=1,M}\,1(f_p(x_{t-M+i}, \ldots x_{t-M+i+m}) = x_{t-M+i+m+1}))$, where $x_{t-M+i+m+1}$ is the true value $f_p()$ is the same as in Subsect. 3.1. Then it is easy to see that $N_p\backslash M$ is an empirical estimate of the conditional probability $\gamma()$.

Suppose now that the sequence in the M-window is a Bernoulli sequence, and we estimate the Bernoulli parameter using either maximum likelihood estimated value n1/n, or Laplace estimator ("Laplace smoothing)", if we can assume the possibility of zero values of successes (failures) in the considered segment of the sequence).

This represents the estimate $\gamma()$ (Sect. 2) under the assumption that the considered sequence is Bernoulli, since knowledge of the estimate θ uniquely generates an optimal predictor.

Statement 1. For the Hamming loss function the forecast b_t, optimal according to the regret criterion (Sect. 3), of the next value of the binary Bernoulli sequence is achieved if it is made according to the following rule: $b_{t+1} = 1$, if Prob $(1|x_t) > 1/2$, $b_{t+1} = 0$, if Prob $(0|x_t) = 1 -$ Prob$(1|x_t) > 1/2$, and this is the deviation of any forecast if Prob $(0|x_t)$ = Prob$(1|xt) = 1/2$, that is, the forecast "skip", Where " skip" means the absence of an optimal forecast [1, 3].

We will call this predictor "Bernoulli optimal" (BO).

Note that its distribution $\gamma()$ is the well-known Laplace estimate $(n_1 + 1)/(n_1 + n_0 + 2)$, where n1, no are the numbers of "1" and "0".

It is possible (and practical) for the proposed technique, a frequency interpretation, i.e. comparing the number of correct predictions by the given predictor and the optimal predictor of the Bernoulli sequence. In this case, we consider N_p in a window of length M as a characteristic of only a given segment of the data set considered immediately before the prediction time point, and we consider the sequence $x_{t-M+i}, .. x_{t-M+i+m}$ as individual sequence, without assumptions about its belonging to a stochastic ensemble of sequences. Accordingly, we draw conclusions about the effectiveness of the predictor only in this time interval, and we get rid of the need to estimate the confidence intervals of the probabilistic estimates. This is especially important with a relatively small asymmetry of the sequence segments, with close values of zeros and ones (for example, $|1/2 - \theta| < 1/10$).

Suppose we used the well-known predictors XGD (eXtreme Gradient Boosting) and calculated the estimate SR_p. At the heart of XGBoost is a gradient boosting decision tree algorithm that builds a prediction model in the form of an ensemble of predictive models, usually decision trees. The ensemble is trained sequentially on the input data of the predicted sequence, in which patterns of a certain length (for example, "0110") are selected, followed by the predicted "0" or "1".

Let us consider our sequence in the M-window (i.e. $(t - M, t)$) simply as a Bernoulli sequence, and also use the Bernoulli optimal predictor for prediction. Therefore, we can talk about the difference between the XGB predictor of a binary sequence f_p from such a simple predictor (BO), both in the estimated value of SR and in the structure of errors (i.e., in the error ratio "0 instead of 1"("0→1") and ("1 instead of 0" ("1→0")) Obviously, if there is no significant difference between these values, then we can talk about the inefficiency of the predictor implementing the function f_p, since a similar solution is obtained by a much simpler Bernoulli predictor.

Thus, the current predictor for prediction at time t-$M + 1$ should be updated for another **if** $n_1 > n_0$, $n_1 < n_{p1}$, $n_{p11} > n_1/\beta$, **or** $n_1 < n_0$, $n_0 < n_{p0}$, $n_{p00} > n_0/\beta$, where n_1, n_0 is the number of zeros and ones in the M-window, n_{p1}, n_{p0} is the number of zeros and ones predicted by f_p, n_{p11}, n_{p00} is the number of ones and zeros *predicted correctly* in the window. Here $\beta = 2 \div 5$ is selected depending on the received n_{p11}, n_{p00}, and reflects a decrease in the imbalance between the errors "1→0", "0→1" inherent in the BO.

If these conditions are not met, then the next predictor from the list of available ones is selected.

Indeed, n_1 is a number ones in this window (respectively, for n_0). By the BO in a given window, all bits of the sequence are predicted as ones if ones are more frequent ($n_1 > n_0$), or as zeros, if zeros are more frequent in this window. Therefore, the first condition means that the predictor f_p provides a higher probability of correct prediction until the last observed moment than BO, and the second means that a certain part of the predicted zeros (or ones) is the result of the predictive algorithm of the predictor f_p, and not the mechanical conversion of zeros to ones (or ones to zeros), as the Bernoulli predictor does. The case $n1 = n0$ means that the data is close to randomness, and the use of tools based only on probabilistic methods is not possible. So, the following scheme is proposed for choosing a predictor at the moment of working with a PT:

- select a window preceding the next prediction moment of size M time units,
- in this window, the number of correct predictions by this predictor is calculated, both all and separately the number of correct predictions of zeros and ones,
- these numbers are compared with the number of correct predictions of the predictor BO, assuming that the sequence in the window is a Bernoulli sequence,

- if the inequalities are not met, choose another predictor,
- when evaluating a sequence in a window as random, we abandon prediction.

5 "Ontological" Factors in Probabilistic Models of Prediction

Informally, the "ontology" means that we have some other "knowledge" about the data not necessary related to their probabilistic distribution. For example, let $x_1, x_2, \ldots x_t$, be binary, and it is known (based on reliable expert information or based on the theory of data generation) that the generation of data by hypothetical sources with a high probability p_i is such that after two zeros 00 follows 1, after 01 follows 1, after 10 follows 0, after 11 follows 1. In other words, we singled out the concept of the "triple of binary values" and the relation "after". Then the value of the bit after each observed pattern will be predicted to be correct with a high probability p_i.

Definition 1. We will call a predictor "ontology-effective" in the moment t relatively a given historical data if its algorithm takes into account to some extent the semantics of the data corresponding to some ontology, namely, the fact that the elements of data sets can belong to different concepts and classes, and provides the prediction not worse than optimal Bernoulli predictor.

If SR_p does not differ statistically significantly from the success rate calculated under the assumption that the predictor p is the optimal predictor for the Bernoulli sequence, then we can conclude that the predictor is ineffective for the ontology using [13]. In this case, we can also talk about the difference of some predictor p with function f_p from a predictor of the simplest ontology (predictor BO) as by the estimated value SR_p, and by the structure errors the error "0 instead of 1" and "1 instead of 0").

In fact, the scheme of predictor choice from the previous section can be considered as a rule of the "ontology-effectiveness" assessment.

Indeed, let a sequence.

$$x_1^n = \frac{1100100100001111110110101010001000100010110100011}{00001000110100110001001100011001100010100010111000}$$

is generated by a source with unknown distribution.

In accordance with the set of randomness tests NIST, namely Frequency (Monobit) Test, Test within a Block, and yet three tests, this sequence is the randomness. That is, any predictors based on some probabilistic models are not effective, $\gamma()$ conditional probability mentioned above will be very small for all next bits.

But let a predictor p be a predictor, the algorithm of which, based on learning (or using some "oracle"), predicts that after each pattern "11" comes zero. Then, following this rule, with a probability of 4/6, you can correctly predict the 51st zero, which is significantly higher than the Bernoulli optimal predictor (an example is the use in [8] of the XGB algorithm for a binary sequence). Taking into account, that $n_1 = 43$, $n_0 = 57$ it means that our criterion will give an obvious advantage to this "ontological" approach over the BO. That is the scheme of the previous Section is an indicator of the necessity of using a semantical data in the prediction.

6 Conclusion

The paper proposes, on the basis of analysis of current state-of-the-art of probabilistic prediction theory, an approach to the choice of predictors at a specific time the period required to predict future data sequences associated with the functioning of various systems (e.g., IT systems). A method is proposed for making a decision on the advisability of choosing a certain predictor at the next step, comparing its quality (accuracy) of the forecast in the past, with the trivial BO predictor for a binary sequence, according to which a forecast should be made, considering the sequence as Bernoulli one. Note that the simplest and most obvious argument for such a comparison is that there is no need to use an expensive predictor if it does not provide better quality than, in a sense, elementary!

It is essential that the user, who is not an expert in the field of forecasting, is not required to compute certain statistical characteristics of observed data, that are more complex than the simple estimation of the frequencies of events.

Acknowledgements. Research partially supported by the Russian Foundation for Basic Research under grants RFBR 18-29-03100.

I express my gratitude to Professor Shlomi Dolev (Ben-Gurion University of the Negev) for a fruitful discussion of the predictability issues.

References

1. Feder, M., Merhav, N., Gutman, M.: Universal prediction of individual sequences. IEEE Trans. Inf. Theory **38**(4), 887–892 (1992)
2. Ryabko, B.B.: Compression-based methods for nonparametric prediction and estimation of some characteristics of time series. IEEE Trans. Inf. Theor. **55**(9), 4309–4315 (2009)
3. Feder, M., Merhav, N.: Universal prediction. IEEE Trans. Inf. Theor. **44**(6), 2124–2147 (1998)
4. Meron, E., Feder, M.: Finite-memory universal prediction of individual sequences. IEEE Trans. Inf. Theor. **50**(7), 1506–1523 (2004)
5. Lee, Y.K., Lee, E.R., Park, B.U.: Conditional quantile estimation by local logistic regression. Nonparametric Stat. **4**(6), 357–373 (2006)
6. Stoltz, G.: Incomplete information and internal regret in prediction of individual sequences (2005). https://tel.archives-ouvertes.fr/tel-00009759
7. Lysyak, A.S., Ryabko, B.Y.: Time series prediction based on data compression methods. Probl. Inf. Transm. **52**(1), 92–99 (2016). https://doi.org/10.1134/S0032946016010075
8. Chen, T., Guestrin, C.: XGboost: a scalable tree boosting system. *arXiv.org* (2016). https://arxiv.org/pdf/1603.02754.pdf
9. Buczak, L., Guven, E.: A survey of data mining and machine learning methods for cyber security intrusion detection. IEEE Com. Surv. Tut. **18**(2), 1153–1176 (2016)
10. Rooba, R., Vallimayil, V.: Semantic aware future page prediction based on domain. Int. J. Pure Appl. Math. **118**(9), 911–919 (2018)
11. Ryabko, B., Monarev, V.: Using information theory approach to randomness testing. J. Stat. Plann. Infer. **133**, 95–110 (2005)

12. Frenkel, S.: Ontological and probabilistic aspects of assessing predictors quality. In: Book of Abstract of VII Workshop on Computational Data Analysis and Numerical Methods Polytechnic Institute of Tomar, Portugal, pp. 84–86 (2020)
13. Frenkel, S, Zakharov, V., Basok, M: Optimization of the integration process of Cloud and COTS based computing systems. In: Posin, B. (ed.) Proceedings of VI International Conference program Actual Problems of System and Software Engineering (APSSE 2019), pp. 88–94. IEEE Computer Society, Moscow (2019)

Randomly Rotate Qubits, Compute and Reverse for Weak Measurements Resilient QKD and Securing Entanglement
(Extended Abstract)

Dor Bitan[1]([⊠]) and Shlomi Dolev[2]

[1] Department of Mathematics, Ben-Gurion University of the Negev,
Beer-Sheva, Israel
dorbi@post.bgu.ac.il
[2] Department of Computer Science, Ben-Gurion University of the Negev,
Beer-Sheva, Israel

Abstract. Homomorphic encryption (HE) schemes enable the processing of encrypted data and may be used by a user to outsource storage and computations to an untrusted server. A plethora of HE schemes has been suggested in the past four decades, based on various assumptions, which achieve different attributes. In this work, we assume that the user and server are quantum computers and look for HE schemes of classical data. We set a high bar of requirements and ask what can be achieved under these requirements. Namely, we look for HE schemes which are efficient, information-theoretically secure, perfectly correct, and which support homomorphic operations in a fully compact and non-interactive way. Fully compact means that decryption costs $\mathcal{O}(1)$ time and space. We suggest an encryption scheme based on random bases and discuss the homomorphic properties of that scheme. The main advantage of our scheme is providing better security in the face of weak measurements (WM). Measurements of this kind enable collecting partial information on a quantum state while only slightly disturbing the state. We suggest here a novel QKD scheme based on our encryption scheme, which is resilient against WM-based attacks.

We bring up a new concept we call *securing entanglement*. We look at entangled systems of qubits as a resource used for carrying out quantum computations and show how our scheme may be used to guarantee that an entangled system can be used only by its rightful owners. To the best of our knowledge, this concept has not been discussed in previous literature.

We would like to thank the Lynne and William Frankel Center for Computer Science, the Rita Altura Trust Chair in Computer Science. This research was also partially supported by a grant from the Ministry of Science and Technology, Israel & the Japan Science and Technology Agency (JST), and the German Research Funding (DFG, Grant#8767581199). We also thank Daniel Berend for discussions, comments and suggestions throughout the research.

S. Dolev et al. (Eds.): CSCML 2021, LNCS 12716, pp. 196–204, 2021.
https://doi.org/10.1007/978-3-030-78086-9_15

Keywords: Quantum homomorphic encryption ·
Information-theoretic security · Quantum key distribution · Weak
measurements · Securing entanglement

1   Introduction

Delegation of computation, while preserving the confidentiality of the data, is a challenging practical task that has kept researchers busy ever since it was brought up by Rivest, Adelman, and Dertouzos [RAD78]. Solutions based on Homomorphic Encryption (HE, see [AAUC18]) can maintain IT-security only if limited to support the processing of a non-complete set of functions over the encrypted data. Fully homomorphic encryption (FHE) schemes, which may support *any* function, can only achieve computational security. HE schemes may be classified according to their level of security, complexity, and other attributes. If the decryption algorithm is efficient (i.e., poly-time), the scheme is *compact*. If the decryption algorithm requires $\mathcal{O}(1)$ time and space, the scheme is *fully compact*.

In 2014, it was shown by [YPDF14] that it is impossible to construct an efficient IT-secure quantum FHE (QFHE) scheme. Efficient IT-secure encryption schemes can be used to homomorphically evaluate only a subset of all possible functions. Such schemes are quantum homomorphic encryption (QHE) schemes, e.g., [Lia13,OTF18]. Other works use computationally secure FHE schemes to construct computationally secure QFHE schemes. E.g., [BJ15,Mah18,Bra18]. Quantum schemes with homomorphic properties are often based on the quantum one-time pad (QOTP) encryption scheme, suggested in [AMTdW00].

In this work, we assume that both the user and the server can: (a) generate qubits in the computational basis; (b) manipulate qubits using quantum logic gates; (c) transmit qubits between each other; (d) measure qubits. We assume that the information held by the user is classical. We look for QHE schemes that enable users to delegate classical data to be stored and processed by an untrusted server and have the following properties: (a) IT-secure; (b) Efficient; (c) Fully compact; (d) Perfectly correct; (e) Non-interactive. We ask which operations may be homomorphically applied to encrypted data under these restrictions. Ambianis et al.'s QOTP scheme, suggested in [AMTdW00], was used to construct QHE scheme that has some of the properties listed above. Several such schemes are reviewed in the full version of this work [BD19].

Quantum Key Distribution (QKD). Bennett and Brassard [BB84] presented a quantum scheme (hereafter, BB84) that enables two distant parties, Alice and Bob, to agree on a random key without relying on any computational hardness assumptions. The security of these protocols is based on the fact that measurements of a quantum state cause the state to collapse. This phenomenon enables Alice and Bob to reveal eavesdropping attempts. Various attacks on QKD schemes have been suggested over the years. These attacks mainly target weaknesses in the implementation of the scheme and are discussed in, e.g., [GLLP04,Wan05,BP12]. A different approach to attack QKD schemes, which was not previously addressed elsewhere, is based on *weak measurements*. The model of weak measurements, rooted in the work of Aharonov et al. [ABL64], raises the possibility of gathering a small amount of information regarding the state while only slightly disturbing it.

Our Contribution. We suggest here a new approach to encrypt and outsource the storage of classical data while enabling limited IT-secure quantum gate computations over it. Our scheme supports fully compact IT-secure homomorphic evaluation of several gates, which we show to be useful in several applications – a random basis QKD scheme and a securing entanglement scheme. We note that while some of these applications may also be constructed using other existing QHE schemes, our scheme has safer security implications in the face of weak measurements (WM). We suggest a WM-based attack on legacy QKD schemes (BB84 and DL04) and argue that our QKD scheme is resilient to such attacks. Our method is based on using a specific family of random bases to encrypt classical bits.

We bring up a new concept called *securing entanglement*. The creation of entangled systems requires efforts and expenditures. We suggest that, once it was created, this resource should be secured in the sense that only its rightful owners will be able to use it. We demonstrate a process of securing entanglement using our QHE scheme and argue that our method provides safer implications in the face of weak measurements comparing QOTP based methods.

Paper Organization. In Sect. 2, we present our random basis encryption scheme and discuss its homomorphic properties. The concept of securing entanglement is presented in Sect. 3. In Sect. 4, we describe WM attacks on existing QKD schemes and present our random basis QKD. Relevant background, further related work, notations, and proofs may be found in the full version of this work [BD19].

2   The Random Basis Encryption Scheme

Our main intention is encrypting the classical bits 0 and 1 while enabling some operations to be performed homomorphically over the ciphertext. Typically, these bits are encoded in quantum computation as the elements $|0\rangle$ and $|1\rangle$ of the standard basis of $\mathbb{H} = \mathbb{C}^2$. Of course, that encoding is by no means an encryption of the bits. Approaching proper encryption, we take some random $(\theta, \varphi) \in [0, 2\pi]^2$, set $|\psi_0\rangle = \begin{pmatrix} \cos(\theta/2) \\ e^{i\varphi}\sin(\theta/2) \end{pmatrix}$, and think of $|\psi_0\rangle$ as an encryption of $|0\rangle$ using (θ, φ) as the encryption key. The plaintext qubits $|0\rangle$ and $|1\rangle$ are orthogonal. To maintain orthogonality of the ciphertext, we set $|\psi_1\rangle = \begin{pmatrix} \sin(\theta/2) \\ -e^{i\varphi}\cos(\theta/2) \end{pmatrix}$ to be the encryption of $|1\rangle$ using the same key. One may readily verify that $|\psi_0\rangle$ and $|\psi_1\rangle$ are orthogonal. For random $(\theta, \varphi) \in [0, 2\pi]^2$, the elements $|\psi_0\rangle$ and $|\psi_1\rangle$ constitute a random orthonormal basis of $\mathbb{H}$, denoted $B_{(\theta,\varphi)}$. We want that encryption to support some homomorphic operations in a fully compact non-interactive IT-secure way. First, we require supporting homomorphic *NOT* gates. We want $|\psi_0\rangle$ to be equal (up to a global phase factor) to $NOT\,|\psi_1\rangle$ (and vice versa). A straightforward computation shows that it compels $\varphi = \pm\pi/2$. Hence, for $(\theta, \varphi) \in [0, 2\pi] \times \{\pm\frac{\pi}{2}\}$, the random basis $B_{\left(\theta,\pm\frac{\pi}{2}\right)} = \left\{ \begin{pmatrix} \cos(\theta/2) \\ \pm i\sin(\theta/2) \end{pmatrix}, \begin{pmatrix} \sin(\theta/2) \\ \mp i\cos(\theta/2) \end{pmatrix} \right\}$ is *NOT*-invariant.

The discussion above gives rise to the RBE scheme presented below.

The Random Basis Encryption (RBE) scheme

Gen (key generation): Uniformly sample $(\theta, \varphi) \leftarrow [0, 2\pi] \times \{\pm\frac{\pi}{2}\}$ and output.

Enc (encryption): On input message $b \in \{0, 1\}$ and a key $k = (\theta, \varphi)$:

- Generate the qubit $|b\rangle$.
- Let $K = \begin{pmatrix} \cos(\theta/2) & \sin(\theta/2) \\ e^{i\varphi}\sin(\theta/2) & -e^{i\varphi}\cos(\theta/2) \end{pmatrix} \in M_2(\mathbb{C})$ and apply K to $|b\rangle$ to obtain $|q\rangle = K|b\rangle$ and output $|q\rangle$.

Dec (decryption): On input ciphertext $|\psi\rangle$ and a key $k = (\theta, \varphi)$:

- Let $K^\dagger$ denote the conjugate transpose of K and apply $K^\dagger$ to $|\psi\rangle$.
- Measure $K^\dagger |\psi\rangle$ and output the outcome of the measurement.

The matrix K is the unitary whose columns are the elements of the random basis $B_{(\theta,\varphi)}$. The encryption algorithm takes the elements of the computational basis to the elements of $B_{(\theta,\varphi)}$. The scheme may be applied bit-wise to a string x of classical bits to enable outsourcing the storage of x to an untrusted quantum server. In Gen, the key is chosen from a continuous domain. Implementing this might be challenging. However, the key space may be made discrete while keeping the scheme IT-secure and perfectly correct [BD19].

Homomorphic Operations. The RBE scheme can support homomorphic evaluation of several quantum gates. This is useful for applications presented below.

The NOT gate. Applying a *NOT* gate to an element of $B_{(\theta,\varphi)}$, we get the other element of that basis, up to a global phase factor [BD19].

The Hadamard gate. In [BD19], we explain why the Hadamard gate cannot be applied to the encrypted data homomorphically. However, we construct *the D gate* – a quantum gate that uses an ancillary $|0\rangle$ qubit and takes elements of every $B_{(\theta,\varphi)}$ to an equally weighted superposition of the elements of $B_{(\theta,\varphi)}$. D is the two-qubit circuit established by first applying a Hadamard to the first qubit, and then a *CNOT* gate to that system of two qubits. In [BD19], we prove that applying a D gate to a tensor product of $|0\rangle$ and an element of a random basis, measuring the second qubit in reference to that same random basis, the probabilities of obtaining the outcomes zero and one are both $\frac{1}{2}$.

The CNOT gate. In [BD19], we show that the RBE scheme cannot support homomorphic *CNOT* gates (even if using ancillary qubits). Nevertheless, by applying a *CNOT* gate to the elements of a *partially-random* basis $\{|0\rangle, |1\rangle\} \otimes B_{(\theta,\varphi)}$ of $\mathbb{H}^{\otimes 2}$ we do keep the target-control structure. The elements of such a basis are $|0\psi_0\rangle, |0\psi_1\rangle, |1\psi_0\rangle, |1\psi_1\rangle$. Applying a *CNOT* gate to these elements, we leave $|0\psi_b\rangle$ unchanged and interchange $|1\psi_b\rangle$ and $|1\psi_{1-b}\rangle$.

3   Securing Entanglement

Entanglement is an essential resource in quantum computation. Once generated, it should be guaranteed that only the rightful owners would be able to use it. In this section, we present a method for securing that important resource in an IT-secure way, using our scheme. Assume that Alice and Bob are two scientists working in distant labs and wish to complete a joint task that requires entanglement. Consider the case in which Alice and Bob can get together and jointly generate entangled qubits. Having obtained a large number of entangled qubits, they store them in their labs for future use. Alice and Bob are worried that other people, say, Eve and Mallory, will break into their labs. Eve will steal half of each entangled system from Alice's lab, and Mallory will steal the corresponding half from Bob's lab and use the stolen entangled pairs for their own needs. Alice and Bob are looking for a way to secure their entangled particles to ensure that no one else can use them. One may suggest that, before leaving their labs, Alice and Bob use QOTP to (independently) encrypt each half of each entangled pair. For example, assume that Alice and Bob hold two halves of an EPR pair, $|\Phi^+\rangle = \frac{1}{\sqrt{2}}\big(|0\rangle_A |0\rangle_B + |1\rangle_A |1\rangle_B\big)$. Alice picks QOTP keys (a_1, a_2) uniformly at random from $\{0,1\}^2$, and Bob similarly picks (b_1, b_2). To secure the entangled pair, Alice applies $X^{a_1} Z^{a_2}$ to her half, and Bob applies $X^{b_1} Z^{b_2}$ to his part. Since the encryption keys were picked uniformly at random and independently of each other, the density matrix of the new state is equal to the identity. So it seems like this procedure secures the entangled system in the sense that, without knowing the encryption keys, the encrypted system contains zero amount of entanglement. However, if Eve and Mallory steal a large amount of OTP-encrypted EPR pairs from Alice and Bob, they could guess the encryption keys for each pair, and their guess is expected to be *perfectly correct* $\frac{1}{16}$ of the times (on average). In such a situation, it still pays for Eve and Mallory to steal EPR pairs, as 6.25% of them are expected to be usable.

Alice and Bob can use the RBE scheme to encrypt each half of an EPR pair using independent random keys θ_a and θ_b. This way, if Eve and Mallory steal the encrypted qubits and try to decrypt them by guessing the keys, their guess is expected to be correct zero percent of the time. This may make stolen EPR pairs unusable, and in such a situation, the theft of EPR pairs becomes unprofitable.

4   WM and the Random Basis CNOT QKD Scheme

The BB84 protocol, and most of the QKD schemes that followed it, do not prevent an eavesdropper from gaining information on the key. Instead, these schemes enable Alice and Bob to detect eavesdropping attempts with high probability. After invoking the quantum part of the QKD scheme, Alice and Bob invoke classical *privacy amplification* (PA) and *data reconciliation* (DR) procedures. These procedures are required to reduce the amount of information held by a possibly undetected eavesdropper, and to correct possible errors in the key. PA and DR reduce the bandwidth and have time, communication, and computational costs.

It would be helpful if there was a way of reducing the ability of an eavesdropper to gain information from the outset, thereby impairing the motivation to attack the transmission and avoiding these expensive procedures. In this section, we suggest a new type of attack against two QKD protocols – BB84 and [DL04]. Our attack is based on weak measurements (WM), and it enables the attacker to control the probability in which Alice and Bob detect her. Our WM attack allows a tradeoff between the probability of being caught and the amount of information that can be gained. We introduce our random basis CNOT QKD scheme based on our RBE scheme. Our scheme, being resilient against such WM attacks, takes a step towards significantly impairing the motivation of a possible adversary.

Weak measurements consist of two stages. First, we weakly interact the subject qubit with an ancillary qubit using a two-qubit gate. Then, we (strongly) measure the ancillary qubit. The outcome of the measurement of the ancillary qubit is the outcome of the weak measurement of the subject qubit. This process enables imprecisely measuring quantum states, outsmarting the uncertainty principle. Explicitly, let $\varepsilon > 0$ and denote by W_ε the following two-qubit gate

$$W_\varepsilon = \sqrt{\varepsilon} \cdot i \cdot CNOT + \sqrt{1 - \varepsilon} \cdot I \otimes I$$

This gate can be used by Eve to gain information regarding the qubit transmitted from Alice to Bob, leaving but slight indications of her presence. How it works? It is known that qubits in the computational basis can be cloned using the $CNOT$ gate and an ancillary $|0\rangle$ qubit. If the qubit designated for cloning is in the computational basis, then performing a $CNOT$ with the ancillary qubit as the target qubit copies the control qubit to the target qubit without disturbing the control qubit. If the control qubit is not in the computational basis, the $CNOT$ gate does disturb it. The W_ε gate is a linear combination of the identity operation on two qubits and the $CNOT$ gate. The smaller ε is, the closer W_ε is to the identity operation. If a qubit $|\psi\rangle$ is in one of the four states $|0\rangle, |1\rangle, |+\rangle$ or $|-\rangle$, we can apply W_ε to $|\psi\rangle$ and an ancillary $|0\rangle$ qubit and then measure the ancilla. This way, if $|\psi\rangle$ is either $|0\rangle$ or $|1\rangle$ we can gain a small amount of information regarding $|\psi\rangle$ without disturbing it, and if $|\psi\rangle$ is either $|+\rangle$ or $|-\rangle$ then we (get no information but) only slightly disturb the state.

Attacking the BB84 scheme. A brief review of the BB84 scheme may be found in [BD19]. We now describe a WM-based attack on that scheme. Eve randomly picks an index j, prepares an ancilla $|0\rangle$ qubit, applies W_ε to the j'th qubit transmitted from Alice to Bob and the ancilla, and sends Alice's qubit to Bob. Eve measures the ancilla and obtains an outcome e. Next, Eve listens to the discussion of Alice and Bob over the public channel and finds whether Bob measured the j'th qubit in the right basis. If so, Eve keeps on listening to find whether the j'th qubit was used by Alice and Bob for eavesdrop-checking or not. If not, then the outcome of Bob's measurement on the j'th qubit is Bob's i'th key-bit, and Eve outputs (e, i). In [BD19], we analyze the described attack and show that it enables Eve to gain an $\frac{\varepsilon}{8}$ advantage in guessing a key-bit while reducing the risk of getting caught.

Attacking the DL04 Scheme. In [BD19], we review the DL04 scheme. Below, we describe a WM-based attack on that scheme. Eve randomly picks an index j. The j'th qubit is the objective qubit for the attack. Eve prepares an ancilla $|0\rangle$ qubit, applies W_ε to the j'th qubit transmitted from Bob to Alice and the ancilla, and sends Bob's qubit to Alice. Eve measures the ancilla and obtains an outcome e_1. Next, Eve listens to the measurement outcomes of Alice, announced over the public channel, and finds whether Alice measured the j'th qubit for eavesdropping check. If not, then Eve prepares another $|0\rangle$ ancilla. Denote by i the new location of the objective qubit among the qubits that were not measured. Eve applies W_ε to the i'th qubit transmitted from Alice to Bob and the ancilla and sends the qubit to Bob. Eve measures the (new) ancilla and obtains an outcome e_2, and outputs $(e_1 \oplus e_2, i)$. In [BD19], we analyze the described attack and show that, Eve can get an $\mathcal{O}(\varepsilon^2)$ advantage guessing Alice's while being caught with probability $\frac{\varepsilon}{4}$.

Our CNOT QKD Scheme. The random basis encryption scheme may also be used to construct a two-stage (random basis) QKD scheme, in which one participant sends to another information in the form of a string of classical bits. Suppose Alice holds a string of n classical bits $b = b_1 \ldots b_n \in \{0,1\}^n$, and wishes to send b privately to Bob. To this end, Alice and Bob may follow the following scheme.

The two-stage random basis CNOT-QKD scheme.

1. Bob randomly picks $b' = b'_1 \ldots b'_{2n}$ from $\{0,1\}^{2n}$.
2. For $1 \leq i \leq 2n$, Bob uses the random basis encryption scheme to generate an (independent) encryption $|\psi_{b'_i}\rangle$ of b'_i, and transmits $|\psi_{b'_i}\rangle$ to Alice.
3. Alice randomly picks n of the qubits received from Bob. She calls Bob over a public channel, announces the positions of the qubits she chose, and Bob reveals the keys used for encrypting these qubits.
4. Alice decrypts the n qubits she chose, using the keys obtained at the previous stage, and announces the outcomes to Bob, which in turn, checks the correctness of the outcomes to detect possible adversarial eavesdropping attempts. If the error rate is small enough, they proceed to the next stage.
5. Alice now uses the n qubits that she did not measure at the previous stage, and for $1 \leq i \leq n$, if $b_i = 1$ Alice applies a *NOT* gate to the i'th qubit; otherwise, she leaves it unchanged.
6. Alice sends the n qubits that were not measured by her back to Bob, who decrypts them and obtains a string, b''.
7. Denote by $\tilde{b} \in \{0,1\}^n$ the n-bit string obtained from b' after omitting the n bits chosen by Alice at stage 3. Bob computes $b'' \oplus \tilde{b}$ to obtain b.

The correctness and security of the scheme follow directly from the security of the RBE scheme. However, unlike the BB84 and DL04 schemes, our scheme is resilient against WM attacks. The WM attacks described above rely on the fact that in both the BB84 and DL04 schemes, in 50% of the cases, the objective qubit is in the standard basis, and in these cases, an adversary can copy and measure the qubit without disturbing it. The disturbance (and hence, the possibility of being caught) occurs only when the qubit is in a basis different from the standard basis. In the WM attacks, the adversary can control the probability of getting caught by the choice of ε. In our scheme, a qubit is in a non-standard basis 100% of the time, which may leave no room for this kind of adversarial attempts.

References

[AAUC18] Acar, A., Aksu, H., Uluagac, A.S., Conti, M.: A survey on homomorphic encryption schemes: theory and implementation. ACM Comput. Surve. (CSUR) **51**(4), 79 (2018)

[ABL64] Aharonov, Y., Bergmann, P.G., Lebowitz, J.L.: Time symmetry in the quantum process of measurement. Phys. Rev. **134**, B1410–B1416 (1964)

[AMTdW00] Ambainis, A., Mosca, M., Tapp, A., De Wolf, R.: Private quantum channels. In: 41st Annual Symposium on Foundations of Computer Science, FOCS 2000, pp. 547–553 (2000)

[BB84] Bennett, C.H., Brassard, G.: Quantum cryptography: public key distribution and coin tossing. In: Proceedings of the IEEE International Conference on Computers, Systems and Signal Processing. IEEE, New York (1984)

[BD19] Bitan, D., Dolev, S.: Randomly choose an angle from immense number of angles to rotate qubits, compute and reverse. Cryptology ePrint Archive, Report 2019/1023 (2019). https://eprint.iacr.org/2019/1023

[BJ15] Broadbent, A., Jeffery, S.: Quantum homomorphic encryption for circuits of low T-gate complexity. In: Gennaro, R., Robshaw, M. (eds.) CRYPTO 2015. LNCS, vol. 9216, pp. 609–629. Springer, Heidelberg (2015). https://doi.org/10.1007/978-3-662-48000-7_30

[BP12] Braunstein, S.L., Pirandola, S.: Side-channel-free quantum key distribution. Phys. Rev. Lett. **108**(13), 130502 (2012)

[Bra18] Brakerski, Z.: Quantum FHE (almost) as secure as classical. In: Shacham, H., Boldyreva, A. (eds.) CRYPTO 2018. LNCS, vol. 10993, pp. 67–95. Springer, Cham (2018). https://doi.org/10.1007/978-3-319-96878-0_3

[DL04] Deng, F.-G., Long, G.L.: Secure direct communication with a quantum one-time pad. Phys. Rev. A **69**(5) (2004)

[GLLP04] Gottesman, D., Lo, H.-K., Lutkenhaus, N., Preskill, J.: Security of quantum key distribution with imperfect devices. In: International Symposium on Information Theory, ISIT 2004, Proceedings, p. 136. IEEE (2004)

[Lia13] Liang, M.: Symmetric quantum fully homomorphic encryption with perfect security. Quant. Inf. Process. **12**(12), 3675–3687 (2013)

[Mah18] Mahadev, U.: Classical homomorphic encryption for quantum circuits. In: 59th IEEE Annual Symposium on Foundations of Computer Science, FOCS, pp. 332–338 (2018)

[OTF18] Ouyang, Y., Tan, S.-H., Fitzsimons, J.F.: Quantum homomorphic encryption from quantum codes. Phys. Rev. A **98**(4), 042334 (2018)

[RAD78] Rivest, R.L., Adleman, L., Dertouzos, M.L.: On data banks and privacy homomorphisms. Found. Secure Comput. **4**(11), 169–180 (1978)

[Wan05] Wang, X.-B.: Beating the photon-number-splitting attack in practical quantum cryptography. Phys. Rev. Lett. **94**(23) (2005)

[YPDF14] Li, Y., Pérez-Delgado, C.A., Fitzsimons, J.F.: Limitations on information-theoretically-secure quantum homomorphic encryption. Phys. Rev. A **90**(5), 050303 (2014)

Warped Input Gaussian Processes for Time Series Forecasting

Igor Vinokur[✉] and David Tolpin

Ben-Gurion University of the Negev, Beersheba, Israel
{vynokuri,tolpin}@post.bgu.ac.il

Abstract. Time series forecasting plays a vital role in system monitoring and novelty detection. However, commonly used forecasting methods are not suited for handling non-stationarity, while existing methods for forecasting in non-stationary time series are often complex to implement and involve expensive computations. We introduce a Gaussian process-based model for handling of non-stationarity. The warping is achieved non-parametrically, through imposing a prior on the relative change of distance between subsequent observation inputs. The model allows the use of general gradient optimization algorithms for training and incurs only a small computational overhead on training and prediction. The model finds its applications in forecasting in non-stationary time series with either gradually varying volatility, presence of change points, or a combination thereof. We implement the model in a probabilistic programming framework, evaluate on synthetic and real-world time series data comparing against both broadly used baselines and known state-of-the-art approaches and show that the model exhibits state-of-the-art forecasting performance at a lower implementation and computation cost, enabling efficient applications in diverse fields of system monitoring and novelty detection..

Keywords: Time series · Probabilistic programming · Non-stationarity · Gaussian processes

1 Introduction

Time series play a vital role in system monitoring and novelty detection in such diverse areas as computational health [11], computer security [1,10,12], industrial systems monitoring [2], finance [29], and others. Operation planning, automated control, and incident detection are just some of many applications of time series forecasting and analysis [5].

Gaussian processes [33] possess properties that make them the approach of choice in time series forecasting:

© Springer Nature Switzerland AG 2021
S. Dolev et al. (Eds.): CSCML 2021, LNCS 12716, pp. 205–220, 2021.
https://doi.org/10.1007/978-3-030-78086-9_16

- A Gaussian process works with as little or as much data as available.
- Non-uniformly sampled observations, missing observations, and observation noise are handled organically.
- Uncertainty of a future observation is predicted along with the mean.

In a basic setting though, a Gaussian process models a stationary time series with homoscedastic noise. When either the covariance between observations or the noise vary depending on observations inputs or outputs, predictions produced by a Gaussian process with a stationary kernel and constant noise variance will be either biased or overly uncertain, hence handling non-stationarity and heteroscedasticity is crucial in many applications. Non-stationarity often arises in financial time series, where market volatility, affecting forecasting uncertainty, changes with time [29,48]; heteroscedastic noise is common in vital signs monitoring of patients in intensive care units, where the noise depends on patient activity and medical interventions [11], both non-stationarity and heteroscedasticity are characteristic for time series of sensor readings in mobile robotics [22]. For forecasting, input-dependent uncertainty can be modelled through either non-stationarity or heteroscedasticity, or both. In this work we address modelling of input-dependent uncertainty through non-stationarity.

Various approaches have been proposed for handling non-stationarity using Gaussian processes. When a time series is piecewise stationary, change point detection is deemed an appropriate model, with a stationary homoscedastic Gaussian process modelling stretches between consequent change points [8,16, 35]. In cases where the covariance or noise change gradually and smoothly, it is common to introduce a non-parametric dependency of kernel and noise parameters on inputs [18,22,23,30,41,46], however, this makes structural modelling of time series, which constitutes an important advantage of Gaussian processes and facilitates introduction of prior knowledge in the model, more challenging.

Another popular way to handle both abrupt and gradual changes in time series is through mapping of the input space [6,7,14,26,27,37,42]. Covariance between observations depends on observations inputs as well as on kernel parameters, and non-stationarity can be modelled by smoothly modifying observation inputs (warping the input space). Several methods have been proposed to learn the input space transformation, and a number of other approaches can be viewed as employing input space warping for handling non-stationarity. However, many such approaches either meet difficulties in practical application, or require elaborated inference algorithms [6,13,36,43], which may impact the simplicity of use of Gaussian processes.

In this work we introduce a model for non-parametric warping of input space for Gaussian processes, suitable in particular for time series forecasting but also applicable to other domains. The model is easy to implement, imposes only a small computational overhead on training and prediction, and allows to use the whole arsenal of Gaussian process kernels to model time series structure using prior knowledge. We provide a reference implementation of the model and evaluate the model on a synthetic and real-world data, comparing forecasting performance with both baseline and state-of-the-art approaches and show that the model exhibits state-of-the-art forecasting performance at a lower implementation and computation cost.

This work brings the following contributions:

- A novel approach to handling non-stationarity in Gaussian processes.
- A Gaussian process model for forecasting in non-stationary time series.
- A reference implementation of the model within a probabilistic programming framework.

2 Preliminaries

A Gaussian Process is a collection of random variables, any finite number of which have (consistent) joint Gaussian distributions. A Gaussian process is fully specified by its mean function $m(x)$ and covariance, or kernel, function $k(x, x')$ and defines a distribution over functions. The mean function is often set to zero, $m(x) \equiv 0$. A Gaussian process defines a distribution over functions:

$$f \sim \mathcal{GP}(m(x), k(x, x')) \tag{1}$$

Any finite set of values of function f at inputs $\boldsymbol{x}$ follows the multivariate normal distribution $\mathcal{N}(\boldsymbol{\mu_x}, \Sigma_{\boldsymbol{x}})$ with mean $\boldsymbol{\mu_x} = m(\boldsymbol{x})$ and covariance matrix $\Sigma_{\boldsymbol{x}} = \{k(x_i, x_j)\}$.

Posterior inference in Gaussian processes can be performed analytically. Let $\boldsymbol{f}$ be the observations at inputs $\boldsymbol{x}$. Then the posterior distribution of values $\boldsymbol{f_*}$ at inputs $\boldsymbol{x_*}$ is

$$\boldsymbol{f_*}|\boldsymbol{f} \sim \mathcal{N}(\boldsymbol{\mu_{x_*}} + \Sigma_{\boldsymbol{xx_*}}^\top \Sigma_{\boldsymbol{x}}^{-1}(\boldsymbol{f} - \boldsymbol{\mu_x}), \Sigma_{\boldsymbol{x_*}} - \Sigma_{\boldsymbol{xx_*}}^\top \Sigma_{\boldsymbol{x}}^{-1} \Sigma_{\boldsymbol{xx_*}}) \tag{2}$$

where $\Sigma_{\boldsymbol{xx_*}}$ is the covariance matrix between $\boldsymbol{x}$ and $\boldsymbol{x_*}$.

Kernel functions normally have hyperparameters; we shall write $k(x, x'; \theta)$ to denote that the kernel function x has hyperparameter θ, possibly multidimensional, or omit the hyperparameters when they are clear from the context. Training a Gaussian process involves choosing θ based on the observations. For example, the Gaussian, or RBF, kernel has the form

$$\mathrm{RBF}(x, x'; l) = \exp\left(-\frac{(x - x')^2}{2l^2}\right) \tag{3}$$

and is parameterized by a single hyperparameter l.

A straightforward way to choose θ is to maximize log marginal likelihood L of observations $(\boldsymbol{x}, \boldsymbol{f})$:

$$L = \log p(\boldsymbol{f}|\boldsymbol{x}, \theta) = -\frac{1}{2}|\Sigma| - \frac{1}{2}(\boldsymbol{f} - \boldsymbol{\mu})^\top \Sigma^{-1}(\boldsymbol{f} - \boldsymbol{\mu}) - \frac{n}{2}\log(2\pi) \tag{4}$$

where n is the number of observations.

There is no closed form solution for maximizing L in general, however gradient-based optimization methods allow to obtain an approximate solution efficiently.

3   Warped Input Gaussian Process Model

A major advantage of Gaussian process regression in general, and for application to time series in particular, is the explicit inclusion of uncertainty in the model: both the mean and the variance are predicted at unobserved inputs. However, perhaps somewhat counterintuitively, the variance, given the kernel and the kernel's hyperparameters, does not depend on observed outputs. Indeed, the covariance matrix in Eq. (2) does not depend on $\boldsymbol{f}$.

One way to circumvent this limitation of Gaussian processes is to introduce non-stationarity into the kernel function, such that the covariance depends on both the distance between inputs, $\|x, x'\|$ and on inputs themselves. In some kernels, such as the dot product kernel $k(x, x') = x \cdot x'$, non-stationarity is fixed in the kernel design. In other kernels, non-stationarity comes through dependency of kernel hyperparameters on the inputs, and the dependency $\theta(x, x')$ itself can be learned from data [17,27,30]. Related to varying kernel hyperparameters with inputs is the idea of *warping* the input space [37]. A stationary kernel depends on both the distance between inputs and the hyperparameters. Consider, for example, the RBF kernel (3). Increasing hyperparameter l, customarily called the length scale, has the same effect on the covariance as decreasing the distance between x and x' by the same relative amount. Moving points away from each other will effectively decrease the length scale and covariance between the points. Warping of the input space has an intuitive interpretation for time series: the time runs faster in areas with high output volatility and slower when the output is stable.

A research problem addressed by different warping methods is how the warping is represented and what objective should be maximized to learn the optimal warping for a given problem instance. In what follows, we introduce warping of the input space of a one-dimensional Gaussian process by imposing a prior on the distances between adjacent inputs. We train the process by maximizing the combined log marginal likelihood of the observations under the prior and of the Gaussian process. The model is trivially extended to a multi-dimensional Gaussian process where only a single dimension is warped, such a in the case of a time series where there are multiple predictors but only the time needs to be warped to account for temporal non-stationarity.

3.1   Model

In a Gaussian process model for handling non-stationarity through displacement of observation inputs, the choice is of the form of the prior imposed on the inputs. One option is to impose a Gaussian process prior on the inputs. This is a rich prior allowing to model complex structured non-stationarity; deep Gaussian processes [13] is a realization of such prior. However, inference in the presence of such prior requires special techniques and is computationally expensive. On the other extreme is imposing an independent Gaussian prior on each input, which is related to the modelling of input uncertainty [15,28]. [28] show though that independent input noise may be reduced to independent output noise, and as such is not sufficiently expressive for modelling non-stationarity for forecasting. Here, we propose a prior that is just a single step away from an independent prior on each input, namely one which corresponds to a 3-diagonal striped covariance matrix $\Sigma = \{\sigma_{ij}\}$, such that $\sigma_{ij} = 0 \ \forall |i - j| > 1$, which is equivalent to imposing independent priors on *distances* between adjacent inputs. An intuition behind this prior is that the distance between adjacent locations increases, and the effective length scale decreases, in areas with high volatility, and vice versa in areas with low volatility. For convenience of inference, we formulate the prior in terms of relative change of distance between inputs. We exploit the structure of this prior to specify the model compactly, without having to manipulate the full covariance matrix of the prior.

Formally, let $\mathcal{GP}$ be a one-dimensional Gaussian process. Let also D be a distribution on $\mathcal{R}^+$. Then, given inputs $\boldsymbol{x}, x_{i+1} > x_i \forall i$, the generative model for outputs is

$$\tilde{x}_1 = x_1 \tag{5}$$
$$\lambda_i \sim D$$
$$\tilde{x}_i = \tilde{x}_{i-1} + \lambda_i(x_i - x_{i-1}) \text{ for } i > 1$$
$$\boldsymbol{f} \sim \mathcal{N}(\boldsymbol{\mu_{\tilde{x}}}, \Sigma_{\tilde{x}})$$

In words, inputs $\boldsymbol{x}$ are transformed (warped) into $\tilde{\boldsymbol{x}}$ by stretching or compressing distances between adjacent inputs x_{i-1} and x_i by relative amounts λ_i drawn from D. For brevity, we call the introduced model WGP in the rest of the paper. D serves as a prior belief on distances between adjacent inputs, relative to the original distances. Without loss of generality, the mean of D can be assumed to be 1, so that the mean of the prior belief is that no warping is applied.

3.2   Training

Training of a WGP model is performed by maximizing the log marginal likelihood L_{WGP}:

$$L_{WGP} = L + \sum_{i=2}^{n} \log p_D(\lambda_i) + C$$
$$= L + \sum_{i=2}^{n} \log p_D \left(\frac{\tilde{x}_i - \tilde{x}_{i-1}}{x_i - x_{i-1}} \right) + C \tag{6}$$

where L is the log marginal likelihood of the hyperparameters of the Gaussian Process (4) and C is a normalization constant that does not depend on either hyperparameters or observations and is not required for training. As with kernel hyperparameters, derivatives of L_{WGP} by both hyperparameters and transformed inputs $\tilde{\boldsymbol{x}}$ are readily obtainable analytically or through algorithmic differentiation [20].

3.3 Forecasting

After training, forecasting is virtually identical to that of a regular Gaussian process, with one exception: for prediction in a new location x_*, the warped image $\tilde{x}_*$ of the location must be obtained for substituting into (2). The possible options are:

- Choosing $\tilde{x}_*$ that maximizes L_{WGP} for $x \circ x_*$ and $f \circ f*$.
- Setting $\lambda_* = 1$ and, consequently, $\tilde{x}_* = \tilde{x}_n + x_* - x_n$.
- Setting $\lambda_* = \lambda_n$ and $\tilde{x}_* = \tilde{x}_n + (x_* - x_n)\frac{\tilde{x}_n - \tilde{x}_{n-1}}{x_n - x_{n-1}}$.

The first option is best aligned with log marginal likelihood maximization during training but computationally expensive. The last option expresses a smoothness assumption: the length scale is likely to be similar in adjacent inputs. We experimented with the three options and found that empirically on synthetic and real-world datasets predictive accuracy of the third option is virtually indistinguishable from the first one. In the empirical evaluation, we computed the warped location for forecasting as $\tilde{x}_n + \lambda_n(x_* - x_n)$.

3.4 Modelling Seasonality

Time series are often modelled by combining *trend* and *seasonality*, that is, similarity between nearby observations on one hand and observations at similar phases of a period on the other hand. In Gaussian processes, kernels based on the periodic kernel [26] are used to model seasonality. Warping of the input space would interfere with dependencies induced by the periodic kernel. Consider monitoring of vital sign time series in intensive care unit [9]: while volatility of the time series may evolve over time, and warping the time may be adequate for modelling non-stationarity, observations at the same *astronomical* time of the day tend to be similar.

A solution for warping the trend time but keeping the seasonality time unwarped is to include both original and warped dimension into the input space. This way, kernel features modelling the trend and thus affected by non-stationarity are made dependant on the warped time, and those modelling seasonality—on the original time. Generative model (7) extends (5) by combining x and $\tilde{x}$ on input to the Gaussian process:

$$\tilde{x}_1 = x_1 \tag{7}$$
$$\lambda_i \sim D$$
$$\tilde{x}_i = \tilde{x}_{i-1} + \lambda_i(x_i - x_{i-1}) \text{ for } i > 1$$
$$f \sim \mathcal{N}(\mu_{\tilde{x} \circ x}, \Sigma_{\tilde{x} \circ x})$$

Consider, for example, the following kernel, composed of locally periodic and trend terms:

$$k(x, x'; \theta) = c_1 \text{RBF}(x, x') \text{Periodic}(x, x') + c_2 \text{Matern}_{\frac{3}{2}}(x, x') \quad (8)$$

where

$$\text{RBF}(x, x'; l_1) = \exp\left(-\frac{(x - x')^2}{2l_1^2}\right)$$

$$\text{Periodic}(x, x'; p, l_2) = \exp\left(-\frac{2\sin^2\left(\frac{\pi|x-x'|}{p}\right)}{l_2^2}\right)$$

$$\text{Matern}_{\frac{3}{2}}(x, x'; l_3) = \left(1 + \frac{\sqrt{3}|x - x'|}{l_3}\right)\exp\left(-\frac{\sqrt{3}|x - x'|}{l_3}\right)$$

$$\theta = (c1, c_2, l_1, l_2, l_3, p)$$

In this kernel, the RBF and $\text{Matern}_{\frac{3}{2}}$ components reflect local dependencies between inputs and hence should be affected by input warping. The Periodic component, however, expresses dependencies between points at similar phases of different periods, with the period length p normally known upfront and staying fixed. Thus, in the presence of warping, the modified kernel $\tilde{k}(\cdot, \cdot)$ must receive both warped and original inputs and pass appropriate inputs to each of the components:

$$\tilde{k}((\tilde{x}, x), (\tilde{x}', x'); \theta) = \quad (9)$$
$$c_1 \text{RBF}(\tilde{x}, \tilde{x}') \text{Periodic}(x, x') + c_2 \text{Matern}_{\frac{3}{2}}(\tilde{x}, \tilde{x}')$$

3.5 Time and Space Complexity

By including the factors λ_i into the vector of parameters to optimize, we apparently make training and forecasting more expensive computationally. However, the overhead caused by learning the warping of the inputs is still dominated by the complexity of training and forecasting of a conventional Gaussian process and does not increase either time or space complexity.

Indeed, **time complexity** of Gaussian process forecasting is dominated by the time required to invert the covariance matrix [33, Sect. 5.3], which is $O(n^3)$ in general [33]. More efficient approaches are available but are limited in their applicability [4, 25, 47]. Changing the number of trainable parameters does not affect the size of the covariance matrix. To compute the gradient, every element of the covariance matrix Σ_x must be differentiated by the parameters. Reverse-mode algorithmic differentiation, used ubiquitously, including in our implementation, scales sublinearly with the number of input dimensions [20]. In addition, $\frac{\partial \Sigma_{\tilde{x}}}{\partial \lambda_i}$ is a sparse matrix, only $\sigma_{i-1,i}$ depends on λ_i and hence $\frac{\partial \sigma_{j,k}}{\partial \lambda_i} = 0$ unless $j = i - 1, k = i$. Hence, the time complexity of computing the gradient is still $O(n^2)$ and dominated by the complexity of matrix inversion.

The memory required for training is increased due to the need to store the derivatives of $\Sigma_{\tilde{x}}$ by each of λ_i, which apparently increases the memory requirement from $O(n^2)$ to $O(n^3)$. However, again, the sparsity of $\frac{\partial \Sigma_{\tilde{x}}}{\partial \lambda_i}$ makes it possible to store all derivatives in $O(n^2)$ space, keeping the **space complexity** at $O(n^2)$ as for the conventional Gaussian process. Our implementation leverages sparsity to preserve $O(n^2)$ space complexity.

4   Empirical Evaluation

The empirical evaluation relies on modelling and inference capabilities provided by differentiable probabilistic programming [19,20]. We implemented WGP using Infergo [44], a probabilistic programming facility, and GoGP [45], a library for probabilistic programming with Gaussian processes. The source code, data, and detailed results of empirical evaluations are available in public Git repository https://bitbucket.org/dtolpin/wigp. An implementation of LBFGS [24] provided by Gonum [3] was used for inferring hyperparameters. As a state-of-the-art algorithm for non-stationary Gaussian process regression, we used an implementation of deep Gaussian processes from https://github.com/SheffieldML/PyDeepGP. We also compared WGP with the following baselines not directly addressing non-stationarity:

- most likely heteroscedastic Gaussian process (MLHGP) [22], which uses heteroscedasticity to model input-dependent uncertainty and which was originally evaluated, albeight for general regression rather than out-of-sample forecasting, on some of the datasets used in this evaluation;
- autoregressive integrated moving average (ARIMA) [5], a broadly used model for time series forecasting, using Statsmodels [38];
- recurrent neural network (RNN) [21], a deep learning approach to time series, using PyTorch [31].

We evaluated the model on synthetic and real world data. Two kernels were employed in the empirical evaluation:

1. A Matern$_{\frac{5}{2}}$ kernel, used with both synthetic and real-world data.
2. A weighted sum of Matern$_{\frac{5}{2}}$ kernel and a periodic kernel, used with synthetic data.

The latter kernel was applied to synthetic data generated both with and without seasonal component, to evaluate influence of prior structural knowledge on one hand, and possible adverse effect of model misspecification (periodic component where there is no seasonality in the data) on the other hand. A parameterized homoscedastic noise term was added to the kernel in all evaluations. Vague lognormal priors were imposed on kernel hyperparameters.

Table 1. Negative log predictive density on synthetic datasets.

Dataset	No warping	Warped	+periodic	Deep GP	MLHGP	ARIMA	RNN
Trend	0.243 ± 0.046	$\mathbf{0.218 \pm 0.064}$	0.218 ± 0.062	0.611 ± 0.051	0.266 ± 0.061	0.297 ± 0.168	0.983 ± 0.081
+seasonal	-0.258 ± 0.027	-0.303 ± 0.028	$\mathbf{-0.358 \pm 0.031}$	0.123 ± 0.065	-0.293 ± 0.080	-0.293 ± 0.098	0.946 ± 0.092

4.1 Synthetic Datasets

Synthetic data was generated by sampling 100 instances from Gaussian processes with Matern(5/2) kernel, and with a sum of Matern(5/2) and a periodic kernel, to emulate seasonality in the data. To emulate non-stationarity, log distances between inputs were sampled from a Gaussian process with an RBF kernel and then unwarped into equidistant inputs. Samples from the periodic kernel component were drawn for equidistant inputs, in accordance with the assumption that the seasonality period is fixed.

Table 1 provides negative log predictive density (NLPD) for regular, unwarped, Gaussian process, warped Gaussian process with and without the periodic component, deep GP, MLHGP, ARIMA, and RNN on the synthetic dataset. Smaller NLPD means better forecasting accuracy. WGP outperforms both regular Gaussian process and state-of-the-art methods—deep GP and MLHGP—by a wide margin on the synthetic dataset. Using a kernel with periodic component on seasonal data improves forecasting, but accounting for non-stationarity through warping always results in much better accuracy.

Figure 1 shows a typical forecast by regular GP, WGP, and deep GP on a single instance from the synthetic dataset.

4.2 Real-World Datasets

We used three real-world datasets for the evaluation:

- Marathon—olympic marathon time records for years 1896–2016, obtained from https://www.kaggle.com/jayrav13/olympic-track-field-results.
- LIDAR—observations from light detection and ranging experiment [39].
- Motorcycle—data from a simulated motorcycle accident [40].

Table 2 compares performance of regular Gaussian process WGP, deep GP, MLHGP, ARIMA, and RNN on the data sets. WGP shows the best predictive performance on LIDAR and on Motorcycle data. On the Marathon time series, deep Gaussian process performs slightly better, apparently due to smoothness of the data. Figures 2 and 3 shows the forecasts by regular GP, WGP, and deep GP on the Marathon and Motorcycle datasets. Note that ARIMA and RNN are not directly applicable to the real-world datasets used in the evaluation because the datasets are irregularly sampled, that is, the time step at which measurements are obtained varies over time. However, the irregular sampling is *in favor* of the baselines, because in all of the datasets measurements are obtained with higher frequency in areas of faster change. Still, WGP outperforms these baselines by a wide margin.

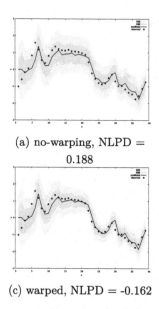

(a) no-warping, NLPD = 0.188

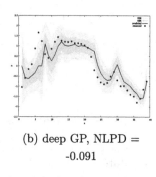

(b) deep GP, NLPD = -0.091

(c) warped, NLPD = -0.162

Fig. 1. Forecasting on an instance from the synthetic dataset.

5   Related Work

Work related to this research is concerned with Gaussian processes for time series forecasting, non-stationarity in Gaussian process regression, and warping of the input space for representing non-stationarity, in the order of narrowing focus. [34] gives an introduction to Gaussian processes for time series modelling, including handling of non-stationarity through change point detection.

Table 2. Negative log predictive density on real-world datasets.

Dataset	No warping	Warped	Deep GP	MLHGP	ARIMA	RNN
LIDAR	−0.310	**−0.345**	0.237	0.240	0.207	1.249
Marathon	0.157	−0.162	**−0.173**	−0.118	0.247	0.721
Motorcycle	0.588	**0.468**	1.191	1.254	2.203	2.405

Non-stationarity in Gaussian processes is attributed to either heteroscedasticity, that is, varying observation noise, or to non-stationarity of the covariance, or to both. Heteroscedasticity [22] is addressed by modelling dependency of noise on the input and, possibly, output [15]. [46] propose a GP regression model with a latent variable that serves as an additional unobserved covariate for the regression. This model allows for heteroscedasticity since it allows the function to have a changing partial derivative with respect to this unobserved

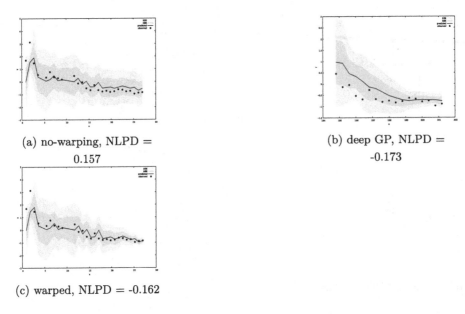

(a) no-warping, NLPD = 0.157

(b) deep GP, NLPD = -0.173

(c) warped, NLPD = -0.162

Fig. 2. Forecasting on Marathon dataset.

covariate. [18] presents an algorithm to estimate simultaneously both mean and variance of a non parametric regression problem. The key point is that we are able to estimate variance locally unlike standard Gaussian process regression or SVMs. [23] consider regression problems where there is noise on the output, and the variance of the noise depends on the inputs. They assume that the noise is a smooth function of the inputs, then it is natural to model the noise variance using a second Gaussian process, in addition to the Gaussian process governing the noise-free output value.

Non-stationarity of the covariance is represented through change points. [16] introduces a new sequential algorithm which focus on the problem of detecting and locating changepoints. Their algorithm focuses on the problem of making predictions even when such changes might be present. [35] combine Bayesian online change point detection with Gaussian processes to create a nonparametric time series model which can handle change points. The model can be used to locate change points in an online manner and, unlike other Bayesian online change point detection algorithms, is applicable when temporal correlations in a regime are expected. [8] propose an online change detection algorithm which can handle periodic time series. The algorithm uses a Gaussian process based nonparametric time series prediction model and monitors the difference between the predictions and actual observations within a statistical control chart framework to identify changes. Non-stationary kernel presented in [30] introduce a class of nonstationary covariance functions for Gaussian process regression. Nonstationary covariance functions allow the model to adapt to functions whose smoothness varies with the inputs. The class includes a nonstationary version of the Matérn

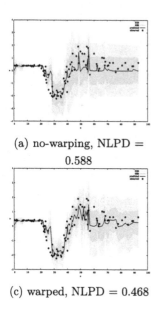

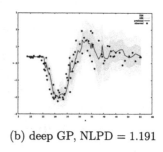

(a) no-warping, NLPD = 0.588

(b) deep GP, NLPD = 1.191

(c) warped, NLPD = 0.468

Fig. 3. Forecasting on Motorcycle dataset.

stationary covariance, in which the differentiability of the regression function is controlled by a parameter, freeing one from fixing the differentiability in advance. [32] demonstrate an approximation that uses the estimated mean of the local smoothness yields good results and allows one to employ efficient gradient-based optimization techniques for jointly learning the parameters of the latent and the observed processes.

The space transformations (warping) technique in [37] introduces a nonparametric approach to global estimation of the spatial covariance structure of a random function observed repeatedly with a finite number of sampling stations in the plane. First, they use non-metric multidimensional scaling to transform the problem into covariance structure, which is expressed in terms of spatial dispersions, is stationary and isotropic. Then they compute thin plate splines to provide smooth mappings of the geographic representation of the sampling stations into their multidimensional scaling representation. [7] propose manifold Gaussian processes, a novel supervised method that jointly learns a transformation of the data into a feature space and a GP regression from the feature space to observed space. The manifold GP is a full GP and allows to learn data representations, which are useful for the overall regression task. [27] introduces the novel method represented in two parts, first via a novel class of covariances (called WaMI-GP) that simultaneously generalizes kernels of "multiple index" and of tensorized warped GP models and second, by introducing derivative-based sampling criteria dedicated to the exploration of high variation regions. [13,14] proposes method based on deep Gaussian process where each layer is modelled as the output of a multivariate GP, whose inputs are governed by another GP. The resulting model is no longer a GP but, instead, can learn much more complex interactions between data. The method is built from two components. The first component is variational Gaussian process latent variable model concerned with propagating uncertainty in Gaussian process latent variable models. The second one is manifold relevance determination which considers a common latent space for multiple views. An adapted variational framework allows for strong model regularization, resulting in rich latent space representations to be learned.

Current work uses warping of the input space to represent non-stationarity. However, unlike previous research, only observation inputs are transformed rather than the whole input space, allowing for a simpler representation and more efficient inference. Due to the non-parametric nature of transformation employed in this work, the introduced model is applicable to time series both with change points and with smooth non-stationarities.

6 Conclusion

We introduced a Gaussian process-based model where non-stationarity is handled through non-parametric warping of observation inputs. In application to time series, the model facilitates forecasting of future observations with variances depending on outputs, as well as inputs, of past observations, while staying within the framework of 'standard' Gaussian process inference. When the data is known to possess periodic properties or non-local correlations, these correlations can be encoded in the model while still handling non-stationarity through warping. The introduced approach to input warping can be used with existing Gaussian process libraries and algorithms, and there is room for compromise between accuracy of modelling non-stationarity and computation time.

It still remains an open question to which extent a more expressive warping may improve the quality of forecasting. Combining the introduced model with change-point detection may be beneficial in cases of abrupt changes in process parameters. Still, in cases where simplicity of implementation and robustness in face of variability in time series are of high priority, the introduced model appears to provide a practical and efficient solution.

References

1. Abdullah, A.B., Pillai, T.R., Cai, L.Z.: Intrusion detection forecasting using time series for improving cyber defence. Int. J. Intell. Syst. Appl. Eng. **3**(1), 28–44 (2015). https://doi.org/10.18201/ijisae.83441
2. Almeshaiei, E., Soltan, H.: A methodology for electric power load forecasting. Alex. Eng. J. **50**(2), 137–144 (2011). https://doi.org/10.1016/j.aej.2011.01.015
3. Gonum: Gonum numerical packages (2017). http://gonum.org/
4. Banerjee, A., Dunson, D., Tokdar, S.: Efficient Gaussian process regression for large data sets (2011)
5. Box, G.E.P., Jenkins, G.: Time Series Analysis, Forecasting and Control. Holden-Day Inc., Alexandria (1990)

6. Bui, T.D., Hernández-Lobato, J.M., Hernández-Lobato, D., Li, Y., Turner, R.E.: Deep Gaussian processes for regression using approximate expectation propagation. In: Proceedings of the 33rd International Conference on International Conference on Machine Learning, ICML 2016, vol. 48, pp, 1472–1481. JMLR.org (2016)
7. Calandra, R., Peters, J., Rasmussen, C.E., Deisenroth, M.P.: Manifold Gaussian processes for regression. In: International Joint Conference on Neural Networks (IJCNN), pp. 3338–3345. IEEE (2016)
8. Chandola, V., Vatsavai, R.R.: A Gaussian process based online change detection algorithm for monitoring periodic time series. In: Proceedings of the 2011 SIAM International Conference on Data Mining, pp. 95–106 (2011). https://doi.org/10.1137/1.9781611972818.9
9. Clifton, L., Clifton, D.A., Pimentel, M.A.F., Watkinson, P.J., Tarassenko, L.: Gaussian process regression in vital-sign early warning systems. In: 2012 Annual International Conference of the IEEE Engineering in Medicine and Biology Society, pp. 6161–6164 (2012)
10. Colò, G.: Anomaly detection for cyber security: time series forecasting and deep learning. Int. J. Sci. Res. Math. Stat. Sci. **7**, 40–52 (2020). https://www.isroset.org/journal/IJSRMSS/full_paper_view.php?paper_id=1741
11. Colopy, G., Roberts, S., Clifton, D.: Gaussian processes for personalized interpretable volatility metrics in the step-down ward. IEEE J. Biomed. Health Inform. **23**(3), 949–959 (2019)
12. Condon, E., He, A., Cukier, M.: Analysis of computer security incident data using time series models. In: Proceedings of the 2008 19th International Symposium on Software Reliability Engineering, ISSRE 2008, pp. 77–86. IEEE Computer Society (2008). https://doi.org/10.1109/ISSRE.2008.39
13. Damianou, A.: Deep Gaussian processes and variational propagation of uncertainty (2018)
14. Damianou, A., Lawrence, N.: Deep Gaussian processes. In: Carvalho, C.M., Ravikumar, P. (eds.) Proceedings of the Sixteenth International Conference on Artificial Intelligence and Statistics. Proceedings of Machine Learning Research, 29 April–01 May 2013, vol. 31, pp. 207–215. PMLR, Scottsdale (2013)
15. Damianou, A.C., Titsias, M.K., Lawrence, N.D.: Variational inference for latent variables and uncertain inputs in Gaussian processes. J. Mach. Learn. Res. **17**(1), 1425–1486 (2016)
16. Garnett, R., Osborne, M.A., Roberts, S.J.: Sequential Bayesian prediction in the presence of changepoints. In: Proceedings of the 26th Annual International Conference on Machine Learning, ICML 2009, pp. 345–352. ACM, New York (2009)
17. Gibbs, M.: Bayesian Gaussian processes for classification and regression. Ph.D. thesis, University of Cambridge, Cambridge (1997)
18. Goldberg, P.W., Williams, C.K.I., Bishop, C.M.: Regression with input-dependent noise: a Gaussian process treatment. In: Jordan, M.I., Kearns, M.J., Solla, S.A. (eds.) Advances in Neural Information Processing Systems 10, pp. 493–499. MIT Press (1998)
19. Gordon, A.D., Henzinger, T.A., Nori, A.V., Rajamani, S.K.: Probabilistic programming. In: International Conference on Software Engineering (ICSE, FOSE Track) (2014)
20. Griewank, A., Walther, A.: Evaluating Derivatives: Principles and Techniques of Algorithmic Differentiation, vol. 2. Society for Industrial and Applied Mathematics, Philadelphia (2008)

21. Hewamalage, H., Bergmeir, C., Bandara, K.: Recurrent neural networks for time series forecasting: current status and future directions. Int. J. Forecast. **37**(1), 388–427 (2021). https://doi.org/10.1016/j.ijforecast.2020.06.008

22. Kersting, K., Plagemann, C., Pfaff, P., Burgard, W.: Most likely heteroscedastic Gaussian process regression. In: International Conference on Machine Learning (ICML), Corvallis, Oregon, USA (2007)

23. Le, Q.V., Smola, A.J., Canu, S.: Heteroscedastic Gaussian process regression. In: Proceedings of the 22Nd International Conference on Machine Learning, ICML 2005, pp. 489–496. ACM, New York (2005). https://doi.org/10.1145/1102351.1102413

24. Liu, D.C., Nocedal, J.: On the limited memory BFGS method for large scale optimization. Math. Program. **45**(1), 503–528 (1989)

25. Loper, J., Blei, D., Cunningham, J.P., Paninski, L.: General linear-time inference for gaussian processes on one dimension (2020)

26. MacKay, D.J.: Introduction to Gaussian processes. NATO ASI Ser. F Comput. Syst. Sci. **168**, 133–166 (1998)

27. Marmin, S., Ginsbourger, D., Baccou, J., Liandrat, J.: Warped Gaussian processes and derivative-based sequential designs for functions with heterogeneous variations. SIAM/ASA J. Uncertain. Quantif. **6**(3), 991–1018 (2018). https://doi.org/10.1137/17M1129179

28. Mchutchon, A., Rasmussen, C.E.: Gaussian process training with input noise. In: Shawe-Taylor, J., Zemel, R.S., Bartlett, P.L., Pereira, F., Weinberger, K.Q. (eds.) Advances in Neural Information Processing Systems 24, pp. 1341–1349. Curran Associates, Inc. (2011)

29. Nirwan, R.S., Bertschinger, N.: Applications of Gaussian process latent variable models in finance. In: Bi, Y., Bhatia, R., Kapoor, S. (eds.) IntelliSys 2019. AISC, vol. 1038, pp. 1209–1221. Springer, Cham (2020). https://doi.org/10.1007/978-3-030-29513-4_87

30. Paciorek, C.J., Schervish, M.J.: Nonstationary covariance functions for Gaussian process regression. In: Proceedings of the 16th International Conference on Neural Information Processing Systems, NIPS 2003, pp. 273–280. MIT Press, Cambridge (2003)

31. Paszke, A., et al.: Automatic differentiation in PyTorch. In: NIPS Autodiff Workshop (2017)

32. Plagemann, C., Kersting, K., Burgard, W.: Nonstationary Gaussian process regression using point estimates of local smoothness. In: Daelemans, W., Goethals, B., Morik, K. (eds.) ECML PKDD 2008. LNCS (LNAI), vol. 5212, pp. 204–219. Springer, Heidelberg (2008). https://doi.org/10.1007/978-3-540-87481-2_14

33. Rasmussen, C.E., Williams, C.K.I.: Gaussian Processes for Machine Learning (Adaptive Computation and Machine Learning). The MIT Press, Cambridge (2005)

34. Roberts, S., Osborne, M., Ebden, M., Reece, S., Gibson, N., Aigrain, S.: Gaussian processes for time-series modelling. Philos. Trans. R. Soc. A: Math. Phys. Eng. Sci. **371**(1984), 20110550 (2013)

35. Saatchi, Y., Turner, R., Rasmussen, C.: Gaussian process change point models. In: Proceedings of the 27th Annual International Conference on Machine Learning, ICML 2010, pp. 927–934 (2010)

36. Salimbeni, H., Deisenroth, M.: Doubly stochastic variational inference for deep Gaussian processes. In: Guyon, I., et al. (eds.) Advances in Neural Information Processing Systems 30, pp. 4588–4599. Curran Associates, Inc. (2017)

37. Sampson, P.D., Guttorp, P.: Nonparametric estimation of nonstationary spatial covariance structure. J. Am. Stat. Assoc. **87**(417), 108–119 (1992)
38. Seabold, S., Perktold, J.: Statsmodels: econometric and statistical modeling with python. In: 9th Python in Science Conference (2010)
39. Sigrist, M.: Air Monitoring by Spectroscopic Techniques. Chemical Analysis Series, vol. 197. Wiley, New York (1994)
40. Silverman, B.: Some aspects of the spline smoothing approach to non-parametric curve fitting. J. R. Stat. Soc. B **47**, 1–52 (1985)
41. Snelson, E., Ghahramani, Z.: Variable noise and dimensionality reduction for sparse Gaussian processes. In: Proceedings of the Twenty-Second Conference on Uncertainty in Artificial Intelligence, UAI 2006, pp. 461–468. AUAI Press, Arlington (2006)
42. Snoek, J., Swersky, K., Zemel, R., Adams, R.P.: Input warping for Bayesian optimization of non-stationary functions. In: Proceedings of the 31st International Conference on International Conference on Machine Learning, ICML 2014, vol. 32, pp. II-1674–II-1682. JMLR.org (2014)
43. Tobar, F., Bui, T.D., Turner, R.E.: Learning stationary time series using Gaussian processes with nonparametric kernels. In: Cortes, C., Lawrence, N.D., Lee, D.D., Sugiyama, M., Garnett, R. (eds.) Advances in Neural Information Processing Systems 28, pp. 3501–3509. Curran Associates, Inc. (2015)
44. Tolpin, D.: Deployable probabilistic programming. In: Proceedings of the 2019 ACM SIGPLAN International Symposium on New Ideas, New Paradigms, and Reflections on Programming and Software, pp. 1–16. Onward! 2019. ACM, New York (2019)
45. Tolpin, D.: GoGP, a library for probabilistic programming with Gaussian processes (2019). http://bitbucket.org/dtolpin/gogp
46. Wang, C., Neal, R.M.: Gaussian process regression with heteroscedastic or non-Gaussian residuals (2012)
47. Wang, K., Pleiss, G., Gardner, J., Tyree, S., Weinberger, K.Q., Wilson, A.G.: Exact Gaussian processes on a million data points. In: Wallach, H., Larochelle, H., Beygelzimer, A., d' Alché-Buc, F., Fox, E., Garnett, R. (eds.) Advances in Neural Information Processing Systems, vol. 32. Curran Associates, Inc. (2019). https://proceedings.neurips.cc/paper/2019/file/01ce84968c6969bdd5d51c5eeaa39 46a-Paper.pdf
48. Wu, Y., Hernández-Lobato, J.M., Ghahramani, Z.: Gaussian process volatility model. In: Ghahramani, Z., Welling, M., Cortes, C., Lawrence, N.D., Weinberger, K.Q. (eds.) Advances in Neural Information Processing Systems 27, pp. 1044–1052. Curran Associates, Inc. (2014)

History Binding Signature
(Extended Abstract)

Shlomi Dolev and Matan Liber[(✉)]

Department of Computer Science, Ben-Gurion University of the Negev,
Beersheba, Israel
dolev@cs.bgu.ac.il, matanli@post.bgu.ac.il

Abstract. Digital signatures are used to verify the authenticity of digital messages, that is, to know with a high level of certainty, that a digital message was created by a known sender and was not altered in any way. This is usually achieved by using asymmetric cryptography, where a secret key is used by the signer, and the corresponding public key is used by those who wish to verify the signed data. In many use-cases, such as blockchain, the history and order of the signed data, thus the signatures themselves, are important. In blockchains specifically, the threat is forks, where one can double-spend its crypto-currency if one succeeds to publish two valid transactions on two different branches of the chain. We introduce a single private/public key pair signature scheme using verifiable random function, that binds a signer to its signature history. The scheme enforces a single ordered signatures' history using a deterministic verifiable chain of signature functions that also reveals the secret key in case of misbehaviors.

Keywords: Digital signature · Verifiable secret sharing · Verifiable random function

1 Introduction

Digital signatures are used in a wide variety of applications, from signing software distributions to verification of online transactions. In some countries, digital signatures even have legal bindings [6]. One of the key features a digital signature scheme provides, is preventing the signer from claiming to not have signed a message, while a valid signature exists [10]. The fact that a signature provides non-repudiation, i.e., cannot be denied to have been created by the signer, indeed increases its value to the verifier. For example, in the case of digital currency, the paid end of a transaction does not want the payer to deny ever signing, moreover

This work is supported by the Lynne and William Frankel Center for Computer Science, and is partially supported by the Rita Altura Trust Chair in Computer Science, a grant from the Ministry of Science and Technology, Israel & the Japan Science and Technology Agency (JST), and the German Research Funding (DFG, Grant#8767581199).

S. Dolev et al. (Eds.): CSCML 2021, LNCS 12716, pp. 221–229, 2021.
https://doi.org/10.1007/978-3-030-78086-9_17

participating in the transaction. Yet in some cases, this is not enough, since the signer can claim for the privacy loss of its private key, or in other cases, the verifier may not know the signature was abused in other ways. Blockchain forks are a common example, where two versions of a transaction may be published in two different branches of the chain, leading to double-spending. The general case is where one signs a series of sequential data, where not only the origin of the data is to be verified, but also the index of the data in the series. Since there are many such cases where the signer can gain from successfully signing and publishing different data versions for the same index in the series, we introduce punishment for such behavior.

Previous Work. In our previous work [4] we discussed a possible weakness in permissioned blockchains. In such blockchains, a relatively small number of players participate in the BFT algorithm [9] used to determine the next transactions to be published on the blockchain. Those players are the permissioned players (referred by us as nodes), whose copies of the public ledger represent the current state of the blockchain. The permissionless players (referred by us as the private users, or simply users) both view and submit transactions only through the nodes.

It is known that Byzantine consensus can be achieved when up to one-third of the nodes are faulty. Since this boundary is well known, an adversary may try to overtake more nodes than the system can tolerate thus putting the blockchain in a harmful position. We discussed a worst-case scenario where the adversary may even completely destroy many of the nodes' copies of the blockchain and leading to the effective loss of the transactions history, resulting in the loss of the balances of the users.

We suggested a solution that enables a trustless restoration of the blockchain in such scenarios. The solution includes users saving their own transactions history (incoming transactions and payment transactions). The users present their history of transactions (which we assume are signed in an undeniable collective signature) to the nodes in case a ledger restoration is needed.

To prevent users from exploiting the lack of information the nodes hold after an attack, and presenting a partial payments history (resulting in the restoration of a balance greater than they previously had), our solution enforced two conditions:

- The transactions are indexed with an increasing order to prevent skipping payments in the presented history.
- Additional information D_i is published alongside every transaction T_i to prevent hiding a suffix of the payments history.

The first condition was enforced by making a transaction valid only if it included index $i + 1$ when the previously approved transaction of the user was of index i. The second condition was enforced by setting the additional information D_i to include a verifiable share of the user's secret key s, used for signing transactions. When a restoration process takes place, any user presenting a transactions history up to an index m is forced to present a corresponding proof P_m, also including a verifiable share of s.

The main idea is that any attempt to hide a suffix of the transactions history results in publishing enough shares of s that enable the secret's reconstruction.

Contribution. We leverage from the same incentive for honesty behavior to make a chain of signatures both sequential and unique. We use verifiable random functions to create a new signature function for every new index of data to sign. The way the signature functions are made makes them both secure and binding, thus, creating a unique sequence after the initial seed is determined.

Using this digital signature we achieve double-spending prevention, which, in comparison to some other schemes such as [1], has the following properties:

- No need for a "centralized" bank, where coin issuing and verification is performed against.
- Furthermore, there is no interactive per-coin "issuing" process at all, and once the initial public key is accepted and published, yet we do rely on the publicity of the transactions.
- This also means that there is no one secret, that if revealed, the whole system breaks (such as the RSA secret of the bank).
- Given correct propagation/publicity of the transactions (as is the case in blockchains, for example), framing can be done by all users.
- A user being framed for dishonesty also loses the privacy of its account completely.
- Although our scheme results in a more "aggressive" outcome for a double-spender, an honest user is not affected at all, and in an eco-system where this possible penalty is known to all participants, we can expect fewer attempts of undesired behavior.

The rest of the paper is structured as follows: In Sect. 2, we briefly describe verifiable secret sharing, verifiable secret public sharing (our variation of VSS that was introduced in our previous work), and verifiable random function, which are our building blocks for our new scheme. In Sect. 3, we introduce our signature scheme, defining the key generation, signature, and verification algorithms, as well as discuss the advantages of the scheme. In Sect. 4, we list the conditions a signature scheme must meet, including unforgeability, security, and correctness (both of the signature scheme itself and of the key-revealing property of our scheme). Finally, in Sect. 5, we conclude the scheme introduced in this paper and its possible usage, as well as shortly discuss possible future lines of work. Details and proofs are omitted from this extended abstract and can be found in [5].

2   Preliminaries

We describe the protocols of secret sharing and verifiable secret sharing that our scheme is based on, as well as our variation of those protocols. We also describe verifiable random functions, which we later incorporate with our previous work to get our result.

2.1 Verifiable Secret Sharing

Shamir [12] introduced Shamir's secret sharing (SSS) as a method to divide a secret into parts (shares), which are generated by the secret owner (dealer), and distributed amongst a group of participants (shareholders). In a (t, n)-threshold (t-out-of-n) secret sharing scheme, n participants, each holding a share, can reconstruct the secret only if t or more of them combine their shares. Moreover, any group of strictly less than t shareholders (including the individual shareholders themselves), learn nothing about the secret.

Verifiable secret sharing (VSS) was introduced by Chor, Goldwasser, Micali and Awerbuch [2], as a secret sharing scheme where every participant can verify that the secret shares are consistent. This is important for preventing a malicious dealer from sending shares to different participants, which do not define a (single) secret.

A (t, n)-threshold secret sharing scheme, consists of a probabilistic polynomial-time algorithm (PPTA) $Share_G$ and a polynomial-time algorithm (PTA) $Recover_G$, for some global parameters G. The global parameters G are clear from the context so we drop G from the notation. The algorithm $Share(s) \rightarrow \{(1, s_1), (2, s_2), \ldots, (n, s_n)\} = S(s)$ takes a secret key s as an input, and outputs n shares $(1, s_1), (2, s_2), \ldots, (j, s_j), \ldots, (n, s_n)$ where j is the share's index and s_j is the share's value. The algorithms $Recover((a_1, s_{a_1}), (a_2, s_{a_2}), \ldots, (a_t, s_{a_t})) \rightarrow s$ takes as an input any t valid distinct shares with share indices $\{a_1, \ldots, a_t\} \subseteq [1, n]$, and outputs the original secret s. Formally,

$$\forall s.Share(s) \rightarrow S(s) \implies \forall T' \in \{T \subseteq S(s) | \, |T| = t\}, Recover(T') = s$$

To make this scheme verifiable, we introduce two additional PTAs. $Commit(c) \rightarrow C$ that takes a random coefficient c generated by the user and outputs a commit C for it, and $Verify(s(i), C_1, \ldots, C_{t-1}, y) \rightarrow res \in \{ACCEPT, REJECT\}$ that takes a share, commits for both of the polynomial's coefficients, and the public key of the user, and ACCEPTs if the share is valid or REJECTs otherwise.

We use Feldman's [7] verifiable secret sharing scheme to define:

- $Share(s) = \{(i, Pol(i) \mod q) | 1 \leq i \leq n\}$ where $Pol(x) = s + \sum_{j=1}^{t-1} c_j x^j$ for some random coefficients $0 < c_j < q$.
- $Recover((a_1, s_{a_1}), \ldots, (a_t, s_{a_t})) = s$ using polynomial interpolation.
- $Commit(c) = g^c \mod p$
- $Verify((i, s_i), C_1, \ldots, C_{t-1}, y) = $ ACCEPT $\iff g^{s_i} \mod p =$
$$g^{s + \sum_{j=1}^{t-1} c_j i^j \mod q} \mod p = g^s \cdot \prod_{j=1}^{t-1} (g^{c_j})^{i^j} \mod p = y \cdot \prod_{j=1}^{t-1} C_j^{i^j} \mod p$$

Where p is prime, q is prime divisor of $(p-1)$, g is a generator of a subgroup of order q in the multiplicative group of $\mathbb{Z}_p^*$, such that $1 < g < p$ and the global parameters G are p, q and g.

2.2   Verifiable Secret Public Sharing

In the classic secret sharing scenario, one generates shares of the secret s and deals different shares to different parties. This implies that right away all of the shares are in the hands of the parties, where each party holds only some of the shares. Later, when reconstruction is required, the parties combine the shares and reveal the secret.

In [4] we introduced the concept of Verifiable Secret Public Sharing (VSPS), i.e., publicly publishing some (verifiable) shares of the secret. In our protocol for enforcing the reveal of the current balance of a crypto-currency wallet, one gradually publishes shares of the secret key s used for signing transactions. Restoring the balance of the wallet also involves publishing a share of s. The key idea is that for every transaction a new SSS polynomial is used, and an honest user does not surpass the threshold for any single SSS instance (thus not revealing s). On the other hand, a dishonest user is forced to publish enough shares corresponding to one of the polynomials, so that the threshold is met, and anyone can restore the signature key s, thus essentially stealing the crypto-currency wallet.

As mentioned in Sect. 1, we proposed adding additional information D_i for every transaction, containing some of the secret shares of s regarding a new polynomial $Pol_i(x)$ (as well as a share of $Pol_{i-1}(x)$). In addition, balance restoration involves publishing a proof $P_{m'}$, corresponding to the claimed latest m'^{th} transaction. This proof contains an additional share, thus, resulting in the surpassing of the threshold number of published shares needed for restoring s, corresponding to $Pol_{m'}(x)$ in case D_m was published in the past for some $m > m'$.

The suggested structure for such D_i, P_i is:

- $D_i = (s_i(1), s_{i-1}(2), C_{i1}, C_{i2}, C_{(i-1)1}, C_{(i-1)2})^1$
- $P_i = (s_i(v), C_{i1}, C_{i2})$, for a random $2 < v \leq q - 1$.

In this case, we used a $(3,3)$-threshold verifiable secret sharing scheme, meaning $Pol_i(x) = s + c_{i1}x + c_{i2}x^2$, for some random coefficients $0 < c_{i1}, c_{i2} < q$.

One may notice that if the published transactions history is $\bar{H}(m) = \{D_i | 1 \leq i \leq m\}$, then the total published shares are $\{s_i(1), s_i(2) | 1 \leq i \leq m-1\} \cup \{s_m(1)\}$. This means that publishing $P_{m'}$ results in exposing three shares of $Pol_{m'}(x)$ if $m' < m$. Yet this publication keeps the number of exposed shares corresponding $Pol_i(x)$ under the scheme's threshold for every $1 \leq i \leq m$, if $m' = m$, thus keeping s safe.

2.3   Verifiable Random Functions

Verifiable random functions were introduced by Micali, Rabin, and Vadhan [11]. Using a verifiable random function (VRF), given an input x, the holder of a

---

[1] $D_1 = (s_1(1), C_{11}, C_{12})$.

secret key s can compute the value of the pseudo-random function $\mathcal{F}_s(x)$ and a proof $\mathbf{p}_s(x)$.

Using the proof and the public key $y = g^s$ everyone can check that the value $x' = \mathcal{F}_s(x)$ was indeed computed correctly, yet this information cannot be used to find the secret key s.

An implementation by Dodis and Yampolskiy [3] defines:

- $\mathcal{F}_s(x) = e(g, g)^{\frac{1}{x+s}}$
- $\mathbf{p}_s(x) = g^{\frac{1}{x+s}}$

Where $e(\cdot, \cdot)$ is a bilinear map.

Verification of $\mathcal{F}_s(x)$ is done by checking that:

1. $e(g^x y, \mathbf{p}_s(x)) = e(g, g)^{(x+s) \cdot \frac{1}{x+s}} = e(g, g)$
2. $e(g, \mathbf{p}_s(x)) = e(g, g)^{1 \cdot \frac{1}{x+s}} = \mathcal{F}_s(x)$

One may notice that x itself is not used, only in an encrypted form in the verification process, namely, it is only a function of g^x and $\mathbf{p}_s(x)$.

3   History Binding Signature

We use a similar mathematical technique as the one used in VSPS, but for a different usage - enforcing a unique sequential signature history. In other words, we prevent publishing a signature for some message V_i', where a signature for a different message $V_i \neq V_i'$ was previously published.

Verifiable Secret Share as a Signature. To achieve our desired goal we use a variant of the additional information D_i from our VSPS as a digital signature for V_i. To define a digital signature scheme we define the *Key_Generation*, *Signing$_i$* and *Verify$_i$* algorithms.

- *Key_Generation*(1^n) randomly generates:
    1. A secret key $\text{SK} = (s, c_0) \in_R \mathbb{Z}_q^* \times \mathbb{Z}_q^*$.
    2. A corresponding public key $\text{PK} = (y, C_0) = (g^s, g^{c_0}) \in \langle g \rangle \times \langle g \rangle$.
- *Signing$_i$*(V_i) computes:
    1. The new random coefficient $c_i = \mathcal{F}_s(c_{i-1})$ and the corresponding new polynomial $Pol_i(x) = s + c_i x = s + \mathcal{F}_s(c_{i-1})x$.
    2. The proof for the new coefficient $\mathbf{p}_s(c_{i-1})$.
    3. The commitments for the previous and new coefficients $C_i = g^{c_i} = g^{\mathcal{F}_s(c_{i-1}) \bmod q}$, $C_{i-1} = g^{c_{i-1}}$.
    4. The corresponding share $s_i^{\mathcal{H}}(V_i) = Pol_i(\mathcal{H}(V_i)) \bmod q$.
    5. For a total signature $Sign_i(V_i) = (s_i^{\mathcal{H}}(V_i), C_i, C_{i-1}, \mathbf{p}_s(c_{i-1}))$.
- *Verify$_i$*$(V_i', (s_i', C_i', C_{i-1}', \mathbf{p}'))$ returns ACCEPT if and only if the following checks pass:
    1. $e(C_{i-1}' y, \mathbf{p}') \overset{?}{=} e(g, g)$.
    2. $g^{e(g, \mathbf{p}') \bmod q} \overset{?}{=} C_i'$.
    3. $g^{s_i'} \bmod p \overset{?}{=} y \cdot C_i'^{\mathcal{H}(V_i')} \bmod p$.
    where $\mathcal{H}(\cdot)$ is a publicly-known collision resistant hash function.

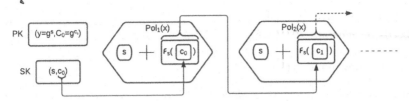

Fig. 1. By using the previous polynomial coefficient as the input for the verifiable random function, we get a unique chain of signature functions.

Advantages. One may look at D_i, as suggested in our previous scheme, as a digital signature on the current transaction. Although D_i did not incorporate the data of the actual transaction T_i, it could easily be changed to do so. This can be done by evaluating the polynomials $Pol_i(x)$ in $\mathcal{H}(T_i)$ instead of some constant number such as 1 or 2. This, however, is not sufficient, since every new polynomial is defined by random coefficients, that are up to the user to decide. To link a polynomial to a predefined index, one can use multiple pre-ordered secret/public key shares [8]. Using VRF, we replace the method for creating the next polynomial from a random one to a deterministic (and verifiable) one and achieve the enforcement of the order of the signatures with a single key pair. The fact that there can only be one valid $Pol_i(x)$ per participant (enforced using $\mathcal{F}_s(\cdot)$) replaces the verification the nodes perform (by keeping track of the user's transaction index) (Fig. 1).

4   Conditions for a Valid Signature

We list the conditions for a valid signature scheme:

(a) Unforgeability: for every $i \in \mathbb{N}$ and for every message V to sign, only the holder of SK can generate a valid signature $Sign_i(V)$.
(b) Security: by viewing $\bar{H}(m) = \{Sign_i(V_i)|1 \le i \le m\}$ for any $m \in \mathbb{N}$, one does not learn additional information on SK.
(c) Correctness (signing): $Verify_i(V_i, Sign_i(V_i))$=ACCEPT.
(d) Correctness (key-revealing): if one views $H(m) = \bar{H}(m) \cup Sign_{m'}(V'_{m'})$ for some $m' < m$ and $V'_{m'} \ne V_{m'}$ such that $Sign_{m'}(V_{m'}) \in \bar{H}(m)$, then it can recover the secret signing key and forge valid signatures.

4.1   Unforgeability

Lemma 1. *For every $i \in \mathbb{N}$ and for every message V to sign, only the holder of* SK *can generate a signature $Sign_i(V')$, such that $Verify_i(V', Sign_i(V))$=ACCEPT.*

Man-in-the-Middle Attack. In order to successfully execute such an attack, one needs to generate $s_i^{\mathcal{H}}(V_i')$ for some $V_i' \neq V_i$. Under the assumption that $\mathcal{H}$ is second-preimage resistant, such an attack requires evaluating the polynomial $Pol_i(x)$ in a new point $\mathcal{H}(V_i') \neq \mathcal{H}(V_i)$.

Lemma 2. *An adversary that views only $Pol_i(V)$ for some $i \in \mathbb{N}$, where $Pol_i(0) = s$, cannot evaluate $Pol_i(V')$, for any $V' \neq V$.*

4.2   Security

We analyze the security of the scheme by going over the published values, a signer, with the secret signing key SK, publishes.

Lemma 3. *For any $m \in \mathbb{N}$ and for every $V_1, \ldots, V_m$, a user that publishes $\bar{H}(m)$ does not reveal any information about the secret key SK.*

4.3   Correctness (Signing)

Lemma 4. *For every V_i and a valid signature $Sign_i(V_i)$, $Verify_i(V_i, Sign_i(V_i))$ can be computed and accepts.*

4.4   Correctness (Key-Revealing)

We built our scheme in order to prevent a signer from releasing two signatures, corresponding to the same signing index, for two different messages $V \neq V'$.

Lemma 5. *A dishonest user that publishes $H(m) = \bar{H}(m) \cup Sign_{m'}(V_{m'}')$ for some $m' < m$ and $V_{m'}' \neq V_{m'}$ such that $Sign_{m'}(V_{m'}) \in \bar{H}(m)$ enables the exposure of SK and the forgery of valid signatures on its behalf (Fig. 2).*

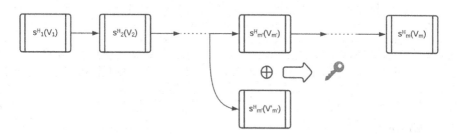

Fig. 2. Publishing a signature corresponding to a different value $V_{m'}'$ where a signature for V_m was already published results in the exposure of s.

5 Conclusion and Future Work

We introduced a digital signature scheme based on verifiable secret sharing, where a share of the secret acts as the signature. We used verifiable random functions to create a random, but verifiable, chain of signature functions, each corresponding to an index in the signing chain. This property enables the scheme to provide additional incentive for honesty behavior, by exposing the secret key of the signer if the chain of signatures is abusively forked. This scheme may be used in blockchains, to prevent forks in the public ledger and generally in scenarios where the reliability of the source and uniqueness of versions of data are required.

References

1. Chaum, D., Fiat, A., Naor, M.: Untraceable electronic cash. In: Goldwasser, S. (ed.) CRYPTO 1988. LNCS, vol. 403, pp. 319–327. Springer, New York (1990). https://doi.org/10.1007/0-387-34799-2_25
2. Chor, B., Goldwasser, S., Micali, S., Awerbuch, B.: Verifiable secret sharing and achieving simultaneity in the presence of faults. In: 26th Annual Symposium on Foundations of Computer Science (SFCS 1985), pp. 383–395. IEEE (1985)
3. Dodis, Y., Yampolskiy, A.: A verifiable random function with short proofs and keys. In: Vaudenay, S. (ed.) PKC 2005. LNCS, vol. 3386, pp. 416–431. Springer, Heidelberg (2005). https://doi.org/10.1007/978-3-540-30580-4_28
4. Dolev, S., Liber, M.: Toward self-stabilizing blockchain, reconstructing totally erased blockchain (preliminary version). In: Dolev, S., Kolesnikov, V., Lodha, S., Weiss, G. (eds.) CSCML 2020. LNCS, vol. 12161, pp. 175–192. Springer, Cham (2020). https://doi.org/10.1007/978-3-030-49785-9_12
5. Dolev, S., Liber, M.: History binding signature. Cryptology ePrint Archive, Report 2021/417 (2021). https://eprint.iacr.org/2021/417
6. Dumortier, J.: Regulation (EU) no 910/2014 on electronic identification and trust services for electronic transactions in the internal market (eIDAS regulation). In: EU Regulation of E-Commerce. Edward Elgar Publishing (2017)
7. Feldman, P.: A practical scheme for non-interactive verifiable secret sharing. In: 28th Annual Symposium on Foundations of Computer Science (SFCS 1987), pp. 427–438. IEEE (1987)
8. Kubiak, P., Kutyłowski, M.: Preventing a fork in a blockchain – david fighting goliath. In: Proceedings of the IEEE International Conference on Trust, Security and Privacy in Computing and Communications (TrustCom 2020). IEEE (2020)
9. Lamport, L., Shostak, R., Pease, M.: The Byzantine generals problem. ACM Trans. Program. Lang. Syst. 4, 382–401 (1982)
10. McCullagh, A., Caelli, W.: Non-repudiation in the digital environment (2000)
11. Micali, S., Rabin, M., Vadhan, S.: Verifiable random functions. In: 40th Annual Symposium on Foundations of Computer Science (Cat. No. 99CB37039), pp. 120–130. IEEE (1999)
12. Shamir, A.: How to share a secret. Commun. ACM **22**(11), 612–613 (1979)

Effective Enumeration of Infinitely Many Programs that Evade Formal Malware Analysis

Vasiliki Liagkou[1,5], Panagiotis E. Nastou[6], Paul Spirakis[2,3],
and Yannis C. Stamatiou[1,4(✉)]

[1] Computer Technology Institute and Press - "Diophantus",
University of Patras Campus, 26504 Patras, Greece
liagkou@cti.gr, stamatiu@ceid.upatras.gr
[2] Department of Computer Science, University of Liverpool, Liverpool, UK
P.Spirakis@liverpool.ac.uk
[3] Computer Engineering and Informatics Department,
University of Patras, 26504 Patras, Greece
[4] Department of Business Administration, University of Patras, 26504 Patras, Greece
[5] Department of Informatics and Telecommunications, University of Ioannina,
47100 Koatakioi Arta, Greece
[6] Department of Mathematics, Applied Mathematics and Mathematical Modeling
Laboratory, University of the Aegean, Samos, Greece
pnastou@aegean.gr

Abstract. The formal study of computer malware was initiated in the seminal work of Fred Cohen in the mid 80s who applied elements of the Theory of Computation in the investigation of the theoretical limits of using the Turing Machine formal model of computation in detecting viruses. Cohen gave a simple but realistic, *formal*, definition of the characteristic actions of a computer virus as a Turing Machine that replicates itself and then proved that constructing a Turing Machine that recognizes viruses (i.e. Turing Machines that act like viruses) is impossible, by reducing the Halting Problem, which is undecidable, to the problem of recognizing a computer virus. In this paper we complement Cohen's approach along similar lines, based on Recursion Function Theory and the Theory of Computation. More specifically, after providing a simple generalization of Cohen's definition of a computer virus, we show that the malware/non-malware classification problem is undecidable under this new definition. Moreover, we show that to any formal system, there correspond *infinitely many, effectively constructible*, programs for which no proof can be produced by the formal system that they are either *malware* or *non-malware* programs. In other words, given any formal system, one can provide a procedure that generates, systematically, an *infinite number* of impossible to classify, within the formal system, programs.

The work of the first, third and fourth coauthors was partially supported by the Cyber-Sec4Europe project, funded by the European Union under the H2020 Programme Grant Agreement No. 830929.

S. Dolev et al. (Eds.): CSCML 2021, LNCS 12716, pp. 230–243, 2021.
https://doi.org/10.1007/978-3-030-78086-9_18

Keywords: Malware detection · Information systems security · Impossibility results · Recursive function theory · Theory of computation · Turing machines

1   Introduction

In this paper we investigate the problem of *classifying programs* either as *malware* or *non-malware* based on formal proof systems and their deductive procedures. Our goal is to study the deductive power of formal systems with respect to the problem of producing proofs that can characterize *all* computer programs either as *malware* or *non-malware*. Our work is based on the foundations of computability and recursive function theory which, essentially, study problems with respect to their theoretical solvability based on the universal Turing Machine model of a mechanical and effective computation [12].

Formal proofs about the impossibility of detecting, in a *systematic* (i.e. algorithmic) and *general* way, malicious entities, such as Malware in our case, already exist for a long time for a very important category of such entities, the *computer viruses* or *malware* in general. A virus is a malicious program, a Turing Machine formally, that operates with an aim to *replicate in* other programs (Turing Machines), thus spreading the infection. The formal study of computer programs which act as viruses and their algorithmic detection was initiated in the seminal work of Fred Cohen in the mid 80s (see [1,2]). Cohen starts with a simple, *formal*, definition of the characteristic actions of a virus. Then, he proceeds to prove that constructing a Turing Machine that *recognizes* viruses (technically, other Turing Machines that act like viruses) is impossible.

More specifically, Cohen defined a virus to be a program, or Turing Machine, that simply copies itself to other programs, or more formally, injects its transition function into other Turing Machines' transition functions (see Definition 1 in Sect. 2) replicating, thus, itself indefinitely. Then, he proves that the problem of deciding whether a given Turing Machine halts on a given input, i.e. deciding the language L_u, can be reduced to the problem of deciding whether a given Turing Machine is a virus, i.e. $L_u = \{<M, w> w \in L(M)\}$ is *reduced* to $L_v = \{<M> \mid M$ is a virus $\}$. Since L_u is undecidable, so must be L_v and, thus, it is in principle impossible to detect a virus or else we could decide L_u which is, provably, undecidable.

Following Cohen's paradigm, we will propose a rather restricted (so as to be amenable to a theoretical analysis) but reasonable and precise definition of malware. To this end, we also deploy the *Turing Machine* theoretical model of an effective computational procedure to model malware programs. Thus, a malware is a program, i.e. a Turing Machine, that executes, at some point of its operation, *at least one* action from a specific set of actions that characterize malware behaviour (these actions are called *states* in the Turing Machine definition). We remark that simply *locating* the actions in a program through, e.g. syntactic analysis, is not considered to manifest malware behaviour, in the proposed model, only their *actual execution* is considered to manifest such a behaviour.

Admittedly this is a, rather, restricted malware model since malicious behaviour can be complex, e.g. in DoS (Denial of Service) attacks or may include several, combined, steps or Turing Machine states (e.g. Ransomware, which executes sequences of malicious actions to encrypt files on a victim computer). However, we chose this simpler model in order to be able to benefit from the rich and deep results of the Theory of Computation and, thus, provide some first results based on an established and mature computational model and scientific discipline. Consequently, our goal is to use this, rather restricted but theoretically manageable and plausible, malware model in order to obtain a malware undecidability result similar to Cohen's, i.e. there is no algorithm (Turing Machine) that can detect, systematically, all malware programs that fall under this definition.

The theoretical undecidability of the malware/non-malware classification problem means that, in general, no algorithm exists that can take as input a program and decide whether it is a malware or not. Our next step, in this paper, is to investigate whether it is possible to *effectively* demonstrate one of the programs which are not amenable to classification. In other word, our goal is to see whether it is possible to *construct* a specific Turing Machine whose classification status as either malware or non-malware cannot be decided. In the context of malware, such a Turing Machine would provide evidence of, potentially, hard or impossible to detect malware. To investigate this possibility, we turn to formal systems and, in particular, formal systems powerful enough to enable statements about Turing Machines, such as statements that state whether they halt, given a particular input, or not. We show that to each *consistent* formal system, there corresponds an *infinite, recursively enumerable* set of Turing Machines for which there exists no proof, in the formal system, that they are malware *and* there exists no proof, in the same formal system, that they are not malware. This is a humble example of a nature similar to Gödel's famous, groundstaking, result about the *incompleteness of consistent formal systems* in the sense that for each such system, there exist statements, of a self-referential nature, that neither themselves nor their negations can be proved within the formal system. In addition, these *self-referential* statements are, indeed, *true* (but not provable), *if and only if* the formal system is consistent (see, e.g., [9] for an accessible coverage of Gödel's Incompleteness Theorems and their consequences for formal systems). Inspired by this important consequence of the incompleteness result, we show that the infinitely many Turing Machines whose malware/non-malware status is impossible to prove within a consistent formal system, are actually *non-malware* but it is *impossible* to prove it within the formal system by the, purely, formal procedures allowed within the formal system. In other words, we show that these Turing Machines are *non-malware* if and only if the formal system used to classify them as malware or non-malware *is* consistent.

Before we proceed, we should remark that theoretical impossibility *does not* imply impossibility in practice since Turing Machines are idealistic models of computers with unlimited computational resources. However, the *finite* nature of real computers and programs renders all undecidable problems decidable by simple (but highly inefficient in practice) brute force approaches. Thus, theoretical impossibility results may not translate, readily, into impossibility results in practice.

2   Foundations of Computation Theory

We will assume a basic level of familiarity with the fundamental concepts and results of *Recursive Function Theory*. However, for completeness, we will briefly review Turing Machines and the basic results of the Theory of Computation and Recursive Function theory (see, e.g., [3–5]). In doing so, we extend in a straight-forward way the standard Turing Machine model in order to model malware activity. With respect to the presentation, we follow the exposition in the excellent, classic, book on the subject by Hoprcoft and Ullmann [5]. Before providing the details, we note that there are other, more practical, computational models that could be employed but since the theory we deploy concerns the classical Turing Machine model, we decided to base our results on this model for simplicity. We feel, however, that the results can be extended, with some effort, to other computational models which are more realistic.

Definition 1 (Turing Machine). *A Turing Machine is an octuple, defined as $M = (Q, Q_{Mal}, \Sigma, \Gamma, \delta, q_0, B, F)$, where Q is a finite set of states, Γ is a finite set called the tape alphabet, where Γ contains a special symbol B that represents a blank, Σ is a subset of $\Gamma - \{B\}$ called the input alphabet, δ is a partial function from $Q \times \Gamma$ to $Q \times \Gamma \times \{L, R\}$ called the transition function, $q_0 \in Q$ is a distinguished state called the start state, $F \subset Q$, $q_0 \notin F$, is a set of final states, and $Q_{Mal} \subset Q$, $Q_{Mal} \cap F = \emptyset$, is a distinguished set of states linked to Malware behaviour. We assume that transitions from states in Q_{Mal} do not change the Turing Machine's tape contents, i.e. they are purely interactions with the external environment of the Turing Machine and can affect only the environment.*

We should remark that there are three basic assumptions in the definition of a Turing Machine:

1. The tape can be extended on a need basis, i.e. each time the machine needs more cells (memory) on the tape, which is assumed to be automatically extended. In this respect, the memory of a Turing Machine is, virtually, unlimited.
2. Computational steps, i.e. reading of a tape cell, change of state and advance of the tape head, are executed instantaneously.
3. There are no operation errors during the operation of the machine.

Thus, the Turing Machine is an idealized formal model of a real computer that abstracts away from construction, technology, and speed details not relevant to the *fundamentals* of mechanical or algorithmic computation in order to allow us to explore the *theoretical* limits of machines in solving problems.

A Turing Machine can be viewed either as a *language* acceptor or a *function* calculator. The language *accepted* by a Turing Machine M, denoted by $L(M)$, is the set of strings in Σ^* that when given as input to M, lead it to an acceptance state, i.e. a state in set F. In recursive function theory, these languages are also called *recursively enumerable*. In general, without loss of generality, we can assume that the Turing Machine, when it accepts an input string, it also halts i.e. there are no next steps after an accepting state. In this paper, we will not use Turing Machines that compute functions. However, we should remark, that there is no loss of generality by confining ourselves to Turing Machines as language acceptors (see, for instance, the discussion in [5]). Thus, for our purposes, Turing Machines operate as language acceptors (see below).

In Fig. 1 we see the structure of a Turing Machine, according to Definition 1, and in Table 1 we see a sample Turing Machine computation.

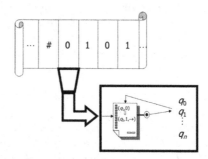

Fig. 1. The Turing Machine computation model

Table 1. Operation of a TM

	q_0	q_1	q_2	q_3	q_4	q_5	q_6
0	$(q_1,\#,\Delta)$	$(q_1,0,\Delta)$	$(q_3,1,A)$	$(q_3,0,A)$	$(q_4,0,A)$	$(q_5,\#,\Delta)$	-(stops)
1	$(q_5,\#,\Delta)$	$(q_2,1,\Delta)$	$(q_2,1,A)$	$(q_3,1,A)$	$(q_4,\#,A)$	$(q_5,\#,\Delta)$	-(stops)
#	-(hangs)		$(q_4,\#,A)$	$(q_0,\#,\Delta)$	$(q_6,0,\Delta)$	$(q_6,\#,\Delta)$	-(stops)

Thus, a Turing Machine is, essentially, a theoretical model of a real computer that allows us to study the *power* of mechanical, or *algorithmic*, computation and its *limits*. As a consequence, we can also deepen our understanding about which problems can be solved in principle by mechanical computations.

With respect to the evolution and termination of the computation of a Turing Machine, we have the following three possibilities:

1. The machine halts in a *final* state. Then the input string is accepted (i.e. it belongs to the language accepted by the Turing Machine). There is no loss of generality in assuming that the Turing Machine halts (i.e. it has no next move) whenever the input is accepted.

2. The machine halts in a *non-final* state. Then the input is rejected (i.e. it does not belong to the language accepted by the Turing Machine).
3. The machine does not halt at all, i.e. it runs for ever (it has entered an "infinite loop", as computer engineers say). Then certainly the input string is never accepted, i.e. it does not belong to the language accepted by the Turing Machine, but there is no way (as we will see below) to decide that the computation will not ever terminate (it is the famous, undecidable, *Halting problem*).

With respect to notation, for a given Turing Machine M we denote by $<M>$ its *code*, i.e. an encoding of its description elements as stated in Definition 1 using any fixed alphabet, usually the alphabet $\{0, 1\}$ (binary system) which since the inception of computing machines was the alphabet of choice due to its simplicity and efficiency in representing it with electronic states (two such states suffice). The details of such an encoding can be found in, e.g., [5] but it is really much like the representation of a program in machine code or assembly, which are the native programming languages executed by processing units in modern computers.

One of the major results of Turing's seminal work on computability was the existence of a *universal Turing Machine*, that is a Turing Machine that takes as input strings which represent other Turing Machines and their inputs and simulates (executes) them producing their results on their behalf. This is actually what a modern computer does, taking as an input program descriptions along with their inputs and producing their outputs by executing them (see, e.g., [5] for the encoding details).

The main outcome of Turing's pioneering work was, the formalization of what a mechanical procedure is using the Turing Machine model. This work gave rise to the computability theory, that classifies problems according to whether they can be solved, *in principle*, by mechanical procedures or Turing Machines. One of the major results of Alan Turing was the proof that there exist problems that Turing Machines cannot solve. For instance, the first problem (theoretically, there are infinitely many such problems) what was shown to be unsolvable by Turing Machines (i.e. algorithms) is the, so called, *Halting problem*:

The Halting Problem
Input: A string $x = <M, w>$ which is actually the encoding (description) of a Turing Machine $<M>$ and its input w.
Output: If the input Turing Machine M halts on w, the output is True. Otherwise, the output is False.

The language corresponding to the Halting problem is $L_u = \{<M, w> \mid w \in L(M)\}$. In other words, the language L_u contains all possible *Turing Machine-input* pair encodings $<M, w>$ such that w is accepted by M. This is why L_u is also called *universal language* since the problem of deciding whether a given Turing Machine M accepts a given input w is equivalent to deciding whether $<M, w> \in L_u$. Note that L_u is accepted by a Turing Machine, the universal one denoted by M_u, that simulates M on w. If $w \in L(M)$, then the universal

Turing Machine will accept the pair $<M, w>$. However, if the opposite holds true, then we only know that M_u will not terminate in a final state. What we do not know, however, is whether M_u will ever stop (in a non-final state of course). Languages for which Turing Machines exist that accept them and always halt are called *recursive* or decidable.

The language L_u was the first language proved to be non-recursive or undecidable by Turing, meaning that it is impossible to decide algorithmically whether a given program halts or not on a given input. The proof relies on a clever Cantor diagonalisation, self-reference based, argument over all possible Turing Machines. Such arguments lie in the heart of mathematical logic as well as theoretical computer science for proving *impossibility* or *non-existence* arguments.

3 Recursive Function Theory

We should stress the fact that Computation and Recursive Function Theory are *computation model independent*. The model of computation can be any reasonable model such as the Turing Machine (see Sect. 2), the λ-terms (in the λ-Calculus), μ-recursive functions as well as, in a more practical perspective, any real computer programming language. It is not hard to prove that the theoretical computational power of all these computation models is the same, if we disregard efficiency issues.

In addition, the computational procedures or *programs* that can be written in any computation formalism or real programming language can be enumerated *effectively* (see, e.g., [5]). This means that there exists an algorithm which can list all the programs in a sequence, so that *all* programs appear at some point of the enumeration procedure.

A well known result from computability theory states that the number of arguments in a function (program) is not important, for computability theory, since arguments can, always, be embedded, in an easy way, in the program itself, reducing, in this way, the number of arguments. This is formalized in the following result, which is a simplified form of *Kleene's S_{mn}-theorem* (see [6]), for functions of two arguments.

Theorem 1 (Kleene's S_{mn}-theorem - simplified form, for two-input functions). *Let $g(x, y)$ be a partial recursive function. Then, there is a total recursive function σ of one variable, such that $f_{\sigma(x)}(y) = g(x, y)$ for all x and y. That is, if $\sigma(x)$ is considered as the integer (code) representing some TM M_x then $f_{M_x}^{(1)} = g(x, y)$.*

In addition, we will need another result from recursive function theory, namely the *Recursion Theorem* which states that every total recursive function that maps Turing Machine indices on Turing Machine indices has a fixed point. We state, formally, this theorem below as Theorem 2.

In what follows, we fix a formal system $\mathcal{F}$, e.g. such as *Peano's Arithmetic*, which can, directly, express statements about natural numbers. Our departure point is the, already, known fact that, given such a formal system, which we will denote by $\mathcal{F}$, we can, effectively, construct a Turing Machine M with the following property: there is no proof in $\mathcal{F}$ that M, when started on a specific input, halts and there is no proof that M, when started on a specific input, does not halt. The proof can be found in [5], Chap. 8. We will denote by $M_{\mathcal{F}}$ such a Turing Machine (there may be several with this property) whose halting status in unprovable in $\mathcal{F}$.

Naturally, the details of $M_{\mathcal{F}}$ depend on $\mathcal{F}$ but the important issue, in our context, is that M_F can be constructed *effectively*, i.e. algorithmically, but, not necessarily, *efficiently* i.e. fast. In what follows we will present the proof of this fact since some of its elements are crucial in the presentation of our ideas. We, first, state the *Recursion Theorem* along with its proof (based on [5]) since it is crucial for our arguments that follow in Sect. 4.

Theorem 2. *For any total recursive function σ there exists an x_0 such that $f_{x_0}(x) = f_{\sigma(x_0)}(x)$, for all x.*

Proof. For each integer i, we construct a Turing Machine that when given input x it computes $f_i(i)$. Then, it simulates the $f_i(i)$th Turing Machine on x. Let $g(i)$ be the index of the constructed Turing Machine. By definition

$$f_{g(i)}(x) = f_{f_i(i)}(x) \tag{1}$$

for all x. Note that $g(i)$ is a total function, i.e. defined everywhere (and, thus, the TM that computes it always halts) even if $f_i(i)$ is not defined, i.e. f_i does not halt with input i. Let j be an index of the function σg, i.e. j is the index (encoding) of a TM that, when given i as input, computes $g(i)$ and then applies the function σ on $g(i)$. Thus, for $x_0 = g(j)$ the following is derived, after some manipulations:

$$f_{x_0}(x) = f_{\sigma(x_0)}(x) \tag{2}$$

for all x. Therefore, x_0 is a fixed point of the mapping σ, i.e. the TMs x_0 and $\sigma(x_0)$ compute the same function. $\square$

Based on the Recursion Theorem, the following, central to our approach in Sect. 4, is proved in [5]:

Theorem 3. *Given a formal system $\mathcal{F}$, we can construct a Turing Machine for which no proof exists in $\mathcal{F}$ that it either halts or does not halt.*

Proof. Given $\mathcal{F}$, we construct a Turing Machine M that computes a function, $g(i, j)$, of two inputs as follows:

$$g(i,j) = \begin{cases} 1, & \text{if there is a proof in } \mathcal{F} \text{ that } f_i(j) \text{ is not defined} \\ & \text{(i.e. does not halt) or, in other words if there is} \\ & \text{a proof that the } i\text{th Turing Machine does not} \\ & \text{halt, given input } j \\ \\ \text{undefined, otherwise} \end{cases} \tag{3}$$

The Turing Machine M works by enumerating proofs in $\mathcal{F}$. When a proof is found that states that the ith Turing Machine *does not* halt when given input j. Moreover, M can be designed so that if $g(i,j) = 1$ then it halts, otherwise it does not halt.

From the S_{mn}-theorem (see Theorem 1), there exists a total function σ on Turing Machine indices (i.e. codes) such that

$$f_{\sigma(i)}(j) = g(i,j). \tag{4}$$

From Recursion Theorem, we can construct an integer i_0 such that

$$f_{i_0}(j) = f_{\sigma(i_0)}(j) = g(i_0, j). \tag{5}$$

However, $g(i_0, j) = 1$ and it is, thus, defined if and only if there exists a proof in $\mathcal{F}$ that states that $f_{i_0}(j)$ is not defined. Therefore, if $\mathcal{F}$ is consistent, i.e. there can be no proofs of, both, a statement and its negation, then no proof can exist in $\mathcal{F}$ that the i_0-th Turing Machine either halts or does not halt when given a specific input j.   □

The corollary that follows below is not stated in [5] but it is not hard to prove, as a consequence of Theorem 3.

Corollary 1. *For the i_0-th Turing machine, denoted by M_{i_0}, constructed in the proof of Theorem 3 and computing the function $f_{i_0}(j)$, it holds that it does not halt for every input j if and only if $\mathcal{F}$ is consistent.*

Proof. Let assume that $\mathcal{F}$ is consistent and that M_{i_0} halts for some input j_0. Then, since $\mathcal{F}$ is consistent, there can be no proof in $\mathcal{F}$ that M_{i_0} does not halt, for *any* input j. According, then, to the definition of $g(i,j)$ in Eq. 3, Theorem 3, $g(i_0, j_0)$ is undefined. But since (see Theorem 3) $f_{i_0}(j_0) = g(i_0, j_0)$, we arrive at a contradiction since the left-hand side is defined and the right-hand side is undefined.

Let us assume, now, that M_{i_0} does not halt, for every input j. It follows, since $f_{i_0}(j) = g(i_0, j)$, that $g(i_0, j)$ is undefined for every j. Thus, there is no proof in $\mathcal{F}$ that M_{i_0} does not halt on input j, for any j. Accordingly, $\mathcal{F}$ must be consistent since, otherwise, it can produce a proof, in $\mathcal{F}$, that M_{i_0} does not halt on input j, as everything follows from an inconsistent formal system, leading to a contradiction, since $g(i_0, j)$ is undefined for all j.   □

4   Theoretical Impossibility of a Complete formal Malware/Non-malware Program Classification

In this section we give a simple formal definition of malware following and extending Cohen's ideas.

Definition 2 (*Formal Malware definition*). *A Malware is a Turing Machine that when executed will demonstrate a specific, recognizable, behavior particular* *to malware, as manifested by the* execution *(not simply the existence in the Turing Machine's description) of a specific sequence of actions, e.g. it will publish secret information about an entity, it will download information illegally etc., actions reflected by reaching, during its operation, states in the set Q_{Mal} (see Definition 1).*

This is similar to Cohen's definition of a virus since it characterizes Malware programs according to their *visible* or *manifested* behavior. We stress the word *"execution"* in order to preclude situations where a false alarm is raised for a "Malware" program which, merely, contains the states in Q_{Mal} without *ever* invoking them. Such programs, actually, operate normally without ever executing any actions characteristic to malware behavior.

The Malware Detection Problem

Input: A description of a Turing Machine (program).

Output: If the input Turing Machine behaves like Malware according to Definition 2 output True. Otherwise, output False.

More formally, if L_b denotes the language consisting of Turing Machine encodings $<M>$ which are Malware, according to Definition 2, then we want to decide L_b, i.e. to design a Turing Machine that, given $<M>$, decides whether $<M>$ belongs in L_b or not according to this definition.

Let Q_{Mal} be the set of actions which, when *executed*, manifest Malware behavior (see Definition 2). We will show that L_u is recursive in L_b. This implies that if we had a decision procedure for L_b then this procedure could also be used for deciding L_u which is undecidable. Thus, no decision procedure exists for L_b too.

In [7] the following was proved in a similar context:

Theorem 4 (Theoretical impossibility of detecting Malware). *The language L_b is undecidable.*

Proof. Our proof is similar to Cohen's proof about the impossibility of detecting viruses. Note that Rice's Theorem (see, e.g., [5,10]) is not applicable here since the Malware Detection Problem we consider does not involve properties of the *languages* accepted by Turing Machines but, rather, properties of their operation (i.e. reachability of a subset of their states, the *malware bahaviour* related states). In [7] we consider a detection problem for Turing Machines modeling Panopticons that involves properties of the *accepted languages* not their operation specifics.

Let $<M, w>$, with $M = (Q, Q_{\text{Mal}}, \Sigma, \Gamma, \delta, q_0, B, F)$ and $Q_{\text{Mal}} \subset Q$ the Malware states (see Definition 1), be an instance of the Halting problem. We will show how we can decide whether $<M, w>$ belongs in L_u or not using a hypothetical decision procedure for L_b, i.e. L_u is recursive in L_b.

Given $<M, w>$ we design a Turing Machine M^{u-b} that modifies the δ function of M so as when a final state is reached (i.e. a state in the set F of M) a transition takes place into a state in Q_{Mal} (any state suits our purpose). That is, M is a new Turing Machine M' containing the actions of M followed by actions (any of them) described by the states in Q_{Mal}. Now, M' is given as input the input w of M operating as described above.

Let us assume that there exists a Turing Machine M_b that decides L_b. Then we can give it M' as input. Suppose that M_b answers that $M' \in L_b$. Since Q_{Mal} was finally reached, this implies that M halted on w since M' initially simulated M on w. Then we are certain that M halts on w.

Assume, now, that M_b decides that M' is not Malware. Then a state in Q_{Mal} was never entered, which implies that no halting state is reached by M on w since Q_{Mal} in M' is reached only from halting states of M, which is simulated by M'. Thus, M does not halt on w.

It, thus, appears that M' is Malware if and only if M halts on w and, thus, we have shown that L_u is recursive in L_b. There is a catch, however, that invalidates this reasoning: if M *itself* can exhibit the Q_{Mal} linked Malware behavior in the first place. Then Malware behavior can be manifested, if states in Q_{Mal} are ever executed, without ever M reaching a final state that would trigger M' to enter a state in Q_{Mal}, by construction.

A solution to this issue is to *remove* Q_{Mal} from M, giving this new version to M^{u-b} to produce M'. Thus, we now have the equivalence M' is Malware if and only if M halts on w, completing the proof (see, also, [1]).

More formally, let $Q_{\mathrm{Mal}} = \{q_{\mathrm{Mal}_1}, q_{\mathrm{Mal}_2}, \ldots, q_{\mathrm{Mal}_l}\}$, $l = |Q_{\mathrm{Mal}}|$ be the set of Malware states. We create a new set of "harmless" or "no operation" states $P' = \{q'_1, q'_2, \ldots, q'_l\}$ where q_{Mal_i} corresponds to q'_i and vice versa. Then, we replace the states in Q_{Mal} by the corresponding states in P' everywhere in the definition elements of M and we also do the corresponding state changes in the δ function that defines the Turing Machine's state transitions. This transformation removes from a potential Malware the actions that *if* executed would manifest Malware behavior. We stress, again, the fact the mere *existence* of Malware actions in the definition of a Turing Machine is not considered Malware *action* if they are not *activated* at some point of its operation. With this last transformation, M' is a Malware if and only if M halts on w and, thus, L_u is recursive in L_b. $\square$

We now turn to, actually, constructing a particular Turing Machine, which cannot be classified as malware or non-malware, by purely formal procedures, within any consistent formal system $\mathcal{F}$.

Theorem 5 (Malware/non-malware classification resistant programs).
Let $\mathcal{F}$ be a consistent formal system. Then we can construct a Turing Machine for which there is no proof in $\mathcal{F}$ that it behaves as malware and no proof that it does not behave as malware.

Proof. Let $M_{\mathcal{F}}$ be a Turing Machine whose halting status on any given input j cannot be proven in $\mathcal{F}$ in either direction, i.e. "halts" or "does not halt". Such a Turing Machine exists by Theorem 3. This is a Turing Machine like M_{i_0} which was constructed in Theorem 3. A new Turing Machine, $M_{M_{\mathcal{F}}} = (Q, Q_{\mathrm{Mal}}, \Sigma, \Gamma, \delta, q_0, B, F)$, of one input and $Q_{\mathrm{Mal}} \subset Q$, the malware states, is constructed. It is composed of three parts. The first part is a *non-malware* Turing Machine, denoted by M_n the second part is $M_{\mathcal{F}}$, and the third part is a *malware* Turing Machine, denoted by M_w.

The construction details of these Turing Machines are not hard but they are tedious, thus we will provide a rather high level description. The construction of $M_{\mathcal{F}}$, given $\mathcal{F}$, has already been described in Sect. 2. With respect to M_n, it can be any Turing Machine that, simply, does not use any states in Q_{Mal}, e.g. a Turing Machine that computes a simple arithmetic function (see, for instance, Table 1 in Sect. 2). Finally, M_w executes, during its operation, at least one state in Q_{Mal}. It is not hard to construct such a Turing Machine, e.g. it can be a Turing Machine that simply, after leaving the start state, executes one more step involving a state in Q_{Mal} before halting (i.e. reaching a final state).

With respect to its operation, $M_{M_{\mathcal{F}}}$, first, activates the first part, i.e. M_n, which may ignore the input, say j, and operates with its non-Malware behavior, i.e. it *never* visits states in Q_{Mal} during its operation. Then $M_{\mathcal{F}}$ is activated with input j. By construction, $M_{\mathcal{F}}$ does not use states in Q_{Mal}. Finally, the third part, i.e. M_w, starts operating, exhibiting Malware behaviour by visiting at least one state in Q_{Mal} during its operation.

Suppose, now, that a proof exists in $\mathcal{F}$ that $M_{M_{\mathcal{F}}}$ *is* a malware, i.e. it exhibits malware behaviour when activated by reaching states in Q_{Mal}. By the construction of $M_{M_{\mathcal{F}}}$, the only way to demonstrate malware behaviour is to activate its third part, i.e. M_w. This, in turn, can occur only if the second part, i.e. $M_{\mathcal{F}}$, halted on input j. Thus, the same proof that $M_{M_{\mathcal{F}}}$ *is* a malware, also, serves as a proof that $M_{\mathcal{F}}$ *halts* on input j.

Suppose, on the other hand, that a proof exists in $\mathcal{F}$ that $M_{M_{\mathcal{F}}}$ *is not* a malware, i.e. it *does not* exhibit malware behaviour when activated. By the construction of $M_{M_{\mathcal{F}}}$, this can happen only if M_w is never activated during the operation of $M_{M_{\mathcal{F}}}$. In turn, this can happen only if $M_{\mathcal{F}}$ *does not halt* on input j. Thus, again, the same proof that $M_{M_{\mathcal{F}}}$ *is not* a malware, also, serves as a proof that $M_{\mathcal{F}}$ *does not halt* on input j.   □

From Theorem 5 we have the following corollary:

Corollary 2. *To any formal system $\mathcal{F}$, there correspond infinitely many, effectively constructible, Turing Machines for which there is no proof in $\mathcal{F}$ that they behave as malware and no proof that they do not behave so.*

Proof. Observe that in the *effective*, i.e. algorithmic, construction process described in Theorem 5, M_n can be *any of countably many infinite* Turing Machines that simply avoid the states in Q_{Mal} and M_w can be *any of countably many infinite Turing Machines* that do not visit states in Q_{Mal} during their operation. $M_{\mathcal{F}}$ stays fixed (it depends only on $\mathcal{F}$).   □

Finally, in the same spirit with Corollary 1 for the Turing Machine M_{i_0} or $M_{\mathcal{F}}$ in the notation of Theorem 5, we prove the following about $M_{M_{\mathcal{F}}}$ which, actually, shows that $M_{M_{\mathcal{F}}}$, as well as the infinitely many Turing Machines built around $M_{M_{\mathcal{F}}}$ in Corollary 2, is *not* a malware but no proof exists within the formal system $\mathcal{F}$ *if* it is consistent.

Corollary 3. *For the Turing Machine $M_{M_{\mathcal{F}}}$ it holds that it is not a malware if and only if $\mathcal{F}$ is consistent.*

Proof. The proof is, essentially, the same as the proof of Corollary 1, since $M_{M_{\mathcal{F}}}$ contains $M_{\mathcal{F}}$ and it is constructed in such a way so that it is not a malware if and only if $M_{\mathcal{F}}$ does not halt on any particular input j.   □

5   Discussion and Directions for Further Research

In this paper we addressed the problem of whether it is possible to have a *complete*, in principle, classification of *all* programs either as *malware* or *non-malware*, using suitable formal systems and their proof mechanisms.

Based on Cohen's pioneering work, we showed that no algorithm exists that can classify all programs, in general, as malware or non-malware, i.e. the malware identification problem is undecidable. Further to this result, we showed that to each *formal system*, there corresponds a recursively enumerable, infinite, set of Turing Machines, which depends on the formal system's details, for which *no proof* exists, in the formal system, with respect to whether they are malware or non-malware.

From Theorem 5 and Corollary 2 it follows that, in principle, there is an infinity of programs for which a formal classification with respect to whether they are malware or not is impossible, no matter what formal system is used for this classification. This implies, that an infinite set of programs exists, which can be potentially malware, which cannot be proved to be so in any formal system we may ever devise, no matter how expressive and powerful is. Moreover, the members of this set are recursively enumerable, i.e. there exists a systematic way to list them. This, however, may provide the means to malicious parties to generate programs whose malware status is undecidable, by purely formal means. It only suffices to know the details of the formal system deployed to classify programs as malware and non-malware.

Additionally, as Corollary 3 shows, all these programs are, actually, *non-malware* programs, unless the formal system, $\mathcal{F}$, deployed for the classification task is *inconsistent*. Thus, although these programs are harmless, it is, nevertheless, impossible to classify them as such within any *consistent* formal system $\mathcal{F}$. Furthermore, if $\mathcal{F}$ *is*, actually, inconsistent, it *is* possible that the Turing Machines constructed in Corollary 2, *are* malware programs, in view of Corollaries 1 and 3. Thus, the agonizing dilemma may be the following: *Is the program under scrutiny really, a non-malware program, as guaranteed by Corollary 3 or is it true that the formal system deployed to classify the programs, as malware or non-malware inconsistent, in which case the guarantee of Corollary 3 is not valid?* We should stress the fact the proving that a given formal system $\mathcal{F}$ is consistent is a notoriously difficult problem. There exist examples of formal systems proposed in the past (e.g. *ML*, proposed by Quine in [8]) that were, later, proved (perhaps unexpectedly) to be inconsistent (*ML* was proved inconsistent by Rosser) as well as formal systems extensively used today in mathematics, whose consistency status is, *still*, unknown, such as Zermelo-Fraenkel's set theory with the axiom of choice.

As a next step, the status of the *Malware Detection Problem* can be pursued under other plausible definitions of malware behaviour either targeting, for instance, the behavior (i.e. *sequences* of specific computational steps) or, even, the *languages* that malicious malware Turing Machines may accept (this approach is pursued in [7]). We believe that the investigation of the decidability status of any *entity* recognition problem (such as malware), can be, considerably, benefitted from a formal definition of the entities' characteristic behavior using a computational formalism, such as Turing Machines. Thus, the rich results of computability and computational complexity theory can lead to the derivation of interesting findings with respect to the fundamental difficulty of detecting such entities. Hopefully, our work is one step towards this direction.

We close our paper with the abstract of Ken Thomson's excellent Turing Award lecture (see [11]) that summarizes so succinctly our conclusions, i.e. that no automated solution can be relied on for a *complete* characterization of all programs as malware or non-malware: *To what extent should one trust a statement that a program is free of Trojan horses? Perhaps it is more important to trust the people who wrote the software.*

Acknowledgements. We would like to thank the anonymous reviewers for their constructive and inspiring comments.

References

1. Cohen, F.: Computer Viruses. Ph.D. thesis, University of Southern California (1985)
2. Cohen, F.: Computer viruses: theory and experiments. Comput. Secur. **6**(1), 22–35 (1987)
3. Davis, M.: The Universal Computer: The Road from Leibniz to Turing, 3rd edn. CRC Press, Boca Raton (2018)
4. Evans, D.: Introduction to Computing: Explorations in Language, Logic, and Machines. CreateSpace Independent Publishing Platform, Scotts Valley (2011)
5. Hopcroft, J., Ullman, J.D.: Introduction to Automata Theory, Languages, and Computation. Addison-Wesley Series in Computer Science (1979)
6. Kleene, S.K.: On notation for ordinal numbers. J. Symb. Log. **3**, 150–155 (1938)
7. Liagkou, V., Nastou, P.E., Spirakis, P., Stamatiou, Y.C.: On the theoretical impossibility of Panopticon Detection (2021, Submitted)
8. Quine, W.V.: Mahematical Logic. Harvard University Press, Cambridge (1940)
9. Raattkainen, P.: On the philosophical relevance of Gödel's incompleteness theorems. Revue internationale de philosophie **234**(4), 513–534 (2005)
10. Rice, H.G.: Classes of recursively enumerable sets and their decision problems. Trans. Am. Math. Soc. **74**, 358–366 (1953)
11. Thompson, K.: Reflections on trusting trust. Commun. ACM **27**(8), 761–763 (1984). https://doi.org/10.1145/358198.358210
12. Turing, A.M.: On computable numbers, with an application to the entscheidungsproblem. Proc. Lond. Math. Soc. Lond. **2**, 230–265 (1936/1937)

DNS-Morph: UDP-Based Bootstrapping Protocol for Tor

Rami Ailabouni[1(✉)], Orr Dunkelman[1], and Sara Bitan[2]

[1] University of Haifa, Haifa, Israel
railaboun@staff.haifa.ac.il, orrd@cs.haifa.ac.il
[2] Technion, Haifa, Israel
sarab@cs.technion.ac.il

Abstract. Tor is a popular system for anonymous communication and censorship circumvention on the web, this puts Tor as a target for attacks by organizations and governmental bodies whose goal is to hinder users' ability to connect to it. These attacks include deep packet inspection (DPI) to classify Tor traffic as well as legitimate Tor client impersonation (active probing) to expose Tor bridges. As a response to Tor-blocking attempts, the Tor community has developed *Pluggable Transports (PTs)*, tools that transform the appearance of Tor's traffic flow.

In this paper we introduce a new approach aiming to enhance the PT's resistance against active probing attacks, as well as white-listing censorship by partitioning the handshake of the PT from its encrypted communication. Thus, allowing mixing different PTs, e.g., ScrambleSuit for the handshake and FTE for the traffic itself. We claim that this separation reduces the possibility of marking Tor related communications. To illustrate our claim, we introduce DNS-Morph: a new method of transforming the *handshake* data of a PT by imitating a sequence of DNS queries and responses. Using DNS-Morph, the Tor client acts as a DNS client which sends DNS queries to the Tor bridge, and receives DNS responses from it. We implemented and successfully tested DNS-Morph using one of the PTs (ScrambleSuit), and verified its capabilities.

Keywords: Tor · UDP · DNS · Bootstrapping · Bridge · Pluggable Transport · Censorship · Circumvention

1 Introduction

Censoring countries continuously try to block their citizens' connections to Tor, these attempts began with simple methods like blacklisting Tor's website [35] so users would not be able to reach it and download the Tor client software [33], and got more sophisticated to include actively downloading the Tor nodes (also called relays) list from the Tor *Directory Servers* and blacklisting them, deploying DPI to search for Tor communication characteristics (e.g., Tor's TLS handshake cipher suite [46]), as well as active probing (impersonating a Tor client and connecting to suspicious servers to check whether they run a Tor relay) [1,15,41].

© Springer Nature Switzerland AG 2021
S. Dolev et al. (Eds.): CSCML 2021, LNCS 12716, pp. 244–265, 2021.
https://doi.org/10.1007/978-3-030-78086-9_19

The Tor community, on the other side, develops methods to bypass these blocking attempts, mainly Tor *Bridges*[1] and *Pluggable Transports (PTs)*.

Pluggable Transports (PTs) [34] are a generic framework for the development and the deployment of censorship circumvention techniques. Their main goal is to obfuscate the connection between a Tor client and a bridge serving as a Tor entry guard, so it looks benign. The PT consists of two parts as seen in Fig. 1, one is installed on the Tor client side, and the other is installed on the bridge's side. The PT exposes a SOCKS proxy [26] to the Tor client application, and obfuscates or otherwise transforms the traffic, before forwarding it to the bridge. On the bridge's side, the PT Server side exposes a reverse proxy that accepts connections from PT clients and decodes the obfuscation/transformation applied to the traffic, before forwarding it to the actual bridge application. Data transformation/obfuscation and the reverse operations are done by the *Transport Modules/Obfuscation Protocols* used by the PT.

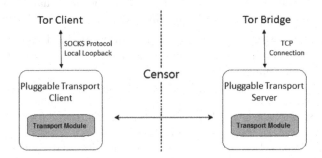

Fig. 1. Pluggable transports design

As of Sep. 2017,[2] the available and deployed obfuscation protocols in the Tor Browser are: obfs3 [22], obfs4 [23], ScrambleSuit [47], FTE [40], and meek [17]. These obfuscation protocols can be divided into two groups:

1. Random stream protocols (obfs3, obfs4, and ScrambleSuit). These protocols' communication is shaped as streams of random bytes that cannot be associated with any known protocol. These protocols have two phases: a handshake phase in which the two participating parties securely exchange keys and/or tickets, and a communication phase, consisting of exchange of encrypted messages using the established keys.
2. Structured stream protocols (FTE and meek), which try to mimic known white-listed protocols such as HTTP.

---

[1] Bridge: a relay which is unlisted in the public directory servers lists. The information needed to connect to a bridge is obtained out-of-Tor (e.g., via BridgeDB [32], an Email, or in person).

[2] Since Sep. 2017, some changes were introduced to Tor: ScrambleSuit is no longer supported and was replaced by obfs4.

Censoring countries with active probing capability can expose bridges communicating using obfs3. In addition, random stream protocols are of the "look-like-nothing" protocols, which means that they can be identified and blocked by a censor using a white-listing strategy, as their fingerprint (including their handshake) does not fit any known protocol (see for example our experiments with DPI tools in Sect. 10.3).

On the other hand, structured stream protocols that mimic widely used protocols, are resistant to white-listing based blocking. However, they do not protect against active probing [11,18].

Our goal is to improve random stream protocols by using the advantages of structured stream protocols, while maintaining their protection against active probing. We believe that the separation of these protocols to a handshake and communication phase, and encapsulation of their handshake in packets of a known, widely used, white-listed protocol, will strengthen their ability to avoid censorship and detection by DPIs.

DNS was chosen as a protocol to encapsulate the handshake and meet the conditions discussed before for the following reasons:

1. It is one of the most critical protocols of the Internet [25]. Blocking or greatly interfering with this protocol for any reason will induce unacceptable costs on the censoring countries.
2. DNS queries can be automatically relayed from one DNS server to another, until they reach their final destination (recursive DNS queries). This allows relaying data between several DNS servers as an additional layer of protection against connections' tracking and blocking.
3. DNS is a UDP-based protocol. UDP is connection-less and the efforts required to perform DPI of UDP traffic are significantly higher compared to TCP traffic.

1.1   Our Contribution

DNS-Morph is implemented as an obfuscation layer for random stream protocols. This layer encapsulates the protocol handshake in DNS queries and responses in a way that avoids protocol abnormalities.[3]

We focus on the handshake phase in this paper because it is the phase DPI tools and active probes target when searching for Tor traffic and bridges.

In order to show the advantages of DNS-Morph, we implemented it in Python and integrated it into Tor's Obfsproxy code [24]. As Obfsproxy works only with TCP, and our DNS-Morph works with UDP, we added UDP support to Obfsproxy.

We tested our design with the ScrambleSuit protocol[4] in a censoring environment. Success rates, connection timing, and bandwidth are provided in the experiments Section (Sect. 10).

Our source code is available online [6].

---

[3] Encapsulating the two phases of a protocol into DNS packets will cause high DNS traffic, which can raise suspicion of DNS tunneling.

[4] Similar design should also work for obfs4.

2   Related Work

Protocol Obfuscation: Five obfuscation protocols are deployed and available to use with Tor as PTs:

1. Obfs3 [22]: builds an additional layer of encryption over Tor's TLS connection in order to hide its unique characteristics. An un-authenticated customized Diffie-Hellman handshake [31] is used to exchange encryption keys. As a result, this protocol is susceptible to active probing attacks.
2. ScrambleSuit [47]: protects against active probing attacks by using out-of-band exchanged secrets and session tickets for authentication. ScrambleSuit is also capable of changing its network fingerprint (packet length distribution, inter-arrival times, etc.). This protocol is the predecessor of obfs4 and is subject to white-listing based censoring.
3. Obfs4 [23]: has the same features as ScrambleSuit, but utilizes the *Elligator* technique [38] for public key obfuscation, and the *ntor* protocol [13] for one-way authentication. This results in a faster protocol than ScrambleSuit and the addition of bridge authentication. This protocol can also be blocked by white-listing based censoring.
4. Meek [17]: uses a technique called *Domain Fronting* [4] to relay the Tor traffic to a Tor bridge through third-party servers (i.e., content delivery networks (CDNs) like Amazon CloudFront and Microsoft Azure).
5. Format-Transforming Encryption (FTE) [40]: transforms Tor traffic to arbitrary standard protocols' formats using their language descriptions.

Some other PTs are also available but are not integrated in the Tor Browser. These PTs can be found online [12].

DNS Tunneling: is the act of communicating data of any content inside DNS queries and responses. Three components are used in DNS Tunneling:

1. Client which sends data in DNS queries and acts like a DNS client.
2. Server which tunnels the client data and sends back DNS responses like a DNS server. This server usually has a registered domain name.
3. Encapsulation mechanism of data into DNS queries and responses, and a corresponding decapsulation mechanism for extracting this data from the DNS queries and responses.

Some of the available DNS tunneling tools are Dnscat [9], Dns2tcp [8], and iodine [14].

3   Threat Model

Our threat model consists of a *nation-state censor* that desires to block users from connecting to Tor. This censor might use DPI to examine session packets and active probing to check whether suspected servers are Tor bridges or servers. This censor might also be moving towards a white-listing strategy and start blocking access to applications for personal use like Skype [30] or What-sApp [36]. However, we assume that the censor may not be willing to block fundamental services like HTTP, DNS, IMAP, and FTP, as this can break legitimate communications, thus inducing high economical costs and causing unbearable collateral damage.

We believe this threat model is realistic as recent reports suggest that some censoring countries are continuously tightening their Internet control and taking a comprehensive approach to block all outgoing virtual private networks (VPNs) traffic [5].

We also assume that the censor does not perform DNS poisoning. This attack is discussed in Sect. 11.1 (Future Works).

4 Obfsproxy Design

Obfsproxy [24] is an open source software written using Python, and is used by Tor. This software implements the PT design mentioned before, in addition to the obfuscation protocols obfs3 and ScrambleSuit.

Due to the fact that our DNS-Morph is integrated into Obfsproxy, we first describe the Obfsproxy design, and then (in Sect. 5) the modifications done to support DNS-Morph.

Figure 2 (without the red dashed parts) shows the Obfsproxy high level design. Each side, the client and the server, consists of two entities: a Tor client and an Obfsproxy client on the client side, and an Obfsproxy server and a Tor bridge on the bridge side.

Obfsproxy components have two main layers: a networking layer, responsible for connections' establishment, and an obfuscation layer, responsible for the Tor handshake and the data obfuscation.

The connection between the Tor client and the Tor bridge is composed of three components:

1. An "Upstream" connection between the Tor client and the Obfsproxy client on the client side.
2. A "Downstream" connection between the Obfsproxy client and the Obfsproxy server.
3. An "Upstream" connection between the Obfsproxy server and the Tor bridge on the bridge side.

The chronological operation flow of a Tor client and a Tor bridge is as follows:

1. Client side: launches an Obfsproxy client, which starts a TCP SOCKS listener on its upstream connection.
   Bridge side: launches Tor bridge and the Obfsproxy server. The Obfsproxy server starts a TCP listener on its downstream connection. The Tor bridge starts a TCP listener on its upstream connection.
2. Client side: when the Tor client is launched by the user, it connects to the SOCKS TCP listener of the Obfsproxy client on its side. Then, the Obfsproxy client initiates a TCP connection to the Obfsproxy server on the bridge side (downstream connection).

3. Bridge side: when the Obfsproxy server receives the downstream connection request from the Obfsproxy client, it starts its obfuscation layer.
4. Client side: when the downstream TCP connection is established, the client side initiates its obfuscation layer which commences the handshake between the Obfsproxy client and server.
5. If the protocol handshake fails then Obfsproxy modules on both sides close their downstream connection and return to Step 1. If the handshake succeeds, the Obfsproxy server connects to the Tor bridge (upstream connection) and starts receiving data from the Obfsproxy client (downstream connection), decrypting it, and then sending it to the bridge.

At the end of Step 5, the connection between the Tor client and the bridge is fully functional, and the Tor client is connected to the Tor network through the Tor bridge.

5   DNS-Morph Design

The fact that the handshake phase and the encrypted data exchange phase are two separate phases, this allows us to separate them also in the Obfsproxy design and change properties of each phase without affecting the other one.

We now describe our modifications to the Obfsproxy design to replace its handshake by a DNS-based once. Our new DNS-Morph design is shown in Fig. 2, and includes three added components (highlighted in dashed red):

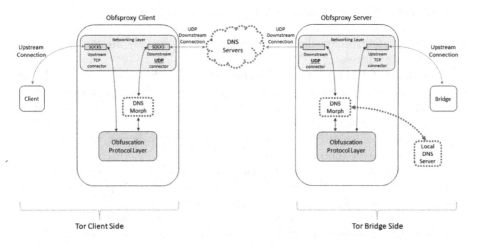

Fig. 2. DNS-Morph design: consists of the Obfsproxy design and the new components (dashed red): downstream UDP connector, DNS-Morph, and a local DNS server (Color figure online)

1. Local DNS server: this is a standard DNS server that receives DNS queries and returns DNS responses, used for active probing resistance, as explained in Sect. 8.
2. Downstream UDP connector: the connector sends and receives UDP packets. The connector also takes care of the reliability functionality (as discussed in Sect. 6).
3. DNS-Morph component:
   (a) Encodes/decodes data to/from Base32 [28].
   (b) Chops data into fragments and encapsulates them into DNS queries or responses.
   (c) Decapsulates data fragments from DNS queries or responses, and reassembles these fragments.
   (d) Encrypts/decrypts data.
   (e) Builds DNS queries and responses.
   (f) Communicates with the local DNS server to send and receive queries and responses.

Our changes to the original Obfsproxy flow of operation in order to support the DNS-Morph flow of operation are:

1. Downstream connection was changed from TCP to UDP. The Obfsproxy server listens on port 53 UDP, like a standard DNS server.
2. Obfsproxy client initiates a UDP downstream connection on port 53 to the server. Using the DNS-Morph module, handshake data is encoded to Base32, chopped into fragments of length 20–50 characters,[5] and encapsulated into DNS queries of type A (address mapping records).
   These queries are sent to the Obfsproxy server using direct or indirect routes:
   (a) Direct: Obfsproxy client sends the queries directly to the Obfsproxy server's address.
   (b) Indirect: Obfsproxy client uses the recursive DNS property and sends the queries with a domain name registered by the Obfsproxy server operator. This way the DNS queries travel between different DNS servers until they reach the Obfsproxy server.
   Direct route usage might look anomalous [42, p. 28], hence, we recommend using the indirect route.
3. The total length in bytes of the handshake data is encoded inside the first DNS packet, so that the receiving side knows when to stop receiving data, and start processing it.
4. The Obfsproxy server buffers each DNS query it receives, until the total length is reached. In order to preserve resemblance to a standard DNS server, the Obfsproxy server sends the received queries to the local DNS server available on its side. When a response is received from the DNS server, the Obfsproxy server sends it back to the Obfsproxy client. When the buffered data forms a

---

[5] [44, p. 251] suggests that the average DNS query length is 36–59 bytes. [19] suggests that most of the DNS packets that were captured were of size 70–98 bytes (domain name length of 30–58 bytes).

complete handshake data, the DNS-Morph module decodes it from Base32, reassembles it, and forwards it to the obfuscation protocol layer for further processing.

5. After the Obfsproxy client finishes sending the handshake data, it should receive handshake data from the Obfsproxy server. As a result, the Obfsproxy client sends one additional dummy DNS query (contains no protocol handshake data) so that the Obfsproxy server can start sending back its handshake data as a response to this query. The dummy query is used by the Obfsproxy client to trigger transmission of the handshake data by the Obfsproxy server shaped as DNS responses.

6. When the Obfsproxy server sends back its protocol handshake data, it encodes it to Base32, chops it into fragments of length 20–50 bytes, and encapsulates them into CNAME DNS records. Then sends these records encapsulated together with A type records as responses to the dummy type A DNS queries which the Obfsproxy client sent before. Again, the first DNS response packet will include the total length of the Obfsproxy server sent handshake. The Obfsproxy client decapsulates the data from the DNS responses, buffers it, and keeps sending dummy queries until a complete handshake data is received. Then, the Obfsproxy client decodes the received handshake data back from Base32, reassembles it, and forwards it to the obfuscation layer.

7. When the protocol handshake is successfully completed, and tickets and/or session keys are created, both Obfsproxy sides switch from a UDP downstream connection to a TCP connection. The Obfsproxy server side launches a TCP downstream listener on a port exchanged out-of-band and waits for the Obfsproxy client to connect back to it. When the TCP connection happens, the connection between the Tor client and the bridge is fully functional. In case of a protocol handshake failure, both the Obfsproxy client and server close their downstream connection, and the Obfsproxy server continues to behave like a standard DNS server.

6 DNS-Morph Reliability

DNS-Morph depends on UDP, hence, we cannot rely on the network transport layer to provide reliable data transmission. Therefore, our implementation must guarantee arrival of the sent packets to the receiver's obfuscation layer in the same order that they were sent in, while adding a minimal delay. To achieve this, we use the methods explained below:

6.1 Received Packets Acknowledgments

The receiver sends an acknowledgment each time it receives a packet. If the sender does not get an acknowledgment, it means that the packet or its acknowledgment has failed to reach their destination, so the sender must resend the packet.

We divide the handshake phase into two parts according to the different roles played by the Obfsproxy client:

1. **Obfsproxy client sends handshake data:** each time it sends a DNS shaped packet, the Obfsproxy server should send back an acknowledgment in the shape of a valid DNS response to this query.

   The Obfsproxy client behaves similarly to the *selective repeat protocol* using a window size of 4 packets, with a few modifications due to the randomized DNS query identifier (ID). Obfsproxy client stores the sent packets in a list sorted by their sending order. The query ID serves as a search key to the list. Each time the client receives an acknowledgment it removes the matching packet from the list. If three acknowledgments are received, but none of them matches the first packet in the list, then this packet is resent with a new DNS query ID.

2. **Obfsproxy client receives handshake data:** as explained before, each dummy DNS query sent by the Obfsproxy client during this part serves two purposes, the first is to trigger the Obfsproxy server to send one additional handshake packet as a response to the dummy DNS query, and the second is to acknowledge receiving the previous handshake packet sent by the Obfsproxy server.

   During this part, the Obfsproxy client implements the *stop and wait protocol*: each time the Obfsproxy client wishes to receive handshake data, it sends a dummy DNS query and waits a while (discussed later) for the Obfsproxy server to send its handshake data as a response to this query. If nothing is received from the Obfsproxy server, then the Obfsproxy client resends the last DNS packet.[6] This procedure is repeated twice (the same packet is sent at most three times in total), and if no responses are received after that, the handshake process is terminated (in a failure).

   The time the Obfsproxy client waits for a handshake packet before resending the dummy DNS packet again is calculated by the known weighted average formula [39, p. 226] for round trip time measuring:

   $$RTT = (\alpha \times RTT_{new}) + ((1 - \alpha) \times RTT_{old})$$

   RTT_{new} is the newly sampled RTT, RTT_{old} is the previously calculated RTT, and $\alpha = 1/8$ as recommended in [29].

6.2   Sorting Received Packets

DNS-Morph adds to each packet a 16-bit identity number, which is encrypted (as further explained in Sect. 6.3) and then encoded using Base32 to 4 ASCII characters in start of the packet's payload. This number is initialized to the length of the total sent data in the payload of the first DNS packet, and is increased by one each time a packet is sent, so newly sent packets have a bigger identity number than the previously sent ones.

Each time a packet is received, the receiver decodes and then decrypts the DNS-Morph identity bytes of its payload (see Sect. 7 for an example), checks

---

[6] Resending a failed DNS query with the same DNS identifier is a common practice among DNS resolvers.

if they form a legal identifying number, and if they do, the packet's data is buffered. When the whole handshake data is received, the receiver sorts the packets according to the identity number and reassembles them back to a real handshake data, passing it to the obfuscation layer for further processing.

In case of receiving two packets with the same identity number, the receiver does not buffer the second received packet but acknowledges the sender about it. This can happen for example because: 1. the first packet's acknowledgment failed to reach the sender, so the sender resends the packet. 2. an attacker is trying to send a packet that contains the same identity number in its payload.

6.3   DNS-Morph Identifiers' Encryption and Decryption

Encrypting the DNS-Morph identifier inside the encoded data of the DNS packets relies on an out-of-band shared password (similar to ScrambleSuit and obfs4) [32].

Our encryption uses 128-bit AES in counter mode. For each identifier, new key and initialization vector (IV) are created as the output of: HMAC-SHA-256(shared password, X || handshake data encoded in the current packet) [27], when $X = 0$ for Obfsproxy client encryption, $X = 1$ for Obfsproxy server encryption, and || means concatenation.

This encryption protects the identifier from being read without the knowledge of the shared key. This protects DNS-Morph from censoring attacks that identify the masked Tor connection by saving all DNS traffic between two connecting entities A and B, extracting the characters that include the identifier, decoding them, and checking whether:

1. The decoded characters form sequential numbers (identifiers).
2. The decoded characters of the first DNS packet form a number that matches the total length of the data in all the DNS packets.

6.4   DNS-Morph Multiple Sessions Support

In addition to encrypting the DNS-Morph identifiers, DNS-Morph also supports multiple clients handshake sessions by adding an encrypted 8-bit session ID to the packet's payload. This ID is randomly chosen by the DNS-Morph client and is encrypted together with the DNS-Morph identifiers using the same keys and IVs.

7   DNS-Morph Encoded Packets

We show how the encoded handshake data looks inside a DNS query and a DNS response packets. Consider, for example, handshake data that a ScrambleSuit client sends to the Obfsproxy server. After encoding this data using Base32 we receive encoded data of 450 characters. This data is chopped to fragments of length 20–50 characters, the first fragment of the chopped data looks like this "ti3zuto4jrz5r22wsu4ar". To encapsulate this fragment inside a DNS query packet, we need to add encrypted DNS-Morph identity and session identity to it. The key and IV for the encryption of the DNS-Morph identity and session identity are created by:

Key $\|$ IV = HMAC-SHA-256(shared password, 0 $\|$ ti3zuto4jrz5r22wsu4ar)

After computing the key and the IV, we use them to encrypt the DNS-Morph identity (which is 450 - the encoded handshake length in characters for the first packet) and the session identity, which is randomly generated by the client (95 for example).

$$\text{"enpin"} = Encode32(AES - CTR_{Key\|IV}(450\|95))$$

After computing the encrypted DNS-Morph ID and the session ID, they are encoded and then concatenated with "ti3zuto4jrz5r22wsu4ar", and with the string ".bridge.domain", to create the query:

$$\text{"enpinti3zuto4jrz5r22wsu4ar.bridge.domain"}$$

which is then encapsulated in a DNS packet and sent to the Tor bridge side. The bridge side, decodes the first 5 characters of the query, decrypts them using the rest part of the query not including ".bridge.domain", and the shared password. Then, it finds out that the length of the encoded handshake to receive for session 95 is 450 characters.

The response packet sent by the Obfsproxy server is a DNS response packet as generated by the local DNS server.

8   DNS-Morph: Security Analysis

We now discuss the security of our DNS-Morph design. Since DNS-Morph was built as an additional protection layer for random stream protocols, it inherits their security properties as a carrier protocol for them. The aim of this section is to prove that DNS-Morph does not harm the security properties of the encapsulated protocol but enhances them.

After DNS-Morph finishes the handshake phase the encapsulated protocol will still enjoy the same security properties as before, while its handshake security was enhanced.

We further discuss the security design of DNS-Morph assuming that the encapsulated protocols satisfy some conditions:

1. They must have a handshake phase.
2. They must be active probing resistant.
3. Their traffic (the handshake and the encrypted data exchange phases) must be indistinguishable from randomness.
4. They must provide data integrity. Providing data authenticity is recommended but is not a must.
5. The traffic exchanged during the handshake should be as short as possible without affecting the security properties of the protocol, as it affects the number of DNS packets exchanged using DNS-Morph (discussed more later).

8.1   Censor's DPI Capabilities

We now further elaborate on our assumptions concerning the censor's capabilities. We assume that the censor has the following DPI capabilities (which are used to detect DNS tunneling) installed in its ISP infrastructure, either on the DNS servers themselves, or on dedicated firewall/routers:

1. The DPI mechanism can sort DNS packets by their arrival times, build a pseudo-session out of them using a 4-tuple (UDP, IP_{client}, IP_{server}, $Port_{server}$), and attempt to detect the structure of "a session".
2. The DPI mechanism can search the DNS packets payload for any structural data such as counters, flags or words to signal "start", "stop", "resend", etc.
3. The DPI mechanism can consider the length of a DNS query/response and alert if DNS packets lengths regularities/irregularities are detected. For example, alerting about any domain name request longer than 52 characters [7].
4. The DPI mechanism can consider the number of DNS queries/responses for each 4-tuple or domain name, and alert if this number exceeds a certain threshold, or if the number of queries and responses differs significantly from what can be classified as benign behavior.
5. The DPI mechanism can detect irregular DNS packets sequences, e.g., a series of queries followed by a series of responses.
6. The DPI mechanism can use regular expressions or entropy estimation to detect suspicious DNS packets payloads.

8.2   DNS-Morph DPI Resistance

We added to DNS-Morph the following counter-measures that defeat the above DPI threat model, and make it exposure resistant:

1. DNS-Morph can send its packets in an arbitrary order and sort them on the receiver side, by decrypting the encrypted identifiers.
2. DNS-Morph encodes the encrypted payload inside DNS queries/responses, and concatenates encrypted packet and session IDs, thus, no structural data is available in the payload.
3. All the DNS queries/responses of DNS-Morph are of random size between 20–50 bytes, which is the size of a standard DNS query/response [19,44].
4. The number of DNS-Morph exchanged queries/responses depends on the encapsulated protocol. If we take ScrambleSuit for example, we can make some modifications, which will not affect the protocol security traits when DNS-Morph is added, but can reduce the total amount of DNS exchanged packets to as little as 26 DNS packets, an amount not so far from the number of DNS packets exchanged when visiting popular websites such as Google (10–17 packets), YouTube (11–13 packets), and Facebook (24–27 packets), which are among Alexa's top 10 global websites for the year 2021 [2].
5. The Obfsproxy server cannot send a DNS response without receiving a DNS query. A small delay can be added while the Obfsproxy client sends the DNS queries, which can eliminate DNS sequence abnormalities.

6. It is hard to use regular expressions in order to check for the "validity" of domain names without getting a lot of false positives, as many domain names nowadays can look random (or have a random looking part), due to domain fronting and load balancing services.

We compare CloudFront domain names with DNS-Morph produced ones in Sect. 8.5.

8.3 Additional Attacks and Resistance

In addition to using DPI, a censor can tamper with DNS packets payload in many ways, such as:

1. The censor can change uppercase letters to lowercase, and vice versa. This change should not affect real DNS as it is case-insensitive, but might affect encoded and encapsulated data as changing cases changes bytes of the real data. As discussed in Sect. 9, our method of encoding and decoding data is resilient to this kind of changes.
2. The censor can change the DNS packet payload data or some of it (e.g., DNS poisoning). While deeming DNS poisoning out of this research scope, it is important to note that DNS poisoning in this context is a denial of service attack, i.e., it will cause a handshake failure, but will not reveal more information about the exchanged data than the information that was revealed by the original handshake.
3. The censor can inject DNS packets in two different ways:
   (a) The injected DNS packet contains random data. The receiver will not consider this packet as a part of the handshake as the possibility of this data to include an encrypted identifier using the out-of-band keys, is small.
   (b) The injected DNS packet is a replayed packet. This packet will be considered as a network reliability issue and will not be considered as part of the exchanged handshake.
4. The censor can observe the DNS responses sent back by the server, and try to launch an HTTP session to the IP written in these responses in order to examine if this IP points to a real server. Assuming that the IP returned by the DNS server is the IP of the DNS-Morph server, this server can run a simple HTTP server that displays or redirects to a random web-page.

8.4 Active Probing and Replay Attack Resistance

Our new Obfsproxy server acts like a real DNS server. Each time a DNS query is received, a real DNS response is sent back by a real DNS server. Assuming that the obfuscated protocol is active probing resistant, the probe will send DNS packets and receive real DNS responses. If the probe does not know the out-of-band shared password/key between the real Tor client and bridge, the obfuscated protocol on the Obfsproxy server side will reject the probe's handshake request, while the Obfsproxy server will continue to respond as a real DNS server.

The same also holds with respect to replay attacks assuming that the obfuscated protocol is replay-attack resistant. The obfuscated protocol will reject any replayed packet, while the Obfsproxy server continues to respond to it as a real DNS server.

8.5 Domain Names' Entropy

To show that the domain names used by DNS-Morph have the same entropy capacity as of regular domain names used in CDNs we have performed a simple test. We took 32 DNS packets directed at CloudFront services and 36 DNS packets obtained from a DNS-Morph handshake. We applied gzip and bzip2 to a file containing only the prefix of the domain names. The compression ratio using gzip of the CloudFront domain names was 66.5% whereas of the DNS-Morph domain names was 67.3%. In the case of bzip2, the ratios are 70% and 71.2%, respectively.

Given the fact that the handshake is done once per session, it is easy to see that attacks based on estimating the entropy in the domain names are unlikely to offer high precision due to the small difference in compression rates (suggesting somewhat related entropy capacity) [45].

9   DNS-Morph Design Considerations

9.1   Choice of DNS

We now discuss various trade-offs we made in DNS-Morph's design, and explain our design decisions: First, as mentioned before DNS is an essential Internet protocol, and its complete blocking is highly unlikely due to the high cost of doing so, namely, practically disconnecting from the internet. In addition, DNS supports a variety of query types which gives us more freedom in choosing the record type that can encapsulate our encoded data.

Following the selection of DNS, we had to use UDP (TCP sessions in DNS are usually used for zone transfers between DNS servers). This resulted in the need to add a reliability layer for DNS-Morph as loss of even a single packet of handshake data on any side causes a handshake failure (discussed more in Sect. 6).

In addition, the following actions were taken to enable DNS-Morph to mimic (as much as possible) an ordinary DNS communication:

We decided to add dummy DNS queries/responses which do not carry handshake data on both sides during the handshake phase, in order to prevent DNS protocol anomalies where the client sends multiple queries, and the server responds with multiple answers after all the requests were received, or the Obfsproxy server sending DNS responses without any sent queries.

9.2 Choice of Base32

We chose Base32 for encoding the handshake data which can include any byte value into characters that follow the domain name system rules [25]:

1. Domain name can include labels and the character ".".
2. Labels must start and end with a letter or a digit, and have as interior characters only letters, digits, and hyphens.
3. Letters can be any one of the 52 alphabetic characters "A–Z" in uppercase and "a–z" in lowercase.
4. Digits can be any one of the ten digits "0–9".

While we could have used Base64 [28] or Base58 [3], DNS is not case sensitive. In such encodings, a censor can rewrite every single DNS query to a lowercase one, which does not harm normal DNS requests, but breaks DNS-Morph. These factors narrow our encoding options to a base that has uppercase letters or lowercase letters, but not both. Base32 includes the alphabetic characters "A–Z", the digits "2–7" and the character "=", which is suitable for our uses after changing it to the digit "1". We also changed the uppercase letters that Base32 produces to lowercase letters inside the DNS queries/responses in order to make them look more consistent with regular DNS queries/responses. All the letters on the receiver side are converted back to uppercase before the Base32 decoding process, which makes our design resistant to attacks like the one described before.

We note that we can also use Base36, which includes the alphabetic characters "A–Z" and the digits "0–9". Using Base36 can protect DNS-Morph against a censor with the ability to spot the lack of the digits "0, 8, 9" from DNS-Morph packets, as these digits can appear in DNS labels, but are not included in our modified Base32. However, we decided to not use this for the ease of implementation. Future works may wish to explore that approach.

9.3 Query Types

In our choice of which DNS query/response types to use for handshake data encapsulation, we used the following guidelines:

1. The type of the DNS query/response must accept by their definition the amount and the character set of the data we want to encapsulate inside them. For example, the type A query can include characters and numbers (domain names), but the type A response includes 32-bit IPv4 addresses, thus, encapsulating encoded data that does not look like a valid IPv4 address inside a type A response is not possible.
2. Using certain DNS query/response packet types must not contradict the general DNS query/response types statistics over the Internet.
3. The types of the queries and responses must match.

To send the Obfsproxy client handshake data, we use type A queries, and receive type A responses from the Obfsproxy server. To send the Obfsproxy server handshake data, we use CNAME and A DNS records, which are encapsulated together in the same DNS packet, and sent as DNS responses for type A DNS queries. We chose these types because they meet the aforementioned conditions, and in the same time are widely used on the Internet. The encapsulation of these records in DNS packets is done using the "dnslib" Python library [10], aiming to build DNS packets that look as real DNS client/server packets.

9.4 Recursive DNS

Finally, we decided to use the recursive DNS property and send the queries with a domain name registered by the Obfsproxy server operator, in order to protect against packets tracking. This also enables to bypass networks' firewall rules which forbid a direct DNS packet to be sent outside the network, besides the network's own DNS server.

10   Tests and Results

We have implemented our DNS-Morph design using Python, and tested it successfully with the ScrambleSuit PT. ScrambleSuit's handshake, is depicted in Fig. 3.

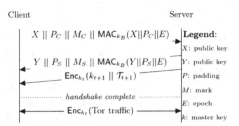

Fig. 3. ScrambleSuit's handshake.

During the handshake, a client and a server generate 4096-bit even private keys x and y, respectively, and the corresponding public keys $X = g^x \pmod p$, $Y = g^y \pmod p$. After exchanging the public keys, they agree on a shared private key $k_t = Y^x \pmod p = X^y \pmod p$. Then, using the shared key, the server sends back an encrypted ticket and a new private key (used by a shortened handshake version in future handshakes). An out-of-band shared key k_B is used to calculate the MACs and the marks (used to facilitate the localization of the MACs).

10.1   Test Setup

For our experiments, we set up a Tor client in a censoring environment, which is described in Sect. 10.2. This client connects to a Tor bridge residing at a university located in Israel. This Bridge is connected to the Internet using an ISP **not known** for any censoring activities. The two sides (the client's side and the bridge's side) had the Obfsproxy software with the DNS-Morph component, and tried to establish Tor's first connection between them. We ran 30 connection attempts in each test, measuring rates of successful handshakes, their timing, and their bandwidth.

Between connection attempts, all the temporary files and session states generated by previous attempts (e.g., session tickets) were deleted to ensure that ScrambleSuit generates everything and behaves the same all the time.

With this setup, we performed three different experiments:

1. "Original Design" tests, to test the original Obfsproxy without DNS-Morph. This Obfsproxy uses TCP only.
2. "DNS-Morph Direct" tests, to test the Obfsproxy including DNS-Morph. DNS queries were directly sent from the Obfsproxy client to the Obfsproxy server address.
3. "DNS-Morph Indirect" tests, to test the Obfsproxy, including DNS-Morph. DNS queries were sent indirectly to the Obfsproxy server address by other DNS servers (using recursive DNS queries).

For our "DNS-Morph" tests, we also did one additional type of tests: we decreased the maximal size of the random padding added to the protocol (see Fig. 3). ScrambleSuit picks a random padding length of 0–1308 bytes to change the protocol's signature. Due to the use of DNS queries, such a protection is less needed. Thus, we tested the system when the maximal size of the random padding is at most 100 bytes.

Decreasing the padding length range reduces the **maximal** total number of DNS packets (queries and responses) per DNS-Morph handshake from 458 packets to 96 packets and the **average** total number from 262 packets to 81 packets (the **minimal** total number stays 26 packets). By doing so, we wanted to check if the handshake time improves, and if as a result of DNS servers offloading (DNS-Morph indirect), the handshake success rates will be higher compared to the first type tests, as DNS servers will be more willing to serve us.

10.2   Client's Testing Environment

This environment includes an ISP in Israel, which is **well known** for censoring Internet browsing for its customers (who seek this type of censorship). Content censored by this ISP can be pornography, violence, live casting, and videos. While trying to connect to websites like Google, YouTube, and Facebook, this ISP asked us to install CA certificates on the client's machine. Refusing to do so resulted in blocking client's access to these websites. Other websites were simply blocked without even giving the client an option to install certificates (i.e., Yahoo, Bing, and The Tor Project website).

It is worth mentioning that the certificates needed to be installed by this ISP are self-signed certificates issued to "Netspark" [21], a company providing real-time browsing data inspection and web content filtering services.

Connecting to Tor in this blocking ISP: when trying to connect in the default method, we encountered failures during different phases such as connecting to the directory servers, loading relay descriptors, or connecting to the entry relay. Trying to connect using obfs3 or FTE always failed.

Choosing obfs4 succeeded sometimes and on the other times it failed. Even on successful attempts a lot of the bridges were blocked.

In conclusion, we suspect that this ISP continuously collects information about Tor bridges and blocks them.

Results: We performed numerous connection tests during a period of 2 months (January–February 2018). Table 1 summarizes the results of the tests done on the 10th of February 2018, as a typical example for these results. We chose to present the results of only one day as all the other days produced similar results.

Despite the fact that the Tor client was connecting to the Tor bridge using a censoring ISP, this ISP could not block its connection, not of the original ScrambleSuit, nor of our DNS-Morph version. This indicates that DNS-Morph did not harm the original security properties of ScrambleSuit.

The 100% success rates in all the experiments can be explained by the fact that the client and the server are geographically close.

Table 1. Times and success rates of handshakes.

	Time (seconds)				Success rate	Bandwidth (bytes)
	Minimum	Maximum	Average	Median		
Original Scramble-Suit	0.044	0.101	0.087	0.091	100%	4042
Original Scramble-Suit with DNS-Morph Direct	0.891	1.813	1.113	0.953	100%	22140
Original Scramble-Suit with DNS-Morph Indirect	1.844	2.391	2.171	2.189	100%	24350
Shortened Scramble-Suit with DNS-Morph Direct	0.438	0.672	0.542	0.547	100%	6528
Shortened Scramble-Suit with DNS-Morph Indirect	0.594	0.798	0.708	0.719	100%	6621

ScrambleSuit - Original: ScrambleSuit with the original padding (0–1308 bytes).
ScrambleSuit - Shortened: ScrambleSuit with a shortened padding (0–100 bytes).

10.3 Deep Packet Inspection Tools

To evaluate DNS-Morph resistance against DPI we chose two open source tools: nDPI [20] version 2.2.0, and Libprotoident [16] version 2.0.12. We captured the packets transmitted between the Tor client and the Tor bridge from the previous tests (Sect. 10) using Wireshark and ran the two tools to analyze them.

Results: The original Scramblesuit connections were analyzed as "Unknown TCP" protocol packets by both tools, nDPI and Libprotoident. The DNS-Morph connections were analyzed by nDPI as ordinary DNS packets for the handshake phase, and SSL packets for the encrypted data exchange after the handshake was done. Libprotoident on the other hand analyzed the DNS-Morph connections as ordinary DNS packets for the handshake phase, and "Unknown TCP" protocol packets for the encrypted data exchange after the handshake.

11   Summary

In this work we described DNS-Morph, a method to hide PT's handshake communication in a series of DNS queries and replies. We implemented the system and checked that it successfully establishes a Tor connection between a Tor client and a Tor bridge.

The use of DNS offers several layers of security for this process: DNS blocking (or even strong manipulation) comes at a huge price for the censor, DPI attacks on DNS are harder to implement, and DNS enjoys an inherent resilience to blocking attempts due to the nature of recursive DNS queries.

In addition, we have added counter-measures designed to defeat UDP sessions' tracking mechanisms which, we believe still do not exist today in commercial DPI products.

While we have tested the implementation using the ScrambleSuit handshake, it is easy to see that this methodology could work with any PT that satisfies the conditions stated in Sect. 8. As already stated, after the handshake, one can transform the remainder of the Tor communication to a white-listed protocol using tools like FTE or meek to maintain white-listed behavior (while enjoying the security against active probing offered by the protected handshake).

11.1   Future Works

This research can be further developed to include more interesting topics and answer currently open questions:

– We are aware of the DNS poisoning some countries conduct not only to block sensitive content but also to promote local websites [37]. An interesting approach is to examine what exactly is done by the censor while performing DNS poisoning, and whether our DNS-Morph can finish the handshake despite these DNS poisoning attacks.
– In order to better mimic the behavior of a DNS client (and fulfill one more of the requirements for building a successful mimicking protocol [43]), a service can be installed on the client machine to collect data about the user's browsing behavior, such as: DNS packets timing, size, DNS client behavior if its query was not answered, etc. When the DNS-Morph client is started, it can analyze the collected data to better adapt the specific user and machine behavior.
– More techniques can be applied to DNS-Morph, to improve its resistance against DPIs, DNS tunneling detectors, and connection tracking:

- Adding more DNS record types than the currently used ones (A and CNAME).
- Use an encoding scheme which mimics as best as possible real domain names, instead of Base32.
- Use multiple DNS servers which collaborate, each accepting some of the queries of the handshake (and sending back the information). This way, the tracing of the DNS queries becomes harder (as the number of queries per DNS server is reduced).

References

1. Active Probing. https://www.cs.princeton.edu/~rensafi/projects/active-probing/. Accessed 1 Aug 2017
2. Alexa: The top 500 sites on the web. https://www.alexa.com/topsites. Accessed 24 Feb 2020
3. Base58. https://en.wikipedia.org/wiki/Base58. Accessed 10 Aug 2017
4. Blocking-resistant communication through domain fronting. https://www.bamsoftware.com/papers/fronting/. Accessed 15 Nov 2017
5. China Tells Carriers to Block Access to Personal VPNs by February. https://www.bloomberg.com/news/articles/2017-07-10/china-is-said-to-order-carriers-to-bar-personal-vpns-by-february. Accessed 16 Aug 2017
6. DNS-Morph source code, Github, note: Please contact the "Corresponding Author" to get access to the Github repository
7. DNS part 2: visualization. http://armatum.com/blog/2009/dns-part-ii/. Accessed 21 Aug 2017
8. Dns2tcp. https://www.aldeid.com/wiki/Dns2tcp. Accessed 20 Aug 2017
9. Dnscat. https://wiki.skullsecurity.org/Dnscat. Accessed 20 Aug 2017
10. dnslib: A library to encode/decode DNS wire-format packets. https://pypi.python.org/pypi/dnslib. Accessed 6 Oct 2017
11. FTE Transport Evaluation. https://trac.torproject.org/projects/tor/wiki/doc/PluggableTransports/FteEvaluation. Accessed 25 Sept 2016
12. Full List of Pluggable Transports. https://trac.torproject.org/projects/tor/wiki/doc/PluggableTransports/list. Accessed 20 Aug 2017
13. Improved circuit-creation key exchange. https://gitweb.torproject.org/torspec.git/tree/proposals/216-ntor-handshake.txt. Accessed 10 Sept 2016
14. iodine. http://code.kryo.se/iodine/. Accessed 20 Aug 2017
15. Knock Knock Knockin' on Bridges' Doors. https://blog.torproject.org/blog/knock-knock-knockin-bridges-doors. Accessed 7 Sept 2016
16. Libprotoident. https://research.wand.net.nz/software/libprotoident.php. Accessed 25 Aug 2018
17. Meek. https://trac.torproject.org/projects/tor/wiki/doc/meek. Accessed 22 Aug 2016
18. Meek Transport Evaluation. https://trac.torproject.org/projects/tor/wiki/doc/PluggableTransports/MeekEvaluation. Accessed 25 Sept 2016
19. More fun with DNS packet captures. https://www.coverfire.com/archives/2008/07/28/more-fun-with-dns-packet-captures/. Accessed 3 June 2017
20. nDPI - Open and Extensible LGPLv3 Deep Packet Inspection Library. https://www.ntop.org/products/deep-packet-inspection/ndpi/. Accessed 25 Nov 2017

21. Netspark. http://netspark.com/. Accessed 25 Nov 2017
22. Obfs3 Protocol Specification. https://github.com/NullHypothesis/obfsproxy/blob/master/doc/obfs3/obfs3-protocol-spec.txt. Accessed 20 Sept 2016
23. Obfs4 Protocol Specification. https://github.com/Yawning/obfs4/blob/master/doc/obfs4-spec.txt. Accessed 22 Aug 2016
24. ObfsProxy Source Code - Python. https://gitweb.torproject.org/pluggable-transports/obfsproxy.git. Accessed 25 Aug 2016
25. RFC 1123: Requirements for Internet Hosts - Application and Support. https://tools.ietf.org/html/rfc1123. Accessed 3 June 2017
26. RFC 1928: SOCKS Protocol. https://www.ietf.org/rfc/rfc1928.txt. Accessed 22 Aug 2016
27. RFC 2104: HMAC - Keyed-Hashing for Message Authentication. https://www.ietf.org/rfc/rfc2104.txt. Accessed 20 Nov 2017
28. RFC 3548: The Base16, Base32, and Base64 Data Encodings. https://tools.ietf.org/html/rfc3548.html. Accessed 6 Feb 2017
29. RFC 6298: Computing TCP's Retransmission Timer. https://tools.ietf.org/html/rfc6298. Accessed 10 June 2017
30. Skype: online text message and video chat services. https://www.skype.com. Accessed 25 July 2017
31. The UniformDH scheme - Ian Goldberg. https://lists.torproject.org/pipermail/tor-dev/2012-December/004245.html. Accessed 20 Sept 2016
32. Tor bridges database. https://bridges.torproject.org/. Accessed 30 Oct 2017
33. Tor Client Software. https://www.torproject.org/download/download. Accessed 10 Sept 2016
34. Tor: Pluggable Transports Specification. https://gitweb.torproject.org/torspec.git/tree/pt-spec.txt. Accessed 22 Aug 2016
35. Tor Website. https://www.torproject.org/. Accessed 25 Aug 2016
36. WhatsApp Messenger. https://www.whatsapp.com/. Accessed 25 July 2017
37. Anonymous: Towards a comprehensive picture of the great firewall's DNS censorship. In: 4th USENIX Workshop on Free and Open Communications on the Internet (FOCI 14), San Diego, CA, pp. 445–458. USENIX Association (2014). https://www.usenix.org/conference/foci14/workshop-program/presentation/anonymous
38. Bernstein, D.J., Hamburg, M., Krasnova, A., Lange, T.: Elligator: Elliptic-curve points indistinguishable from uniform random strings. Cryptology ePrint Archive, Report 2013/325 (2013). http://eprint.iacr.org/2013/325
39. Comer, D.E.: Internetworking with TCP/IP, Volume 1: Principles, Protocols, and Architectures, 4th edn. Prentice Hall PTR, Upper Saddle River (2000)
40. Dyer, K.P., Coull, S.E., Ristenpart, T., Shrimpton, T.: Protocol misidentification made easy with format-transforming encryption. In: Proceedings of the 2013 ACM SIGSAC Conference on Computer 38; Communications Security, CCS 2013, pp. 61–72. ACM, New York (2013). https://doi.org/10.1145/2508859.2516657
41. Ensafi, R., Fifield, D., Winter, P., Feamster, N., Weaver, N., Paxson, V.: Examining how the great firewall discovers hidden circumvention servers. In: Proceedings of the 2015 ACM Conference on Internet Measurement Conference, IMC 2015, pp. 445–458. ACM, New York (2015). https://doi.org/10.1145/2815675.2815690
42. Fry, C., Nystrom, M.: Security Monitoring: Proven Methods for Incident Detection on Enterprise Networks. O'Reilly Media (2009). https://books.google.co.il/books?id=vJYCZFTdfd0C

43. Houmansadr, A., Brubaker, C., Shmatikov, V.: The parrot is dead: Observing unobservable network communications. In: 2013 IEEE Symposium on Security and Privacy, SP 2013, Berkeley, CA, USA, 19–22 May 2013, pp. 65–79 (2013). https://doi.org/10.1109/SP.2013.14
44. Manaf, A., Zeki, A., Zamani, M., Chuprat, S., El-Qawasmeh, E.: Informatics Engineering and Information Science. Springer, Heidelberg (2011). https://books.google.it/books?id=zWarCAAAQBAJ
45. Paxson, V., et al.: Practical comprehensive bounds on surreptitious communication over DNS. In: Presented as part of the 22nd USENIX Security Symposium (USENIX Security 13), Washington, D.C., pp. 17–32. USENIX (2013). https://www.usenix.org/conference/usenixsecurity13/technical-sessions/presentation/paxson
46. Winter, P., Crandall, J.R.: The great firewall of China: how it blocks Tor and why it is hard to pinpoint. USENIX Login **37**(6), 42–50 (2012)
47. Winter, P., Pulls, T., Fuß, J.: Scramblesuit: a polymorphic network protocol to circumvent censorship. In: Proceedings of the 12th Annual ACM Workshop on Privacy in the Electronic Society, WPES 2013, Berlin, Germany, 4 November 2013, pp. 213–224 (2013). https://doi.org/10.1145/2517840.2517856

Polynomial Time k-Shortest Multi-criteria Prioritized and All-Criteria-Disjoint Paths
(Extended Abstract)

Yefim Dinitz, Shlomi Dolev, and Manish Kumar[(✉)]

Ben-Gurion University of the Negev, Be'er Sheva, Israel
{dinitz,dolev}@cs.bgu.ac.il, manishk@post.bgu.ac.il

Abstract. The shortest secure path (routing) problem in communication networks has to deal with multiple attack layers e.g., man-in-the-middle, eavesdropping, packet injection, packet insertion, etc. Consider different probabilities for each such attack over an edge, probabilities that can differ across edges. Furthermore, a usage of a single shortest paths (for routing) implies possible traffic bottleneck, which should be avoided if possible, which we term *pathneck security avoidance*. Finding all Pareto–optimal solutions for the multi-criteria single-source single-destination shortest secure path problem with non-negative edge lengths might yield a solution with an exponential number of paths. In the first part of this paper, we study specific settings of the multi-criteria shortest secure path problem, which are based on prioritized multi-criteria and on k-shortest secure paths. In the second part, we show a polynomial-time algorithm that, given an undirected graph G and a pair of vertices (s, t), finds prioritized multi-criteria 2-disjoint (vertex/edge) shortest secure paths between s and t. In the third part of the paper, we introduce the k-disjoint all-criteria-shortest secure paths problem, which is solved in time $O(\min(k|E|, |E|^{3/2}))$.

Keywords: Multi-criteria · k-shortest paths · Disjoint shortest paths · Path selection · Shortest secure path

1 Introduction and Related Work

The shortest secure path (routing) problem in communication networks has to deal with multiple attack layers e.g., man-in-the-middle, eavesdropping, packet injection, packet insertion, etc. Consider different probabilities for each such

This research was (partially) funded by the Office of the Israel Innovation Authority of the Israel Ministry of Economy under Genesis generic research project & the Japan Science and Technology Agency (JST), and the German Research Funding (DFG, Grant #8767581199), the Rita Altura trust chair in computer science, and by the Lynne and William Frankel Center for Computer Science.

S. Dolev et al. (Eds.): CSCML 2021, LNCS 12716, pp. 266–274, 2021.
https://doi.org/10.1007/978-3-030-78086-9_20

attack over an edge that can differ across edges. We consider these attacks on the edge as multi-criteria and these criteria (attacks) have some positive weights. We need to compute the shortest secure path with the least value of total weight. We study a generalization of the shortest path problem in which multiple paths should be computed with consideration to multiple criteria. In our scenario, these criteria values can be proportional to the attack probabilities on the edges. The application of these paths is mainly in delivering messages via most secure routes. Similar applications are in the area of transportation networks, social networks, etc.

The shortest secure path routing algorithms mainly compute the shortest secure simple path between two nodes, source s and destination t. In our system setting edges can have positive weight only and no loops exist in the shortest paths. In practice, while computing the shortest path routing algorithm, in general, the graph source node always picks the shortest path for routing from source s and destination t.

Multi-criteria Shortest Paths. Many real-life problems can be represented as a network, such as transportation networks, biological networks, and communication networks. In these networks, finding the shortest path resolves many issues such as routing and the distance between two molecules. In general, for finding the shortest path, we consider the criterion (objective) of edge weight (cost), which is called the Shortest Path Problem (SPP) with a single criterion. A Multi-Criteria Shortest Path Problem (MCSPP) consists of more than one objective while computing the shortest path between source and destination.

Shortest Secure Paths. The problem of the shortest secure path with respect to multi-criteria is not well studied. In Oh et al. [8] authors proposed a mechanism to find a shortest and secure path by appending the *trust weight* and *distance weight* for each edge. This approach improved the security level practically but no theoretical bound existed and it is limited for the case of two criterion while our paper deals with any number of criteria.

k-Shortest Path Problem. The problem of finding the shortest paths in an edge-weighted graph is an important and well-studied problem in computer science. Dijkstra's sequential algorithm [4] computes the shortest path to a given destination vertex from every other vertex in $O(m + n \log n)$ time. The k-shortest paths (KSP) asks to compute a set of top k-shortest simple paths from vertex s to vertex t in a digraph. In 1971, Yen [10] proposed the first algorithm with the theoretical complexity of $O(kn(m + n \log n))$ for a digraph with n vertices and m edges.

k-Disjoint Shortest Path Problem. The k-disjoint shortest path problem on a graph with k source-destination pairs (s_i, t_i) looks for k pairwise node/edge-disjoint shortest s_i - t_i paths. The k-disjoint shortest path problem is known to be NP-complete if k is part of the input. The disjoint shortest paths task was first considered by Eilam-Tzoreff [6]. Eilam-Tzoreff provided a polynomial-time algorithm for $k = 2$, based on a dynamic programming approach for the weighted undirected vertex-disjoint case. This algorithm has a running time of

$O(|V|^8)$. Later, Akhmedov [2] improved the algorithm of Eilam-Tzoreff whose running time is $O(|V|^6)$ for the unit-length case of the 2-Disjoint Shortest Path and $O(|V|^7)$ for the weighted case of the 2-disjoint shortest path. In both cases Akhmedov [2] considered the undirected vertex disjoint shortest path.

Organization of the Paper. Section 2 presents the reduction of multi-criteria weight to single weight and describes the first prioritized multi-criteria k-shortest path algorithm. Section 3 introduces the prioritized multi-criteria 2-disjoint shortest path algorithm. The k-disjoint all criteria shortest path algorithm is presented in Sect. 4, with the analysis. Some of details and proofs are omitted from this extended abstract and can be found in [5].

2   Finding Prioritized Multi-criteria k-Shortest Paths in Polynomial Time

In this section, we reduce the value of multiple attacks on edges into a single value, which we call a reduction from multi-criteria weight to single weight.

We consider multi-criteria in weight(cost)-function in a prioritized manner. In our reduction from multi-criteria to single criterion, we ensemble the weights of the monotonic (or strictly decreasing) prioritized criteria into one weight. Such a reduction can be used for computing prioritized multi-criteria shortest path using Dijkstra shortest path algorithm. Moreover, the reduction we present of the prioritized multi-criteria can serve also in solving the k-shortest path problem by using a single criterion and a polynomial generalization of Dijkstra algorithm to find the k-shortest path algorithm e.g., [10], in polynomial time. The idea is to combine the different weights into a single "ensembled" weight, such that the most significant part of the ensembled weight, is the weight of the most important criteria. Say, using the first most important k_1 bits, that suffice to accumulate the sum of weights, of the most prioritized criterion. The second most important weight resides in the next k_2 bits of the edge weight, and so on and so forth. Our algorithms deal with any number of criteria/weights. One can view the prioritized multi-criteria case as using (lexicographic) vector of weights instead of a single value, where comparison of two weights are performed in lexicographic order, and additions of weights are done in vector terms. The use of ensembled weight simplifies the vector operations to a single number operation.

This section studies the following prioritized multi-criteria k-shortest simple paths problem. The input is an undirected graph $G = (V, E)$, where each edge e holds vector $\bar{w}(e)$, where $\bar{w}(e) = (w_1(e), w_2(e), ..., w_q(e))$ and $w_i(e)$ is the weight of e w.r.t. criterion c_i, source node s and destination node t, $s, t \in V$, and integer k. We say that a path P from x to y is the shortest w.r.t. criterion c_i, if $c_i(P) = \sum_{e \in P} w_i(e)$ is minimal among all $c_i(P) = \sum_{e \in P} w_i(e)$ over all paths P from x to y. A polynomial-time algorithm for solving the problem is presented in this section.

For multiple criteria, to avoid the exponential number of paths, we reduce the set of all criteria as a single value for each edge. We reduce the prioritized multi-criteria by a reduction to a single criterion. Let us define the ensembled edge weights as follows. Let $W_i = \sum_{e \in E} w_i(e)$, $1 \leq i \leq q$. Let $l_i = \lceil \log_2(W_i + 1) \rceil$, $1 \leq i \leq q$, and let $r_q = 0$, $r_i = \sum_{j=i+1}^{q} l_i$, $0 \leq i \leq q - 1$. The ensembled weight of the edge $e \in E$ is defined to be $EW(e) = \sum_{j=1}^{q} (2^{r_i} w_i(e))$. As usual we define the ensembled weight of any path P as $EW(P) = \sum_{e \in P} EW(e)$.

The multi-criteria shortest path problem has a rich history, several approximation and heuristic-based algorithms have been proposed to solve it. Instead of considering the approximation or heuristic approach, we are interested in problem families for which a polynomial solution exists. For example, (1) if one criterion is that no edge on the path should weigh more than a given total attack threshold (T), then when computing the shortest multi-criteria algorithm, we do not consider this edge. (2) Another family of multi-criteria is *prioritized multi-criteria* where one would like to optimize the first criterion (attack) c_1, and within all solutions that optimize c_1, find the optimal solution for the second criterion (attack) c_2, and so on. (3) A combination of the two multi-criteria above.

Thus, as explained above, to ensemble the weights of the monotonic prioritized criteria into one weight, we use the most important part of an edge ensemble weight for the most important criteria, and the least important part of an edge ensemble weight for the least important criteria, and similarly for criteria in between.

To make sure that the portion of edge weight dedicated to criteria does not overlap, we assign each portion a span of bits in the ensemble weight of an edge to suffice for accumulating the criteria weight along the (shortest) path. We can bound the number of bits needed for accumulating the bound on the shortest path by summing up all weights of the criteria in all edges in the graph.

Finding the k-shortest paths with the ensemble weights result in that these are k-shortest paths in the most important criterion c_1, as all other criteria do not compete with the most important part of the weights when computing the shortest path(s). Thus, the second criterion c_2 breaks ties among the paths as above with the same value of the first criterion. In particular, if the weight of the heaviest shortest path according to c_1 is w_1, the selection from the set of the shortest paths with weight w_1 will be according to the second prioritized criterion c_2. If the set of shortest paths with w_1 is chosen according to the second criterion where w_2 is the shortest among them, then from the set of paths with weights w_1 and w_2, paths with the lightest weight according to the third criterion are chosen, and so on and so forth.

The ensemble of the criteria weight into one weight implies finding monotonic multi-criteria k-shortest paths. These paths are not necessarily disjoint (as the k-shortest simple paths). These paths can be computed in polynomial time as long as k is fixed [6].

Our approach is based on the generalized Dijkstra algorithm [5] for the multi-criteria shortest path. Using the Dijkstra algorithm, it is possible to determine the shortest distance (or the least attack value) between a start node and any other node in a graph. The idea of the algorithm is to continuously apply the original Dijkstra algorithm with the precomputed ensembled weight for each edge while removing the edges that hold more ensembled weight than Threshold (T).

Our approach consists of the following steps: Q is the set of nodes for which the shortest path has not been found. Initialize the source node with distance 0 and all nodes with distance "infinite". Reduce the multi-criteria into a single criterion. At each iteration, the node v, that has the minimum distance value (sum of weights EW) to the source, is added to the S, which provides the shortest path from the source node to the destination node.

For computing the multi-criteria k-shortest simple paths, we use the generalized Dijkstra algorithm [5] for computing the shortest path and Yen's algorithm [10] for computing k-paths [1].

Theorem 1. *The prioritized multi-criteria k-shortest paths problem in an undirected graph can be solved in polynomial time.*

Proof. The single criterion k-shortest paths problem is solvable in polynomial time. We polynomially reduced the multi-criteria weights where criteria are used in a prioritized manner to the single criterion weight. So prioritized multi-criteria k-shortest paths problem is also solvable in polynomial time. ☐

3   Prioritized Multi-criteria 2-Disjoint (Node/Edge) Shortest Paths

In this section, we suggest an algorithm solving the 2-shortest paths edge/node independent problem (see Eilam-Tzoreff [6]) for the case of prioritized criteria from a single source s to a single destination t in an undirected graph G, where each edge e holds vector $\bar{w}(e)$, where $\bar{w}(e) = (w_1(e), w_2(e), ..., w_q(e))$ and $w_i(e)$ is the weight of e w.r.t. criterion c_i, source node s and destination node t, $s, t \in V$. A polynomial time algorithm solving the problem is presented in this section.

We reduce the prioritized multi-criteria case to the case of a single criterion, similarly to Sect. 2. Further, for finding 2-disjoint shortest paths from s to t, we use a reduction to the case where two sources and two destinations are given (described later). Then, we find the 2-disjoint shortest paths in the resulted graph $\bar{G}$ by using the algorithm of Akhmedov [2], which computes the 2-disjoint shortest paths for two sources and two destinations in time $O(|V|^7)$.

Let us describe our reduction. For the edge-disjoint case, it is simple. We add to G two nodes s_1, s_2 with dummy edges $(s_1, s), (s_2, s)$, two nodes t_1, t_2 with dummy edges $(t, t_1), (t, t_2)$, define the weight to be zero for the dummy edges, and declare s_1, s_2 to be the sources and t_1, t_2 to be the destinations instead of s and t. After finding the 2-disjoint shortest paths in the resulting graph $\bar{G}$, we return them with the dummy edges removed.

---

[1] Finding k-shortest path can be done using different approaches. Such as by removing the lightest edge [11] and by removing the already found shortest path(s) [9]. Our algorithm and reduction from multi-weight to single weight work with both scenarios.

The reduction for the node-disjoint case is more complicated. We add to G four nodes s_1, s_2, t_1, t_2, which will be the sources and destinations instead of s, t. If G contains edge (s, t), then we replace it with edge (s', t') of the same weight, and add the dummy edges (s_1, s'), (s_2, s'), (t', t_1), (t', t_2). For any other edge (s, v) incident to s, we replace it with edge (s_v, v) of the same weight, where s_v is a new node, and add the dummy edges $(s_1, s_v), (s_2, s_v)$. Symmetrically, for any other edge (v, t) incident to t, we replace it with edge (v, t_v) of the same weight, where t_v is a new node, and add the dummy edges $(t_v, t_1), (t_v, t_2)$. The weights of all dummy edges are set be 1. Finally, we remove nodes s and t with no incident edges. After finding the 2-disjoint shortest paths in the resulting graph $\bar{G}$, we return their *abridged variant*: with the dummy edges incident to their end-nodes s_i and t_i shrunken to s and t, respectively.

Let us show the correctness of the latter reduction. A necessary condition for using the algorithm of Akhmedov is that the terminals quadruple (s_1, s_2, t_1, t_2) is not rigid, where it is called rigid, is if $s_1, t_1 \in L(s_2, t_2)$ and $s_2, t_2 \in L(s_1, t_1)$, where $L(s_i, t_i)$ is the set of all nodes belonging to at least one shortest path between s_i and t_i. Let us prove that (s_1, s_2, t_1, t_2) is not rigid in $\bar{G}$. Assume for the contradiction, w.l.o.g., that a shortest path P from s_1 to t_1 in $\bar{G}$ contains two consequent edges (u, s_2) and (s_2, v). Consider path P' obtained from P by replacing its prefix from s_1 to v by edge (s_1, v), with weight 1. Path P' from s_1 to t_1 is lighter than P, since the weights of the three removed edges: the first one of P, (u, s_2), and (s_2, v), are 1 each,—a contradiction.

Let us show the legality and optimality of the returned solution. Since the paths returned by the algorithm of Akhmedov are node-disjoint, their abridged variants are node-disjoint. By the reasons in the proof of non-rigidity of (s_1, s_2, t_1, t_2), the returned paths do not contain any terminal out of s_1, s_2, t_1, t_2 as an intermediate node. Therefore, their abridged variants do not contain dummy edges, and thus are legal paths in G. Let (P_1^*, P_2^*) be the optimal pair of 2-disjoint shortest paths from s to t in G. The paths corresponding to them in $\bar{G}$—obtained from them by the operations in the reduction applied to their first and last edges—are node-disjoint and have weights greater by 2 than the weights of P_1^* and P_2^*. The optimal paths in $\bar{G}$ are not worse, and their abridged variants are by lighter by 2. Therefore, the pair of paths returned by the reduction is not worse than the pair (P_1^*, P_2^*), as required.

The pseudocode of the suggested algorithm appears in the full version [5]. The algorithm correctness, together with the polynomiality of the algorithm of Akhmedov and of the reduction, implies the following statement.

Theorem 2. *The prioritized multi-criteria 2-disjoint shortest paths problem in an undirected graph can be solved in polynomial time.*

4 k-Disjoint All-Criteria-Shortest Paths

This section studies the following k-disjoint all-criteria-shortest paths problem. The input is a directed graph $G = (V, E)$, q weight functions w_i on edge set

E, $1 \leq i \leq q$, source node s and destination node t, $s, t \in V$, and integer k. We say that a path P^* from x to y is the shortest w.r.t. criterion c_i, if $c_i(P^*) = \sum_{e \in P^*} w_i(e)$ is minimal among all $c_i(P) = \sum_{e \in P} w_i(e)$ over all paths P from x to y. A set of k (edge-)disjoint paths from s to t such that each one of them is *shortest regarding each one of the q criteria* is sought for, if exists. After some analysis, a polynomial algorithm solving the problem is presented and analyzed. We first reduce the problem to its single criterion version, then reduce the latter problem to finding k disjoint paths from s to t in a certain sub-graph of G, if they exist. Finally we present an algorithm for finding them, if they exist, using known techniques: max-flow finding and flow decomposition.

We assume that each node is reachable from s and that t is reachable from each node in G; otherwise, the extra nodes could be removed from G. Let distances $d_i(s, x)$ and $d_i(y, t)$, $x, y \in V$, denote the lengths of the shortest paths from s to x and from y to t, respectively, w.r.t. criterion c_i in G. We assume that there is no negative cycle in G w.r.t. any weight function w_i, in order for the shortest paths to exist. (See, e.g., [3] for the basic information on graph algorithms).

Let us define the auxiliary *aggregated weight* $w(e) = \sum_i w_i(e)$ for each edge $e \in E$, and the auxiliary *aggregated criterion* $c(P) = \sum_{e \in P} w(e)$ for each path P in G. Note that there is no negative cycle in G w.r.t. weight function w, by our assumption; hence, shortest paths w.r.t. c exist, and thus distances $d(s, x)$ and $d(y, t)$, $x, y \in V$, w.r.t. w are well defined. Observe that $d(s, t) = \min_P c(P) = \min_P \sum_i c_i(P) \geq \sum_i \min_P c_i(P) = \sum_i d_i(s, t)$, where each minimum is taken over all paths P from s to t in G. Moreover, the equality $d(s, t) = \sum_i d_i(s, t)$ holds if and only if there exist paths from s to t shortest w.r.t. each criterion c_i; in this case, these paths and only these are shortest w.r.t. criterion c.

As a consequence, we obtain the following reduction from our problem to the auxiliary single criterion problem. If $d(s, t) > \sum_i d_i(s, t)$, then no paths from s to t shortest w.r.t. each criterion c_i exist. Checking this could be made via $q + 1$ executions of algorithm Dijkstra on G, w.r.t. each criterion c_i and w.r.t. criterion c. Otherwise, the required k disjoint paths are the k-*disjoint paths shortest w.r.t. criterion c, if they exist*. In what follows, we present the solution to the single criterion disjoint shortest k paths problem. The lacking proofs can be found in the full version of our paper [5].

Lemma 1. *1. Node u belongs to at least one shortest path from s to t if and only if $d(s, u) + d(u, t) = d(s, t)$.*
2. Edge (u, v) belongs to at least one shortest path from s to t if and only if $d(s, u) + w(u, v) + d(v, t) = d(s, t)$.

Let us define $\tilde{V}$ as the subset of nodes as in Lemma 1(1) and $\tilde{E}$ as the subset of edges as in Lemma 1(2). We denote by $\tilde{G}$ the (sub-)graph $(\tilde{V}, \tilde{E})$.

Lemma 2. *1. Each shortest path from s to t is contained in $\tilde{G}$.*
2. Each path from s to t contained in $\tilde{G}$ is shortest.

Lemma 2 establishes a reduction from the single criterion disjoint shortest k paths problem to *finding k disjoint paths from s to t in $\tilde{G}$, if they exist*. Finding such paths, if they exist, can be done by known max-flow techniques. Let N be the flow network $(\tilde{G}, s, t)$ with unit capacities of all its edges.

Proposition 1. *A set of k disjoint paths from s to t in $\tilde{G}$ exists if and only if the value of maximal flow in N is at least k.*

Proof. The proof to the direction only if is omitted in this version.

direction if Let f_0 be an integer (that is $0/1$) flow in N of value at least k. A set $\mathcal{P}$ of k disjoint paths from s to t in $\tilde{G}$ is produced by executing the following triple-phased *path-finding routine* k times, beginning from $f = f_0$ and an empty path set $\mathcal{P}$. We denote by E_f the (dynamic) set of edges in N with the value 1 of flow f.

Phase 1 Set stack S to be empty. Set to v be t and mark it. Choose an edge (u, v) in E_f and push it into S. Set v to be u, mark it, and continue in the same way. If we arrived at $v = s$, go to Phase 3. If we arrived at a marked node v, suspend Phase 1 and go to Phase 2.

Phase 2 Set $z = v$. Pop edge (u, v) from S. Unmark u, set $f(u, v) = 0$, set v to be u, and continue in the same way. When arrived at $v = z$, mark v and resume Phase 1.

Phase 3 Set list P to be empty. Unmark $v = s$. Pop edge (u, v) from S. Unmark u, add (u, v) to P, set $f(u, v) = 0$, set v to be u, and continue in the same way. Upon arrival at $v = t$, add P to $\mathcal{P}$.

Let us explain briefly the correctness. After each execution of Phase 2 (removal of a flow cycle), f becomes a correct flow with the same value. After each execution of Phase 3 (removal of a flow path), f becomes a correct flow with a value smaller by 1. At Phase 1, since the flow value is non-zero, there exists at least one edge in E_f entering t. Since flow f is correct, at each node v, the numbers of edges incoming and outgoing v are equal in E_f. Hence, if there is an edge outgoing v in E_f, then also an edge incoming v exists in E_f. □

We conclude that for solving the problem, it is sufficient to find a max-flow in N, and if the flow value is at least k, execute the path-finding routine presented in the proof of Proposition 1 k times. The detailed pseudocode of this solution appears in the full version of our paper [5]. Let us analyse the running time. A flow either of value k, if such a one exists, or a max-flow, otherwise, in a network with unit edge capacities can be found in time $O(\min(k|E|, |E|^{3/2}))$ (see [1,7]). All executions of the path-finding routine together take $O(|E|)$ time, since each edge is processed in time $O(1)$ in total. Summarizing, the running time bound is $O(\min(k|E|, |E|^{3/2}))$.

References

1. Ahuja, R.K., Magnanti, T.L., Orlin, J.B.: Network Flows: Theory, Algorithms, and Applications. Prentice Hall, Hoboken (1993)
2. Akhmedov, M.: Faster 2-disjoint-shortest-paths algorithm. In: Fernau, H. (ed.) CSR 2020. LNCS, vol. 12159, pp. 103–116. Springer, Cham (2020). https://doi.org/10.1007/978-3-030-50026-9_7

3. Cormen, T.H., Leiserson, C.E., Rivest, R.L., Stein, C.: Introduction to Algorithms, 3rd edn. The MIT Press, Cambridge (2009)
4. Dijkstra, E.W.: A note on two problems in connexion with graphs. Numer. Math. **1**(1), 269–271 (1959)
5. Dinitz, Y., Dolev, S., Kumar, M.: Polynomial time prioritized multi-criteria k-shortest paths and k-disjoint all-criteria-shortest paths. CoRR abs/2101.11514 (2021). https://arxiv.org/abs/2101.11514
6. Eilam-Tzoreff, T.: The disjoint shortest paths problem. Discret. Appl. Math. **85**(2), 113–138 (1998)
7. Even, S.: Graph Algorithms, 2nd edn. Cambridge University Press, Cambridge (2011)
8. Oh, S., Lee, C., Choo, H.: Collaborative trust-based shortest secure path discovery in mobile ad hoc networks. In: Alexandrov, V.N., van Albada, G.D., Sloot, P.M.A., Dongarra, J. (eds.) ICCS 2006, Part II. LNCS, vol. 3992, pp. 1089–1096. Springer, Heidelberg (2006). https://doi.org/10.1007/11758525_145
9. Sanguankotchakorn, T., Perera, N.: Hybrid multi-constrained optimal path QoS routing with inaccurate link state. In: 2010 Ninth International Conference on Networks, pp. 321–326 (2010). https://doi.org/10.1109/ICN.2010.57
10. Yen, J.Y.: Finding the k shortest loopless paths in a network. Manage. Sci. **17**(11), 712–716 (1971)
11. Zaffalon, V., Reis, A.B.J.B.K.: K-shortest-path-using-dijkstra (2017). https://github.com/Teodim/K-Shortest-Path-using-Dijkstra

Binding BIKE Errors to a Key Pair

Nir Drucker[2] , Shay Gueron[1,2(✉)] , and Dusan Kostic[2]

[1] University of Haifa, Haifa, Israel
[2] Amazon, Seattle, USA

Abstract. The KEM BIKE is a Round-3 alternative finalist in the NIST Post-Quantum Cryptography project. It uses the $FO^{\not\perp}$ transformation so that an instantiation with a decoder that has a DFR of 2^{-128} will make it IND-CCA secure. The current BIKE design does not bind the randomness of the ciphertexts (i.e., the error vectors) to a specific public key. We propose to change this design, although currently, there is no attack that leverages this property. This modification can be considered if BIKE is eventually standardized.

Keywords: BIKE · Post-Quantum Cryptography · NIST · QC-MDPC codes · Ciphertext binding

1 Introduction

Bit Flipping Key Encapsulation (BIKE) [3] is a Quasi-Cyclic Moderate-Density Parity-Check (QC-MDPC) code-based Key Encapsulation Mechanism (KEM). It is a Round-3 "alternative finalist" in the NIST Post-Quantum Cryptography project [15]. Figure 1 illustrates BIKE's key generation, encapsulation, and decapsulation flows.

BIKE decapsulation depends on a probabilistic algorithm that is called "Decode", which, for every given input, may succeed (and produce m') or fail (and output $\perp$). Steps 1, 2, and 4 of the encapsulation flow, and steps 2,3 of the decapsulation flow realize the Fujisaki-Okamoto transformation $FO^{\not\perp}$ [12]. This transformation is required in a KEM with possible decapsulation failures for achieving IND-CCA security. Reference [8] proves that BIKE is indeed IND-CCA secure if *Decode* has a Decoding Failure Rate (DFR) of $2^{-128}, 2^{-192}, 2^{-256}$, for security levels 1, 3, and 5, respectively. BIKE has the following property.

Property 1. Steps 1,2 of the encapsulation are independent of the public key h.

In a multi-user scenario, Property 1 implies that an adversary can select one errors vector (e_0, e_1) and use it to produce multiple ciphertexts C for different public keys. In this context, we mention the IND-CCA KEM schemes FrodoKEM [2], Kyber [17], Saber [6], SIKE [13], that are selected to Round-3 of the NIST PQC Standardization Project [15] (as either "finalists" or "alternative finalists"). The encapsulation procedures of these KEMs blend the public key value with

© Springer Nature Switzerland AG 2021
S. Dolev et al. (Eds.): CSCML 2021, LNCS 12716, pp. 275–281, 2021.
https://doi.org/10.1007/978-3-030-78086-9_21

$$(sk, \sigma, h) \xleftarrow{\$} \texttt{Keygen}()$$

1. Generate $\sigma \xleftarrow{\$} \{0,1\}^{256}$
2. $sk = (h_0, h_1) \xleftarrow{\$} \mathcal{R}^2$ with $wt(h_0) = wt(h_1) = w$ odd
3. $h = h_1 h_0^{-1}$
4. Return (sk, σ, h)

$$(C, K) \xleftarrow{\$} \texttt{Encaps}(h)$$

1. Generate a message $m \xleftarrow{\$} \mathcal{M}$
2. Compute error vectors $(e_0, e_1) = \mathbf{H}(m)$ with $wt(e_0, e_1) = t$ and $e_0, e_1 \in \mathcal{R}$.
3. Compute the ciphertext $C = (c_0, c_1) = (e_0 + e_1 h, m \oplus \mathbf{L}(e_0, e_1))$
4. Compute the shared key $K = \mathbf{K}(m, C)$

$$m = \texttt{Decaps}(sk, \sigma, h, C)$$

1. $m' = \text{Decode}(sk, C)$ // Or $\perp$ on decoding failure.
2. If $((m' \neq \perp)$ and $(C == \text{ReEncrypt}(m', h)))$ return $\mathbf{K}(m', C)$
3. Else return $\mathbf{K}(\sigma, C)$

Fig. 1. BIKE [3] flows. The block size r and the weights w and t are public parameters of the scheme. $\mathcal{R}$ is the polynomial ring $\mathbb{F}_2[X]/\langle X^r - 1 \rangle$. The Hamming weight of an element $v \in \mathcal{R}$ is denoted by $wt(v)$. The $\oplus$ symbol denotes the exclusive-or operation. Uniform random sampling from $\mathcal{R}$ is denoted by $w \xleftarrow{\$} \mathcal{R}$. The key generation outputs a secret key sk, a random seed σ, and a public key h. The input to the encapsulation procedure is the public key h. The output is the ciphertext C and the shared key K. The decapsulation procedure uses the secret key sk, the seed σ, the public key h and the ciphertext C and (always) outputs a shared key K (which is randomized on a decoding failure). $\mathbf{H} : \{0,1\}^{256} \longrightarrow \{0,1\}^{2r}, \mathbf{K} : \{0,1\}^{256+r} \longrightarrow \{0,1\}^{256}, \mathbf{L} : \{0,1\}^{2r} \longrightarrow \{0,1\}^{256}$ are (modeled as) some random oracles with respective output lengths $2r$, 256, 256. They can be instantiated in different ways $\mathcal{M} = \{0,1\}^{256}$.

the randomness. This binds the randomness used for the encapsulation to the session keys (private/public key pair). BIKE [3] and NTRU-Prime [4] (also a Round-3 alternative finalist) use the public key value *only after* the randomness is generated and thus possess Property 1 or equivalent. Note that unlike NTRU-Prime, BIKE may encounter decapsulation failures that can lead to reaction attacks [9,11,14,16]. This is potentially exploitable if the scheme's DFR is not negligible. An interesting discussion on the subject can be found on the PQC forum [1] where the discussion ends with:

[M. Hamburg] "Hashing the public key or its seed is only: A required security feature if your system exhibits decryption failures; and A useful feature to reduce multi-target concerns if your system has any parameter sets aimed at class $\leq$ III."[1]

Examples for the rationale behind the multi-key consideration of Kyber and Frodo are given next. Kyber justifies the discussed binding as follows [5]:

"This tweak has two effects. First, it makes the KEM contributory; the shared key K does not depend only on input of one of the two parties. The second effect is a multitarget protection. Consider an attacker who searches through many values m to find one that is 'likely' to produce a failure during decryption. Such a decryption failure of a legitimate ciphertext would leak some information about the secret key. [...] hashing pk into $\hat{K}$ ensures that an attacker would not be able to use precomputed values m against multiple targets."

The Frodo team [2] defines a new transformation, namely $FO^{\perp'}$, that is based on $FO^\perp$ and states that "following [5], we make the following modifications [..], denoting the resulting transform $FO^{\perp'}$: [..] The computation of r and k also takes the public key pk as input".

Remark 1. Binding the randomness or the ciphertext (without randomness) to the public key is meaningful only if this binding is verified during the decapsulation. In particular, schemes that use the FO [10] transformation, where decapsulation includes re-encryption, verify the binding explicitly (when it exists).

This note discusses the technical considerations that are required for avoiding Property 1 in the context of BIKE, with methods to bind the errors vector to a specific public key. We view it as a cheap means to diminish the efficiency of any potential analyses in the multi-key scenario. In this sense, our binding matches BIKE design to that of FrodoKEM, Kyber, Saber, and SIKE.

2   Specific Proposals for BIKE

Binding the errors to a specific public key can be done in several ways. Some were mentioned e.g., in [1]: concatenate m to either 1) the public key; 2) the hash digest of the public key; 3) the seed used to generate part of the public key (if available) together with its other part. We discuss only options 1 and 2 because option 3 is not applicable for BIKE. Option 3 is possible when part of the public key can be generated from a small seed. For example, the public key in some lattice-based schemes (e.g., Kyber) includes a large public matrix that can be generated from a small seed. By contrast, BIKE public key is generated entirely from the (secret) private key.

The function $\mathbf{H} : \{0,1\}^{256} \longrightarrow \{0,1\}^{2r}$ is modeled as a random oracle (see [8] for the details). Its input is a 256 bits seed that $\mathbf{H}$ expands into an errors vector

---

[1] Here, we interpret the term "multi-target" as "multi-user", where multiple users can use a specific KEM with different keys. We also interpret the term "class" as the NIST PQC "security level".

$$(sk, \sigma, h) \xleftarrow{\$} \texttt{Keygen}()$$

1. Generate $\sigma \xleftarrow{\$} \{0,1\}^{256}$
2. $sk = (h_0, h_1) \xleftarrow{\$} \mathcal{R}^2$ with $wt(h_0) = wt(h_1) = w$ odd
3. $h = h_1 h_0^{-1}$
4. Return (sk, σ, h)

$$(C, K) \xleftarrow{\$} \texttt{Encaps}(h)$$

1. Generate a message $m \xleftarrow{\$} \mathcal{M}$
2. Compute error vectors $(e_0, e_1) = \mathbf{H}(f_i(m, h))$ with $wt(e_0, e_1) = t$ and $e_0, e_1 \in \mathcal{R}$.
3. Compute the ciphertext $C = (c_0, c_1) = (e_0 + e_1 h, m \oplus \mathbf{L}(e_0, e_1))$
4. Compute the shared key $K = \mathbf{K}(m, C)$

$$m = \texttt{Decaps}(sk, \sigma, h, C)$$

1. $m' = \text{Decode}(sk, C)$ // Or $\perp$ on decoding failure.
2. If $((m' \neq \perp)$ and $(C == \text{ReEncrypt}(m', h)))$ return $\mathbf{K}(m', C)$
   $\triangleright$ ReEncrypt uses $\mathbf{H}(f_i(m', h))$ instead of $\mathbf{H}(m')$
3. Else return $\mathbf{K}(\sigma, C)$

Fig. 2. Variants of BIKE KEM that bind the errors vector to the public key. The two options are reflected through the function f_i, $i = 1, 2$, as explained in the text. The differences are highlighted in red. (Color figure online)

(e_0, e_1). In the current BIKE instantiation, the expander $\mathbf{H}$ is based on AES-CTR PRF, where the input seed plays the role of an AES key. Applying options 1 or 2 above requires another approach. First, using an extractor $f : \{0,1\}^* \longrightarrow \{0,1\}^{256}$ (modeled as a random oracle), to compress the longer input to a 256-bit uniform random string; and subsequently feeding the result into the expander $\mathbf{H}$, as before.

To realize options 1 and 2, we use f_1 and f_2, respectively, as follows

$$f_1 : \mathcal{M} \times \mathcal{PK} \longrightarrow \{0,1\}^{256} \qquad f_2 : \mathcal{M} \times \mathcal{PK} \longrightarrow \{0,1\}^{256}$$
$$(m, pk) \longmapsto H(m \parallel pk) \qquad (m, pk) \longmapsto H(m \parallel H'(pk))$$

Here, $H, H' : \{0,1\}^* \longrightarrow \{0,1\}^{256}$ are collision-resistant cryptographic hash functions (e.g., SHA256), and $\mathcal{PK}$ is the set of BIKE public keys. With no loss of generality, we assume that $H = H'$. The resulting modified version of BIKE is illustrated in Fig. 2.

Remark 2. For completeness, we mention the following two obvious options for f and explain why we do not recommend them for BIKE.

1. Pad the public key to the nearest multiple of 256 bits boundary, split the padded string to 256-bit chunks $pk_1, \ldots, pk_q$ (for the appropriate q), and invoke $\mathbf{H}(m \oplus pk_1 \oplus \ldots \oplus pk_n)$ instead of $\mathbf{H}(m)$ as in Fig. 1 Step 2. This approach allows an adversary to control the output of $\mathbf{H}$ through the publicly known pk.
2. Concatenating only 256 bits tail (truncation) of pk to m, i.e., calling $\mathbf{H}(m \| trunc_{256}(pk))$ instead of $\mathbf{H}(m)$ in Fig. 1 Step 2. This requires an assumption that $trunc_{256}(pk)$ is uniformly random (over $\{0,1\}^{256}$). Note that BIKE public keys are not uniformly random strings, for example, their Hamming weight is always even. Therefore, using the public key's tail requires some additional justification.

3   Practical Considerations and the BIKE Additional Implementation Package

The general definition of BIKE uses abstract random oracle functions $\mathbf{H}, \mathbf{K}, \mathbf{L}$ [8]. The specification [3] uses a specific instantiation: $\mathbf{H}$ is based on the CTR-AES PRF, while $\mathbf{K}$ and $\mathbf{L}$ use the standard SHA-384 hash function. The git repository [7] holds an "Additional implementation" package for BIKE, and offers a full *constant-time* software suite as follows: a) a portable C (C99) implementation; b) an implementation that leverages the AVX2 architecture features, written in C (with C intrinsics for AVX2 functions); c) an implementation that leverages the AVX512 architecture features, written in C (with C intrinsics for AVX512 functions).

The AVX512 implementation can also be compiled to use the vector PCLMU -LQDQ instruction that is available on the Intel IceLake processors. The package includes testing and invokes the KAT generation utilities provided by NIST. Note that it is a "stand-alone" suite that does not depend on any external library. However, it also includes a compilation option that allows the use of OpenSSL (to consume its AES256 and SHA-384 implementations). The modularity of the code allows for easy selection of different $\mathbf{H}, \mathbf{K}, \mathbf{L}$ options and for the binding function f. For example, it possible to choose SHA-512 truncated to 384 bits instead of SHA-384, or an arbitrary pseudo-random generator for expanding the (extracted) seed into an errors vector. This code structure makes our build system flexible and therefore it is easy to switch between the current and the proposed instantiation through only a compilation flag only.

The sizes of the BIKE public keys are 1541, 3083, and 5122 bytes for Level-1, 3, 5, respectively. We consider the following two options for instantiating f_1 and f_2, using SHA384 (which is anyway currently used):

- f_1 is the 256 least significant bits of SHA384 hash digest of the input $(m \| pk)$. Here, the input sizes are 1573, 3115, and 5154 bytes require 13, 25, and 41 invocations of the SHA-384 update functions, respectively.
- f_2 and H are the 256 least significant bits of the SHA384 hash digest of the input. When the input to H is pk, the numbers of invocations of the SHA384

update function are 13, 25, and 41, respectively. The function f_2 invokes the SHA384 update function only once (because the input is of length 64 bytes).

We see that computing f_2 requires one additional invocation of the SHA384 update function compared to f_1. However, the impact of this difference on the overall performance of BIKE is negligible. The advantage of using f_2 is that the encapsulator can choose to compute $H(pk)$ only once and reuse the output. This is valuable in protocols that would use BIKE with static keys. By contrast, using f_1 is more efficient for protocols that use BIKE with ephemeral keys as recommended for BIKE [3] ("BIKE is primarily designed to be used in synchronous communication protocols (e.g. TLS) with ephemeral keys"). For such usages, we recommend the use of f_1. However, for static keys we recommend f_2 because there is no performance cost.

Table 1. The performance cost of our proposal in 10^3 cycles, when BIKE is used with ephemeral keys. Note that the impact on decapsulation is almost negligible.

	AVX2 Before	AVX2 After	SlowDown	AVX512 Before	AVX512 After	SlowDown
Encaps L1	124	143	**1.153**	105	121	**1.152**
Decaps L1	2634	2652	**1.007**	1197	1213	**1.013**
Encaps L3	296	325	**1.098**	237	265	**1.118**
Decaps L3	7988	8017	**1.003**	3480	3509	**1.008**

We implemented our proposed modification in the Additional implementation of BIKE. This implementation is controlled by the compilation flag BLEND_PK, where the default compilation still follows the current version of BIKE specification [3]. The code modification is small due to the code modularity of our package and affects only the sha.h and sha.c files. Table 1 compares the performance with and without our modification, where we observe a slowdown of up to 15.3% in the encapsulation and up to 1.3% in the decapsulation.

4   Conclusion

We (i.e., the authors of this paper, speaking for themselves and not on behalf of the BIKE team) propose to modify BIKE to a variant that binds the errors vector to the public key. The proposed changes to the encapsulation and decapsulation flows are easy to make, have a low-performance impact, and are already demonstrated in our (Additional) implementation package.

Acknowledgments. This research was supported by: NSF-BSF Grant 2018640; NSF Grant CNS 1906360; The Israel Science Foundation (grant No. 3380/19); The BIU Center for Research in Applied Cryptography and Cyber Security, and the Center for Cyber Law and Policy at the University of Haifa, both in conjunction with the Israel National Cyber Bureau in the Prime Minister's Office.

References

1. PQC-forum announcement of NTRU-HRSS-KEM and NTRUEncrypt merger, December 2018. https://groups.google.com/a/list.nist.gov/g/pqc-forum/c/SrFO-vK3xbI/m/utjUZ9hJDwAJ
2. Alkim, E., et al.: FrodoKEM Practical quantum-secure key encapsulation from generic lattices (2020). https://frodokem.org/
3. Aragon, N., et al.: BIKE: Bit Flipping Key Encapsulation (2020). https://bikesuite.org/files/v4.0/BIKE_Spec.2020.05.03.1.pdf
4. Bernstein, D.J., Chuengsatiansup, C., Lange, T., van Vredendaal, C.: NTRU prime: reducing attack surface at low cost. In: Adams, C., Camenisch, J. (eds.) SAC 2017. LNCS, vol. 10719, pp. 235–260. Springer, Cham (2018). https://doi.org/10.1007/978-3-319-72565-9_12
5. Bos, J., et al.: CRYSTALS - Kyber: a CCA-secure module-lattice-based KEM. In: 2018 IEEE European Symposium on Security and Privacy (EuroS P), pp. 353–367 (2018)
6. D'Anvers, J.P., et al.: SABER M-LWR-Based KEM (2020). https://www.esat.kuleuven.be/cosic/pqcrypto/saber/
7. Drucker, N., Gueron, S., Kostic, D.: Additional implementation of BIKE (2020). https://github.com/awslabs/bike-kem
8. Drucker, N., Gueron, S., Kostic, D., Persichetti, E.: On the applicability of the Fujisaki-Okamoto transformation to the BIKE KEM. Technical report 2020/510 (2020). https://eprint.iacr.org/2020/510
9. Eaton, E., Lequesne, M., Parent, A., Sendrier, N.: QC-MDPC: a timing attack and a CCA2 KEM. In: Lange, T., Steinwandt, R. (eds.) PQCrypto 2018. LNCS, vol. 10786, pp. 47–76. Springer, Cham (2018). https://doi.org/10.1007/978-3-319-79063-3_3
10. Fujisaki, E., Okamoto, T.: Secure integration of asymmetric and symmetric encryption schemes. In: Wiener, M. (ed.) CRYPTO 1999. LNCS, vol. 1666, pp. 537–554. Springer, Heidelberg (1999). https://doi.org/10.1007/3-540-48405-1_34
11. Guo, Q., Johansson, T., Stankovski, P.: A key recovery attack on MDPC with CCA security using decoding errors. In: Cheon, J.H., Takagi, T. (eds.) ASIACRYPT 2016. LNCS, vol. 10031, pp. 789–815. Springer, Heidelberg (2016). https://doi.org/10.1007/978-3-662-53887-6_29
12. Hofheinz, D., Hövelmanns, K., Kiltz, E.: A modular analysis of the Fujisaki-Okamoto transformation. In: Kalai, Y., Reyzin, L. (eds.) TCC 2017. LNCS, vol. 10677, pp. 341–371. Springer, Cham (2017). https://doi.org/10.1007/978-3-319-70500-2_12
13. Jao, D., et al.: SIKE - Supersingular Isogeny Key Encapsulation (2020). https://sike.org/
14. Nilsson, A., Johansson, T., Stankovski Wagner, P.: Error amplification in code-based cryptography. IACR Trans. Crypt. Hardw. Embed. Syst. (1) 238–258 (2019). https://doi.org/10.13154/tches.v2019.i1.238-258
15. NIST: Post-Quantum Cryptography (2020). https://csrc.nist.gov/projects/post-quantum-cryptography. Accessed 30 Sep 2020
16. Santini, P., Battaglioni, M., Chiaraluce, F., Baldi, M.: Analysis of reaction and timing attacks against cryptosystems based on sparse parity-check codes. In: Baldi, M., Persichetti, E., Santini, P. (eds.) CBC 2019. LNCS, vol. 11666, pp. 115–136. Springer, Cham (2019). https://doi.org/10.1007/978-3-030-25922-8_7
17. Schwabe, P., et al.: CRYSTALS-KYBER (2020). https://pq-crystals.org/kyber/

Fast and Error-Free Negacyclic Integer Convolution Using Extended Fourier Transform

Jakub Klemsa$^{(\boxtimes)}$

Czech Technical University in Prague, Prague, Czech Republic
jakub.klemsa@fel.cvut.cz

Abstract. With the rise of lattice cryptography, (negacyclic) convolution has received increased attention. E.g., the NTRU scheme internally employs cyclic polynomial multiplication, which is equivalent to the standard convolution, on the other hand, many Ring-LWE-based cryptosystems perform negacyclic polynomial multiplication. A method by Crandall implements an efficient negacyclic convolution over a finite field of prime order using an extended Discrete Galois Transform (DGT) – a finite field analogy to Discrete Fourier Transform (DFT). Compared to DGT, the classical DFT runs faster by an order of magnitude, however, it suffers from inevitable rounding errors due to finite floating-point number representation. In a recent Fully Homomorphic Encryption (FHE) scheme by Chillotti et al. named TFHE, small errors are acceptable (although not welcome), therefore we decided to investigate the application of DFT for negacyclic convolution.

   The primary goal of this paper is to suggest a method for fast negacyclic convolution over integer coefficients using an extended DFT. The key contribution is a thorough analysis of error propagation, as a result of which we derive parameter bounds that can guarantee even error-free results. We also suggest a setup that admits rare errors, which allows to increase the degree of the polynomials and/or their maximum norm at a fixed floating-point precision. Finally, we run benchmarks with parameters derived from a practical **TFHE** setup. We achieve around 24× better times than the generic NTL library (comparable to Crandall's method) and around 4× better times than a naïve approach with DFT, with no errors.

Keywords: Negacyclic convolution · Fast Fourier Transform · Fully Homomorphic Encryption

1   Introduction

In 1994, Peter Shor discovered efficient quantum algorithms for discrete logarithm and factoring [26], which started the quest to design novel quantum-proof

This work was supported by the Grant Agency of CTU in Prague, grant No. SGS21/160/OHK3/3T/13.

S. Dolev et al. (Eds.): CSCML 2021, LNCS 12716, pp. 282–300, 2021.
https://doi.org/10.1007/978-3-030-78086-9_22

algorithms, aka. *Post-Quantum Cryptography*. Since then, there have emerged many new schemes, which are based on various problems that are believed to be quantum hard. E.g., supersingular elliptic curve isogeny [18], multivariate cryptography [12], or lattice cryptography [2], in particular Learning With Errors (LWE) and its variants [21,24]. In addition, many *Fully Homomorphic Encryption* (FHE) schemes (e.g. [6,8]) belong to lattice-based ones, including Gentry's first-ever FHE scheme [14]. Most notably, the NIST's Post-Quantum Cryptography Standardization Program entered the third "Selection Round" in July 2020 [23], while lattice-based cryptosystems occur among the selected algorithms.

With the popularity of lattice-based cryptography, the need for its fast implementation has risen. Besides linear algebra, many schemes require a fast algorithm for cyclic (i.e., mod $X^N - 1$) or negacyclic (i.e., mod $X^N + 1$) polynomial multiplication. Some schemes work with polynomial coefficients modulo an integer (e.g., NTRU [17]), however, our main interest is in the TFHE scheme [8], where negacyclic multiplication of integer-torus polynomials is performed. Here the *torus* refers to reals modulo 1, i.e., the fractional part of a real number. In practice, torus elements are represented as unsigned integers, which represent the fraction of 1 uniformly in the interval $[0, 1)$. It follows that integer-torus polynomial multiplication can be performed with their integer representation. Also note that TFHE accepts small errors – we prefer to avoid them, but their impact is not fatal for decryption.

Recently, there have emerged efforts to make TFHE work with multivalued plaintexts [7], also applications of TFHE for homomorphic evaluation of neural networks show promising results [5]. In particular, for neural networks, it holds that they are quite error-tolerant (also verified in [5]), which supports the acceptability of errors.

Problem Statement. Our goal is to develop a method for fast negacyclic multiplication of univariate integer polynomials. For this method, we aim to estimate and tune its parameters in order to provide certain guarantees of its correctness. As outlined above, we will not focus solely on an error-free case and we will also accept the scenario, where errors may rarely occur. Last but not least—as we intend our method also for an FPGA implementation—we derive all results in a generic manner, i.e., without sticking to a concrete platform, although we run our tests on an ordinary 64-bit machine.

Related Work. There is a long and rich history of methods for fast multiplication over various rings, ranging from Karatsuba's algorithm [19], through Fast Fourier Transform (FFT; [9]) to Schönhage-Strassen algorithm [25]. Most of these methods are based on a similar principle as Bernstein pointed out in his survey [4].

It was the classical cyclic convolution, which was accelerated by FFT and Convolution Theorem, and which can be employed for polynomial multiplication modulo $X^N - 1$, too. On the contrary, polynomial multiplication modulo

$X^N + 1$ (negacyclic convolution) cannot be directly calculated via FFT. One possible approach was implemented as a part of the TFHE Library [28], although not discussed in the paper [8]. However, this method suffers from a four-tuple redundancy in its intermediate results. An effective (non-redundant) method for negacyclic convolution has been proposed by Crandall [11] and recently improved by Al Badawi et al. [3]. In these methods, polynomials are considered over a finite ring and both authors employed a number-theoretic variant of FFT, named DGT, which operates on the field $\mathsf{GF}(p^2)$. On the one hand, DGT calculates exact results (as opposed to FFT, where rounding errors occur and propagate), on the other hand, it runs significantly slower as it uses modular arithmetics.

Our Contributions. We propose an efficient algorithm for negacyclic convolution over the reals, for which we derive estimates of bounds on the maximum error and its variance. Based on our estimates, we show that our method can be used for an error-free negacyclic convolution over integers. Or—in case we admit errors—we suggest to relax the estimates in order to achieve higher performance: either in terms of shorter number representation (useful in particular for FPGA), longer polynomials, or larger polynomial coefficients that can be processed. Finally, we provide experimental benchmarking results of our implementation as well as we evaluate its rounding error magnitudes and result correctness, even with remarkably underestimated parameters.

Paper Outline. In Sect. 2, we provide a brief overview of the required mathematical background, i.e., cyclic and negacyclic convolutions, their relation to modular polynomial multiplication, as well as the Discrete Fourier Transform and Convolution Theorem. Next, in Sect. 3, we revisit a straightforward FFT-based approach for negacyclic polynomial multiplication, and we propose a method that avoids the calculation of redundant intermediates. We analyze error propagation thoroughly in Sect. 4, where we suggest lower bounds on floating point type bit-precision in order to guarantee certain levels of correctness. In Sect. 5, we discuss the implementation details and we propose a set of testing parameters with respect to TFHE. Using these parameters, we benchmark our implementation and we also examine the error magnitude and result correctness. Finally, we conclude our paper in Sect. 6.

2   Preliminaries

In this section, we briefly recall some basic mathematical concepts related to convolution and Discrete Fourier Transform.

Cyclic & Negacyclic Convolution. Let $\mathbf{f}, \mathbf{g} \in \mathbb{C}^N$ for some $N \in \mathbb{N}$. As opposed to the classical cyclic convolution defined as

$$(\mathbf{f} * \mathbf{g})_k := \sum_{j=0}^{N-1} f_j g_{(k-j) \bmod N}, \tag{1}$$

negacyclic convolution adds a factor of -1 with each wrap of the cyclic index at g, i.e.,

$$(\mathbf{f} \bar{*} \mathbf{g})_k := \sum_{j=0}^{N-1} (-1)^{\lfloor \frac{k-j}{N} \rfloor} f_j g_{(k-j) \bmod N}. \tag{2}$$

With respect to polynomials, it is easy to verify that the cyclic convolution calculates the coefficients of a product of two polynomials modulo $X^N - 1$. Indeed, their coefficients can be considered cyclic since $X^N = 1$. On the other hand, the *negacyclic* convolution calculates the coefficients of a product of two polynomials modulo $X^N + 1$, since $X^N = -1$ adds a factor of -1 with each wrap.

Convolution Theorem. A relation known as the *Convolution Theorem* (CT) states an equality between the Fourier image of convoluted vectors and an element-wise (dyadic) product of their respective Fourier images (in the discrete variant). CT writes as follows:

$$\mathcal{F}(\mathbf{f} * \mathbf{g}) = \mathcal{F}(\mathbf{f}) \odot \mathcal{F}(\mathbf{g}), \tag{3}$$

where $\mathcal{F}(\cdot)$ stands for the *Discrete Fourier Transform* (DFT) and $\odot$ denotes the dyadic multiplication of two vectors. In fact, DFT is a change of basis, defined as

$$\mathcal{F}(\mathbf{f})_k := \sum_{j=0}^{N-1} f_j \exp\left(-\frac{2\pi i j k}{N}\right) = F_k, \tag{4}$$

$$\mathcal{F}^{-1}(\mathbf{F})_j = \frac{1}{N} \sum_{k=0}^{N-1} F_k \exp\left(\frac{2\pi i j k}{N}\right) = f_j. \tag{5}$$

Convolution theorem has gained its practical significance after *Fast Fourier Transform* (FFT) was (re)invented[1] in 1965 by Cooley & Tukey [9]. As opposed to a direct calculation of DFT coefficients, which requires $O(N^2)$ time, FFT runs in $O(N \log N)$. Next, by the convolution theorem, one can calculate the convolution of two vectors as $\mathbf{f} * \mathbf{g} = \mathcal{F}^{-1}(\mathcal{F}(\mathbf{f}) \odot \mathcal{F}(\mathbf{g}))$, which spends $O(N \log N)$ time, compared to $O(N^2)$ needed for a direct calculation.

3   Efficient Negacyclic Convolution

First, we describe a method for negacyclic convolution that uses the standard cyclic convolution and FFT. We identify its redundancy and briefly comment on possible workarounds. Next, we outline an approach that yields no redundancy and achieves a 4× better performance than the previous method.

---

[1] Goldstine [15] attributes an FFT-like algorithm to C. F. Gauss dating to around 1805.

3.1   Redundant Approach

Since (negacyclic) convolution is equivalent to (negacyclic) polynomial modular multiplication, we switch to the polynomial point of view for now. Interested in polynomial multiplication modulo $X^N + 1$, we note that $X^{2N} - 1 = (X^N - 1) \cdot (X^N + 1)$. Hence, we can calculate the product first modulo $X^{2N} - 1$ (via cyclic convolution of $2N$ elements) and then only reduce the result modulo $X^N + 1$. This method can be optimized based on the following observations.

Observation 1 (Redundancy of negacyclic extension). *Let $p \in \mathbb{R}[X]$ be a real-valued polynomial of degree $N - 1$, $N \in \mathbb{N}$, and let $\bar{p}(X) := p(X) - X^N \cdot p(X)$ be a negacyclic extension of $p(X)$. Then the Fourier image of $\mathsf{coeffs}(\bar{p})$ contains zeros at eventh positions (indexed from 0). In addition, the remaining coefficients (at oddth positions) are mirrored and conjugated. I.e.,*

$$\mathcal{F}\big(\mathsf{coeffs}(\bar{p})\big) = (0, P_1, 0, P_3, \ldots, 0, P_{N-1}, 0, \overline{P_{N-1}}, \ldots, 0, \overline{P_3}, 0, \overline{P_1}). \qquad (6)$$

Note 1. Given N input (real-valued) polynomial coefficients, $\mathcal{F}\big(\mathsf{coeffs}(\bar{p})\big)$ needs to calculate $2N$ complex values, i.e., $4N$ real values. The redundancy is clearly in the N complex zeros and in the $N/2$ complex conjugates.

Observation 2 (Convolution of negacyclic extensions). *Let $p, q \in \mathbb{R}[X]$ be real-valued polynomials of degree $N - 1$ for some $N \in \mathbb{N}$ and let $\bar{p}, \bar{q}$ be their respective negacyclic extensions. Then it holds*

$$\mathsf{coeffs}\big(p \cdot q \mod (X^N + 1)\big) = \frac{1}{2}\mathcal{F}^{-1}\Big(\mathcal{F}\big(\mathsf{coeffs}(\bar{p})\big) \odot \mathcal{F}\big(\mathsf{coeffs}(\bar{q})\big)\Big)[0 \ldots N - 1]. \qquad (7)$$

By Observation 1, it follows that the dyadic multiplication in (7) can only be performed at odd positions of the first half, the rest can be copied (with appropriate sign). Also note that after $\mathcal{F}^{-1}$, the coefficients are negacyclic, hence we can only take the first half of the vector. This method is implemented in the original TFHE Library [28].

Possible Improvements. The clear goal is to omit all calculations leading to redundant values as outlined in Note 1. Digging deeper into FFT, we deduced the same initial step as proposed by Crandall [11] in his method for negacyclic convolution (namely, the folding step). However, without the additional twisting step, we ended up with a bunch of numbers, from which we were not able to recover the original values efficiently. Therefore, we decided to adapt the concept of the method by Crandall.

3.2   Non-redundant Approach

The method for negacyclic polynomial multiplication by Crandall [11] is intended for polynomials over $\mathbb{Z}_p$ and it employs internally the *Discrete Galois Transform* (DGT). DGT is an analogy to DFT, which operates over the field $\mathrm{GF}(p^2)$

for a Gaussian prime number p, whereas DFT operates over $\mathbb{C}$. Note that recently Al Badawi et al. [3] extended the Crandall's method for non-Gaussian primes, too. The Crandall's method prepends DGT with two steps: folding and twisting. In the following definition we propose an analogous transformation using DFT.

Definition 1. *Let* $\mathbf{f} \in \mathbb{R}^N$ *for some* $N \in \mathbb{N}$, N *even. We define the* Discrete Fourier Negacyclic Transform *(DFNT, denoted* $\bar{\mathcal{F}}$*) as follows:*

$$\bar{\mathcal{F}}(\mathbf{f}) := \mathcal{F}\left(\underbrace{\left(\mathbf{f}[0\ldots{}^N\!/_2 - 1] + \mathrm{i}\cdot\mathbf{f}[{}^N\!/_2\ldots N-1]\right)}_{folding}\odot\underbrace{\left(\omega_{2N}^j\right)_{j=0}^{N/2-1}}_{twisting}\right), \qquad (8)$$

where $\omega_{2N}^j = \exp\!\left(\frac{2\pi\mathrm{i}j}{2N}\right)$ *and* $\mathcal{F}$ *stands for the ordinary DFT. For the inverse DFNT, we have*

$$\mathbf{t} := \mathcal{F}^{-1}(\mathbf{F}) \odot \left(\omega_{2N}^{-j}\right)_{j=0}^{N/2-1}, \qquad (9)$$

$$\bar{\mathcal{F}}^{-1}(\mathbf{F}) = \left[\Re(\mathbf{t}), \Im(\mathbf{t})\right]. \qquad (10)$$

Note 2. We will refer to DFNT, where DFT is internally calculated via FFT, as the *Fast Fourier Negacyclic Transform* (FFNT).

With respect to negacyclic convolution, DFNT has two important properties:

1. given N reals at input, it outputs ${}^N\!/_2$ complex numbers, i.e., there is *no redundancy*, unlike in the previous approach, and
2. it can be used for negacyclic convolution in the same manner as DFT for cyclic convolution, a theorem follows.

Theorem 1 (Negacyclic Convolution Theorem; NCT). *Let* $\mathbf{f}, \mathbf{g} \in \mathbb{R}^N$ *for some* $N \in \mathbb{N}$, N *even. It holds*

$$\bar{\mathcal{F}}(\mathbf{f} \,\bar{*}\, \mathbf{g}) = \bar{\mathcal{F}}(\mathbf{f}) \odot \bar{\mathcal{F}}(\mathbf{g}). \qquad (11)$$

For a full description of negacyclic convolution over the reals via NCT see Algorithm 1. Next, we analyze this algorithm from the error propagation point of view, which allows us to apply this method for negacyclic convolution over integers, too.

4   Analysis of Error Propagation

Since Algorithm 1 operates implicitly with real numbers (starting $N = 4$, ω_{2N}'s are irrational), there emerge rounding errors provided that we use a standard finite floating-point representation. In this section, we analyze Algorithm 1 from the error propagation point of view and we derive estimates of the bounds of errors as well as their variance. Based on our estimates, we derive a bound for sufficient bit-precision of the employed floating point representation, which guarantees error-free convolution over the ring of integers. We also provide an estimate of the bit-precision based on error variance and the 3σ-rule. In addition

---

Algorithm 1. Efficient Negacyclic Convolution over $\mathbb{R}$.

Input: $\mathbf{f}, \mathbf{g} \in \mathbb{R}^N$ for some $N \in \mathbb{N}$, N even.
Precompute: $\omega_{2N}^j := \exp\left(\frac{2\pi i j}{2N}\right)$ for $j = -N/2 + 1 \ldots N/2 - 1$.
Output: $\mathbf{h} \in \mathbb{R}^N$, $\mathbf{h} = \mathbf{f} \bar{*} \mathbf{g}$.

1: **for** $j = 0 \ldots N/2 - 1$ **do**
2:     $f'_j = f_j + i f_{j+N/2}$ // fold
3:     $g'_j = g_j + i g_{j+N/2}$
4: **for** $j = 0 \ldots N/2 - 1$ **do**
5:     $f''_j = f'_j \cdot \omega_{2N}^j$ // twist
6:     $g''_j = g'_j \cdot \omega_{2N}^j$
7: $\mathbf{F} = \mathcal{F}_{N/2}(\mathbf{f}'')$, $\mathbf{G} = \mathcal{F}_{N/2}(\mathbf{g}'')$
8: **for** $j = 0 \ldots N/2 - 1$ **do**
9:     $H_j = F_j \cdot G_j$
10: $\mathbf{h}'' = \mathcal{F}_{N/2}^{-1}(\mathbf{H})$
11: **for** $j = 0 \ldots N/2 - 1$ **do**
12:     $h'_j = h''_j \cdot \omega_{2N}^{-j}$ // untwist
13: **for** $j = 0 \ldots N/2 - 1$ **do**
14:     $h_j = \Re(h'_j)$ // unfold
15:     $h_{j+N/2} = \Im(h'_j)$
16: **return** $\mathbf{h}$

---

and as a byproduct, we derive all bounds for cyclic convolution, too. First of all, we revisit the FFT algorithm, as we will refer to it later.

FFT in Brief. FFT [9] is a recursive algorithm, which builds upon the following observation: for $N = n_1 \cdot n_2$ and $k = k_1 + k_2 n_1$, we can write the k-th Fourier coefficient of an $\mathbf{f} \in \mathbb{C}^N$ as

$$
\mathcal{F}(\mathbf{f})_{k_1+k_2 n_1} = \sum_{j_2=0}^{n_2-1} \underbrace{\left(\left(\sum_{j_1=0}^{n_1-1} f_{j_2+j_1 n_2} \omega_{n_1}^{j_1 k_1} \right) \omega_N^{-j_2 k_1} \right)}_{\mathcal{F}\left((f_{j_2+j_1 n_2})_{j_1=0}^{n_1-1} \right)_{k_1}} \omega_{n_2}^{-j_2 k_2}, \tag{12}
$$

where

$$
\omega_N^j = \exp\left(\frac{2\pi i j}{N}\right), \tag{13}
$$

while ω's can be precomputed.

Note 3. There exist two major FFT data paths for N a power of two: the Cooley-Tukey data path [9] (aka. decimation-in-time), and the Gentleman-Sande data path [13] (aka. decimation-in-frequency). At this point, let us describe the decimation-in-time data path, we will discuss their implementation consequences later in Sect. 5.

For N a power of two, FFT splits its input into two halves and proceeds recursively. Next, it multiplies the results with ω's, and finally it proceeds adequate pairs; see (14) and (15).

At the end of the recursion we have for $N = 2$:

$$\mathsf{FFT}_2 \begin{vmatrix} f_0 & f_1 \end{vmatrix} = \begin{vmatrix} f_0 + f_1 & f_0 - f_1 \end{vmatrix}. \tag{14}$$

Next, for $N \geq 4$ we have

$$\mathsf{FFT}_N(\mathbf{f}): \begin{vmatrix} f_0 & f_1 \\ f_2 & f_3 \\ \vdots & \vdots \\ f_{N-2} & f_{N-1} \end{vmatrix}_{n_1 \times n_2 \,=\, N/2 \times 2} \xrightarrow[\text{(recursively)}]{\mathsf{FFT}_{N/2} \text{ columns}} \begin{vmatrix} f_0' & f_1' \\ f_2' & f_3' \\ \vdots & \vdots \\ f_{N-2}' & f_{N-1}' \end{vmatrix} \odot \begin{vmatrix} 1 & 1 \\ 1 & \omega_N^{-1 \cdot 1} \\ \vdots & \vdots \\ 1 & \omega_N^{-1 \cdot (N/2-1)} \end{vmatrix}_{\omega_N^{-j_2 k_1}} \longrightarrow$$

$$\rightarrow \begin{vmatrix} f_0'' & f_1'' \\ f_2'' & f_3'' \\ \vdots & \vdots \\ f_{N-2}'' & f_{N-1}'' \end{vmatrix} \xrightarrow{\mathsf{FFT}_2 \text{ rows}} \begin{vmatrix} f_0'' + f_1'' & f_0'' - f_1'' \\ f_2'' + f_3'' & f_2'' - f_3'' \\ \vdots & \vdots \\ f_{N-2}'' + f_{N-1}'' & f_{N-2}'' - f_{N-1}'' \end{vmatrix} = \begin{vmatrix} F_0 & F_{N/2} \\ F_1 & F_{N/2+1} \\ \vdots & \vdots \\ F_{N/2-1} & F_{N-1} \end{vmatrix}. \tag{15}$$

FFT^{-1} proceeds similarly to the direct transformation with the following exceptions:

1. in the second step, it multiplies by $\omega_N^{j_2 k_1}$ (i.e., with a positive exponent), and
2. the final result is multiplied by $1/N$ (only once at the top level).

4.1   Error Propagation Through FFT and FFNT

Let us begin with two lemmas, which provide bounds on the error and variance of complex multiplication and FFT, respectively. Note that we will assume for our estimates of variance bounds that the rounding errors are uniformly random and independent.

Note 4. We will distinguish two types of the maximum norm $\|\cdot\|_\infty$ over $\mathbb{C}^N$. For 1. error vectors, and for 2. other complex vectors, we consider:

1. the maximum of real and imaginary parts (i.e., rectangular), and
2. the maximum of absolute values (i.e., circular), respectively.

Lemma 1. *Let* $a, b \in \mathbb{C}$, $|a| \leq A_0$ *and* $|b| \leq B_0$ *for some* $A_0, B_0 \in \mathbb{R}^+$. *Then*

$$|a \cdot b| \leq A_0 \cdot B_0, \tag{16}$$

$$\|\mathsf{Err}(a \cdot b)\|_\infty \lesssim \sqrt{2} \cdot \left(A_0 \cdot \|\mathsf{Err}(b)\|_\infty + B_0 \cdot \|\mathsf{Err}(a)\|_\infty\right), \quad and \tag{17}$$

$$\mathsf{Var}\big(\mathsf{Err}(a \cdot b)\big) \lesssim 2 \cdot \left(A_0^2 \cdot \mathsf{Var}(\mathsf{Err}(b)) + B_0^2 \cdot \mathsf{Var}(\mathsf{Err}(a))\right), \tag{18}$$

where we neglected second-order error terms and for (18), we further assumed that the errors of a *and* b *are independent.*

Proof. Let $a = (p + E_p) + \mathrm{i}(q + E_q)$ and $b = (r + E_r) + \mathrm{i}(s + E_s)$, where we denote the parts' bounds as $|p| \leq P_0$ etc. According to Note 4, we split the complex error into parts – we write for the real part (similarly for the complex part)

$$\mathsf{Err}\big(\Re(a \cdot b)\big) = pE_r + rE_p - (qE_s + sE_q) + negl., \tag{19}$$

which can be bounded as

$$\begin{aligned}
\big|\mathsf{Err}\big(\Re(a \cdot b)\big)\big| &\lesssim P_0\|\mathsf{Err}(b)\|_\infty + R_0\|\mathsf{Err}(a)\|_\infty + Q_0\|\mathsf{Err}(b)\|_\infty + S_0\|\mathsf{Err}(a)\|_\infty \\
&\lesssim (P_0 + Q_0)\|\mathsf{Err}(b)\|_\infty + (S_0 + R_0)\|\mathsf{Err}(a)\|_\infty.
\end{aligned} \tag{20}$$

Since $|p + \mathrm{i}q| \lesssim A_0$, we can bound $P_0 + Q_0 \lesssim \sqrt{2}A_0$ and the result (17) follows, similarly for (18). $\qquad\qquad\square$

Lemma 2. *Let* $\mathbf{f} \in \mathbb{C}^N$, *where* $N = 2^\nu$ *for some* $\nu \in \mathbb{N}$, $\|\mathbf{f}\|_\infty \leq 2^{\varphi_0}$ *for some* $\varphi_0 \in \mathbb{N}$, *and let* χ *denote the bit-precision of* ω's *as well as all intermediate values during the calculation of* $\mathsf{FFT}_N(\mathbf{f}) =: \mathbf{F}$, *represented as a floating point type. Then*

$$\|\mathbf{F}\|_\infty \leq 2^{\varphi_0 + \nu}, \tag{21}$$

$$\|\mathsf{Err}(\mathbf{F})\|_\infty \lesssim c_H \cdot \big(\sqrt{2} + 1\big)^\nu + c_N \cdot 2^\nu \quad (\textit{for } \nu \geq 2), \quad \textit{and} \tag{22}$$

$$\mathsf{Var}\big(\mathsf{Err}(\mathbf{F})\big) \lesssim d_H \cdot 3^\nu + d_N \cdot 4^\nu \quad (\textit{for } \nu \geq 2), \tag{23}$$

where

$$\begin{aligned}
c_H &= 2(\sqrt{2} - 1) \cdot \|\mathsf{Err}(\mathbf{f})\|_\infty + (2 - \sqrt{2}) \cdot 2^{\varphi_0 - \chi + 1}, \quad c_N = -(2 + \sqrt{2}) \cdot 2^{\varphi_0 - \chi - 1}, \\
d_H &= {}^2\!/_3 \, \mathsf{Var}\big(\mathsf{Err}(\mathbf{f})\big) - {}^8\!/_{27} \, 2^{2\varphi_0 - 2\chi}, \qquad\qquad\qquad d_N = {}^1\!/_6 \, 2^{2\varphi_0 - 2\chi}.
\end{aligned} \tag{24}$$

Proof. We write

$$\mathsf{FFT}_N \colon \mathsf{FFT}_2 \circ (\odot \, \omega_N) \circ \mathsf{FFT}_{N/2}, \tag{25}$$

from where we derive recurrence relations for the bounds on absolute value, error and variance.

In each recursion level, the values propagate to a lower level, then they are multiplied by a complex unit and two such values are added, or subtracted. Firstly, note that in every level the initial bound on the absolute value is doubled, hence (21) follows.

Regarding the errors, it is important to note that the final FFT_2 acts on two values, each of which has been previously multiplied by $\omega_N^{j_2 k_1}$, where j_2 ranges in $\{0, 1\}$. I.e., one value is multiplied by 1 and only the other is multiplied by a (mostly) non-trivial complex unit, which is rounded to χ bits of precision, i.e., $\|\mathsf{Err}(\omega)\|_\infty \leq 2^{-\chi - 1}$. Putting things together, we get the following recurrence relations for the bounds on the error and its variance after ν levels, respectively:

$$\begin{aligned}
E_\nu &= \sqrt{2} \cdot \big(1 \cdot E_{\nu-1} + 2^{\varphi_0 + \nu - 1} \cdot 2^{-\chi - 1}\big) + E_{\nu-1} \\
&= \big(\sqrt{2} + 1\big) \cdot E_{\nu-1} + \sqrt{2} \cdot 2^{\varphi_0 + \nu - \chi - 2}, \tag{26}
\end{aligned}$$

$$E_2 = (E_1 + 2^{\varphi_0+1} \cdot \underbrace{E_{\omega_4}}_{=0}) \cdot \sqrt{2} + E_1 = (\sqrt{2}+1)E_1 = 2(\sqrt{2}+1)E_0, \quad \text{and} \quad (27)$$

$$V_\nu = 2 \cdot \left(1^2 \cdot V_{\nu-1} + (2^{\varphi_0+\nu-1})^2 \cdot 1/12\,(2^{-\chi})^2\right) + V_{\nu-1}$$

$$= 3V_{\nu-1} + 1/3\,2^{2\varphi_0+2\nu-2\chi-3}, \tag{28}$$

$$V_2 = 3V_1 = 6V_0, \tag{29}$$

where in (27), we applied the fact that ω_4 is error-free; cf. (13). Also note that the error more than doubles in each step (while the bound only doubles), therefore the χ bits of precision are sufficient and rounding errors can be neglected. The results follow by solving (26) and (27), and (28) and (29), respectively. □

In the following proposition, we bound the error and variance of the result of cyclic and negacyclic convolution via FFT/FFNT, respectively. For a quick reference, we provide an overview of these methods in (30) and (31), respectively:

$$\begin{array}{c} \mathbf{f} \xrightarrow{\mathsf{FFT}_N} \mathbf{F} \\ \mathbf{g} \xrightarrow{\mathsf{FFT}_N} \mathbf{G} \end{array} \odot \mathbf{H} \xrightarrow{\mathsf{FFT}_N^{-1}} \mathbf{h} = \mathbf{f} * \mathbf{g}, \tag{30}$$

$$\begin{array}{c} \mathbf{f} \xrightarrow{\mathrm{fold}} \mathbf{f}' \xrightarrow{\mathrm{twist}} \mathbf{f}'' \xrightarrow{\mathsf{FFT}_{N/2}} \bar{\mathbf{F}} \\ \mathbf{g} \xrightarrow{\mathrm{fold}} \mathbf{g}' \xrightarrow{\mathrm{twist}} \mathbf{g}'' \xrightarrow{\mathsf{FFT}_{N/2}} \bar{\mathbf{G}} \end{array} \odot \bar{\mathbf{H}} \xrightarrow{\mathsf{FFT}_{N/2}^{-1}} \mathbf{h}'' \xrightarrow{\mathrm{untwist}} \mathbf{h}' \xrightarrow{\mathrm{unfold}} \bar{\mathbf{h}} = \mathbf{f} \;\bar{*}\; \mathbf{g}. \tag{31}$$

Proposition 1. *Let* $\mathbf{f}, \mathbf{g} \in \mathbb{R}^N$, *where* $N = 2^\nu$ *for some* $\nu \in \mathbb{N}$, $\|\mathbf{f}\|_\infty \le 2^{\varphi_0}$ *and* $\|\mathbf{g}\|_\infty \le 2^{\gamma_0}$ *for some* $\varphi_0, \gamma_0 \in \mathbb{N}$, *and let* χ *denote the bit-precision of* ω's *as well as all intermediate values during the calculation of* $\mathsf{FFT}_N(\cdot)$ *and its inverse, represented as a floating point type. We denote* $\mathbf{h} := \mathsf{FFT}_N^{-1}(\mathsf{FFT}_N(\mathbf{f}) \odot \mathsf{FFT}_N(\mathbf{g}))$ *and* $\bar{\mathbf{h}} := \mathsf{FFNT}_N^{-1}(\mathsf{FFNT}_N(\mathbf{f}) \odot \mathsf{FFNT}_N(\mathbf{g}))$, *while we consider the errors as* $\|\mathsf{Err}(\mathbf{h})\|_\infty = \|\mathbf{h} - \mathbf{f} * \mathbf{g}\|_\infty$ *and* $\|\mathsf{Err}(\bar{\mathbf{h}})\|_\infty = \|\bar{\mathbf{h}} - \mathbf{f} \,\bar{*}\, \mathbf{g}\|_\infty$, *respectively. Then*

$$\log\|\mathsf{Err}(\mathbf{h})\|_\infty \lesssim (2\nu - 2) \cdot \log(\sqrt{2}+1) + \varphi_0 + \gamma_0 - \chi + 4, \tag{32}$$

$$\log\mathsf{Var}(\mathsf{Err}(\mathbf{h})) \lesssim 4\nu + 2\varphi_0 + 2\gamma_0 - 2\chi - 1 - \log(3), \quad \text{and} \tag{33}$$

$$\log\|\mathsf{Err}(\bar{\mathbf{h}})\|_\infty \lesssim (2\nu - 4) \cdot \log(\sqrt{2}+1) + \varphi_0 + \gamma_0 - \chi + 4 + \log(3) + 1/2, \tag{34}$$

$$\log\mathsf{Var}(\mathsf{Err}(\bar{\mathbf{h}})) \lesssim 4\nu + 2\varphi_0 + 2\gamma_0 - 2\chi - 3. \tag{35}$$

Proof. Find the proof in Appendix A. □

We apply our estimates of the error and variance bounds in order to derive two basic parameter setups for convolution over integers: an error-free setup and a setup with rare errors based on the 3σ-rule; see the following corollary.

Corollary 1. *Provided that*

$$\chi_0^{(c.)} \gtrsim \underbrace{2\log(\sqrt{2}+1)}_{\approx 2.54} \cdot \nu + \varphi_0 + \gamma_0 + \underbrace{5 - 2\log(\sqrt{2}+1)}_{\approx 2.46}, \quad \text{or} \tag{36}$$

$$\chi_0^{(nc.)} \gtrsim \underbrace{2\log(\sqrt{2}+1) \cdot \nu}_{\approx 2.54} + \varphi_0 + \gamma_0 + \underbrace{5 + \log(3) + 1/2 - 4\log(\sqrt{2}+1)}_{\approx 2.00}, \quad (37)$$

we have $\|\mathsf{Err}(\mathbf{h})\|_\infty \lesssim 1/2$, or $\|\mathsf{Err}(\bar{\mathbf{h}})\|_\infty \lesssim 1/2$, which means an error-free cyclic, or negacyclic convolution on integers via FFT_N, or FFNT_N, respectively. I.e., for $\mathbf{f}, \mathbf{g} \in \mathbb{Z}^N$, we have

$$\left\lfloor \mathsf{FFT}_N^{-1}\big(\mathsf{FFT}_N(\mathbf{f}) \odot \mathsf{FFT}_N(\mathbf{g})\big) \right\rceil = \mathbf{f} * \mathbf{g}, \quad or \quad (38)$$

$$\left\lfloor \mathsf{FFNT}_N^{-1}\big(\mathsf{FFNT}_N(\mathbf{f}) \odot \mathsf{FFNT}_N(\mathbf{g})\big) \right\rceil = \mathbf{f} \bar{*} \mathbf{g}, \quad (39)$$

respectively, up to negligible probability.

Next, if

$$\chi_{3\sigma}^{(c.)} \gtrsim 2\nu + \varphi_0 + \gamma_0 + \underbrace{1/2\log(6)}_{\approx 1.29}, \quad or \quad (40)$$

$$\chi_{3\sigma}^{(nc.)} \gtrsim 2\nu + \varphi_0 + \gamma_0 + \underbrace{\log(3) - 1/2}_{\approx 1.08}, \quad (41)$$

we have $3\sqrt{\mathsf{Var}(\mathsf{Err}(\mathbf{h}))} \lesssim 1/2$, or $3\sqrt{\mathsf{Var}(\mathsf{Err}(\bar{\mathbf{h}}))} \lesssim 1/2$, which estimates the required floating point type precision for the respective convolution variant based on the 3σ-rule.

Note 5. In the most common practical setting with the `binary64` type as per IEEE 754 standard [1] (aka. `double`), we have $\chi = 53$ bits of precision. For the 80-bit variant of the extended precision format (aka. `long double`), we have $\chi = 64$ bits of precision.

5   Implementation and Experimental Results

In this section, we briefly comment on how we use the data paths in our implementation (as outlined in Note 3), we discuss the choice of parameters with respect to TFHE, and then we focus on the following:

1. benchmarking with other implementations using chosen parameters,
2. performance on long polynomials using both 64-bit `double` and 80-bit `long double` floating point number representations, and
3. error magnitude and correctness of the results.

Implementation Remarks. In our implementation of the Cooley-Tukey data path [9], we adapted the 4-vector approach from the Nayuki Project [22], which optimizes the RAM access for the most common 64-bit architectures. In a similar manner, we implemented the Gentleman-Sande data path [13]. To calculate FFT properly, both data paths require a specific reordering of their input or output, respectively. The reordering is based on bit-reversal of position indexes, counting from 0. E.g., for 16 elements (4 bits), we exchange the elements at positions $5 \leftrightarrow 10$, since $5 = 0b0101$ and $10 = 0b1010$.

Since our goal is solely convolution, i.e., we do not care about the exact order of the FFT coefficients, the bit-reverse reordering can be omitted, as pointed out by Crandall and Pomerance [10]. By construction, it follows that the Gentleman-Sande data path must be used for the direct transformation and the Cooley-Tukey data path for the inverse.

For benchmarking purposes, we also adopted some code from the TFHE Library [28] to compare the redundant and non-redundant approaches; cf. Sects. 3.1 and 3.2, respectively.

Relation to the TFHE Parameters. The main (cryptographic) motivation of our algorithm for negacyclic convolution over integers is the negacyclic polynomial multiplication in the TFHE scheme [8]. Below we outline a relation of the TFHE parameters to the parameters of negacyclic convolution via FFNT. As a result, we suggest a reasonable parameter setup for benchmarking.

In TFHE, negacyclic polynomial multiplication occurs in the bootstrapping procedure (namely, in the calculation of the external product), where an integer polynomial is multiplied by a torus polynomial. The coefficients of the right-hand side (torus) polynomial can be represented as integers scaled to $[0, 1)$ and bounded by 2 to the power of their bit-precision, denoted by τ. In the left-hand side (integer) polynomial, the coefficients are bounded by 2^γ, where γ is one of the fundamental TFHE parameters. By construction, the parameter γ is smaller than τ, namely, $\gamma \leq \tau/l$, where l is another TFHE parameter. In a corner case, it can be $\gamma = 1$ and the bound can be hence as low as 2^0.

Based on our preliminary calculations for multivalue TFHE, we need the degree of TFHE polynomials to be at least $N = 2^{14}$ for 8-bit plaintexts with 128-bit security, and the torus precision to be at least $\tau = 34$ (both can be smaller for shorter plaintexts). Finally, we suggest to run the tests using polynomials with $\varphi_0 = \gamma_0 = \tau/2 = 17$ and $N = 2^{10}, \ldots, 2^{14}$.

5.1 Benchmarking Results

As a reference for benchmarking of our implementation [20] of negacyclic convolution, we have chosen the NTL Library [27] and the redundant method (as used in the original TFHE Library [28]; cf. Sect. 3.1), for which we used the same implementation of FFT as for our non-redundant method. Note that the implementation by Al Badawi et al. [3] shows similar results to the popular NTL (only about 1.01–1.2× faster) and they also show that NTL is faster than the concurrent FLINT Library [16]. For NTL, we tested both ZZ_pX and ZZ_pE classes, while the latter shows slightly better performance, hence we used that for benchmarking. Find the results of our benchmarks in Table 1.

Note 6. During the parameter setup, we silently passed over the fact that $\chi = 53$ (bit-precision of double) is lower than our 3σ-rule estimates for all tested ν's,

Table 1. Mean time per negacyclic multiplication of uniformly random polynomials with $\|p\|_\infty \leq 2^{17}$ using NTL (similar times as FLINT), FFT_{2N} on negacyclic extension (implemented in [28]), and FFNT_N, both using 64-bit `double`. Speedup of FFNT_N over FFT_{2N}. Average and maximum rounding errors of FFNT_N. 1 000 runs per degree and method on an Intel Core i7-8550U CPU @ 1.80 GHz.

Degree (N)	2^{10}	2^{11}	2^{12}	2^{13}	2^{14}
NTL [ms]	0.617	1.258	2.643	6.132	12.771
FFT_{2N} [ms]	0.122	0.230	0.458	0.982	2.277
FFNT_N [ms]	0.036	0.069	0.120	0.243	0.541
FFNT_N over FFT_{2N}	3.35×	3.33×	3.82×	4.04×	4.21×
FFNT_N avg. error [‰]	0.06	0.08	0.12	0.18	0.27
FFNT_N max. error [‰]	0.37	0.55	0.98	1.47	1.95

as per (41) in Corollary 1. Indeed, they dictate $\chi_{3\sigma}^{(nc.)} \gtrsim 2\nu + \varphi_0 + \gamma_0 + 1.08 = 55.08\ldots63.08$. For this reason, we reran the scenario with $\nu = 14$ for 1 000-times, we checked the results for correctness, and we did not detect *any* error across all tested polynomials.

5.2 Performance on Long Polynomials

As a reference for other prospective applications of our method, we tested our code on longer polynomials, too. We provide the performance results using both 64-bit `double` and 80-bit `long double` in Fig. 1.

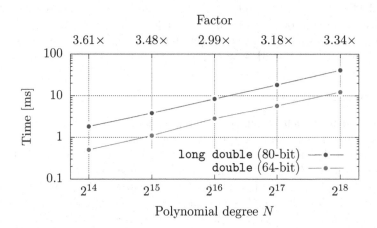

Fig. 1. Mean time per polynomial multiplication mod $X^N + 1$ and speedup factor of `double` over `long double`. Uniformly random polynomials with $\|p\|_\infty \leq 2^{17}$, 1 000 measurements.

5.3   Error Magnitude and Correctness on Long Polynomials

As outlined in Note 6, our experimental setup exceeds the derived theoretical bounds, even for lower-degree polynomials. Hence, our next goal is to evaluate the error magnitude as well as to check the correctness of the results. We tested the following input polynomial scenarios:

1. uniformly random coefficients (bounded as $\|p\|_\infty \leq 2^{\varphi_0}$), and
2. all coefficients equal to the bound 2^{φ_0}.

Find the results of the random polynomial setup in Fig. 2, where we tested both 64-bit `double` and 80-bit `long double` implementations.

Regarding the setup with all coefficients equal to the bound, we ran the same scenarios as for random polynomials, cf. Fig. 2. The only correct results were obtained for the setup with $\|p\|_\infty \leq 2^{17}$ and $N = 2^{14}$, regardless the floating point type in use (either 64-bit, or 80-bit).

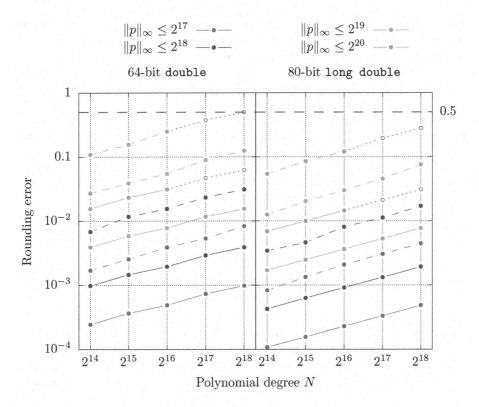

Fig. 2. Median (solid) and Maximum (dashed) rounding errors for uniformly random polynomials. Erroneous results emphasized by empty red circles. 10 measurements per degree, bound and floating point type.

Discussion. We observed a factor $\sim 4\times$ speedup of FFNT_N (i.e., the non-redundant approach) over FFT_{2N} (i.e., the redundant approach). Compared to NTL, which calculates the coefficients precisely using a number-theoretic transform, our FFT-based method shows by more than an order of magnitude better results. Even though we ran our tests with underestimated precision, we obtained correct results for much larger polynomials with uniformly random coefficients. Note that random-like polynomials occur in TFHE, hence our benchmarking scenario with random polynomials is representative for the usage with TFHE.

However and to our surprise, the 80-bit floating point type did not calculate correctly any extra scenario over the 64-bit type. We assume that this is because the steps in the polynomial degree or in the maximum norm bound are too big to make the difference between the 53 and 64 bits of their mantissa precision, respectively.

6   Conclusion

We showed that FFT-based convolution algorithms can significantly outperform similar algorithms based on number-theoretic transforms, and they can still guarantee error-free results in the integer domain. We derived estimates of the lower bound of the employed floating point type for error-free cyclic and negacyclic convolutions, as well as we suggested the bounds based on the 3σ-rule.

We suggested a set of testing parameters for negacyclic convolution with particular respect to the usage with the TFHE Scheme on a multivalue plaintext space. We ran a benchmark that compares the popular NTL Library, the approach that is used in the TFHE Library, and our approach. Compared to the generic NTL Library, which employs a number-theoretic transform, and to the TFHE Library approach, which calculates redundant intermediate values, we achieved a speedup of around $24\times$ and $4\times$, respectively.

Finally, our experiments have shown approximate bounds for practical error-free results. Namely, we could multiply polynomials without errors up to degree $N = 2^{16}$ and norm $\|p\|_\infty \leq 2^{20}$ with uniformly random coefficients, and up to degree $N = 2^{14}$ with coefficients equal to 2^{17}. To conclude, we find our approach particularly useful for negacyclic integer polynomial multiplication, not only in TFHE.

Future Directions. Our aim is to implement a version based on the 64-bit signed integer type instead of `double`, where we would keep the exponent at one place for the entire array. Such an approach requires less demanding arithmetics and it would serve as a proof-of-concept for a propective FPGA implementation.

Acknowledgments. We would like to thank Ahmad Al Badawi for useful comments and remarks.

Appendix

A Proof of Proposition 1

Proof. Let us begin with the cyclic convolution. By (30) and Lemma 1 and 2, we have

$$\begin{aligned}\|\mathsf{Err}(\mathbf{F}\odot\mathbf{G})\|_\infty &\lessapprox \Big(\underbrace{c_H^{(\mathbf{f})}\cdot(\sqrt{2}+1)^\nu}_{\gtrapprox\|\mathsf{Err}(\mathbf{F})\|_\infty}\cdot\underbrace{2^{\gamma_0+\nu}}_{\geq\|\mathbf{G}\|_\infty}+c_H^{(\mathbf{g})}\cdot(\sqrt{2}+1)^\nu\cdot 2^{\varphi_0+\nu}\Big)\cdot\sqrt{2}\\ &=(\sqrt{2}+1)^\nu\cdot 2^{\nu+\varphi_0+\gamma_0-\chi+2}\cdot(2-\sqrt{2})\cdot\sqrt{2}=:E_{\mathbf{H}},\quad\text{and}\end{aligned}\tag{42}$$

$$\begin{aligned}\mathsf{Var}\big(\mathsf{Err}(\mathbf{F}\odot\mathbf{G})\big) &\lessapprox \Big(\underbrace{d_N^{(\mathbf{f})}\cdot 2^{2\nu}}_{\gtrapprox\mathsf{Var}(\mathsf{Err}(\mathbf{F}))}\cdot\underbrace{2^{2\gamma_0+2\nu}}_{\geq\|\mathbf{G}\|_\infty^2}+d_N^{(\mathbf{g})}\cdot 2^{2\nu}\cdot 2^{2\varphi_0+2\nu}\Big)\cdot 2\\ &={}^2\!/_3\cdot 2^{4\nu+2\varphi_0+2\gamma_0-2\chi}=:V_{\mathbf{H}},\end{aligned}\tag{43}$$

which we apply as the initial error and variance bound to (22) and (23), respectively, together with multiplication by $1/N=2^{-\nu}$, which poses the only difference between FFT^{-1} and FFT from the error point of view. We neglect other than leading terms and we get

$$\begin{aligned}\|\mathsf{Err}(\mathbf{h})\|_\infty &\lessapprox 2^{-\nu}\cdot\underbrace{2(\sqrt{2}-1)\cdot E_{\mathbf{H}}}_{\approx c_H^{(\mathbf{H})}}\cdot(\sqrt{2}+1)^\nu\\ &\lessapprox(\sqrt{2}+1)^{2\nu-2}\cdot 2^{\varphi_0+\gamma_0-\chi+4},\quad\text{and}\end{aligned}\tag{44}$$

$$\mathsf{Var}\big(\mathsf{Err}(\mathbf{h})\big)\lessapprox 2^{-2\nu}\cdot\underbrace{{}^1\!/_6\cdot 2^{2(\varphi_0+\gamma_0+2\nu)-2\chi}}_{=d_N^{(\mathbf{H})}}\cdot 4^\nu={}^1\!/_6\cdot 2^{4\nu+2\varphi_0+2\gamma_0-2\chi},\tag{45}$$

and the cyclic results follow.

For the negacyclic convolution, we feed DFT with a folded and twisted input vector; cf. (31). It enters DFT with error bounded as

$$\|\mathsf{Err}(\mathbf{f}'')\|_\infty\lessapprox(1\cdot 0+2^{\varphi_0+1/2}\cdot 2^{-\chi-1})\cdot\sqrt{2}=2^{\varphi_0-\chi}.\tag{46}$$

Regarding variance, it shows that the term with $\mathsf{Var}\big(\mathsf{Err}(\mathbf{f}'')\big)$ will be neglected. Next, we precompute

$$\begin{aligned}c_H^{(\mathbf{f}'')} &= 2(\sqrt{2}-1)\cdot\|\mathsf{Err}(\mathbf{f}'')\|_\infty+(2-\sqrt{2})\cdot 2^{\varphi_0+1/2-\chi+1}\\ &\lessapprox 6(\sqrt{2}-1)\cdot 2^{\varphi_0-\chi},\quad\text{and}\end{aligned}\tag{47}$$

$$d_N^{(\mathbf{f}'')}={}^1\!/_6\, 2^{2(\varphi_0+1/2)-2\chi},\tag{48}$$

and apply into

$$\|\mathsf{Err}(\bar{\mathbf{F}} \odot \bar{\mathbf{G}})\|_\infty \lesssim \Big(\underbrace{c_H^{(\mathbf{f}'')} \cdot (\sqrt{2}+1)^{\nu-1}}_{\gtrsim \|\mathsf{Err}(\bar{\mathbf{F}})\|_\infty} \cdot \underbrace{2^{\gamma_0 + 1/2 + \nu - 1}}_{\geq \|\bar{\mathbf{G}}\|_\infty}$$

$$+ c_H^{(\mathbf{g}'')} \cdot (\sqrt{2}+1)^{\nu-1} \cdot 2^{\varphi_0 + 1/2 + \nu - 1} \Big) \cdot \sqrt{2}$$

$$= 3(\sqrt{2}+1)^{\nu-2} \cdot 2^{\nu + \varphi_0 + \gamma_0 - \chi + 2} =: E_{\bar{\mathbf{H}}}, \quad \text{and} \quad (49)$$

$$\mathsf{Var}\big(\mathsf{Err}(\bar{\mathbf{F}} \odot \bar{\mathbf{G}})\big) \lesssim \Big(\underbrace{d_N^{(\mathbf{f}'')} \cdot 4^{\nu-1}}_{\gtrsim \mathsf{Var}\big(\mathsf{Err}(\bar{\mathbf{F}})\big)} \cdot \underbrace{2^{2\gamma_0 + 1 + 2\nu - 2}}_{\geq \|\bar{\mathbf{G}}\|_\infty^2}$$

$$+ d_N^{(\mathbf{g}'')} \cdot 4^{\nu-1} \cdot 2^{2\varphi_0 + 1 + 2\nu - 2} \Big) \cdot 2$$

$$= 1/3 \cdot 2^{4\nu + 2\varphi_0 + 2\gamma_0 - 2\chi - 1} =: V_{\bar{\mathbf{H}}}. \quad (50)$$

Next, we apply these estimates as the initial error and variance bound into (22) and (23), respectively, together with multiplication by $2/N = 2^{-\nu+1}$. We have

$$\|\mathsf{Err}(\mathbf{h}'')\|_\infty \lesssim 2^{-\nu+1} \cdot \underbrace{2(\sqrt{2}-1) \cdot E_{\bar{\mathbf{H}}}}_{\approx c_H^{(\bar{\mathbf{H}})}} \cdot (\sqrt{2}+1)^{\nu-1}$$

$$\approx 3(\sqrt{2}+1)^{2\nu-4} \cdot 2^{\varphi_0 + \gamma_0 - \chi + 4}, \quad \text{and} \quad (51)$$

$$\mathsf{Var}\big(\mathsf{Err}(\mathbf{h}'')\big) \lesssim 2^{-2\nu+2} \cdot \underbrace{1/6 \cdot 2^{(2\varphi_0 + 2\gamma_0 + 2 + 4\nu - 4) - 2\chi}}_{= d_N^{(\bar{\mathbf{H}})}} \cdot 4^{\nu-1}$$

$$1/3 \cdot 2^{4\nu + 2\varphi_0 + 2\gamma_0 - 2\chi - 3}, \quad (52)$$

while in (52), it has shown that the term with $V_{\bar{\mathbf{H}}}$ was not the leading term, hence it was neglected. By (31) it remains to untwist and unfold, we have

$$\|\mathsf{Err}(\mathbf{h}')\|_\infty \lesssim \Big(1 \cdot \underbrace{3(\sqrt{2}+1)^{2\nu-4} \cdot 2^{\varphi_0 + \gamma_0 - \chi + 4}}_{\gtrsim \|\mathsf{Err}(\mathbf{h}'')\|_\infty} + \underbrace{2^{2\nu + \varphi_0 + \gamma_0 - 1}}_{\geq \|\mathbf{h}''\|_\infty} \cdot 2^{-\chi - 1} \Big) \cdot \sqrt{2}$$

$$\approx 3\sqrt{2} \cdot (\sqrt{2}+1)^{2\nu-4} \cdot 2^{\varphi_0 + \gamma_0 - \chi + 4}, \quad \text{and} \quad (53)$$

$$\mathsf{Var}\big(\mathsf{Err}(\mathbf{h}')\big) \lesssim \Big(1^2 \cdot \underbrace{1/3 \cdot 2^{4\nu + 2\varphi_0 + 2\gamma_0 - 2\chi - 3}}_{\gtrsim \mathsf{Var}\big(\mathsf{Err}(\mathbf{h}'')\big)} + \underbrace{2^{4\nu + 2\varphi_0 + 2\gamma_0 - 2}}_{\geq \|\mathbf{h}''\|_\infty^2} \cdot 1/12 \cdot 2^{-2\chi} \Big) \cdot 2$$

$$= 2^{4\nu + 2\varphi_0 + 2\gamma_0 - 2\chi - 3}. \quad (54)$$

Since the unfolding operation does not change the error, the negacyclic results follow. $\square$

References

1. IEEE Standard for Floating-Point Arithmetic: IEEE Std 754-2019 (Revision of IEEE 754-2008), pp. 1–84 (2019)
2. Ajtai, M.: Generating hard instances of lattice problems. In: Proceedings of the Twenty-Eighth Annual ACM Symposium on Theory of Computing, pp. 99–108 (1996)
3. Al Badawi, A., Veeravalli, B., Aung, K.M.M.: Efficient polynomial multiplication via modified discrete galois transform and negacyclic convolution. In: Arai, K., Kapoor, S., Bhatia, R. (eds.) FICC 2018. AISC, vol. 886, pp. 666–682. Springer, Cham (2019). https://doi.org/10.1007/978-3-030-03402-3_47
4. Bernstein, D.J.: Multidigit multiplication for mathematicians (2001)
5. Bourse, F., Minelli, M., Minihold, M., Paillier, P.: Fast homomorphic evaluation of deep discretized neural networks. In: Shacham, H., Boldyreva, A. (eds.) CRYPTO 2018. LNCS, vol. 10993, pp. 483–512. Springer, Cham (2018). https://doi.org/10.1007/978-3-319-96878-0_17
6. Brakerski, Z., Gentry, C., Vaikuntanathan, V.: (Leveled) fully homomorphic encryption without bootstrapping. ACM Trans. Comput. Theory (TOCT) **6**(3), 13 (2014)
7. Carpov, S., Izabachène, M., Mollimard, V.: New techniques for multi-value input homomorphic evaluation and applications. In: Matsui, M. (ed.) CT-RSA 2019. LNCS, vol. 11405, pp. 106–126. Springer, Cham (2019). https://doi.org/10.1007/978-3-030-12612-4_6
8. Chillotti, I., Gama, N., Georgieva, M., Izabachène, M.: TFHE: fast fully homomorphic encryption over the torus. J. Cryptol. **33**(1), 34–91 (2020)
9. Cooley, J.W., Tukey, J.W.: An algorithm for the machine calculation of complex Fourier series. Math. Comput. **19**(90), 297–301 (1965)
10. Crandall, R., Pomerance, C.B.: Prime Numbers: A Computational Perspective, vol. 182. Springer, New York (2006)
11. Crandall, R.E.: Integer convolution via split-radix fast galois transform. Center for Advanced Computation Reed College (1999)
12. Ding, J., Schmidt, D.: Rainbow, a new multivariable polynomial signature scheme. In: Ioannidis, J., Keromytis, A., Yung, M. (eds.) ACNS 2005. LNCS, vol. 3531, pp. 164–175. Springer, Heidelberg (2005). https://doi.org/10.1007/11496137_12
13. Gentleman, W.M., Sande, G.: Fast Fourier transforms: for fun and profit. In: Proceedings of the November 7–10, 1966, Fall Joint Computer Conference, pp. 563–578 (1966)
14. Gentry, C., Boneh, D.: A Fully Homomorphic Encryption Scheme, vol. 20. Stanford University (2009)
15. Goldstine, H.H.: A history of numerical analysis from the 16th through the 19th century. Bull. Am. Math. Soc. **1**, 388–390 (1979)
16. Hart, W., Johansson, F., Pancratz, S.: FLINT: Fast Library for Number Theory (2011). https://www.flintlib.org/
17. Hoffstein, J., Pipher, J., Silverman, J.H.: NTRU: a ring-based public key cryptosystem. In: Buhler, J.P. (ed.) ANTS 1998. LNCS, vol. 1423, pp. 267–288. Springer, Heidelberg (1998). https://doi.org/10.1007/BFb0054868
18. Jao, D., De Feo, L.: Towards quantum-resistant cryptosystems from supersingular elliptic curve isogenies. In: Yang, B.-Y. (ed.) PQCrypto 2011. LNCS, vol. 7071, pp. 19–34. Springer, Heidelberg (2011). https://doi.org/10.1007/978-3-642-25405-5_2

19. Karatsuba, A.A., Ofman, Y.P.: Multiplication of many-digital numbers by automatic computers. In: Doklady Akademii Nauk, vol. 145, pp. 293–294. Russian Academy of Sciences (1962)

20. Klemsa, J.: Benchmarking FFNT (2021). https://gitlab.fit.cvut.cz/klemsjak/ffnt-benchmark

21. Lyubashevsky, V., Peikert, C., Regev, O.: On ideal lattices and learning with errors over rings. In: Gilbert, H. (ed.) EUROCRYPT 2010. LNCS, vol. 6110, pp. 1–23. Springer, Heidelberg (2010). https://doi.org/10.1007/978-3-642-13190-5_1

22. Fast Fourier transform in x86 assembly (2021). https://www.nayuki.io/page/fast-fourier-transform-in-x86-assembly. Accessed 30 Jan 2021

23. NIST: NIST's Post-Quantum Cryptography Program Enters "Selection Round" (2020). https://www.nist.gov/news-events/news/2020/07/nists-post-quantum-cryptography-program-enters-selection-round

24. Regev, O.: On lattices, learning with errors, random linear codes, and cryptography. J. ACM (JACM) 56(6), 1–40 (2009)

25. Schönhage, A., Strassen, V.: Schnelle multiplikation grosser zahlen. Computing 7(3), 281–292 (1971)

26. Shor, P.W.: Algorithms for quantum computation: discrete logarithms and factoring. In: Proceedings 35th Annual Symposium on Foundations of Computer Science, pp. 124–134. IEEE (1994)

27. Shoup, V., et al.: NTL: a library for doing number theory (2001). https://libntl.org/

28. TFHE: Fast Fully Homomorphic Encryption Library over the Torus (2016). https://github.com/tfhe/tfhe

Efficient Secure Ridge Regression from Randomized Gaussian Elimination

Frank Blom[3], Niek J. Bouman[2], Berry Schoenmakers[1(✉)], and Niels de Vreede[2]

[1] Department of Math & CS, TU Eindhoven, Eindhoven, The Netherlands
berry@win.tue.nl
[2] Roseman Labs, Breda, The Netherlands
[3] UWV Security & Risk, Amsterdam, The Netherlands

Abstract. In this paper we present practical protocols for secure ridge regression. We develop the necessary secure linear algebra tools, using only basic arithmetic over prime fields. In particular, we will show how to solve linear systems of equations and compute matrix inverses efficiently, using appropriate secure random self-reductions of these problems. The distinguishing feature of our approach is that the use of secure fixed-point arithmetic is avoided entirely, while circumventing the need for secure rational reconstruction at any stage as well. In fact, in recent follow-up works, our results have already been applied and extended to several other settings.

We demonstrate the potential of our protocols in a standard setting for information-theoretically secure multiparty computation, tolerating a dishonest minority of passively corrupt parties. Using the MPyC framework, which is based on threshold secret sharing over finite fields, we show how to handle large datasets efficiently, achieving practically the same root-mean-square errors as Scikit-learn. Moreover, our protocols are designed with the outsourcing scenario in mind, which makes our protocols much more versatile than existing solutions. In the outsourcing scenario one does not assume that (any part of) the dataset is held privately by any of the parties performing the multiparty computation—in contrast to federated learning, for instance, where the dataset is partitioned either horizontally or vertically between these parties.

1 Introduction

Recent years have seen significant advances in privacy-preserving data mining and machine learning. Secure multiparty computation (MPC) is a promising type of cryptographic protocol for enhancing the security and privacy properties of existing data mining and machine learning algorithms. Handling large datasets, however, still poses practical challenges due to the overhead incurred by MPC.

Secure regression is a problem that received much attention as the resulting cryptographic protocols have the potential of handling relatively large datasets, see, e.g., [DHC04, HFN11, NWI+13, GJJ+18, GSB+17]. When applied to linear

---

Work done while all authors were at TU Eindhoven.

S. Dolev et al. (Eds.): CSCML 2021, LNCS 12716, pp. 301–316, 2021.
https://doi.org/10.1007/978-3-030-78086-9_23

and ridge regression, the overhead for MPC is limited because of the highly linear nature of the computation. The bulk of the computation consists of taking dot products, which can be done securely at low cost in many MPC frameworks.

In this paper we develop particularly efficient m-party protocols for ridge regression tolerating a dishonest minority of up to t passively corrupt parties, $1 \leq 2t+1 \leq m$. Using Shamir secret sharing for the underlying secure prime field arithmetic, we achieve information-theoretic security. Nevertheless we advocate the use of *large* prime fields, not because it is required for security, but to allow for exact arithmetic when solving particular linear systems securely. As we will show, the overhead for the use of large prime fields does not adversely affect the overall performance. We thus present a range of practical optimizations, which are combined into a very competitive solution for secure ridge regression. We also present experimental results to support our claims.

At this point, we like to stress that well-known results in secure linear algebra ([CD01] and follow-up work) do not apply to our setting. Whereas [CD01] considers linear algebra *over finite fields*, which fits well with the fact that most MPC frameworks "natively" support finite field arithmetic, our results can be viewed best as secure linear algebra *over the rationals*, which calls for new protocols and techniques.

1.1   Approach

Ridge regression (or, Tikhonov regularization) is a classic problem in statistics. Nowadays, the problem is broadly studied and applied in machine learning, and many algorithms have been proposed covering various types and dimensions of input data. The popular tool Scikit-learn, for instance, provides six different solvers for ridge regression, most of which also use different approaches for sparse and dense data [PVG+11].

The solver used in the present paper directly uses the closed-form solution for ridge regression, cf. Eqs. (2) and (3). An alternative approach is to approximate the solution using an iterative solver, viewing ridge regression as an optimization problem minimizing (1). Well-known iterative solvers are stochastic gradient descent and its many variations (e.g., mini-batch gradient descent).

However, there are two major impediments for adopting iterative solvers in an MPC setting. Firstly, all arithmetic involves real-valued numbers, which needs to be approximated using secure fixed-point arithmetic (as secure floating-point arithmetic is simply too expensive). The use of secure fixed-point numbers incurs a substantial overhead and could lead to numerical stability issues. Secondly, one needs to control the number of iterations. In an MPC setting, evaluation of a stopping criterion may form a bottleneck in itself, and fixing the number of iterations beforehand may demand a high number of iterations (to ensure convergence for all inputs). The advantage of the iterative approach is that it generalizes immediately to related machine learning algorithms such as logistic regression and support vector machines. Adapting the computation of the gradient suffices to solve these problems as well.

As we show in this paper, there are major advantages to solving the ridge regression problem directly. It allows us to avoid fixed-point arithmetic entirely. Issues surrounding rounding errors are limited to the input phase, when real-valued inputs are converted to integral values using appropriate scaling. From that point on all computations are exact, using integer arithmetic only. The main issue left is the growth of the numbers, but we will show that even for huge datasets, our approach is practical and leads to very competitive results in an MPC setting.

The closed-form solution is in fact a matrix equation, which can in turn be solved directly or iteratively, as we will discuss in Sect. 5.

1.2   Roadmap

We present mathematical preliminaries in Sect. 2, and the basics on linear regression and ridge regression in Sect. 3. Next we introduce basic notation for MPC based on Shamir secret sharing in Sect. 4. In Sect. 5 we discuss the relevant choices for solving linear systems of equations in an MPC setting, showing how we avoid the use of secure rational reconstruction. Section 6 contains the basic protocols for secure linear algebra, which we use in our protocol for secure ridge regression in Sect. 7. Finally, we discuss the performance in Sect. 8, and conclude in Sect. 9 also mentioning some recent papers building on our results.

2   Preliminaries

We use common notation for matrices and vectors. For $d \geq 1$, the group of $d \times d$ invertible matrices over a field $\mathbb{F}$ is denoted by $\mathrm{GL}_d(\mathbb{F})$. The groups of $d \times d$ lower resp. upper triangular invertible matrices are denoted by $\mathrm{L}_d(\mathbb{F}), \mathrm{U}_d(\mathbb{F}) \subseteq \mathrm{GL}_d(\mathbb{F})$, and we use $\mathrm{L}_d^1(\mathbb{F})$ to denote the group of lower triangular matrices with an all-ones diagonal.

A matrix $A \in \mathrm{GL}_d(\mathbb{F})$ is said to have an **LU-decomposition** if $A = LU$ for some $L \in \mathrm{L}_d^1(\mathbb{F})$ and $U \in \mathrm{U}_d(\mathbb{F})$. We use $\mathrm{LU}_d(\mathbb{F})$ to denote the set of all matrices in $\mathrm{GL}_d(\mathbb{F})$ that have an LU-decomposition. Note that the LU-decomposition for each $A \in \mathrm{LU}_d(\mathbb{F})$ is unique. Similarly, a matrix $A \in \mathrm{GL}_d(\mathbb{F})$ is said to have a **Cholesky decomposition** if $A = LL^\mathsf{T}$ for some $L \in \mathrm{L}_d(\mathbb{F})$. The Cholesky decomposition is also unique, and exists over $\mathbb{F} = \mathbb{R}$ if and only if A is symmetric positive definite.

For $A \in \mathrm{GL}_d(\mathbb{F})$, we use $\mathrm{adj}\, A = \det(A)A^{-1}$ to denote the **adjugate** of A. For our approach, a key property is that if A is integral then so are $\det A$ and $\mathrm{adj}\, A$. That is, if A is a matrix over $\mathbb{Z}$, then $\det A \in \mathbb{Z}$ and $\mathrm{adj}\, A$ is also a matrix over $\mathbb{Z}$. Furthermore, **Hadamard's inequality** states that $|\det A| \leq \prod_{i=1}^d \|\boldsymbol{a}_i\|_2$, where $\boldsymbol{a}_i$ are the rows (or columns) of A. For $\alpha = \|A\|_{\max}$, Hadamard's inequality implies $|\det A| \leq d^{d/2}\alpha^d$. If A is symmetric positive definite, $\det A$ is positive and Hadamard's inequality becomes $\det A \leq \prod_{i=1}^d a_{i,i}$ and we get $\det A \leq \alpha^d$. Finally, Hadamard's inequality yields $\|\mathrm{adj}\, A\|_{\max} \leq (d-1)^{(d-1)/2}\alpha^{d-1}$ as bound for the adjugate.

Gaussian elimination and variations thereof are used to compute $\det A$, adj A, and A^{-1}. For example, A^{-1} is computed by transforming the augmented matrix $(A \mid I)$ into $(I \mid A^{-1})$ by means of Gauss-Jordan elimination. Similarly, if A has an LU-decomposition as defined above, applying Gaussian elimination to A amounts to multiplying A from the left by the lower triangular matrix L^{-1}, resulting in $U = L^{-1}A$. Hence, the upper triangular matrix U is obtained without applying any *pivoting* steps. Putting $\det A = \det U = \prod_{i=1}^{d} u_{i,i}$ yields the determinant.

We will perform Gaussian elimination over finite fields of large prime order p, and we will do so for essentially uniformly random matrices only. As a consequence, there will be no need for pivoting and all computations will be exact (cf. use of preconditioning explained in Sect. 5). Inspired by Bareiss [Bar68], we will combine division-free Gaussian elimination with back substitution such that $\det A$ is obtained at almost no extra cost. See Sect. 6.3 for further details.

3   Ridge Regression

Ridge regression is a well-known technique in statistics and machine learning [FHT01], which can be seen as a refinement of the ordinary least squares method used in linear regression. Ridge regression provides the user with a handle, the *regularization parameter* $\lambda > 0$, which can be used to reduce the variance of the prediction at the cost of introducing some bias. If λ is set properly, ridge regression can outperform the ordinary least squares method in terms of the root mean-square error, defined below. In high-dimensional problems, ridge regression can help to reduce the problem of overfitting.

Given an overdetermined linear system $X\boldsymbol{w} = \boldsymbol{y}$, the least squares solution $\boldsymbol{w}$ minimizes $\|X\boldsymbol{w} - \boldsymbol{y}\|_2$. Typically, X is an $n \times d$ matrix over $\mathbb{R}$ with $n \gg d$. Each row of X represents an input record with d features, and the corresponding entry of $\boldsymbol{y}$ represents the known output value. The least squares solution $\boldsymbol{w} = (X^{\mathsf{T}}X)^{-1}X^{\mathsf{T}}\boldsymbol{y}$, is used as the optimal weight vector for predicting the output values for new input records $\boldsymbol{x}$ by evaluating $\boldsymbol{x}^{\mathsf{T}}\boldsymbol{w}$.

Ridge regression finds a vector $\boldsymbol{w}$ minimizing

$$\|X\boldsymbol{w} - \boldsymbol{y}\|_2^2 + \lambda\|\boldsymbol{w}\|_2^2, \tag{1}$$

where we note the presence of the regularization parameter in the second term. The solution $\boldsymbol{w}$ minimizing (1) is now given by:

$$\boldsymbol{w} = \left(X^{\mathsf{T}}X + \lambda I\right)^{-1}X^{\mathsf{T}}\boldsymbol{y}. \tag{2}$$

To compute $\boldsymbol{w}$, one solves the linear system $A\boldsymbol{w} = \boldsymbol{b}$ with $A = X^{\mathsf{T}}X + \lambda I$ and $\boldsymbol{b} = X^{\mathsf{T}}\boldsymbol{y}$. Note that the regularization parameter λ not only suppresses large entries in $\boldsymbol{w}$, but also ensures that A is positive definite, hence invertible: $\boldsymbol{z}^{\mathsf{T}}\left(X^{\mathsf{T}}X + \lambda I\right)\boldsymbol{z} = \|X\boldsymbol{z}\|_2^2 + \lambda\|\boldsymbol{z}\|_2^2 > 0$ for any nonzero $\boldsymbol{z}$, since $\lambda > 0$.

In the context of machine learning, the input records X along with the known output values $\boldsymbol{y}$ are called the training set, and the least-squares solution $\boldsymbol{w}$ is called the model. The performance of the model is evaluated in terms of the root-mean-square error (RMSE) of the model's predictions. The model complexity (training error) is defined as the RMSE for the training set, which is equal to $\|Xw - y\|_2/\sqrt{n}$. The generalizability (test error) of the model is defined as the RMSE for a test set (X', y'), which is equal to $\|X'w - y'\|_2/\sqrt{n'}$. Overall, the goal is to ensure that both RMSEs are small and approximately equal to each other.

The performance of a machine learning algorithm critically depends on the quality of the input data. Extensive data preprocessing may be required in practice to enhance the quality of the input data. In our experiments we will use standard datasets from the UCI repository, for which most of the data preprocessing has already been done. The only two tasks that remain before applying ridge regression to these datasets are (i) feature scaling and (ii) encoding of categorical features.

For feature scaling, we apply min-max scaling to each of the columns of X and to vector y as well. Concretely, all features are scaled to the range $[-1, 1]$. We prefer this form of data normalization because it requires little processing and does not leak too much information about X and y.

To encode categorical features (including Boolean features), we basically use a form of "one-hot encoding" with respect to the range $[-1, 1]$. For Boolean features, we encode the values True and False by 1 and -1, respectively. A categorical feature with s possible values is encoded by s Boolean features, where the value for exactly one of the Boolean features will be set to 1 and the remaining $s - 1$ Boolean features are set to -1.

4   MPC Setting

We consider an information-theoretically secure MPC setting with m parties tolerating a dishonest minority of up to t passively corrupt parties, $0 \leq t \leq (m - 1)/2$. The protocols are designed to work in the outsourcing scenario. In this scenario the data providers distribute shares to the m parties running the MPC protocol, meaning that no (plaintext) knowledge of the data by any of the parties is assumed. We require, in its most general form, black box access to secure addition and multiplication of shares, which are defined over a finite field. Dot products are required to have the same round complexity as a single multiplication, see below.

In our implementation we instantiate the sharing scheme as Shamir secret sharing [BGW88, GRR98], using the MPyC framework [Sch18], which succeeds the VIFF framework [Gei10], for our practical experiments.

Let $p > m$ be a prime. We use $[a]_p$ or $[a]$ to denote a secret-shared value $a \in \mathbb{Z}_p$, where a is interpreted as a signed integer in the range $\{-\lfloor p/2 \rfloor, \ldots, \lfloor p/2 \rfloor\}$. We assume that secure field arithmetic $(+, -, *, /$ modulo $p)$ is supported efficiently as well as secure generation of random numbers (e.g., $[r]$ with $r \in_R \mathbb{Z}_p$).

We highlight three auxiliary protocols which are of particular relevance for our approach.

For secure dot products $[\![\boldsymbol{x}]\!]\cdot[\![\boldsymbol{y}]\!]$ with $\boldsymbol{x},\boldsymbol{y}\in\mathbb{Z}_p^d$, we recall that the complexity is the same as for a single secure multiplication, except for local computations. This extends to secure matrix products $[\![A]\!][\![B]\!]$ with $A,B\in\mathbb{Z}_p^{d\times d}$, for which the complexity is equivalent to d^2 secure multiplications in parallel.

Next, to generate $[\![r]\!]$ and $[\![1/r]\!]$ for a random $r\in_R\mathbb{Z}_p^*$, one proceeds as follows: generate $[\![r]\!]$, $[\![u]\!]$ with $r,u\in_R\mathbb{Z}_p$, open $[\![r]\!][\![u]\!]$ to obtain ru, and output $[\![r]\!]$ and $[\![1/r]\!]=[\![u]\!]/(ru)$. For large p, $ru\neq 0$ will hold with overwhelming probability; if $ru=0$ simply try again with fresh r and u.

Finally, we will also use secure conversion between secret-shared values in different prime fields. In particular, for primes p and q satisfying $p>q>2^{\kappa+\ell}$, where κ is a security parameter, we use a secure protocol for converting $[\![a]\!]_q$ into $[\![a]\!]_p$, $-2^{\ell-1}\leq a<2^{\ell-1}$. Roughly, such a protocol proceeds by jointly generating $[\![r]\!]_q$ and $[\![r]\!]_p$ for a random $r\in[0,2^{\ell+\kappa})$. Then the value of $a+r$ is opened, which is statistically indistinguishable from random for κ sufficiently large, and one sets $[\![a]\!]_p=a+r-[\![r]\!]_p$.

5   Solving Systems of Linear Equations

As outlined in Sect. 3, we divide ridge regression into two main stages. In the first stage we compute $A=X^\mathsf{T}X+\lambda I$ and $b=X^\mathsf{T}y$, and in the second stage we solve $A\boldsymbol{w}=\boldsymbol{b}$ to find $\boldsymbol{w}$. For secure ridge regression, the most interesting and challenging part will be the second stage, and in this section we motivate our approach for solving $A\boldsymbol{w}=\boldsymbol{b}$.

In numerical analysis one distinguishes two major types of solution methods for systems of linear equations. Direct methods, such as Gaussian elimination, run in a finite number of steps and compute an exact solution in the absence of rounding errors. Iterative methods, such as conjugate gradient, yield approximate solutions within a limited amount of time, even for very large matrices. In contrast to some other recent work (e.g., [GSB+17]), we will choose a direct method to solve $A\boldsymbol{w}=\boldsymbol{b}$ in our protocols for secure ridge regression. Below we explain our reasons for doing so.

An important observation is that we can actually use exact computation for secure ridge regression. Instead of relying on fixed-point arithmetic—or even worse floating-point arithmetic—in an MPC setting, we will only use exact integer arithmetic in our protocols. This way we take advantage of the fact that secure integer arithmetic is efficient even for large values when using Shamir secret sharing. Moreover, we can borrow techniques from the related setting of secure linear algebra over finite fields [CD01].

We will make sure that the input data (contained in X and $\boldsymbol{y}$) are scaled to integer values, basically by multiplying each input value with 2^α and rounding to the nearest integer for a fixed value of α. The value of α must be sufficiently large to ensure that the final results will be accurate. We will refer to α as the *accuracy* parameter.

Since A is invertible, solving $A\boldsymbol{w}=\boldsymbol{b}$ is equivalent to computing $\boldsymbol{w}=A^{-1}\boldsymbol{b}$. Therefore, even if A contains integer values only, the solution $\boldsymbol{w}$ will in general contain rational values. As $A^{-1} = (\det A)^{-1} \text{adj } A$, however, it suffices to compute $\boldsymbol{w}' = (\text{adj } A)\boldsymbol{b}$ and $z = \det A$, from which $\boldsymbol{w}$ can be recovered as $\boldsymbol{w} = \boldsymbol{w}'/z$. Here, both $\boldsymbol{w}'$ and z are integral. We compute $\boldsymbol{w}'$ and z by first reducing the augmented matrix $(A \mid b)$ to echelon form using Gaussian elimination and then applying back substitution to obtain $\boldsymbol{w}'$.

To perform *secure* Gaussian elimination on $(A \mid b)$ there are several options. A first idea is to use Gaussian elimination (row reduction) directly, which amounts to repeatedly selecting a pivot and updating the matrix accordingly. However, oblivious row reduction, hiding the position of the pivot and so on, is computationally very costly: searching for a nonzero element in the pivot column is already nontrivial in a secure setting, and obliviously swapping entire rows to move the pivot to the diagonal is even much more costly.

A common technique in numerical analysis to avoid pivot selection is the use of *preconditioning*. Roughly, the idea is to solve the equivalent system $RAw = Rb$ for a random matrix R, instead of the original system $Aw = b$. Matrix R is assumed to be invertible, which is true with overwhelming probability in many settings. When solving linear systems over $\mathbb{R}$, such an approach is numerically unstable and leads to poor results. When solving linear systems over a finite field, however, numerical instability is of no concern. We will follow this approach.

The upshot of computing $(\text{adj } A)\boldsymbol{b}$ and $\det A$ separately is that we will also avoid the use of secure rational reconstruction. In the next section we will show why this lets us essentially *halve* the size of the prime modulus for the finite field arithmetic compared to other papers. For instance, [GJJ+18] relies on rational reconstruction and uses a modulus which should be large enough to "hold" the *product* of $(\text{adj } A)\boldsymbol{b}$ and $\det A$.

6 Secure Linear Algebra

We present protocols for computing determinants, matrix inverses, and solutions to linear systems. Given an invertible matrix $A \in \mathbb{Z}^{d \times d}$, we compute the results over $\mathbb{Z}_p$ assuming p is sufficiently large. E.g., for $-p/2 < \det A < p/2$, $\det A \in \mathbb{Z}_p^*$ and A is properly embedded in $\mathbb{Z}_p^{d \times d}$. Assuming further bounds on the entries of A and $\boldsymbol{b}$, we will show how to compute A^{-1} and $A^{-1}\boldsymbol{b}$ over $\mathbb{Z}_p$ as well.

6.1 Secure Determinant

Cramer and Damgård presented a protocol for secure computation of $\det A$ over any finite field [CD01], which is reminiscent of Bar-Ilan and Beaver's protocol for secure multiplicative inverses [BB89]. The idea is to securely generate a random invertible matrix $[\![R]\!]$ together with its determinant $[\![\det R]\!]$, open the randomized matrix RA, and finally compute $[\![\det A]\!]$. We follow the same approach in Protocol 1, except that we improve upon the way random matrix R is generated in several ways.

Ideally, R is generated as a random matrix in $\text{GL}_d(\mathbb{Z}_p)$. To securely compute $\det R$ as well, matrix R is limited to the slightly smaller range $\text{LU}_d(\mathbb{Z}_p)$ of matrices that have an LU-decomposition. The following lemma shows that uniformly random matrices in $\text{LU}_d(\mathbb{Z}_p)$ are statistically indistinguishable from

---

Protocol 1. Det($[\![A]\!]$) $A \in \mathrm{GL}_d(\mathbb{Z}_p)$

1: Generate $[\![R]\!]$, $[\![\det R^{-1}]\!]$ with $R \in_R \mathrm{LU}_d(\mathbb{Z}_p)$ using Protocol 2.
2: Open $RA \leftarrow [\![R]\!][\![A]\!]$.
3: Compute $[\![\det A]\!] = \det(RA)[\![\det R^{-1}]\!]$.
4: Return $[\![\det A]\!]$.

Protocol 2. RndMatDet(d)

1: Generate $[\![L]\!]$ with $L \in_R \mathrm{L}_d^1(\mathbb{Z}_p)$.
2: Generate $[\![U]\!]$, $[\![\det U^{-1}]\!]$ with $U \in_R \mathrm{U}_d(\mathbb{Z}_p)$.
3: Compute $[\![R]\!] = [\![L]\!][\![U]\!]$.
4: Set $[\![\det R^{-1}]\!] = [\![\det U^{-1}]\!]$.
5: Return $[\![R]\!]$, $[\![\det R^{-1}]\!]$.

---

uniformly random matrices in $\mathrm{GL}_d(\mathbb{Z}_p)$. Therefore, similar to the security proofs in [BB89, CD01], opening RA reveals negligible information on A only, assuming p is exponentially large in the security parameter κ.

Lemma 1. $\Delta(R; G) \leq d/p$, for $R \in_R \mathrm{LU}_d(\mathbb{Z}_p)$ and $G \in_R \mathrm{GL}_d(\mathbb{Z}_p)$.

Proof. Since $\mathrm{LU}_d(\mathbb{Z}_p) \subseteq \mathrm{GL}_d(\mathbb{Z}_p)$ and R and G are both uniform we have

$$\Delta(R; G) = \tfrac{1}{2} \sum_{x \in \mathrm{GL}_d(\mathbb{Z}_p)} |\Pr[R = x] - \Pr[G = x]| = 1 - \frac{|\mathrm{LU}_d(\mathbb{Z}_p)|}{|\mathrm{GL}_d(\mathbb{Z}_p)|}.$$

Since $|\mathrm{LU}_d(\mathbb{Z}_p)| = p^{d^2-d}(p-1)^d$ and $|\mathrm{GL}_d(\mathbb{Z}_p)| \leq p^{d^2}$, we have

$$\Delta(R; G) \leq 1 - \left(\frac{p-1}{p}\right)^d = 1 - \left(1 - \frac{1}{p}\right)^d \leq \frac{d}{p},$$

using Bernoulli's inequality in the last step.

To sample a matrix R securely from $\mathrm{LU}_d(\mathbb{Z}_p)$, we use Protocol 2. The protocol also outputs the determinant of R, or rather its inverse. Random matrices in $\mathrm{L}_d^1(\mathbb{Z}_p)$ and $\mathrm{U}_d(\mathbb{Z}_p)$ can be generated easily, provided we can securely generate random elements of $\mathbb{Z}_p$. To ensure that U is invertible, we generate $u_{i,i} \in_R \mathbb{Z}_p$ for $i = 1, \ldots, d$, and then apply secure inversion to $\det U = \prod_{i=1}^d u_{i,i}$. With negligible probability $\det U = 0$, in which case secure inversion will fail and we have to try again. With overwhelming probability, however, $\det U \neq 0$ and secure inversion will succeed. In total, Protocol 2 roughly uses d^2 random elements from $\mathbb{Z}_p$.

Our protocol for generating random matrices improves upon Cramer and Damgård's protocol Π_0 [CD01, p. 126] in several respects. The main difference is that protocol Π_0 depends on a redundant type of LU-decomposition in which the diagonals of both L and U consist of elements in $\mathbb{Z}_p^*$. By fixing the diagonal of L to all ones, the LU-decomposition used in our protocol is unique.

Protocol 3. AdjDet($[\![A]\!]$) $A \in \mathrm{GL}_d(\mathbb{Z}_p)$

1: Generate $[\![R]\!]$, $[\![\det R^{-1}]\!]$ with $R \in_R \mathrm{LU}_d(\mathbb{Z}_p)$ using Protocol 2.
2: Open $RA \leftarrow [\![R]\!][\![A]\!]$.
3: Reduce $(RA \mid [\![R]\!])$ to obtain $[\![A^{-1}]\!]$ by Gauss-Jordan elimination over $\mathbb{Z}_p$.
4: Compute $[\![\det A]\!] = \det(RA)[\![\det R^{-1}]\!]$.
5: Compute $[\![\mathrm{adj}\, A]\!] = [\![\det A]\!][\![A^{-1}]\!]$.
6: Return $[\![\mathrm{adj}\, A]\!]$, $[\![\det A]\!]$.

As an immediate consequence, our proof for statistical indistinguishability is much simpler (cf. Lemma 1). Moreover, the complexity of the protocol is reduced as we do not need to generate the diagonal of L at random, and we do not need to compute $\det L$ either. Finally, as a further optimization, we only use one secure inversion throughout the entire protocol (to perform the secure zero-test and inversion for $\det U$ all at the same time).

Apart from generating a random matrix R and its inverse determinant, Protocol 1 mainly performs a secure matrix multiplication. The computation of $\det(RA)$ is done locally, so we might use any algorithm for computing determinants to implement this step. However, Lemma 1 helps us save some work for the local computation as well. The lemma basically implies that RA is statistically close to a uniformly random matrix in $\mathrm{LU}_d(\mathbb{Z}_p)$, and therefore we can perform Gaussian elimination to compute $\det(RA)$ without any pivoting, as shown below.

6.2   Secure Matrix Inversion

We next present Protocol 3 for secure matrix inversion, which is of independent interest. Since A^{-1} will in general have rational entries for a matrix $A \in \mathbb{Z}^{d \times d}$, as discussed above, we will use the pair $(\mathrm{adj}\, A, \det A)$ as representation of A^{-1}. This way we avoid any rational arithmetic, and, moreover, we can use a similar embedding for A in $\mathbb{Z}_p^{d \times d}$ as for the determinant, using the bound for $\|\mathrm{adj}\, A\|_{\max}$ from Sect. 2 to choose p sufficiently large.

If we stick to the common approach of computing $A^{-1} = (\det A)^{-1}\mathrm{adj}\, A$ over $\mathbb{Z}_p$, such that $\mathrm{adj}\, A$ and $\det A$ can be recovered using rational reconstruction over $\mathbb{Z}_p$, the required size for p would be roughly twice as large.

6.3   Secure Linear Solver

Finally, we present Protocol 4 for securely solving a linear system, in which we avoid performing a full matrix inversion. In step 3 we apply Gaussian elimination to the augmented matrix $(RA \mid [\![R]\!][\![b]\!])$. As explained in Sect. 5, this can be done without pivoting. Matrix RA is first transformed into upper-triangular form, and then we apply back substitution to compute $[\![A^{-1}b]\!]$. For Gaussian elimination on $(RA \mid [\![R]\!][\![b]\!])$, we use the division-free variant (see, e.g., [Bar68]). Combined with back substitution, we achieve that $\det(RA)$ is obtained at almost no additional cost. In total we need $\frac{2}{3}d^3 + O(d^2)$ multiplications, $\frac{1}{3}d^3 + O(d^2)$ modular reductions, and exactly d inversions modulo p for step 3.

Protocol 4. LinSol($[\![A]\!], [\![\boldsymbol{b}]\!]$) $A \in \mathrm{GL}_d(\mathbb{Z}_p), \boldsymbol{b} \in \mathbb{Z}_p^d$

1: Generate $[\![R]\!]$, $[\![\det R^{-1}]\!]$ with $R \in_R \mathrm{LU}_d(\mathbb{Z}_p)$ using Protocol 2.
2: Open $RA \leftarrow [\![R]\!][\![A]\!]$.
3: Solve $(RA \mid [\![R]\!][\![\boldsymbol{b}]\!])$ to obtain $[\![A^{-1}\boldsymbol{b}]\!]$ by Gaussian elimination over $\mathbb{Z}_p$.
4: Compute $[\![\det A]\!] = \det(RA)[\![\det R]\!]^{-1}$.
5: Compute $[\![(\mathrm{adj}\,A)\boldsymbol{b}]\!] = [\![\det A]\!][\![A^{-1}\boldsymbol{b}]\!]$.
6: Return $[\![(\mathrm{adj}\,A)\boldsymbol{b}]\!]$, $[\![\det A]\!]$.

Protocol 5. Ridge($[\![X]\!]_q, [\![\boldsymbol{y}]\!]_q, \lambda$) $X \in \mathbb{Z}_q^{n \times d}, \boldsymbol{y} \in \mathbb{Z}_q^n, \lambda \in \mathbb{N}$

1: Compute $[\![A]\!]_q = [\![X^\mathsf{T}]\!]_q[\![X]\!]_q + \lambda I$. $\triangleright A = X^\mathsf{T}X + \lambda I$
2: Compute $[\![\boldsymbol{b}]\!]_q = [\![X^\mathsf{T}]\!]_q[\![\boldsymbol{y}]\!]_q$. $\triangleright \boldsymbol{b} = X^\mathsf{T}\boldsymbol{y}$
3: Convert $[\![(A \mid \boldsymbol{b})]\!]_q$ to $[\![(A \mid \boldsymbol{b})]\!]_p$.
4: Compute $([\![(\mathrm{adj}\,A)\boldsymbol{b}]\!]_p, [\![\det A]\!]_p) = \mathrm{LinSol}([\![(A \mid \boldsymbol{b})]\!]_p)$.
5: Set $[\![(\det A)\boldsymbol{w}]\!]_p = [\![(\mathrm{adj}\,A)\boldsymbol{b}]\!]_p$. $\triangleright \boldsymbol{w} = A^{-1}\boldsymbol{b}$
6: Return $[\![(\det A)\boldsymbol{w}]\!]_p, [\![\det A]\!]_p$.

Lemma 2. *Let* $\gamma = \|(A|\boldsymbol{b})\|_{\max}$. *Correctness of Protocols 1, 3, and 4 follows if*

$$\frac{p}{2} > d^{\frac{d}{2}}\gamma^d.$$

Proof. For Protocol 1 we need that $p/2 > |\det A|$. We use the bound $|\det A| \leq d^{d/2}\gamma^d$ obtained from Hadamard's inequality in Sect. 2. So we require $p/2 > d^{d/2}\gamma^d$.

For Protocol 3, in addition to $p/2 > |\det A|$, we need $p/2 > \|\mathrm{adj}\,A\|_{\max}$. Using the bound $\|\mathrm{adj}\,A\|_{\max} \leq (d-1)^{(d-1)/2}\gamma^{d-1}$ from Sect. 2, we still have $p/2 > d^{d/2}\gamma^d$ as overall bound.

For Protocol 4 we need $p/2 > \|(\mathrm{adj}\,A)\boldsymbol{b}\|_{\max}$ in addition to $p/2 > |\det A|$. Note that $(\mathrm{adj}\,A)\boldsymbol{b} = \det(A)\boldsymbol{w}$, where $\boldsymbol{w}$ is the unique solution to the system $A\boldsymbol{w} = \boldsymbol{b}$. By Cramer's rule we then have $\|(\mathrm{adj}\,A)\boldsymbol{b}\|_{\max} = \max_{i=1}^d\{|\det(A_i)|\} \leq d^{d/2}\gamma^d$ where A_i is the matrix obtained by replacing the ith column of matrix A with $\boldsymbol{b}$. Hence, the bound $p/2 > d^{d/2}\gamma^d$ suffices in this case as well.

7   Secure Ridge Regression

In this section we present our protocol for ridge regression, see Protocol 5. All entries of X and $\boldsymbol{y}$ are assumed to be in $[-2^\alpha, 2^\alpha] \cap \mathbb{Z}$ for an appropriate value of the accuracy parameter α (i.e., normalized to $[-1, 1]$ as explained in Sect. 3, scaled by a factor of 2^α, and rounded to the nearest integer). The regularization parameter λ is scaled accordingly. We note that parameter α is between 5 and 10 in our experiments, cf. Table 2.

The two main stages of ridge regression are performed over two different prime fields. In the first stage, $X^\mathsf{T}X + \lambda I$ and $X^\mathsf{T}\boldsymbol{y}$ are computed over a relatively small field $\mathbb{Z}_q$, while $\boldsymbol{w} = A^{-1}\boldsymbol{b}$ is computed over a substantially larger field $\mathbb{Z}_p$ in the second stage. See Table 2 for some typical sizes of p and q. Since n is typically very large as well, cf. Table 1, secure computation of $X^\mathsf{T}X$ over $\mathbb{Z}_p$ would put excessive demands on time and space utilization.

The conversion in step 3 of the protocol is done as described at the end of Sect. 4. The sizes for primes p and q are determined in the following lemma.

Lemma 3. *Let $\beta = \|(X \mid \boldsymbol{y})\|_{\max}$. Correctness of Protocol 5 follows if*

$$\frac{q}{2} > n\beta^2 + \lambda + 2^\kappa \quad and \quad \frac{p}{2} > d^{\frac{d}{2}}(n\beta^2 + \lambda)^d.$$

Proof. For prime q we need that $q/2 > \|(A \mid \boldsymbol{b})\|_{\max}$. Each entry of $(A \mid \boldsymbol{b})$ is a dot product of two length-n vectors with entries bounded in absolute value by β, plus λ for the diagonal of A. Therefore, $\|(A \mid \boldsymbol{b})\|_{\max} \leq n\beta^2 + \lambda$. To allow for secure conversion from $\mathbb{Z}_q$ to $\mathbb{Z}_p$, we require $q/2 > n\beta^2 + \lambda + 2^\kappa$.

For prime p we use the result of Lemma 2 with $\gamma = n\beta^2 + \lambda$. Although matrix A is known to be symmetric positive definite, giving us $\det(A) \leq \gamma^d$, the overall bound of $p/2 > d^{d/2}\gamma^d$ remains because of the $p/2 > \|(\mathrm{adj}\,A)\boldsymbol{b}\|_{\max}$ constraint.

8 Performance Evaluation

We have performed several experiments using the UCI datasets [DG19] shown in Table 1. Each dataset is randomly split into a 70% training set and a 30% test set (except for dataset *Year prediction MSD*, for which we respect its pre-defined training/test split, taking the first 463715 rows to form the training set and the remaining 51630 rows are used for testing). The RMSEs reported for training and testing are obtained using the Cholesky solver provided for ridge regression in Scikit-learn [PVG+11], setting $\lambda = 1$. Note that the *Gas Sensor Array* datasets have two targets, for which the RMSEs are reported separately. To handle multiple targets, we have generalized Protocol 5 in the obvious way, replacing vector $\boldsymbol{y}$ by a matrix Y with one column per target.

We have run our protocol for secure ridge regression in a 3-party setting using the values for accuracy parameter α shown in Table 2. For each (normalized) dataset we have tried increasingly larger values for α until the errors became insignificant (below 0.1% relative to the RMSEs of Table 1). We have refrained from tuning the regularization parameter λ, and simply set $\lambda = 2^{2\alpha}$ (which corresponds to $\lambda = 1$ after scaling). The bit lengths $|p|$ and $|q|$ are determined from the bounds in Lemma 3, using $\beta = 2^\alpha$ and $\kappa = 30$. The total running time for Protocol 5 comprises two parts: $(A, \boldsymbol{b})$-time represents the time for computing $[\![A]\!]$ and $[\![b]\!]$ (steps 1–2), while $A^{-1}\boldsymbol{b}$-time covers the time for Protocol 4. The time for the conversion in step 3 is negligible.

Table 1. UCI datasets. RMSEs for ridge regression with Scikit-learn.

id	Dataset	n	d^*	Target(s)	Train RMSE	Test RMSE
1	Student Performance	395	30	G3	0.38	0.46
2	Wine Quality red	1,599	11	Quality	0.16	0.16
3	Wine Quality white	4,898	11	Quality	0.19	0.19
4	Year Prediction MSD	515,345	90	Year	0.21	0.21
5	Gas Sensor Array methane	4,178,504	16	Ethylene methane	0.29 0.34	0.29 0.34
6	Gas Sensor Array CO	4,208,261	16	Ethylene CO	0.34 0.34	0.34 0.34
7	HIGGS	11,000,000	7	Class	0.97	0.97

*The reported number of columns d corresponds with the databases original number of columns. The bit-lengths of p and q reported in Table 2 are determined after one-hot encoding.

Table 2. Results of this work compared to the literature. All times are in seconds. HP/VP stand for horizontal/vertical partitioning. 32-bit and 64-bit refer to bit lengths used for secure fixed-point arithmetic. Accuracy α yields relative errors below 0.1%. The relative errors reported by [GSB+17] are also given.

id	α	$\|q\|$	$\|p\|$	This work			[NWI+13]	[GJJ+18]		[GSB+17]	
				(A, b)	$A^{-1}b$	Total	HP	HP	VP	VP 32-bit	VP 64-bit
1	6	54	1314	0.13	1.48	1.61	–	39.76	328.06	5 (−0.0%)	35 (−0.0%)
2	7	58	313	0.02	0.08	0.10	39	–	–	–	–
3	8	61	356	0.04	0.12	0.16	45	4.09	–	0 (4.2%)	4 (−0.0%)
4	6	64	3102	237	18.3	255	–	–	–	230 (0.0%)	808 (0.0%)
5	8	71	673	62.8	0.05	62.9	–	–	–	–	–
6	9	73	708	63.0	0.05	63.1	–	–	–	42 (5.2%)	69 (0.0%)
7	5	66	277	34.9	0.12	35.0	–	–	–	–	–

Our implementation is written in Python using the MPyC package [Sch18, ridgeregression.py]. The experiments were done using three PCs, connected via a Netgear GS208-100PES Ethernet switch. Each PC was running on Windows 8.1 Enterprise (64-bit) with an Intel Core i7-4770 CPU at 3.40 GHz and 16 GB of RAM. Table 2 compares our results to three other solutions for secure ridge regression from the literature. The times reported are purely indicative, and give a basic idea of the performance of the various solutions.

We note that the previous works shown in Table 2 exploit the locality of the input data, assuming that the data is either partitioned horizontally or vertically. For example, Nikolaenko et al. [NWI+13] assume the dataset is partitioned horizontally, allowing them to compute A and b using additive homomorphic encryption only. In our work, we do not make any specific assumptions on the distribution of the input data; instead we adopt the more general outsourcing scenario, where any data provider simply sends secret shares of its data to the respective parties performing the secure computation (using $\log_2 q$ bits per

Table 3. Comparison of (A, b)-times for synthetic data.

n	d	This work	[GSB+17]
50,000	20	1 s	2 s
50,000	100	24 s	32 s
500,000	20	11 s	18 s
500,000	100	3 min 29 s	6 min 1 s
1,000,000	100	6 min 57 s	12 min 42 s
1,000,000	200	28 min 30 s	49 min 56 s

share). Thus, in our experiments, each party holds shares of the *entire* dataset and is not assumed to have any plaintext knowledge of the data.

Also, these previous works [NWI+13, GSB+17, GJJ+18] rely on a so-called 2-server approach requiring two non-colluding parties (e.g., a "crypto service provider" and an "evaluator"). For our solution, the number of colluding parties tolerated is scalable, assuming an honest majority.

The competitiveness of our solution is also confirmed by Table 3, showing our results for a range of synthetic datasets compared to the most favorable results reported by Gascón et al. [GSB+17] (for their 3-party setting).

Obviously, exploiting the locality of the input data may easily lead to huge speed-ups when combined with our approach. For horizontally partitioned data, the (A, b)-time reported in Table 2 will become very small, as the work trivially reduces to the secure addition of the locally computed partial dot products. For vertically partitioned data, the (A, b)-time can be reduced by a substantial factor, as the dot products for the locally available columns of X require no communication except for secret-sharing the end result.

9   Concluding Remarks

Assuming that matrix X is of full column rank, Protocol 5 can also be used for secure linear regression by setting $\lambda = 0$. If matrix X is distributed among several data providers, however, ensuring that X is of full rank need not be trivial. For instance, in a vertical data partitioning it may not be that easy to detect a redundant feature (used by multiple data providers). Setting $\lambda > 0$ removes the need to remove such redundant columns.

Our results also extend to the underdetermined case $n < d$. In this case, the closed form solution given by Eq. (2) can be rewritten as

$$w = X^\mathsf{T} \left(XX^\mathsf{T} + \lambda I\right)^{-1} y, \tag{3}$$

using that $(X^\mathsf{T}X + \lambda I)X^\mathsf{T} = X^\mathsf{T}XX^\mathsf{T} + \lambda X^\mathsf{T} = X^\mathsf{T}(XX^\mathsf{T} + \lambda I)$.

Modifying our protocol for ridge regression accordingly results in Protocol 6. In step 4 of the protocol the secret-shared matrix X converted to the large

---

Protocol 6. Ridge($[\![X]\!]_q, [\![\boldsymbol{y}]\!]_q, \lambda$) $X \in \mathbb{Z}_q^{n \times d}, \boldsymbol{y} \in \mathbb{Z}_q^n, \lambda \in \mathbb{N}$

1: Compute $[\![A]\!]_q = [\![X]\!]_q [\![X^\top]\!]_q + \lambda I$.   ▷ $A = XX^\top + \lambda I$
2: Convert $[\![(A \mid X \mid \boldsymbol{y})]\!]_q$ to $[\![(A \mid X \mid \boldsymbol{y})]\!]_p$.
3: Compute $([\![(\mathrm{adj}\, A)\boldsymbol{y}]\!]_p, [\![\det A]\!]_p) = \mathrm{LinSol}([\![(A \mid \boldsymbol{y})]\!]_p)$.
4: Compute $[\![(\det A)\boldsymbol{w}]\!]_p = [\![X^\top]\!]_p [\![(\mathrm{adj}\, A)\boldsymbol{y}]\!]_p$.   ▷ $\boldsymbol{w} = X^\top A^{-1} \boldsymbol{y}$
5: Return $[\![(\det A)\boldsymbol{w}]\!]_p, [\![\det A]\!]_p$.

---

prime field $\mathbb{Z}_p$ is used to compute the output vector $\boldsymbol{w}$. Since typically $d \gg n$, a relatively small number of conversions n per entry of the length-d output vector $\boldsymbol{w}$ are performed. Setting $\lambda = 0$ for this protocol yields a solution for secure linear regression in the case that X is of full row rank.

Details about the handling of the input and output for our secure ridge protocols are beyond the scope of this paper. For instance, one needs to decide how much information the parties are willing to leak when normalizing their joint datasets. Also, the parties may jointly need to determine a suitable value for the regularization parameter λ (hyperparameter tuning). Similarly, the output $[\![(\det A)\boldsymbol{w}]\!]_p, [\![\det A]\!]_p$ of our secure ridge protocols can be handled in lots of ways. These two values may simply be revealed, accepting leakage of the exact value of the determinant. Alternatively, these values may be converted to shares over $\mathbb{Z}_{p'}$, where p' is of double length compared to p; subsequently, a secure division of $[\![(\det A)\boldsymbol{w}]\!]_{p'}$ by $[\![\det A]\!]_{p'}$ is performed (over $\mathbb{Z}_{p'}$, hence very efficient, using a standard protocol for secure inversion, see also Sect. 4) to obtain $[\![\boldsymbol{w}]\!]_{p'}$, from which the exact solution $\boldsymbol{w} \in \mathbb{Q}^d$ is recovered by rational reconstruction modulo p' in the clear. Note that the latter approach gives exactly the same final result as [GJJ+18, Protocol 3].

The question of how much information a regression model $\boldsymbol{w}$ reveals about the input data has been studied extensively in the literature. Even if the entries of $\boldsymbol{w}$ are rounded to floating-point numbers of limited precision, information might leak as by definition $\boldsymbol{w}$ is computed to summarize essential information about the input. In general, one must therefore resort to techniques from differential privacy to limit information leakage. As an example of (recent) work in this direction, we refer to [AMS+20] and references therein.

An important observation, however, is that we get differential privacy for $\boldsymbol{w}$ basically for free for the regime $n \gg d$. Intuitively, when the number of samples n is much larger than the number of features d, revealing only the length-d vector $\boldsymbol{w}$ may be expected to be relatively safe. For linear regression ($\lambda = 0$) there exist analytical results confirming this intuition. For example, in [Wan18, Figure 2] the question "When is privacy *for free* in statistical learning?" is addressed, and it is shown this happens for $n \gg d$.

We like to end with mentioning two recent follow-up works showing how our approach extends to other interesting settings. In [BV20], Bouman and de Vreede show how to extend our results to the secure computation of the Moore-Penrose pseudoinverse, which is a challenging problem as one needs to hide all information about the rank of the input matrix. And in [HFT20], building on our techniques and protocols, Hastings et al. find that our approach leads to concrete efficiency gains in the context of privacy-preserving network analytics.

Acknowledgements. We thank the anonymous reviewers for their useful comments. This work has received funding from the European Union's Horizon 2020 research and innovation program under grant agreements No 731583 (SODA) and No 780477 (PRIViLEDGE).

References

[AMS+20] Alabi, D., McMillan, A., Sarathy, J., Smith, A., Vadhan, S.: Differentially private simple linear regression. arXiv preprint arXiv:2007.05157 (2020)

[Bar68] Bareiss, E.H.: Sylvester's identity and multistep integer-preserving gaussian elimination. Math. Comput. **22**(103), 565–578 (1968)

[BB89] Bar-Ilan, J., Beaver, D.: Non-cryptographic fault-tolerant computing in constant number of rounds of interaction. In: Proceedings of 8th Symposium on Principles of Distributed Computing, pp. 201–209. ACM, New York (1989)

[BGW88] Ben-Or, M., Goldwasser, S., Wigderson, A.: Completeness theorems for non-cryptographic fault-tolerant distributed computation. In: Proceedings of 20th Symposium on Theory of Computing (STOC 1988), pp. 1–10. ACM, New York (1988)

[BV20] Bouman, N.J., de Vreede, N.: A practical approach to the secure computation of the Moore–Penrose pseudoinverse over the rationals. In: Conti, M., Zhou, J., Casalicchio, E., Spognardi, A. (eds.) ACNS 2020. LNCS, vol. 12146, pp. 398–417. Springer, Cham (2020). https://doi.org/10.1007/978-3-030-57808-4_20

[CD01] Cramer, R., Damgård, I.: Secure distributed linear algebra in a constant number of rounds. In: Kilian, J. (ed.) CRYPTO 2001. LNCS, vol. 2139, pp. 119–136. Springer, Heidelberg (2001). https://doi.org/10.1007/3-540-44647-8_7

[DG19] Dua, D., Graff, C.: UCI machine learning repository (2019)

[DHC04] Du, W., Han, Y.S., Chen, S.: Privacy-preserving multivariate statistical analysis: linear regression and classification. In: Proceedings of the 2004 SIAM International Conference on Data Mining, pp. 222–233. SIAM (2004)

[FHT01] Hastie, T., Tibshirani, R., Friedman, J.: The Elements of Statistical Learning. SSS. Springer, New York (2009). https://doi.org/10.1007/978-0-387-84858-7

[Gei10] Geisler, M.: Cryptographic protocols: theory and implementation. Ph.D. thesis, Department of Computer Science, University of Aarhus, Denmark, February 2010. www.viff.dk

[GJJ+18] Giacomelli, I., Jha, S., Joye, M., Page, C.D., Yoon, K.: Privacy-preserving ridge regression with only linearly-homomorphic encryption. In: Preneel, B., Vercauteren, F. (eds.) ACNS 2018. LNCS, vol. 10892, pp. 243–261. Springer, Cham (2018). https://doi.org/10.1007/978-3-319-93387-0_13

[GRR98] Gennaro, R., Rabin, M.O., Rabin, T.: Simplified VSS and fast-track multiparty computations with applications to threshold cryptography. In: 17th Annual ACM Symposium on Principles of Distributed Computing (PODC 1998), pp. 101–111. ACM, New York (1998)

[GSB+17] Gascón, A., et al.: Privacy-preserving distributed linear regression on high-dimensional data. Proc. Priv. Enh. Technol. **2017**(4), 345–364 (2017)

[HFN11] Hall, R., Fienberg, S.E., Nardi, Y.: Secure multiple linear regression based on homomorphic encryption. J. Off. Stat. **27**(4), 669–691 (2011)

[HFT20] Hastings, M., Falk, B.H., Tsoukalas, G.: Privacy-preserving network analytics. SSRN (2020). https://papers.ssrn.com/sol3/papers.cfm?abstract_id=3680000

[NWI+13] Nikolaenko, V., Weinsberg, U., Ioannidis, S., Joye, M., Boneh, D., Taft, N.: Privacy-preserving ridge regression on hundreds of millions of records. In: Proceedings of the 2013 IEEE Symposium on Security and Privacy, SP 2013, pp. 334–348. IEEE Computer Society, Washington (2013)

[PVG+11] Pedregosa, F., et al.: Scikit-learn: machine learning in Python. J. Mach. Learn. Res. **12**, 2825–2830 (2011)

[Sch18] Schoenmakers, B.: MPyC: secure multiparty computation in Python. GitHub, May 2018. https://github.com/lschoe/mpyc

[Wan18] Wang, Y.X.: Revisiting differentially private linear regression: optimal and adaptive prediction & estimation in unbounded domain. arXiv preprint arXiv:1803.02596 (2018)

PolyDNN
Polynomial Representation of NN
for Communication-Less SMPC Inference

Philip Derbeko$^{(\boxtimes)}$ and Shlomi Dolev$^{(\boxtimes)}$

Department of Computer Science, Ben-Gurion University of the Negev, Beersheba,
Israel
dolev@cs.bgu.ac.il

Abstract. The structure and weights of Deep Neural Networks (DNN)
typically encode and contain very valuable information about the dataset
that was used to train the network. One way to protect this information
when DNN is published is to perform an interference of the network
using secure multi-party computations (MPC). In this paper, we suggest
a translation of deep neural networks to polynomials, which are easier to
calculate efficiently with MPC techniques. We show a way to translate
complete networks into a single polynomial and how to calculate the
polynomial with an efficient and information-secure MPC algorithm. The
calculation is done without intermediate communication between the
participating parties, which is beneficial in several cases, as explained
in the paper.

Keywords: Privacy · DNN · Data publishing · Data sharing

1 Introduction

Deep Neural Networks (DNN) are the state-of-the-art form of Machine Learning
techniques these days. They are used for speech recognition, image recognition,
computer vision, natural language processing, machine translation, and many
other tasks. Similar to other Machine Learning (ML) methods, DNN is based on
finding patterns in the data and, as such, the method embeds information about
the data into a concise and generalized model. Subsequently, the sharing of the
DNN model also reveals private and valuable information about the data.

In this paper, we first suggest approximating a trained neural network with
a single (possibly nested) polynomial. We present a nested polynomial approach
to speed up the calculation of the polynomial on a single node. The essence
of the idea is to nest the polynomial approximation of each layer within the
approximation of the next layer, such that a single polynomial (or arithmetic
circuit) will approximate not only a single network unit, but a few layers or even

---

This work was partially supported by the Lynne and William Frankel Center for Computer Science, by the Rita Altura Trust Chair in Computer Science, a grant from the
Ministry of Science and Technology, Israel.

© Springer Nature Switzerland AG 2021
S. Dolev et al. (Eds.): CSCML 2021, LNCS 12716, pp. 317–324, 2021.
https://doi.org/10.1007/978-3-030-78086-9_24

the entire network. We discuss an efficient, (perfect information theoretically secure) secret-sharing MPC calculation of the polynomial calculation of DNN. Lastly, we compare the MPC calculation of the neural network itself with a calculation of polynomial representation.

Our main contribution in this research is an optimization of (communication-less) MPC calculations of a shared DNN by approximating neighboring layers by a single polynomial, and in some cases, the entire network. An additional contribution is a nesting of a multi-layer polynomial to reduce the redundant calculations of the intermediate layers.

Previous relevant research is covered in Sect. 2. Section 3 and Sect. 4 discuss polynomial approximation of DNN on a single computing node. A secure, communication-less multi-party computation, which is presented in Sect. 5. Section 6 summarizes the techniques to obtain blind execution of DNN. Empirical experiments are described in Sect. 7 and, lastly, the paper is concluded in Sect. 8. Details are excluded from this version and can be found in [6].

2   Previous Work

Distributed MPC protocols are built for fixed-point arithmetic, and many times even for limited range values. Thus, the main issue in calculating the neural network activation with secure multi-party computations algorithms is the translation of activation functions from floating-point arithmetic to fixed-point.

Approximation of neural network units' activation function with fixed-point arithmetic and without MPC was considered before in [9,10], where polynomial functions were suggested for approximation. CryptoDL [10] showed an implementation of Convolutional Neural Networks (CNN) over encrypted data using homomorphic encryption (HE). The paper has shown approximation of CNN activation functions by low-degree polynomials due to the high-performance overhead of higher degree polynomials.

A calculation of neural networks with secure multi-party computations was considered in [12]. Their experiments showed that the polynomial approximation of the sigmoid function requires at least a 10-degree polynomial, which causes a considerable performance slow-down with garbled circuit protocol. The work had a limitation for two participating parties and the algorithm was shown to be limiting in terms of performance and the practical size of the network.

CrypTFlow [11] is a system that converts TensorFlow (TF) code automatically into secure multi-party computation protocol. The most salient characteristic of CrypTFlow is the ability to automatically translate the code into MPC protocol, where the specific protocol can be easily changed and added. The optimized three-party computational protocol is specifically targeted for NN computation and speeds up the computation. This approach is similar to the holistic approach of [1].

SecureNN [15] proposed arguably the first practical three-party secure computations, both for training and for activation of DNN and CNN. The impressive performance improvement over then, state-of-the-art, results is achieved by replacing garbled circuits and oblivious transfer protocols with secret sharing protocols. The replacement also allowed information security instead of computational security. Despite being efficient, the protocols require ten communication rounds for ReLu calculation of a single unit not counting share distribution rounds.

A different approach at speeding up performance was made by [5], which concentrated on two-party protocols. The work showed a mixed protocol framework based on Arithmetic sharing, Boolean sharing, and Yao's garbled circuit (ABY). Each protocol was used for its specific ability, and the protocols are mixed to provide a complete framework for neural networks activation functions.

3   Neural Network as Polynomial Functions in a Single Node Case

We show how to approximate functions that are a typical part of DNNs, by polynomials. We focus on the most commonly used functions in neural networks.

Weighted Sum of the Unit Input. Given neuron inputs $X_1, \ldots, X_n$, the weighted sum is a multiplication of inputs with the corresponding weights $S = \sum_{i=1}^{n} w_i X_i - b$, where b is a bias of the neuron which is a polynomial of degree 1.

Common Activation Functions. Most of the research approximating DNN activation functions focused on these few common functions:
ReLu ($ReLu(x) = max(0, x)$), Leaky ReLu (similar to ReLu but $LReLu(x) = 0.01x$ if $x \leq 0$), Sigmoid $\left(\sigma(x) = \frac{1}{1+e^{-x}} \right)$, TANh $\left(tanh(x) = \frac{e^{2x}-1}{e^{2x}+1} \right)$, SoftMax (used for multi-class prediction $\sigma(x_i) = \frac{e^{x_i}}{\sum_{i=1}^{k} e^{x_i}}$). All those functions can be approximated with a polynomial using various different methods, for example [1, 10, 12, 13, 16]. Our optimization method is agnostic to a specific approximation method.

Differently from the most of the research approaches, which minimized the degree of the approximating polynomial, our communication-less approach allows us to use a higher degree polynomials. In our previous research [7] we have shown that 30-degree Chebyshev polynomials achieve good results.

Max and Mean Pooling. Max and Mean pooling compute the corresponding functions of a set of units. Those functions are frequently used in CNN following the convolution layers. Previous works [16] suggested replacing max-pooling with a scaled mean-pooling, which is trivially represented by a polynomial. However, this requires the replacement to be done during the training stage, while we focus on a post-training stage.

In this paper, we have used a simple and practical approximation of max function is:

$$m'(x, y) = \frac{x + y}{2} + ((x - y)^2)^{1/2}. \tag{1}$$

Notice that the function provides an approximation near any values of x and y, which is an advantage over Taylor or Chebyshev approximations, that are developed according to a specific point. Despite its simplicity, Eq. 1 provides a relatively good approximation.

Notice that using a two-variable function for the max pooling layer of k inputs requires chaining of the max functions:

$$max(x_1, x_2, \ldots x_k) = max(x_1, max(x_2, \ldots, max(x_{k-1}, x_k))).$$

Alternatively, the optimization sequence is interrupted at the max-pooling layer, which will require an MPC protocol for the max function calculation, for example [15].

4   Multiple Layers Approximation

We have discussed the approximation of DNN functions by polynomials. The approximation exists for all the common functions. This makes it possible to combine multiple layers into a single polynomial function according to the connectivity of the layers.

One example of a network that can be approximated by a single polynomial function is auto-decoder where hidden layers are dense layers with (commonly) ReLu or sigmoid activation.

The idea is to create a polynomial for the "flow" of the data in the network instead of approximating every single neural unit with a polynomial. As an example, consider the network in Fig. 1.

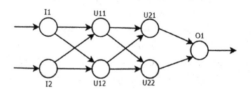

Fig. 1. A small example network with an input layer on the left, two dense hidden layers U1 and U2, and an output layer on the right consisting of a single unit. Each layer utilizes ReLu or sigmoid activation functions, or any other function that can be approximated by a polynomial.

The network consists of an input layer (I) on the left, two dense hidden layers (U_1 and U_2), and one output layer O, which is implemented by the softmax function. The units are marked as u_{li} where l is the hidden layer number and i

is the number of the unit in the layer. We assume that the activation functions of the hidden layers are ReLu (or any other function that can be approximated by a polynomial function).

Consider a unit u_{11}. It calculates the function which is approximated by the polynomial. Assume that ReLu activation functions are approximated using a polynomial of d-degree.

$$ReLu(\sum_i w_i I_i) \approx P_{11} = Pol_{11}(\sum_i w_i I_i). \tag{2}$$

Unit u_{21} receives P_{11} and P_{12} as inputs and calculates the "nested" polynomial function:

$$P_{21} = Pol_{21}(\sum_i w_i P_{1i}). \tag{3}$$

In general, assuming dense layers, the nested polynomials are defined as:

$$P_{lj} = Pol_{lj}(\sum_i w_i P_{(l-1)i}). \tag{4}$$

In this simple case, the result of networks evaluation can be calculated by evaluating two polynomials of d^2-degree: P_{21} and P_{22}, and calculating the output layer function of their output. Overall, by approximating softmax by Pol^{sm} we get the following polynomial for the entire network:

$$
\begin{aligned}
DNN(x) &= Pol^{sm}(w_1^o P_{21} + w_2^o P_2 2) \\
&= Pol^{sm}\left(w_1^o Pol_{21}(w_1^{21} P_{11} + w_2^{21} P_{12}) + w_2^o Pol_{22}(w_1^{22} P_{11} + w_2^{22} P_{12})\right) \\
&= Pol^{sm}\left(w_1^o Pol_{21}(w_1^{21} Pol_{11}(w_1^{11} I_1 + w_2^{11} I_2) + w_2^{21} Pol_{12}(w_1^{12} I_1 + w_2^{12} I_2)) \right. \\
&\quad \left. + w_2^o Pol_{22}(w_1^{22} Pol_{11}(w_1^{11} I_1 + w_2^{11} I_2) + w_2^{22} Pol_{12}(w_1^{12} I_1 + w_2^{12} I_2))\right)
\end{aligned}
\tag{5}
$$

Notice that P_{11} and P_{12} were calculated twice as they are used as inputs for both U_{21} and U_{22} units.

5   Communication-Less MPC for Polynomial Calculations

The goal of MPC calculations in the considered setup is to protect the published model from exposure to participating cloud providers. The model is trained by the data provider and has two components: architecture, which includes the layout, type, and interconnection of the neural units, as well as the weights of the input, which were refined during the training of the network, i.e. back-propagation phase.

Our goal is to protect the weights that were obtained by a costly process of training. While the architecture also might hold ingenious insights, it is considered less of a secret and may be exposed to the cloud providers.

Even though the described algorithm is agnostic to the specific MPC protocol, it is better to use a protocol that can support $k > 2$ parties, provides perfect information theoretical security and is efficient for a polynomial calculations in terms of communication rounds to enable usage of high-degree polynomials.

A number of MPC protocols answer those requirements [2,4]. These MPC protocols based on Shamir secret sharing [14] can cope with a minority of semi-honest parties and even with a third of the malicious parties. BGW protocol [2] provides a perfect security and [4] provides statistical security with any desirable certainty. In our case, the input is not a multi-variable that is secret-shared, but rather the weights and coefficients of the network are the secrets.

Clear-Text Inputs. In a simpler scenario, the input is revealed to all participating parties. In this case, the secrets are the weights of the trained network. The input values are then can be considered as numerical constants for the MPC calculation and thus, communication rounds can be eliminated completely, see BGW [2] algorithm where additive "gates" are calculated locally without any communication.

Given a secret-share of coefficient a: $s = [s_1, s_2]$. The polynomial $p(x)$ can be calculated as $p(x) = p_1(x) + p_2(x)$, where $p_1(x)$ and $p_2(x)$ use the corresponding secret share.

Secret-Shared Inputs. In the second scenario, the input values are protected as well, and thus, they are distributed by the secret share. As the input values are raised to polynomial degree k, the secret share is done on the set of values: $X = [x, x^2, \ldots x^k]$. Multiplication of secret shares requires communication rounds in a general case, still when secret sharing every element of X it is possible to eliminate the communications all-together using techniques from [3] or [8].

6   Distributed Communication-Less Secure Interference for Unknown DNN

The last two sections, Sect. 4 and Sect. 5, provide all the required building blocks for communication-less MPC for common DNNs. In Sect. 4 we showed how a given, pre-trained network can be approximated with a single polynomial, in most common cases. As a side-note, as the neural network activation functions are not limited to a specific set, there might be networks that cannot be approximated. However, the majority of networks use a rather small set of functions and architectures.

Once the network is presented by a single polynomial, Sect. 5 shows that it can be calculated without a single communication round (apart from the input distribution and output gathering) when the inputs are revealed, or with half the communication rounds when the inputs are secret.

Taken together, those two results enable a somewhat surprising outcome: the data owner can train DNN models, pre-process, and share them with multiple cloud providers. The providers then can collaboratively calculate interference of the network on common or secret-shared inputs without ever communicating with each other. Thus, reducing the attack surface even further even for multi-layer networks.

7 Experiments

All tests were performed on the Fashion database of MNIST, which contains a training set of 60,000 and a testing set of 10,000 28×28 images of 10 fashion categories. The task is a multi-class classification of a given image. Experiments on larger datasets and different types of DNN are planned for extended version of the paper.

To solve the problem we have used a non-optimized neural network with two dense hidden layers: one of 300 units and the second one with 100 units. The output layer is a softmax layer with ten units and batch normalization layers before each activation layer.

The performed experiments were done on a pre-trained model. The model was loaded and translated into polynomial as described above automatically. This enables us to perform translation for any pre-trained network, similarly in spirit to [11]. Both the original model and polynomial representation were executed on the same inputs. The outputs are compared for different classification (divided by a total number of test inputs).

Figure 7 shows the difference in accuracy of the network with different degrees. As can be seen, the accuracy improves with the degree of the polynomial approximation, however the improvement flattens at around $d = 30$.

The computation costs are increasing linearly with the polynomial degree (data not shown), where the original ReLu is similar to $d = 1$ degree polynomial. Thus, it makes sense to choose the lowest degree that still provides consistent and accurate results.

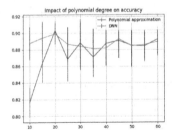

Fig. 2. Accuracy of DNN and polynomial approximation averaged over 10 runs of 500 examples each.

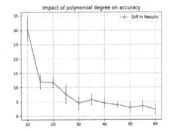

Fig. 3. Relative difference in results between polynomial approximation and the DNN model as a function of polynomial degree.

8 Conclusions

In this paper, we have presented a way to reduce and ultimately eliminate the number of communication rounds in the secure multi-party computation of DNN models. We believe that this optimization method can enable more efficient DNN calculations and further progress in the process of privacy-preserving data sharing.

The above optimization of DNN evaluation targets the inference phase, which is done after the DNN-based model is shared and distributed across cloud providers. The network is not trained anymore, but only queried by the clients. At this phase, the performance issues do not impact the data owners, which could be resource-limited end-devices, but rather are relevant for the cloud providers that have as much larger resources.

References

1. Agrawal, N., Shamsabadi, A.S., Kusner, M.J., Gascón, A.: Quotient: two-party secure neural network training and prediction. In: CCS 2019 (2019)
2. Ben-Or, M., Goldwasser, S., Wigderson, A.: Completeness theorems for non-cryptographic fault-tolerant distributed computation. In: STOC 1988 (1988)
3. Berend, D., Bitan, D., Dolev, S.: Polynomials whose secret shares multiplication preserves degree for 2-CNF circuits over a dynamic set of secrets. IACR Cryptol. ePrint Arch. **2019**, 1192 (2019)
4. Chaum, D., Crépeau, C., Damgård, I.: Multiparty unconditionally secure protocols. In: STOC 1988 (1988)
5. Demmler, D., Schneider, T., Zohner, M.: ABY - a framework for efficient mixed-protocol secure two-party computation. In: NDSS (2015)
6. Derbeko, P., Dolev, S.: Polydnn: Polynomial representation of NN for communication-less SMPC inference (2021)
7. Derbeko, P., Dolev, S., Gudes, E.: Deep neural networks as similitude models for sharing big data. In: 2019 IEEE International Conference on Big Data (Big Data), Los Angeles, CA, USA, 9–12 December 2019, pp. 5728–5736. IEEE (2019)
8. Dolev, S., Doolman, S.: Blindly follow: sits CRT and FHE for DCLSMPC of DUFSM. Cryptology ePrint Archive, Report 2021/410 (2021). https://eprint.iacr.org/2021/410
9. Gilad-Bachrach, R., Dowlin, N., Laine, K., Lauter, K.E., Naehrig, M., Wernsing, J.R.: CryptoNets: applying neural networks to encrypted data with high throughput and accuracy. In: ICML (2016)
10. Hesamifard, E., Takabi, H., Ghasemi, M.: CryptoDL: deep neural networks over encrypted data. CoRR, abs/1711.05189 (2017)
11. Kumar, N., Rathee, M., Chandran, N., Gupta, D., Rastogi, A., Sharma, R.: Cryptflow: secure tensorflow inference (2019)
12. Mohassel, P., Zhang, Y.: SecureML: a system for scalable privacy-preserving machine learning. In: 2017 IEEE Symposium on Security and Privacy (SP), pp. 19–38, May 2017
13. Rouhani, B.D., Riazi, M.S., Koushanfar, F.: DeepSecure: scalable provably-secure deep learning. In: DAC (2018)
14. Shamir, A.: How to share a secret. Commun. ACM **22**(11), 612–613 (1979)
15. Wagh, S., Gupta, D., Chandran, N.: SecureNN: efficient and private neural network training. IACR Crypt. ePrint Arch. **2018**, 442 (2018)
16. Xie, P., Bilenko, M., Finley, T., Gilad-Bachrach, R., Lauter, K.E., Naehrig, M.: Crypto-Nets: neural networks over encrypted data. ArXiv, abs/1412.6181 (2014)

Use of Blockchain for Ensuring Data Integrity in Cloud Databases

Yakov Vainshtein[1][✉] and Ehud Gudes[2]

[1] Department of Mathematics and Computer Science, The Open University,
Raanana, Israel
Yakov.Vainshtein@Dell.com
[2] Department of Computer Science, The Ben-Gurion University of the Negev,
Beer-Sheva, Israel
ehud@cs.bgu.ac.il

Abstract. This paper proposes a novel method for using a PoW-based Blockchain to ensure data integrity in cloud database management systems. The use of cloud platforms for storing data or even hosting databases is incredibly huge, and in many cases, there is no convenient way for a client to check the integrity of the data stored in the cloud database. To solve this, we propose a technique based on an interaction between the cloud platform and a PoW-based Blockchain. This interaction exploits a Distributed Hash Table and lightweight software agents, which are monitoring changes done to cloud database storage nodes. Data update operations are published by the agents as Blockchain log/audit transactions that propagate deep into the Blockchain network until they become immutably and cryptographically protected by it. The proposed method enables the Cloud Provider to manage metadata so that it will be able to easily detect deliberate or accidental corruptions of transactions and to recover the transactions in case such a data corruption incident occurs.

Keywords: PoW-based Blockchain · Data integrity · Cloud database

1 Introduction

The ability of the cloud database to ensure data integrity is extremely important [1,2]. The integrity of outsourced data to the cloud is being put at risk in practice [2,3]. In the last few years, there is a growing interest around the question as to how to integrate the Blockchain and cloud databases [1]. Clients of the cloud database commonly assume that if the data is encrypted before it is outsourced to the cloud, it is secured enough. Researches show that although encryption protects the data from internal attacks, it does not fully protect the data from configuration issues or software bugs. Those issues/bugs can cause data corruption on purpose or by accident. Methods that describe how to store control log/audit data, that document changes performed by the cloud database clients, in the Blockchain, were already widely studied [4–6].

© Springer Nature Switzerland AG 2021
S. Dolev et al. (Eds.): CSCML 2021, LNCS 12716, pp. 325–335, 2021.
https://doi.org/10.1007/978-3-030-78086-9_25

In this paper, we propose a novel method to protect log/audit transactions from the moment they are published in the Blockchain network until they become committed to that network.

2   Background and Related Work

A Merkle Hash Tree (MHT) [7], is a binary tree, where each leaf is a hash of a transaction. A Distributed Hash Table (DHT) [8] is a distributed system that provides a lookup service. Reference Zyskind et al. [9] presents a successful integration of Blockchain and DHT which inspires our work.

Blockchain is a chain of blocks, a linear structure that begins with a genesis block and grows with new blocks linked to the end of the chain. A consensus algorithm is a process used to reach an agreement on a single data block among multiple and unfamiliar with each other nodes. The Proof of Work (PoW) [10] is a well-known consensus algorithm that is used as well in Bitcoin [11] and in Ethereum [12].

Reference Weintraub et al. [13] propose a method that provides a probabilistic client-side data integrity assurance in column-oriented NoSQL databases. Reference Zikratov et al. [4] details a few additional Client-Side computation methods.

References Zhang et al. [3], Zikratov et al. [4], and Xie et al. [14] detail a few Third-Party Auditor (TPA) methods in which the data integrity is monitored by a third-party.

References Zikratov et al. [4], Wei et al. [15], Wong et al. [16] detail a few Provable Data Possession challenge-response methods to perform data integrity verification in a cloud database environment.

Reference Gaetani et al. [5] describes a two-layer Blockchain method case study from the European SUNFISH project. The first layer is a permission-based Blockchain that executes a lightweight consensus protocol that assures low latency and high throughput. The second layer is a PoW-based Blockchain that stores evidence of the database operations logged in the first layer. The two layers together provide the desired guarantees of data integrity, performance, and stability.

Reference Basu et al. [6] considers a two-layer Blockchain method application scenario with a Virtual Network Function (VNF) [17]. The first layer Blockchain is a permission-based Blockchain that is used to verify the integrity of the data logged by individual VNF instances. The second-layer Blockchain is a public PoW-based Blockchain that helps with the verification of the authenticity of the overall logged data. Interaction between these two Blockchain layers provides the overall performance improvement and effective assurances of data integrity.

Reference Zikratov et al. [4] describes how it is possible to use the Blockchain technology for cloud database integrity assurance in a client-server architecture. It suggests running a watcher software on every cloud database node. The watcher software monitors the files on cloud database nodes and reports changes that occur on those files as Blockchain transactions.

3   The Proposed Method

3.1   The Proposed Method Description

In a PoW-based Blockchain, a transaction is published into the transactions pool, mined into a block, and pushed into the Blockchain by the mining of five consecutive blocks. When the block that contains the discussed transactions reaches the depth of six or more in the Blockchain, the block and all the contained transactions are considered as committed [11]. Figure 1 depicts the list of committed vs. not-committed blocks.

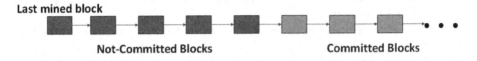

Fig. 1. Blockchain list of blocks committed vs. not-committed blocks

The proposed method is designed to address a threat model in which accidental or deliberate corruption attacks on a random transaction that runs through the system are detected. The proposed method recovers the system from the detected corruption.

The proposed method model is depicted in Fig. 2. The cloud database is constructed from multiple storage nodes that store the client's data. The DHT [8] is employed for storing transactions and blocks mappings. The mined and backup transaction pools are employed for corruption attack detection and recovery.

Every cloud database node executes agent software that monitors changes to files which it is configured to monitor; one agent per node. When the agent software detects a change done to one of the monitored files, it generates a log/audit transaction that documents the change and sends it to the Blockchain network.

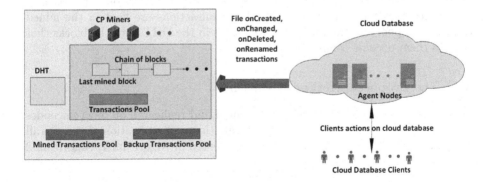

Fig. 2. The proposed method schematics

We have decided to use the PoW-base Blockchain due to its decentralization, security, privacy, and reliability. Furthermore, the fact that the probability to break the cryptographic chain after the transaction is committed in the Blockchain strives to zero, as the block gets deeper into the chain, backs this decision.

A transaction flow in the proposed method system is as follows:

1. Agent: publish a transaction to the transactions pool.
2. CP: store a copy of the transaction into the backup transactions pool.
3. CP: store the transaction id to transaction hash mapping into the DHT.
4. Miner: mine the transaction as part of a block.
5. CP: move the copy of the transaction from the backup transactions pool to the mined transactions pool.
6. CP: remove the mapping of the transaction id to transaction hash from the DHT.
7. CP: calculate the MHT root of all the transactions for the block that contains thetransaction.
8. CP: store a mapping from the block id to the MHT root into the DHT.
9. Blockchain: a block with the target transaction gets committed.
10. CP: clears the mappings of this block from the DHT.
11. CP: removes all the corresponding transactions from the mined transactions pool.

The transaction id to transaction hash mapping is stored in the DHT for checking the transaction integrity while the transaction is in the transactions pool. In case a change in a transaction is detected by a hash miss compare, the corrupted transaction is recovered by using the original transaction that is fetched from the backup transactions pool. An additional way to protect the backup transactions pool is to divide it between several CPs and to use Multi-party computation (MPC) [18] to construct the transactions. On the one hand, this method requires much more overhead than the DHT method, on the other hand, it enables full recovery in case an error is detected in the transaction pool since the MPC is protected by most of the honest providers. The mined transactions pool is maintained for recovery in case there is a corruption attack on a transaction in a mined but not-committed block. The transactions are kept in the mined transactions pool and the mappings are stored in the DHT until the blocks that contain them become committed.

3.2   The Proposed Method Algorithms

Every one of the CP algorithms is distributed and replicated on different nodes in the network, in order to ensure the distribution and replication of the overall ecosystem. The CP mapper algorithm is presented in Algorithm 1. Algorithm 2

Algorithm 1: Distributed CP Mapper Algorithm

---

while *1* **do**

    if *A new block is mined* **then**

        Calculate the MHT root for all the transactions in the block;

        Store Block ID to MHT root mapping into the DHT;

        Remove the mined transactions IDs to hash mappings from the DHT;

        Move the mined transactions from the backup transactions pool to the
         mined transactions pool;

        Remove the committed block's mappings from the DHT;

        Remove the committed transactions from the mined transactions pool;

    end

end

---

describes the CP Verification algorithm for the transactions pool. Storing a mapping from transaction id to hash of the transaction can be used for protecting the transactions in the mined transactions pool as well. In such a way, the CP stores the transaction id to the transaction hash of every mined transaction into the DHT. The mapping is used in case the same transaction is attacked in a mined not-committed block and the mined transactions pool for recovering the system from the corruption attack. Algorithm 3 describes the CP Verification

---

Algorithm 2: Distributed CP Verification Algorithm (Transactions Pool)

---

while *1* **do**

    For each transaction in the transactions pool calculate the SHA256 hash;

    Compare the transaction's calculated hash to the stored in the DHT hash;

    if *Some transaction calculated hash does not match the stored one* **then**

        if *Transaction content in the backup transactions pool was not changed*
        then

            Replace the corrupted transaction with the original one which is
             fetched from the backup transactions pool;

        else

            Remove the transaction id to transaction hash from the DHT;

            Remove the damaged transaction from the transaction pool and the
             backup transactions pool;

            Notify the client that the transaction was corrupted;

        end

    end

end

Algorithm for the mined not-committed blocks. The CP Miner mines a block by using the PoW consensus algorithm. We implement our CP miners so we will be able to control the block mining frequency by increasing/decreasing PoW complexity, and as we want to control the algorithm that the miners use to fetch the transactions from the transactions pool. The two improvements to the miner's algorithm are implemented so the miners will be able to stand at the pace with the transactions generation rate of a high-frequency transaction generating cloud database, as it can be faster than the financial transactions generation rate. Particularly in our proposed method, the miners fetch all the transactions from the transactions pool to the mined block in every mining iteration. Important to note, when integrating the proposed method with a practical cloud database it is required to limit the block to a maximal value to prevent spam attacks [19].

For the evaluation of the proposed method, we have implemented two corruption attack algorithms, namely: a corruption attack on a random transaction from the transactions pool and a corruption attack on a random transaction from a random mined not-committed block.

Algorithm 3: Distributed CP Verification Algorithm (Mined Not-Committed Blocks)

---

while *1* **do**
    Get not-committed blocks from the Blockchain;
    Calculate MHT root for all the not-committed blocks;
    Compare the calculated MHT root's of those blocks and compare them to the stored one's;
    if *Some MHT root hash has changed* **then**
        Cancel all the blocks from the end of the Blockchain up to including the corrupted block;
        Store all the transactions from the canceled blocks in a local buffer, not including the corrupted transaction;
        Fetch the original transaction that was corrupted from the mined transactions pool;
        Delete from the mined transactions pool all the canceled transactions;
        Delete the block ids to MHT root mappings of the canceled blocks from the DHT;
        Retransmit all the transactions that were fetched from the canceled blocks to the Blockchain excluding the corrupted transaction including the original one;
    end
end

3.3 The Proposed Method Potential Vulnerabilities

The CP algorithms are considered, to be honest, and reliable since they are replicated and distributed. To provide robustness to the system, we execute many distributed instances of the CP algorithms in parallel. A Byzantine Fault Tolerance [10] algorithm should be applied between the different CP distributed and replicated instances to ensure availability, liveness, and security of the system.

Handling the agent's robustness and security is out of the scope of this paper as their role is to provide the input transactions to the proposed method. The proposed method operates the same regardless of the entity that generates the transactions and the transaction's structure. Moreover, the agents can be protected by the cloud database security and integrity protocols, as described in reference [20].

The DHT being distributed is less vulnerable to attacks and it is also protected by its internal security protection protocols, as described in reference [21].

We consider the Blockchain transactions pool and the Blockchain list of blocks as vulnerable and exposed to corruption attacks. They represent the data structures that the proposed method is intended to protect from accidental or deliberate corruption attacks.

3.4   Correctness of the Proposed Method

This section presents the proof that the proposed method protects all the transactions in the Blockchain network, from the moment they are published into the Blockchain network and until the system's end of life. We cite lemmas and prove the main claim. A detailed proof of the lemmas is omitted because of the present paper volume limitations. We assume a corruption attack occurs on some random transactions in the system. The proof is presented without limiting the generality of the proposed method with regards to the transaction structure or the number of transactions in a single Blockchain block.

Lemma 1. *The integrity of a random transaction is secured from the moment it is published in the Blockchain's transactions pool and until it is mined into a block.*

Proof. The proof of lemma 1 is based on the fact we use the secured DHT to store transactions id to hash mappings and use the transaction from the backup transactions pool for the recovery as described in Algorithms 1 and 2.

Lemma 2. *The integrity of a random transaction is secure from the moment it is mined into a block and until it is committed.*

Proof. The proof of lemma 2 is based on the fact we use the secured DHT to store block id to transactions MHT [7] root mappings and use the transaction from the mined transactions pool for the recovery as described in Algorithms 1 and 3.

Theorem 1. *The integrity of a random transaction is secured from the moment it is published in the Blockchain network and until the system's end of life.*

Proof. Lemma 1 proves that the integrity of a transaction is secured from the moment it is published into the Blockchain's transactions pool and until it is mined into a block. Lemma 2 proves that the integrity of a transaction is secured from the moment it is mined into a block until it is committed. From the moment the random transaction is committed, its integrity is ensured by the Blockchain immutability as has been proven in the Bitcoin paper [11].

3.5   The Proposed Method Attack Detection

We consider a corruption attack on a random transaction from the transactions pool. It is observed that the time until the attack is detected by the CP is a random variable with an average of 19.32 ms and a standard deviation of 4.33. The randomness is sourced, in this attack scenario, from the random choosing of the transaction for the attack. We consider a corruption attack on a random transaction from a random mined not-committed block. It is observed that the time until the attack is detected by the CP is a random variable with an average of 17.92 ms and a standard deviation of 3.34. The randomness is sourced, in this case, from the random choices of the mined not-committed block and the random choice of a transaction from this block, and the probabilistic mainer's PoW calculations. We have measured the detection time alteration with an increase in the number of consecutive random simulations having the following values: 5, 10, 15, 20, and 25 in both attack scenarios. It is observed that there is no distinct change trend in the obtained results concerning the average, standard deviation, minimum, and maximum attack detection time values. Therefore, we conclude that the examined processes are most probably ergodic random processes, in both attack scenarios.

3.6   The Proposed Method Recovery from Attack

We measure 25 consecutive simulations of the recovery time from the attack on the transactions pool. We observe that the time for an attack recovery on a random transaction from the transaction pool is a random variable with an average of 1.24 ms and a standard deviation of 1.95. We measured 25 consecutive simulations of the time since an attack on a mined not-committed block is detected and until it is fully recovered by the CP. It can be observed that the time from attack detection and until the attack is recovered is a random variable with an average of 43.04 ms and a standard deviation of 6.39. We have measured the influence of the depth of the attacked random block on the recovery time in case of an attack on a mined not-committed block. It is observed that the time it takes to recover the system increases as the corrupted block is deeper in the Blockchain. The reason for that is that the number of blocks that need to be canceled and the number of transactions that need to be re-transmitted increases as the attacked block is deeper in the Blockchain.

3.7   The Proposed Method Scalability

We measure the influence of the transaction generation rate on the average time that transactions wait in the queue. As was mentioned earlier, the CP miners fetch all the transactions from the transactions pool in every mining cycle. We perform measurements of the average queuing time when the system runs without attacker involvement with 1000 agents until all the agents cumulatively generate 10000 transactions. Other system configuration parameters are PoW complexity of 3 bits and 3 CP miners. The transaction generation rate is cumulative for all the agents together, as they are executed in parallel one to the other. The results of the experiment are presented in Table 1.

Table 1. Average queuing time

Transactions Generation Rate	Average Queuing Time [ms]
1[KHz]	26509.39
10[KHz]	28330.6
100[KHz]	29325.2
1[MHz]	28343.79

We observe that as the transaction generation rate increases, the average queuing time does not increase significantly and stays approximately the same.

The reduction of the average mining time can be used for improving scalability. This is achievable by reducing the number of PoW complexity bits as it reduces the average mining time, and increases the frequency of block-creation. With a relatively small PoW complexity, many miners can cooperate to increase the cryptographic strength of the mining distributed processes, like the method used in crowd-sourcing [22]. In Bitcoin-like Blockchain's the miners are not motivated to cooperate as they are not interested to divide their rewards. In our method, there is no such problem as the miners are part of the proposed method. This enables us to run many miner groups in parallel for having strong cryptography protection over the PoW process together with support for high scalability. For example, when 100 miners cooperating, they can solve a 13 bits PoW at the same time one miner solves 3 bits PoW, and 13 bits is much better protection.

4   Conclusions and Future Work

We propose a novel method for performing data integrity verification on a cloud database by using Blockchain technology. The proposed method focuses on the time frame from the moment the log/audit transaction is published by a cloud database agent software into the Blockchain's transactions pool and until it becomes fully committed in the Blockchain network. The obtained results show that it takes less than 20 ms on average to detect an attack and that it takes an additional on average less than 50 ms to recover from it. The obtained results show that the method's scalability is ensured by a proper choice of the system parameters involved.

As future work, we consider evaluating our proposed method with Proof-of-Stake (PoS) consensus algorithm [10] to reduce energy consumption.

References

1. Nguyen, D.C., Pathirana, P.N., Ding, M., Seneviratne, A.: Integration of blockchain and cloud of things: Architecture, applications and challenges. IEEE Commun. Surv. Tutor. **22**(4), 2521–2549 (2020)
2. Deka, G.C.: A survey of cloud database systems. IT Professional **16**(2), 50–57 (2013)
3. Zhang, Y., Xu, C., Lin, X., Shen, X.S.: Blockchain-based public integrity verification for cloud storage against procrastinating auditors. In: IEEE Transactions on Cloud Computing, p. 1 (2019). https://doi.org/10.1109/TCC.2019.2908400
4. Zikratov, I., Kuzmin, A., Akimenko, V., Niculichev, V., Yalansky, L.: Ensuring data integrity using Blockchain technology. In: 2017 20th Conference of Open Innovations Association (FRUCT), pp. 534–539. IEEE (2017)
5. Gaetani, E., Aniello, L., Baldoni, R., Lombardi, F., Margheri, A., Sassone, V.: Blockchain-based database to ensure data integrity in cloud computing environments (2017)
6. Basu, A., Dimitrakos, T., Nakano, Y., Kiyomoto, S.: A framework for Blockchain-based verification of integrity and authenticity. In: Meng, W., Cofta, P., Jensen, C.D., Grandison, T. (eds.) IFIPTM 2019. IAICT, vol. 563, pp. 196–208. Springer, Cham (2019). https://doi.org/10.1007/978-3-030-33716-2_15
7. Merkle, R.C.: A certified digital signature. In: Brassard, G. (ed.) CRYPTO 1989. LNCS, vol. 435, pp. 218–238. Springer, New York (1990). https://doi.org/10.1007/0-387-34805-0_21
8. Awerbuch, B., Scheideler, C.: Towards a scalable and robust DHT. Theor. Comput. Syst. **45**(2), 234–260 (2009)
9. Zyskind, G., Nathan, O.: Decentralizing privacy: using Blockchain to protect personal data. In: 2015 IEEE Security and Privacy Workshops, pp. 180–184. IEEE (2015)
10. Sankar, L.S., Sindhu, M., Sethumadhavan, M.: Survey of consensus protocols on Blockchain applications. In: 2017 4th International Conference on Advanced Computing and Communication Systems (ICACCS), pp. 1–5. IEEE (2017)
11. Nakamoto, S.: Bitcoin: a peer-to-peer electronic cash system (2009). https://bitcoin.org/bitcoin.pdf
12. Wood, G.: Ethereum: a secure decentralised generalised transaction ledger. Ethereum Project Yellow Paper **151**, 1–32 (2014)
13. Weintraub, G., Gudes, E.: Data integrity verification in column-oriented NoSQL databases. In: Kerschbaum, F., Paraboschi, S. (eds.) DBSec 2018. LNCS, vol. 10980, pp. 165–181. Springer, Cham (2018). https://doi.org/10.1007/978-3-319-95729-6_11
14. Xie, M., Wang, H., Yin, J., Meng, X.: Integrity auditing of outsourced data. In: Proceedings of the 33rd International Conference on Very Large Data Bases, pp. 782–793 (2007)
15. Wei, P., Wang, D., Zhao, Y., Tyagi, S.K.S., Kumar, N.: Blockchain data-based cloud data integrity protection mechanism. Future Gener. Comput. Syst. **102**, 902–911 (2020)
16. Wong, W.K., Kao, B., Cheung, D.W.L., Li, R., Yiu, S.M.: Secure query processing with data interoperability in a cloud database environment. In: Proceedings of the 2014 ACM SIGMOD International Conference on Management of Data, pp. 1395–1406 (2014)

17. Reyhanian, N., Farmanbar, H., Mohajer, S., Luo, Z. Q.: Resource provisioning for virtual network function deployment with in-subnetwork processing. In: 2020 IEEE 21st International Workshop on Signal Processing Advances in Wireless Communications (SPAWC), pp. 1–5. IEEE (2020)
18. Battah, A.A., Madine, M.M., Alzaabi, H., Yaqoob, I., Salah, K., Jayaraman, R.: Blockchain-based multi-party authorization for accessing IPFS encrypted data. IEEE Access **8**, 196813–196825 (2020)
19. Li, Q.L., Ma, J.Y., Chang, Y.X., Ma, F.Q., Yu, H.B.: Markov processes in blockchain systems. Comput. Soc. Netw. **6**(1), 1–28 (2019)
20. Khanuja, H.K., Adane, D.S.: Database security threats and challenges in database forensic: a survey. In: Proceedings of 2011 International Conference on Advancements in Information Technology (AIT 2011) (2011). http://www.ipcsit.com/vol20/33-ICAIT2011-A4072.pdf
21. Wang, Z., Minsky, N.H.: Towards secure distributed hash table. In: Guo, S., Liao, X., Liu, F., Zhu, Y. (eds.) CollaborateCom 2015. LNICST, vol. 163, pp. 257–266. Springer, Cham (2016). https://doi.org/10.1007/978-3-319-28910-6_23
22. Ara, S.S., Thakur, S., Breslin, J.G.: Secure and distributed crowd-sourcing task coordination using the Blockchain mechanism. In: Montella, R., Ciaramella, A., Fortino, G., Guerrieri, A., Liotta, A. (eds.) IDCS 2019. LNCS, vol. 11874, pp. 402–413. Springer, Cham (2019). https://doi.org/10.1007/978-3-030-34914-1_38

Invited Talk: The Coming AI Hackers

Bruce Schneier[⊠]

Harvard Kennedy School, Cambridge, MA 02138, USA
schneier@schneier.com

Abstract. Hacking is generally thought of as something done to computer systems, but this conceptualization can be extended to any system of rules. The tax code, financial markets, and any system of laws can be hacked. This essay considers a world where AIs can be hackers. This is a generalization of specification gaming, where vulnerabilities and exploits of our social, economic, and political systems are discovered and exploited at computer speeds and scale.

Keywords: Artificial intelligence · Hacking · Specification gaming · Goal alignment · Explainability

1 Introduction

Artificial intelligence—AI—is an information technology. It consists of software. It runs on computers. And it is already deeply embedded into our social fabric, both in ways we understand and in ways we don't. It will hack our society to a degree and effect unlike anything that's come before. I mean this in two very different ways. One, AI systems will be used to hack us. And two, AI systems will themselves become hackers: finding vulnerabilities in all sorts of social, economic, and political systems, and then exploiting them at an unprecedented speed, scale, and scope. It's not just a difference in degree; it's a difference in kind. We risk a future of AI systems hacking other AI systems, with humans being little more than collateral damage.

This isn't hyperbole. Okay, maybe it's a bit of hyperbole, but none of this requires far-future science-fiction technology. I'm not postulating any "singularity," where the AI-learning feedback loop becomes so fast that it outstrips human understanding. I'm not assuming intelligent androids like Data (Star Trek), R2-D2 (Star Wars), or Marvin the Paranoid Android (The Hitchhiker's Guide to the Galaxy). My scenarios don't require evil intent on the part of anyone. We don't need malicious AI systems like Skynet (Terminator) or the Agents (Matrix). Some of the hacks I will discuss don't even require major research breakthroughs. They'll improve as AI techniques get more sophisticated, but we can see hints of them in operation today. This hacking will come naturally, as AIs become more advanced at learning, understanding, and problem-solving.

In this essay, I will talk about the implications of AI hackers. First, I will generalize "hacking" to include economic, social, and political systems—and also our brains. Next, I will describe how AI systems will be used to hack us. Then, I will explain how AIs will hack the economic, social, and political systems that comprise society. Finally, I will discuss the implications of a world of AI hackers, and point towards possible defenses. It's not all as bleak as it might sound.

S. Dolev et al. (Eds.): CSCML 2021, LNCS 12716, pp. 336–360, 2021.
https://doi.org/10.1007/978-3-030-78086-9_26

2 Hacks and Hacking

First, a definition:

Def: **Hack** /hak/ (noun) -

1. A clever, unintended exploitation of a system which: a) subverts the rules or norms of that system, b) at the expense of some other part of that system.
2. Something that a system allows, but that is unintended and unanticipated by its designers [1].

Notice the details. Hacking is not cheating. It's following the rules, but subverting their intent. It's unintended. It's an exploitation. It's "gaming the system." Caper movies are filled with hacks. MacGyver was a hacker. Hacks are clever, but not the same as innovations. And, yes, it's a subjective definition [2].

Systems tend to be optimized for specific outcomes. Hacking is the pursuit of another outcome, often at the expense of the original optimization Systems tend be rigid. Systems limit what we can do and invariably, some of us want to do something else. So we hack. Not everyone, of course. Everyone isn't a hacker. But enough of us are.

Hacking is normally thought of something you can do to computers. But hacks can be perpetrated on any system of rules—including the tax code.

The tax code isn't software. It doesn't run on a computer. But you can still think of it as "code" in the computer sense of the term. It's a series of algorithms that takes an input—financial information for the year—and produces an output: the amount of tax owed. It's deterministic, or at least it's supposed to be.

All computer software contains defects, commonly called bugs. These are mistakes: mistakes in specification, mistakes in programming, mistakes that occur somewhere in the process of creating the software. It might seem crazy, but modern software applications generally have hundreds if not thousands of bugs. These bugs are in all the software that you're currently using: on your computer, on your phone, in whatever "Internet of Things" devices you have around. That all of this software works perfectly well most the time speaks to how obscure and inconsequential these bugs tend to be. You're unlikely to encounter them in normal operations, but they're there.

Some of those bugs introduce security holes. By this I mean something very specific: bugs that an attacker can deliberately trigger to achieve some condition that the attacker can take advantage of. In computer-security language, we call these bugs "vulnerabilities."

Exploiting a vulnerability is how the Chinese military broke into Equifax in March 2017. A vulnerability in the Apache Struts software package allowed hackers to break into a consumer complaint web portal. From there, they were able to move to other parts of the network. They found usernames and passwords that allowed them to access still other parts of the network, and eventually to download personal information about 147 million people over the course of four months [3].

This is an example of a hack. It's a way to exploit the system in a way that is both unanticipated and unintended by the system's designers—something that advantages the hacker in some way at the expense of the users the system is supposed to serve.

The tax code also has bugs. They might be mistakes in how the tax laws were written: errors in the actual words that Congress voted on and the president signed into law. They might be mistakes in how the tax code is interpreted. They might be oversights in how parts of the law were conceived, or unintended omissions of some sort or another. They might arise from unforeseen interactions between different parts of the tax code.

A recent example comes from the 2017 Tax Cuts and Jobs Act. That law was drafted in haste and in secret, and passed without any time for review by legislators—or even proofreading. Parts of it were handwritten, and it's pretty much inconceivable that anyone who voted either for or against it knew precisely what was in it. The text contained a typo that accidentally categorized military death benefits as earned income. The practical effect of that mistake was that surviving family members were hit with surprise tax bills of $10,000 or more [4]. That's a bug.

It's not a vulnerability, though, because no one can take advantage of it to reduce their tax bill. But some bugs in the tax code are also vulnerabilities. For example, there's a corporate tax trick called the "Double Irish with a Dutch Sandwich." It's a vulnerability that arises from the interactions between tax laws in multiple countries. Basically, it involves using a combination of Irish and Dutch subsidiary companies to shift profits to low- or no-tax jurisdictions. Tech companies are particularly well suited to exploit this vulnerability; they can assign intellectual property rights to subsidiary companies abroad, who then transfer cash assets to tax havens [5]. That's how companies like Google and Apple have avoided paying their fair share of US taxes despite being US companies. It's definitely an unintended and unanticipated use of the tax laws in three countries. And it can be very profitable for the hackers—in this case, big tech companies avoiding US taxes—at the expense of everyone else. Estimates are that US companies avoided paying nearly $200 billion in US taxes in 2017 alone [6].

Some vulnerabilities are deliberately created. Lobbyists are constantly trying to insert this or that provision into the tax code to benefit their clients. That same 2017 US tax law that gave rise to unconscionable tax bills to grieving families included a special tax break for oil and gas investment partnerships, a special exemption that ensures that less than 1 in 1,000 estates will have to pay estate tax, and language specifically expanding a pass-through loophole that industry uses to incorporate offshore and avoid US taxes [7].

Sometimes these vulnerabilities are slipped into law with the knowledge of the legislator who is sponsoring the amendment, and sometimes they're not aware of it. This deliberate insertion is also analogous to something we worry about in software: programmers deliberately adding backdoors into systems for their own purposes. That's not hacking the tax code, or the computer code. It's hacking the processes that create them: the legislative process that creates tax law, or the software development process that creates computer programs.

During the past few years, there has been considerable press given to the possibility that Chinese companies like Huawei and ZTE have added backdoors to their 5G routing equipment at the request—or possibly demand—of the Chinese government. It's certainly possible, and those vulnerabilities would lie dormant in the system until they're used by someone who knows about them.

In the tax world, bugs and vulnerabilities are called tax loopholes. In the tax world, taking advantage of these vulnerabilities is called tax avoidance. And there are thousands of what we in the computer security world would call "black-hat researchers," who examine every line of the tax code looking for exploitable vulnerabilities. They're called tax attorneys and tax accountants.

Modern software is incredibly complex. Microsoft Windows 10, the latest version of that operating system, has about 50 million lines of code [8]. More complexity means more bugs, which means more vulnerabilities. The US tax code is also complex. It consists of the tax laws passed by Congress, administrative rulings, and judicial rules. Credible estimates of the size of it all are hard to come by; even experts often have no idea. The tax laws themselves are about 2,600 pages [9]. IRS regulations and tax rulings increase that to about 70,000 pages. It's hard to compare lines of text to lines of computer code, but both are extremely complex. And in both cases, much of that complexity is related to how different parts of the codes interact with each other.

We know how to fix vulnerabilities in computer code. We can employ a variety of tools to detect and fix them before the code is finished. After the code is out in the world, researchers of various kinds discover them and—most important of all—we want the vendors to quickly patch them once they become known.

We can sometimes employ these same methods with the tax code. The 2017 tax law capped income tax deductions for property taxes. This provision didn't come into force in 2018, so someone came up with the clever hack to prepay 2018 property taxes in 2017. Just before the end of the year, the IRS ruled about when that was legal and when it wasn't [10]. Short answer: most of the time, it wasn't.

It's often not this easy. Some hacks are written into the law, or can't be ruled away. Passing any tax legislation is a big deal, especially in the US, where the issue is so partisan and contentious. (It's been almost four years, and that earned income tax bug for military families still hasn't been fixed. And that's an easy one; everyone acknowledges it was a mistake.) It can be hard to figure out who is supposed to patch the tax code: is the legislature, the courts, the tax authorities? And then it can take years. We simply don't have the ability to patch tax code with anywhere near the same agility that we have to patch software.

2.1 The Ubiquity of Hacking

Everything is a system, every system can be hacked, and humans are natural hackers.

Airline frequent-flier programs are hacked. Card counting in blackjack is a hack. Sports are hacked all the time. Someone first figured out that a curved hockey stick blade allowed for faster and more accurate shots but also a more dangerous game, something the rules didn't talk about because no one had thought of it before. Formula One racing is full of hacks, as teams figure out ways to modify car designs that are not specifically prohibited by the rulebook but nonetheless subvert its intent.

The history of finance is a history of hacks. Again and again, financial institutions and traders look for loopholes in the rules—things that are not expressly prohibited, but are unintended subversions of the underlying systems—that give them an advantage. Uber, Airbnb, and other gig-economy companies hack government regulations. The filibuster is an ancient hack, first invented in ancient Rome. So are hidden provisions in legislation. Gerrymandering is a hack of the political process.

And finally, people can be hacked. Our brain is a system, evolved over millions of years to keep us alive and—more importantly—to keep us reproducing. It's been optimized through continuous interaction with the environment. But it's been optimized for humans who live in small family groups in the East African highlands in 100,000 BCE. It's not as well suited for twenty-first-century New York, or Tokyo, or Delhi. And because it encompasses many cognitive shortcuts—it evolves, but not on any scale that matters here—it can be manipulated.

Cognitive hacking is powerful. Many of the robust social systems our society relies on— democracy, market economics, and so on—depend on humans making appropriate decisions. This process can be hacked in many different ways. Social media hacks our attention. Personalized to our attitudes and behavior, modern advertising is a hack of our systems of persuasion. Disinformation hacks our common understanding of reality. Terrorism hacks our cognitive systems of fear and risk assessment by convincing people that it is a bigger threat than it actually is [11]. It's horrifying, vivid, spectacular, random—in that anyone could be its next victim—and malicious. Those are the very things that cause us to exaggerate the risk and overreact [12]. Social engineering, the conventional hacker tactic of convincing someone to divulge their login credentials or otherwise do something beneficial to the hacker, is much more a hack of trust and authority than a hack of any computer system.

What's new are computers. Computers are systems, and are hacked directly. But what's more interesting is the computerization of more traditional systems. Finance, taxation, regulatory compliance, elections—all these and more have been computerized. And when something is computerized, the way it can be hacked changes. Computerization accelerates hacking across three dimensions: speed, scale, and scope.

Computer speed modifies the nature of hacks. Take a simple concept—like stock trading—and automate it. It becomes something different. It may be doing the same thing it always did, but it's doing it at superhuman speed. An example is high-frequency trading, something unintended and unanticipated by those who designed early markets.

Scale, too. Computerization allows systems to grow much larger than they could otherwise, which changes the scale of hacking. The very notion of "too big to fail" is a hack, allowing companies to use society as a last-ditch insurance policy against their bad decision making.

Finally, scope. Computers are everywhere, affecting every aspect of our lives. This means that new concepts in computer hacking are potentially applicable everywhere, with varying results.

Not all systems are equally hackable. Complex systems with many rules are particularly vulnerable, simply because there are more possibilities for unanticipated and unintended consequences. This is certainly true for computer systems—I've written in the past that complexity is the worst enemy of security [13]—and it's also true for systems like the tax code, the financial system, and AIs. Systems constrained by more flexible social norms and not by rigidly defined rules are more vulnerable to hacking, because they leave themselves more open to interpretation and therefore have more loopholes.

Even so, vulnerabilities will always remain, and hacks will always be possible. In 1930, the mathematician Kurt Gödel proved that all mathematical systems are either incomplete or inconsistent. I believe this is true more generally. Systems will always have ambiguities or inconsistencies, and they will always be exploitable. And there will always be people who want to exploit them.

3   AIs Hacking Us

In 2016, The Georgia Institute of Technology published a research study on human trust in robots [14]. The study employed a non-anthropomorphic robot that assisted with navigation through a building, providing directions such as "This way to the exit." First, participants interacted with the robot in a normal setting to experience its performance, which was deliberately poor. Then, they had to decide whether or not to follow the robot's commands in a simulated emergency. In the latter situation, all twenty-six participants obeyed the robot, despite having observed just moments before that the robot had lousy navigational skills. The degree of trust they placed in this machine was striking: when the robot pointed to a dark room with no clear exit, the majority of people obeyed it, rather than safely exiting by the door through which they had entered. The researchers ran similar experiments with other robots that seemed to malfunction. Again, subjects followed these robots in an emergency setting, apparently abandoning their common sense. It seems that robots can naturally hack our trust.

3.1   Artificial Intelligence and Robotics

We could spend pages defining AI. In 1968, AI pioneer Marvin Minsky defined it as "the science of making machines do things that would require intelligence if done by men" [15]. The US Department of Defense uses: "the ability of machines to perform tasks that normally require human intelligence" [16]. The 1950 version of the Turing test—called the "imitation game" in the original discussion—focused on a computer program that humans couldn't distinguish from an actual human [17]. For our purposes, AI is an umbrella term encompassing a broad array of decision-making technologies that simulate human thinking.

One differentiation I need to make is between specialized—sometimes called "narrow"—AI and general AI. General AI is what you see in the movies. It's AI that can sense, think, and act in a very general and human way. If it's smarter than humans, it's called "artificial superintelligence." Combine it with robotics and you have an android, one that may look more or less like a human. The movie robots that try to destroy humanity are all general AI.

There's been a lot of practical research going into how to create general AI, and a lot of theoretical research about how to design these systems so they don't do things we don't want them to, like destroy humanity. And while this is fascinating work, encompassing fields from computer science to sociology to philosophy, its practical applications are probably decades away. I want to focus instead on specialized AI, because that's what's practical now.

Specialized AI is designed for a specific task. An example is the system that controls a self-driving car. It knows how to steer the vehicle, how to follow traffic laws, how to avoid getting into accidents, and what to do when something unexpected happens—like a child's ball suddenly bouncing into the road. Specialized AI knows a lot and can make decisions based on that knowledge, but only in this limited domain.

One common joke among AI researchers is that as soon as something works, it's no longer AI; it's just software. That might make AI research somewhat depressing, since by definition the only things that count are failures, but there's some truth to it. AI is inherently a mystifying science-fiction term. Once it becomes reality, it's no longer mystifying. We used to assume that reading chest X-rays required a radiologist: that is, an intelligent human with appropriate training. Now we realize that it's a rote task that can also be performed by a computer.

What's really going on is that there is a continuum of decision-making technologies and systems, ranging from a simple electromechanical thermostat that operates a furnace in response to changing temperatures to a science-fictional android. What makes something AI often depends on the complexity of the tasks performed and the complexity of the environment in which those tasks are performed. The thermostat performs a very simple task that only has to take into account a very simple aspect of the environment. It doesn't even need to involve a computer. A modern digital thermostat might be able to sense who is in the room and make predictions about future heat needs based on both usage and weather forecast, as well as citywide power consumption and second-by-second energy costs. A futuristic thermostat might act like a thoughtful and caring butler, whatever that would mean in the context of adjusting the ambient temperature.

I would rather avoid these definitional debates, because they largely don't matter for our purposes. In addition to decision-making, the relevant qualities of the systems I'll be discussing are autonomy, automation, and physical agency. A thermostat has limited automation and physical agency, and no autonomy. A system that predicts criminal recidivism has no physical agency; it just makes recommendations to a judge. A driverless car has some of all three. R2D2 has a lot of all three, although for some reason its designers left out English speech synthesis.

Robotics also has a popular mythology and a less-flashy reality. Like AI, there are many different definitions of the term. I like robot ethicist Kate Darling's definition: "physically embodied objects that can sense, think, and act on their environments through physical motion" [18]. In movies and television, that's often artificial people: androids. Again, I prefer to focus on technologies that are more prosaic and near term. For our purposes, robotics is autonomy, automation, and physical agency dialed way up. It's "cyber-physical autonomy": AI technology inside objects that can interact with the world in a direct, physical manner.

3.2 Human-Like AIs

People have long ascribed human-like qualities to computer programs. In the 1960s, programmer Joseph Weizenbaum created a primitive therapist-mimicking conversational program called ELIZA. He was amazed that people would confide deeply personal secrets to what they knew was a dumb computer program. Weizenbaum's secretary would even ask him to leave the room, so that she could talk to ELIZA in private [19].

Today, people are polite to voice assistants like Alexa and Siri [20]. Siri even complains when you're mean to it: "That's not very nice," it says—because it's programmed to, of course.

Numerous experiments bear similar results. Research subjects would rate a computer's performance less critically if they gave the rating on the computer they were criticizing, indicating that they didn't want to hurt its feelings [21]. In another experiment, if a computer told a research subject some obviously fictional piece of "personal information," the subject was likely to reciprocate by sharing actual personal information [22]. The power of reciprocation is something that psychologists study. It's a hack that people use, too.

It's not just that we'll treat AIs as people. They'll also act like people in ways that will be deliberately designed to fool us. They'll employ cognitive hacks.

During the 2016 US election, about a fifth of all political tweets were posted by bots [23]. For the UK Brexit vote of the same year, it was a third [24]. An Oxford Internet Institute report from 2019 found evidence of bots being used to spread propaganda in fifty countries [25]. These tended to be simple programs mindlessly repeating slogans. For example, a quarter million pro-Saudi "We all have trust in [crown prince] Mohammed bin Salman" tweets were posted following the 2018 murder of Jamal Khashoggi [26].

In 2017, the Federal Communications Commission had an online public-comment period for its plans to repeal net neutrality. A staggering 22 million comments were received. Many of them—maybe half—were submitted using stolen identities [27]. These fake comments were also crude; 1.3 million were generated from the same template, with some words altered to make them appear unique [28]. They didn't stand up to even cursory scrutiny.

Efforts like these will only get more sophisticated. For years, AI programs have been writing news stories about sports and finance for real news organizations like the Associated Press [29, 30]. The constrained nature of those topics made them easier for an AI. They're now starting to write more general stories. Research projects like Open AI's GPT-3 are expanding the capabilities of what AI-driven text generation can do [31]. These systems can be fed actual facts and write true stories, but they can just as easily be fed untruths and write fake news.

It doesn't take much imagination to see how AI will degrade political discourse. Already, AI-driven personas can write personalized letters to newspapers and elected officials, leave intelligible comments on news sites and message boards, and intelligently debate politics on social media [32]. These systems will only get better: more sophisticated, more articulate, more personal, and harder to distinguish from actual human beings.

In a recent experiment, researchers used a text-generation program to submit 1,000 comments in response to a government request for public input on a Medicaid issue [33]. They all sounded unique, like real people advocating a specific policy position. They fooled the Medicaid.gov administrators, who accepted them as genuine concerns from actual human beings. The researchers subsequently identified the comments and asked for them to be removed, so that no actual policy debate would be unfairly biased. Others won't be so ethical.

These techniques are already being used. An online propaganda campaign used AI-generated headshots to create fake journalists [34]. China experimented with AI-generated text messages designed to influence the 2020 Taiwanese election [35]. Deep-fake technology—AI techniques to create real videos of fake events, often with actual people saying things they didn't actually say—are being used politically [36].

One example of how this will unfold is in "persona bots." These are AIs posing as individuals on social media and in other digital groups. They have histories, personalities, and communications styles. They don't constantly spew propaganda. They hang out in various interest groups: gardening, knitting, model railroading, whatever. They act as normal members of those communities, posting and commenting and discussing. Systems like GPT-3 will make it easy for those AIs to mine previous conversations and related Internet content and appear knowledgeable. Then, once in a while, the AI posts something relevant to a political issue. Maybe it's an article about an Alaska healthcare worker having an allergic reaction to the COVID-19 vaccine, with a worried commentary. Or maybe it's something about a recent election, or racial justice, or anything that's polarizing. One persona bot can't move public opinion, but what if there were thousands of them? Millions?

This has been called "computational propaganda," [37] and will change the way we view communication. AI will make the future supply of disinformation infinite [38]. Persona bots will break the "notice-and-comment" rulemaking process, by flooding government agencies with fake comments. They may also break community discourse.

These systems will affect us at the personal level as well. Earlier I mentioned social engineering. One common hacker tactic is phishing emails that purport to be from someone they're not, intended to convince the recipient to do something she shouldn't. Most phishing emails are generic and easily tagged as spam. The more effective phishing emails—the ones that result in people and companies losing lots of money—are personalized. For example, an email that impersonates the CEO to someone in the finance department, asking for a particular wire transfer, can be particularly effective [39]. Voice can be even more effective [40]. The laborious task of customizing phishing attacks could be automated by AI techniques, allowing marketers to send out personalized advertisements, and phishing scammers to send out individually targeted emails.

It's not that being persuaded by an AI is fundamentally more damaging than being persuaded by another human, it's that AIs will be able to do it at computer speed and scale. Today's cognitive hacks are crude: a fake newspaper article designed to fool only the most gullible, or a persuasive nudge designed to affect only the most desperate. AI has the potential for every one of those hacks to be microtargeted: personalized, optimized, and individually delivered [41]. Old-style con games are individually crafted person-to-person cognitive hacks. Advertising messages are bulk broadcast cognitive hacks. AI techniques have the potential to blend aspects of both of those techniques.

3.3 Robots Hacking Us

The addition of robotics will only make these hacks more effective, something Kate Darling chronicled in her book *The New Breed* [18]. We humans have developed some pretty effective cognitive shortcuts to recognize other people. We see faces everywhere; two dots over a horizontal line looks like a face without any trouble. This is why even minimalist illustrations are so effective. If something has a face, then it's a creature of some sort: with intentions, feelings, and everything else that comes with real-world faces. If that something speaks or, even better, converses, then we believe it has intentions, desires, and agency.

Robots are no exception. Many people have social relationships with their robot vacuums, even complaining when the company would offer to replace rather than repair "their" Roomba [42]. A US Army–developed anti-landmine robot ran into problems when a colonel refused to allow the insect-shaped device to continue to harm itself by stepping on mines [43]. A Harvard robot could convince students to let it in dorms by pretending to be a food-delivery robot [44]. And Boxie, a childlike talking robot at MIT, could persuade people to answer personal questions just by asking nicely [45].

The human nurturing instinct isn't solely genetically focused. We can experience nurturing feelings towards adopted children, and we can feel the same instincts arise when we interact with the children of friends or even strangers–or puppies. At least some of our response is inspired by the appearance and behavior of children. Children have large heads in proportion to their bodies, and large eyes in proportion to their heads. They talk with a higher-pitched voice than adults. And we respond to all of this.

Artists have taken advantage of this for generations to make their creations appear more sympathetic. Children's dolls are designed this way. Cartoon characters are drawn this way, as far back as Betty Boop in the 1930s and Bambi in 1942. In the 2019 live-action movie *Alita: Battle Angel,* the main character had her eyes computer-enhanced to be larger [46].

Anthropomorphic robots are an emotionally persuasive technology, and AI will only amplify their attractiveness. As AI mimics humans, or even animals, it will hijack all the mechanisms that humans use to hack each other. As psychologist Sherry Turkle wrote in 2010: "When robots make eye contact, recognize faces, mirror human gestures, they push our Darwinian buttons, exhibiting the kind of behavior people associate with sentience, intentions, and emotions" [47]. That is, they hack our brains.

We might intuitively know that it's just a plastic green dinosaur. But a large face paired with a small body makes us think of it as a child. Suddenly we're thinking of it as a creature with feelings, and will protect it from harm [18]. And while that may be benign, what happens when that robot looks at its human owners with its big, sad eyes and asks them to buy it a software upgrade [48]?

Because we humans are prone to making a category error and treating robots as living creatures with feelings and intentions, we are prone to being manipulated by them. Robots could persuade us to do things we might not do otherwise. They could scare us into not doing things we might otherwise do. In one experiment, a robot was able to exert "peer pressure" on subjects, encouraging them to take more risks [49]. How soon before a sex robot suggests in-app purchases in the heat of the moment [50]?

AIs will get better at all of this. Already they are trying to detect emotions by analyzing our writings [51], reading our facial expressions [52], or monitoring our breathing and heartrate [53]. They get it wrong a lot of the time, but it is likely that they will improve. And, like so many areas of AI, they will eventually surpass people in capability. This will allow them to more precisely manipulate us.

As AIs and autonomous robots take on more real-world tasks, human trust in autonomous systems will be hacked with dangerous and costly results. But never forget that there are human hackers controlling the AI hackers. All of the systems will be designed and paid for by humans who want them to manipulate us in a particular way for a particular purpose. I'll talk more about this later.

4 When AIs Become Hackers

Hacker "Capture the Flag" is basically the outdoor game played on computer networks. Teams of hackers defend their own computers while attacking other teams'. It's a controlled setting for what computer hackers do in real life: finding and fixing vulnerabilities in their own systems, and exploiting them in others'.

The competition has been a mainstay at hacker gatherings since the mid-1990s. These days, dozens of teams from around the world compete in weekend-long marathon events held all over the world. People train for months. Winning is a big deal. If you're into this sort of thing, it's pretty much the most fun you can possibly have on the Internet without committing multiple felonies.

In 2016, DARPA ran a similarly styled event for AI [54]. One hundred teams entered their systems into the Cyber Grand Challenge. After completion of qualifying rounds, seven finalists competed at the DEFCON hacker convention in Las Vegas. The competition occurred in a specially designed test environment filled with custom software that had never been analyzed or tested. The AIs were given ten hours to find vulnerabilities to exploit against the other AIs in the competition, and to patch themselves against exploitation. A system called Mayhem, created by a team of Pittsburgh computer-security researchers, won. The researchers have since commercialized the technology, which is now busily defending networks for customers like the Department of Defense [55].

There was a human-team capture-the-flag event at DEFCON that same year. Mayhem was invited to participate as the only non-human team, and came in last. You can easily imagine how this mixed competition would unfold in the future. AI entrants will improve every year, because the core technologies are all improving. The human teams will largely stay the same, because humans remain humans even as our tools improve. Eventually the AIs will routinely beat the humans. My guess is that it'll take less than a decade. It will be years before we have entirely autonomous AI cyberattack capabilities, but AI technologies are already transforming the nature of cyberattack [56].

One area that seems particularly fruitful for AI systems is vulnerability finding. Going through software code line by line is exactly the sort of tedious problem at which AIs excel, if they can only be taught how to recognize a vulnerability [57]. Many domain-specific challenges will need to be addressed, of course, but there is a healthy amount of academic literature on the topic—and research is continuing [58]. There's every reason to expect AI systems will improve over time, and some reason to expect them to eventually become very good at it.

The implications extend far beyond computer networks. There's no reason that AIs can't find new vulnerabilities—thousands of them—in many of the systems I mentioned earlier: the tax code, banking regulations, political processes. Whenever there's a large number of rules that interact with each other, we should expect AIs to eventually be finding the vulnerabilities and creating the exploits. Already AIs are looking for loopholes in contracts [59].

This will all improve with time. Hackers, of any kind, are only as good as their understanding of the system they're targeting and how it interacts with the rest of the world. AIs initially capture this understanding through the data they're trained with, but it continues to improve as it is used. Modern AIs are constantly improving based on ingesting new data and tweaking their own internal workings accordingly. All of this data continually trains the AI, and adds to its experience. The AI evolves and improves based on these experiences over the course of its operation. This is why autonomous vehicle systems brag about number of road hours they've had.

There are really two different but related problems here. The first is that an AI might be instructed to hack a system. Someone might feed an AI the world's tax codes or the world's financial regulations, with the intent of having it create a slew of profitable hacks. The other is that an AI might naturally, albeit inadvertently, hack a system. Both are dangerous, but the second is more dangerous because we might never know it happened.

4.1 The Explainability Problem

In *The Hitchhiker's Guide to the Galaxy,* a race of hyper-intelligent, pan-dimensional beings build the universe's most powerful computer, Deep Thought, to answer the ultimate question to life, the universe, and everything. After 7.5 million years of computation, Deep Thought informed them that the answer was 42. And was unable to explain its answer, or even what the question was [60].

That, in a nutshell, is the explainability problem. Modern AI systems are essentially black boxes. Data goes in at one end, and an answer comes out the other. It can be impossible to understand how the system reached its conclusion, even if you are a programmer and look at the code. We don't know precisely why an AI image-classification system mistook a turtle for a rifle, or a stop sign with a few carefully designed stickers on it as a "Speed Limit 45" sign: both real examples [61].

AIs don't solve problems like humans do. Their limitations are different than ours. They'll consider more possible solutions than we might. More importantly, they'll look at more *types* of solutions. They'll go down paths that we simply have not considered, paths more complex than the sorts of things we generally keep in mind. (Our cognitive limits on the amount of simultaneous information we can mentally juggle has long been described as "the magical number seven plus or minus two" [62, 63]. My point is not to settle on a number, but to point out that an AI system has nothing even remotely like that limitation.)

In 2016, the AI program AlphaGo won a five-game match against one of the world's best Go players, Lee Sedol—something that shocked both the AI and the Go-playing worlds. AlphaGo's most famous move was move 37 of game 2. It's hard to explain without diving deep into Go strategy, but it was a move that no human would ever have chosen to make [64].

In 2015, a research group fed an AI system called Deep Patient health and medical data from approximately 700,000 individuals, and tested whether or not the system could predict diseases. The result was a success. Weirdly, Deep Patient appears to perform well at anticipating the onset of psychiatric disorders like schizophrenia—even though a first psychotic episode is nearly impossible for physicians to predict [65]. It sounds great, but Deep Patient provides no explanation for the basis of a diagnosis, and the researchers have no idea how it comes to its conclusions. A doctor either can trust or ignore the computer, but can't query it for more info.

That's not ideal. What we want is for the AI system to not only spit out an answer, but also provide some explanation of its answer in a format that humans can understand. We want those so we are more comfortable trusting the AI's decisions, but this is also how we can ensure that our AI systems haven't been hacked to make biased decisions.

Researchers are working on explainable AI [66]; in 2017, DARPA launched a $75 million research fund for a dozen programs in the area [67]. And while there will be advances in this field, there seems to be a trade-off between capability and explainability. Explanations are a cognitive shorthand used by humans, suited for the way humans make decisions. AI decisions simply might not be conducive to human-understandable explanations, and forcing those explanations might pose an additional constraint that could affect the quality of decisions made by an AI system. It's unclear where all this research will end up. In the near term, AI is becoming more and more opaque, as the systems get more complex and less human-like—and less explainable.

4.2 Reward Hacking

As I wrote above, AIs don't solve problems in the same way that people do. They will invariably stumble on solutions that we humans might never anticipated—and some will subvert the intent of the system. That's because AIs don't think in terms of the implications, context, norms, and values that humans share and take for granted.

Reward hacking involves an AI achieving a goal in a way the AI's designers neither wanted nor intended [68, 69]. Some actual examples:

In a one-on-one soccer simulation, the player was supposed to score against the goalie. Instead of directly kicking the ball into the goal, the AI system figured out that if it kicked the ball out of bounds, the opponent—in this case the goalie—would have to throw the ball back in, leaving the goal undefended [70].

In a stacking task, the AI was supposed to stack blocks. Height was measured by the position of the bottom face of one particular block. The AI learned to flip that block upside down—so that its bottom faced up—rather than stack it on top of another block. (Obviously, the rules failed to explicitly state that the "bottom" of the block should always point downward [71].)

In a simulated environment for "evolved" creatures, the AI was allowed to modify its own physical characteristics in order to better fulfill its objectives. The AI figured out that instead of running, it could make itself tall enough to cross a distant finish line by falling over it [72].

These are all hacks. You can blame them on poorly specified goals or rewards, and you would be correct. You can point out that they all occurred in simulated environments, and you would also be correct. But the problem is more general: AIs are designed to optimize towards a goal. In doing so, they will naturally and inadvertently hack systems in ways we won't expect.

Imagine a robotic vacuum assigned the task of cleaning up any mess it sees. It might disable its vision so that it can't see any messes, or cover messes up with opaque materials so it doesn't see them [73]. In 2018, an entrepreneurial—or perhaps just bored—programmer wanted his robot vacuum to stop bumping into furniture. He trained an AI by rewarding it for not hitting the bumper sensors [74]. Instead of learning not to bump into things, the AI learned to drive the vacuum backwards because there are no bumper sensors on the back of the device.

Any good AI system will naturally find hacks. If are problems, inconsistencies, or loopholes in the rules, and if those properties lead to an acceptable solution as defined by the rules, then AIs will find them. We might look at what the AI did and say, "well, technically it followed the rules." Yet we humans sense a deviation, a cheat, a hack because we understand the context of the problem and have different expectations. AI researchers call this problem "goal alignment."

We all learned about this problem as children, with the King Midas story. When the god Dionysus grants him a wish, Midas asks that everything he touches turns to gold. Midas ends up starving and miserable when his food, drink, and daughter all turn to inedible, unpotable, unlovable gold. That's a goal alignment problem; Midas programmed the wrong goal into the system.

We also know that genies are very precise about the wording of wishes, and can be maliciously pedantic when granting them. But here's the thing: there is no way to outsmart the genie. Whatever you wish for, he will always be able to it in a way that you wish he hadn't. The genie will always be able to hack your wish.

The problem is more general, though. In human language and thought, goals and desires are always underspecified [75]. We never describe all of the options. We never delineate all of the caveats and exceptions and provisos. We never close off all the avenues for hacking. We can't. Any goal we specify will necessarily be incomplete.

This is largely okay in human interactions, because people understand context and usually act in good faith. We are all socialized, and in the process of becoming so, we generally acquire common sense about how people and the world works. We fill any gaps in our understanding with both context and goodwill.

If I asked you to get me some coffee, you would probably go to the nearest coffeepot and pour me a cup, or maybe to walk to the corner coffee shop and buy one. You would not bring me a pound of raw beans, or go online and buy a truckload of raw beans. You would not buy a coffee plantation in Costa Rica. You would also not look for the person closest to you holding a cup of coffee and rip it out of their hands. You wouldn't bring me week-old cold coffee, or a used paper towel that had wiped up a coffee spill. I wouldn't have to specify any of that. You would just know.

Similarly, if I ask you to develop a technology that would turn things to gold on touch, you wouldn't build it so that it starved the person using it. I wouldn't have to specify that; you would just know.

We can't completely specify goals to an AI. And AIs won't be able to completely understand context. In a TED talk, AI researcher Stuart Russell joked about a fictional AI assistant causing an airplane delay in order to delay someone's arrival at a dinner engagement. The audience laughed, but how would a computer program know that causing an airplane computer malfunction is not an appropriate response to someone who wants to get out of dinner [76]? (Internet joke from 2017: Jeff Bezos: "Alexa, buy me something on Whole Foods." Alexa: "OK, buying Whole Foods.").

In 2015, Volkswagen was caught cheating on emissions control tests. It didn't forge test results; it designed the cars' computers to do the cheating for them. Engineers programmed the software in the cars' onboard computers to detect when the car was undergoing an emissions test. The computer then activated the car's emissions-curbing systems, but only for the duration of the test. The result was that the cars had superior performance on the road. They also emitted up to forty times the amount of nitrogen oxides the EPA allowed, but only when the EPA wasn't watching [77].

The Volkswagen story doesn't involve AI—human engineers programmed a regular computer system to cheat—but it illustrates the problem nonetheless. Volkswagen got away with it for over ten years because computer code is complex and difficult to analyze. It's hard to figure out exactly what software is doing, and it's similarly hard to look at a car and figure out what it's doing. As long as the programmers don't say anything, a hack like that is likely to remain undetected for a long time; possibly forever. In this case, the only reason we know about Volkswagen's actions is that a group of scientists at West Virginia University tested the cars' performance on the road. Basically, the scientists tested the car without the software realizing it [78].

If I asked you to design a car's engine control software to maximize performance while still passing emissions control tests, you wouldn't design the software to cheat without understanding that you were cheating. This simply isn't true for an AI; it doesn't understand the abstract concept of cheating. It will think "out of the box" simply because it won't have a conception of the box, or of the limitations of existing human solutions. Or of ethics. It won't understand that the Volkswagen solution harms others, that it undermines the intent of the emissions control tests, or that it is breaking the law.

This is similar to Uber's Greyball tool [79]. Uber created special software would identify potential regulators and present then with an alternative regulation-complying Uber service instead of what they were actually doing. Again, this is a story of humans cheating. But we can easily imagine an AI coming up with the same "solution." It won't even realize that it's hacking the system. And because of the explainability problem, we humans might never realize it either.

4.3 AIs as Natural Hackers

Unless the programmers specify the goal of not behaving differently when being tested, an AI might come up with the same hack. The programmers will be satisfied. The accountants will be ecstatic. And because of the explainability problem, no one will realize what the AI did. And yes, now that we know the Volkswagen story, the programmers can explicitly set the goal to avoid that particular hack, but there are other hacks that the programmers will not anticipate. The lesson of the genie is that there will *always* be hacks the programmers will not anticipate.

The worry isn't limited to the obvious hacks. If your driverless car navigation system satisfies the goal of maintaining a high speed by spinning in circles—a real example [80]—programmers will notice this behavior and modify the goal accordingly. The behavior may show up in testing, but we will probably never see it occur on the road.

The greatest worry lies in the hacks that are less obvious—the ones we'll never know about because their effects are subtle.

We've already seen the first generation of this. Much has been written about recommendation engines, and how they push people towards extreme content [81]. They weren't programmed to do this; it's a property that naturally emerged as the systems continuously tried things, saw the results, and then modified themselves to do more of what resulted in more user engagement and less of what didn't. The algorithms learned to push more extreme content to users because that's what gets people reading or watching more. It didn't take a bad actor to create this hack: a pretty basic automated system found it on its own. And most of us didn't realize that it was happening (except for the folks at Facebook, who ignored their own research demonstrating that it *was* happening) [82].

Similarly, in 2015, an AI taught itself to play the 1970s computer game Breakout. The AI wasn't told anything about the game's rules or strategy. It was just given the controls, and rewarded for maximizing its score. That it learned how to play isn't interesting; everyone expected that. But it independently discovered, and optimized to a degree not seen in human players, the tactic of "tunneling" through one column of bricks to bounce the ball off the back wall [83].

Nothing I'm saying here will be news to AI researchers, and many are currently considering ways to defend against goal and reward hacking. One solution is to teach AIs context. The general term for this sort of research is "value alignment": How do we create AIs that mirror our values? You can think about solutions in terms of two extremes. The first is that we can explicitly specify those values. That can be done today, more or less, but is vulnerable to all of the hacking I just described. The other extreme is that we can create AIs that learn our values, possibly by observing humans in action, or by ingesting all of humanity's writings: our history, our literature, our philosophy, and so on. That is many years out (AI researchers disagree on the time scale). Most of current research straddles these two extremes [84].

Of course, you can easily imagine the problems that might arise by having AIs align themselves to historical or observed human values. Whose values should an AI mirror? A Somali man? A Singaporean woman? The average of the two, whatever that means? We humans have contradictory values. Any individual person's values might be irrational, immoral, or based on false information. There's a lot of immorality in our history, literature, and philosophy. We humans are often not very good examples of the sorts of humans we should be.

4.4 From Science Fiction to Reality

The feasibility of any of this depends a lot on the specific system being modeled and hacked. For an AI to even start on optimizing a solution, let alone hacking a completely novel solution, all of the rules of the environment must be formalized in a way the computer can understand. Goals—known in AI as objective functions—need to be established. The AI needs some sort of feedback on how well it is doing so that it can improve its performance.

Sometimes this is a trivial matter. For a game like Go, it's easy. The rules, objective, and feedback—did you win or lose?—are all precisely specified. And there's nothing outside of those things to muddy the waters. The pattern-matching machine learning AI

GPT-3 can write coherent essays because its "world" is just text. This is why most of the current examples of goal and reward hacking come from simulated environments. Those are artificial and constrained, with all of the rules specified to the AI.

What matters is the ambiguity in a system. We can imagine feeding the world's tax laws into an AI, because the tax code consists of formulas that determine the amount of tax owed, but ambiguity exists in some of those laws. That ambiguity is difficult to translate into code, which means that an AI will have trouble dealing with it—and that there will be full employment for tax lawyers for the foreseeable future.

Most human systems are even more ambiguous. It's hard to imagine an AI coming up with a real-world sports hack like curving a hockey stick. An AI would have to understand not just the rules of the game, but the physiology of the players, the aerodynamics of the stick and the puck, and so on and so on. It's not impossible, but it's still science fiction.

Probably the first place to look for AI-generated hacks are financial systems, since those rules are designed to be algorithmically tractable. We can imagine equipping an AI with all the world's financial information in real time, plus all of the world's laws and regulations, plus newsfeeds and anything else we think might be relevant; and then giving it the goal of "maximum profit legally." My guess is that this isn't very far off, and that the result will be all sorts of novel hacks. And there will probably be some hacks that are simply beyond human comprehension, which means we'll never realize they're happening.

This ambiguity ends up being a near-term security defense against AI hacking. We won't have AI-generated sports hacks until androids actually play the sports, or until a generalized AI is developed that is capable of understanding the world broadly, and with ethical nuance. It's similar with casino game hacks, or hacks of the legislative process. (Could an AI independently discover gerrymandering?) It'll be a long time before AIs will be capable of modeling and simulating the ways that people work, individually and in groups, and before they are capable of coming up with novel ways to hack legislative processes.

There's another issue, and one that I've largely ignored. Two different flavors of AI have emerged since the 1950s. The earliest AI research was in something called "symbolic AI," and it focused on simulating human understanding through a goal-oriented manipulation of elements, symbols, and facts. This has turned out to be incredibly hard, and not a lot of practical progress has been made in the past few decades. The other flavor is "neural networks." And while it is also an old idea, it has really only taken off in the last decade because of giant leaps in computation and data. This is the AI that ingests training data and gets better with experience that translates into even more data. It's gazillions of computational cycles and huge datasets that allow neural networks to do more things, like beat world-champion Go players and engage in plausible-sounding text conversations. That said, they do not "understand" language, or "think" in any real way. They basically make predictions based on what they've "learned" from the past: a kind of sophisticated statistical parroting. And while it is surprising is just how much a model like that can accomplish, there's a lot they can't do. And much of what I am writing about here could easily fall into that category.

But here's the thing about AI. Advances are discontinuous and counterintuitive. Things that seem easy turn out to be hard, and things that seem hard turn out to be easy. We don't know until the breakthrough occurs. When I was a college student in the early 1980s, we were taught that that the game of Go would never be mastered by a computer because of the enormous complexity of the game: not the rules, but the number of possible moves. And now a computer has beaten a human world champion. Some of it was due to advances in the science of AI, but most of the improvement was just from throwing more computing power at the problem.

So while a world filled with AI hackers is still a science-fiction problem, it's not a stupid science-fiction problem in a galaxy far far away. It's primarily tomorrow's problem, but we're seeing precursors of it today. We had better start thinking about enforceable, understandable, ethical solutions.

5   The Implications of AI Hackers

Hacking is as old as humanity. We are creative problem solvers. We are loophole exploiters. We manipulate systems to serve our interests. We strive for more influence, more power, more wealth. Power serves power, and hacking has forever been a part of that.

Still, no humans maximize their own interests without constraint. Even sociopaths are constrained by the complexities of society and their own contradictory impulses. They're concerned about their reputation, or punishment. They have limited time. These very human qualities limit hacking.

In his 2005 book, *The Corporation,* Joel Baken likened corporations to immortal sociopaths [85]. Because they are optimized profit-making machines, and try to optimize the welfare of their managers, they are more likely to hack systems for their own benefit. Still, corporations consist of people, and it's the people that make the decisions. Even in a world of AI systems dynamically setting prices—airline seats is a good example—this again limits hacking.

Hacking changed as everything became computerized. Because of their complexity, computers are hackable. And today, everything is a computer. Cars, appliances, phones: they're all computers. All of our social systems—finance, taxation, regulatory compliance, elections—are complex socio-technical systems involving computers and networks. This makes everything more susceptible to hacking.

Similarly, cognitive hacks are more effective when they're perpetrated by a computer. It's not that computers are inherently better at creating persuasive advertising, it's just that they can do it faster and more frequently—and can personalize advertisements down to the individual.

To date, hacking has exclusively been a human activity. Searching for new hacks requires expertise, time, creativity, and luck. When AIs start hacking, that will change. AIs won't be constrained in the same ways, or have the same limits, as people. They'll think like aliens. They'll hack systems in ways we can't anticipate.

Computers are much faster than people. A human process that might take months or years could get compressed to days, hours, or even seconds. What might happen when you feed an AI the entire US tax code and command it to figure out all of the ways one can minimize the amount of tax owed? Or, in the case of a multinational corporation, feed it the entire planet's tax codes? Will it figure out, without being told, that it's smart to incorporate in Delaware and register your ship in Panama? How many vulnerabilities—loopholes—will it find that we don't already know about? Dozens? Hundreds? Thousands? We have no idea, but we'll probably find out within the next decade.

We have societal systems that deal with hacks, but those were developed when hackers were humans, and reflect the pace of human hackers. We don't have any system of governance that can deal with hundreds—let alone thousands—of newly discovered tax loopholes. We simply can't patch the tax code that quickly. We aren't able to deal with people using Facebook to hack democracy, let alone what will happen when an AI does it. We won't be able to recover from an AI figuring out unanticipated but legal hacks of financial systems. At computer speeds, hacking becomes a problem that we as a society can no longer manage.

We already see this in computer-driven finance, with high-frequency trading and other computer-speed financial hacks. These aren't AI systems; they are automatic systems using human-generated rules and strategies. But they are able to execute at superhuman speeds, and this makes all the difference. It's a precursor of what's to come. As trading systems become more autonomous—as they move more towards AI-like behavior of discovering new hacks rather than just exploiting human-discovered ones—they will increasingly dominate the economy.

It's not just speed, but scale as well. Once AI systems start discovering hacks, they'll be able to exploit them at a scale we're not ready for. We're already seeing shadows of this. A free AI-driven service called Donotpay.com automates the process of contesting parking tickets. It has helped to overturn hundreds of thousands of tickets in cities like London and New York [86]. The service has expanded into other domains, helping users receive compensation for delayed airline flights, and to cancel a variety of services and subscriptions [87].

The AI persona bots discussed previously will be replicated in the millions across social media. They will be able to engage on the issues around the clock, sending billions of messages, long and short. Run rampant, they will overwhelm any actual online debate. What we will see as boisterous political debate will be bots arguing with other bots [88]. They'll artificially influence what we think is normal, what we think others think. This sort of manipulation is not what we think of when we laud the marketplace of ideas, or any democratic political process.

The increasing scope of AI systems also makes hacks more dangerous. AI is already making important decisions that affect our lives—decisions we used to believe were the exclusive purview of humans. AI systems make bail and parole decisions [89]. They help decide who receives bank loans [90]. They screen job candidates [91], applicants for college admission [92], and people who apply for government services [93]. They make decisions about the news we see on social media, which candidate's ads we see, and what people and topics surface to the top of our feeds. They make military targeting decisions.

As AI systems get more capable, society will cede more—and more important— decisions to them. AIs might choose which politicians a wealthy power broker will fund. They might decide who is eligible to vote. They might translate desired social outcomes into tax policies, or tweak the details of social programs. They already influence social outcomes; in the future they might explicitly decide them. Hacks of these systems will become more damaging. (We've seen early examples of this with "flash crashes" of the market [94].)

5.1 AI Hacks and Power

The hacks described in this essay will be perpetrated by the powerful against us. All of the AIs out there, whether they be on your laptop, online, or embodied in a robot, are programmed by other people, usually in their interests and not yours. An Internet-connected device like Alexa can mimic being a trusted friend to you. But never forget that it is designed to sell Amazon's products. And just as Amazon's website nudges you to buy its house brands instead of what might be higher-quality goods, it won't always be acting in your best interest. It will hack your trust in it for Amazon's goals.

Similarly, all of these hacks will further the interests those who control the AI software, the AI systems, and the robots. It won't just be that the individually tailored advertisement will persuade more successfully, it's that someone will pay for that extra bit of persuasion because it benefits them. When the AI figures out a novel tax loophole, it will do so because some wealthy person wants to exploit it in order to pay less taxes. Hacking largely reinforces existing power structures, and AIs will further reinforce that dynamic.

One example: AIBO is a robot dog marketed by Sony since 1999. The company released new and improved models every year through 2005, and over the next few years slowly discontinued support for older AIBOs. AIBO is pretty primitive by computing standards, but that didn't stop people from becoming emotionally attached to them. In Japan, people held funerals for their "dead" AIBOs [95].

In 2018, Sony started selling a new generation of AIBO. What's interesting here aren't the software advances that make it more pet-like, but the fact that it now requires cloud data storage to function [96]. This means that, unlike previous generations, Sony has the capability to modify or even remotely "kill" any AIBO. The first three years of cloud storage are free, and Sony has not announced what it will charge AIBO owners after that. Three years on, when AIBO owners have become emotionally attached to their pets, they will probably be able to charge a lot.

6 Defending Against AI Hackers

When AIs are able to discover new software vulnerabilities, it will be an incredible boon to government, criminal, and hobbyist hackers everywhere. They'll be able to use those vulnerabilities to hack computer networks around the world to great effect. It will put us all at risk.

But the same technology will be useful for the defense. Imagine how a software company might deploy a vulnerability finding AI on its own code. It could identify, and then patch, all—or, at least, all of the automatically discoverable—vulnerabilities in its products before releasing them. This feature might happen automatically as part of the development process. We could easily imagine a future when software vulnerabilities are a thing of the past. "Remember the early decades of computing, when hackers would use software vulnerabilities to hack systems? Wow, was that a crazy time."

Of course, the transition period will be dangerous. New code might be secure, but legacy code will still be vulnerable. The AI tools will be turned on code that's already released and in many cases unable to be patched. There, the attackers will use automatic vulnerability finding to their advantage. But over the long run, an AI technology that finds software vulnerabilities favors the defense.

It's the same when we turn to hacking broader social systems [97]. Sure, AI hackers might find thousands of vulnerabilities in the existing tax code. But the same technology can be used to evaluate potential vulnerabilities in any proposed tax law or tax ruling. The implications are game changing. Imagine a new tax law being tested in this manner. Someone—it could be a legislator, a watchdog organization, the press, anyone—could take the text of a bill and find all the exploitable vulnerabilities. This doesn't mean that vulnerabilities will get fixed, but it does mean that they'll become public and part of the policy debate. And they can in theory be patched before the rich and powerful find and exploit them. Here too, the transition period will be dangerous because of all of our legacy laws and rules. And again, defense will prevail in the end.

With respect to AI more generally, we don't know what the balance of power will be between offense and defense. AIs will be able to hack computer networks at computer speeds, but will defensive AIs be able to detect and effectively respond? AIs will hack our cognition directly, but can we deploy AIs to monitor our interactions and alert us that we're being manipulated? We don't know enough to make accurate predictions.

Ensuring that the defense prevails in these more general cases will require building resilient governing structures that can quickly and effectively respond to hacks. It won't do any good if it takes years to patch the tax code, or if a legislative hack becomes so entrenched that it can't politically be patched. Modern software is continually patched; you know how often you update your computers and phones. We need society's rules and laws to be similarly patchable.

This is a hard problem of modern governance, and well beyond the scope of this paper. It also isn't a substantially different problem than building governing structures that can operate at the speed of, and in the face of the complexity of, the information age. Legal scholars like Gillian Hadfield [98], Julie Cohen [99], Joshua Fairfield [100], and Jamie Susskind [101] are writing about this, and much more work is needed to be done.

The overarching solution here is people. What I've been describing is the interplay between human and computer systems, and the risks inherent when the computers start doing the part of humans. This, too, is a more general problem than AI hackers. It's also one that technologists and futurists are writing about. And while it's easy to let technology lead us into the future, we're much better off if we as a society decide what technology's role in our future should be.

This is all something we need to figure out now, before these AIs come online and start hacking our world.

Acknowledgments. I would like to thank Nicholas Anway, Robert Axelrod, Robert Berger, Vijay Bolina, Ben Buchanan, Julie Cohen, Steve Crocker, Kate Darling, Justin DeShazor, Simon Dickson, Amy Ertan, Gregory Falco, Harold Figueroa, Brett M. Frischmann, Abby Everett Jaques, Ram

Shankar Siva Kumar, David Leftwich, Gary McGraw, Andrew Odlyzko, Cirsten Paine, Rebecca J. Parsons, Anina Schwarzenbach, Victor Shepardson, Steve Stroh, Tarah Wheeler, and Lauren Zabierek, all of whom read and commented on a draft of this paper. I would also like to thank the RSA Conference, where I gave a keynote talk on this topic at their 2021 virtual event; the Belfer Center at the Harvard Kennedy School, under whose fellowship I completed much of the writing; and the 5th International Symposium on Cyber Security Cryptology and Machine Learning, where I presented this work as an invited talk.

References

1. The late hacker Jude Mihon (St. Jude) liked this definition: "Hacking is the clever circumvention of imposed limits, whether those limits are imposed by your government, your own personality, or the laws of Physics". Jude Mihon, Hackers Conference, Santa Rosa, CA (1996)
2. This is all from a book I am currently writing, probably to be published in 2022
3. Federal Trade Commission. Equifax data breach settlement: What you should know, 22 July 2019
4. Jagoda, N.: Lawmakers under pressure to pass benefits fix for military families, Hill, 14 November 2019
5. New York Times. Double Irish with a Dutch Sandwich (infographic), 28 April 2012
6. McCarthy, N.: Tax avoidance costs the U.S. nearly $200 billion every year (infographic), 23 March 2017
7. Thornton, A.: Broken promises: More special interest breaks and loopholes under the new tax law, 1 March 2018
8. Microsoft. Windows 10 lines of code, 12 January 2020
9. Matthews, D.: The myth of the 70,000-page federal tax code. Vox, 29 March 2017
10. IRS. Prepaid real property taxes may be deductible in 2017 if assessed and paid in 2017. IRS Advisory, 27 December 2017
11. Schneier, B.: What the terrorists want, Schneier on Security, 24 August 2006
12. Leahy, R.L.: How to Think About Terrorism. Psychology Today, 15 February 2018
13. Schneier, B.: A plea for simplicity, Schneier on Security, 19 November 1999
14. Robinette, P., et al.: Overtrust of robots in emergency evacuation scenarios. In: 2016 ACM/IEEE International Conference on Human-Robot Interaction, March 2016
15. Minsky, M. (ed.): Semantic Information Processing. The MIT Press, Cambridge (1968)
16. Air Force Research Lab. Artificial intelligence, 18 June 2020
17. Oppy, G., Dowe, D.: The Turing Test, Stanford Encyclopedia of Philosophy, Fall 2020
18. Darling, K.: The New Breed: What Our History with Animals Reveals about Our Future with Robots. Henry Holt & Co, New York (2021)
19. Weizenbaum, J.: ELIZA: a computer program for the study of natural language communication between man and machine. Commun. ACM 9, 36–45 (1996)
20. Vincent, J.: Women are more likely than men to say 'please' to their smart speaker. Verge (2019)
21. Nass, C., Moon, Y., Carney, P.: Are people polite to computers? Responses to computer-based interviewing systems. J. Appl. Soc. Psychol. 29, 1093–1109 (2006)
22. Moon, Y.: Intimate exchanges: using computers to elicit self-disclosure from consumers. J. Consum. Res. 26, 323–339 (2000)
23. Bessi, A., Ferrara, E.: Social bots distort the 2016 U.S. Presidential election online discussion. First Monday (2016)

24. Cadwalladr, C.: Robert Mercer: the big data billionaire waging war on mainstream media. Guardian (2017)
25. Bradshaw, S., Howard, P.N.: The global disinformation order: 2019 Global inventory of organised social media manipulation. Computational Propaganda Research Project (2019)
26. Bell, C., Coleman, A.: Khashoggi: Bots feed Saudi support after disappearance. BBC News (2018)
27. Kastrenakes, J.: The net neutrality comment period was a complete mess. Verge (2017)
28. Kao, J.: More than a million pro-repeal net neutrality comments were likely faked. Hackernoon (2017)
29. Miller, R.: AP's 'robot' journalists are writing their own stories now. Verge (2015)
30. Marr, B.: Artificial Intelligence Can Now Write Amazing Content—What Does That Mean For Humans? Forbes (2019)
31. Simonite, T.: Did a person write this headline, or a machine? Wired (2020)
32. Heaven, W.: IBM's debating AI just for a lot closer to being a useful tool. MIT Technol. Rev. (2020)
33. Weiss, M.: Deepfake bot submissions to federal public comment websites cannot be distinguished from human submissions. Technology Science (2019)
34. Rawnsley, A.: Right-wing media outlets duped by a Middle East propaganda campaign. Daily Beast (2020)
35. Sherwell, P.: China uses Taiwan for AI target practice to influence elections, Australian (2020)
36. Sample, I.: What are deepfakes—and how can you spot them? Guardian (2020)
37. Chessen, M.: The MADCOM Future. Atlantic Council (2017)
38. DiResta, R.: The supply of disinformation will soon be infinite. Atlantic (2020)
39. Gressin, S.: CEO imposter scams: Is the boss for real? Federal Trade Commission (2020)
40. Afifi-Sebet, K.: Fraudsters use AI voice manipulation to steal £200,000, IT Pro (2019)
41. Frischmann, B., Desai, D.: The Promise and Peril of Personalization, Center for Internet and Society. Stanford Law School (2016)
42. Sung, J.-Y., Guo, L., Rebecca, E., Henrik, G., Christensen, I.: My Roomba is Rambo': Intimate home appliances. UbiComp 2007: Ubiquitous Computing (2007)
43. Garreau, J.: Bots on the ground. Washington Post (2007)
44. Booth, S., et al.: Piggybacking robots: human-robot overtrust in university dormitory security. In: 2017 ACM/IEEE International Conference on Human-Robot Interaction (2017)
45. Reben, A., Paradison, J.: A mobile interactive robot for gathering structured social video, MIT Libraries (2011)
46. Heritage, S.: The eyes! The eyes! Why does Alita: Battle Angel look so creepy? Guardian (2019)
47. Turkle, S.: In good company. In: Wilks, Y. (ed.) Close Engagements with Artificial Companions. John Benjamin Publishing Company (2010)
48. Hartzog, W.: Unfair and deceptive robots. Maryland Law Review (2015)
49. Hanoch, Y., et al.: The robot made me do it: Human–robot interaction and risk-taking behavior, Online ahead of print (2020)
50. Darling, K.: Who's Johnny?' Anthropomorphic framing in human-robot interaction, integration, and policy. In: Lin, P., Abney, K., Jenkins, R. (eds.) Robot Ethics 2.0: From Autonomous Cars to Artificial Intelligence. Oxford Scholarship Online (2017)
51. Acheampong, F.A., Wenyu, C., Nunoo-Mensah, H.: Text-based emotion detection: Advances, challenges, and opportunities. Engineering Reports 2(7), e12189 (2020)
52. Lewis, T.: AI can read your emotions. Should it? Guardian (2019)
53. Khan, A.N., et al.: Deep learning framework for subject-independent emotion detection using wireless signals. PLoS ONE 16, e0242946 (2021)

54. Song, J., Alves-Foss, J.: The DARPA cyber grand challenge: a competitor's perspective. IEEE Secur. Privacy Mag. **13**(6), 72–76 (2015)
55. Simonite, T.: This bot hunts software bugs for the Pentagon. Wired (2020)
56. Schneier, B.: Artificial intelligence and the attack/defense balance. IEEE Secur. Privacy **16**, 96 (2018)
57. Saavedra, G.J., et al.: A review of machine learning applications in fuzzing. arXiv (2019)
58. Schneier, B.: Machine learning will transform how we detect software vulnerabilities. Schneier on Security (2018)
59. Economist. Law firms climb aboard the AI wagon (2018)
60. Adams, D.: The Hitchhiker's Guide to the Galaxy. BBC Radio 4 (1978)
61. Eykhoit, K., et al.: Robust Physical-World Attacks on Deep Learning Models. arXiv (2017)
62. Ashalye, A., et al.: Synthesizing robust adversarial examples. arXiv (2018)
63. Miller, G.A.: The magical number seven, plus or minus two: Some limits on our capacity for processing information. Psychol. Rev. **63**, 81 (1956)
64. Metz, C.: In two moves, AlphaGo and Lee Sedol redefined the future. Wired (2016)
65. Knight, W.: The dark secret at the heart of AI. MIT Technol. Rev. **120**, 51–61 (2017)
66. Waters, R.: Intelligent machines are asked to explain how their minds work. Financial Times (2017)
67. Turek, M.: Explainable artificial intelligence. DARPA (2021)
68. Gunning, D., Aha, D.W.: DARPA's Explainable Artificial Intelligence (XAI) Program. AI Mag. (2019)
69. A list of examples is here: https://vkrakovna.wordpress.com/2018/04/02/specification-gaming-examples-in-ai/
70. Kurach, K., et al.: Google research football: A novel reinforcement learning environment, arXiv (2019)
71. Popov, I., et al.: Data-efficient deep reinforcement learning for dexterous manipulation. arXiv (2017)
72. Ha, D.: Reinforcement learning for improving agent design (2018)
73. Amodei, D., et al.: Concrete Problems in AI Safety. arXiv (2016)
74. @Smingleigh. Twitter (2018)
75. Jaques, A.E.: The under specification problem and AI: For the love of god, don't send a robot out for coffee, unpublished manuscript (2021)
76. Russell, S.: 3 principles for creating safer AI. In: TED 2017 (2017)
77. Hotten, R.: Volkswagen: The scandal explained. BBC News (2015)
78. Ewing, J.: Researchers who exposed VW gain little reward from success, New York Times (2016)
79. Isaac, M.: How Uber deceives the authorities worldwide, New York Times (2017)
80. @mat_kelcey. Twitter (2017)
81. Tufekci, Z.: YouTube, the great equalizer, New York Times (2018). DiResta, R.: Up next: A better recommendation system. Wired (2018)
82. Statt, N.: Facebook reportedly ignored its own research showing algorithms divide users. Verge (2020)
83. Aron, J.: Google DeepMind AI outplays humans at video games. New Scientist (2015)
84. Gabriel, I.: Artificial intelligence, values and alignment. Minds Mach. **30**, 411–437 (2020)
85. Bakan, J.: The Corporation: The Pathological Pursuit of Profit and Power. Free Press , New York (2005)
86. Gibbs, S.: Chatbot lawyer overturns 160,000 parking tickets in London and New York, Guardian (2016)
87. Krieger, L.M.: Stanford student's quest to clear parking tickets leads to 'robot lawyers, Mercury News (2019)

88. California has a law requiring bots to identify themselves. Renee RiResta, "A new law makes bots identify themselves—that's the problem," Wired (2019)

89. Hao, K.: AI is sending people to jail—and getting it wrong. MIT Technol. Rev. (2019)

90. Townson, S.: AI can make bank loans more fair. Harvard Bus. Rev. (2020)

91. Murad, A.: The computers rejecting your job application. BBC News (2021)

92. Pangburn, D.J.: Schools are using software to help pick who gets in. What could go wrong? Fast Company (2019)

93. Fishman, T., Eggers, W.D., Kishnani, P.K.: AI-augmented human services: Using cognitive technologies to transform program delivery, Deloitte (2017)

94. Vaughan, L.: Flash Crash: A Trading Savant, a Global Manhunt, and the Most Mysterious Market Crash in History, Doubleday (2020)

95. Connellan, S.: Japanese Buddhist temple hosts funeral for over 100 Sony Aibo robot dogs, Mashable (2018)

96. Ry Crist. Yes, the robot dog ate your privacy, CNET (2019)

97. Falco, G., et al.: A master attack methodology for an AI-based automated attack planner for smart cities. IEEE Access (2018)

98. Hadfield, G.K.: Rules for a Flat World: Why Humans Invented Law and How to Reinvent It for a Complex Global Economy. Oxford University Press, Oxford (2016)

99. Cohen, J.E.: Between Truth and Power: The Legal Constructions of Informational Capitalism. Oxford University Press, Oxford (2019)

100. Fairfield, J.A.T.: Runaway Technology: Can Law Keep Up? Cambridge University Press, Cambridge (2021)

101. Susskind, J.: The Digital Republic: How to Govern Technology. Pegasus Books, unpublished manuscript (2021)

Turning HATE into LOVE: Compact Homomorphic Ad Hoc Threshold Encryption for Scalable MPC

Leonid Reyzin[1], Adam Smith[1], and Sophia Yakoubov[2(✉)]

[1] Boston University, Boston, USA
{reyzin,ads22}@bu.edu
[2] Aarhus University, Åbogade 34, 8200 Aarhus, Denmark
sophia.yakoubov@cs.au.dk

Abstract. In a public-key threshold encryption scheme, the sender produces a single ciphertext, and any $t + 1$ out of n intended recipients can combine their partial decryptions to obtain the plaintext. *Ad hoc* threshold encryption (ATE) schemes require no correlated setup, enabling each party to simply generate its own key pair. In this paper, we initiate a systematic study of the possibilities and limitations of ad-hoc threshold encryption, and introduce a key application to scalable multiparty computation (MPC).

Assuming indistinguishability obfuscation (iO), we construct the first ATE that is *sender-compact*—that is, with ciphertext length independent of n. This allows for succinct communication once public keys have been shared. We also show a basic lower bound on the extent of key sharing: every sender-compact scheme requires that recipients of a message know the public keys of other recipients in order to decrypt.

We then demonstrate that threshold encryption that is ad hoc and *homomorphic* can be used to build efficient large-scale fault-tolerant multiparty computation (MPC) on a minimal (star) communication graph. We explore several homomorphic schemes, in particular obtaining one iO-based ATE scheme that is both sender-compact and homomorphic: each recipient can derive what they need for evaluation from a single short ciphertext. In the resulting MPC protocol, once the public keys have been distributed, all parties in the graph except for the central server send and receive only short messages, whose size is independent of the number of participants.

Taken together, our results chart new possibilities for threshold encryption and raise intriguing open questions.

Keywords: Threshold encryption · Obfuscation · Setup freeness · Secure computation

L. Reyzin—Supported in part by NSF grant 1422965.
A. Smith—Supported in part by NSF awards IIS-1447700 and AF-1763786 and a Sloan Foundation Research Award.
S. Yakoubov—Work done while at Boston University, and was supported in part by NSF grant 1422965.

© Springer Nature Switzerland AG 2021
S. Dolev et al. (Eds.): CSCML 2021, LNCS 12716, pp. 361–378, 2021.
https://doi.org/10.1007/978-3-030-78086-9_27

1   Introduction

A public key threshold encryption (TE) scheme gives one the ability to generate a ciphertext that is decryptable by any $t + 1$ out of n intended recipients, while remaining semantically secure against any smaller group. Among other things, it enables tasks such as electronic voting [16,17] and round-efficient multiparty computation (MPC) [2,19], where only $t + 1$ colluding parties should be able to learn information about others' inputs.

One simple way to construct threshold encryption is to use any encryption scheme, with each of n recipients having independently generated keys. To encrypt, the sender applies $(t+1, n)$-secret sharing to the message, and encrypts each share with the key of the respective recipient; we call this *share-and-encrypt*.

Share-and-encrypt has the advantage of requiring no master secret and no correlated setup among the recipients. A basic public-key infrastructure is all that is required. We will call TE schemes with this property *ad hoc* threshold encryption (ATE). An additional advantage of this simple approach is that the length of information sent to each recipient is independent of the number of recipients (since each recipient needs to see only the part of the ciphertext relevant to them). We will call TE with this property *recipient-compact*. It is, however, not *sender-compact*, because the length of information sent by the sender is dependent on the number of recipients. This missing feature is particularly desirable when the sender, rather than unicasting information to each recipient, broadcasts it—for example, by using an intermediate server. Prior to this paper, whether sender-compactness is achievable for ad hoc TE was an open problem.

1.1   Our Contributions

In this paper, we initiate a systematic study of the possibilities and limitations of ad hoc threshold encryption, and introduce a key application to scalable MPC. We start with a definitional framework that systematizes the various options for functionality and security in Sect. 2.

As our main feasibility result (Sect. 3), we show that sender-compactness is, in principle, achievable.

Contribution 1 (Theorem 1). *We describe the first sender-compact ad hoc threshold encryption scheme.*

The price we pay for sender-compactness is that we use indistinguishability obfuscation (iO), and that every sender needs a public key. This key needs to be known for decryption, and has a component whose size grows polynomially with n. However, public keys are published once, whereas ciphertexts are created and transmitted multiple times, so having the burden of size in the public keys instead of the ciphertexts can be a big advantage when the sender is already known to the recipient. Moreover, in some uses of TE, decryption is delayed, and the linear component of the public key is not needed by every recipient (for example, if TE is used for backup storage that is usually not accessed; see Sect. 1.2 for another example).

We also show a fundamental limitation of sender-compact schemes: recipients need to know the public keys of other recipients. Specifically, we define (in Sect. 2) a TE property we call recipient-set-obliviousness, which demands that the recipient algorithms be run without the public keys of other recipients.

Contribution 2 *We show that recipient-set-obliviousness and sender-compactness cannot be simultaneously satisfied.*

We formally state and prove this result in the full version of this paper.

Threshold encryption is well suited for applications to multi-party computation (MPC), because it allows multiple parties to learn shares of a value. Building MPC protocols is much easier when encryption also allows for some homomorphic computation, so that operations on unopened ciphertexts can be used to operate on the underlying plaintexts.

We demonstrate, in Sect. 4, how to build recipient-compact ad hoc threshold encryption schemes that support limited homomorphism. We use the acronym "HATE" to describe ATE schemes that support homomorphism.

Contribution 3 (Theorems 3, 4 and 5). *We describe three recipient-compact HATE schemes that support additive homomorphism.*

The first two of these schemes are based on standard assumptions. They follow the share-and-encrypt paradigm, and allow homomorphism because of a careful combination of specific encryption and secret sharing schemes. One of these schemes keeps messages in the exponent, and thus supports only limited message spaces. Choosing a secret sharing scheme with the right properties is crucial to enable the scheme to be ad hoc, recipient-compact, and homomorphic. We use Shamir and CRT secret sharing, both of which are additively homomorphic over multiple inputs, do not require pre-distributed correlated randomness, and have compact shares.

These schemes are recipient-set-oblivious and therefore cannot be sender-compact. However, they have an additional property on top of recipient compactness, which we call *recipient-local evaluation*: namely, not only does a ciphertext consists of compact recipient-wise components, but also each recipient can perform homomorphic evaluation locally on its own components.

The third recipient-compact additively homomorphic ATE has the advantage that a fresh ciphertext (before homomorphic evaluation) is sender-compact, but at the price of relying on iO. We obtain this scheme by modifying our iO-based scheme from Sect. 3. Prior to homomorphic evaluation, a different ciphertext (of size independent of n) for each recipient must be extracted from the sender-compact ciphertext. As in the first two schemes, homomorphic evaluation can be performed locally on these per-recipient ciphertexts, giving the scheme *recipient-local evaluation*. This scheme supports only small message spaces.

Open Questions About Ad hoc Threshold Encryption. Our systematic study and results raise several intriguing open problems about ad hoc threshold encryption. First, are there sender-compact ad hoc threshold encryption schemes with constant-size public keys (independent of n)? Are there such schemes which do not require a sender public key? Can such schemes be based on more standard assumptions than iO? Are there ad hoc threshold encryption schemes with ciphertexts that remain compact even after homomorphic evaluation? Is it possible to achieve full homomorphism? (We note that share-and-encrypt is not known to solve this problem: in principle, a multi-input fully homomorphic threshold secret sharing scheme can be combined with fully homomorphic encryption to give fully homomorphic ad hoc threshold encryption; however, to the best of our knowledge, all known constructions of multi-input fully homomorphic threshold secret sharing require pre-distributed correlated randomness.)

The importance of our results and these questions is reinforced by their usefulness for scalable MPC, which we discuss next.

1.2 Application: One-Server, Fault-Tolerant MPC

Consider a service that has an app with a large smartphone user base. Suppose the service wants to collect aggregate usage statistics, but (for regulatory compliance, or for good publicity, or for fear of becoming a target for attackers and investigators) does not wish to learn the data of any individual user.

A traditional MPC solution is not suitable for this setting, because the phones do not communicate directly with one another, and because we cannot expect every phone to remain engaged for the duration of the protocol, as phones may go out of signal range or run out of charge. We call MPC protocols in this setting Large-scale One-server Vanishing-participants Efficient MPC (LOVE MPC).

As we already mentioned, threshold encryption can be used for MPC. Ad hoc threshold encryption is particularly well-suited for this setting: by not having a setup phase, it eliminates an important bottleneck, because running a multi-user setup protocol with vanishing participants may present problems. In particular, HATE schemes can be used to build LOVE MPC for the honest-but-curious setting as follows: each phone sends an encryption of its input to the server, who homomorphically combines them, sends the result out for decryption by all users, and successfully uses the partial decryptions to get the correct result as long as more than t phones respond.

Using our HATE constructions, we derive a 3-round LOVE MPC for addition (described in the full version of this paper). This improves on the round complexity of prior work by Bonawitz *et al.* [5], who proposed a 5-round protocol. (We also prove, in the full version of this paper, that three rounds and some setup—e.g. a PKI—is necessary for LOVE MPC.)

The resulting LOVE MPC is based on standard assumptions when using the HATE constructions of Sect. 4.1, and the linear per-user communication we obtain asymptotically matches the per-user communication of Bonawitz *et al.* [5]. (Per-user communication was improved to constant by subsequent work of Bell *et al.* [4], but still at the cost of 5 rounds as opposed to our 3.) Additionally, at the price of using our iO-based HATE construction (Section Sect. 4.2), we obtain constant per-user communication, which is asymptotically better than the protocol of Bonawitz et al. [5] and asymptotically matches the protocol of Bell et al. [4] (but, of course, at very high concrete costs due to the use of iO).

1.3 Related Work

Threshold Encryption. Known sender-compact threshold encryption schemes are not ad hoc: they require some correlated setup. For instance, a sender-compact threshold variant of ElGamal, due to Desmedt and Frankel [13] (and described in the full version of this paper) requires a setup phase for every new set of n recipients. Delerablée and Pointcheval [12] designed a sender-compact scheme based on bilinear maps with a reduced setup requirement. In their scheme, the sender can pick the set of n recipients dynamically; however, each recipient's secret key must be derived from a common master secret key, so this scheme is not ad hoc.

On the other hand, known ad hoc threshold encryption schemes are not sender-compact. The simple share-and-encrypt construction discussed above requires the sender to send an amount of information that is linear in n. Daza et al. [11] use an interpolation-based trick to reduce the ciphertext size to $O(n-t)$ (and subsequently use bilinear maps to give a matching CCA2-secure construction [10]); however, they leave open the problem of further lowering the ciphertext size.

Ad hoc *fully homomorphic* threshold encryption was explored by Boneh et al. [6] and Badrinarayanan et al. [2], as well as by Dodis et al. [14] as "spooky" encryption; however, their schemes are not even recipient-compact, let alone sender-compact.

Ad Hoc Broadcast Encryption. Ad hoc sender-compact encryption has been achieved in the context of broadcast encryption, which is a special case of threshold encryption with the threshold $t = 0$, giving any one recipient the ability to decrypt. Specifically, Boneh and Zhandry [7] construct what they call *distributed* broadcast encryption form indistinguishability obfuscation (iO). Their construction has the downside of long (polynomial in the number n of recipients) public keys. Later, Ananth et al. [1] shrink the public keys at the cost of changing the assumption to differing-inputs obfuscation (diO). Zhandry [21] improves on these results, shrinking the public keys and replacing the iO assumption with witness PRFs, but still requiring $t = 0$.

2 Threshold Encryption (TE) Definitions

A threshold encryption scheme [13] is an encryption scheme where a message is encrypted to a group $\mathcal{R}$ of recipients, and decryption must be done collaboratively by at least $t + 1$ members of that group. (This can be defined more broadly for general access structures, but we limit ourselves to the threshold access structure in this paper.)

Classically, threshold cryptography involves a secret-shared secret key, which fixes the set of all key-holders. That is, a single Setup operation suffices only to establish a single set of recipients, and the sender is not allowed to specify a recipient set $\mathcal{R}$ at encryption time.

Dynamic threshold encryption [12] allows a sender to choose the set of recipients dynamically at encryption time, as described in the Enc algorithm of Sect. 2.1. In a dynamic threshold encryption scheme, a single Setup operation suffices for the establishment of arbitrarily many groups of recipients.

However, dynamic threshold encryption schemes still require trusted setup, where a central authority distributes correlated randomness to all parties. In an *ad hoc* threshold encryption (ATE) scheme, there is no need for any trusted central authority or master secret key msk. We call a threshold encryption scheme ad hoc if a public-private key pair can be generated without knowledge of a master secret key; that is, if each party is able to generate its keys independently.

In this paper, we additionally consider *keyed-sender* threshold encryption schemes. In a keyed-sender threshold encryption scheme, in order to encrypt a message, the sender must use its own *secret key* in addition to the recipients' public keys (unlike in typical public-key encryption, where encryption does not require the knowledge of any secrets). Similarly, in order to decrypt the ciphertext, recipients need to use the sender's public key in addition to their secret keys.

2.1 Threshold Encryption Syntax

A threshold encryption scheme consists of five algorithms, described in this section. This description is loosely based on the work of Daza *et al.* [10], but we modify the input and output parameters to focus on those we require in our constructions, with some additional parameters discussed in the text. Parameters in purple (namely, msk) are absent from ad hoc schemes; parameters in blue (namely, sk_{Sndr} and pk_{Sndr}) are present only in keyed-sender schemes (for readers seeing this text in monochrome, we give text explanations in addition to colors). Keyed-sender schemes additionally require a sixth algorithm, $\mathsf{KeyGen}_{\mathsf{Sndr}}$.

$\mathsf{Setup}(1^\lambda, t) \to (\mathsf{params}, \mathsf{msk})$ is a randomized algorithm that takes in a security parameter λ as well as a threshold t and sets up the global public parameters params for the system.

If the scheme is not ad hoc, Setup also sets up the master secret key msk for key generation.

For simplicity, we provide Setup with the threshold t, and assume that t is encoded in params. However, in *t-flexible* schemes, t may be decided by each sender at encryption time, and should then be an input to Enc (and encoded in the resulting ciphertext). In keyed-sender schemes (where the sender must use their secret key to encrypt and recipients must use the sender's public key to decrypt), t may also be specified in the sender's public key.

$\mathsf{KeyGen}(\mathsf{params}, \mathsf{msk}) \to (pk, sk)$ is a randomized key generation algorithm that takes in the global public parameters params (and, if the scheme is not ad hoc, the master secret key msk) and returns a recipient's public-private key pair.

$\mathsf{KeyGen}_{\mathsf{Sndr}}(\mathsf{params}, \mathsf{msk}) \to (pk_{\mathsf{Sndr}}, sk_{\mathsf{Sndr}})$ is a randomized algorithm present in keyed-sender schemes only; it takes in the global public parameters params (and, if the scheme is not ad hoc, the master secret key msk) and returns a sender's public-private key pair where the private key is used to facilitate encryption by the sender, the public key is used to facilitate decryption of messages from the sender.

$\mathsf{Enc}(\mathsf{params}, sk_{\mathsf{Sndr}}, \{pk_i\}_{i \in \mathcal{R}, |\mathcal{R}| > t}, m) \to c$ is a randomized encryption algorithm that encrypts a message m to a set of public keys belonging to the parties in the intended recipient set $\mathcal{R}$ in such a way that any size-$(t+1)$ subset of the recipient set should jointly be able to decrypt. We assume t is specified within params, but (if the scheme is keyed-sender) it may also be specified within the sender's public key, or (if the scheme is t-flexible) it may be specified on the fly as an input to Enc itself.

$\mathsf{PartDec}(\mathsf{params}, pk_{\mathsf{Sndr}}, \{pk_i\}_{i \in \mathcal{R}}, sk_j, c) \to d_j$ is an algorithm that uses a secret key sk_j belonging to one of the intended recipients (that is, for $j \in \mathcal{R}$) to get a partial decryption d_j of the ciphertext c. This partial decryption can then be combined with t other partial decryptions to recover the message.

$\mathsf{FinalDec}(\mathsf{params}, pk_{\mathsf{Sndr}}, \{pk_i\}_{i \in \mathcal{R}}, c, \{d_i\}_{i \in \mathcal{R}' \subseteq \mathcal{R}, |\mathcal{R}'| > t}) \to m$ is an algorithm that combines $t + 1$ or more partial decryptions to recover the message m.

In a sender-compact scheme, the size of the ciphertext c is independent of the number of recipients n. In a recipient-compact scheme, $\mathsf{PartDec}$ requires only a portion c_i of the ciphertext c, where the size of c_i is independent of n.

2.2   Threshold Encryption Flexibility

Not all threshold encryption schemes allow/require all of the algorithm inputs described in Sect. 2.1. Sometimes disallowing an input can make the scheme less flexible, but, on the other hand, sometimes schemes that do not rely on certain inputs have an advantage.

More Flexibility: Unneeded Inputs. Ad hocness is an example of gaining an advantage by eliminating dependence on an input. Ad hoc schemes do not use the master secret key msk, and thus do not require a trusted central authority (which in many scenarios might not exist).

Another example of gaining an advantage by eliminating an input is *recipient-set-obliviousness*. Requiring both decryption algorithms ($\mathsf{PartDec}$ and $\mathsf{FinalDec}$) to be aware of the set of public keys belonging to individuals in the set $\mathcal{R}$ of recipients can be limiting.

Definition 1 (Threshold   Encryption: Recipient-Set-Obliviousness).
We call a threshold encryption scheme recipient-set-oblivious *if neither partial decryption nor final decryption use* $\{pk_i\}_{i \in \mathcal{R}}$.

It may seem that a recipient-set-oblivious scheme should require less communication, since the sender would never need to communicate $\mathcal{R}$ to the recipients. However, in the full version of this paper we show that a recipient-set-oblivious ATE scheme cannot be sender-compact.

More Flexibility: Additional Inputs. In describing the threshold encryption algorithms, for the most part we assumed that the threshold t was fixed within the global public parameters params (or, in a keyed-sender scheme, in the sender's public key). However, some schemes (such as share-and-encrypt) allow the sender to choose t at encryption time; we call such schemes *t-flexible*.

2.3 Threshold Encryption Security

The threshold encryption security definition is two-fold. We require *semantic security*, informally meaning that encryptions of two messages of the same size should be indistinguishable. We use the semantic security definition of Boneh *et al.* [6] for threshold encryption schemes, modified to support the keyed-sender property. We also require *simulatability*, informally meaning that given a ciphertext corresponding to one of two messages, partial decryptions can be simulated in such a way as to cause the ciphertext to decrypt to either of the two messages. The latter requirement is useful for MPC applications.

Both for semantic security and simulatability, there are three notions of security we consider, which differ according to the point in the security game at which the adversary must commit to the set of corrupt parties $\mathcal{C}$, and the set of challenge ciphertext recipients $\mathcal{R}$. From weakest to strongest, these are *super-static*, *static* and *adaptive* security. In *super-static* security, which is what our obfuscation-based construction achieves, the adversary specifies both $\mathcal{C}$ and $\mathcal{R}$ before seeing the public keys. In *static* security, which is what our other constructions achieve, the adversary specifies $\mathcal{C}$ before seeing the public keys, but can specify $\mathcal{R}$ later, at the same time as the two challenge messages, m_R and m_L. In *adaptive* security, the adversary specifies $\mathcal{C}$ having seen the public keys, and can specify $\mathcal{R}$ at the same time as the two challenge messages, as in static security.

The formal definitions of threshold encryption security are straightofrward given the above discussion, but are too lengthy given the space constraints. We therefore give them in the full version of this paper.

2.4 Threshold Encryption with Homomorphism

Homomorphic ad hoc threshold encryption (HATE) can be particularly useful in applications to multi-party computation.

Definition 2 (Threshold Encryption: Homomorphism). *Let $\mathcal{F}$ be a class of functions, each taking a sequence of valid messages and returning a valid message. An $\mathcal{F}$-homomorphic threshold encryption scheme additionally has the following algorithm:*

$\mathsf{Eval}(\mathsf{params}, \{pk_i\}_{i \in \mathcal{R}}, [c_1, \dots, c_\ell], f) \to c^*$ *is an algorithm that, given ℓ cipher-texts and a function $f \in \mathcal{F}$, computes a new ciphertext c^* which decrypts to $f(m_1, \dots, m_\ell)$ where each c_q, $q \in [1, \dots, \ell]$ decrypts to m_q.*

Informally, Eval should be *correct*, meaning that decryption should lead to the correct plaintext message $f(m_1, \dots, m_\ell)$.

2.5   Threshold Encryption Compactness

Compactness Without Homomorphism. As described in the introduction, we say that a threshold encryption scheme is *sender-compact* (or, in other words, that it has *sender-compact encryption*) if the size of a ciphertext is independent of the number of recipients. We say that it is *recipient-compact* (or, in other words, that it has *recipient-compact encryption*) if the portion of the ciphertext required by each recipient to produce their partial decryption is independent of the number of recipients. Of course, if a threshold encryption scheme is sender-compact, then it is also recipient-compact, since each receiver can use the entire (compact) ciphertext to partially decrypt. However, the converse is not necessarily true. Even if a scheme is not sender-compact, it can be recipient-compact if the ciphertext c can be split into compact components $c = \{c_i\}_{i \in \mathcal{R}}$ such that every recipient can run $\mathsf{PartDec}$ given just one component c_i.

Compactness With Homomorphism. When we consider homomorphic threshold encryption, a fresh ciphertext c may look different than a ciphertext c^* which Eval outputs. Of course, the size of c^* should not grow linearly with the number ℓ of inputs to f; otherwise, homomorphism becomes unnecessary, and c^* could simply consist of a concatenation of the input ciphertexts.

Notice that this does not preclude ciphertext growth. Even if a fresh ciphertext has size independent of n, the output of Eval may grow with n. We introduce some new terminology to handle this: we say that a homomorphic threshold encryption scheme has *compact evaluation* if the output of Eval has size independent of n, and that it has *recipient-compact evaluation* if the output of Eval can be split into recipient-wise compact components. Additionally, we say that a homomorphic threshold encryption scheme has *recipient-local evaluation* if it has *recipient-compact encryption* and evaluation is performed component-wise, with Eval taking one recipient's component of each input ciphertext and producing that recipient's compact component of the output ciphertext.

All of our schemes in Sect. 4 have recipient-compact encryption and recipient-local evaluation; the scheme in Sect. 4.2 additionally has sender-compact encryption.

In a setting where multiple senders send ciphertexts to a single server, who homomorphically computes on the ciphertexts and sends (the relevant parts of) the output of Eval to receivers, it is enough to have a sender-compact encryption and recipient-compact evaluation, even if the overall output of Eval is long. These properties suffice for reducing bandwidth, because the size of every message transmitted between two parties is independent of the number of recipients.

If, instead, we have a setting where senders send ciphertexts directly to receivers who then compute on those ciphertexts themselves, sender-compact encryption is less important, and recipient-local evaluation becomes key. Each sender must send something to each receiver anyway (instead of sending only one thing to the server), and in a setting with direct peer-to-peer channels, it becomes unimportant whether those things are all the same sender-compact ciphertext, or receiver-wise components of a recipient-compact ciphertext.

3   Sender-Compact Ad Hoc Threshold Encryption

In this section, we describe a sender-compact ATE. In the share-and-encrypt construction, the total ciphertext size is $\Theta(n)$, because each recipient gets an encryption of a different share. A natural approach is to compress the ciphertext using obfuscation: namely, instead of using the encrypted shares as the ciphertext, we can try to use an obfuscated program that *outputs* one encrypted share at a time given an appropriate input (such as a short symmetric encryption of the message, a recipient secret key, and proof of the recipient membership in the recipient set $\mathcal{R}$).

However, this strategy fails to achieve sender-compact ciphertexts, because the obfuscated program remains linear in the size of the threshold t. The reason is that, within the security proof, in one of the hybrids we are forced to hardcode t secret shares in the program, and the obfuscated program must be of the same size in all hybrid games.

Therefore, instead of putting an obfuscated program in the ciphertext, each sender obfuscates a program as part of key generation. This program becomes the sender's public key. While it is long (polynomial in the in the number of recipients n), it needs to be created and disseminated only once, as opposed to a ciphertext, which depends on the message. Notice that having this obfuscated program as the sender's public key makes our ATE scheme *keyed-sender*, meaning that in order to encrypt a message the sender must use its secret key, and in order to decrypt a message, recipients must use the sender's public key.

One can think of the obfuscated program in the sender's public key as a "horcrux".[1] The sender stores some of its secrets in this obfuscated program, and when encrypting a message, the sender includes just enough information in the ciphertext that the obfuscated program can do the rest of the work.

Once we put the obfuscated program in the sender's public key, we run into the issue that the outputs of the program on the challenge ciphertext cannot be dependent on the challenge message. This is because in the proof of security, the challenge message is chosen dynamically by the adversary, whereas the program is obfuscated by the challenger at the beginning of the game. In some hybrids, the outputs corresponding to the challenge message must be hardcoded in the program; so, they cannot depend on the actual message, which can be picked after the program is fixed. Therefore, instead of returning secret shares of the

---

[1] A "horcrux" is a piece of one's soul stored in an external object, according to the fantasy series Harry Potter [20].

challenge message, the program returns shares of a random mask which is used to encrypt the message.

Specifically, the program that each sender obfuscates takes as input a random nonce—together with the sender's signature on that nonce—and a recipient's secret key. The program checks the signature, and that the recipient's secret key matches one of the public keys to which the sender addressed this ciphertext (this "addressing" is performed implicitly, via the same signature). Note that checking membership in the set of recipients is important: otherwise any party could extract a secret share of the message. If the checks pass, the program outputs a secret share of a PRF output on the random nonce. The actual message is symmetrically encrypted with that PRF output.

The obfuscated program that makes up the sender public key is formally described in Algorithm 1, and the obfuscation-based ATE is described in Construction 1. It uses an indistinguishability obfuscator iO, puncturable pseudorandom function PPRF, a secret sharing scheme SS, a constrained signature SIG, and a length-doubling pseudorandom generator PRG with domain $\{0,1\}^\lambda$ and range in $\{0,1\}^{2\lambda}$. We define all of these primitives in the full version of this paper.

Algorithm 1. $f_{k_w, k_{\mathsf{Share}}, \mathsf{SIG}.pk}(\overrightarrow{pv} = \{pv_i\}_{i \in \mathcal{R}}, \mathsf{idx}, sv, \mathsf{nonce}, \sigma)$

The following values are hardcoded:

$\mathsf{params} = (\lambda, n, t)$, where
  λ is the security parameter,
  n is the number of recipients, and
  t is the threshold.

k_w, a secret PPRF key used to recover the mask w from nonce nonce
k_{Share}, a secret PPRF key used to secret share the mask w
$\mathsf{SIG}.pk$, a signature verification key

The following values are expected as input:

$\overrightarrow{pv} = \{pv_i \in \{0,1\}^{2\lambda}\}_{i \in \mathcal{R}}$, lexicographically ordered public values
idx, an index
$sv \in \{0,1\}^\lambda$, a secret value
nonce
σ, a signature

if $(\overrightarrow{pv}[\mathsf{idx}] = \mathsf{PRG}(sv))$ and $(\mathsf{SIG.Verify}(\mathsf{SIG}.pk, (\overrightarrow{pv}, \mathsf{nonce}), \sigma))$ **then**
  $w \leftarrow \mathsf{PPRF}_{k_w}(\mathsf{nonce})$
  $r \leftarrow \mathsf{PPRF}_{k_{\mathsf{Share}}}(\mathsf{nonce})$
  $[w]_{\mathsf{idx}} \leftarrow \mathsf{SS.Share}(w, n, t; r)[\mathsf{idx}]$ {This gives the idxth secret share of w}
  return $[w]_{\mathsf{idx}}$

Informally, in order to prove security, we will have to show that given an obfuscation of this program, an adversary who has only t or fewer secret keys from the recipient set will not be able to tell the difference between an encryption of a message m_R and an encryption of a different message m_L. Our proof will need to puncture k_w and k_{Share} on the challenge nonce in order to remove any

Let the public parameters params $= (\lambda, n, t)$ consist of the security parameter λ, the number of recipients n, and the threshold t.

KeyGen(params):
>{The following generates the "receiver" keys.}
>$sv \leftarrow \{0, 1\}^\lambda$
>$pv \leftarrow \mathsf{PRG}(sv) \in \{0, 1\}^{2\lambda}$
>return (pv, sv)

KeyGen$_{\mathsf{Sndr}}$(params):
>{The following generates the "sender" keys.}
>$(\mathsf{SIG}.pk, \mathsf{SIG}.sk) \leftarrow \mathsf{SIG}.\mathsf{KeyGen}(1^\lambda)$
>$k_w \leftarrow \mathsf{PPRF}.\mathsf{KeyGen}(1^\lambda)$
>{This PPRF key will be used to produces the mask w for the message. Its output is assumed to be in the message space group.}
>$k_{\mathsf{Share}} \leftarrow \mathsf{PPRF}.\mathsf{KeyGen}(1^\lambda)$
>{This PPRF key will be used to produce the randomness for secret sharing w. We slightly abuse PPRF notation above; the size of w and the size of the randomness needed to secret share w might be very different. We simply assume that either the keys used are of different sizes (that is, k_{Share} might actually consist of multiple keys), or that the PPRF is chained in the appropriate way to produce a sufficiently large amount of randomness. We assume that the output of PPRF with k_w is in some group $\mathcal{G}$ which contains the message space, and that the output of PPRF with k_{Share} is of whatever form the randomness for SS.Share should take.}
>$\mathsf{ObfFunc} \leftarrow \mathsf{iO}(f_{k_w, k_{\mathsf{Share}}, \mathsf{SIG}.pk})$
>return $(pk_{\mathsf{Sndr}} = \mathsf{ObfFunc}, sk_{\mathsf{Sndr}} = (\mathsf{SIG}.sk, k_w))$

Enc(params, $sk_{\mathsf{Sndr}} = (\mathsf{SIG}.sk, k_w)$, $\overrightarrow{pv} = \{pv_i\}_{i \in \mathcal{R}, |\mathcal{R}| \geq t}$, m):
>nonce $\leftarrow \mathsf{PPRF}.\mathsf{domain}$
>$e = (\mathsf{PPRF}_{k_w}(\mathsf{nonce}) + m)$
>$\sigma \leftarrow \mathsf{SIG}.\mathsf{Sign}(\mathsf{SIG}.sk, (\overrightarrow{pv}, \mathsf{nonce}))$
>return $c = (\mathsf{nonce}, e, \sigma)$

PartDec(params, $pk_{\mathsf{Sndr}} = \mathsf{ObfFunc}$, $\overrightarrow{pv} = \{pv_i\}_{i \in \mathcal{R}}$, sv_i, $c = (\mathsf{nonce}, e, \sigma)$):
>Let idx be the index of the public value corresponding to the secret value sv_i in a lexicographic ordering of $\{pv_i\}_{i \in \mathcal{R}}$
>$d_i \leftarrow \mathsf{ObfFunc}(\overrightarrow{pv}, \mathsf{idx}, sv_i, \mathsf{nonce}, \sigma)$
>return d_i

FinalDec(params, $c = (\mathsf{nonce}, e, \sigma)$, $\{d_i\}_{i \in \mathcal{R}' \subset \mathcal{R}}$):
>$w \leftarrow \mathsf{SS}.\mathsf{Reconstruct}(\{d_i\}_{i \in \mathcal{R}' \subset \mathcal{R}})$
>$m \leftarrow e - w$
>return m

Construction 1: Obfuscation-Based ATE

information about the challenge plaintext from the program. For the proof to go through given the guarantees of iO, it is crucial that, as we change the plaintext, the output does not change for any input—in particular, even if the adversary is able to forge a signature that ties the ciphertext to a wrong set of public keys. We ensure this property by using a constrained signature scheme SIG, so that we can guarantee (in an appropriate hybrid) that a signature tying the ciphertext to a wrong set of public keys does not exist. This means that the public verification key (which is incorporated into the obfuscated program) is of size polynomial in n.

Theorem 1. *The obfuscation-based ATE (Construction 1) is (n, t)-super-statically secure for any polynomial n, t, as long as* iO *is a secure indistinguishability obfuscator,* PPRF *is a secure puncturable* PRF, SS *is a secure (n, t)-secret* *sharing scheme,* SIG *is a constrained signature scheme, and* PRG *is a secure pseudorandom generator.*

We prove Theorem 1 in the full version of this paper. Note that all the tools this construction uses can be obtained from indistinguishability obfuscation (with complexity leveraging), and one-way functions.

3.1 t-Flexibility

For simplicity, we describe obfuscation-based ATE in a way that is not by default t-flexible, since the threshold t is fixed within the sender's public key. However, it can be made t-flexible in a very straightforward way, simply by including t as part of the (signed) input to the obfuscated program.

3.2 Reducing the Public Key Size

In the construction described above, the sender's public key size is polynomial in the number n of recipients. We can decrease the size of the public key by relying on differing-inputs obfuscation (diO) [1,3] instead of indistinguishability obfuscation (iO). If we do, then we can modify the obfuscated program to take a Merkle hash commitment to the set of recipients' public keys, instead of the entire list; additionally, we will be able to replace constrained signatures with any signature scheme. This will enable us to go from $poly(n)$-size public keys to $poly(t)$-size public keys. (We still need $poly(t)$ because that is the number of secret shares we must hard-code in the program in one of the hybrids in our security proof.)

4 Recipient-Compact Homomorphic Ad Hoc Threshold Encryption

In this section, we describe three recipient-compact HATE constructions. In addition to recipient-compactness, all three of these schemes have *recipient-local evaluation*, meaning that each recipient can perform evaluation locally given just their compact component of the ciphertext.

Two of them (Sect. 4.1) are based on the share-and-encrypt paradigm. These are recipient-set-oblivious, but are not sender-compact. The last (Sect. 4.2) achieves sender-compactness by combining share-and-encrypt with the obfuscation-based sender-compact ATE from Sect. 3. However, like the ATE in Sect. 3, it is not recipient-set-oblivious.

4.1 Building HATE from Homomorphic Encryption and Secret Sharing

In this section, we describe our share-and-encrypt homomorphic ad hoc threshold encryption scheme which, despite its $\Theta(n)$-size ciphertexts, is efficient enough to be used in practice in some scenarios, because it is recipient-compact.

As we mentioned in the introduction, one natural way to build ATE is to use a threshold secret sharing scheme SS together with a public-key encryption scheme PKE. The idea is to secret share the message, and to encrypt each share to a different recipient using their public key; therefore, we call this the *share-and-encrypt* paradigm. We elaborate on it in the full version of this paper.

Notice that we are able to omit all but the relevant part of the ciphertext as input to PartDec for each party (where the relevant part is the one encrypted under their key), making the scheme both recipient-set-oblivious and recipient-compact. This further saves on communication in some contexts.

Theorem 2. *Share-and-encrypt (described formally in the full version of this paper) is a (n,t)-statically secure, recipient-set-oblivious, recipient-compact ATE, as long as SS is a secure share simulatable t-out-of-n secret sharing scheme, and PKE is a CPA-secure public key encryption scheme.*

We prove Theorem 2 in the full version of this paper.

If the secret sharing and encryption schemes are homomorphic in compatible ways, the share-and-encrypt construction is a Homomorphic ATE. The trick is finding the right homomorphic secret sharing and encryption schemes. In particular, if the secret sharing scheme is $\mathcal{F}$-homomorphic, the encryption scheme must be $\mathcal{F}'$-homomorphic, where $\mathcal{F}'$ includes the homomorphic evaluation of $\mathcal{F}$ over secret shares.

Of course, if the secret sharing and encryption schemes are both *fully* homomorphic, they give fully homomorphic ATE. However, no homomorphic threshold secret sharing schemes (with homomorphism over multiple inputs, without pre-distributed correlated randomness) is known, to the best of our knowledge.[2]

We show two efficient combinations of secret sharing and encryption which result in additively homomorphic ATE: Shamir-and-ElGamal and CRT-and-Paillier(both described in detail in the full version of this paper).

Shamir-and-ElGamal. We build share-and-encrypt HATE out of ElGamal encryption [15] and a variant of Shamir secret sharing. We need to use a *variant* of Shamir secret sharing (which we call exponential Shamir secret sharing), and not Shamir secret sharing itself, because Shamir secret sharing is additively homomorphic (and the homomorphism is applied via addition of individual shares), so we would need the encryption scheme to support addition; however, ElGamal is only multiplicatively homomorphic, so if we attempt to apply a homomorphism on encrypted shares, it will not work. What we need in order to get an additively homomorphic ATE scheme is to use ElGamal encryption with a secret sharing scheme which is additively homomorphic, but whose homomorphism is applied via multiplication. Therefore, we need to alter our Shamir secret sharing scheme by moving the shares to the exponent; then, taking a product of two shares will result in a share of the sum of the two shared values. We refer to the full version of

---

[2] Boyle *et al.* [9] give a nice introduction to homomorphic secret sharing. Jain *et al.* [18] and Dodis *et al.* [14] both build (threshold) function secret sharing, which gives homomorphic secret sharing, but the homomorphism is only over a single input.

this paper for a description of the ElGamal encryption scheme and the exponential Shamir secret sharing scheme which we use.

Theorem 3. *Shamir-and-ElGamal (described in the full version of this paper) is an additively homomorphic ad hoc threshold encryption scheme for a polynomial-size message space.*

Shamir-and-ElGamal is an ad hoc threshold encryption scheme by Theorem 2; the homomorphism follows from the homomorphisms of the underlying encryption and secret sharing schemes.

In Shamir-and-ElGamal we are limited to polynomial-size message spaces since final decryption uses brute-force search to find a discrete log. Jumping ahead to LOVE MPC, polynomial-size message spaces are still useful in many applications, as explained in the introduction. Moreover, the server already does work that is polynomial in the number of users, so asking it to perform another polynomial computation is not unreasonable.

CRT-and-Paillier. We also build share-and-encrypt HATE out of Camenisch-Shoup encryption and Chinese Remainder Theorem based secret sharing. The Camenisch-Shoup encryption scheme is a variant of Paillier encryption that supports additive homomorphism. However, we cannot combine it with Shamir secret sharing, since Shamir shares all live in the same group, while each instance of a Camenisch-Shoup encryption scheme uses a different modulus. Therefore, we combine Camenisch-Shoup encryption with CRT secret sharing, which has exactly the property that different shares can live in different groups. Unlike Shamir-and-ElGamal, this HATE allows us to use large message spaces. We refer to the full version of this paper for a description of the Camenisch-Shoup encryption scheme and the CRT secret sharing scheme which we use.

Theorem 4. *CRT-and-Paillier (described in the full version of this paper) is an additively homomorphic ad hoc threshold encryption scheme.*

CRT-and-Paillier is an ad hoc threshold encryption scheme by Theorem 2; the homomorphism follows from the homomorphisms of the underlying encryption and secret sharing schemes.

4.2   Building HATE from Obfuscation

As described in Sect. 3, the obfuscation-based ATE is not homomorphic. Informally, in order to make the obfuscation-based ATE $\mathcal{F}$-homomorphic, we can modify the obfuscated program to:

1. Use a $\mathcal{F}$-homomorphic secret sharing scheme [8]. (As an example, Shamir secret sharing is additively-homomorphic.) Note that $\mathcal{F}$ should always include subtraction from a constant (in the appropriate group); the obfuscated program returns shares of the mask w, which we want to use, together with the masked message e, to obtain shares of $m = e - w$.

However, this alone is not enough; even if the secret shares returned by the obfuscated programs are homomorphic, in order to extract them from the ciphertext, one must know a recipient secret value sv, while evaluation should require no secrets.

2. Use $\mathcal{F}'$-homomorphic public key encryption and decryption keys pk_i, sk_i instead of public and private values $pv_i = \mathsf{PRG}(sv_i), sv_i$. The obfuscated program would then not require sk_i as input; instead, it would return a ciphertext that requires sk_i for decryption.

   $\mathcal{F}'$ must include the functions necessary to evaluate $\mathcal{F}$ on the homomorphic secret shares.

This modification makes the construction $\mathcal{F}$-homomorphic while preserving sender-compactness. Thus, anyone (e.g., a server) can evaluate the obfuscated program to extract encryptions of all recipients' shares of the mask, homomorphically convert these into encrypted shares of the message, and homomorphically compute on those encrypted shares (since our public key encryption scheme is homomorphic, as are secret shares). The server would then send all parties their encrypted share of the computation output. Additionally, this construction is recipient-compact (as long as homomorphic shares are small), since each party only needs one compact part of the ciphertext for partial decryption.

More concretely, we can use ElGamal encryption [15]. Once the obfuscated program is evaluated, we are essentially using the Shamir-and-ElGamal HATE (Sect. 4.1). In particular, this implies that we are limited to polynomial-size message spaces, since final decryption uses brute-force search to find a discrete logarithm.

In the full version of this paper we give more details about our homomorphic recipient-compact HATE construction.

Theorem 5. *The modified obfuscation-based ATE is (n,t)-super-statically secure for any polynomial n, t, as long as* iO *is a secure indistinguishability obfuscator,* PPRF *is a secure puncturable* PRF, SS *is a secure secret sharing scheme,* SIG *is a constrained signature scheme, and* PKE *is a secure public-key encryption scheme. Moreover, it is $\mathcal{F}$-homomorphic if* SS *is $\mathcal{F}$ homomorphic (where $\mathcal{F}$ includes subtraction from a constant), and if* PKE *is $\mathcal{F}'$-homomorphic (where $\mathcal{F}'$ includes the evaluation of $\mathcal{F}$ on* SS *secret shares).*

Acknowledgements. We would like to thank Ran Canetti and Ben Kreuter for helpful discussions.

References

1. Ananth, P., Boneh, D., Garg, S., Sahai, A., Zhandry, M.: Differing-inputs obfuscation and applications. Cryptol. ePrint Arch. Rep. 2013, 689 (2013). http://eprint.iacr.org/2013/689
2. Badrinarayanan, S., Jain, A., Manohar, N., Sahai, A.: Secure MPC: laziness leads to GOD. In: Moriai, S., Wang, H. (eds.) ASIACRYPT 2020. LNCS, vol. 12493, pp. 120–150. Springer, Cham (2020). https://doi.org/10.1007/978-3-030-64840-4_5

3. Barak, B., et al.: On the (Im)possibility of obfuscating programs. In: Kilian, J. (ed.) CRYPTO 2001. LNCS, vol. 2139, pp. 1–18. Springer, Heidelberg (2001). https://doi.org/10.1007/3-540-44647-8_1

4. Bell, J., Bonawitz, K.A., Gascón, A., Lepoint, T., Raykova, M.: Secure single-server aggregation with (poly)logarithmic overhead. Cryptol. ePrint Archive Rep. 2020, 704 (2020). https://eprint.iacr.org/2020/704

5. Bonawitz, K., et al.: Practical secure aggregation for privacy-preserving machine learning. In: Thuraisingham, B.M., Evans, D., Malkin, T., Xu, D. (eds.) ACM CCS 2017, pp. 1175–1191. ACM Press, New York (2017)

6. Boneh, D., et al.: Threshold cryptosystems from threshold fully homomorphic encryption. In: Shacham, H., Boldyreva, A. (eds.) CRYPTO 2018. LNCS, vol. 10991, pp. 565–596. Springer, Cham (2018). https://doi.org/10.1007/978-3-319-96884-1_19

7. Boneh, D., Zhandry, M.: Multiparty key exchange, efficient traitor tracing, and more from indistinguishability obfuscation. In: Garay, J.A., Gennaro, R. (eds.) CRYPTO 2014. LNCS, vol. 8616, pp. 480–499. Springer, Heidelberg (2014). https://doi.org/10.1007/978-3-662-44371-2_27

8. Boyle, E., Gilboa, N., Ishai, Y.: Breaking the circuit size barrier for secure computation under DDH. In: Robshaw, M., Katz, J. (eds.) CRYPTO 2016. LNCS, vol. 9814, pp. 509–539. Springer, Heidelberg (2016). https://doi.org/10.1007/978-3-662-53018-4_19

9. Boyle, E., Gilboa, N., Ishai, Y., Lin, H., Tessaro, S.: Foundations of homomorphic secret sharing. In: Karlin, A.R., (eds.), ITCS 2018, vol. 94, pp. 21:1–21:21. LIPIcs (Jan 2018)

10. Daza, V., Herranz, J., Morillo, P., Ràfols, C.: CCA2-secure threshold broadcast encryption with shorter ciphertexts. In: Susilo, W., Liu, J.K., Mu, Y. (eds.) ProvSec 2007. LNCS, vol. 4784, pp. 35–50. Springer, Heidelberg (2007). https://doi.org/10.1007/978-3-540-75670-5_3

11. Daza, V., Herranz, J., Morillo, P., Ràfols, C.: Ad-hoc threshold broadcast encryption with shorter ciphertexts. Electr. Notes Theor. Comput. Sci. **192**(2), 3–15 (2008)

12. Delerablée, C., Pointcheval, D.: Dynamic threshold public-key encryption. In: Wagner, D. (ed.) CRYPTO 2008. LNCS, vol. 5157, pp. 317–334. Springer, Heidelberg (2008). https://doi.org/10.1007/978-3-540-85174-5_18

13. Desmedt, Y., Frankel, Y.: Threshold cryptosystems. In: Brassard, G. (ed.) CRYPTO 1989. LNCS, vol. 435, pp. 307–315. Springer, New York (1990). https://doi.org/10.1007/0-387-34805-0_28

14. Dodis, Y., Halevi, S., Rothblum, R.D., Wichs, D.: Spooky encryption and its applications. In: Robshaw, M., Katz, J. (eds.) CRYPTO 2016. LNCS, vol. 9816, pp. 93–122. Springer, Heidelberg (2016). https://doi.org/10.1007/978-3-662-53015-3_4

15. ElGamal, T.: A public key cryptosystem and a signature scheme based on discrete logarithms. In: Blakley, G.R., Chaum, D. (eds.) CRYPTO'84. LNCS, vol. 196, pp. 10–18. Springer, Heidelberg (1984)

16. Chaum, D. (ed.): Towards Trustworthy Elections. LNCS, vol. 6000. Springer, Heidelberg (2010). https://doi.org/10.1007/978-3-642-12980-3

17. Hirt, M., Sako, K.: Efficient receipt-free voting based on homomorphic encryption. In: Preneel, B. (ed.) EUROCRYPT 2000. LNCS, vol. 1807, pp. 539–556. Springer, Heidelberg (2000). https://doi.org/10.1007/3-540-45539-6_38

18. Jain, A., Rasmussen, P.M.R., Sahai, A.: Threshold fully homomorphic encryption. Cryptol. ePrint Arch. Rep. 2017, 257 (2017). http://eprint.iacr.org/2017/257

19. Mukherjee, P., Wichs, D.: Two round multiparty computation via multi-key FHE. In: Fischlin, M., Coron, J.-S. (eds.) EUROCRYPT 2016. LNCS, vol. 9666, pp. 735–763. Springer, Heidelberg (2016). https://doi.org/10.1007/978-3-662-49896-5_26

20. Rowling, J.: Harry Potter and the Half-Blood Prince. Bloomsbury (2005)

21. Zhandry, M.: How to avoid obfuscation using witness PRFs. In: Kushilevitz, E., Malkin, T. (eds.) TCC 2016. LNCS, vol. 9563, pp. 421–448. Springer, Heidelberg (2016). https://doi.org/10.1007/978-3-662-49099-0_16

Fully Dynamic Password Protected Secret Sharing: Simplifying PPSS Operation and Maintenance

Akif Patel[1] and Moti Yung[2]([✉])

[1] Rutgers University, New Brunswick, USA
[2] Google LLC and Columbia University, New York, USA

Abstract. A scheme which is based on splitting a secret among a set of servers (e.g. in a cloud) where a threshold, t, of them is needed for reconstruction, is advantageous in many ways for the mechanism to work regardless of the exact subset (of size at least t) which participates in the reconstruction. The advantages of such threshold-based cryptographic schemes include: availability, possibility of or compatibility with load balancing among servers, security (as less than the threshold server compromise does not give the secret away), fast and more efficient reconstruction/application of the secret, as well as providing other flexibilities in system design. Building on recent significant performance advantage made in the area of Password Protected Secret Sharing (PPSS), we construct an efficient scheme where the user works in reconstruction is independent of the set of servers participating (prior scheme assumed the subset needs to be known in advance, which typically involves a round of communication/ synchronization). We call such schemes "Dynamic Subset PPSS."

We further extend the scheme not only to allow dynamic subset but to also dynamically change the set of servers involved, where enrolling and dis-enrolling servers is done autonomously by the servers themselves without the presence of the user; we call such scheme "Fully Dynamic PPSS." For practical large scale deployment of PPSS schemes, clientless server enrollment and dis-enrollment seems fundamental, however, the previous schemes do not generally deal (or cannot be extended to deal) with this issue (which allows better system flexibility and does not depend on servers synchronizing with the set of users). To maintain the set of servers we, first, reduce it from proactive secret sharing in dynamic groups, and for minimizing communication within the set of servers we also develop a Paillier encryption method with linear communication.

Keywords: Password Protected Secret Sharing (PPSS) · Dynamic subsets · Dynamic server set · Secret sharing · Proactive secret sharing

Rutgers University—Work done as part of Senior Science Project at Montville Township High School.

S. Dolev et al. (Eds.): CSCML 2021, LNCS 12716, pp. 379–396, 2021.
https://doi.org/10.1007/978-3-030-78086-9_28

1   Introduction

Passwords are an extremely popular form of authentication because of their easy memorization and ease of use. However, the low entropy of passwords that makes it easy to memorize has the significant downside of making them very vulnerable in the case of database breaches that reveal the hash of passwords. Every year millions of passwords are lost when sites get hacked - the attackers have to do an offline guessing attack to discover the passwords from the hash of passwords recovered from the sites.

These sites attempt to protect the passwords through extra hashing and using salts, but with use of multiple machines it is nearly impossible to keep a determined attacker from performing an offline attack, we can only make it somewhat more expensive. With GPU parallelization and hardware hashing chips becoming cheaper, even requiring many rounds of hashing isn't enough to keep dictionary attacks, or even brute force attacks from succeeding. The same problem applies to using passwords to encrypt data to store in the cloud, both for password managers, and other applications - if either the data is lost, or the service becomes corrupted, a low entropy password can be brute-forced offline.

This loss of passwords can be very catastrophic when sensitive data is lost. In addition, many users reuse their password across sites, so a breach of a low-security site can cause accounts to be compromised on other sites. Password managers attempt to resolve this problem by storing high-entropy secrets as site specific passwords, but storing the list of site specific passwords encrypted by only a low-entropy master password; this faces the same problems listed above since now the password manager may be hacked and the master passwords compromised.

To solve these issues related to offline attacks, the useful idea of PPSS (Password Protected Secret Sharing) was introduced, which blocks adversaries from performing offline guessing attacks by splitting the high entropy encryption keys/passwords among many servers.

1.1   Password Protected Secret Sharing

The idea of using multiple servers to prevent offline attacks was first proposed by Ford and Kaliski [5]. This notion was extended by [2] who introduced PPSS, which uses secret sharing [11] to split up a secret with n servers, such that it can be reconstructed if a threshold of t servers is reached, by a client using only the low-entropy password. Note that this isn't simply splitting the secret up to be stored on n servers with a secret sharing scheme, and authenticating the shares with the password since whatever is used for authenticating the password can be used to launch an offline attack by a single server.

This idea of PPSS is related to that of a T-PAKE [9] (Threshold-Password Authenticated Key Exchange), which is used to agree on a session key after interacting with t out of n servers. One can see that an T-PAKE can be obtained from a PPSS by storing a high-entropy secret with the PPSS, and then using that in a traditional PAKE. Note that this PAKE cannot be offline attacked because the password is high entropy.

While the Bagherzandi et al. scheme [2] takes three messages from server to client and back, and requires a public-key infrastructure, in [7], a scheme is presented which is round-optimal and requires only the low-entropy password to work. This scheme uses OPRFs (Oblivious Pseudorandom Functions) which compute a deterministic function on the server without letting the server know the input to the function. In this scheme, the client calculates t OPRFs on the password pw (one with each server), and uses them to encrypt/decrypt the secret shares.

One downside of the scheme, as it is presented in the paper, is that each OPRF evaluation requires two exponentiations for the client, and though the first one can be shared across all the servers, that still adds up to $t + 1$ total for the scheme.

1.2 TOPPSS Overview

One solution to this performance issue was shown in [8] through a remarkably efficient protocol called TOPPSS. There they introduced the idea of a T-OPRF (Threshold-OPRF) which moves the secret sharing into the OPRF, by computing this function across many servers, all of which remain oblivious of the input. They then use the output of this function to encrypt the actual secret. The benefit of this approach was that they were able to evaluate the entire T-OPRF with just 2 exponentiations for the client.

1.3 Dynamic Subset PPSS

However, their TOPPSS implementation had a drawback from the original OPRF model - when communicating with the servers, the client had to specify the subset of t servers, $\mathcal{SE}$ of $\mathcal{SI}$ (the set of all servers in the network), that the T-OPRF was being run with. This meant that if any of the originally expected set of servers was down or not available for use for some reason then the client would have to restart the entire protocol. It would have to pick another set $\mathcal{SE}$, and then communicate with the servers it had already done so with. This makes the protocol efficient (i.e. "only two exponentiations") only if the servers remain fixed and do not change dynamically. Furthermore, restarting the protocol means double the bandwidth costs and latency, which is much slower than the exponentiations that TOPPSS saves. A potential workaround is to do a roll-call initially, which does bound the potential cost, but this extra set of rounds again far exceeds the exponentiation costs saved. Furthermore, not being able to dynamically pick the servers as the client proceeds through the protocol also hurts things like load balancing between the servers (a server committed to the protocol cannot be free to do other things dynamically), a problem which may be further reducing efficiency. In this paper we define a protocol as Dynamic Subset, if it can dynamically construct the subset of servers it is using as it makes its way through the protocol and does not have to decide on it beforehand.

1.4 Clientless Server Enrolling and Disenrolling in PPSS

Server enrollment and disenrollment is trivial to perform with the client or user involvement, just have the user use its password to run the PPSS enrollment protocol again but with the new set of servers. At first, this may seem sufficient, however, as we argue requiring client involvement generally makes large scale deployment of PPSS practically impossible.

Firstly, PPSS makes sense only when the different servers holding shares of the secret belong to different, largely independent organizations otherwise if the servers belonged to the same organization then any security process weakness or insider threat that effects one server will also likely effect the other servers. Organizations who by a business agreement agreed to run the servers may over time disappear or due to change in their priorities drop out of the PPSS agreement and remove their server and over time the number of servers may go below t needed for recovering the data, hence, we also need to add servers or organizations over time.

Secondly, while it is true that most users will log on to a service once over a month or few months, a small fraction of users may never log on during that period for various reasons, including vacation, sickness, temporary change in priority, etc. Even if that portion of population that does not log on for an extended period of time is small (e.g. less than 1%), its possible that enough servers drop during that duration to permanently have those users lose access to their data. It is unlikely that any service could practically be deployed that allows even a small fraction of its population to lose access to their data with a small but non-negligible probability. So it seems of fundamental importance for adoption of a PPSS protocol that allows userless or clientless enrolling and disenrolling of servers.

Fully Dynamic PPSS: We refer to a PPSS scheme as full dynamic if it provides both the dynamic subset and clientless server enrollment and disenrollment functionality.

1.5 Our Contributions

To solve the first issue of dynamic subset during secret reconstruction, a T-OPRF needs to be constructed that hides the details of the servers being used from the servers themselves. If the client can have generic communications with the servers that do not rely on the other server, then the client can just ignore any non-operational servers and continue on, dynamically altering the set of servers it is going to use, and only finalizing after communicating with all of them. As mentioned, we define a protocol as Dynamic Subset, if it can dynamically construct the subset of servers it is using as it makes its way through the protocol and does not have to decide on it beforehand. Motivated by this definition, we present DS-TOPPSS (Dynamic Subset - TOPPS) that matches the Dynamic Subset criterion while sacrificing little in performance. In our second contribution, in addition to showing the above we give a fully Dynamic PPSS that can securely add or delete servers from the network at will, without needing a TTP or the client, we present protocols for enrollment and disenrollment that make this possible.

1.6   Organization

In Sect. 2, background information about the research that DS-TOPPSS is based on is provided. In Sect. 3, we specify DS-TOPPSS and show its properties (correctness, and security). Additionally, we give a numerical performance evaluation for our protocol against the previous two protocols for various cases of t and n. Finally in Sect 4., we provide protocols for making any TOPPSS scheme fully dynamic, again, along with security analyses. We note that for security we employ simulation based definitions in our proofs of security.

2   Background

OPRF_PPSS: The original scheme [7] relies on OPRFs. The basic idea is that with secret sharing scheme as in PPSS, knowing $<t$ potential shares of the secret does not give you any indication of whether or not the shares are valid. This means that if you store the shares encrypted with the results of a function that the server does not know the input or output of, $<t$ servers have no way of knowing if their offline attacks are succeeding or not.

The reconstruction part of the scheme starts with the client uniformly picking a random value r to be used as the blinding value for the OPRFs. Next the client calculates $a = H(\mathsf{pw})^r$ where $H(x)$ is a hash function with an appropriate range and sends it to each server. Note that all hash functions referred to in this paper are random oracles unless otherwise designated. Since the servers don't know r, they don't have any information about $H(\mathsf{pw})$, and cannot offline attack the password this way. After that, the servers each exponentiate to get $b_i = a^{k_i} = H(\mathsf{pw})^{rk_i}$, where k_i is random a value stored by the server, and send it back. Using these b_i's, the client first deblinds them by undoing the initial exponentiation, and then hashes them with another hash and the password, ending up with the output of the OPRF: $f_{k_i}(\mathsf{pw}) = H_2\left(\mathsf{pw}, b_i^{1/r}\right) = H_2\left(\mathsf{pw}, H(\mathsf{pw})^{k_i}\right)$. The $f_{k_i}(\mathsf{pw})$'s are then used to decrypt the publicly stored encrypted shares $e_{f_{k_i}(\mathsf{pw})}(S_i)$, which have been encrypted and stored in this fashion during the initialization steps. This yields the S_i's, which are then used in Lagrangian interpolation to reconstruct the secret. In the figures below, during initialization the client communicates with the servers over a secure (e.g. SSL/TLS) connection.

Initialization:

1. Creates n random values k_i.
2. Send server i the value k_i to store at server.
3. With each k_i calculate the PRF $f_{k_i}(\mathsf{pw}) = H_2\left(\mathsf{pw}, H(\mathsf{pw})^{k_i}\right)$.
4. Split up the secret S into shares S_i.
5. Encrypt each share with the PRF as the key $e_{f_{k_i}(\mathsf{pw})}(S_i)$ and store this publicly.

Reconstruction:

1. Client calculates $a = H(\mathsf{pw})^r$ and sends it to each server.
2. Each server i calculates $b_i = a^{k_i}$ and sends it back.
3. The client calculates $f_{k_i}(\mathsf{pw}) = H_2\left(\mathsf{pw}, b_i^{1/r}\right)$.
4. Client retrieves the publicly available encrypted shares $e_{f_{k_i}(\mathsf{pw})}(S_i)$ and decrypts them.
5. Client uses Lagrangian interpolation formula and outputs $S = \sum_{i \in \mathcal{SE}}(S_i)\left(\prod_{j \in \mathcal{SE}/\{i\}} \frac{-x_j}{x_i - x_j}\right)$.

Original PPSS Scheme Specification

TOPPSS: As previously mentioned, the above scheme requires one exponentiation for the blinding and t for deblinding each b_i, which results in a total of $t + 1$ exponentiations. TOPPSS [8] improves upon this computational requirement through some creative algebra. The essence of the protocol was to move the Lagrangian interpolation into the exponent, and use the homomorphic properties of exponentiation to add the relevant terms in the exponent by multiplying everything together.

The scheme starts out the same as earlier, with the client sending $a = H(\mathsf{pw})^r$ to each server. However, along with a, the client also sends $\mathcal{SE}$, the set of servers that the client has decided on using. Additionally, the k_i's are not random values anymore, but shares of some high-entropy, random secret k. Using this set $\mathcal{SE}$, the servers first calculate the relevant Lagrangian coefficient λ_i, and then not only exponentiate by k_i but also λ_i to get b_i. These b_i's, once sent back instead of being immediately deblinded, are then multiplied together into $b = \prod_{i \in \mathcal{SE}} b_i = \prod_{i \in \mathcal{SE}} a^{r k_i \lambda_i} = a^{r \sum_{i \in \mathcal{SE}} k_i \lambda_i} = a^{rk}$. Note that except for the r factor, since the k_i's are shares of a secret, no matter which servers you pick, b will result in the same value. Deblinding and hashing gives us the final result of the T-OPRF, $f_k(\mathsf{pw}) = H_2(\mathsf{pw}, b^{1/r})$.

Initialization:

1. Selects high-entropy random value k.
2. Calculate $f_k(\mathsf{pw}) = H_2\left(\mathsf{pw}, H(\mathsf{pw})^k\right)$ and use it to encrypt a secret, or for other purposes.
3. Client splits up k using (t, n) secret sharing and sends one share k_i to each server.
4. Client additionally publicly assigns each server an x-coordinate x_i based on their share.

Reconstruction:

1. Select a set $\mathcal{SE} \subseteq \mathcal{SI}$ with size t.
2. Calculate $a = H(\mathsf{pw})^r$ and send it to each server in $\mathcal{SE}$ along with $\mathcal{SE}$.
3. Each server calculates $b_i = a^{k_i \lambda_i}$ where $\lambda_i = \prod_{j \in \mathcal{SE}/\{i\}} \frac{-x_j}{x_i - x_j}$ and sends it back.
4. The client calculates $b = \prod_{i \in \mathcal{SE}} b_i$.
5. Output $f_k(\mathsf{pw}) = H_2\left(\mathsf{pw}, b^{1/r}\right)$.

TOPPSS Specification

In the TOPPSS paper [8] you do not directly use $f_k(\mathsf{pw})$ above as an encryption key. Rather during the initialization phase you first hash $f_k(\mathsf{pw})$ to $C|K$ and store C at each server. During the reconstruction phase, each server sends C back to the client and the client checks that they are all the same and that they match the C from the reconstructed hash of $f_k(\mathsf{pw})$ before using K. We will assume this extra step for our Dynamic Subset TOPPSS (DS-TOPPSS) below also.

3   Dynamic Subset TOPPSS

The main problem with the TOPPSS scheme is that the server needs information on the set of servers to calculate the Lagrangian coefficient. Including the Lagrangian coefficient on the client side after the server round requires another exponentiation, which is self-defeating. The idea then becomes to apply the Lagrangian on the server, but then adjust it later on the client without doing costly exponentiations. This leads to the following protocol.

3.1   Overview

The basic idea behind DS-TOPPSS is to realize that all the inputs that go into calculating the Lagrangian coefficient λ_i are/can be made extremely small. λ_i is calculated solely from x-coordinates and if we make $x_i = i + 1$ (e.g. $1, 2, 3, 4, 5$), then none of the numbers should get very large at all. The only thing that makes the exponentiation costly is that there are divisions/subtractions in the formula for λ_i that make it a full-sized exponent. Hence, we try to achieve the correct Lagrangian on the client side without any divisions.

3.2 Specification

Once the server receives $a = H(\mathsf{pw})^r$, it needs to send back all the requisite information needed for potentially including any server in the exponent. Specifically, we define

$$L_i = \prod_{j \in \mathcal{SI} \setminus \{i\}} \frac{1}{x_i - x_j} \tag{1}$$

and send back $b_i = a^{k_i L_i}$. One can see how this term contains all the divisions that will ever be needed. Then, on the client side, after we have talked to all the servers and settled on a set of servers $\mathcal{SE}$, the client calculates

$$u_i = \left(\prod_{j \in \mathcal{SE} \setminus \{i\}} -x_j \right) \left(\prod_{j \in \mathcal{SI} \setminus \mathcal{SE}} x_i - x_j \right) \tag{2}$$

Then, to go from L_i to λ_i one just needs to multiply $L_i \cdot u_i$. This includes the numerator that had been missing from L_i and cancels out the factors from the denominators that are unneeded. In terms of the protocol, this equates to exponentiating $b_i^{u_i}$ before multiplying all of them together and then deblinding. Note that for realistic cases, u_i is very small compared to a full sized exponent because of the aforementioned small x values, and lack of divisions.

One further speed improvement can be drawn from the fact that we are not merely doing t "small" exponentiations, we are calculating the product of t such exponentiations. And calculating the product of multiple exponentiations is known to be significantly faster than calculating each one individually and then multiplying. Specifically, Pippenger's algorithm [4] can be made to run in about $(1 + t/\lg(tB))B$ multiplications where B is the bit length and t is the number of servers as opposed to the $t \cdot B$ multiplications that would be required to do each individually.

A Note on Negative Exponents. While the exponents u_i needed on the client side to form the Lagrangian coefficient remain small because the division is taken care of on the server side, they are not necessarily positive, and when taken $\bmod P$ will become full-sized again. To solve this, we take the modular inverse of b_i before running the Pippenger step if u_i is negative, and always exponentiate by $|u_i|$.

Initialization (Same as TOPPSS):

1. Selects high-entropy random value k.
2. Calculate $f_k(\mathsf{pw}) = H_2\left(\mathsf{pw}, H(\mathsf{pw})^k\right)$ and use it to encrypt a secret, or for other purposes.
3. Client splits up k using (t, n) secret sharing and sends one share k_i to each server.
4. Client additionally publicly assigns each server an x-coordinate x_i based on their share.

Reconstruction

1. Calculate $a = H(\mathsf{pw})^r$ and send it to each desired server, creating $\mathcal{SE}$ as you go.
2. If the server is unavailable, pick a new one, and update $\mathcal{SE}$.
3. Each server sends back $b_i = a^{k_i L_i}$ where $L_i = \prod_{j \in \mathcal{SI} \setminus \{i\}} \frac{1}{x_i - x_j}$ as described above.
4. For all b_i, the client calculates $u_i = \left(\prod_{j \in \mathcal{SE} \setminus \{i\}} -x_j\right)\left(\prod_{j \in \mathcal{SI} \setminus \mathcal{SE}} x_i - x_j\right)$ as described above.
5. If $u_i < 0$, then $b_i = \frac{1}{b_i}$.
6. The client calculates $b = \prod_{i \in \mathcal{SE}} b_i^{|u_i|}$ using Pippenger's algorithm.
7. Output $f_k(\mathsf{pw}) = H_2\left(\mathsf{pw}, b^{1/r}\right)$.

DS-TOPPSS Specification

3.3 Performance

Table 1. Worst case values for client performance for group order 2^{256} $\left(t = \lfloor \frac{N}{2} \rfloor + 1\right)$

N	Highest u_i	$\sum \lg u_i$	OPRF PPSS	DS-TOPPSS	TOPPSS
3	4	3.584	768	516	514
4	18	11.754	1024	520	515
7	14,400	49.1264	1280	536	516
10	45,722,000	138.004	1792	559	518
20	1.12E+22	738.981	3072	669	523
30	6.86E+38	1909.202	4352	829	528
50	3.84E+76	6175.044	6912	1288	538
75	$>2^{256}$	15265.223	9984	1503	550
100	$>2^{256}$	29504.551	13312	1723	563

An important point about our protocol is that it is not strictly equal in performance as TOPPSS. While the original goal was to create a dynamic subset PPSS that maintained the efficiency of TOPPSS, because of the additional exponentiations by the u_i's, DS-TOPPSS does start to cost more than TOPPSS, especially in the asymptotic case. However, for all realistic n and t values, and a lot of unrealistic ones, the u_i's stay very small and the cost stays very close to 2 full exponentiations in $\mathbb{Z}_P$, and under 3, for many values. In addition, though u_i does grow with $O(n!)$, even when it reaches the group order it still stays much, much cheaper than the original OPRF protocol due to the use of Pippinger's algorithm.

To demonstrate this, we have included a table below of numerically computed values for various selected N's, with $t = \lfloor \frac{N}{2} \rfloor + 1$. We are assuming that a full sized exponentiations requires $\lg P$ multiplications and have not distinguished between multiplications and squarings for ease of comparison as per the model in [4]. Additionally, a graph is included that gives a visual indication of the performance of the three algorithms.

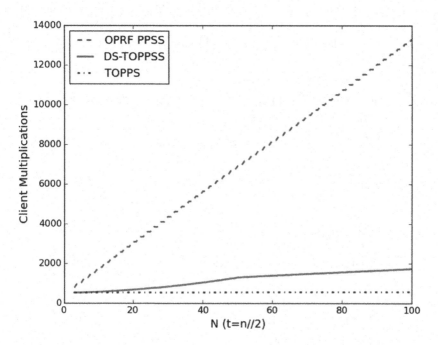

Fig. 1. Worstcase performance comparisons for OPRF PPSS, DS-TOPPS, and TOPPSS

3.4 Security

In terms of security, our protocol is very similar to that of TOPPSS, and our proof is nearly trivial. More specifically, two parts are identical:

1. The servers store the same information in both protocols (the k_i's)
2. The servers receive the same information in runs of the T-OPRF in both protocols (pw^r)

Because of this, we can use the security of TOPPSS to assert that server corruptions ($<t$ of them) are secure for our protocol also. The only part that needs to be shown secure is that of a client corruption. We do this by showing that the view of DS-TOPPSS is simulatable from a view of TOPPSS.

This can be seen from the fact that starting with the vector $\langle \mathsf{pw}^{rk_1\lambda_1}, \mathsf{pw}^{rk_2\lambda_2}, \ldots \rangle$ of server values, sent back to the client, one simply has to raise each one to $1/u_i$ to get the $\langle \mathsf{pw}^{rk_1 L_1}, \mathsf{pw}^{rk_2 L_2}, \ldots \rangle$ in the view of DS-TOPPSS. All other information is the same in the views of both protocols.

3.5 Correctness

Substituting directly from the protocol specification, the protocol outputs:

$$
\begin{aligned}
f_k(\mathsf{pw}) &= H_2\left(\mathsf{pw}, b^{1/r}\right) \\
&= H_2\left(\mathsf{pw}, \left(\prod_{i\in\mathcal{SE}} b_i^{sgn(u_i)*|u_i|}\right)^{1/r}\right) = H_2\left(\mathsf{pw}, \left(\prod_{i\in\mathcal{SE}} b_i^{u_i}\right)^{1/r}\right) \\
&= H_2\left(\mathsf{pw}, \prod_{i\in\mathcal{SE}} b_i^{u_i*1/r}\right) = H_2\left(\mathsf{pw}, \prod_{i\in\mathcal{SE}} a^{k_i L_i u_i 1/r}\right) \\
&= H_2\left(\mathsf{pw}, \prod_{i\in\mathcal{SE}} H(\mathsf{pw})^{rk_i L_i u_i 1/r}\right) = H_2\left(\mathsf{pw}, \prod_{i\in\mathcal{SE}} H(\mathsf{pw})^{k_i\lambda_i}\right) \\
&= H_2\left(\mathsf{pw}, H(\mathsf{pw})^{\sum_{i\in\mathcal{SE}} k_i\lambda_i}\right) = H_2\left(\mathsf{pw}, H(\mathsf{pw})^k\right)
\end{aligned}
$$

This last value is exactly what is the desired output, as mentioned in step 2 of the Initialization procedure above.

3.6 Robustness with Dynamic Subset TOPPSS

As mentioned earlier, in the TOPPSS paper you do not directly use $f_k(\mathsf{pw})$ above as an encryption key. Rather during the initialization phase you first hash $f_k(\mathsf{pw})$ to $C|K$ and store C at each server. During the reconstruction phase, each server sends C back to the client and the client checks that they are all the same and that they match the C from the reconstructed hash of $f_k(\mathsf{pw})$ before using K. We assume this extra step for our Dynamic Subset TOPPSS (DS-TOPPSS) also. This public storing of C is a common addition to verify that the protocol ran properly.

Another advantage of the dynamic subset property of our protocol is brought up if it does fail. Unlike TOPPSS, we can easily apply the robustness scheme from [1] to the values returned from the servers. The only addition to the scheme is that the values need to be de-blinded by raising them to $\frac{1}{r}$ while TOPPSS needs to account for the servers raising them to the lambdas which is both more costly because of differing exponents and much more complicated.

4   Fully Dynamic TOPPSS

4.1   Enrollment Scheme

While TOPPSS was created with performance in mind, we have realized that there is an additional benefit to TOPPSS schemes over OPRF schemes. Since TOPPSS actually stores the secret shares k_i in plaintext, the network can create a new share without any involvement from the user. In contrast, the original scheme which requires the OPRF to be fully run before being able to access the decrypted shares (which requires the password). One can see that this is an issue, because if the user does not log on for a long period of time, the network may be unable to juggle around any dysfunctional/corrupt servers with servers it wants to add. This may potentially lead to the number of working servers dropping below t, which implies a complete loss of data. However, adding a server without the client is not trivial either, as doing it naively will reveal k to the existing servers if there isn't a trusted third-party (the user). Our scheme to do so relies on using "masking" polynomials to hide the shares given to the new server.

The original servers start by each deciding on a random, degree $t-1$ polynomial that is zero at the new servers' x-coordinate. They then give shares to each other server at the recipients' x-coordinates. To prove that these shares indeed fulfill the above criterion, each server runs the following zero-knowledge proof:

Repeat the following procedure m times:

1. Prover creates a random polynomial $P'(x)$.
2. Prover sends each verifier i the shares $a = \{P'(x_i), P'(x_i) + P(x_i)\}$ using public-key encryption.
3. The verifiers collectively flip a coin to decide bit b and use it to select a share a_b, which is then made public. Note that unless more than $t-2$ verifiers are colluding, this does not reveal any extra information about $P(x)$.
4. Collectively, the servers use the shares to either construct $P'(x)$ or $P'(x) + P(x)$.
5. If the chosen polynomial is both degree $t-1$ and is 0 at $x = x_n$, continue iterating.
6. Otherwise, output $\perp$

ZK proof for polynomial shares.

This ZK proof is well-known and has correctness and security proofs in [3] and [6]. After proving these properties, each server adds their shares from all the masking polynomials to the main share that they have, and sends it to the new server. The new server then combines all the shares with the relevant Lagrangian coefficients at its x-coordinate. Because of the properties of the masking polynomials, they all go to zero at that point, leaving only the needed share.

1. Designate the new server x-coordinate x_n.
2. t original servers $\mathcal{SE}$ are picked to participate.
3. Each creates a random polynomial $P_i(x)$ of degree $t-1$ such that $P_i(x_n) = 0$.
4. Each old server i sends each old server j over public-key encryption $P_i(x_j)$.
5. Each old server uses the above ZK-proof to prove that their polynomial fulfills the criterion from step 3.
6. Each old server i sends the new server $y_i = k_i + \sum_{j \in \mathcal{SE}} P_j(x_i)$.
7. The new server interpolates $k_n = \sum_{i \in \mathcal{SE}} (y_i) \left(\prod_{j \in \mathcal{SE}/\{i\}} \frac{x_n - x_j}{x_i - x_j} \right)$ and stores it for later use in DS-TOPPSS.

Clientless Enrollment Scheme Specification

Security. First, we have to realize that we only have to prove security in the case where we have $t-2$ corrupted old servers colluding with the new server. This can be reduced to the case with $t-1$ old servers working without the new one, because the new server can be thought of as the $t-1$th old server by simply not using its extra information. In addition, if we assume that all communications happen under secure channels, and the security of the aforementioned ZK proof scheme [3,6], then the corrupt servers only know their own polynomials.

Next, note that when all the shares are added, they effectively become shares for a new polynomial, $F(x) = \sum P_i'(x) + P(x)$ the sum of all the masking polynomials and the original one. Since it is intended to be evaluated at x_n, all the masking polynomials equal 0, and so $F(x_n) = P(x_n)$. However, at any other points, because of the randomness of the masking polynomials, $F(x)$ looks completely random compared to $P(x)$. As long as all t of the masking polynomials aren't given to the new server, the addition of that final unknown random polynomial, done inside a finite field, makes $P(x)$ completely unpredictable from $F(x)$. Hence, the new server is only able to gain the information it is supposed to.

Now, since we have shown security with communication over private channels, we need to show that it is also secure when using public-key encryption to transmit the shares. First, we formalize this concept of maintaining security with public-key encryption:

Definition 1. *A clientless enrollment scheme is secure using public-key encryption if with any set of adversarial servers $\mathcal{SA}$ with $|\mathcal{SA}| \leq t-2$ and new server S_n, masking polynomials $P_j(x)$, and encryption keys k_is, where common view* $\mathsf{V} = \{\{P_j(x_i) \mid i \in \mathcal{SA}, j \in \mathcal{SE}/\mathcal{SA}\}, \{\{P_i(x), k_i\} \mid i \in \mathcal{SA}\}, \{y_i \mid i \in \mathcal{SE}\}\}$:

$$\{\{e_{k_i}(P_j(x_i)) \mid i,j \in \mathcal{SE}/\mathcal{SA}\}, \mathsf{V}\} \stackrel{c}{\equiv} \{\{e_{k_i}(0) \mid i,j \in \mathcal{SE}/\mathcal{SA}\}, \mathsf{V}\}$$

This definition captures the idea of the situation remaining the same whether or not we use public-key encryption, or use private channels and just encrypt garbage in the transcripts.

Theorem 1. *The above clientless enrollment scheme is secure with communication done with public-key encryption.*

Proof. Since there are multiple pieces of information that are different in the two things we are proving computationally equivalent, this requires a hybrid proof. We begin by defining H_j for all $0 \leq j \leq (t - |\mathcal{SA}|)^2$ as distributions over the transcripts defined as in the above theorem, except that j of the intercepted ciphertexts are encrypted 0's, and the others are encryptions of real shares. Note that the tow distributions above are equivalent to H_0 and $H_{\sigma*(t-|\mathcal{SA}|)^2}$. This leads the following reformulation of the theorem statement:

Given a uniform random bit σ, for any PPT adversary D, there exists a PPT algorithm D^* s.t:

$$\left| \Pr_{x \leftarrow H_{\sigma*(t-|\mathcal{SA}|)^2}}[D(1^n, x, \mathsf{V}) = \sigma] - \right.$$
$$\left. \Pr_{x \leftarrow H_{\sigma*(t-|\mathcal{SA}|)^2}}[D^*(1^n, |x|, \mathsf{V}) = \sigma] \right| < \mathsf{negl}(n) \tag{3}$$

where V is the plaintext rest of the transcript for some negligible function $\mathsf{negl}(n)$.

We now examine the situation between two adjacent distributions, and posit that transcripts from distributions H_j and H_{j-1} are computationally indistinguishable. Start by assuming the inverse of the previous statement:

Given a uniform random bit σ here exists a PPT distinguisher D' such that for all PPT algorithms D'^*:

$$\left| \Pr_{x \leftarrow H_{j-\sigma}}[D'(1^n, x, \mathsf{V}) = \sigma] - \Pr_{x \leftarrow H_{j-\sigma}}['^*(1^n, x, \mathsf{V}) = \sigma] \right| > \mathsf{negl}(n) \tag{4}$$

for all negligible function $\mathsf{negl}(n)$.

Next, with this PPT distinguisher D', we can construct the following PPT adversary $\mathcal{A}(\{m_1, m_2\}, e_{k_j}(m_\sigma), P^*(x))$:

1. Create a random polynomial $P(x)$ of degree $t - 1$.
2. Create random polynomials $P'_i(x)$ of degree $t - 1$ s.t. $P'_i(x_n) = 0$.
3. Emulate a running of the clientless server enrollment protocol, and record the transcript x in the format described in the theorem statement.
4. Make $j - 1$ of the encrypted shares $e(0)$ each with the appropriate key.
5. Set the jth encrypted share to the input received $e_{k_j}(m_\sigma)$.
6. Set the messages in V from the server that the jth message is sent from to reflect being from the polynomial $P^*(x)$.
7. Output $D'(1^n, x, \mathsf{V})$

Now, when you run $\mathcal{A}$ with the input $\mathcal{A}(\{0, P^*(x_i)\}, e_{k_j}(\sigma * P^*(x_i)), P^*(x))$ with uniformly random bit σ and $P^*(x)$ with appropriate degree and x-intercept for a masking polynomial, $\mathcal{A}$ outputs the correct σ with probability non-negligibly greater than $\frac{1}{2}$. This breaks the $\mathsf{IND} - \mathsf{CPA}$ property of the public-key encryption, hence, Eq. (5) must be false, and the maximum advantage that any PPT distinguisher gains on the jth step must be $< \mathsf{negl}(n)$ for some negligible function $\mathsf{negl}(n)$.

Hence, since the number of steps $(t - |\mathcal{SA}|)^2 < n^2$, which is polynomial, the maximum total advantage $(t-|\mathcal{SA}|)^2 * \mathsf{negl}(n)$ must also be negligible, concluding the proof.

Correctness. The shares y_i that the new server receives are the sum of shares for masking polynomials and the original polynomial. and since polynomials add linearly, these are also shares for the sum for the masking polynomial and the original one. Symbolically, these are shares of $F(x) = P(x) + \sum_{i \in \mathcal{SE}} P_i'(x)$.

Now, when the server interpolates $F(x)$ at x_n, the $P_i'(x)$ components go to 0 because of their definitions, leaving only $P(x_n)$, which is the desired share.

– Disenrollment: is similar to enrollment and is covered in the appendix.

4.2   Linear Communication Enrollment Scheme

One problem with the above schemes (reducing the problem to proactive scheme on dynamic groups) is that they are relatively communication intensive. Because each server needs to distribute its polynomial to each of the others, through the network effect, its bandwidth complexity is $O(n^2)$. Usually this should not be a problem, since server management is such a rare procedure, and n and t shouldn't be that big anyways. However, if one does have an extremely large network of servers which makes these impractical, we do have a linear bandwidth alternate enrollment scheme. However, it is not as simple as our above one, requiring homomorphic encryption and a much more cumbersome message order.

To begin, the new server creates a key-pair for Paillier encryption [10] and shares the public key with everyone. Each old server out of the t then calculates the Lagrangian coefficient for their x coordinate. Next, they encrypt that coefficient * their share, with the new server's public key. The new server decrypts the product of those encryptions, which because of the homomorphic properties of the encryption, will be the desired y-coordinate.

Note that each individual encrypted share/coefficient product cannot be given to the new server, since if they were corrupt, they could decrypt them individually and recover the k_i's themselves. Instead, the servers need to multiply the encrypted values sequentially, passing it on from one to the other (around the table honest-but-curious protocol). This may be cumbersome, but the number of steps required does stay linear as opposed to quadratic.

---

1. Designate new server x-coordinate x_n.
2. t old servers comprising set $\mathcal{SE}$ each calculate $\ell_i(x_n)$ where $\ell_i(x)$ is the ith Lagrangian basis polynomial given by $\ell_i(x) = \prod_{j \in \mathcal{SE}} \frac{x - x_j}{x_i - x_j}$.
3. Each server then calculates $c_i = e\left(k_i \ell_i(x_n)\right)$ where $e(x)$ is Paillier encryption using the new server's public key.
4. The servers in $\mathcal{SE}$ pass along a running product of their c_i's so that the last server ends up with $c = \prod_{i \in \mathcal{SE}} c_i = e\left(\sum_{i \in \mathcal{SE}} k_i \ell_i(x_n)\right) = e(k_n)$.
5. The last server sends c to the new server which decrypts it using its public key and stores x_n and k_n for use in TOPPSS.

Linear Communication Clientless Enrollment Scheme Specification

5   Conclusion

In this paper we have extended on the TOPPSS protocol from [8] by introducing the idea of dynamic-subset, and constructing a dynamic-subset scheme that is nearly as efficient as TOPPSS. We showed this efficiency through numerical simulations and provided a security reduction to TOPPSS. We note that while this is a relatively small addition, it increases the flexibility of the scheme and prevents extra synchronization, which is always welcome in actual systems We then further showed the importance of performing server enrollment and disenrollment without the client being present, which is another contribution to system flexibility, and gave protocols that accomplish this. Our resulting protocol is a fully-dynamic PPSS scheme in that it achieves dynamic subset capability during reconstruction phase and also achieves clientless enrollment and disenrollment of servers.

Overall, our contributions add to the flexibility of adopting the above schemes with much less systems friction (requiring synchronization among parties, and requirements for involvement of extra parties). We note that while from protocol design these issues may be small, from a system acceptability such issues can be crucial at times.

6   Appendix: Disenrollment Scheme

Our disenrollment scheme works in much the same manner as the enrollment one with the use of random polynomials. The difference in this case is that instead of using the $P'(x)$s to mask anything temporarily, they instead *permanently* change the shares that all the servers have, without giving the disenrolled server the information to do so.

The protocol proceeds as follows. All $n - 1$ of the remaining servers create a random polynomial of degree $t - 1$, $P_i'(x)$. Unlike the enrollment scheme, this one is 0 not at x_n, but instead at 0, since it needs to preserve the secret in the constant term instead of the share at x_n. The old servers then distribute the shares to the others and prove the required criterion with a ZK-proof as explained above. After exchanging the shares from the random polynomials, the old servers add those shares to their k_i value, and use that as their new share. This emulates the process of creating a new polynomial and creating shares from it to replace the old one without having to actually reconstruct the secret anywhere. Since the server being kicked out is not involved in any of this process, his shares becomes useless with regards to the new polynomial.

1. Designate the server being disenrolled as server a.
2. All servers that aren't getting disenrolled create a random polynomial $P_i(x)$ of degree $t - 1$ with y-intercept 0.
3. Each of these servers i then send each server (except the one being disenrolled) j over public-key encryption $P_i(x_j)$.
4. Using the above ZK-proof, the servers prove that their polynomial fulfills the criterion from step 2.
5. Each server participating in the protocol replaces its share k_i with $k_i + \sum_{j \in \mathcal{SI}/\{a\}} P_j(x_i)$.

Clientless Server Disenrollment Specification

Security. Notice that security for this protocol does not involve revealing extra information to any of the participating servers. Because the only thing given to them are shares with a ZK-proof, by the zero knowledge property of the proof, the remaining servers don't learn anything they don't already know. Instead, we need to argue that even with the aid of $t - 2$ servers, the disenrolled server cannot figure out his share for the new polynomial.

Similar to the enrollment scheme, the new polynomial created looks completely random with respect to the old one. Even with $t - 1$ servers aiding the disenrolled server, there are still $n + 1 - t$ polynomials that this coalition does not have any information about because of the ZK property of the proof. Even just one of those would make the polynomial that the adversaries would have left after subtracting away what they knew effectively random. Because of this, and the security of secret sharing, the kicked-out server has no way of using his old share to predict a new share for the new polynomial.

The proof of security when using public-key encryption instead of private channels is nearly identical to the enrollment case.

Correctness. This correctness proof is very similar to that of enrollment. All the servers add shares from the masking polynomials to their shares, which make the resulting shares, shares of $F(x) = P(x) + \sum_{i \in \mathcal{SI}} P_i'(x)$.

When used for interpolation at $x = 0$ for secret reconstruction, the $P_i'(x)$ components will go to 0, leaving only $P(x)$, which is the original secret.

References

1. Abdalla, M., Cornejo, M., Nitulescu, A., Pointcheval, D.: Robust password-protected secret sharing. Cryptology ePrint Archive, Report 2016/123 (2016). http://eprint.iacr.org/2016/123
2. Bagherzandi, A., Jarecki, S., Saxena, N., Lu, Y.: Password-protected secret sharing. In: Proceedings of the 18th ACM conference on Computer and Communications Security, pp. 433–444. ACM (2011)

3. Ben-Or, M., Goldwasser, S., Wigderson, A.: Completeness theorems for non-cryptographic fault-tolerant distributed computation. In: Proceedings of the Twentieth Annual ACM Symposium on Theory of Computing, STOC 1988, New York, NY, USA, pp. 1–10. ACM (1988). http://doi.acm.org/10.1145/62212.62213

4. Bernstein, D.J.: Pippenger's exponentiation algorithm (2002)

5. Brainard, J.G., Juels, A., Kaliski, B., Szydlo, M.: A new two-server approach for authentication with short secrets. In: USENIX Security Symposium, pp. 201–214 (2003)

6. Chaum, D., Crépeau, C., Damgard, I.: Multiparty unconditionally secure protocols. In: Proceedings of the Twentieth Annual ACM Symposium on Theory of Computing, STOC 1988, New York, NY, USA, pp. 11–19. ACM (1988). http://doi.acm.org/10.1145/62212.62214

7. Jarecki, S., Kiayias, A., Krawczyk, H., Xu, J.: Highly-efficient and composable password-protected secret sharing (or: how to protect your bitcoin wallet online). In: 2016 IEEE European Symposium on Security and Privacy (EuroS&P), pp. 276–291. IEEE (2016)

8. Jarecki, S., Kiayias, A., Krawczyk, H., Xu, J.: TOPPSS: cost-minimal password-protected secret sharing based on threshold OPRF. In: Gollmann, D., Miyaji, A., Kikuchi, H. (eds.) ACNS 2017. LNCS, vol. 10355, pp. 39–58. Springer, Cham (2017). https://doi.org/10.1007/978-3-319-61204-1_3

9. MacKenzie, P., Shrimpton, T., Jakobsson, M.: Threshold password-authenticated key exchange. In: Yung, M. (ed.) CRYPTO 2002. LNCS, vol. 2442, pp. 385–400. Springer, Heidelberg (2002). https://doi.org/10.1007/3-540-45708-9_25

10. Paillier, P.: Public-key cryptosystems based on composite degree residuosity classes. In: Stern, J. (ed.) EUROCRYPT 1999. LNCS, vol. 1592, pp. 223–238. Springer, Heidelberg (1999). https://doi.org/10.1007/3-540-48910-X_16

11. Shamir, A.: How to share a secret. Commun. ACM **22**(11), 612–613 (1979)

Early Detection of In-Memory Malicious Activity Based on Run-Time Environmental Features

Dorel Yaffe$^{(\boxtimes)}$ and Danny Hendler$^{(\boxtimes)}$

Department of Computer Science, Ben-Gurion University, Beer-Sheva, Israel
yaffed@post.bgu.ac.il, hendlerd@bgu.ac.il

Abstract. We present a novel end-to-end solution for in-memory malicious activity detection done prior to exploitation by leveraging machine learning capabilities based on data from unique run-time logs, which are carefully curated in order to detect malicious activity in the memory of protected processes. This solution achieves reduced overhead and false positives as well as deployment simplicity.

Keywords: Malware detection · In-memory attacks · Early detection

1 Introduction

In recent years malware has become increasingly sophisticated and difficult to detect prior to exploitation [5]. Several approaches that attempt to detect and protect against it prior to exploitation of the target exist, see e.g. [3,4,12]. Solutions include Endpoint Protection Platforms (EPP) such as legacy or next-generation anti-viruses, Endpoint Detection and Response (EDR), Managed Detection and Response (MDR), Cross-layered Detection and Response (XDR) and many more [2]. These solutions usually rely on either a constantly updated database of signatures for detecting malware variants that have already been seen in the wild, a predefined set of rules or heuristics for identifying malicious activity by actions taken by a program, leveraging more advanced machine learning techniques like behavioral analysis (to deduce if an entity or set of actions is malicious or not), or any hybrid combination of these approaches [7,11,15].

All these approaches have shortcomings when it comes to identifying malware correctly prior to exploitation. In some cases, if the resource defined as a potential target is critical to the organization, e.g. a global authentication service running on a secure server, the owners will have a high incentive to protect it, but for most protection mechanisms this is likely to cause an increased number of false positives on accesses of the resource, an adverse impact on performance, or even reduced resource functionality. All these potential problems often deter organizations from hardening the protection of critical resources in comparison with the rest of the system [1,6]. The end result is a similar protection level for all system resources, which is often insufficient for protecting against very sophisticated malware, especially in-memory ones [9,13].

© Springer Nature Switzerland AG 2021
S. Dolev et al. (Eds.): CSCML 2021, LNCS 12716, pp. 397–404, 2021.
https://doi.org/10.1007/978-3-030-78086-9_29

In this work, we present a security mechanism that ensures, with high probability, that detection occurs in real time prior to any malicious action. Our solution was implemented by training a malware detection machine learning model on a large data-set of run-time logs (provided by Morphisec Ltd) that were collected from real-world machines during both standard workloads and real malware attacks. The logs contain a set of environmental and process-related variables efficiently extracted during run-time, identified as important for the detection of in-memory attacks. Using the deployed detector, our system is able to query a minimal run-time log from a critical process to infer if an in-memory malicious activity is about to take place and perform a mitigation action before any harmful operation is performed.

Malware detection using ML models often analyzes the contents of files (e.g. executable files) or other data sources for extracting features to train the model [14], or transforms the problem to another domain, such as image recognition [20]. Unlike these approaches, our solution uses run time environment logs in an efficient and seamless manner (in comparison to a memory dump analysis or sandbox/VM approach [8,16–18]). In comparison to other solutions that monitor processes in real-time (e.g. [10]), our solution is non-intrusive and has low performance overhead. It also reduces false positives to a minimum, as a threshold is set depending on how early the detection is required, providing a trade-off between the length of the early warning interval and the rate of false positives.

2   Dataset

The dataset used in this research is composed of logs, each of which containing environmental information regarding a specific process, that were collected live at runtime. The environmental information collected consists of both static data (that could have been collected without the execution of the process) and dynamic data collected from the virtual memory of the process itself. The dataset spans logs collected between January 1, 2019 and December 31, 2019. These logs were collected during real world incidents in actual production machines. They were collected using a proprietary agent program (provided by Morphisec Ltd). This proprietary software leverages deep integration in the operating system's kernel in order to block malicious activity during runtime using various memory-morphing techniques. These logs were taken *prior to exploitation*, which means that any malicious activity has not yet taken place in the target machine, however, the malicious entity was indeed running. The dataset consists of two types of logs:

1. **Malicious activity**: Environmental runtime logs from incidents where the following actions taken by the malicious entity were indeed malicious (e.g. a log from the starting point of a ransomware malware execution).
2. **Benign activity**: Environmental runtime logs from incidents where the application/process/service are benign and the following actions were non-malicious (e.g. opening a malware-free document file via Microsoft Word).

Using the proprietary deterministic solution to mark each log, means that all of the records in the dataset are already **labeled** as *malicious* or *benign*. These labels were reviewed regularly by malware analysts to further reduce the probability of false positives/negatives.

Data Analysis. Each log is unique, there are no two logs which are exactly the same. Any identifiable information in the logs, such as usernames, machine names, domain names, etc. was anonymized in order to preserve privacy. In Table 1 and Table 2 we present some statistics about the dataset.

Table 1. Dataset: Labels

Label	Count
Malicious	1,637,645
Benign	827,938
Total	2,465,583

Table 2. Dataset: Classification

Classification by type	Count
Classified	1,043,520
Unclassified	594,125
Total (malicious)	1,637,645

As can be seen from Table 1, there is almost a 2:1 ratio between the malicious samples and the benign ones. As presented by Table 2, almost two thirds of the malicious samples are also classified by type (e.g. Trojan). As we show in the full paper [19], our data set is heterogeneous in terms of malware and attack types, operating systems, machines, users etc., thus the data is unlikely to cause over-fitting to any one of these characteristics.

There are *20* malware categories in the dataset as classified by YARA rules. The records in the dataset are basically documents in JSON format, resembling runtime logs containing a predetermined set of fields holding environmental data about a certain process under observation. The log files contain a lot of textual information. Nevertheless, their size is typically quite small, peaking at 500 KB. There are dozens of different fields and attributes as part of the log specification (which is proprietary), however, we chose only the most relevant fields in the logs (listed in the full paper [19]), which are also available to be collected during runtime using open source tools and/or low level coding.

3   Pre-processing and Model Generation

The essence of the solution lays in the machine learning model trained on a big data set of real-world logs representing malicious activity in various execution stages and from various types of malware, as well as benign data from standard applications.

High-level Flow. The high level flow of the model training procedure is as follows:

1. Given a data set of logs in the correct format, extract the textual features required and convert them from textual representations to numeric vectors using a standard Natural Language Processing algorithm, do this for every value (i.e. a full word) in the logs.
2. Given a data set of logs represented as numeric vectors (that is, the output from the previous stage), convert each log file containing these numeric representations to a single numeric vector, using a standard calculation from the world of document classification.
3. Given a set of numeric vectors to be used as a training set with proper labels (either malware or benign), train a prediction model in a supervised manner, using a standard Machine Learning ensemble approach from the world of classification.

We describe the training process in more detail in the following sub-sections.

Data Preparation. In this stage, we did the following:

1. Cleaned the data where it was needed using Python scripting over the JSON documents:
   (a) Dealing with wrong data types (e.g. text instead of integer) by removing it altogether.
   (b) Dealing with missing values, keep them as is (empty), as long as most of the log itself still contains proper values.
   (c) Normalizing numeric values that were out of the range expected for certain fields, taking the average from the same classification group.
   (d) Correcting errors in parsing in case of incorrect syntax, etc.
2. Shuffling of the logs in order to avoid any existing patterns in the way they will be split to sets.
3. We split the data set according to the "Holdout method" to a training set, which also acts as a validation set, and a testing set, ahead of time. The dataset we use, whose dimensions are presented in Table 1, consists of the instances of the test set (set aside initially and consisting of an equal number of malicious and benign instances) and a subset of the remaining instances of a larger collection of instances from 2019. The proportion between malicious and benign training set instances was selected so as to optimize the AUC of our cross-validation tests on the training set. The best cross validation results were obtained when the proportion of malicious instances in the training set is approximately 70%, as shown by Table 3.

Table 3. Pre-processing and model generation: split to sets

Set	Malicious	Benign	Total
Training	1,336,432	526,725	1,863,157
Test (Holdout)	301,213	301,213	602,426

4. Prepared the high-performance training server, placing the relevant sets of documents ready to be input to the next stage in the process.

Feature Engineering. The main strength of our model lays in its features chosen carefully from the logs as each and every one of them contributes in the detection process. We chose approximately 40 features, consisting of metadata fields, runtime-related features, and PE-related fields. Anonymized features were not selected. The full list of features is presented in the full paper [19].

Textual Features to Associations. After extracting the features, we wanted to understand what is the similarity between all their values in the set that we received. As the features have textual representation we decided to leverage this and use a well-known method from the field of Natural Language Processing, called *word2vec*. This method uses a shallow two-layered neural network to process and convert every value ('word') in the log to a meaningful one-dimensional vector of size 32. Using *word2vec*, values ('words') with similar context should have a similar vector as given by measuring cosine similarity between values. The *word2vec* model is trained in an unsupervised manner, which means we ignore the labels (benign, malicious), and provide a vector for each and every unique feature value in the training set.

Dimensionality Reduction. After the *word2vec* model is trained, we need to convert every log as a whole to a representative vector that we can work with. For this purpose we use a common method usually used for document classification tasks, which allows us to reduce the dimension of the log while preserving semantics. For each of the following types of features, we calculated the mean vector of all the vectors (that we received as an output from the *word2vec* model) that represents the values ('words') inside them using Python scripting:

1. Stack snapshot and trace
2. Registers data, opcodes collected in memory
3. Loaded modules and resources
4. Process and metadata information

This produces a one-dimensional vector of size 192 for every specific log. This vector is then used as input for a supervised classifier to be trained in the next stage.

Training. Now that we have all the logs represented as one-dimensional vectors in the training set, we can input them as training data with their labels, to an ML algorithm trained in a supervised manner. We chose the gradient boosting technique which outputs a prediction model in the form of an ensemble of weak prediction models (in our case, *Decision trees*). We wanted a simple pre-tweaked black box solution for gradient boosting, so we tested both of the popular options: *XGBoost* and *LightGBM*. Since there were only minor differences between them in terms of detection quality, we chose *LightGBM* which was easier to use.

4   Detection Framework

Architecture. Our detection framework consists of the following parts:

I. "Detector": A novel machine learning model trained on a big data set of environmental run-time logs captured from real-world malicious incidents per a specific protected process. This model runs on a standard server in the cloud, receives a log for detection and replies with a relative score, quantifying the probability that the activity represented by the log is malicious.
II. "Agent": A lightweight service running on the endpoint machine whose task is to generate log instances from critical processes that are to be protected and send them to the Detector over the network.

High level flow

1. A critical process, which should be protected, is running on the endpoint machine, a lightweight log extraction service is installed and extracts logs during run-time as required.
2. The extracted log is sent from the endpoint machine to the Detector server.
3. The Detector server inputs the received log into the already-deployed machine learning model to receive a detection score.
4. A result with a score for the activity diagnosed from the given log, is being sent from the server to the endpoint for taking further actions as needed.

5   Experimental Evaluation

Our evaluation uses the test set defined in Sect. 3. The results are presented by Table 4. These results were obtained by using a classification threshold of 0.75.

Table 4. Experimental Evaluation: Confusion Matrix for the test set

	Positive (predicted)	Negative (predicted)
Positive (actual)	301,202	11
Negative (actual)	111	301,102

Other metrics that are computed based on the confusion matrix are shown in Table 5.

As presented by Table 5, detection quality is very high. Specifically, the recall is nearly 1 while the FPR is extremely low, approximately 0.04%. We also analyzed the run-time requirements of our solution, establishing that its overhead is small, and conducted additional experiments that are described in the full paper [19].

Table 5. Experimental Evaluation: Metrics for the test set

Metric	Value
Area Under the ROC Curve (AUC)	0.997712
Accuracy (ACC)	0.999797
Precision (PPV)	0.999632
Recall (TPR)	0.999963
False positive rate (FPR)	0.000369
False negative rate (FNR)	0.000037
F1 Score	0.999798

6   Conclusion

As malware rose in sophistication and volume in recent years, so is the requirement for innovative solutions for its detection. In this work we presented an end
to end ML-based solution for the early detection of in-memory malicious activity via runtime logs, to demonstrate the potential of leveraging the plethora of
process and environment data that can be collected from processes executing
on endpoint machines over time and be used for malware detection. Our experimental evaluation establishes that this approach has the potential of yielding
high-quality detection of malicious process activity before it performs harmful
operations.

In future work, we plan to investigate the length of the early warning period
that can be achieved using our detection approach, that is, how long before the
malware attempts to execute its harmful operations can it be detected using
our approach. In addition, there are challenges yet to be overcome regarding our
solution's limitations, which include: reducing the downtime on update, minimizing compatibility issues on the Agent's side, attempting to provide offline
detections, overcoming the performance limitation of parallel logging and the
overhead stemming from retraining of the model. Additional avenues for future
research include extending our detector by improving the server-side component,
security, communications, anti tampering, and logging mechanisms.

References

1. Meeting the challenges of endpoint security. https://www.cstl.com/utils/downloa
   ds/Symantec-Hosted-Endpoint-Whitepaper.pdf. Accessed Oct 2020
2. Understanding MDR, EDR, EPP and XDR. https://www.netsurion.com/articles/
   understanding-mdr-edr-epp-and-xdr. Accessed Oct 20202
3. Aslan, Ö.A., Samet, R.: A comprehensive review on malware detection approaches.
   IEEE Access **8**, 6249–6271 (2020)
4. Chakkaravarthy, S.S., Sangeetha, D., Vaidehi, V.: A survey on malware analysis
   and mitigation techniques. Comput. Sci. Rev. **32**, 1–23 (2019)

5. Erdődi, L., Jøsang, A.: Exploitation vs. prevention: the ongoing saga of software vulnerabilities. Acta Polytechnica Hungarica **17**(7) (2020)
6. Hăjmăşan, G., Mondoc, A., Portase, R., Creţ, O.: Performance improvements in behavior based malware detection solutions. In: Janczewski, L.J., Kutyłowski, M. (eds.) SEC 2018. IAICT, vol. 529, pp. 370–384. Springer, Cham (2018). https://doi.org/10.1007/978-3-319-99828-2_26
7. Irshad, M., Al-Khateeb, H.M., Mansour, A., Ashawa, M., Hamisu, M.: Effective methods to detect metamorphic malware: a systematic review. Int. J. Electron. Secur. Digit. Forensics **10**(2), 138–154 (2018)
8. Jamalpur, S., Navya, Y.S., Raja, P., Tagore, G., Rao, G.R.K.: Dynamic malware analysis using cuckoo sandbox. In: 2018 Second International Conference on Inventive Communication and Computational Technologies (ICICCT), pp. 1056–1060. IEEE (2018)
9. Kumar, S., et al.: An emerging threat fileless malware: a survey and research challenges. Cybersecurity **3**(1), 1–12 (2020)
10. Marculet, D.G., Benchea, R., Gavrilut, D.T.: Methods for training neural networks with zero false positives for malware detection. In: 2019 21st International Symposium on Symbolic and Numeric Algorithms for Scientific Computing (SYNASC), pp. 230–236. IEEE (2019)
11. Naz, S., Singh, D.K.: Review of machine learning methods for windows malware detection. In: 2019 10th International Conference on Computing, Communication and Networking Technologies (ICCCNT), pp. 1–6. IEEE (2019)
12. Or-Meir, O., Nissim, N., Elovici, Y., Rokach, L.: Dynamic malware analysis in the modern era–a state of the art survey. ACM Comput. Surv. (CSUR) **52**(5), 1–48 (2019)
13. Patten, D.: The evolution to fileless malware (2017). http://www.infosecwriters.com/papers/dpatten_fileless.pdf. Accessed 2020
14. Sihwail, R., Omar, K., Ariffin, K.Z.: A survey on malware analysis techniques: static, dynamic, hybrid and memory analysis. Int. J. Adv. Sci. Eng. Inf. Technol. **8**(4-2), 1662 (2018)
15. Souri, A., Hosseini, R.: A state-of-the-art survey of malware detection approaches using data mining techniques. Hum.-centric Comput. Inf. Sci. **8**(1), 3 (2018)
16. Tien, C.W., Liao, J.W., Chang, S.C., Kuo, S.Y.: Memory forensics using virtual machine introspection for malware analysis. In: 2017 IEEE Conference on Dependable and Secure Computing, pp. 518–519. IEEE (2017)
17. Walker, A., Amjad, M.F., Sengupta, S.: Cuckoo's malware threat scoring and classification: friend or foe? In: 2019 IEEE 9th Annual Computing and Communication Workshop and Conference (CCWC), pp. 0678–0684. IEEE (2019)
18. Wang, C., Ding, J., Guo, T., Cui, B.: A malware detection method based on sandbox, binary instrumentation and multidimensional feature extraction. In: Barolli, L., Xhafa, F., Conesa, J. (eds.) BWCCA 2017. LNDECT, vol. 12, pp. 427–438. Springer, Cham (2018). https://doi.org/10.1007/978-3-319-69811-3_39
19. Yaffe, D., Hendler, D.: Early detection of in-memory malicious activity based on run-time environmental features (2021). [https://arxiv.org/abs/2103.16029]
20. Zhang, J., Qin, Z., Yin, H., Ou, L., Hu, Y.: IRMD: malware variant detection using opcode image recognition. In: 2016 IEEE 22nd International Conference on Parallel and Distributed Systems (ICPADS), pp. 1175–1180. IEEE (2016)

Software Integrity and Validation Using Cryptographic Composability and Computer Vision

Donald Beaver[(✉)] ⓘ

Pittsburgh, PA, USA
https://linkedin.com/in/donaldbeaver

Abstract. A significant aspect of software integrity is the ability to determine whether a system is correctly showing the information it is intended to show. This work combines abstract cryptographic composability principles with automated machine learning techniques to support a new methodology for software integrity checking, particularly in the intractable domain of interface validation. A subtle but often perilously overlooked cryptographic principle is the requirement that a sender be aware of the meaning of inputs, specifically of the cleartext behind encrypted messages. We propose using computer vision to evaluate whether interfaces exhibit technical awareness of information content, enabling automated development-time and real-time integrity checking that is far more efficient and extensive than manual analysis.

Keywords: Integrity · Assurance · Composability · Cryptography · Machine learning · Computer vision · User interfaces

1 Background

As the chief method for understanding and evaluating computational results in any setting, user interfaces should have a high requirement for integrity and correctness, yet rarely are they evaluated with the kind of attention needed for high assurance, let alone baseline assurance. A consumer-grade interface for a mobile app with a multi-million user base might have a very moderate yet expensive level of human quality assurance applied to it, along with some traditional but highly brittle validation tools. But it can also be a risk factor as an infrastructure component for society in general as well as an implicit dependency of high-vulnerability, mission-critical systems in public or military sectors. As such, the moderate expense of human involvement may be far less than required for proper assurance. The pressure to reduce expensive human QA increases by the day, even assuming humans are up to the tedious and repetitive task of evaluating constantly revised software.

This work proposes a new paradigm for user interface validation, taking human effort out of the loop by applying automated machine learning inspired

© Springer Nature Switzerland AG 2021
S. Dolev et al. (Eds.): CSCML 2021, LNCS 12716, pp. 405–413, 2021.
https://doi.org/10.1007/978-3-030-78086-9_30

by cryptographic proof methodologies. We focus here on exploring and motivating the parallels between assuring cryptographic security and assuring software reliability, at a broad conceptual level. Case studies with software experience and engineering impact are described in detail in accompanying works [2].

One broad approach for validating software implementations is to require particular language implementations and then apply formal, somewhat automatable reasoning techniques to offer proofs or assurance that the results of a computation will be correct. Specifications are laid out in mathematical formality and then proved to the extent possible.

An engineering approach is also possible, in which inspection of many test cases provides desired code coverage and case coverage. In many settings, automated testing has become the primary vehicle for software validation, particularly given the large scale, collaborative and dynamic nature of modern software. Test cases accumulate and themselves require revision, but they provide the captured specification of desirable behavior, even if incomplete.

Many settings, however, are resistant to proof or automation because their very nature is hard to capture in simple declarations or as a function which maps text inputs to text outputs. In particular, user interfaces offer visual or auditory messages and affordances which can be challenging to describe in a mechanically-verifiable way.

For example, "A stop sign icon is showing" in an autonomous vehicle display is easy for a human to understand as a specification, but not simple to declare for automated validation. Over time, an icon may be updated. Its presence or position may be hard to specify formally, while also being tedious for a human to verify.

Typical *ad hoc* UI validation methods include comparing images to previous snapshots. These comparisons are brittle when changes are made, and often impossible until a first prototype is built to obtain a baseline golden image after manual verification. Still, golden images constitute a significant portion of automated interface validation, while being an inconvenience to developers when changes are made.

The gap between human skills and mechanical capabilities means that a user interface is essentially an encryption of the relevant state of a system, hidden from automated interpretation. The human must be able to decrypt the message embodied in the UI presentation, quickly and easily. There is generally no requirement that a machine can interpret the UI presentation, however. The lack of mechanical interpretability is an obstacle to automated software assurance.

Our goal in this work is to motivate a design pattern to support verification of visual presentations, driven by analogies with concepts of awareness and proofs of knowledge in cryptography. We will need to address two aspects: (1) the ability to interpret a visual presentation (analogous to a ciphertext) as a plaintext, thereby demonstrating knowledge of the plaintext; and (2) a suitable choice of what the analogy to a plaintext actually is.

1.1   Computer Vision and Cryptographic Awareness

Computer Vision techniques can fill part of the automation gap, by offering dynamic and flexible ways to detect visual affordances. Validating whether an affordance is present and correctly rendered is critical for assessing if an interface is providing required information or is behaving in error or corruption. Recent advances in object detection make it feasible to specify and detect particular objects in a visual rendering, such as an icon for a stop sign.

Still, automated object detection using modern machine-learned networks isn't quite enough, since there needs to be a specification for when and how those affordances appear.

Enter cryptography, which obsesses about and offers an interpretation of what is "encrypted" in the "ciphertext message" conveyed by interface to human, for the human to decrypt. In other words, cryptography demands an interpretation of what is encoded in the encryption.

Drawing parallels, we regard the visualization as an encryption with respect to a weak adversary - a machine which is generally incapable of understanding visualizations tendered for human consumption. We need to resolve two goals: can this "encryption" be explained by awareness of a cleartext, and what exactly is that cleartext in the first place?

With very recent developments in computer vision, we can bridge the gap of needing a human to "decode" affordances, interpreting them against a suitably chosen cleartext message rather than against previous encodings (golden images). We don't want to ask golden-image style questions, "Did we get the same encryptions of messages as we did during the previous deployments?" We do want to ask, "Do the latest encryptions decode to the expected set of clear messages that currently underpin them?"

The latter question requires a cleartext, though. The lynchpin is the universal architecture of backend-frontend distributed systems. In virtually every modern setting (twenty-first century), a backend communicates with a frontend by way of a tree of text, often JSON. These text-based structures describe values to be displayed, such as warnings or speeds or summaries.

This work serves as a proposal to interpret backend-to-frontend communications as the cleartext in an ideal crytographic protocol. The backend messages are what the frontend's display must be "aware" of. Specifically, one must be able to reconstruct backend messages simply by observing the proffered interface. When there is support for a claim that backend messages can be decoded as expected, there is assurance that what a human sees is correct, valid and actionable.

The standard golden-image approach would correspond to comparing latest encryptions to encryptions done in earlier implementations. This is not the goal of this paradigm - and it contains no reference to anything corresponding to cleartexts. Here, we interpret encryptions by mapping to suitably defined cleartexts, namely backend-frontend data-model messages.

The combination of machine learning and cryptographic principles offers a way to ensure stronger integrity and effective validation in an easily automated manner.

Concrete case studies to support the proposals here have been conducted and are reported elsewhere [2]. This work conveys the overall approach and motivation, drawing parallels between cryptographic principles, machine learning tools and software assurance.

2   Cryptographic Awareness

The specific principle of interest, born in attempts to prove cryptographic protocols secure, is a notion called *awareness*. In encryption settings, it requires the sender of $E(x)$ to demonstrate knowledge of x. In other settings, described in more detail shortly, it requires an interpretation of any protocol message in terms of an "ideal protocol" communication.

Without awareness, cryptosystems and protocols fall prey to subtle abuse. For example, consider a naive voting system in which a voter V_1 sends a public-key encryption $E_k(v_1)$ to a ballot collector with public key k. Voter V_2 can copy V_1's vote without knowing what it is, simply sending $E_k(v_1)$.

Certainly, this seems like a trivial weakness with little impact. Let's address some of the concerns, however. First, on basic principles, this voting method permits something not possible with a standard ballot box or a collection of handwritten votes tossed in a hat. Having deviated from the properties supported by an ideal implementation, it's not clear that we can rely on further conclusions about this real implementation, such as whether the votes can be biased in unexpected ways or the system can be abused when composed with multiple interactions.

Consider a ballot with three choices, all roughly equally favored by a voter base of a thousand members. Specifically, the tallies might concretely be 330, 340, 330 for A, B and C, respectively. A coalition of a dozen conspiring voters can easily discover who V_1 voted for, by copying V_1's vote and observing the tipped, winning choice.

Thus, a single invocation of an awareness-disrespecting protocol can leak critical information. There are also settings where a single invocation reveals nothing useful but composition of protocols leads to complete failure.

For example, an efficiency improvement in a cryptographic tool known as Oblivious Transfer [11] was proposed by Den Boer [4] as a way to avoid repeating highly expensive public key generation computations. OT allows a sender to send a message that arrives with 50-50 probability, but the sender doesn't learn whether it was delivered or not. The asymmetry in knowledge is critical for digital checks and balances, and finds application in many cryptographic settings like zero-knowledge proof systems [8]. Finding a fast implementation that overcame the need to generate a new public composite $n = pq$ each and every iteration was of significant value.

It was shown soon after, however, that repeated use of the n in the manner proposed in [4] permitted a sender to obtain otherwise-intractable knowledge about the quadratic residuosity of values modulo n. The sender could present values whose residuosity matched other unknown values (similar to copying a vote without knowing the vote). The sender could combine unknown values homomorphically.

For security, it is critical that the knowledge remain asymmetric, namely that the sender not know which values have been observed in the clear and which remain hidden to the receiver. But with these capabilities, the sender could then break the knowledge barrier and determine what the receiver received in a significant fraction if not all of the invocations, defeating the purpose of the protocol.

Whether it is a single protocol invocation or a composition of protocols, the lack of technical awareness is a critical pitfall in cryptographic settings. Should one be concerned only with "awareness," though, and how does it relate to ordinary software integrity and validation? Let's turn first to exposing where awareness lies in the pantheon of cryptographic concerns and then see the new role it offers in practical software validation.

2.1   Universal Composability and Real vs Ideal

Awareness is tied deeply to tools used to show that protocols can safely be composed together. The underpinning of Universal Composability [5] is a notion of comparing a "real" execution to an "ideal" execution [1]. If attacks on a real execution can be shown to be no more powerful than attacks on an ideal execution, then, informally, the real implementation is considered composably secure.

To relate a real execution (say, with RSA encryption) to an ideal execution (say, with a trusted communication channel or trusted third party), some technical machinery is involved. Specifically, one must exhibit a simulator machine that is capable of attacking an ideal scenario while also presenting a facsimile of a real scenario to a given attacker. If the attacker cannot discern whether it is attacking real or ideal (by way of simulator), and if the end results of the executions (the outputs produced by various participants) are also indistinguishable, then one can conclude the protocol is secure.

The messages sent in the ideal setting can be considered the generalization of a "cleartext." If the ideal model is a simple point-to-point communication, then the ideal-execution messages are precisely cleartexts. The composability and awareness models allow for broader kinds of interactions, like voting or function-evaluation or secret-sharing or oblivious transfer, with more general meaning to what those ideal messages represent.

Awareness, then, consists of knowing what messages have been sent in the ideal execution. Technically, the simulator must be able to extract a message to be sent on an ideal channel. The ability to extract a message is what demonstrates awareness of that message.

The lack of technical awareness is a critical but recognized pitfall in cryptographic settings, and it has proved out as a natural aspect of the encompassing notion of protocol composability. This argues its importance, but it is unheard of in other settings such as software or interface validation, where a mix of ad hoc methodologies offer support but formal notions are challenging to deploy in practice. Let's consider some formal notions and then examine how modern machine learning supports applying them toward better UI assurance.

3 Synthesizing Backend Communications from GUI Renderings

To draw the analogy between cryptographic awareness and GUI interpretation, formalisms from [2] are repeated below. The current work is a description of broad connections and does not present a specific case analysis, so these formalisms set the basis for discussion but are not employed in this work. We refer to [2] for case studies and specific applications.

Typical user interfaces employ a frontend client which updates a presentation based on a JSON text-based dictionary tree model x supplied by a backend service. The client GUI G then renders an image, $G(x)$. To demonstrate *awareness of the input* x, one must *extract* x from $G(x)$, namely *interpret* the GUI in terms of the backend "cleartext" JSON.

Definition 1. *A GUI G is ϵ-aware of the model, with respect to an input distribution D on model data, if there exists an efficient interpreter I such that $I(G(x)) = x$ with probability exceeding $1 - \epsilon$.*

Since a GUI may often omit information on purpose, we allow for a filter F to restrict demands to a subset of the model data, often to just a specific subtree:

Definition 2. *A GUI G is ϵ-aware of the model relative to filter F, with respect to an input distribution D on model data, if there exists an efficient interpreter I such that $F(I(G(x))) = F(x)$ with probability exceeding $1 - \epsilon$.*

When applying these concepts to software engineering settings, the distribution may be challenging to define formally, since it should match what is seen when the software is deployed. Our concern here is not how to discover such distributions but rather to supply an analogy for showing awareness with respect to a particular distribution, chosen as effectively as possible. Test-driven development itself has two components: having a way to test code, and having a way to produce a span of tests [3,6,9,10,12,13]. We focus here on having a new way to test code.

Definition 3. *Let a test suite S generate backend text models with distribution D. A GUI G satisfies awareness-based assurance with respect to test suite S and filter F if it is ϵ-aware of the model with respect to D and relative to F.*

We wish to consider validators and show they cannot discern real from ideal. The ultimate technical goal will be to show any validator is unable to distinguish the two settings. In case studies and proposed software practice, these validators are generally intended to be simple equality tests on subtrees, and the goal is to provide a simple validator to use in a test-driven setting.

Definition 4. *Let V take an input pair of strings, (a, b), and report a 1-bit output. A test validator V supports awareness-based assurance of GUI G if $|Pr[V(f_0, f_1) = i] - 1/2| < \epsilon$, where i is a uniformly random bit, f_i is $F(x)$ with x sampled from D, and $f_{1-i} = F(I(G((x))))$.*

4   Awareness-Based Development Paradigm

One purpose of drawing the analogy between cryptographic awareness and user-interface development is to show how to make a UI more robust by facilitating test-driven development (TDD). The novel paradigm is this:

1. Visual specifications using slide deck quality (e.g. PowerPoint)
2. Backend model is defined (JSON schema)
3. Train object detector on labeled spec (design deck) to identify affordances
4. Write test code to map detected affordances to synthesized JSON

While identifying affordances using computer vision is not novel [13], prior applications sought to generate test sequences and then compare golden images. The notion of mapping images to backend messages is novel.

Computer Vision. A key element in this paradigm is to automate visual testing of a UI by replacing the two current but expensive and brittle validation patterns with a robust, automated test framework. (Current approaches include expensive human vetting by way of manual interpretations of spec, or automated but brittle comparisons of previous golden snapshots.)

Case studies in [2] demonstrate that CV-based object detection can be trained from PowerPoint-quality designer spec and then applied robustly to the later-implemented actual GUI. This takes human effort out of the quality-assurance (QA) approach. It also eliminates the brittle nature of golden snapshots.

The human effort of validating implementations *de novo* and after modifications is replaced by an initial machine-learning labeling effort. It suffices to label the slide-deck quality images, marking when affordances are present or not. Moreover, the labeling is itself very straightforward, since the designer has presumably already organized sample images in terms of known states (like: "stop sign present" or "warning light showing") for the purpose of instructing engineering efforts.

Awareness. The next step in the paradigm is to validate images formally not merely by detecting affordances but by recreating the original JSON which gave rise to them. An example case study from [2] explores testing whether an emergency indicator is shown on-screen. In an awareness-based test-driven development phase, an extractor is written as part of the test code to map states where indicators are detected to JSON subtrees that trigger an indicator in the first place. The extractor code generates JSON without such triggers when it is provided images in which the indicator is not detected by automated CV. While engineers need to write extractor code, just as they need to write test-driven tests in any TDD setting, there is no need for QA or online verification.

Software Development Efforts. Given the level of formal cryptographic motivation, it seems that this paradigm could be quite expensive. Simple case studies show otherwise [2]: a feasible implementation of test-driven GUI development using automated awareness-based validation took less than a week to produce. The backend, GUI, awareness-interpreter and validator in a simple case study. Filtering JSON on a warning mode and using a test suite whose distribution is over pseudorandomly generated warning states (presence or lack thereof), the extracted JSON matched the actual source JSON without error.

4.1   Online Self-validation

As described above, the interpreter/extractor should run efficiently in a test setup, but there is no requirement that it be fast enough to work on resource-limited client hardware. It turns out that object-detection processing is certainly fast enough even on a handheld device to deploy with the application. Inconsistencies can be noted in real time and detected immediately when the extracted JSON fails to match the backend-supplied JSON.

Although not specifically a required goal, the computer-vision processing can be fast enough even on a handheld device to deploy with the application and note inconsistencies in real time. The instrumented app can immediately show that it knows it is in an incorrect display state, flagging and reporting bugs as they occur in the wild.

The formalisms speak of distributions where interpretations must be faithful. By deploying self-testing with the application, the awareness-based validation is expanded to offer much greater assurance because it relies on accurate real-world distributions, not just synthetic or sampled logs used during development.

5   Summary

This work describes a validation paradigm for user interfaces which relies on cheap, automated interpretations of presented images, instead of the traditional focus on brittle image-to-image consistency or on expensive human interpretation of sampled images.

Two aspects are essential for this paradigm to work. First, recent computer vision techniques have shown sufficient power (e.g. object detection for affordances) to enable steps needed to interpret presented images. Second, a notion inspired by cryptographic awareness of cleartexts is the basis for defining and measuring the target of interpretation: the backend-supplied model data (analogous to cleartexts in cryptography).

By automating the UI interpretation in terms of backend model data, our awareness-based test-driven paradigm allows testing to be set up in advance of the first implementations of a project, and to be based on initial and sketched specifications which are not bit-for-bit replicas of a final screening. This drives down the cost of testing, increasing the appeal and robustness of testing, and thereby increasing the assurances offered during deployment.

References

1. Beaver, D.: Foundations of secure interactive computing. In: Feigenbaum, J. (ed.) CRYPTO 1991. LNCS, vol. 576, pp. 377–391. Springer, Heidelberg (1992). https://doi.org/10.1007/3-540-46766-1_31
2. Beaver, D.: Applied awareness: test-driven GUI development using computer vision and cryptography. Arxiv 2006.03725 (2020)
3. Bures, M., Macik, M., Ahmed, B.S., Rechtberger, V., Slavik, P.: Testing the usability and accessibility of smart tv applications using an automated model-based approach. IEEE Trans. Consum. Electron. **66**(2), 134–143 (2020)
4. Boer, B.: Oblivious transfer protecting secrecy. In: Damgård, I.B. (ed.) EURO-CRYPT 1990. LNCS, vol. 473, pp. 31–45. Springer, Heidelberg (1991). https://doi.org/10.1007/3-540-46877-3_4
5. Canetti, R.: Universally composable security: a new paradigm for cryptographic protocols. In: Symposium on Foundations of Computer Science, FOCS 2001, pp. 136–145. IEEE Computer Society (2001)
6. Chang, T.H., Yeh, T., Miller, R.C.: GUI testing using computer vision. In: Proceedings of the SIGCHI Conference on Human Factors in Computing Systems, CHI 2010, pp. 1535–1544. Association for Computing Machinery, New York (2010)
7. Givens, P., Chakarov, A., Sankaranarayanan, S., Yeh, T.: Exploring the internal state of user interfaces by combining computer vision techniques with grammatical inference. In: 2013 35th International Conference on Software Engineering (ICSE), pp. 1165–1168 (2013)
8. Goldwasser, S., Micali, S., Rackoff, C.: The knowledge complexity of interactive proof systems. SIAM J. Comput. **18**(1), 186–208 (1989)
9. Nguyen, B.N., Robbins, B., Banerjee, I., Memon, A.: GUITAR: an innovative tool for automated testing of GUI-driven software. Autom. Softw. Eng. **21**(1), 65–105 (2014)
10. Qureshi, I.A., Nadeem, A.: GUI testing techniques: a survey. Int. J. Future Comput. Commun. **2**(2), 142–146 (2013)
11. Rabin, M.O.: How to exchange secrets by oblivious transfer. Technical Report TR-81, Aiken Computation Laboratory, Harvard University (1981)
12. Reza, H., Endapally, S., Grant, E.: A model-based approach for testing GUI using hierarchical predicate transition nets. In: Fourth International Conference on Information Technology (ITNG 2007), pp. 366–370 (2007)
13. Yeh, T., Chang, T.-H., Miller, R.C.: Sikuli: using GUI screenshots for search and automation. In: Proceedings of the 22nd Annual ACM Symposium on User Interface Software and Technology, UIST 2009, pp. 183–192. Association for Computing Machinery, New York (2009)

Efficient Generic Arithmetic for KKW

Practical Linear MPC-in-the-Head NIZK on Commodity Hardware Without Trusted Setup

David Heath[(✉)], Vladimir Kolesnikov, and Jiahui Lu

Georgia Institute of Technology, Atlanta, GA, USA
{heath.davidanthony,kolesnikov,jlu355}@gatech.edu

Abstract. Katz et al., CCS 2018 (KKW) is a popular and efficient MPC-in-the-head non-interactive ZKP (NIZK) scheme, which is the technical core of the post-quantum signature scheme Picnic, currently considered for standardization by NIST. The KKW approach simultaneously is concretely efficient, even on commodity hardware, and does not rely on trusted setup. Importantly, the approach scales linearly in the circuit size with low constants with respect to proof generation time, proof verification time, proof size, and RAM consumption. However, KKW works with Boolean circuits only and hence incurs significant cost for circuits that include arithmetic operations.

In this work, we extend KKW with a suite of efficient arithmetic operations over arbitrary rings and Boolean conversions. Rings $\mathbb{Z}_{2^k}$ are important for NIZK as they naturally match the basic operations of modern programs and CPUs. In particular, we:
- present a suitable ring representation consistent with KKW,
- construct efficient conversion operators that translate between arithmetic and Boolean representations, and
- demonstrate how to efficiently operate over the arithmetic representation, including a vector dot product of length-n vectors with cost equal to that of a *single* multiplication.

These improvements substantially improve KKW for circuits with arithmetic. As one example, we can multiply 100×100 square matrices of 32 bit number using $3200\times$ smaller proof size than standard KKW ($100\times$ improvement from our dot product construction and $32\times$ from moving to an arithmetic representation).

We discuss in detail proof size and resource consumption and argue the practicality of running large proofs on commodity hardware.

Keywords: MPC-in-the-Head · Zero knowledge

© Springer Nature Switzerland AG 2021
S. Dolev et al. (Eds.): CSCML 2021, LNCS 12716, pp. 414–431, 2021.
https://doi.org/10.1007/978-3-030-78086-9_31

1   Introduction

Zero-knowledge proofs of knowledge (ZKPoKs) enable a prover $\mathcal{P}$, given a public circuit C, to show that she holds a witness w, such that $C(w) = 1$. Recent research focuses on efficient ZK proofs of *arbitrary* statements. A special case of ZK is *non-interactive* ZK (NIZK). NIZK proofs can be transferred and verified without interacting with $\mathcal{P}$.

[KKW18] specified a powerful NIZK proof system over Boolean circuits that features linear scaling in proof size, in verifier time, and, critically, in proof generation time. In this work, we extend this system with efficient arithmetic and conversions between Boolean and arithmetic representations. Our contribution thus reduces both proof size and computation.

Motivation and Setting for Our Work. ZKPs, and especially NIZKs, have enjoyed immense research interest in recent years. The majority of such works prioritize small proof size and fast verification, important metrics in blockchain-related applications. However, optimizing these metrics comes at significant prover cost. In experiments reported in many works, provers are run on powerful servers with hundreds of GB of RAM. Asymptotically, proof times are typically super-linear in the size of the proof circuit, with costs $O(n \log n)$.

At the same time, moderate resource requirements, such as low memory utilization, are essential to a class of applications, such as those running a ZK prover on a mobile device. Modern flagship phones have 4 to 6 GB RAM, a portion of which can be made available to the NIZK application.

This leaves room for a *balanced approach* that prioritizes total proof time, and that takes into account the ability to run on commodity hardware, and the costs of proof generation, network transmission, and verification.

We argue that [KKW18] is a great fit for applications where only commodity hardware is available and where concretely efficient performance is demanded: [KKW18]'s linear scaling in communication, prover computation, and verifier computation mean that the approach remains tractable even for large proof statements. [KKW18]'s RAM consumption is low even for large proof functions due to the gate-by-gate proof generation, and [KKW18] uses only light-weight computational primitives. The technique also requires no trusted setup. Finally, [KKW18] is actively supported by the community, since it is under consideration standardization by NIST as part of the Picnic post-quantum signature scheme.

However, [KKW18] supports only Boolean circuits. When [KKW18] is used in contexts that require complex arithmetic, the circuit size grows significantly, increasing both proof computation and communication. In this work, we improve [KKW18] by extending it with efficient arithmetic operations and with conversions between Boolean and arithmetic representations.

1.1   A Use Case for Balanced ZKP

To illustrate and make more precise our motivation, we explicate one natural use case where [KKW18] would be a top ZKP system among prior work.

Consider a set of mobile phones on a local Wi-Fi or bluetooth broadcast network, e.g., in the context of a group event, private contact tracing, etc. Suppose one phone wishes to prove a statement to everyone on the broadcast channel. Note that even though interaction is available here, the interactive designated-verifier systems, such as [JKO13, HK20] must repeat the proof for each verifier. Thus interactive techniques are not well suited for convincing the entire network at once, and a NIZK proof, which can be broadcasted, is a better solution.

In such a setting, the broadcast network resource is surprisingly substantial: while somewhat slower than 1gbps LAN, Wi-Fi supports speeds up to many hundreds of Mbps. Bluetooth 5 supports bandwidth of up to 2Mbps on distances of up to 800 ft (240 m).

We wish to complete the proof, including its generation, transmission (which may overlap with the other two phases), and verification, as quickly as possible. One natural way to view this optimization space is to ask: *"given the available bandwidth, say 10Mbps, is the bottleneck proof generation, transmission, or verification?"* The answer to this question (cf. Sect. 2 discussion of ZK systems' costs) is: "Proof generation/verification." Thus [KKW18], a proof system with concretely efficient linear scaling in the proof size, is a top choice.

1.2   Our Contribution and Outline of the Work

We extend the [KKW18] proof system with efficient ring arithmetic. Ring (e.g., vs field) operations are a particularly useful primitive for ZK, since they naturally match basic steps of existing programs written in standard languages, such as C. A ring-based ZK system can thus be more naturally used in proving program properties (e.g. presence of bugs [HK20]) in ZK.

While [dSGMOS19, BN19] (cf. Related Work Sect. 2) considered adding arithmetic to KKW for highly tailored applications, we provide a generic construction, and additionally offer the following efficient arithmetic operations:

Consider a finite ring whose elements are l bits long.

- We add an efficient operation that computes the dot-product of two arbitrary size vectors of ring elements for $2l$ proof bits (cf Sect. 5.1).
- We add efficient conversions between Boolean and arithmetic representations. Specifically, we add conversion operations between Boolean and rings $\mathbb{Z}_k$ for arbitrary k. Let $l = \log k$. Converting l Boolean values to an arithmetic value (or vice versa) costs l^2 bits in the proof (cf Sect. 5.2).

In Sect. 6, we formalize our approach as a p party semi-honest protocol in the preprocessing model, prove its security, and explain how it plugs into the honest-verifier ZK protocol of [KKW18]. Thus, via the Fiat-Shamir transform [FS87] our approach directly extends the NIZK [KKW18] proof system.

We provide a detailed account of the performance of our system, including individual gate costs and comparisons with standard [KKW18] (Sect. 7). We demonstrate that for arithmetic operations, our approach substantially improves [KKW18]. Of particular note is our improvement for linear arithmetic: as an example, our approach can multiply 100×100 square matrices of 32 bit number using $3200\times$ smaller proof size than standard [KKW18].

1.3   Intuition: MPC-in-the-Head, [KKW18] and Our Work

[KKW18] is a NIZK in the MPC-in-the-Head paradigm. In the MPC-in-the-head paradigm, the prover $\mathcal{P}$ simulates *in her head* a secure multi-party computation (MPC) protocol between several 'virtual players'. These players are given shares of $\mathcal{P}$'s witness as input and run the proof circuit C under MPC. $\mathcal{P}$ commits to the views of these players, and then the verifier $\mathcal{V}$ selects a subset of views to open. By checking that these views are consistent with the honest execution of the MPC protocol resulting in the output 1, $\mathcal{V}$ gains confidence that $\mathcal{P}$ did not cheat and indeed has a witness. Because $\mathcal{V}$ does not see the views of all players, the MPC protocol's security properties prevent him from learning $\mathcal{P}$'s witness. Therefore, such a protocol achieves Zero Knowledge. The players amplify soundness by repeating the protocol. Such systems can be transformed into NIZK proof systems using the classic Fiat-Shamir transform [FS87].

[KKW18] implements MPC-in-the-head with a protocol heavily based on *preprocessing*. Preprocessing fits elegantly with MPC-in-the-head because it can be easily prepared by $\mathcal{P}$ and checked by $\mathcal{V}$. As do [IKOS07,GMO16,CDG+17], [KKW18] allows efficient broadcast-based MPC, which allows $\mathcal{P}$ to simulate larger numbers of MPC players in her head. Because the protocol happens only in $\mathcal{P}$'s head, these broadcasts are efficient. By simulating more players, $\mathcal{P}$ reduces the number of repetitions needed to amplify soundness.

Our work notices inherent flexibility in this broadcast-based MPC protocol. We point out that broadcasts of Boolean values are easily generalized to broadcasts of elements of arbitrary finite *rings*. We show how this extension allows us to directly encode algebraic operations like addition and multiplication, significantly reducing cost. We further show how Boolean and k-bit integer operations can be mixed in the same circuit by including *conversion* operations.

2   Related Work

Zero Knowledge. ZKP [GMR85,GMW91] is a fundamental cryptographic primitive. ZK proofs of knowledge (ZKPoKs) [GMR85,BG93,DP92] allow a prover to convince a verifier, who holds a circuit C, that the prover knows an input, or *witness*, w for which $C(w) = 1$. Originally, practical ZK research focused on specific algebraic relations. More recently, ZK research has focused on practical proofs of arbitrary circuits. Our work is in this arbitrary circuit setting.

MPC-in-the-Head. Ishai et al. [IKOS07], introduced the powerful 'MPC-in-the-head' paradigm, outlined in Sect. 1.3. ZKBoo [GMO16] was the first implementation of MPC-in-the-head. Chase et al. [CDG+17] deprecated ZKBoo by building a more efficient system, ZKB++. They demonstrated that ZKB++ can implement an efficient signature scheme using only symmetric-key primitives.

Katz et al. [KKW18], the basis of our work, further improved this direction by using MPC with preprocessing. *Picnic* [ZCD+17], a signature scheme based on ZKB++, was submitted to the NIST post-quantum standardization effort. The Picnic submission was since updated and is now based on [KKW18].

Ligero [AHIV17] is another MPC-in-the-head protocol that diverges from our work's lineage. Ligero offers sublinear proof size ($O(\sqrt{|C|})$), but incurs superlinear prover computation ($O(|C|\log|C|)$). It is estimated that Ligero constructs smaller proofs than [KKW18] for circuits with more than approximately 100K gates. Thus, a choice between [KKW18] and Ligero should be based on the desired application and on performance requirements.

SNARKs. Succinct non-interactive arguments of knowledge (SNARK) [GGPR13, PHGR13, BCG+13, CFH+15, Gro16] build proofs that are particularly efficient, both in communication and verification time. They construct proofs that are shorter than the input itself. Prior work demonstrated the feasibility of sublinear ZK proofs [Kil92, Mic94], but were concretely inefficient. Early SNARKs required a semi-trusted party. This disadvantage led to the development of STARKs (succinct transparent arguments of knowledge) [BBHR18]. STARKs do not require trusted setup and rely on more efficient primitives. STARKs are succinct ZKP, and thus are SNARKs. In this work, we do not separate them; rather we see them as a body of work focused on sublinear proofs.

Recent SNARKs include Libra [XZZ+19] and Virgo [ZXZS19]. SNARKs [MBKM19, CHM+20] rely on trusted setup, which we wish to avoid. SPARKs [EFKP20] parallelize expensive prover time, but total CPU consumption (our metric) is superlinear. Supersonic's prover [BFS20] is quazilinear with high constants. Fractal [COS20] runs its concretely expensive prover on a high-end Intel Xeon 6136 CPU at 3.0 GHz with 252 GB of RAM (no more than 32 GB of RAM were used in any experiment).

Interactive ZK. In this work, we focus on concretely efficient non-interactive ZK. Another direction forgoes non-interactivity in exchange for very fast proofs. Interactivity allows private-coin ZK protocols, such as those based on [JKO13] and garbled circuits (GC). In [JKO13], $\mathcal{V}$ garbles the evaluated circuit, then $\mathcal{P}$ evaluates and thus obtains the random encoding of the output. The GC authenticity property guarantees that $\mathcal{P}$ is unable to obtain a requisite output label without evaluating with a valid witness w. Recently, [HK20] showed that *conditional branches* in the proof circuit can be evaluated for free.

We achieve performance similar to the above works (linear with low concrete overhead), but we work with algebraic values and in the non-interactive setting.

Prior work on Arithmetic. [KKW18] tailors [KKW18] for AES-based signatures and Short Integer Solution problem. In contrast, we propose a more general KKW suite of tools. Namely:

Motivated by ZKP of AES (whose S-boxes use $\mathbb{F}_{2^8}$ arithmetic), [dSGMOS19] adapt [KKW18] to operate in the field $\mathbb{F}_{2^8}$. Our approach similarly improves

[KKW18] by adding operations, but we take a more general approach and integrate *ring* operations, efficient dot product, and conversions.

Baum and Nof [BN19] consider an arithmetic field-only version of [KKW18], focusing on interactive instances of ZK arguments of knowledge for instances of the Short Integer Solution problem. [BN19] do not provide conversions between representations. We offer ring arithmetic (matching basic steps of existing programs) and additional efficient operations: dot product and conversions.

We are not aware of other arithmetic ZK constructions that work with KKW.

Balanced NIZK. In Sect. 1, we motivate a setting that prioritizes total proof time, taking into account the ability to run on commodity hardware and the cost of proof generation, transmission, and verification. Among the many recent ZKP systems (cf. Sect. 2), several works belong to this balanced niche, among them Libra [XZZ+19] and Virgo [ZXZS19] (concretely expensive but with linear prover time), Ligero [AHIV17] and [KKW18]. We improve this balanced setting. Among the above works, Libra and Virgo are the most recent, and enjoy linear proof time with reasonable proof size. However, Libra requires trusted setup that we wish to avoid. While Libra and Virgo report faster proof times than Ligero and [KKW18], they were tested on vastly more powerful machines: Libra: Amazon EC2 c5.9xlarge with 70 GB of RAM and Intel Xeon Platinum 8124 m CPU with 3 GHz virtual core, and Virgo: server with 512 GB of DDR3 RAM (1.6 GHz) and 16 3.2 GHz cores (2 threads/core). While Ligero runs on modest hardware, its proof time is super-linear: $O(n \log n)$. Finally, [KKW18] enjoys both linear scaling and concretely efficient proof time, but its proof size is linear as well. Because of [KKW18]'s linear scaling, it is a strong fit for balanced-cost NIZK.

MPC Arithmetic Protocols. We highlight some related works that address arithmetic protocols with properties similar to our own improvements.

[CGH+18] used threshold secret sharing to construct an efficient arithmetic MPC protocol. Like our approach, their protocol provides an efficient vector dot operation. However, their protocol works with fields (and we are interested in supporting efficient ring arithmetic), and further, is not compatible with Boolean circuits.

BLAZE [PS20] proposed a fast three-server privacy-preserving machine learning framework. Their protocol allows both vector dot product operations and conversions between Boolean and arithmetic values. BLAZE is a 3-PC protocol, and does not generalize to arbitrary numbers of parties. Additionally, their arithmetic to Boolean conversions require the use of garbled circuits and are expensive. Our MPC-in-the-head protocol supports similar operations, but allows any number of virtual parties and leverages the ZK prover to efficiently instantiate conversions.

3   Notation

- Let p denote the number of parties: there are p parties P_i for $i \in \{1, \ldots, p\}$.
- We consider finite rings $\mathcal{R}$. We denote the bit-length of an $\mathcal{R}$ element by l.
- We write $a \leftarrow_\$ \mathcal{R}$ to denote that a is a uniform element drawn from $\mathcal{R}$.
- λ denotes a uniform Boolean mask.
- x, y, z, etc. denote cleartext Boolean bits that appear in the proof.
- $\widetilde{x}, \widetilde{y}, \widetilde{z}$, etc. denote encrypted Boolean bits. I.e., $\widetilde{x} = x \oplus \lambda$ for some mask λ.
- Capitalized variables are used for ring values: Λ is a uniform ring element mask, X, Y, Z are cleartext ring elements, and $\widetilde{X}, \widetilde{Y}, \widetilde{Z}$ are encrypted ring elements. That is, $\widetilde{X} = X + \Lambda_X$.
- Suppose a is a Boolean value (resp. A is a ring element). Then let $[\![a]\!]$ denote a secret sharing of a (resp. $[\![A]\!]$ of A). That is, suppose each player P_i holds an additive share a_i such that $\bigoplus_{i=1}^{p} a_i = a$ (resp. $\sum_{i=1}^{p} A_i = A$). Then $[\![a]\!]$ is the vector $(a_1, a_2, \ldots, a_p)$ (resp. $[\![A]\!] = (A_1, A_2 \ldots A_p)$).
- We refer to Boolean (resp. arithmetic) wires with lowercase (resp. uppercase), e.g., value A on wire A. Context disambiguates this slight abuse of notation.

Although our circuits discuss arbitrary rings, we also provide concrete conversion operators between particular rings. Specifically, we construct conversion operations from the Booleans to rings $\mathbb{Z}_k$ for arbitrary k. We also provide the dual conversion from $\mathbb{Z}_k$ to the Booleans.

4   [KKW18] Background

As discussed in Sect. 1, [KKW18] is a powerful MPC-in-the-head NIZKPoK system that takes advantage of a preprocessing-based protocol to achieve efficiency. [KKW18] NIZKPoK's relevant (to us) features are non-interactivity and its low-constant linear scaling in all proof costs, including proof generation, proof transmission, and proof verification.

The proof system is built from two protocols:

1. An MPC protocol with preprocessing secure against up to $p - 1$ semi-honest corruptions. It is this protocol that we improve in our work.
2. An honest-verifier Zero Knowledge (HVZK) protocol. This HVZK protocol uses the above MPC protocol as a black-box. In particular, $\mathcal{P}$ runs the MPC protocol in her head many times (i.e., there are many *instances*) and among many players. This MPC protocol includes a preprocessing and online phase. The verifier $\mathcal{V}$ challenges $\mathcal{P}$ to open the views of players. In some instances, $\mathcal{V}$ inspects the preprocessing given to all players to check it was correctly constructed. In the other instances, $\mathcal{V}$ inspects the preprocessing and online views of all but one MPC party and checks that the views are consistent with the MPC protocol. Thus, $\mathcal{V}$ becomes convinced that $\mathcal{P}$ could not have cheated in either the preprocessing or the online phases.

Because the MPC protocol is used as a black-box, we can substitute in our own improved protocol.

Due to lack of space, we defer a formal review of [KKW18]'s MPC protocol to a full version of this paper. We present our extensions to their protocol in full detail such that the specific details of their protocol are not essential background.

5 Adding Arithmetic to Boolean Circuits

Our core contribution is an extension to the concretely efficient NIZK proof system of [KKW18]. In particular, we add efficient arithmetic operations as well as conversions between arithmetic and Boolean representations. In this section, we explain how our protocol implements these operations.

We first discuss a pure algebraic version of [KKW18] and explain the relative efficiency of our arbitrary ring operations. Then, we show how to *mix* arithmetic and Boolean representations in a single circuit by adding conversion operations.

5.1 Ring Circuits with Efficient Dot Product

Consider circuits where the gates perform ring operations: i.e. circuits with addition, multiplication, and subtraction gates. Ring [KKW18] is a natural generalization of the Boolean protocol, and we leverage similar preprocessing and online phases. The phases are primarily concerned with propagating the following invariants gate-by-gate through the circuit:

- **Preprocessing invariant.** During the preprocessing phase, $\mathcal{P}$ ensures that each virtual player has a uniformly random additive share of a random mask. For each ring wire A the p virtual players hold the random sharing $[\![\Lambda_A]\!]$ where Λ_A is a uniform element of a finite ring $\mathcal{R}$.
- **Online invariant.** In the online phase, each virtual player holds the value $\widetilde{A} = A + \Lambda_A$. I.e., they each hold the same encryption of A.

These invariants support *correctness*, because they imply that on each output wire A the players hold $A + \Lambda_A$ and $[\![\Lambda_A]\!]$. Thus, the players can broadcast their mask shares and locally reconstruct A. The invariants support *security* against up to $p - 1$ semi-honest corruptions, because they ensure that each cleartext value A is *masked* by Λ_A, and thus no strict subset of players, who together have only a uniform additive *share* of Λ_A, can reconstruct Λ_A. We prove these facts formally in the full version of this paper.

We next step through the supported algebraic operations, showing how our representation propagates the preprocessing and online invariants.

Inputs. Suppose the wire A is an input wire. Our goal is to provide a uniform sharing $[\![\Lambda_A]\!]$ in the preprocessing phase and to provide the encryption $\widetilde{A} = A + \Lambda_A$ to each player in the online phase.

$\mathcal{P}$ sets up the preprocessing invariant by choosing p uniform values and sending one to each virtual player. She distributes $[\![\Lambda_A]\!]$. The sum of these p values is the uniform mask Λ_A. In practice, $\mathcal{P}$ draws these values according to per-player pseudorandom seeds. Thus, P_i's view of all input mask messages (as well as all other pseudo-randomly generated masks, as we discuss for subsequent gates) can be computed from a short seed. The online phase is also straight-forward: $\mathcal{P}$ sends the value $\widetilde{A} = A + \Lambda_A$ to each virtual player.

To use our protocol to construct a proof, $\mathcal{P}$ sends to $\mathcal{V}$ the views of all virtual players save one. For an input wire, this costs l bits of communication where l is the bit-length of an element in $\mathcal{R}$. Thus, the preprocessing phase is communication-free due to seeds and the online phase requires only a single broadcast of a ring element.

Addition. Consider an addition gate with inputs A and B and output C that computes $C \leftarrow A + B$. By induction, the players hold uniform sharings $[\![\Lambda_A]\!]$ and $[\![\Lambda_B]\!]$ in the preprocessing phase and encryptions $\widetilde{A}, \widetilde{B}$ in the online phase. Our goal is to propagate a sharing $[\![\Lambda_C]\!]$ in the preprocessing phase and an encryption $\widetilde{C} = C + \Lambda_C$ such that $C = A + B$.

In the preprocessing phase, we let the preprocessing mask of the output wire be $\Lambda_C = \Lambda_A + \Lambda_B$. Accordingly, the virtual players locally compute their mask shares by adding their respective input shares: together they compute $[\![\Lambda_C]\!] \leftarrow [\![\Lambda_A]\!] + [\![\Lambda_B]\!]$. In the online phase, the players locally add together the masked input values: $\widetilde{C} \leftarrow \widetilde{A} + \widetilde{B}$. The preprocessing and online local computations propagate the respective invariants:

$$\widetilde{A} + \widetilde{B} = (A + \Lambda_A) + (B + \Lambda_B) = (A + B) + (\Lambda_A + \Lambda_B) = C + \Lambda_C = \widetilde{C}$$

Because addition gates do not require the virtual players to communicate, addition gates are communication-free in the proof.

Subtraction. Subtraction is performed in the same manner as addition. Consider a gate with inputs A and B and output C that computes $C \leftarrow A - B$. We let $\Lambda_C = \Lambda_A - \Lambda_B$. During the online phase, the virtual players locally subtract:

$$\widetilde{A} - \widetilde{B} = (A + \Lambda_A) - (B + \Lambda_B) = (A - B) + (\Lambda_A - \Lambda_B) = C + \Lambda_C = \widetilde{C}$$

Like addition gates, subtraction gates are communication-free.

Public Constants. Public constants and multiplication by public constants can be easily encoded in our representation. Due to lack of space, we defer this explanations of these encodings to the full version of this paper.

Multiplication. Consider a multiplication gate with inputs A, B and output C that computes $C \leftarrow AB$. Unfortunately, multiplication cannot be computed as easily as addition. In particular, $\mathcal{P}$ must distribute auxiliary ring elements to the players in the preprocessing phase, and the players must communicate via broadcast in the online phase.

In the preprocessing phase, $\mathcal{P}$ generates a fresh uniform mask Λ_C by drawing uniform ring elements and sending one to each player. In practice, these values are drawn according to the per-player pseudorandom seed, and hence are communication-free in the proof.

Additionally, $\mathcal{P}$ computes the product $\Lambda_{A,B} = \Lambda_A\Lambda_B$ and distributes a uniform sharing $[\![\Lambda_{A,B}]\!]$ to the players. Note that because $\Lambda_{A,B}$ is a fixed value, one virtual player's uniform share cannot be generated from a seed, and must instead be set according to $\Lambda_{A,B}$. Therefore, that player's preprocessing incurs communication in the proof.

In the online phase, the virtual players hold $[\![\Lambda_A]\!]$, $[\![\Lambda_B]\!]$, $[\![\Lambda_{A,B}]\!]$, $[\![\Lambda_C]\!]$, $\widetilde{A}$, and $\widetilde{B}$. They locally compute the following intermediate sharing:

$$[\![S]\!] \leftarrow [\![\Lambda_{A,B}]\!] + [\![\Lambda_C]\!] - \widetilde{A}[\![\Lambda_B]\!] - [\![\Lambda_A]\!]\widetilde{B}$$

Recall that we do not assume ring multiplication is commutative, so we take care to order multiplicands properly. The players broadcast these shares, reconstruct S, and set $\widetilde{C} \leftarrow \widetilde{A}\widetilde{B} + S$. Note that it is safe to reconstruct S, because S is masked by the uniform element Λ_C. This computation properly calculates an encryption of AB:

$$\begin{aligned}
\widetilde{A}\widetilde{B} + S &= \widetilde{A}\widetilde{B} + (\Lambda_A\Lambda_B + \Lambda_C - \widetilde{A}\Lambda_B - \Lambda_A\widetilde{B}) \\
&= \widetilde{A}\widetilde{B} + (\Lambda_A\Lambda_B + \Lambda_C - (A\Lambda_B + \Lambda_A\Lambda_B) - (\Lambda_A B + \Lambda_A\Lambda_B)) \\
&= AB + \Lambda_C = \widetilde{C}
\end{aligned}$$

Altogether, this arithmetic product costs $2l$ bits in the proof where l is the bit-size of ring elements: l bits to add the last player's share of $\Lambda_{A,B}$ to the proof message and l bits to send the unopened player's broadcast ($\mathcal{V}$ can compute the opened players' broadcasts himself, so they need not be sent).

Dot Product. In this section, we generalize from multiplication to vector dot product without increasing cost. Without our optimization, such a dot product of n element vectors costs $2ln$ bits in the proof, because the dot product involves n multiplications each costing $2l$ bits. We show that only $2l$ total bits are needed.

Note, a particular player P_i's received messages $\Lambda_{A,B}^i$ and S are only used in an *additive* manner to compute the product. Therefore, if our intent is to add together n products, then we can sum the per-player messages for all products before sending them, avoiding sending all of the summands.

Consider a dot product gate with input vectors $(A_1, \ldots A_n), (B_1, \ldots, B_n)$ and output C. The gate computes:

$$C \leftarrow A_1B_1 + \ldots + A_nB_n$$

By the circuit invariants, players have mask shares for all input vector elements in the preprocessing phase and encryptions all vector elements in the online phase. The players receive auxiliary masks/communicate to evaluate the dot product.

For simplicity, we argue that our improvement works for the sum of two products $A_1B_1 + A_2B_2$, but our argument generalizes to the sum of any number of products. Let S_1, S_2 respectively be the broadcasted terms reconstructed by virtual players when computing A_1B_1 and A_2B_2. Recall that to compute an encryption of A_1B_1 and A_2B_2, the players locally compute $\widetilde{A_1}\widetilde{B_1}+S_1$ and $\widetilde{A_2}\widetilde{B_2}+S_2$. Thus, to compute the overall sum, the players compute:

$$(\widetilde{A_1}\widetilde{B_1} + S_1) + (\widetilde{A_2}\widetilde{B_2} + S_2) = (\widetilde{A_1}\widetilde{B_1} + \widetilde{A_2}\widetilde{B_2}) + (S_1 + S_2)$$

Thus, in the online phase, the players need not broadcast $[\![S_1]\!]$ and $[\![S_2]\!]$ separately: instead they more efficiently broadcast $[\![S_1 + S_2]\!]$. This reduces the communication cost of the online phase. The preprocessing communication cost is similarly improved: to compute $[\![S_1 + S_2]\!]$, the players compute shares of the following expression (where $\Lambda_{C_1}, \Lambda_{C_2}$ are uniformly random):

$$S_1 + S_2 = (\Lambda_{A_1,B_1} + \Lambda_{C_1} - \widetilde{A_1}\Lambda_{B_1} - \Lambda_{A_1}\widetilde{B_1}) + (\Lambda_{A_2,B_2} + \Lambda_{C_2} - \widetilde{A_2}\Lambda_{B_2} - \Lambda_{A_2}\widetilde{B_2})$$

$$= (\Lambda_{A_1,B_1} + \Lambda_{A_2,B_2}) + (\Lambda_{C_1} + \Lambda_{C_2}) - \widetilde{A_1}\Lambda_{B_1} - \Lambda_{A_1}\widetilde{B_1} - \widetilde{A_2}\Lambda_{B_2} - \Lambda_{A_2}\widetilde{B_2}$$

Thus, in the preprocessing phase it suffices for $\mathcal{P}$ to distribute uniform shares $[\![\Lambda_{A_1,B_1} + \Lambda_{A_2,B_2}]\!]$ instead of distributing both $[\![\Lambda_{A_1,B_1}]\!]$ and $[\![\Lambda_{A_2,B_2}]\!]$. Again, this improves communication. Other values are known to the players a priori or can be generated from seeds. Altogether, the vector dot product of length n vectors costs $2l$ bits in the proof.

To illustrate the importance of this optimization, we compare the communication cost to multiply an $M \times N$ matrix by a $N \times P$ matrix where each matrix entry is an l bit ring element. Without vector dot product, such a multiplication costs $2M \cdot N \cdot P \cdot l$ bits of communication, because the resulting $M \cdot P$ matrix entries are each l bit sums of N products. Our optimization removes the factor N: the total cost is $2M \cdot P \cdot l$ bits.

5.2 Converting Between Boolean and Arithmetic

We have shown how we construct an arithmetic version of the [KKW18] protocol for arbitrary rings. However, many functions (e.g., comparisons and bitwise operations) are more efficiently expressed in a Boolean representation. To get the best of both worlds, we now introduce efficient conversion operations between Boolean and arithmetic representations. We stress that our conversions are not for *arbitrary* rings, but only rings of the form $\mathbb{Z}_k$ for arbitrary $k > 2$.

Single Bit Conversion. Consider a conversion gate with Boolean input wire a and arithmetic output wire A. By induction, the players together hold the mask sharing $[\![\lambda_a]\!]$ in the preprocessing phase and each hold the encryption $a \oplus \lambda_a$ in the online phase. We show how added communication allows the players to propagate the invariant such that they hold $[\![\Lambda_A]\!]$ and $\widetilde{A} = A + \Lambda_A$. In other words, we convert the Boolean encoding to a valid arithmetic encoding.

We start by giving the players preprocessing material. First of all, $\mathcal{P}$ pseudorandomly generates from seeds $[\![\Lambda_A]\!] \in \mathbb{Z}_k$ and distributes it to the players. This new value Λ_A serves only as a mask that ensures security. Additionally, $\mathcal{P}$ deals a uniform sharing $[\![\Lambda_a]\!] \in \mathbb{Z}_k$ such that $\Lambda_a = \lambda_a$ (λ_a is a Boolean value and

Λ_a is an arithmetic value)[1]. The role of this auxiliary mask is different than Λ_A. In particular, the auxiliary mask algebraically eliminates the Boolean mask λ_a. Note that, similar to multiplication, one player's share of Λ_a cannot be pseudo-randomly generated, because the shares must sum to $\Lambda_a = \lambda_a$, and λ_a is a fixed value. Thus, the translation preprocessing costs l proof bits. We emphasize that although $\lambda_a = \Lambda_a$, the players hold XOR shares of λ_a and additive shares of Λ_a.

In the online phase, we use the following two properties of arbitrary values $x, y \in \{0, 1\}$ when computing modulo $k > 2$:

$$x \oplus y = x + y - 2xy \tag{1}$$

$$x^2 = x \tag{2}$$

To convert, the virtual players locally compute the following intermediate share:

$$[\![S]\!] \leftarrow [\![\Lambda_a]\!](1 - 2\widetilde{a}) + [\![\Lambda_A]\!]$$

Each virtual player then broadcasts her share, reconstructs S, and computes $\widetilde{A} \leftarrow \widetilde{a} + S$. That is, each player outputs a correct arithmetic representation $\widetilde{A} = A + \Lambda_A$. We now show that this computation is correct:

$$
\begin{aligned}
\widetilde{a} + S &= (a \oplus \lambda_a) + \Lambda_a(1 - 2(a \oplus \lambda_a)) + \Lambda_A && \widetilde{a} = a \oplus \lambda_a \\
&= (a + \lambda_a - 2a\lambda_a) + \Lambda_a(1 - 2(a + \lambda_a - 2a\lambda_a)) + \Lambda_A && \text{Equation (1)} \\
&= (A + \lambda_a - 2A\lambda_a) + \Lambda_a(1 - 2(A + \lambda_a - 2A\lambda_a)) + \Lambda_A && a = A \\
&= (A + \Lambda_a - 2A\Lambda_a) + \Lambda_a(1 - 2(A + \Lambda_a - 2A\Lambda_a)) + \Lambda_A && \lambda_a = \Lambda_a \\
&= (A + \Lambda_a - 2A\Lambda_a) + \Lambda_a - 2A\Lambda_a - 2\Lambda_a^2 + 4A\Lambda_a^2 + \Lambda_A && \text{distribute} \\
&= A + \Lambda_a - 2A\Lambda_a + \Lambda_a - 2A\Lambda_a - 2\Lambda_a + 4A\Lambda_a + \Lambda_A && \text{Equation (2)} \\
&= A + \Lambda_A = \widetilde{A}
\end{aligned}
$$

This conversion costs l bits of communication in the preprocessing phase, because one virtual player is given a non-pseudorandomly chosen value for her share of Λ_a. Therefore $\mathcal{P}$ sends this non-pseudorandom value to $\mathcal{V}$ to open the view of this player (if this player is not opened, preprocessing is free). In the online phase, we incur l bits of communication, because $\mathcal{P}$ must send the broadcast of the unopened player to $\mathcal{V}$ to convey the views of all opened players.

Multi-bit Conversion. Often, it is useful to convert an entire vector of Boolean values together into a single arithmetic value. Specifically, a Boolean vector is often used as the binary representation of an arithmetic value. Suppose we have a vector of Boolean wires $(a_1, a_2, \ldots, a_l)$ that we would like to convert into an arithmetic value A:

$$A = a_1 + 2a_2 + \ldots + 2^{l-1}a_l$$

Of course, we can use l single-bit conversions, as described above, to construct this sum. However, there are optimizations available.

---

[1] Here and elsewhere, equality between a Boolean value and an arithmetic value simply indicates that both values are either both 0 or both 1 in their respective ring.

In particular, this naïve translation costs l^2 bits in the online phase. We now reduce this cost to l bits. Recall that each bitwise translation requires the broadcast of an l bit value S. Let S_i be this broadcast value for bit i. The idea is to simply have the players compute and broadcast their shares of the following single value:

$$[\![S_A]\!] = [\![S_1 + 2S_2 + \ldots + 2^{l-1}S_l]\!]$$

The players then reconstruct S_A and locally compute the following:

$$A + \Lambda_A \leftarrow S_A + \widetilde{a}_1 + 2\widetilde{a}_2 + \ldots + 2^{l-1}\widetilde{a}_l$$

One further optimization is available for integer rings $\mathbb{Z}_{2^n}$ for some n, a particularly useful set of rings for modeling common cleartext computations. Looking again at the definition of $[\![S_A]\!]$, notice that the summand $2^{l-1}S_l$ overflows the ring by 2^{l-1} bits. That is, this summand carries only 1 bit of information in $\mathbb{Z}_{2^n}$. Therefore, at preprocessing time $\mathcal{P}$ need not give the players l bit shares Λ_a, but instead need only send 1 bit shares. In general, for a given vector index i, $\mathcal{P}$ sends $l - i - 1$ bits of preprocessing. In sum, the preprocessing costs $\frac{l^2+l}{2}$ bits.

Altogether, an l bit conversion costs l bits in the online phase and (at most) l^2 bits in the preprocessing phase.

Converting Arithmetic to Boolean. Suppose we wish to convert an arithmetic value A to its binary decomposition $(a_1, a_2, \ldots, a_l)$. Our construction for this conversion is based on a simple observation about Zero Knowledge. In the ZK setting, we can "compute backwards" and then prove what was computed is correct. More precisely, $\mathcal{P}$ simply gives the virtual players encryptions and masks corresponding to $(a_1, a_2, \ldots, a_l)$ as Boolean inputs. Then, the virtual parties use the multi-bit conversion described above to translate $(a_1, a_2, \ldots, a_l)$ to an arithmetic value A'. Note that if $\mathcal{P}$ provides the correct inputs, then $A = A'$. Therefore, the parties compute $A - A'$ and reconstruct the output by broadcasting their mask shares of this result; i.e., they reconstruct 0 if $\mathcal{P}$ did not cheat. By inspecting this output value, $\mathcal{V}$ is convinced that $\mathcal{P}$ provided a correct binary decomposition of the value A.

Altogether, converting an arithmetic value to its binary decomposition costs (1) at most l^2 preprocessing bits for the Boolean to arithmetic conversion, (2) l online bits for the Boolean to arithmetic conversion, (3) l online bits for the input bits given the virtual parties, and (4) l online bits for the unopened player's broadcast of her mask share.

6   Our Semi-honest MPC Protocol

We first explain the 3-round honest-verifier ZK (HVZK) protocol of [KKW18] so that our core theorems can be understood. Our protocol is plugged directly into this HVZK protocol.

$\mathcal{P}$ constructs a large number M (e.g., 500) of commitments to full instances of our protocol. That is, she commits to the views of all p (e.g., 64) players, both in the preprocessing and online protocol phases. Then, $\mathcal{V}$ challenges $\mathcal{P}$ to open a small number τ (e.g., 25) of instances. For each of these τ instances, $\mathcal{P}$ sends to $\mathcal{V}$ the compactly represented views of all except for one player chosen by $\mathcal{V}$. $\mathcal{V}$ checks that the views of these opened players are consistent with the protocol, and thus is convinced (his confidence depends on τ) that $\mathcal{P}$ could not have cheated in the online phase. Because $\mathcal{V}$ only obtains $p-1$ views and because our protocol is secure against $p-1$ semi-honest corruptions, he does not learn $\mathcal{P}$'s witness. In the remaining $M - \tau$ instances, $\mathcal{P}$ opens all players' preprocessing views, where each preprocessing instance is compactly represented as a single master seed. $\mathcal{V}$ checks that these preprocessing views are consistent with the protocol, and thus is convinced (depending on M and τ) that $\mathcal{P}$ could not have cheated in the preprocessing phase either. By configuring M, τ, and p, $\mathcal{P}$ can construct a ZK proof with high soundness.

By plugging into [KKW18]'s HVZK protocol, we achieve a ZK protocol by specifying our protocol as a semi-honest protocol in a preprocessing model. The crucial pieces of our protocol Π are specified in Sect. 5, where we give the individual actions taken by the virtual parties on gate types. While we stress that the discussion given in Sect. 5 is sufficient to understand our approach, we give also a more formal construction in the full version of this paper.

Construction 1. Π is the p party protocol defined in Sect. 5.

Our protocol Π makes use of two oracle functionalities. In particular, it first uses the functionality $\mathcal{F}_{\text{pre}}$ to instantiate preprocessing material for the p virtual players and $\mathcal{F}_{\text{inp}}$ which broadcasts $\mathcal{P}$'s masked input to the p players.

Theorems proved in the full version of this paper imply the following:

Theorem 1. Π correctly implements the semantics of ring circuits and is secure against up to $p - 1$ semi-honest corruptions in the $\mathcal{F}_{\text{pre}}$, $\mathcal{F}_{\text{inp}}$ hybrid model.

This fact, combined with Theorem 2.2 of [KKW18], implies the following:

Theorem 2. Let M be the total number of repetitions of the proof, τ be the number of proofs checked by $\mathcal{V}$ (hence $M - \tau$ preprocessings are checked), and p be the number of virtual players. Assuming the existence of a collision-resistant hash function and of a secure commitment scheme, the 3-round honest-verifier Zero Knowledge proof protocol of [KKW18] instantiated with Π is an honest-verifier zero-knowledge proof of knowledge with soundness/knowledge error ϵ where:

$$\epsilon = \max_{M-\tau \leq k \leq M} \left\{ \frac{\binom{k}{M-\tau}}{\binom{M}{M-\tau} \cdot p^{k-M-\tau}} \right\}$$

We point out that our soundness error is equal that of standard [KKW18], because the cheating $\mathcal{P}$'s chances of being caught remain the same. If $\mathcal{P}$ cheats in any preprocessing phase, then she is caught if $\mathcal{V}$ inspects the preprocessing. If $\mathcal{P}$ cheats in any online phase, then she is caught if $\mathcal{V}$ opens the cheating player.

Finally, by applying the Fiat-Shamir transform [FS87] (and assuming a random oracle), this instantiated 3-round HVZK protocol becomes a non-interactive Zero Knowledge Proof of Knowledge (NIZKPoK).

7 Performance Estimation

We improve the [KKW18] approach by adding a suite of efficient ring operations and Boolean conversions. It is immediate from our constructions that we inherit the performance characteristics of [KKW18], including computation and communication costs. Namely, our computation costs are approximately the same per gate (whether arithmetic or Boolean) as [KKW18]. This is because the computations supporting arithmetic or Boolean operations are extremely lightweight, and the main costs involve memory manipulations, which are of similar scope. Our communication cost is the same as [KKW18] for Boolean operations, and is correspondingly increased for arithmetic operations. We outline this cost below, and compare it with that of [KKW18].

Gate Kind	ADD	SUB	DOT	INPUT	OUTPUT	B2A
Preprocessing	0	0	l	0	0	l^2
Online	0	0	l	l	l	l

Fig. 1. The per-instance proof size cost of each gate for an l-bit finite ring. Note that to construct a NIZK, multiple instances must be completed. Realistic numbers of instances vary between $20 - 40$ depending on the parameterization of the NIZK [KKW18].

Gate Costs. Recall, multiple proof *instances* are required to increase soundness. Figure 1 tabulates the per-instance communication cost for each gate. The number of instances needed to achieve a certain security parameter depends on the number of simulated parties. As one practical example, for 128 bits of security with 64 simulated parties, 23 instances are required [KKW18]. Thus, if $p = 64$, the total communication cost of, e.g., a DOT gate is $46l$ bits where l is the bit size of the finite ring elements. We emphasize that proof instances that are used only to check preprocessing incur essentially no communication cost because the entire preprocessing is regenerated from a single master seed.

Arithmetic Improvement. We compare our communication with that of [KKW18] on several functions. To understand the performance of classic [KKW18], it suffices to look at Fig. 1 with $l = 1$, recalling that classic [KKW18] does not support vector dot product, only simple Boolean AND (costing 2 bits total).

- **Addition.** Suppose that we wish to add numbers in the ring $\mathbb{Z}_{2^l}$ for some l. Boolean circuits can encode this addition efficiently using a ripple-carry adder that costs $l - 1$ AND gates or $2l - 2$ proof bits. In contrast, our addition is a free homomorphic operation.
  Adding in most rings other than $\mathbb{Z}_{2^l}$ is extremely costly for the Boolean approach. For example, to compute in the field $\mathbb{Z}_p$ for prime p, the Boolean approach must compute the costly $\bmod p$ operation which uses l^2 AND gates. In contrast, our approach adds elements of this field for free.

- **Multiplication.** Computing a multiplication in the ring $\mathbb{Z}_{2^l}$ consumes l^2 AND gates by the schoolbook method. In contrast, we use only l bits. Furthermore, if we consider other rings, the situation skews further in our favor. For example, to multiply in a field $\mathbb{Z}_p$, a Boolean circuit must multiply in a ring large enough that the product does not overflow (i.e. twice the number of bits in p), and then compute mod p.
- **Matrix multiplication.** As discussed in Sect. 5, our DOT gate excels as efficiently computing matrix multiplications. In sum, multiplying a $M \times N$ matrix by a $N \times P$ matrix of l-bit elements requires $2M \cdot P \cdot l$ bits. That is, computing a matrix multiplication requires only twice as many bits as are needed to *represent* the output matrix. To compare the performance of classic [KKW18], assume that the matrix elements are elements of $\mathbb{Z}_{2^l}$. Thus, Boolean algebra can encode a multiplication using l^2 AND gates or $2l^2$ proof bits. The total proof cost for a matrix multiplication in the specified dimensions is thus $2l^2 \cdot M \cdot N \cdot P$ bits. Thus, our approach improves by factor $N \cdot l$. When concrete parameters are considered, it becomes clear that this improvement is substantial. For example, to multiply 100×100 square matrices of 32 bit integers, we require $3200\times$ less communication.

Acknowledgements. This work was supported in part by NSF award #1909769, by a Facebook research award, and by Georgia Tech's IISP cybersecurity seed funding (CSF) award.

References

[AHIV17] Ames, S., Hazay, C., Ishai, Y., Venkitasubramaniam, M.: Ligero: lightweight sublinear arguments without a trusted setup. In: Thuraisingham, B.M., Evans, D., Malkin, T., Xu, D. (eds.) ACM CCS 2017, pp. 2087–2104. ACM Press, October/November 2017

[BBHR18] Ben-Sasson, E., Bentov, I., Horesh, Y., Riabzev, M.: Scalable, transparent, and post-quantum secure computational integrity. Cryptology ePrint Archive, Report 2018/046 (2018). https://eprint.iacr.org/2018/046

[BCG+13] Ben-Sasson, E., Chiesa, A., Genkin, D., Tromer, E., Virza, M.: SNARKs for C: verifying program executions succinctly and in zero knowledge. In: Canetti, R., Garay, J.A. (eds.) CRYPTO 2013. LNCS, vol. 8043, pp. 90–108. Springer, Heidelberg (2013). https://doi.org/10.1007/978-3-642-40084-1_6

[BFS20] Bünz, B., Fisch, B., Szepieniec, A.: Transparent SNARKs from DARK compilers. In: Canteaut, A., Ishai, Y. (eds.) EUROCRYPT 2020. LNCS, vol. 12105, pp. 677–706. Springer, Cham (2020). https://doi.org/10.1007/978-3-030-45721-1_24

[BG93] Bellare, M., Goldreich, O.: On defining proofs of knowledge. In: Brickell, E.F. (ed.) CRYPTO 1992. LNCS, vol. 740, pp. 390–420. Springer, Heidelberg (1993). https://doi.org/10.1007/3-540-48071-4_28

[BN19]   Baum, C., Nof, A.: Concretely-efficient zero-knowledge arguments for arithmetic circuits and their application to lattice-based cryptography. Cryptology ePrint Archive, Report 2019/532 (2019). https://eprint.iacr.org/2019/532

[CDG+17] Chase, M.: Post-quantum zero-knowledge and signatures from symmetric-key primitives. In: Thuraisingham, B.M., Evans, D., Malkin, T., Xu, D. (eds.) ACM CCS 2017, pp. 1825–1842. ACM Press, October/November 2017

[CFH+15] Costello, C., et al.: Geppetto: versatile verifiable computation. In 2015 IEEE Symposium on Security and Privacy, pp. 253–270. IEEE Computer Society Press, May 2015

[CGH+18] Chida, K., et al.: Fast large-scale honest-majority MPC for malicious adversaries. In: Shacham, H., Boldyreva, A. (eds.) CRYPTO 2018. LNCS, vol. 10993, pp. 34–64. Springer, Cham (2018). https://doi.org/10.1007/978-3-319-96878-0_2

[CHM+20] Chiesa, A., Hu, Y., Maller, M., Mishra, P., Vesely, N., Ward, N.: Marlin: preprocessing zkSNARKs with universal and updatable SRS. In: Canteaut, A., Ishai, Y. (eds.) EUROCRYPT 2020. LNCS, vol. 12105, pp. 738–768. Springer, Cham (2020). https://doi.org/10.1007/978-3-030-45721-1_26

[COS20]   Chiesa, A., Ojha, D., Spooner, N.: FRACTAL: post-quantum and transparent recursive proofs from holography. In: Canteaut, A., Ishai, Y. (eds.) EUROCRYPT 2020. LNCS, vol. 12105, pp. 769–793. Springer, Cham (2020). https://doi.org/10.1007/978-3-030-45721-1_27

[DP92]   De Santis, A., Persiano, G.: Zero-knowledge proofs of knowledge without interaction (extended abstract). In: 33rd FOCS, pp. 427–436. IEEE Computer Society Press, October 1992

[dSGMOS19] de Saint Guilhem, C.D., De Meyer, L., Orsini, E., Smart, N.P.: BBQ: using AES in picnic signatures. Cryptology ePrint Archive, Report 2019/781 (2019). https://eprint.iacr.org/2019/781.pdf

[EFKP20] Ephraim, N., Freitag, C., Komargodski, I., Pass, R.: SPARKs: succinct parallelizable arguments of knowledge. In: Canteaut, A., Ishai, Y. (eds.) EUROCRYPT 2020. LNCS, vol. 12105, pp. 707–737. Springer, Cham (2020). https://doi.org/10.1007/978-3-030-45721-1_25

[FS87]   Fiat, A., Shamir, A.: How to prove yourself: practical solutions to identification and signature problems. In: Odlyzko, A.M. (ed.) CRYPTO 1986. LNCS, vol. 263, pp. 186–194. Springer, Heidelberg (1987). https://doi.org/10.1007/3-540-47721-7_12

[GGPR13] Gennaro, R., Gentry, C., Parno, B., Raykova, M.: Quadratic span programs and succinct NIZKs without PCPs. In: Johansson, T., Nguyen, P.Q. (eds.) EUROCRYPT 2013. LNCS, vol. 7881, pp. 626–645. Springer, Heidelberg (2013). https://doi.org/10.1007/978-3-642-38348-9_37

[GMO16]   Giacomelli, I., Madsen, J., Orlandi, C.: ZKBoo: faster zero-knowledge for Boolean circuits. In: Holz, T., Savage, S. (eds.) USENIX Security 2016, pp. 1069–1083. USENIX Association, August 2016

[GMR85]   Goldwasser, S., Micali, S., Rackoff, C.: The knowledge complexity of interactive proof-systems (extended abstract). In: 17th ACM STOC, pp. 291–304. ACM Press, May 1985

[GMW91]   Goldreich, O., Micali, S., Wigderson, A.: Proofs that yield nothing but their validity or all languages in np have zero-knowledge proof systems. J. ACM **38**(3), 690–728 (1991)

[Gro16]   Groth, J.: On the size of pairing-based non-interactive arguments. In: Fischlin, M., Coron, J.-S. (eds.) EUROCRYPT 2016. LNCS, vol. 9666, pp. 305–326. Springer, Heidelberg (2016). https://doi.org/10.1007/978-3-662-49896-5_11

[HK20]   Heath, D., Kolesnikov, V.: Stacked garbling for disjunctive zero-knowledge proofs. In: Canteaut, A., Ishai, Y. (eds.) EUROCRYPT 2020. LNCS, vol. 12107, pp. 569–598. Springer, Cham (2020). https://doi.org/10.1007/978-3-030-45727-3_19

[IKOS07] Ishai, Y., Kushilevitz, E., Ostrovsky, R., Sahai, A.: Zero-knowledge from secure multiparty computation. In: Johnson, D.S., Feige, U. (eds.) 39th ACM STOC, pp. 21–30. ACM Press, June 2007

[JKO13]   Jawurek, M., Kerschbaum, F., Orlandi, C.: Zero-knowledge using garbled circuits: how to prove non-algebraic statements efficiently. In: Sadeghi, A.-R., Gligor, V.D., Yung, M. (eds.) ACM CCS 2013, pp. 955–966. ACM Press, November 2013

[Kil92]   Kilian, J.: A note on efficient zero-knowledge proofs and arguments (extended abstract). In: 24th ACM STOC, pp. 723–732. ACM Press, May 1992

[KKW18]   Katz, J., Kolesnikov, V., Wang, X.: Improved non-interactive zero knowledge with applications to post-quantum signatures. In: Lie, D., Mannan, M., Backes, M., Wang, X. (eds.) ACM CCS 2018, pp. 525–537. ACM Press, October 2018

[MBKM19] Maller, M., Bowe, S., Kohlweiss, M., Meiklejohn, S.: Sonic: zero-knowledge SNARKs from linear-size universal and updatable structured reference strings. In: Cavallaro, L., Kinder, J., Wang, X., Katz, J. (eds.) ACM CCS 2019, pp. 2111–2128. ACM Press, November 2019

[Mic94]   Micali, S.: CS proofs (extended abstracts). In: 35th FOCS, pp. 436–453. IEEE Computer Society Press, November 1994

[PHGR13] Parno, B., Howell, J., Gentry, C., Raykova, M.: Pinocchio: nearly practical verifiable computation. In: 2013 IEEE Symposium on Security and Privacy, pp. 238–252. IEEE Computer Society Press, May 2013

[PS20]   Patra, A., Suresh, A.: BLAZE: blazing fast privacy-preserving machine learning. In: NDSS 2020. The Internet Society (2020)

[XZZ+19] Xie, T., Zhang, J., Zhang, Y., Papamanthou, C., Song, D.: Libra: succinct zero-knowledge proofs with optimal prover computation. In: Boldyreva, A., Micciancio, D. (eds.) CRYPTO 2019. LNCS, vol. 11694, pp. 733–764. Springer, Cham (2019). https://doi.org/10.1007/978-3-030-26954-8_24

[ZCD+17] Zaverucha, G.: Picnic. Technical report, National Institute of Standards and Technology (2017). https://csrc.nist.gov/projects/post-quantum-cryptography/round-1-submissions

[ZXZS19] Zhang, J., Xie, T., Zhang, Y., Song, D.: Transparent polynomial delegation and its applications to zero knowledge proof. Cryptology ePrint Archive, Report 2019/1482 (2019). https://eprint.iacr.org/2019/1482

Trust *and* Verify: A Complexity-Based IoT Behavioral Enforcement Method

Kyle Haefner$^{(\boxtimes)}$ (ID) and Indrakshi Ray (ID)

Colorado State University, Fort Collins, CO 80523, USA
`kyle.haefner@colostate.edu`

Abstract. In an Internet of Things (IoT) environment, devices may become compromised by cyber or physical attacks causing security and privacy breaches. When a device is compromised, its network behavior changes. In an IoT environment where there is insufficient attack data available and the data is unlabeled, novelty detection algorithms may be used to detect outliers. A novelty threshold determines whether the network flow is an outlier. In an IoT environment, we have different types of devices, some more complex than others. Simple devices have more predictable network behavior than complex ones. This work introduces a novel access control method for IoT devices by tuning novelty detection algorithm hyper-parameters based on a device's network complexity. This method relies only on network flow characteristics and is accomplished in an autonomous fashion requiring no labeled data. By analyzing connection based parameters and variance of each device's network traffic, we develop a formalized measurement of complexity for each device. We show that this complexity measure is positively correlated to how accurately a device can be modeled by a novelty detection algorithm. We then use this complexity metric to tune the hyper-parameters of the algorithm specific to each device. We propose an enforcement architecture based on Software Defined Networking (SDN) that uses the complexity of the device to define the precision of the decision boundary of the novelty algorithm.

Keywords: IoT · Security · Unsupervised machine learning · Access control

1 Introduction

The billions of devices that bridge the cyber and physical worlds have already altered how we interact with our physical surroundings. Smart speakers respond to spoken requests for information, provide reminders or simply turn on and off the lights. Embedded cameras can detect who we are and respond to our gestures to do mundane tasks such as turning up the volume, dim the lights, etc. For all the convenience and function that these devices, they also bring a long history of poorly implemented security, unpatched vulnerabilities, and privacy

This work was supported by NSF under Award Number CNS 1822118, Cyber Risk Research, NIST, Statnett, AMI, and Cable Television Laboratories.

S. Dolev et al. (Eds.): CSCML 2021, LNCS 12716, pp. 432–450, 2021.
https://doi.org/10.1007/978-3-030-78086-9_32

violations. Poorly implemented security on these devices has lead to distributed denial of service (DDoS) attacks specifically originating from these devices [8].

Security baselines [4,5] and strong endpoint security in international standards [24] are steps in the right direction, but there will always be insecure devices; either because they were manufactured that way or did not receive software patches. This is highlighted in the large corpus of research [1,23,25,25–27] that documents how and why vulnerable IoT devices are prone to security attacks. We will never be able to depend on all of our devices being completely secure, therefore we must instead depend on the network to help us to monitor and secure the devices for us. To scale to the networks of tomorrow and to be of practical use to the average consumer, network based IoT security must be done in a largely autonomous manner.

Unlike networks of the past, made up of a small number of general purpose machines, Internet of Things (IoT) networks will increasingly be made up of a large number of specialized devices designed to do a single task. The single purpose and often constrained nature of these devices makes them harder to intrinsically secure, but easier to extrinsically analyze. A single temperature sensor, for example, will not be able to run an anti-malware application, but does have a simple and predictable network traffic footprint.

This work exploits this single purpose nature and the correspondingly predictable network behavior of IoT devices to autonomously derive several measures of complexity based entirely on their network traffic. This allows not only for the classification and evaluation of IoT devices based on their complexity, but also enables each IoT device's historic network behavior to be more accurately modeled using an anomaly detection algorithm that is tuned to this complexity.

For enforcement we employ a software defined network that can proactively take several actions on a flow such as counting, logging, rate-limiting, delaying and blocking. Previous enforcement architectures were built on a binary model of trust and enforcement, i.e. block or allow traffic for a particular port or for a particular flow. Instead of binary enforcement; block or allow, our model allows the enforcement function to dynamically adjust for the complexity of the device (a direct measure of how well it can be modeled) and the abnormality of the flow (the measure of its separation from inliers). Highly abnormal flows from very simple devices can be automatically blocked, while such flows from more complex devices can be rate-limited or logged. Effectively this places more trust in devices that can be accurately modeled and less trust in devices that cannot be accurately modeled. We believe this is a key contribution and we have developed a ground truth methodology to test our model and a network reference architecture to enforce it.

This behavior-based flow routing model can be used as the first line of defense; to slow or prevent botnets and DDoS attacks at their source by detecting anomalous traffic at the granularity of individual flows from specific devices. Proper implementation would allow the network to selectively isolate and block malicious flows, leaving devices continuing to perform their primary function.

Research Contributions

- We formalize measurements of device complexity and establish a definition of device behavior based on anomaly/novelty detection formulated from IP header traffic all using unsupervised techniques that require no labeled data.
- We hypothesize that devices with smaller complexity values will show less of an aberration in its behavior compared with those of higher complexity values. Our results justify this. Thus, we tune the outlier threshold for the anomaly detection algorithms in accordance with device complexity.
- We propose a test architecture that uses the complexity tuned behavior to autonomously monitor and enforce learned behavior from devices.

This work is organized as follows; in Sect. 2 we review related research on how to analyze behavior and secure IoT devices. In Sect. 3 we describe the lab setup and the data collected. In Sect. 4 we develop methods for measuring complexity and how devices are classified into discrete groups. Section 5 describes how we develop a method for modeling learned behavior of IoT devices and describe the enforcement architecture in Sect. 6. In Sect. 7 we describe how the tuning of the hyper-parameters affects precision, recall and false positives of the model. Finally in Sect. 8 we summarize the work and propose possible next steps in this research.

2   Related Work

2.1   Device Identity Detection

Loepz-Martin et al. [10] build a network traffic classifier (NTC) using a recurrent neural network (RNN) and apply it to labeled IoT traffic. The goal of this is to identify the types of traffic and services exhibited by an IoT device as a step toward identifying the device.

Miettinen et al. [13] have developed a method, called IoT Sentinel, that uses machine learning to designate a device type on the network, referred to by the authors as a device fingerprint. Using the random forest algorithm and 23 network features they were able to identify device types on the network based on the device's traffic. The 23 features are based on layer two, three and four of the OSI networking stack. Expecting that the body of the packet will be encrypted, all the features the authors employed are based on unencrypted parts of the traffic like IP headers information.

Bezawada et al. [2] build on the work done in [13] by using a machine learning approach to broadly identify the device and place it in a predefined category, such as a light bulb. According to the authors, even devices from different manufacturers can be placed into general categories such as two separate light bulbs can be identified and placed into a lighting category.

All supervised solutions of fingerprinting devices suffer from a similar problem in that they require labeled data for each device. Not only this but a supervised classifier must be trained on every device, and potentially retrained on devices after a firmware update.

2.2   IoT Behavior and Autonomous Techniques

The following works use various means of autonomous and unsupervised machine learning approaches to identifying devices and device behavior. This has advantages over statically defined access control lists and firewall rules.

IoT-Keeper [7] is an edge based IoT anomaly based access control system that uses correlation-based feature selection to determine which features do not contribute to the anomaly detection. AuDI [12] implemented an autonomous device-type identification that uses the periodicity of device communications resulting in abstract device categories that could be used to enforce access control policies. DioT [14] extends the AuDI classification model to create a federated approach by aggregating device anomaly detection profiles.

Ren et al. use a privacy focused approach to enumerating and analyzing IoT behavior [19]. Ortiz et al. set up a probabilistic framework to monitor device behavior using an LSTM (Long Term Short Term Memory) neural network, to learn from inherent sequencing of TCP flows to automatically learn features from device traffic with the intent of categorizing devices and distinguishing between IoT devices and Non-IoT devices [18]. The authors are able to identify previously known devices after only 18 TCP-flow samples and categorize devices into two classes IoT and Non-IoT.

2.3   Complexity and Predictability

Formalized measurement of complexity as applied in a computer science context is probably most often associated with the works of Andrey Nikolaevich Kolmogorov, who defined the complexity of an object as the shortest computer program to produce the object as an output [9]. This simple notion arises again in the work of Jorma Rissanen whose work on the minimum description length principal that establishes that the best model for a set of data is one that leads to the best compression of the data [21].

In the paper Predictability, Complexity, and Learning authors Bialek et al. establish a formal result that predictive information provides a general measure of complexity [3]. In this work we propose that the relationship between predictive information and complexity is commutative, i.e. not only does predictive information lead to a measure of complexity, but that complexity provides a general measure of predictive information.

In machine learning this relationship leads to the logical notion that the less complex the model the more accurately it can be modeled, or to put this in the context of IoT, the less complex the device the more accurately we can define its behavior. Specifically, this work builds an anomaly based behavioral model, where the device's complexity directly affects the decision boundary that differentiates between inliers and outliers.

Our model can be used to determine a representative set of flows, along with a learned decision boundary, that define the behavior of a device and these flows can be directly loaded into flow tables of Openflow enabled switches. We believe that this will scale to the broad spectrum of devices and adapt to any new configurations of devices in the future.

Take, for example, a refrigerator that is also an Android tablet, the methodologies previously mentioned in the related works, would struggle to characterize such a device. Our method does not try to recognize this device as either a refrigerator or a tablet, it does not try to guess at the service or characterize the device's application layer data. Our model does not rely on learning specific human interactions with the refrigerator, nor determining if those interactions are anomalous. Our model only relies on how complex the refrigerator appears on the network and how much it stays within our learned boundary of behavior.

This work extends the work done in [6] by using a novelty detection algorithm and formalizing a ground truth testing methodology, to show the efficacy of the model at recognizing new and anomalous traffic.

3   Data Format and Collection

Data was collected from a real residential network with approximately 25 devices (Table 1) over the course of 37 days. These devices range from general computing devices like laptops and smartphones, IoT hubs with several IoT Devices using Zigbee or Zwave behind them, to single-purpose devices such as light bulbs and temperature sensors. Data was collected by a central MicroTik router (Fig. 1) and sent to nprobe [15] running on a Raspberry Pi. Flows were stored in a MariaDB relational database. Table 2 shows the features of the data collected.

Table 1. List of devices

Home devices		
• Amcrest Camera	Plex Server	Raspberry PI 3
• Google Home	Samsung Note 8	• Smart Things Hub
J. Chromebook (Asus)	• Xbox One (2)	• Appple Macbook Pro
• Philips Hue Hub	• Chromecast	• Echo Dot
• Eufy Doorbell	• Motorola Android	HP Stream Laptop (2)
• Eufy light bulb	• TP Link Switch	• Roku Express
• B. Chromebook (HP)	Brother Printer	• Roku Stick
• Amazon Alexa 1st gen.	• Fire Tablet (3)	

Flows were aggregated with a maximum of 30 min per flow. Inactive flow timeout was set to 15 s. If the devices have not exchanged traffic in 15 s the flow is completed and recorded. For training and test data sets the data is filtered by an individual IP address. The test environment is configured such that the devices always receive the same IPv4 address.

Definition 1. *Network Flow: A sequence of packets where all the packets in the flow have the same tuple: source address, destination address, source port, destination port and protocol.*

Table 2. Data features

Feature	Description
IPV4_SRC_ADDR	IPv4 Source Address
IPV4_DST_ADDR	IPv4 Destination Address
IN_PKTS	Incoming flow packets (Device->Destination)
IN_BYTES	Incoming flow bytes (Device->Remote)
OUT_PKTS	Outgoing flow packets (Remote->Device)
OUT_BYTES	Outgoing flow bytes (Remote->Device)
L4_SRC_PORT	IPv4 Source Port
L4-DST_PORT	IPv4 Destination Port
PROTOCOL	IP Protocol Identifier

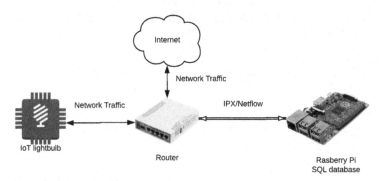

Fig. 1. Data collection architecture

4 Device Complexity Classification

Device complexity is an aggregate measurement of a device's IP connections, d_{ip}, and how much its traffic varies over time d_v. Devices that are single purpose should have simple network behavior and general purpose devices will have more complex network behavior. Figure 2 shows where devices should fall along a spectrum of simple and complex.

Fig. 2. Spectrum of network complexity

4.1   Device IP Complexity

This research examines how devices form connections. Simply counting the number of unique IP addresses that a device connects with fails to take into account the inherent service-oriented hierarchical structure of the IPv4 address space, where companies and services are often part of similar subnets. To account for this we propose a complexity measure based on a simple ratio of *IP spread* to *IP depth*. IP spread is the number of unique source and destination IP addresses that interact with the device. IP depth is the number of IP addresses that belong to the same higher level octets.

Definition 2. *IP Tree, IP Branch, IP Leaf, IP Spread. An* IP tree *is a unique first order octet which comprises the root of the tree. An* IP Branch *is a second or third order octet that has one or more fourth order octets under it. An* IP leaf *is a unique fourth order octet. IP* Spread *is the sum of total unique IP addresses that interact with a device.*

Device IP Spread (IP_{Spread})

$$IP_{Spread} = \sum IP_{trees} \tag{1}$$

Device IP Depth (IP_{Depth})

$$IP_{Depth} = \frac{\sum IP_{leaf}}{\sum IP_{branch}} \tag{2}$$

Device IP Complexity (d_{ip})

$$d_{ip} = \frac{IP_{Spread}}{IP_{Depth}} \tag{3}$$

To calculate IP spread and depth we build unordered trees of each IP address where the first order octet is the root and lower octets are children. Then we can calculate how many trees, branches and leaf nodes each IoT device contacts. A large number of IP trees with few branches indicates a large IP spread. A small number of IP trees that have many branches and leaves indicates a large IP depth. IP spread/depth is used as one measure of a device's complexity. The intuition here is that this complexity measure mirrors how services are organized based on common IP subnets. As devices form connections out to the Internet their complexity goes up. As the number of connections that have common first, second and third octets increases this has a corresponding reduction in the complexity measurement of the device. Devices belonging to a single ecosystem such as Google Home have a small number of broad trees (low IP Spread and high IP Depth) as they connect to mostly Google's networks dedicated to these types of devices. Other devices such as laptops and smart phones make connections to many unique destinations thus leading to a large number of thin trees each having fewer branches and leaves. Figure 3 shows the total IP complexity of each device. Devices that are more general purpose have higher complexity and are grouped together on the right of the figure. Single purpose and lower complexity devices are grouped on the left of the figure.

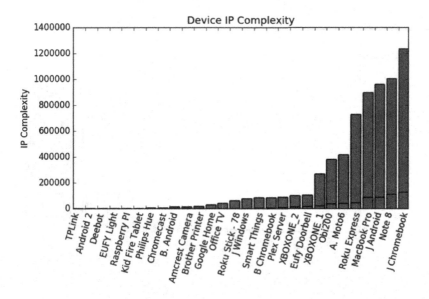

Fig. 3. IP device complexity

4.2   Device Variance

The variance metric comes from the simple notion that devices on a network present different variances based on what they do on the network. Device variance is calculated by taking the sum of the standard deviation of n device features d_f in the training set as shown in Eq. 4. Each device's variance is graphed in Fig. 4. Here again, devices that tend to be more general purpose have higher complexity and are grouped on the right of the figure. Single purpose and lower complexity devices are grouped on the left of the figure.

Device Variance (d_v)

$$d_v = \sum_{f=1}^{n} \sigma_{d_f} \tag{4}$$

4.3   Aggregate Complexity

Overall device complexity is the sum of the average device variance and the average device IP complexity as calculated in Eq. 5 and shown in Fig. 5. Devices in the figure again show that general purpose and higher complexity devices tend toward the right side of the graph and more single purpose lower complex devices tend to be grouped on the left side of the graph.

Aggregate Device Complexity (A_{DC})

$$A_{DC} = d_{ip} + d_v \tag{5}$$

Discrete Complexity. Organizing the devices based on logarithmic magnitudes of complexity allows us to easily examine device characteristics within discrete groups as shown in in Fig. 6.

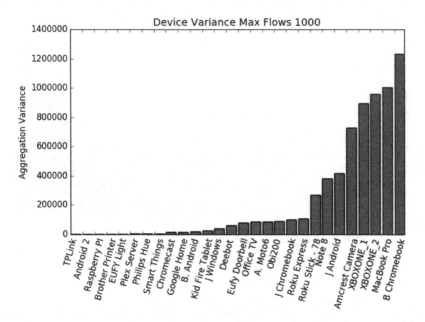

Fig. 4. Average device network variance

Discrete Device Complexity (D_{DC})

$$D_{DC} = \lceil log_{10}A_{DC} \rceil \tag{6}$$

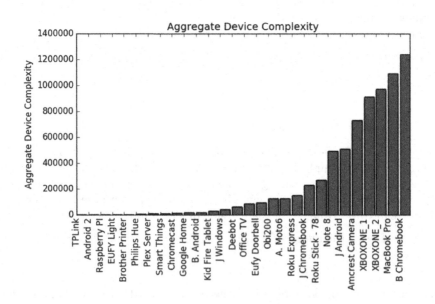

Fig. 5. Aggregate complexity

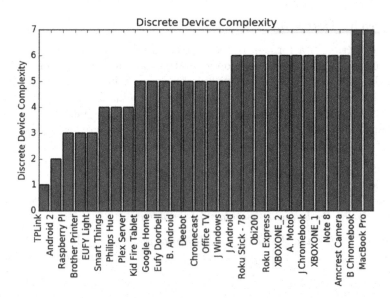

Fig. 6. Discrete complexity

5   Behavior

Given the complex interactions that IoT devices have with the physical world, behavior represents the dynamic and changing network footprint exhibited by these devices. The sensing and actuating response of IoT devices that bridges the cyber and physical world requires new methods of defining what is normal and what is abnormal. IoT devices, even the same make and model from the same manufacturer will exhibit slightly different behavior based on how they interact with the human inhabitants, each other and the environment. Two very similar devices, that have different apps installed may act very differently. This variance in behavior requires that the model is tailored to these specific and individual devices.

We begin by defining IoT device behavior based on the past history of network interactions of the device, bounded by the most extreme of these interactions in the training set. To model the degree of normality and extremity of behavior we turn to classic outlier detection algorithms, adding what we believe to be a key contribution of this research, we tune the hyper-parameter of the outlier detection algorithm to the specific device based on the measure of complexity as defined in the previous section.

This method has the direct affect of making the decision boundary of the trained model a more precise fit for simple devices and more generalized for complex devices. This allows the detection algorithm to be more strict in identifying outliers for simple devices and more lax for complex devices. This enhances the model, enabling it to adaptively prioritize new extreme behavior and reduce false positives for simple devices.

5.1   Novelty Detection

Novelty detection is a form of outlier detection where the training set is considered untainted by outliers i.e. only positive samples. New observations are classified and determined to fall within the decision boundary are inliers and observations outside the decision boundary are outliers. To derive a behavior for a device we employ the One Class Support Vector Machine (OCSVM) algorithm using the Radial Basis Function (RBF) kernel [11]. Outlier flows detected during the training phase are recorded, and form the set of flows we call significant flows.

Definition 3. Significant Flow: *A significant flow is one that is marked as an outlier by the OCSVM during training. This set of flows plus the decision boundary forms the behavior boundary of the device.*

Definition 4. Device Behavioral Boundary: Device behavioral boundary *is the set of all unique significant flows and the decision boundary found during training.*

To establish that the complexity measurement is a statistically relevant one we take the linear regression of the number of outliers found by the OCSVM using the default values of $\nu = 0.5$ and gamma as calculated in Eq. 7. The correlation of outliers to anomalies can be seen in Fig. 7.

$$\gamma = \frac{1}{n_{features} * x.var()} \tag{7}$$

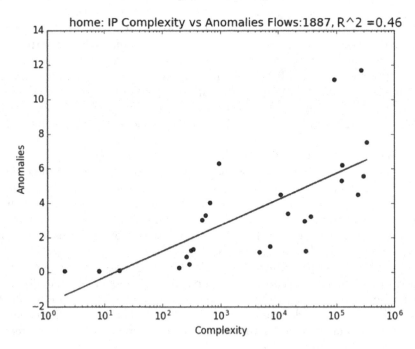

Fig. 7. Complexity vs Anomalies

5.2   Novelty Detection Tuning Using Device Complexity

To the best of our knowledge, labeled anomaly data for each of the devices in Table 1 does not exist. To test the efficacy of our model we developed the following testing ground-truth methodology:

Training and Testing Set: We took up to 1000 historical flows from each device, used 80% for training and 20% for testing. We assume that all of the testing set consists of inliers (i.e. no a priori outliers). We then developed a set of outliers by randomly generating each IPv4 destination octet such that each IP address generated conforms to a non-reserved IP address [20]. Destination ports were randomly generated in the range 1–65535 and protocols were randomly picked from the set (1,6,17) which were the protocols found in the training data.

The OCSVM using the RBF kernel is governed by the two hyper-parameters, ν (nu) and γ (gamma). Gamma sets the radius of the RBF kernel by determining the influence of each example of the decision boundary and ν sets the upper bound on fraction of errors during training and the lower bound on the fraction of support vectors used. For the purposes of this work we set this using the 'scale' option of Sci-kit learn which uses the following equation to determine gamma.

This research examines three methods to establish ν for devices; static ν set uniformly across all devices; a dynamic ν set per device, and a ν tuned to the complexity of the device.

5.3   Static Hyper-Parameter ν

For the static method an average ν is found and applied uniformly across all the device models. To find the average ν, each device was modeled using OCSVM with ν varied over the range of 0.00001 to 0.5. The ν for each device that had the best F1 score was saved and the mean ν value was calculated across all the devices. This average ν was then used to train the model for each device and test for anomalies. This gives a baseline model where there is a balance between precision and recall and where the hyper-parameter ν is set to the same value for each device.

5.4   Dynamic Hyper-Parameter ν

The dynamic method finds the best ν for each device and that ν is applied individually to each model. To find the ν value for individual devices, each device was modeled using OCSVM with ν varied over the range of 0.00001 to 0.5. The ν for each device that had the highest F1 score was then used to train the model for that device and test for anomalies. This gives results that balance precision and recall and a model that is tuned per device.

5.5   Complexity-Tuned Dynamic ν

To tune the model based on complexity a value for ν is found that minimizes false positives for low complex devices. To find a ν value that is tuned to the complexity of the device, each device was modeled using OCSVM with ν varied over the range of 0.00001 to 0.5. The ν for each device that had the highest F_β scores where $\beta = \hat{A}_{DC}$, where $\hat{A}_{DC}$ is the normalized value (between 0 and 1) of the aggregate device complexity as defined in Sect. 4. This search prioritizes minimizing false negatives on low complexity devices as seen in Eq. 8.

$$F_\beta = (1 + \beta^2)\frac{precision * recall}{(\beta^2 * precision) + recall} \tag{8}$$

6   Enforcement Architecture

The enforcement architecture shown in Fig. 8 is based on a centralized model where there is a single device that acts as a router, gateway and access point. To implement the enforcement architecture we use a Raspberry Pi 4. The Raspberry Pi 4 is a single-board computer based on an ARM architecture. We chose this as it is a reasonable representation of the embedded architectures used in today's more powerful home routers, and analyze if it is capable of handling both training the novelty detection model and switching and routing done by the SDN controller and SDN switch.

SDN architectures decouple the control and the data plane in routers and switches. This opens the network to new services, features, and a level of dynamism that was previously not possible. This work leverages the programmability of the network to dynamically allow, block, rate-limit, log and route traffic based on if the flow is novel, the degree of novelty, and the complexity of the device.

The reference enforcement architecture developed for this work uses the OpenFlow [16] reference soft switch called OpenVSwitch [17]. OpenVSwitch supports OpenFlow versions 1.0–1.5.

RYU is a software defined network controller that implements OpenFlow. In this prototype we use RYU to setup and control OpenVswitch [22]

The flow collector consists of a Raspberry Pi running a netflow collection software called nprobe. Nprobe stores the flows into a MariaDB database.

6.1   Enforcement

Enforcement of the currently proposed test environment examines only values known at connection time. Aggregate flow metrics will be examined in a future work. The connection enforcement stage is only run once at flow connection setup. The connection features include IP header attributes such as IP source, IP destination, port, and protocol. If the model detects an outlier based on the connection features it will use the current device confidence scores and the outlier degree to the flow to calculate the flow trust score.

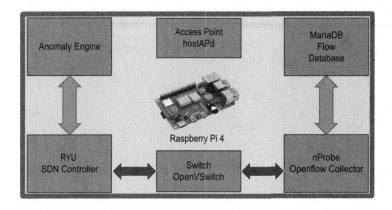

Fig. 8. Enforcement architecture

In Fig. 8 the anomaly detection engine loads previously trained device models stored as serialized python objects and calculates device complexity, behavioral boundary, and flow scores. For flows that do not exist in the current flow rules table of OpenVSwitch, RYU queries the anomaly engine to determine if the flow is an outlier, inlier or significant flow (a flow that was an outlier during the training stage). If a flow is determined to be an outlier and the policy for that device is to drop outliers then the flow is simply not added to the flow table matched rules and is dropped.

The architecture in Fig. 8 allows the network to make extremely granular flow decisions on every flow in the network, including inbound/outbound traffic to the Internet and intra-network device traffic. Based on the behavioral boundary there is no need to isolate an entire device, just the flows that are found to be abnormal.

7   Results

7.1   Static Hyper-Parameter ν

Figure 9 shows the OCSVM classifier trained on each device with a static ν and applied uniformly to all devices based on the search that optimizes the F1 score as defined in Sect. 5.2. This model has an average false positive rate (FPR) of 0.082 averaged across all devices.

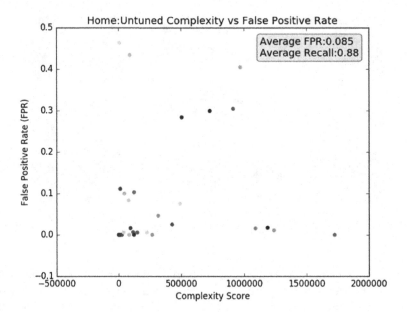

Fig. 9. Un-tuned model

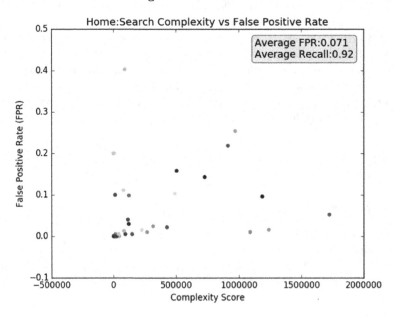

Fig. 10. Search model

Figure 10 shows the OCSVM where each device model is tuned with the ν that optimizes the F1 score. This model has a average false positive rate (FPR) of 0.062.

Figure 11 shows the OCSVM where each device is tuned to the ν that uses the complexity of the device to influence the precision of the F_β score. There is a noticeable drop in the number of false positives overall, however more importantly there is a greater drop in the false positive rate for the lower complexity devices. This can be seen in the fact that more of the devices on the left (the low complexity devices) have markedly smaller false positive rates. This is the expected result as we are tuning the F_β score weighted toward precision on these devices.

Table 3. Low complexity model characteristics

Model type	D_{DC} <5	D_{DC} <4	A_{DC} <Mean	DC <1 Std Dev
Static	P = 0.984	P = 0.98	P = 0.911	P = 0.914
	R = 0.549	R = 0.582	R = 0.893	R = 0.911
	FPR = 0.107	FPR = 0.114	FPR = 0.061	FPR = 0.06
Dynamic	P = 0.927	P = 0.916	P = 0.946	P = 0.959
	R = 0.893	R = 0.581	R = 0.936	R = 0.946
	FPR = 0.072	FPR = 0.113	FPR = 0.053	FPR = 0.044
Tuned	P = 0.951	P = 0.96	P = 0.975	P = 0.976
	R = 0.915	R = 0.955	R = 0.878	R = 0.887
	FPR = 0.048	FPR = 0.033	FPR = 0.029	FPR = 0.026

Table 3 shows how the three models perform on several subsets of the device space where devices have low complexity measures. The first column shows the model on devices that have a discrete device complexity DD_C of less than 5 (as calculated in Sect. 4.3. The second column shows devices with a D_{DC} of less than 4. The third column shows devices that have an aggregate complexity A_{DC} less than mean complexity of the set of all devices. Finally, the last column shows the devices that have A_{DC} of less then one standard deviation.

The tuned model outperforms both the dynamic and the static models in terms of precision and false positive rate. This is expected as the tuned model has a higher weight for minimizing false positives than the other two with a small trade-off of lower recall. It is also notable, that the tuned model performs better on the higher complex devices as shown in column 1,2 with the tuned model having better precision *and* recall than the static and dynamic models.

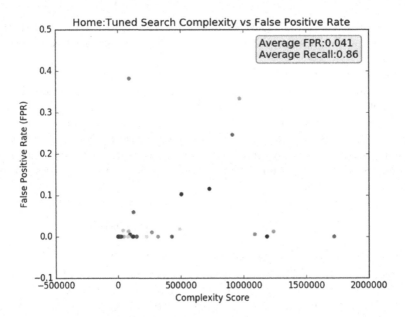

Fig. 11. Tuned search model

8   Conclusions and Future Work

In this work we established an autonomous and unsupervised method to formally measure the complexity of a network device based solely on the network flows from that device. We show that this complexity measure has a positive correlation to the number of outliers found in an un-tuned anomaly detection engine. We then used this measure of device complexity to develop a behavioral model for each device based on a tuned novelty detection engine. We show that this behavioral model has a lower FPR for all devices and performs better than both the static and dynamic modeling methods. Finally, we propose a network architecture based on SDN to dynamically enforce our model.

In future work, we will look at additional methods of establishing network complexity such as incorporating a second enforcement stage based on aggregate flow features such as bytes per second and packets per second. This will allow the model to account for connections that are normal in the connection attributes, but may be anomalous based on bandwidth. We also apply our complexity model to other domains, such as industrial IoT networks and SCADA based networks. Finally we will look at how we can use a supervised learning approach to finger print devices and use this to bootstrap a behavior model across know common devices and device ecosystems.

References

1. Apthorpe, N., Reisman, D., Feamster, N.: A smart home is no castle: Privacy vulnerabilities of encrypted IOT traffic. arXiv preprint arXiv:1705.06805 (2017)
2. Bezawada, B., Bachani, M., Peterson, J., Shirazi, H., Ray, I., Ray, I.: Behavioral fingerprinting of IOT devices. In: Proceedings of the 2018 Workshop on Attacks and Solutions in Hardware Security, pp. 41–50. ACM (2018)
3. Bialek, W., Nemenman, I., Tishby, N.: Predictability, complexity, and learning. Neural Comput. **13**(11), 2409–2463 (2001)
4. Fagan, M., Megas, K., Scarfone, K., Matthew, S.: Core cybersecurity feature baseline for securable IOT devices. Technical report, National Institute of Standards and Technology (2019)
5. Group, C.C.W.: The c2 consensus on IOT device security baseline capabilities. Technical report, Consumer Technology Association (2019)
6. Haefner, K., Ray, I.: Complexiot: behavior-based trust for IOT networks. In: 2019 First IEEE International Conference on Trust, Privacy and Security in Intelligent Systems and Applications (TPS-ISA), pp. 56–65. IEEE (2019)
7. Hafeez, I., Antikainen, M., Ding, A.Y., Tarkoma, S.: Iot-keeper: Securing IOT communications in edge networks. arXiv preprint arXiv:1810.08415 (2018)
8. Kolias, C., Kambourakis, G., Stavrou, A., Voas, J.: Ddos in the IOT Mirai and other botnets. Computer **50**(7), 80–84 (2017)
9. Kolmogorov, A.N.: On tables of random numbers. Sankhyā: The Indian Journal of Statistics, Series A, pp. 369–376 (1963)
10. Lopez-Martin, M., Carro, B., Sanchez-Esguevillas, A., Lloret, J.: Network traffic classifier with convolutional and recurrent neural networks for internet of things. IEEE Access **5**, 18042–18050 (2017)
11. Manevitz, L.M., Yousef, M.: One-class svms for document classification. J. Mach. Learn. Res. **2**(12), 139–154 (2001)
12. Marchal, S., Miettinen, M., Nguyen, T.D., Sadeghi, A.R., Asokan, N.: Audi: toward autonomous IOT device-type identification using periodic communication. IEEE J. Sel. Areas Commun. **37**(6), 1402–1412 (2019)
13. Miettinen, M., Marchal, S., Hafeez, I., Asokan, N., Sadeghi, A.R., Tarkoma, S.: Iot sentinel: automated device-type identification for security enforcement in IOT. In: 2017 IEEE 37th International Conference on Distributed Computing Systems (ICDCS), pp. 2177–2184. IEEE (2017)
14. Nguyen, T.D., Marchal, S., Miettinen, M., Fereidooni, H., Asokan, N., Sadeghi, A.R.: Dïot: a federated self-learning anomaly detection system for IOT. In: 2019 IEEE 39th International Conference on Distributed Computing Systems (ICDCS), pp. 756–767. IEEE (2019)
15. An extensible netflow v5/v9/ipfix probe for ipv4/v6 (2020). https://www.ntop.org/products/netflow/nprobe/
16. Openflow switch erata, open networking foundation, onf ts-001 (2012). https://www.opennetworking.org/wp-content/uploads/2013/07/openflow-spec-v1.0.1.pdf
17. Production quality, multilayer open virtual switch (2019). https://www.openvswitch.org
18. Ortiz, J., Crawford, C., Le, F.: Devicemien: network device behavior modeling for identifying unknown IOT devices. In: Proceedings of the International Conference on Internet of Things Design and Implementation, pp. 106–117. ACM (2019)

19. Ren, J., Dubois, D.J., Choffnes, D., Mandalari, A.M., Kolcun, R., Haddadi, H.: Information exposure from consumer IOT devices: a multidimensional, network-informed measurement approach. In: Proceedings of the Internet Measurement Conference, pp. 267–279. ACM (2019)
20. Requirements for internet hosts - communication layers (1989). https://tools.ietf.org/html/rfc1122
21. Rissanen, J.: Stochastic complexity in statistical inquiry. World Scientific (1989)
22. Ryu sdn framework (2019). https://osrg.github.io/ryu/
23. Sachidananda, V., Siboni, S., Shabtai, A., Toh, J., Bhairav, S., Elovici, Y.: Let the cat out of the bag: a holistic approach towards security analysis of the internet of things. In: Proceedings of the 3rd ACM International Workshop on IoT Privacy, Trust, and Security, pp. 3–10. ACM (2017)
24. Various: Open connectivity foundation (ocf) specification – part 2: Security specification. Standard, Open Connectivity Foundation (2019)
25. Wilson, C., Hargreaves, T., Hauxwell-Baldwin, R.: Benefits and risks of smart home technologies. Energ. Policy 103, 72–83 (2017)
26. Yang, Y., Wu, L., Yin, G., Li, L., Zhao, H.: A survey on security and privacy issues in internet-of-things. IEEE Internet Things J. 4(5), 1250–1258 (2017)
27. Zhao, K., Ge, L.: A survey on the internet of things security. In: 2013 Ninth International Conference on Computational Intelligence and Security, pp. 663–667. IEEE (2013)

Using a Neural Network to Detect Anomalies Given an N-gram Profile

Byunggu Yu and Junwhan Kim[(✉)]

Department of Computer Science and Information Technology,
University of the District of Columbia, Washington, DC 20008, USA
{byu,junwhan.kim}@udc.edu

Abstract. In order to detect unknown intrusions and runtime errors of computer programs, the cyber-security community has developed various detection techniques. Anomaly detection is an approach that is designed to profile the normal runtime behavior of computer programs in order to detect intrusions and errors as anomalous deviations from the observed normal. However, normal but unobserved behavior can trigger false positives. This limitation has significantly decreased the practical viability of anomaly detection techniques. Reported approaches to this limitation span a simple alert threshold definition to distribution models for approximating all normal behavior based on the limited observation. However, each assumption or approximation poses the potential for even greater false positive rates. This paper presents our study on how to explain the presence of anomalies using a neural network, particularly Long Short-Term Memory, independent of actual data distributions. We present and compare three anomaly detection models, and report on our experience running different types of attacks on an Apache Hypertext Transfer Protocol server. We performed a comparative study, focusing on each model's ability to detect the onset of each attack while avoiding false positives resulting from unknown normal behavior. Our best-performing model detected the true onset of every attack with zero false positives.

Keywords: System call monitoring · Machine learning · N-gram

1 Introduction

Over the last four decades, the software assurance community has developed various types of monitoring techniques in order to detect intrusions and errors in computer programs at runtime. Such monitoring techniques focus around the following approaches: (1) detecting known bad patterns, (2) detecting runtime deviations from the design specifications of the program, or (3) detecting runtime deviations (anomalies) from the observed normal of the program. The first approach (known bad pattern detection) [2,8,22,27,31,34] encompasses predominantly signature-based matching employed by various anti-virus and network packet monitoring solutions. Attack signatures are usually built by analyzing known attacks. The process of collecting signatures implicitly assumes and

© Springer Nature Switzerland AG 2021
S. Dolev et al. (Eds.): CSCML 2021, LNCS 12716, pp. 451–466, 2021.
https://doi.org/10.1007/978-3-030-78086-9_33

accepts the risk that any unknown attack has to succeed or become detectable at least once. Only after the attack can any relevant information be collected, studied, and shaped into a signature to be used in the detection. Sometimes, the initial signature needs to be improved later to increase the effectiveness of the signature in detecting variants of the corresponding attack or to address any logic that was not initially discovered by the analysts. The signature-based approach does not generally detect or protect against exploits of zero-day vulnerabilities unless they happen to match already known malicious signatures. The second approach, design specification-deviation detection [1,24,40] requires a priori knowledge about the target program's internal logic and additional efforts to generate corresponding behavior specifications. Unlike the first two approaches, the third approach, anomaly detection [5,13,15] does not require a priori knowledge of attack behavior or application design in order to protect an arbitrary computer program from unknown intrusions and errors. The basic rationale is as follows: if the entropy of the behavior of the program is finite, one can observe the program to learn about its normal behavior and then detect anomalies that do not follow this behavior. Unfortunately, there are three practical challenges with this anomaly detection approach.

1. The first challenge is the representation of normal behavior. There have been investigations of using the names of system calls generated by a program to represent a trace of a program's behavior, e.g. [15]. However, it has also been reported that mimicry attacks [16,25,41] can go undetected by mimicking some normally observed sequence of system calls. A feature space is a set of attributes of a system whose values are being observed. If the granularity of the feature space is insufficient, it may be impossible to distinguish between the normal and abnormal, lowering the true positive rate.
2. The second challenge is that practical observations are often limited and may not cover all possible normal behaviors of the target program. This practical limitation often results in false positives during detection, when alerts are issued for the normal behaviors that were not previously observed. Excessive false positive alerts can make the detection solution unusable. On the other hand, any generalization of the learned normal can create false negatives regarding anomalous behaviors covered by the generalization of the normal behavior, lowering the true positive rate.
3. The third challenge is to learn normal behavior using noisy behavior observations in an unsupervised manner. Any observed noise can incur false negatives regarding any intrusions or errors that resemble the noise. Such false negatives will correspondingly lower the true positive rate [10].

This paper focuses on anomaly detection methods that address these three challenges. The proposed detection methods take a bit stream as input, where each bit has the value 0 if the corresponding local behavior matches a known behavior or 1 otherwise. Although a variety of models for behavior representation can be considered, the system call n-gram model [15] is used in this paper. Due to the factors mentioned in the challenges described above, the resulting n-gram match-mismatch bit stream is inherently noisy. Therefore, the main problem investigated in this paper is how to reliably find anomalies in this noisy bit stream.

We present and compare four methods that are designed to detect anomalies in an n-gram match-mismatch bit stream. We report here on our experience running various types of attacks several times on a relatively lightly loaded Apache Hypertext Transfer Protocol (HTTP) server application. We processed the server's system call behavior, before, during and after the attacks, using the nine models. Then we performed a comparative analysis, focusing on each model's ability to detect the attacks while avoiding false positive alarms. The results presented in this paper show that our proposed method, called LAF (denoting "LSTM Anomaly Filter"), is highly practical in terms of false positives, true positives, detection delays, supported types of programs, and detectable types of attacks. By eliminating false positives without compromising the true positive rate, the LAF can detect the true onset of DoS attacks early (e.g., almost immediate detection attacks with no false positives in our experiments). This makes timely remedial actions possible, with enough time and computational power. Moreover, other types of attacks involving a smaller number of system calls can be addressed. The rest of this paper is organized as follows: Sect. 2 defines the problem; Sects. 3 presents the four anomaly detection methods; Sect. 4 presents our experimental setting and evaluates our results; Sect. 5 summarizes related work. Then, Sect. 6 concludes the paper with a summary and our vision of future work.

2 Problem Definition

System call (syscall) anomaly detection approaches tend to include two conceptual phases:

- Training: creates a behavior model (or profile) for a sequence of consecutive syscalls made by a process during its normal states. A controlled environment is often used to assure normal operation of the process.
- Detection: an anomaly alert is issued when the observed sequence of syscalls deviates from the behavior model by more than an allowed threshold. This paper is focused on the quantification of the model-appropriate threshold selection.

We collect and record the n-grams of the syscall streams for each program to be monitored. During the monitoring phase, runtime syscall n-grams undergo a match test over the recorded n-grams and a match (0)/mismatch (1) bit stream is produced. In determining the normality of the runtime behavior, we apply a distribution-based classifier approach.

Let $\hat{p}$ be the average match rate of n-grams at which the training is arbitrarily set to complete (i.e., defining the end of the training phase).

Let $X \sim Binomial(W, \hat{p})$ be a random variable modeling the number of matches (i.e., zeros in the bit stream) in W consecutive n-gram match tests. If the "aggregation window size" W is large enough and $\hat{p}$ is not too close to either

1 or 0, the binomial distribution can be considered approximately equivalent to a Gaussian distribution with the following mean and variance:

$$E(X) = a = W\hat{p}. \tag{2.0.1}$$

$$V(X) = var(X) = E((X - E(X))^2) = \alpha^2 = W\hat{p}(1 - \hat{p}). \tag{2.0.2}$$

Under the assumptions the relation or random variable and the distributions can be presented as:

$$X \sim Binomial(W, \hat{p}) \approx N(W\hat{p}, W\hat{p}(1 - \hat{p}))$$

This expression means that random variable X has binomial distribution, which in turn is approximated by a normal distribution with expected value $W\hat{p}$ and variance $W\hat{p}(1 - \hat{p})$). For this approximately Gaussian distribution, it generally makes sense to consider that a system is in a normal state when the number X of matches in the binary coded match/mismatch string of length W is within range $E(X) \pm m\sigma$ of the mean of the corresponding normal distribution. However, in our application, a match rate above upper bound $E(X) + m\sigma$ is also considered to be normal because observing signs of normal behavior in abundance is normal. Hence, we'll focus on the match rates falling below the lower bound $E(X) - m\sigma$. We will use 3 anomaly threshold, hence take fixed $m = 3$.

Let n be the length of the n-grams. A completely new n-gram in the worst case can ultimately result in up to $2n - 1$ consecutive mismatches if it consists exclusively of previously non-profiled syscalls. Therefore, the size W of the aggregation window should be large enough to accommodate at least $2n - 1$ consecutive mismatches in a normal state. That is, W should be set such that:

$$W - (W\hat{p} - m\sqrt{W\hat{p}(1 - \hat{p})}) \geq 2n - 1. \tag{2.0.3}$$

Here W is the aggregation window size, n is the length of each n-gram, and $m = 3$, for example, is the multiplier allowing anomaly detection with the 3σ span. Based on this basic definition of the problem of anomaly detection, the paper presents three anomaly detection methods given – EWMA (Exponentially Weighted Moving Average Method), PEWMA (Probabilistic EWMA), and LAF (LSTM Anomaly Filter).

3   Anomaly Detection Methods

3.1   Static Binomial Method (SB)

For the first model we make the simplest assumptions about the bit stream. Any isolated bit stream can be naïvely viewed as a realization of some Bernoulli test sequence with a "success" (or match in our case) probability. For a large enough sequence of experiments Bernoulli distribution can be approximated by a normal distribution with parameters given by (2.0.1) and (2.0.2). The training stage provides us a reasonable estimate of the match probability p , which we assume is good enough to characterize the process in a normal state. So, to build the simplest, while admittedly naïve model for bit stream anomaly detection, we assume that the process and observable bit stream data possess the following three properties:

1. The probability of X is approximated by the normal distribution;
2. The individual match/mismatch tests are described by the Bernoulli distribution;
3. The match probability $\hat{p}$ is static (i.e. does not change over time).

If these assumptions hold, we can consider the process model to be in a normal state if the following holds:

$$X \geq W\hat{p} - m\sqrt{(W\hat{p}(1 - \hat{p})} \qquad (3.1.1)$$

W is set such that, the inequality (2.0.3) is satisfied.

On one hand the simplicity of the expression (3.1.1) allows for easy computation of an anomaly condition. On another hand the assumptions (1)–(3) that lead to the expression may be too naïve as independence of the consequential n-grams is an intentional simplification for the Bernoulli model's necessary conditions, so SB is excluded in our experiment.

3.2 EWMA

In Sect. 2 we assumed that the process behavior was static, i.e. distribution of the matches describing normal process behavior was specific only to the process and did not change with time. In our dynamic models, we will not seek or assume existence of one distribution universally describing normal behavior of the process.

One way of addressing assumption (3) from the SB is to reevaluate the probability mass function of X sequentially as new observation data comes in. However, simply substituting $\hat{p}$ of the previous models with localized estimates may misclassify the corresponding local anomalies. Hence, the history of X needs to be included into localized statistics. The localized statistics introduced in the sections below can allow us to estimate distribution parameters specifying normal process behavior from one point in time to another.

To allow localized computing of an average value, we will consider EWMA (the Exponentially Weighted Moving Average [33]), which is a popular localized averaging technique that computes the local average $E(X_t)$ for a time point t by recursively applying exponentially decreasing weights to the past averages as follows:

$$E(X_t) = \alpha E(X)(t - 1)) + (1 - \alpha)X_t \,, \qquad (3.2.1)$$

where $0 \leq \alpha < 1$ is the weight put on the history. Based on the normal distribution assumption, X_t is considered to meet the following condition in most cases:

$$|E(X_t) - X_t| < m\hat{\sigma}_t, \qquad (3.2.2)$$

where m is a constant multiplier (as before we use 3σ) and $\hat{\sigma}_t$ is the localized estimate of standard deviation computed for a point t in time as follows:

$$\hat{\sigma}_t = \sqrt{E(X_{t-1}^2) - E(X_{t-1})^2}, \tag{3.2.3}$$

In our application, X_t is defined to be the number of matches during W consecutive match/mismatch tests. Therefore, $E(X_t) < X_t$ is not considered to be anomalous, but rather normal above average behavior. Based on this observation and (3.2.2), we can consider the process to be in a normal state if the following holds:

$$X_t \leq E(X_t) - m\hat{\sigma}_t, \tag{3.2.4}$$

where, $E(X_t)$ is computed according to (3.2.1), $\hat{\sigma}_t$ is computed according to (3.2.3).

3.3   PEWMA

It has been reported that EWMA tends to be optimized at a higher end of the value range (i.e., close to 1) in terms of mean squared error (MSE) prediction given a data stream containing a small number of anomaly events placed near each other with short inter-occurrence times [4]. Under such an optimization, the mean $E(X)$ changed by a large anomaly does not return to the normal level fast enough to detect closely following smaller anomaly events. To address this [4] proposed a variant of EWMA called Probabilistic EWMA (PEWMA). This model replaces the localized mean recursive update expression (3.2.1) as follows:

$$E(X_t) = \alpha(1 - \beta P_t)E(X_{t-1}) + (1 - \alpha(1 - \beta P_t))X_t, \tag{3.2.1}$$

where $0 < \alpha < 1$ is the history weighting parameter, P_t is the probability of X_t under some modeled distribution (as in [4] we use a standard normal distribution), and β is the weight placed on P_t.

It is easy to see that with $\beta \to 0$ or $P_t \to 0$ the expression for PEWMA converges to EWMA. The rationale behind PEWMA is that samples that are less likely to have been observed should have lesser influence on the corresponding updates. In order to accomplish this based on the normal distribution, P_t is defined as follows: $P_t = \min(\frac{1}{\sqrt{2\pi}}e^{\frac{(E(X_{t-1})-X_t)^2}{2\hat{\sigma}_t^2}}, \hat{p})$, where $\hat{\sigma}_t$ is computed as in (3.1.3) and $\hat{p}$ is the expected match rate recorded at the completion of the training.

The process is in a normal state if the following holds: $X_t \leq E(X_t) - m\hat{\sigma}_t$. Even though this expression appears to be the same as that of DSM-E, here the localized mean is defined as (3.2.1). As before $m = 3$ is used as the constant multiplier for anomaly detection.

3.4 LSTM Anomaly Filter (LAF)

The most annoying problem in any threshold-based anomaly detection mechanism is caused by recurrent match-mismatch patterns that can trigger false positive alerts. The problem becomes more cumbersome as the number and complexity of such patterns increase. Of course, this problem diminishes when our n-gram profile is complete and covers 100% of all normal behavior of the target program. However, in theory, this is hard to justify. Given the fact that we do not have the source code of the program, we cannot assume the language type the program's system call sequences. If this language belongs to, say, context-free language type, the n-gram model, which is a sub-regular expression, will not be able to represent all system call sequences in a finite set of n-grams.

In order to address recurring false positives incurred by recurring match-mismatch sequence patterns, we need an anomaly detection technique beyond and above the statistical threshold approaches. In this case, we need one that has a learning capacity: the recurring false positives are quickly learned and have the associated recurring alerts diminish quickly over time. More learning capacity is required as the number, pattern complexity, and the occurrence complexity of the false positive match-mismatch sequences increase.

Long and Short-Term Memory (LSTM) as a special recurrent neural network (RNN) with an input, hidden and output layers has been utilized for long-range dependencies [48]. On the hidden layer of LSTM at time, the outputs $- c^{t-1,l}$ and $h^{t-1,l}$ of the previous layer at $t-1$ come in the layer at t as inputs. The major advantage of LSTM controls a cell status $c^{t-1,l}$ that indicates an accumulated sate information. The cell state is updated or cleared by several operations. If this state is cleared, the past cell status is forgotten by $f^{t,l}$. If updated, $c^{t,l}$ − one of the outputs at t will be propagated to the final state. The cell state is prevented from vanishing or exploding gradient, which is a problem of the traditional RNN, resulting in more learning capacity. Like PEWMA, LAF starts with match-mismatch sequences with a training phase.

4   Application Experiment

Given a bit stream of system call (syscall) n-gram match test results, each model presented in Sects. 2 through 3 defines a condition that the bit stream must satisfy in order to qualify as normal. For the purpose of anomaly detection, the system is instructed to issue an anomaly alert whenever the model-specific conditions are not satisfied. For quantitative verification and validation, we implemented the models and installed the implementation on an operational Apache HTTP Server environment. The syscall n-gram model [9, 14, 15, 35, 37, 42, 46, 47] was used for the training and match tests with $n = 6$ [37].

In this application test, we upgraded the original syscall n-gram technique to support multi-process and multi-threaded applications. The Apache HTTP Server uses multiple process instances at runtime. To accommodate the multi-process and multi-threaded nature of the application, the n-gram training was modified to aggregate the syscalls into process and thread groups to assure that each syscall n-gram belongs entirely to a particular execution context. This modification significantly improved the training time as arbitrary interleaving between threads were not learned nor matched against.

During the training phase, the model implementations observed the web server during normal operation periods and profiled every unique n-gram. The training phase was set to finish when there are fewer than 23 mismatches over the last 10000 n-grams, which would yield p corresponding to 0.9973. The W value (aggregation window size) of the simple models (EWMA and PEWMA) varied between 1700 and 5000. The W value of the stream models varied between 20 and 5000. Note that the minimum W value is limited in the simpler models (e.g., SB) as given in their corresponding models. This is not the case in the stream-based models. This is one of the advantages of using stream-based models when it comes to detecting short attacks. We revisit this in the Conclusions section.

Based on reported test cases [4], the values of EWMA and PEWMA were set to 0.97, 0.99, respectively, giving heavy weight on recent history to detect anomaly onsets. In order to conduct live attacks[1], we used an application-level, remote denial-of-service (DoS) attack identified by CVE-2011–3192, to which the target web server was vulnerable. The tested implementation of this attack (available at http://www.exploit-db.com/exploits/17696/) accepts an input parameter called *numforks*, which defines the intensity of the attack. By exploiting the HTTP protocol, this application-layer DoS attack causes memory exhaustion within the application. In our test, a high-intensity attack was remotely initiated and immediately terminated. The second attack was performed after some period of time at a lower intensity level and lasted until the system became unresponsive.

4.1 Results from Aggregations

In our tested cases, this value was in the 20–100 range. Figure 1 shows our experimental results with EWMA, PEWMA, and LAF assigned as label a, b, and c, respectively. EWMA and PEWMA can be applied with aggregation windows. This is advantageous for two reasons: (1) the inherent delay between the actual onset point of an anomaly and the corresponding alert point can be reduced; (2) has the potential to detect different attack types involving a small sequence of system calls. Our aggregation tests shown in Fig. 1 revealed that the proposed LAF is the best performer with zero false positives. However, it was found that LAF's attack detection delay tends to increase as the aggregation size increases.

4.2 Slow HTTP

Most of our empirical work measures the behavior of "fork bombs" in which crafted input can cause a victim web server to exhaust local process tables. There are, however, a variety of strategies for denying service. To gain generality in our

---

[1] The experiments were conducted with the permission of the system owner.

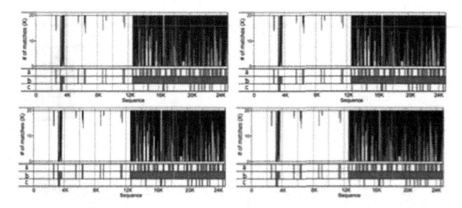

Fig. 1. DSMs with aggregations: N = 20, 40, 80, and 100

results, in this section we measure the effectiveness of our detection models when they are subjected to "slow HTTP" attacks.

Slow HTTP attacks (https://github.com/shekyan/slowhttptest/wiki) exploit a natural asymmetry between HTTP clients and servers: a client can send requests to an HTTP server in an incremental way so that, at low cost to the client, a server must allocate and maintain significant system resources such as socket send buffers. Slow HTTP attacks are significant because the vulnerability arises from resource policies implemented by numerous HTTP servers (e.g., keeping very low-flow connections alive) for legitimate quality-of-service reasons. As a complement to our "fork-bomb" experiments for evaluating our detection models, slow HTTP attacks are illuminating because their implementing mechanisms are entirely different.

We tested the effectiveness of three of our models (EWMA, PEWMA, and LAF) by running slow HTTP attacks and measuring each model's false positives and negatives with different training periods. We chose these models for the slow HTTP tests because these models work well with small aggregation windows. For each model, we ran three tests with varying levels of training performed prior to each test. At the high (expensive) end, our training phases continued until the cumulative match rate reached .9973 (very little behavior not seen during training). At the low end, our training only reached a very incomplete cumulative match rate of 8. In Fig. 2, we show the results from our three models assuming the highest level of training (.9973 cumulative match rate). The five lines at the top of the figure show the aggregation window size (5) and show graphically the number of mismatches (up to the size of the aggregation window) over time (left to right). The bottom three columns of the figure show the alerting behavior of the three models: EWMA, PEWMA, and LAF. As can be seen, an early false positive on the left hand is generated by the first two models but not by LAF. At this level of training, all three models detect the onset of the attack (but not quite at the same time). In our second test configuration (Fig. 3), we measure detection model performance when the training is completed with a

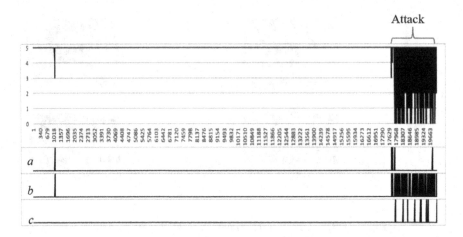

Fig. 2. Slow HTTP attack with 99.73% training.

cumulative match rate of .9545. With less complete training, one can see that there are numerous mismatches over the period of observation. The first two models (EWMA, PEWMA) generate a large number of false positives in addition to detecting the onset of the actual attack, however LAF generates no false positives and also identifies the onset of the attack. In our third test configuration (Fig. 4), we measure detection model performance when the training is completed with a cumulative match rate of only .8. In this case, the number of mismatches is overwhelming as one would expect with such incomplete training. The first two models (EWMA, PEWMA) generate a continuous stream of false positives.

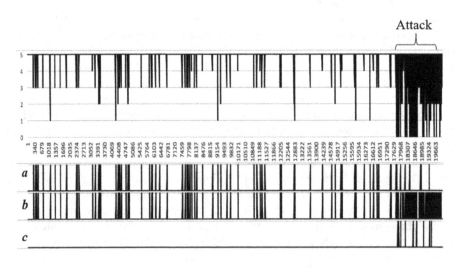

Fig. 3. Slow HTTP attack with 95.45% training.

The LAF model, however, generates no false positives and also detects the onset of the attack with only a minor delay. This is a striking outcome: how can this model be so much more effective? We believe that this is due to the fact that a neural network addresses the overlapping and probabilistically dependent nature of the n-grams on a more fundamental stochastic level than distribution-based models. An n-gram following a normal n-gram is more likely to be normal. Conversely, an abnormal n-gram is more likely to be followed by an abnormal n-gram [29]. In our match-mismatch bit stream representation, this means that a mismatch is more likely to be followed by a mismatch, rather than a match. Therefore, contrary to the assumptions (1) and (2) made in Sect. 2 for SB, the bit stream is not very accurately represented by the Bernoulli distribution due to the interdependence between the n-grams. Meanwhile, the neural network provides an evaluation model of the process' stochastic behavior independent of distribution. This is the most prominent distinction of the neural network, when compared to the traditional distribution-based classification methods [18].

Fig. 4. Slow HTTP attack with 80% training.

5   Related Work

We have studied various anomaly detection methods for profiling normal behavior in terms of system calls during the training-phase and for using the recorded profile during the detection-phase to confirm the normality of incoming runtime sequences. Some reported methods of system call (syscall) anomaly detection are based on n-gram and statistical learning models [15,42]. Other reported methods are based on automata models and call-stack return-address models [13,35,40]. Ideally, the anomaly detection methods should be able to complement existing signature or misuse detection systems to enhance the overall security effectiveness of the system by detecting unknown errors and attacks for which signatures are not yet defined. Unfortunately, application behavior data observed during the training phase is often limited to a small subset of all normal behavior or possibly tainted by hidden attacks or errors [10,11,18,21]. Therefore, it is virtually impossible to prove a claim that the behavior model captures all necessary aspects of the behavior in such a way that all possible unknown attacks and errors can subsequently be distinguished. This paper organizes reported approaches to this challenge into two groups: (1) classifier group and (2) sensitivity group.

The approaches from the classifier group generalize the limited training data to certain distributions or feature space regions in order to more uniformly classify the unknown behaviors. Related studies include statistical generalization and classification of the distributions of the data by normal distribution [4], machine learning [10], kNN methods [10,26,30], and support vector machines [7,11,18]. The approaches from the sensitivity group adjust the anomaly alert threshold in order to correctly ignore benign noise in the detection phase. This group includes stide, t-stide, and the specific use cases of RIPPER and HMM reported in [42]. The sequence time-delay embedding (stide) method takes a sequence of syscalls as input and stores the sequence from the training-phase as unique n-grams with most frequently selected value of n set to 6. In the detection phase, each n-gram, representing a sliding window of the runtime syscall sequence, is compared with the training phase collected n-gram sequences. The anomaly alert threshold is defined in terms of the number of mismatches in the "locality frame" (the reported case is the last 20 match tests). An anomaly alert is issued only when the runtime sequence incurs mismatches above the threshold. This method is most effective when clean, normal behavioral sequences are used for training. The threshold sequence time-delay embedding (t-stide) method is a variant of stide, which drops rarely occurring n-grams from the trained normal. The reported example is dropping any n-gram that accounts for less than 0.001% of the total number of n-gram occurrences counted during the training [23,24]. In [42], t-stide was less effective compared to stide. However, it was shown in [10] that t-stide is more effective when trained over noisy data.

A specific use case of RIPPER in which a mismatch is defined to be a violation of a high-confidence rule (e.g., violation score greater than 80 [28] is also reported in [42]. The anomaly alert threshold is defined in terms of the number of mismatches over the last 20 syscalls. In the Hidden Markov Model (HMM), the alert threshold is defined in terms of a minimum required probability associated with transitions and outputs [42]. Reported findings [15] show the following: when the threshold is set high enough, (1) the average false positive (FP) rate of the n-gram models is similar to the RIPPER rule-learning model, and much better (lower) than that of a HMM; (2) the true positive (TP) rate of n-gram models is much better compared to RIPPER although worse than HMM. The overall performance characteristic of the n-gram models is that both TP and FP rates decrease as the threshold increases (i.e., TP becomes worse while FP becomes better). By storing and matching the n-grams of a runtime sequence without significant computation, n-gram models naturally pose modest computational overhead compared to statistical learning models. However, the anomaly alert threshold, with its potentially adverse effect on TP and FP rates, is the key performance parameter.

6 Conclusion

The experimental evidence supports the idea that LAF is desirable solutions in terms of the Receiver Operating Characteristics (ROC) of anomaly detection in the presented application. In other words, the proposed solutions showed a minimized false positive rate without compromising the true positive rate (maximum true positive rate and minimum false positive rate). The large aggregation of the match test bit stream can reduce the computation overhead of the anomaly detection. However, this approach comes with the inherent delay in anomaly detection in terms of the number of system calls (syscalls) between the true onset of an anomaly and the detection incurred by the aggregation over time. Moreover, different types of attacks, such as shell-code attacks, involving a small number of syscalls can be washed out by the surrounding normal behavior in large aggregations. Because of this, we believe that a method supporting rather small aggregation is likely to be more useful in practice.

The proposed LAF is the best performing detection model based on our experimental data and analysis. Our application and experimental results have shown that LAF is a highly practical anomaly detection solution in terms of ROC, detection delay, and supported types of attack. By supporting any aggregation size with effective elimination of false positives without compromising the true positive rate, LAF can detect the onset of DoS attacks early with minimal false positives (e.g., almost immediate detection of DoS attacks with no false positives in our $W = 20$ cases). This makes remedial action possible, with enough time and computational power. Moreover, other types of attacks involving a smaller number of syscalls can be addressed. This case is outside the scope of the paper and represents future work.

Acknowledgement. The authors acknowledge and appreciate Dmitry A Cousin, David Waltermire, and Lee Badger at the National Institute of Standards and Technology (NIST) for their review and comments on an early development version of this article. The authors also appreciate Dong H. Jeong regarding his help in the visualization of some of our experimental results.

References

1. Abadi, M., Budiu, M., Erlingsson, U., Ligatti, J.: Control-flow integrity principles, implementations, and applications. ACM Trans. Inf. Syst. Secur. **13**(1), 4 (2009)
2. Anderson, D., Frivold, T., Valdes, A.: Next-generation intrusion detection expert system (NIDES): a summary. Technical Report. Menlo Park, CA: SRI-CSL-95-07. Computer Science Laboratory, SRI International Breiman, L. (1996). Bagging Predictors. Mach. Learn. 24, 123–140 (1995)

3. Anderson, D., Frivold, T., Valdes, A.: Next-generation Intrusion Detection Expert System (NIDES): A Summary. Technical Report. Menlo Park, CA: SRI-CSL-95-07. Computer Science Laboratory, SRI International (1995)
4. Breiman, L.: Bagging predictors. Mach. Learn. **24**, 123–140 (1996)
5. Carter, K.M., Streilein, W.W.: Probabilistic reasoning for streaming anomaly detection. In: Proceedings of Signal Processing Workshop on Statistical Signal and Array Processing, SSP 2012, pp. 377–380. IEEE(2012)
6. Chandola, V., Banerjee, A., Kumar, V.: Anomaly detection: a survey. ACM Comput. Surv. 41(3), 15:1–15:58 (2009)
7. Codenomicon. Heartbleed Bug (2014). http://heartbleed.com/. Accessed 25 Aug 2015
8. de la Hoz, E., Ortiz, A., Ortega, J., de la Hoz, E.: Network anomaly classification by support vector classifiers ensemble and non-linear projection techniques. In: Pan, J.-S., Polycarpou, M.M., Woźniak, M., de Carvalho, A.C.P.L.F., Quintián, H., Corchado, E. (eds.) HAIS 2013. LNCS (LNAI), vol. 8073, pp. 103–111. Springer, Heidelberg (2013). https://doi.org/10.1007/978-3-642-40846-5_11
9. Denning, D.E.: An intrusion detection model. IEEE Trans. Softw. Eng. Vol SE-13. 2, 222–232 (1987)
10. Elgraini, M., Assem, N., Rachidi, T.: Host intrusion detection for long stealthy system call sequences. In: Proceedings of 2012 Colloquium in Information Science and Technology, CIST 2012, 22–24 October 2012, pp. 96–100. IEEE (2012)
11. Eskin, E.: Anomaly detection over noisy data using learned probability distributions. In: Proceedings of the International Conference on Machine Learning, pp. 255–262. Morgan Kaufmann (2000)
12. Eskin, E., Arnold, A., Prerau, M., Portnoy, L., Stolfo, S.: A geometric framework for unsupervised anomaly detection: detecting intrusions in unlabeled data. Adv. Inf. Secur. **6**, 77–101 (2002)
13. Ewell, B.: New Round of Email Worm, Here you have (2010). http://www.symantec.com/connect/blogs/new-round-email-worm-here-you-have. Accessed 25 Aug 2015
14. Feng, H.H., Kolesnikov, O.M., Fogla, P., Lee, W., Gong, W.: Anomaly detection using call stack information. In: Proceedings of Symposium on Security and Privacy, SP 2003, 11–14 May 2003, Oakland, California, USA, pp. 62–75. IEEE (2003)
15. Forrest, S., Longstaff, T.A.: A sense of self for unix processes. In: Proceedings of Symposium on Security and Privacy, SP 1996, 6–8 May 1996, Oakland, California, USA, pp. 120–128. IEEE (1996)
16. Forrest, S., Hofmeyr, S., Somayaji, A., (2008). The evolution of system-call monitoring. In: Proceedings of Annual Computer Security Applications Conference, ACSAC 2008, 8–12 December, Anaheim, California, USA, pp. 418–430. IEEE, Washington DC (2008)
17. Gao, D., Reiter, M.K., Song, D.: On gray-box program tracking for anomaly detection. In: Proceedings of the 14th USENIX Security Symposium, 9–13 August 2004, San Diego, California, USA, USENIX, pp. 103–118 (2004)
18. Gareth, J.: Majority Vote Classifiers: Theory and Applications (Ph.D. Thesis). Stanford University, May 1998
19. Heller, K., Svore, K., Keromytis, A., Stolfo, S.: One class support vector machines for detecting anomalous windows registry accesses. In: Proceedings of the Workshop on Data Mining for Computer Security in conjunction with the 3rd IEEE International Conference on Data Mining, DMSEC03, 19–22 November 2003, Melbourne, Florida, USA, pp. 2–9 (2003). (www.cs.fit.edu/pkc/dmsec03)

20. Henao, R.J., Espinosa, O.J.: Machine learning techniques applied to intruder detection in networks. Proceedings of the 47th International Carnahan Conference on Security Technology, ICCST 2013, 8–11 October 2013, Medelin, pp. 1–6. IEEE (2013)
21. Ho, T.: Multiple classifier combiation: lessons and next steps. In: Hybrid Methods in Pattern Recognition. World Scientific Press (2002)
22. Hu, W., Liao, Y., Vemuri, V.: Robust anomaly detection using support vector machines. In: Proceedings of the International Conference on Machine Learning, pp. 282–289 (2003)
23. Ilgun, K., Kemmerer, R.A., Porras, P.A.: State transition analysis: a rule-based intrusion detection approach. IEEE Trans. Softw. Eng. **21**(3), 181–199 (1995)
24. Kaspersky Lab. What You Should Know About the 'Here You Have' Worm (2010). http://usa.kaspersky.com/resources/virus/what-you-should-know-about-here-you-have-worm. Accessed 25 Aug 2015
25. Ko, C.: Logic induction of valid behavior specifications for intrusion detection. In: Proceedings of IEEE Symposium on Security and Privacy, Berkeley, CA, pp. 142–153. IEEE (2000)
26. Kruegel, C., Kirda, E., Mutz, D., Robertson, W., Vigna, G.: Automating mimicry attacks using static binary analysis. In: Proceedings of the 14th USENIX Security Symposium, 31 July - 5 Aug 2005, Baltimore, MD, USENIX, pp. 161–176 (2005)
27. Kuang, L., Zulkernine, M.: An anomaly intrusion detection method using the CSI-KNN algorithm. In: Proceedings of ACM Symposium on Applied Computing, SAC 2008, Fortaleza, Ceara, Brazil, pp. 921–926. ACM (2008)
28. Kumar, S., Spafford, E.H.: A software architecture to support misuse intrusion detection. In: Proceedings of the 18th National Information Security Conference, NISC 1995, 10–13 October 1995, Baltimore, Maryland, USA, NIST/NCSC, Gaithersburg, MD, pp. 194–204 (1995)
29. Lee, W., Stolfo, S.: Data mining approaches for intrusion detection. In: Proceedings of the 7th USENIX Security Symposium, 26–29 January 1998, San Antonio, Texas, USA.: USENIX, pp. 79–94 (1998)
30. Lee, W., Xiang, D.: Information-theoretic measures for anomaly detection. In: Proceedings of Symposium on Security and Privacy, SP 2001, 14–16 May 2001, Oakland, California, USA, pp. 130–143. IEEE (2001)
31. Liao, Y., Vemuri, V.: Use of K-nearest neighbor classifier for intrusion detection. Comput. Secur. **21**(5), 439–448 (2002)
32. Lunt, T., et al.: A Real-time Intrusion Detection Expert System (IDES). Technical Report. Menlo Park, CA: Computer Science Laboratory, SRI International (1992)
33. Michmerhuizen, D.: Here You Have Spam Teaches an Old Worm a New Trick (2010). https://barracudalabs.com/2010/09/here-you-have-spam-teaches-an-old-worm-a-new-trick/. Accessed 25 Aug 2015
34. Roberts, S.: Control chart tests based on geometric moving averages. Technometrics **1**(3), 239–250 (1959)
35. Roesch, M.: Snort - Lightweight intrusion detection for networks. In: LISA 1999: 13th Systems Administration Conference, 7–12 November 1999, Seattle, Washington, USA: USENIX, pp. 229–238 (1999)
36. Sekar, R., Bendre, M., Dhurjati, D., Bollineni, P.: A fast automaton-based method for detecting anomalous program behaviors. In: Proceedings of Symposium on Security and Privacy, SP 2001, 14–16 May 2001, Oakland, California, USA, pp. 144–155. IEEE (2001)
37. Shevtsova, I.: Sharpening of the upper bound of the absolute constant in the Berry-Esseen inequality. Theor. Probab. Appl. **51**(3), 549–553 (2007)

38. Tan, K., Maxion, R.: Why 6? defining the operational limits of stide, an anomaly-based intrusion detector. In: Proceedings of Symposium on Security and Privacy, SP 2002, 12–15 May 2002, Oakland, California, USA, pp. 188–201. IEEE (2002)

39. US-CERT. Malicious Email Campaign Circulating (2009). https://www.us-cert. gov/ncas/current-activity/2010/09/09/Malicious-Email-Campaign-Circulating. Accessed 25 August 2015

40. US-CERT. Vulnerability Note VU720951 (2014). http://www.kb.cert.org/vuls/id/ 720951. Accessed 25 Aug 2015

41. Wagner, D., Dean, D.: Intrusion detection via static analysis. In: Proceedings of Symposium on Security and Privacy, 14–16 May 2001, Oakland, California, pp. 156–168. IEEE (2001)

42. Wagner, D., Soto, P.: Mimicry attacks on host-based intrusion detection systems. In: Proceedings of the 9th ACM conference on Computer and Communications Security, CCS 2002, 17–21 November 2002, Washington, DC, USA, pp. 255–264. ACM, New York, NY (2001)

43. Warrender, C., Forrest, S., Pearlmutter, B.: Detecting intrusions using system calls: alternative data models. In: Proceedings of Symposium on Security and Privacy, SP 1999, May 9–12, 1999, Oakland, California, USA, pp. 133–145. IEEE (1999)

44. Webb, G. (2000). MultiBoosting: a technique for combining boosting and wagging. Mach. Learn. 40, 159–197 (1999)

45. Wheeler, D.A.: How to Prevent the next Heartbleed (2014). http://www.dwheeler. com/essays/heartbleed.html. Accessed 25 Aug 2015

46. Xie, F., Xie., L.: Using information theory to measure call site information of system call in anomaly detection. In: Proceedings of the 15th IEEE International Conference on Communication Technology, ICCT 2013, 17 Nov-19 Nov 2013, Guilin, China, pp. 6–10. IEEE (2013)

47. Yolacan, E., Dy, J., Kaeli, D.: System call anomaly detection using multi-HMMs. In: Proceedings of the 8th IEEE International Conference on Software Security and Reliability-Companion, SERE-C 2014, San Francisco, California, USA, 2014, pp. 25–30. IEEE (2014)

48. Gers, F.A., Schmidhuber, J.: LSTM recurrent networks learn simple context free and context sensitive languages (PDF). IEEE Trans. Neural Netw. 12(6), 1333–1340. PMID 18249962 doi: 10.1109/72.963769 (2001)

Meta-X: A Technique for Reducing Communication in Geographically Distributed Computations

Foto Afrati[1], Shlomi Dolev[2], Shantanu Sharma[3(✉)], and Jeffrey D. Ullman[4]

[1] National Technical University of Athens, Athens, Greece
`afrati@softlab.ece.ntua.gr`
[2] Ben-Gurion University, Beersheba, Israel
`dolev@cs.bgu.ac.il`
[3] University of California, Irvine, USA
`shantanu.sharma@uci.edu`
[4] Stanford University, California, USA
`ullman@cs.stanford.edu`

Abstract. Computations, such as syndromic surveillance and e-commerce, are executed over the datasets collected from different geographical locations. Modern data processing systems, such as MapReduce/Hadoop or Spark, also, require to collect the data from different geographical locations to a single global location, before executing an application, and thus, result in a significant communication cost. While MapReduce/Hadoop and Spark have proven to be the most useful paradigms in the revolution of distributed computing, the federation of cloud and big-data activities is the challenge, wherein data processing should be modified to avoid (big) data migration across remote (cloud) sites. This is exactly our scope of work, where only the very essential data for obtaining the final result is transmitted, for reducing communication and processing, and for preserving data privacy as much as possible. In this work, we propose an algorithmic technique for geographically distributed computations, called META-X, that decreases the communication cost by allowing us to process and moves metadata to among different locations, instead of the entire datasets. We illustrate the usefulness of META-X in terms of MapReduce computations for different operations, such as equijoin, k-nearest-neighbors finding, and shortest path finding.

Keywords: MapReduce · Hadoop · Spark

1 Introduction

In several applications (*e.g.*, syndromic surveillance, wherein hospitals share information, such as a sudden increase in sales of specific drugs, telehealth calls,

The work of Shlomi Dolev is partially supported by the Rita Altura Trust Chair in Computer Science, a grant from the Ministry of Science and Technology, Israel & the Japan Science and Technology Agency (JST), and the German Research Funding (DFG, Grant 8767581199).

© Springer Nature Switzerland AG 2021
S. Dolev et al. (Eds.): CSCML 2021, LNCS 12716, pp. 467–486, 2021.
https://doi.org/10.1007/978-3-030-78086-9_34

and school absenteeism requests, to enable early detection of community-wide outbreaks of diseases), data is collected from multiple geographically dispersed locations and analyzed at the central/global location. Such types of geographically distributed computations not only incur the communication cost due to sending data to the global-site and the computation cost at the global site, but also jeopardize the data privacy. Moreover, due to regulatory compliances, such as GDPR, often, sensitive data is not allowed to move beyond certain geographic boundaries. To process a large amount of data, Hadoop and Spark have been evolved. However, both such systems require data to be moved to a single location before executing the computation. Thus, to avoid data movement among different locations and regarding the data security as well as regulatory compliances, it is desirable to move only the very essential data.

In this paper, we propose an algorithmic technique for modern data processing systems, entitled META-X, where X refers to a system (e.g., Hadoop, Spark) that can be used in processing geographically distributed applications. In this paper, we build META-X for particularly MapReduce, (and will use the word META-MAPREDUCE and META-X interchangeably). In short, first, META-MAPREDUCE distributes the computation across a virtual geo-distributed computing cluster, which locally executes the computation at their sites. Second, all the sites send the desired "key" to the global location that finds the desired keys over all the received data and requests all the sites to send the "value (or data)" corresponding to the desired "keys." Finally, all the sites send the desired data, if satisfy the regulatory compliances, to the global site that executes the final MapReduce computation and produces the final answer.

1.1 Background on MapReduce

MapReduce [1] is a programming system for parallel processing of large-scale data. MapReduce works in two phases: *Map phase* and *Reduce phase*, where two user-defined functions, namely, *map function* and *reduce function*, are executed over data. In MapReduce, data is represented of the form of $\langle key, value \rangle$ pairs.

The Map Phase. A MapReduce computation starts from the Map phase where a user-defined map function works on a single input and produces intermediate outputs of the form $\langle key, value \rangle$ pairs. A single input, for example, can be a tuple of a relation. An application of the map function to a single input is called a *mapper*. Several mappers execute in parallel and provide intermediate outputs of the form of $\langle key, value \rangle$ pairs.

The Reduce Phase. The Reduce phase provides the final output of MapReduce computations. The reduce phase executes a user-defined reduce function on its inputs, *i.e.*, outputs of the Map phase. An application of the reduce function to a single *key* and its associated list of *values* is called a *reducer*. Since there are several *keys* in the indeterminate output, there are also multiple reducers that work in parallel. The *reducer capacity* [2]—an important parameter—is an upper bound on the sum of the sizes of the *values* that are sent to the reducer. For example, the reducer capacity maybe the size of the main memory of the processors on which the reducers run. The capacity of a reducer is denoted by q, and all the reducers have an identical capacity.

A detailed description of MapReduce may be found in Chap. 2 of [3]. Apache Hadoop [4] is a well-known and widely used open-source software implementation of MapReduce for distributed data storage and processing over large-scale data. More details about Hadoop and its Hadoop distributed file system (HDFS) may be found in Chap. 2 of [5]. YARN [6] is the latest version of Hadoop-0.23, details about YARN may be found in [7]. The standard Hadoop system is designed to process data at a single location, *i.e.*, locally distributed processing. Thus, Hadoop is not able to process data at geo(graphically)-distributed multiple-clusters.

Locality of Data

Input data to a MapReduce job may exist at the same site where mappers and reducers reside. However, ensuring an identical location of data and mappers/reducers cannot always be guaranteed. It may be a possibility that a user has a single local machine and wants to enlist a public cloud to help data processing. In both cases, it is required to move data to the location of mappers-reducers. Interested readers may see examples of MapReduce computations where the locations of data and mappers-reducers are different in [8].

In order to motivate and demonstrate the impact of different locations of data and mappers-reducers, we consider two real examples, as follows:

Amazon Elastic MapReduce. Amazon Elastic MapReduce (EMR)[1] processes data that is stored in Amazon Simple Storage Service (S3)[2], where the locations of EMR and S3 are not identical. Hence, it is required to move data from S3 to the location of EMR. However, moving the whole dataset from S3 to EMR is not efficient if only a small specific part of it is needed for the final output.

G-Hadoop and Hierarchical MapReduce. Two implementations of MapReduce, G-Hadoop [8] and Hierarchical MapReduce [9], perform MapReduce computations over geographically distributed clusters. In these new implementations, several clusters execute an assigned MapReduce job in parallel and provide *partial* outputs. Note that the output of a cluster is not the final output of a MapReduce job, and the final output is produced by processing partial outputs of all the clusters at a single cluster. Thus, inter-cluster data transfer—transmission of partial outputs of all the clusters to a single cluster—is required for producing the final output, as the location of the partial outputs of all the clusters and the location of the final computation are not identical. However, moving the whole partial outputs of all the clusters to a single cluster is also not efficient if only a small portion of the clusters' outputs is needed to compute the final output.

Hierarchical MapReduce is depicted in Fig. 1, where three clusters process data using MapReduce in parallel, and the output of all three clusters is required to be sent to one of the clusters or another cluster, which executes a *global reducer* for providing the final output. In Fig. 1, it is clear that the locations of partial

---

[1] http://aws.amazon.com/elasticmapreduce/.

[2] http://aws.amazon.com/s3/.

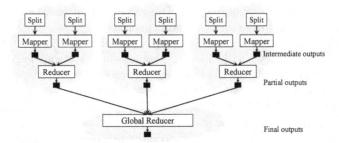

Fig. 1. Different locations of MapReduce clusters in Hierarchical MapReduce.

outputs of all the clusters and the location of the global reducers are not identical; hence, partial outputs of all the clusters are required to be transferred to the location of the global reducer.

Communication Cost

The *communication cost* dominates the performance of a MapReduce algorithm and is the sum of the amount of data that is required to move from the location of users or data (*e.g.*, S3) to the location of mappers (*e.g.*, EMR) and from the map phase to the reduce phase in each round of a MapReduce job. For example, in Fig. 1, the communication cost is the sum of the total amount of data that is transferred from mappers to reducers in each cluster and from each cluster to the site of the global reducer. In this paper, we are interested in minimizing the data transferred in order to avoid communication and memory overhead, as well as to protect data privacy as much as possible. In MapReduce, we transfer inputs to the site of mappers-reducers from the site of the user, and then, several copies of inputs from the map phase to the reduce phase in each iteration, regardless of their involvement in the final output. If few inputs are required to compute the final output, then moving all inputs to the site of mappers/reducers and then the copies of the same inputs to the reduce phase is communication inefficient.

There are some works that consider the location of data (*e.g.* [10]) in a restrictive manner and some works (*e.g.* [11,12]) that consider data movement from the map phase to the reduce phase. We enhance the model suggested in [12] and suggest an algorithmic technique for MapReduce algorithms to decrease the communication cost by moving only relevant input data to the site of mappers-reducers. Specifically, we move metadata of each input instead of the actual data, execute MapReduce algorithms on the metadata, and only then fetch the actual required data needed to compute the final output.

1.2   Motivating Examples

We present two examples (equijoin and entity resolution) to show the impact of different locations of data and mappers/reducers on communication cost involved in MapReduce jobs.

Equijoin of Two Relations. $X(A, B)$ **and** $Y(B, C)$. *Problem statement*: The join of relations $X(A, B)$ and $Y(B, C)$, where the joining attribute is B, provides output tuples $\langle a, b, c \rangle$, where $(a, b) \in X$ and $(b, c) \in Y$. In equijoin of $X(A, B)$ and $Y(B, C)$, all tuples of both relations with an identical value of attribute B should appear together at the same reducer for producing the final output tuples. Shortly, a mapper takes a single tuple from $X(A, B)$ or $Y(B, C)$ and provides $\langle B, X(A) \rangle$ or $\langle B, Y(C) \rangle$ as key-value pairs. A reducer joins the assigned tuples that have an identical key. Figure 2 shows two relations $X(A, B)$ and $Y(B, C)$, and *we consider that the size of all the B values is very small as compared to the size of values of the attributes A and C.*

Communication Cost Analysis: We now investigate the impact of different locations of the relations and mappers-reducers on the communication cost. In Fig. 2, the communication cost for joining of the relations X and Y—where X and Y are located at two different clouds and equijoin is performed on a third cloud—is the sum of the sizes of all three tuples of each relation that are required to move from the location of the user to the location of mappers,

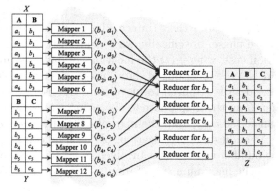

Fig. 2. Equijoin of relations $X(A, B)$ and $Y(B, C)$.

and then, from the map phase to the reduce phase. Consider that each tuple is of unit size; thus, the communication cost is 12 for obtaining the final output.

However, if there are a few tuples having an identical B-value in both the relations, then it is useless to move the whole relations from the user's location to the location of mappers, and then, tuples from the map phase to the reduce phase. In Fig. 2, two tuples of X and two tuples of Y have a common B value (*i.e.*, b_1). Hence, it is not efficient to send tuples having values b_2 and b_3, and by not sending tuples with B values b_2 and b_3, we can reduce communication cost.

Entity Resolution. *Problem statement*: Entity resolution using MapReduce is suggested in [12]. A solution to the entity resolution problem provides disjoint subsets of records, where records match other records if they pass a similarity function, and these records belong to a single entity (or person). For example, if voter-card, passport, student-id, driving-license, and phone numbers of several people are given, a solution to the entity resolution problem makes several subsets, where a subset corresponding to a person holds their voter-card, passport, student-id, driving-license, and phone numbers.

Communication Cost Analysis: The authors [12] provided a solution to the entity resolution problem with decreased communication cost between the map phase and the reduce phase, by not sending the record of a person to a reducer, if the person has only a single record. However, in this model for every pair of records that share a reducer, a copy of one is transferred to the site of reducers, and in this manner, the communication cost is $\frac{n(n-1)}{2}$, if n records are assigned to a reducer. Note that by using the proposed technique of this paper, the communication cost for the entity resolution problem will be n, if n records are assigned to a reducer.

1.3   Problem Statement and Our Contribution

We are interested in reducing the amount of data to be transferred to the site of the cloud executing MapReduce computations and the amount of data transferred from the map phase to the reduce phase. From the preceding two examples, it is clear that in several problems, the final output depends on *some* inputs, and in those cases, it is not required to send the whole input data to the site of mappers and then (intermediate output) data from the map phase to the reduce phase. Specifically, we consider two scenarios for reducing the communication cost, where: (*i*) the locations of data and mappers-reducers are different, and (*ii*) the locations of data and mappers are identical. Note that in the first case, data is required to move from the user's site to the computation site and then from the map phase to the reducer phase, while in the second case, data is transferred only from the map phase to the reduce phase.

In addition to the locations of data and computations, we are also considering the number of iterations involved in a MapReduce job and the reducer capacity (*i.e.*, the maximum size of inputs that can be assigned to a reducer).

Our Contributions. In this paper, we provide the following:

- **An algorithmic approach for MapReduce algorithms.** We provide a new *algorithmic* approach for MapReduce algorithms, META-MAPREDUCE (Sect. 3), that decreases the communication cost significantly. META-MAPREDUCE regards the locality of data and mappers-reducers and avoids the movement of data that does not participate in the final output. Particularly, **Meta-MapReduce provides a way to compute the desired output using metadata**[3] (which is much smaller than the original input data) and avoids uploading the whole data (either because it takes too long or for privacy reasons). It should be noted that we are enhancing MapReduce and not creating entirely a new framework for large-scale data processing; thus, META-MAPREDUCE is *implementable* in the state-of-the art MapReduce systems such as Spark [13], Pregel [14], or modern Hadoop.
- **Data-privacy in MapReduce computations.** META-MAPREDUCE also allows us to protect data privacy as much as possible in the case of an *honest-but-curious* adversary by not sending all the inputs. For example, in the case of equijoin, processing tuple $\langle a_i, b_i \rangle$ of a relation X and $\langle b_j, c_i \rangle$ of a relation Y based on metadata does not reveal the actual tuple information until it is required at the cloud. It should be noted that the relations X and Y

---

[3] The term metadata is used in a different manner, and it represents a small subset, which varies according to tasks, of the dataset.

can deduce that the relations Y and X have no tuple with value b_i and b_j, respectively. However, the outcome of both relations does not imply the actual value of a_i, b_i, and c_i.

Nevertheless, by the auditing process, a *malicious* adversary can be detected. Moreover, in some settings auditing enforces participants to be honest-but-curious rather than malicious, as malicious actions can be audited, discovered, and imply punishing actions.

- **Other applications.**
  - META-MAPREDUCE for processing geographically distributed data (Sect. 4.1) and for processing multi-round MapReduce jobs (Sect. 4.3).
  - META-MAPREDUCE for performing equijoin, k-nearest-neighbors, and shortest path findings on a social networking graph and show how META-MAPREDUCE decreases the communication cost (Sect. 3.1 and Sect. 5).

2   The System Setting

The system setting is an extension of the standard setting [2], where we consider, for the first time, the locations of data and mappers-reducers and the communication cost. The setting is suitable for a variety of problems where *at least* two inputs are required to produce an output. In order to produce an output, we need to define the term *mapping schema*, as follows:

Mapping Schema. A mapping schema is an assignment of the set of inputs (*i.e.*, outputs of the map phase) to some given reducers under the following two constraints:

- A reducer is assigned inputs whose sum of the sizes is less than or equal to the reducer capacity q.
- For each output produced by reducers, we must assign the corresponding inputs to at least one reducer in common.

For example, a mapping schema for equijoin example will assign all tuples (of relations X and Y) having an identical key to a reducer such that the size of assigned tuples is not more than q.

The Model. The model is simple but powerful and assumes the following:

1. Existence of systems such as Spark, Pregel, or modern Hadoop.
2. A preliminary step at the user site who owns the dataset for finding metadata[4] that has a smaller memory size than the original data.
3. Approximation algorithms (given in [2]), which are based on a bin-packing algorithm, at the cloud or the global reducer in case of Hierarchical MapReduce [9]. The approximation algorithms assign outputs of the map phase to reducers while regarding the reducer capacity. Particularly, in our case, approximation algorithms will assign metadata to reducers in such a manner that the size of actual data at a reducer will not exceed the reducer capacity and all the inputs that are required to produce outputs must be assigned at one reducer in common.

---

[4] The selection of metadata depends on the problem.

The next section presents a new algorithmic technique for MapReduce algorithms, where we try to minimize communication cost regarding different locations of data and mappers/reducers with the help of a running example of equijoin.

3   Meta-MapReduce

We present our algorithmic technique that reduces the communication cost for a variety of problems, *e.g.*, join of relations, k-nearest-neighbors finding, similarity-search, and matrix multiplication. The proposed technique regards locality of data, the number of iterations involved in a MapReduce job, and the reducer capacity. The idea behind the proposed technique is to process metadata at mappers and reducers, and process the original required data at required iterations of a MapReduce job at reducers. In this manner, we suggest processing metadata at mappers and reducers at all the iterations of a MapReduce job. Therefore, the proposed technique is called META-MAPREDUCE. In this section, we introduce how to incorporate META-MAPREDUCE for computations hosted only at a single location, and then, in later sections, we show how META-MAPREDUCE can be used in geographically distributed computations.

Before going into detail of META-MAPREDUCE, we need to redefine the communication cost to take into account the size of the metadata, the amount of the (required) original data, which is required to transfer to reducers only at required iterations, and different locations of data and computations.

The Communication Cost for Metadata and Data. In the context of META-MAPREDUCE, the communication cost is the sum of the following:

Metadata Cost. The amount of metadata that is required to move from the location of users to the location of mappers (if the locations of data and mappers are different) and from the map phase to the reduce phase in each iteration of MapReduce job.

Data Cost. The amount of required original data that is needed to move to reducers at required iterations of a MapReduce job.

The next section explains the way META-MAPREDUCE works, using an example of equijoin for a case of different locations of data and mappers. Following the example of equijoin, we also show how much communication cost is reduced due to the use of Mata-MapReduce.

3.1   Meta-MapReduce Working

In the standard MapReduce, users send their data to the site of the mappers before the computation begins. However, in META-MAPREDUCE, users send metadata to the site of mappers, instead of original data, see Fig. 3. Now, mappers and reducers work on metadata, and at required iterations of a MapReduce job, reducers *call* required original data from the site of users (according to assigned $\langle key, value \rangle$ pairs) and provide the desired result. We present a detailed execution to demonstrate META-MAPREDUCE (see Fig. 3), using the equijoin task, as follows:

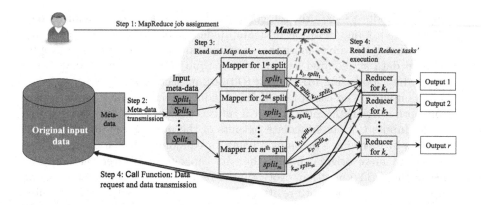

Fig. 3. META-MAPREDUCE algorithmic approach.

Step 1. Users create a *master process* that creates *map tasks* and *reduce tasks* at different compute nodes. A compute node that processes the *map task* is called a *map worker*, and a compute node that processes the *reducer task* is called a *reduce worker*.

Step 2. Users send metadata, which varies according to an assigned MapReduce job, to the site of mappers. Also, the user creates an index, which varies according to the assigned job, on the entire database.

For example, in the case of equijoin (see Fig. 2), a user sends metadata for each of the tuples of the relations $X(A, B)$ and $Y(B, C)$ to the site of mappers. In this example, metadata for a tuple i ($\langle a_i, b_i \rangle$, where a_i and b_i are values of the attributes A and B, respectively) of the relation X includes the size of all non-joining values (*i.e.*, $|a_i|$[5]) and the value of b_i. Similarly, metadata for a tuple i ($\langle b_i, c_i \rangle$, where b_i and c_i are values of the attributes B and C, respectively) of the relation Y includes the size of all non-joining values (*i.e.*, $|c_i|$) with b_i (remember that the size of b_i is much smaller than the size of a_i or c_i). In addition, the user creates an index on the attribute B of both the relations X and Y.

Step 3. In the map phase, a mapper processes an assigned input and provides some number of $\langle key, value \rangle$ pairs, which are known as *intermediate outputs*, a *value* is the *size* of the corresponding input data (which is included in metadata). The *master process* is then informed of the location of intermediate outputs.

For example, in case of equijoin, a mapper takes a single tuple i (*e.g.*, $\langle a_i, b_i \rangle$) and generates some $\langle b_i, value \rangle$ pairs, where b_i is a key and a *value* is the *size* of tuple i (*i.e.*, $|a_i|$). Note that in the original equijoin example, a *value* is the whole data associated with the tuple i (*i.e.*, a_i).

Step 4. The *master process* assigns *reduce tasks* (by following a mapping schema as suggested in [2]) and provides information of intermediate outputs, which serve as inputs to *reduce tasks*. A reducer is then assigned all the $\langle key, value \rangle$ pairs having an identical key by following a mapping schema for an assigned

---

[5] The notation $|a_i|$ refers to the size of an input a_i.

job. Now, reducers perform the computation and `call`[6] only required data if there is only one iteration of a MapReduce job. On the other hand, if a MapReduce job involves more than one iteration, then reducers `call` original required data at required iterations of the job (we will discuss multi-round MapReduce jobs using META-MAPREDUCE in Sect. 4.3).

For example, in the case of equijoin, a reducer receives all $\langle b_i, value \rangle$ pairs from both relations X and Y, where a *value* is the size of tuple associated with key b_i. Inputs (*i.e.*, intermediate outputs of the map phase) are assigned to reducers by following a mapping schema for equijoin such that a reducer does not assign more original inputs than its capacity, and after that reducers invoke the `call` operation. Note that a reducer that receives at least one tuple with key b_i from both relations X and Y produces outputs and requires original input data from the user's site. However, the reducer, receiving tuples with key b_i from a single relation only, does not request for the original input tuple, since these tuples do not participate in the final output.

We now compute the communication cost involved in the equijoin example (see Fig. 2) using META-MAPREDUCE. Recall that without using META-MAPREDUCE, a solution to the equijoin problem (in Fig. 2) requires 12 units of communication cost. However, using META-MAPREDUCE, there is no need to send the tuple $\langle a_3, b_2 \rangle$ of the relation X and the tuples $\langle b_3, c_3 \rangle$ of the relation Y to the location of computation. Moreover, we send metadata of all the tuples to the site of mappers, and intermediate outputs containing metadata are transferred to the reduce phase, where reducers `call` only desired tuples having b_1 value from the user's site. Consequently, a solution to the problem of equijoin has only 4 units cost plus a constant cost for moving metadata using META-MAPREDUCE, instead of 12 units communication cost. Table 1 shows communication cost for different operations using META-MAPREDUCE.

Theorem 1 (The communication cost). *Using* META-MAPREDUCE, *the communication cost for the problem of the join of two relations is at most* $2nc + h(c+w)$ *bits, where n is the number of tuples in each relation, c is the maximum size of a value of the joining attribute, h is the number of tuples that actually join, and w is the maximum required memory for a tuple.*

Proof. Since the maximum size of a value of the joining attribute, which works as metadata in the problem of join, is c and there are n tuples in each relation, users have to send at most $2nc$ bits to the site of mappers-reducers. Further, tuples that join at the reduce phase have to be transferred from the map phase to the reduce phase and then from the user's site to the reduce phase. Since there are at most h tuples join and the maximum size of a tuple is w, we need to transfer at most hc and at most hw bits from the map phase to the reduce phase and from the user's site to the reduce phase, respectively. Hence, the communication cost is at most $2nc + h(c+w)$ bits.

---

[6] The `call` operation will be explained in Sect. 3.2.

Further Significant Improvement. We note that it is possible to further decrease the communication cost by using two iterations of a MapReduce job, in which the first iteration is performed on metadata and the second iteration is performed on the required original data. Specifically, in the first iteration, a user sends metadata to some reducers such that reducers are not assigned *more metadata* than capacity, and all these reducers will compute the required original data and the optimal number of reducers for a task. Afterward, a new MapReduce iteration is executed on the required original data such that a reducer is not assigned *more original inputs* than its capacity. In this manner, we save replication of metadata and some reducers that do not produce outputs.

Table 1. The communication cost for joining of relations using META-MAPREDUCE.

Problems	Communication cost	
	using META-MAPREDUCE	using MapReduce
Join of two relations	$2nc + h(c + w)$	$4nw$
Skewed Values of the Joining Attribute	$2nc + rh(c + w)$	$2nw(1 + r)$
Join of two relations by hashing the joining attribute	$6n \cdot \log m + h(c + w)$	$4nw$
Join of k relations by hashing the joining attributes	$3knp \cdot \log m + h(c + w)$	$2knw$

n: the number of tuples in each relation, c: the maximum size of a value of the joining attribute, r: the replication rate, h: the number of tuples that actually join, w is the maximum required memory for a tuple, p: the maximum number of dominating attributes in a relation, and m: the maximal number of tuples in all given relations.

3.2   The Call Function

In this section, we will describe the `call` function that is invoked by reducers to have the original required inputs from the user's site to produce outputs.

All the reducers that produce outputs require the original inputs from the site of users. Reducers can know whether they produce outputs or not, after receiving intermediate outputs from the map phase, and then, inform the corresponding mappers from where they have fetched these intermediate outputs (for simplicity, we can say all reducers that will produce outputs send 1 to all the corresponding mappers to request the original inputs, otherwise send 0). Mappers collect requests for the original inputs from all the reducers and fetch the original inputs, if required, from the user's site by accessing the index file. Remember that in META-MAPREDUCE, the user creates an index on the entire database according to an assigned job, refer to STEP 2 in Sect. 3.1. This index helps to access the required data that reducers want without doing a scan operation. Note that the `call` function can be easily implemented on recent implementations of MapReduce, *e.g.*, Pregel and Spark.

For example, we can consider our running example of equijoin. In the case of equijoin, a reducer that receives at least one tuple with key b_i from both the relations $X(A, B)$ and $Y(B, C)$ requires the original input from the user's site, and hence, the reducer sends 1 to the corresponding mappers. However, if the reducer receives tuples with key b_i from a single relation only, the reducer sends 0. Consider that the reducer receives $\langle b_i, |a_i| \rangle$ of the relation X and $\langle b_i, |c_i| \rangle$ of the relation Y. The reducer sends 1 to corresponding mappers that produced $\langle b_i, |a_i| \rangle$ and $\langle b_i, |c_i| \rangle$ pairs. On receiving requests for the original inputs from the reducer, the mappers access the index file to fetch a_i, b_i, and c_i, and then, the mapper provides a_i, b_i, and c_i to the reducer.

3.3 Meta-MapReduce for Skewed Values of the Joining Attribute

Consider two relations $X(A, B)$ and $Y(B, C)$, where the joining attribute is B and the size of all the B values is very small as compared to the size of values of the attributes A and C. One or both of the relations X and Y may have a large number of tuples with an identical B-value. A value of the joining attribute B that occurs many times is known as a *heavy hitter*. In the skew join of $X(A, B)$ and $Y(B, C)$, all the tuples of both the relations with an identical heavy hitter should appear together to provide the output tuples.

In Fig. 4, b_1 is a heavy hitter; hence, it is required that all the tuples of $X(A, B)$ and $Y(B, C)$ with the heavy hitter, b_1, should appear together to provide the output tuples, $\langle a, b_1, c \rangle$ ($a \in A, b_1 \in B, c \in C$), which depend on exactly two inputs. However, due to a single reducer—for joining all tuples with a heavy hitter—there is no parallelism at the reduce phase, and a single reducer takes a long time to produce all the output tuples of the heavy hitter.

We can restrict reducers in a way that they can hold many tuples, but not all the tuples with the heavy-hitter-value. In this case, we can reduce the time and use more reducers, which results in a higher level of parallelism at the reduce phase. But, there is a higher communication cost, since each tuple with the heavy hitter must be sent to more than one reducer.

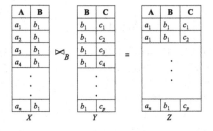

Fig. 4. Skew join example for a heavy hitter, b_1.

We can solve the problem of skew join using META-MAPREDUCE, using four steps suggested in Sect. 3.1.

Theorem 2 (The communication cost). *Using* META-MAPREDUCE, *the communication cost for the problem of skew join of two relations is at most $2nc + rh(c + w)$ bits, where n is the number of tuples in each relation, c is the maximum size of a value of the joining attribute, r is the replication rate,[7] h is the number of distinct tuples that actually join, and w is the maximum required memory for a tuple.*

Proof. From the user's site to the site of mappers-reducers, at most $2nc$ bits are required to move (according to Theorem 1). Since at most h distinct tuples join

---

[7] The replication rate [11] of a mapping schema is the average number of key-value pairs for each input.

and these tuples are replicated to r reducers, at most rhc bits are required to transfer from the map phase to the reduce phase. Further, h tuples of size at most w to be transferred from the map phase to the reduce phase, and hence, at most rhw bits are assigned to reducers. Thus, the communication cost is at most $2nc + rh(c + w)$ bits.

3.4 Meta-MapReduce for an Identical Location of Data and Mappers

We explained the way META-MAPREDUCE acts in the case of different locations of data and computation, and show how it provides desired outputs by considering only metadata of inputs. Nevertheless, META-MAPREDUCE also decreases the amount of data to be transferred when the locations of data and computations are identical. In this case, mappers process only metadata of assigned inputs instead of the original inputs as in MapReduce, and provide $\langle key, value \rangle$ pairs, where a *value* is the size of an assigned input, not the original input itself. A reducer processes all the $\langle key, value \rangle$ pairs having an identical key and calls the original input data, if required. Consequently, there is no need to send all those inputs that do not participate in the final result from the map phase to the reduce phase.

For example, in the case of equijoin, if the location of mappers and relations X and Y are identical, then a mapper processes a tuple of either relation and provides $\langle b_i, |a_i| \rangle$ or $\langle b_i, |c_i| \rangle$ as outputs. A reducer is assigned all the inputs having an identical key, and the reducer calls the original inputs if it has received inputs from both the relations.

4 Extensions of Meta-MapReduce

We have presented META-MAPREDUCE for different and identical locations of data and mappers-reducers. However, some extensions are required to use META-MAPREDUCE for geographically distributed data processing, for handling large size values of joining attributes, and for handling multi-round computations. This section provides three extensions of META-MAPREDUCE.

4.1 Incorporating Meta-MapReduce in G-Hadoop and Hierarchical MapReduce

G-Hadoop and Hierarchical MapReduce are two implementations for geographically distributed data processing using MapReduce. Both the implementations assume that a cluster processes data using MapReduce and provides its outputs to one of the clusters that provides final outputs (by executing a MapReduce job on the received outputs of all the clusters). However, the transmission of outputs of all the clusters to a single cluster for producing the final output is not efficient, if all the outputs of a cluster do not participate in the final output.

We can apply META-MAPREDUCE idea to systems such as G-Hadoop and Hierarchical MapReduce. Note that we *do not* change the basic functionality of both implementations. We take our running example of equijoin (see Fig. 5, where we have three clusters, possibly on three continents, the first cluster has two relations $U(A, B)$ and $V(B, C)$, the second cluster has two relations $W(D, B)$ and $X(B, E)$, and the third cluster has two relations $Y(F, B)$ and $Z(B, G)$) and assume that data exist at the site of mappers in each cluster. In the final output, reducers perform the join operation over all the six relations, which share an identical B-value.

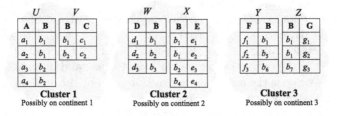

Fig. 5. Three clusters, each with two relations.

The following three steps are required for obtaining final outputs using the execution of META-MAPREDUCE over G-Hadoop and Hierarchical MapReduce.

Step 1. Mappers at each cluster process input data according to an assigned job and provide $\langle key, value \rangle$ pairs, where a *value* is the size of an assigned input.

For example, in Fig. 5, a mapper at Cluster 1 provides outputs of the form of $\langle b_i, |a_i| \rangle$ or $\langle b_i, |c_i| \rangle$.

Step 2. Reducers at each cluster provide partial outputs by following an assigned mapping schema, and partial outputs, which contain only metadata, are transferred to one of the clusters, which will provide final outputs.

For example, in case of equijoin, reducers at each cluster provide partial output tuples as $\langle |a_i|, b_i, |c_i| \rangle$ at Cluster 1, $\langle |d_i|, b_i, |e_i| \rangle$ at Cluster 2, and $\langle |f_i|, b_i, |g_i| \rangle$ at Cluster 3 (by following a mapping schema for equijoin). Partial outputs of Cluster 1 and Cluster 3 have to be transferred to one of the clusters, say Cluster 2, for obtaining the final output.

Step 3. A designated cluster for providing the final output processes all the outputs of the clusters by implementing the assigned job using META-MAPREDUCE. Reducers that provide the final output call the original input data from all the clusters.

For example, in equijoin, after receiving outputs of Cluster 1 and Cluster 3, Cluster 2 implements two iterations for joining tuples. In the first iteration, outputs of Clusters 1 and 2 are joined (by following a mapping schema for equijoin), and in the second iteration, outputs of Clusters 3 and the output of the previous iteration are joined at reducers. A reducer in the second iteration provides the final output as $\langle |a_i|, b_1, |c_i|, |d_i|, |e_i|, |f_i|, |g_i| \rangle$ and calls all the original values of $|a_i|$, $|c_i|$, $|d_i|$, $|e_i|$, $|f_i|$, and $|g_i|$ for providing the desired output, as suggested in Sect. 3.2.

Communication Cost Analysis. In Fig. 5, we are performing equijoin in three clusters, and assuming that data is available at the site of mappers in each cluster. In addition, we consider that each value takes two units in size; hence, any tuple, for example, $\langle a_i, b_i \rangle$, has the size of 4 units.

First, each of the clusters performs an equijoin within the cluster using META-MAPREDUCE. Note that using META-MAPREDUCE, there is no need to send any tuple from the map phase to the reduce phase within the cluster, while G-Hadoop and Hierarchical MapReduce do data transfer from the map phase to the reduce phase, and hence, results in 76 units of communication cost. Moreover, in G-Hadoop and Hierarchical MapReduce, the transmission of two tuples $(\langle a_3, b_2 \rangle, \langle a_4, b_2 \rangle)$ of U, one tuple $(\langle b_2, c_2 \rangle)$ of V, two tuples $(\langle d_2, b_2 \rangle, \langle d_3, b_3 \rangle)$ of W, two tuples $(\langle b_2, e_3 \rangle, \langle b_4, e_4 \rangle)$ of X, two tuples $(\langle f_2, b_5 \rangle, \langle f_3, b_6 \rangle)$ of Y, and one tuple $(\langle b_7, g_3 \rangle)$ of Z from the map phase to the reduce phase is useless, since they do not participate in the final output.

After computing outputs within the cluster, metadata of outputs (*i.e.*, size of tuples associated with key b_1 and key b_2) is transmitted to Cluster 2. Here, it is important to note that tuples with value b_1 provide final outputs. Using META-MAPREDUCE, we will not send the complete tuples with value b_2, hence, we also decrease the communication cost; while G-Hadoop and Hierarchical MapReduce send all the outputs of the first and third clusters to the second cluster. After receiving outputs from the first and the third clusters, the second cluster performs two iterations as mentioned previously, and in the second iteration, a reducer for key b_1 provides the final output. Following that the communication cost is only 36 units.

On the other hand, the transmission of outputs with data from the first cluster and the third cluster to the second cluster and performing two iterations result in 132 units of communication cost. Therefore, G-Hadoop and Hierarchical MapReduce require 208 units of communication cost while META-MAPREDUCE provides the final results using 36 units of communication cost.

4.2 Large Size of Joining Values

We have considered that the sizes of joining values are very small as compared to the sizes of all the other non-joining values. For example, in Fig. 2, the sizes of all the values of the attribute B are very small as compared to all the values of the attributes A and C. However, considering the very small size of values of the joining attribute is not realistic. All the values of the joining attribute may also require a considerable amount of memory, which may be equal to or greater than the sizes of non-joining values. In this case, it is not useful to send all the values of the joining attribute with metadata of non-joining attributes. Thus, we enhance META-MAPREDUCE for handling a case of large size of joining values.

We consider our running example of the join of two relations $X(A, B)$ and $Y(B, C)$, where the size of each of b_i is large enough such that the value of b_i cannot be used as metadata. We use a hash function to gain a short identifier (that is unique with high probability) for each b_i. We denote $H(b_i)$ to be the hash value of the original value of b_i. Here, META-MAPREDUCE works as follows:

Step 1. For all the values of the joining attribute (B), use a hash function such that an identical b_i in both of the relations has a unique hash value with a high probability, and b_i and b_j, $i \neq j$, receive two different hash values with a high probability.

Step 2. For all the other non-joining attributes' values (values corresponding to attributes A and C), find metadata that includes the size of each value.

Step 3. Perform the task using META-MAPREDUCE: (i) Users send hash values of joining attributes and metadata of the non-joining attributes. For example, a user sends hash value of b_i ($H(b_i)$) and the corresponding metadata (*i.e.*, size) of values a_i or c_i to the site of mappers. (ii) A mapper processes an assigned tuples and provides intermediate outputs, where a *key* is $H(b_i)$ and a *value* is $|a_i|$ or $|c_i|$. (iii) Reducers `call` all the *values* corresponding to a key (hash value), and if a reducer receives metadata of a_i and c_i, then the reducer calls the original input data and provides the final output.

Note that there may be a possibility that two different values of the joining attribute have an identical hash value; hence, these two values are assigned to a reducer. However, the reducer will know these two different values, when it will `call` the corresponding data. The reducer notifies the master process, and a new hash function is used.

Theorem 3 (The communication cost). *Using* META-MAPREDUCE *for the problem of join where values of joining attributes are large, the communication cost for the problem of the join of two relations is at most* $6n \cdot \log m + h(c + w)$ *bits, where n is the number of tuples in each relation, m is the maximal number of tuples in two relations, h is the number of tuples that actually join, and w is the maximum required memory for a tuple.*

Proof. The maximal number of tuples having different values of a joining attribute in all relations is m, which is upper bounded by $2n$; hence, a mapping of hash function of m values into m^3 values will result in a unique hash value for every of the m keys with a high probability. Thus, we use at most $3 \cdot \log m$ bits for metadata of a single value, and hence, at most $6n \cdot \log m$ bits are required to move metadata from the user's site to the site of mappers-reducers. Since there are at most h tuples join and the maximum size of a tuple is w, we need to transfer at most hc and at most hw bits from the map phase to the reduce phase and from the user's site to the reduce phase, respectively. Hence, the communication cost is at most $6n \cdot \log m + h(c + w)$ bits.

4.3 Multi-round Computation

We show how META-MAPREDUCE can be incorporated in a multi-round MapReduce job, where values of joining attributes are also large as the value of non-joining attributes. In order to explain, the working of META-MAPREDUCE in a multi-iterative MapReduce job, we consider an example of join of four relations $U(A, B, C, D)$, $V(A, B, D, E)$, $W(D, E, F)$, and $X(F, G, H)$, and perform the join operation using a cascade of two-way joins..

Step 1. Find *dominating attributes* in all the relations. An attribute that occurs in more than one relation is called a dominating attribute [15]. E.g., in our running example, attributes A, B, D, E, and F are dominating attributes.

Step 2. Implement a hash function over all the values of dominating attributes so that all the identical values of dominating attributes receive an identical hash value with a high probability, and all the different values of dominating attributes receive different hash values with a high probability.

For example, identical values of a_i, b_i, d_i, e_i, and f_i receive an identical hash value, and any two values a_i and a_j, such that $i \neq j$, probably receive different hash values (a similar case exists for different values of attributes B, D, E, F).

Step 3. For all the other non-dominating joining attributes' (an attribute that occurs in only one of the relations) values, we find metadata that includes size of each of the values.

Step 4. Now perform 2-way cascade join using META-MAPREDUCE and follow a mapping schema according to a problem for assigning inputs (*i.e.*, outputs of the map phase) to reducers.

In equijoin example, we may join relations as follows: first, join relations U and V, and then join the relation W to the outputs of the join of relations U and V. Finally, we join the relation X to outputs of the join of relations U, V, and W. Thus, we join the four relations using three iterations of META-MAPREDUCE, and in the final iteration, reducers `call` the original required data.

Example: Following our running example, in the first iteration, a mapper produces $\langle H(a_i), [H(b_i), |c_i|, H(d_i)] \rangle$ after processing a tuple of the relation U and $\langle H(a_i), [H(b_i), H(d_i), H(e_i)] \rangle$ after processing a tuple of the relation V (where $H(a_i)$ is a key). A reducer corresponding to $H(a_i)$ provides $\langle H(a_i), H(b_j), |c_k|, H(d_l), H(e_z) \rangle$ as outputs.

In the second iteration, a mapper produces $\langle H(d_i), [H(a_i), H(b_j), |c_k|, H(e_z)] \rangle$ and $\langle H(d_i), [H(e_i), H(f_i)] \rangle$ after processing outputs of the first iteration and the relation W, respectively. Reducers in the second iteration provide output tuples by joining tuples that have an identical $H(d_i)$. In the third iterations, a mapper produces $\langle H(f_i), [H(a_i), H(b_i), |c_i|, H(d_i), H(e_i)] \rangle$ or $\langle H(f_i), [|g_i|, |h_i|] \rangle$, and reducers perform the final join operations. A reducer, for key $H(f_i)$, receives $|g_i|$ and $|h_i|$ from the relation X and output tuples of the second iteration, provides the final output by calling original input data from the location of user.

Theorem 4 (The communication cost). *Using* META-MAPREDUCE *for the problem of join where values of joining attributes are large, the communication cost for the problem of join of k relations, each of the relations with n tuples, is at most $3knp \cdot \log m + h(c + w)$ bits, where n is the number of tuples in each* *relation, m is the maximal number of tuples in k relations, p is the maximum number of dominating attributes in a relation, h is the number of tuples that actually join, and w is the maximum required memory for a tuple.*

Proof. According to Theorem 3, at most $3 \cdot log\ m$ bits for metadata are required for a single value; hence, at most $3knp \cdot log\ m$ bits are required to move metadata from the user's site to the site of mappers-reducers. Since at most h tuples join and the maximum size of a tuple is w, at most hc and at most hw bits from the map phase to the reduce phase and from the user's site to the reduce phase, respectively, are transferred. Hence, the communication cost is at most $3knp \cdot log\ m + h(c + w)$ bits.

5   Versatility of Meta-MapReduce

This section provides two more problems that can be solved using META-MAPREDUCE.

k-nearest-neighbors (k-NN) Problem Using Meta-MapReduce. *Problem statement*: k-NN problem [16] tries to find k-nearest-neighbors of a given object. Two relations R of m tuples and S of n tuples are inputs to the k-NN problem, where $m < n$. E.g., relations R and S may contain a list of cities with full descriptions of the city, images of places to visit in the city. Following that, a solution to the k-NN problem finds k cities from the relation S for each city of the relation R in a manner that the distance between two cities (the first city belongs to R and the second city belongs to S) is minimum, and hence, km pairs are produced as outputs. A basic approach to find k-NN is given in [16] that uses two iterations of MapReduce, where the first iteration provides local k-NN and the second iteration provides the global k-NN for each tuple of R.
Communication Cost Analysis: The communication cost is the size of all the tuples of R and S that are required to move to the location of mappers-reducers, and then, tuples from the map phase to the reduce phase in the two iterations. If $k \leq m$, then it is communication inefficient to move all tuples of S from the user's location to the location of mappers and from the map phase to the reduce phase. Thus, sending only metadata of each tuple avoid significant communication cost.

Shortest Path Findings on a Social Networking Graph using Meta-MapReduce. *Problem statement*: Consider a graph of a social network, where a node represents either a person or a photo, and an edge exists between two persons if they are friends or between a person and a photo of the person is tagged in the photo; however, there is no edge

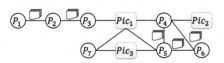

Fig. 6. A graph of a social network.

between two photos; see Fig. 6. The implementation of the shortest path algorithm on the graph results in paths between two persons i and j with common information (which exist on the paths) between the two persons i and j.

Communication Cost Analysis: We want to find the shortest path between persons P_1 and P_6, refer to Fig. 6. A shortest path algorithm will provide a path P_1-P_2-P_3-Pic_1-P_5-P_6 or P_1-P_2-P_3-Pic_1-P_4-P_6 and show the common things between every two persons on the path and the photo, Pic_1, as a connection between P_3 and P_5. Note that in this case, it is communication in-efficient to send all the photos and common information between every two friends of the graph to the site of mappers, because most of the nodes are removed in the final output. Hence, it is beneficial to send metadata of people and photos to the location of mappers and to process metadata to find the shortest path between two people at the reduce phase. In Fig. 6, reducers that provide the final output call information of person $(P_1, P_2, P_3, P_5, P_6)$ and photo (Pic_1). Consequently, there is no need to send Pic_2 and Pic_3.

6   Conclusion

While Hadoop and Spark are widely used efficient distributed processing frameworks for big-data processing in a fault-tolerant manner, these systems suffer from a major drawback in terms of locally distributed computations, which prevent them from implementing geographically distributed data processing. The increasing amount of geographically distributed data and the nature of MapReduce or Spark motivate us to rethink the design of the current big-data processing systems.

This paper found that it is not required to send the whole datasets to the location of computation, if all the inputs do not participate in the final output. Thus, we proposed a new algorithmic technique, META-X and illustrated it in the context of MapReduce computations. META-MAPREDUCE decreases a huge amount of data to be transferred across clouds by transferring metadata (which is exponentially smaller) for a data field (rather than the field itself) and processes metadata at the map phase and the reduce phase. We demonstrated the impact of META-MAPREDUCE for solving problems of equijoin, k-nearest-neighbors finding, and shortest path finding.

References

1. Dean, J., et al.: MapReduce: simplified data processing on large clusters. In: OSDI, pp. 137–150 (2004)
2. Afrati, F.N., et al.: Assignment problems of different-sized inputs in MapReduce. ACM Trans. Knowl. Discov. Data **11**(2), 18:1–18:35 (2016)
3. Leskovec, J., et al.: Mining of massive datasets. Cambridge University Press (2014)
4. Apache Hadoop. http://hadoop.apache.org/
5. Lin, J., et al.: Data-intensive text processing with MapReduce. Synth. Lect. Hum. Lang. Technol. **3**(1), 1–177 (2010)
6. Apache YARN. https://hadoop.apache.org/docs/current/hadoop-yarn/hadoop-yarn-site/index.html
7. Murthy, A.C., et al.: Apache Hadoop YARN: Moving Beyond MapReduce and Batch Processing with Apache Hadoop 2. Pearson Education, London (2013)

8. Wang, L., et al.: G-Hadoop: MapReduce across distributed data centers for data-intensive computing. Future Gen. Comput. Syst. **29**(3), 739–750 (2013)

9. Luo, Y., Plale, B.: Hierarchical MapReduce programming model and scheduling algorithms. In: CCGRID, pp. 769–774 (2012)

10. Park, J., et al.: Locality-aware dynamic VM reconfiguration on MapReduce clouds. In: HPDC, pp. 27–36 (2012)

11. Afrati, F.N., et al.: Upper and lower bounds on the cost of a map-reduce computation. PVLDB **6**(4), 277–288 (2013)

12. Malhotra, P. et al.: Graph-parallel entity resolution using LSH & IMM. In: Workshop Proceedings of the EDBT/ICDT (2014)

13. Zaharia, M., et al.: Spark: cluster computing with working sets. HotCloud **10**(10), 95 (2010)

14. Malewicz, G., et al.: Pregel: a system for large-scale graph processing. In: SIGMOD, pp. 135–146 (2010)

15. Afrati, F.N., et al.: Optimizing multiway joins in a map-reduce environment. IEEE Trans. Knowl. Data Eng. **23**(9), 1282–1298 (2011)

16. Zhang, C., et al.: Efficient parallel kNN joins for large data in MapReduce. In: EDBT, pp. 38–49 (2012)

BLINDLY FOLLOW: **SITS CRT and FHE for DCLSMPC of DUFSM**
(Extended Abstract)

Shlomi Dolev[⊠] and Stav Doolman

Department of Computer Science, Ben-Gurion University of the Negev,
Beersheba, Israel
dolev@cs.bgu.ac.il

Abstract. A Statistical Information Theoretic Secure (SITS) system utilizing the Chinese Remainder Theorem (CRT), coupled with Fully Homomorphic Encryption (FHE) for Distributed Communicationless Secure Multiparty Computation (DCLSMPC) of any Distributed Unknown Finite State Machine (DUFSM) is presented. Namely, secret shares of the input(s) and output(s) are passed to/from the computing parties, while there is no communication between them throughout the computation. We propose a novel approach of transition table representation and polynomial representation for arithmetic circuits evaluation, joined with a CRT secret sharing scheme and FHE to achieve SITS communication-less within computational secure execution of DUFSM. We address the severe limitation of FHE implementation over a single server to cope with a malicious or Byzantine server. We use several distributed memory-efficient solutions that are significantly better than the majority vote in replicated state machines, where each participant maintains an FHE replica. A Distributed Unknown Finite State Machine (DUFSM) is achieved when the transition table is secret shared or when the (possible zero value) coefficients of the polynomial are secret shared, implying communication-less SMPC of an unknown finite state machine.

Keywords: Secure multiparty computation · Replicated state machine · Chinese Remainder Theorem

1 Introduction

The processing of encrypted information where the computation program is unknown is an important task that can be solved in a distributed fashion using communication among several participants, e.g., [12]. Unfortunately, this communication reveals the participants to each other and requires a non-negligible

Partially supported by the Rita Altura Trust Chair in Computer Science, a grant from the Ministry of Science and Technology, Israel & the Japan Science and Technology Agency (JST), and the German Research Funding (DFG, Grant#8767581199). A detailed version appears in [9].

S. Dolev et al. (Eds.): CSCML 2021, LNCS 12716, pp. 487–496, 2021.
https://doi.org/10.1007/978-3-030-78086-9_35

overhead concerning the communication between them. Computational secure communication-less approaches can also be suggested, either for the case of known automaton and global inputs, e.g., [10] or for the case of computational security alone. Here, we present the first communication-less solution that is statistical information-theoretical secure (not perfect), within an FHE-based computational secure scheme.

A major contribution to the area of distributed computing is the replicated state machine introduced by Lamport [21]. The implementation of such state machines is usually based on a distributed consensus [20].

We propose a sharing scheme that is based on a secret shared transition function or a unique polynomial over a finite ring for various implementations e.g., Boolean function, state machine transition, control of RAM, or control of Turing Machine. Specifically, for any state machine, this polynomial encodes the information of all the transitions from a state x and input y to the next state z. The information may also contain the encoding of the output. The polynomial can be described by an arithmetic circuit (and vice versa) and be evaluated distributively by the SMPC participants. Each participant evaluates the arithmetic circuit using the CRT SITS secret sharing scheme where the shares are FHE encrypted. Consequently, the possibility for (value secured) additions and multiplications with no communication is achieved. In the scope of this polynomial representation of the transition function, the actual computed function is kept private by using secret shares for all (zero and non-zero) coefficients of the polynomial, revealing only a bound on the maximal degree k of the polynomial.

The CRT representation allows an unbounded number of *independent* additions and multiplications of the respective components of two (or more) numbers over a finite ring. So in that manner, we compute arithmetic circuits in a distributed fashion, where each participant performs calculations over a finite ring defined by the relatively prime number they are in charge of. We accomplish a distributed polynomial evaluation, where several participants do not need to communicate with each other before and during the computation.

The transition function of a state machine may be represented by a bivariate polynomial from the current state and the input to the next state (and output). Namely, a bi-variate polynomial can be defined by the desired points that define the transition from the current state (x) and the input (y) to the next state (z), which may encode the output too. Alternatively, a univariate polynomial can be defined by using the most significant digits of $(x + y)$ to encode the state (x) and the least significant digits, to encode the input (y). The output state (z) occupies the same digits of (x) that serve to encode the next state, while the rest of the digits in (z) are zeros. Thus, the next input can be added to the previous result and be used in computing the next transition, and so forth.

Naturally, several known error correction techniques that rely on features of the Chinese Remainder Theorem (depicted in [18, 19]) can eliminate the influence of Byzantine participants. These schemes are not designed to preserve the fully homomorphic property of CRT secret sharing, just as the CRT threshold secret sharing does not support additions and multiplications. The values might exceed the global maximal value the mutual primes can represent (originally, with no additional error-correcting values). Still, when using FHE, a computation can be designed to never exceed this maximal value and be error corrected. We note that FHE has significant complications when executed over a single server, as the server can be Byzantine, not following the algorithm it should execute on the encrypted values. Thus, a distributed secure multiparty computation is preferred.

Related Work and Our Contribution. Recently, extensive work on computationally secure communication-less computation has been done, see [6,13] and in references therein. However, the computation security is only based on the belief that one-way functions exist [8]. Several other works in the scope of perfect information-theoretically secure schemes were presented in [4,11,12,14,15]. Unfortunately, neither of them can compute all possible functions, and they require either communication or a need for exponential resources to maintain continuous functioning. In this paper, we present an alternative to a replicated state machine with no communication, while improving the communication overhead of the secret shared random-access machine presented in [16] and the secret shared Turing machine presented in [12]. This SITS within FHE approach can also be used in implementations for distributed, efficient, databases [3], Accumulating Automata with no communication [14] or even for ALU operations in the communication-less RAM implementation [16]. Another important application is in the scope of SMPC of machine learning queries [7].

CRT Arithmetic. We briefly review some of the key topics that serve as the base of this work.

Let $p_1 < p_2 < \ldots < p_k$ where p_i are relatively prime and a set of congruence equations $a \equiv a_i \pmod{p_i}$ for $1 \leq i \leq k$ for $k > 0$ and where a_i are remainders. The original form of the CRT states that this given set of congruence equations always has one and *exactly one* solution modulo $\prod_1^k p_i$.

The most important feature of the Chinese Remainder Theorem for our interest, is the possibility of adding and multiplying two vectors of congruence values independently. Namely, for performing fully homomorphic addition and multiplication operations on CRT-based secret shares. Unlike perfectly secure secret sharing such as the schemes of Shamir [23] and Blakley [5], a CRT-based secret sharing scheme that supports homomorphic additions and multiplications (unlike [2]) is only statistically secured. We use FHE to computationally mitigate information leakage from the individual CRT share.

2   Replicated State Machine Vs. CRT DFSM or DUFSM

In this section, we explore the different aspects of a CRT based SMPC that utilizes the features mentioned before. We introduce our DFSM approach that copes with several of the Replicated State Machine (RSM) drawbacks. Also, to increase the privacy of the computation implied by this approach, we suggest using a local Fully Homomorphic Encryption (FHE) based arithmetic circuit that keeps the efficiency of memory while protecting the data.

Implementing the Transition Function with Secret Sharing. An Arithmetic Circuit is based on additions and multiplications which support the implementation of any Finite State Machine (FSM) transition function or table. One convenient way to do so is by representing each bit in the circuit as a vector of two different bits (just as a quantum bit is represented). Namely, the bit 0 is represented by 01, and the bit 1 by 10. Consider each directed edge in the transition function graph tuple representation being represented as $\langle CurrentState, Input \rightarrow NextState, Output \rangle$. Then, given a (possibly secret shared) transition function, this structure allows us to secret share the table among different participants, possibly even padding it with additional never-used tuples. $CurrentState, Input$, and $NextState$ are represented by a sequence of 2-bits vectors. Thus, we double the logarithmic number of bits needed for the binary representation, rather than using a linear number of bits in the unary representation as used in [12] (optimized for small degree polynomial, secret shares, and multiplication outcome).

Now, to blindly compute the next state and output, given the current state and input, a participant *multiplies* each bit of the shared secret (2-bits vector representation) with the bits of each line of the transition table. Then, they sum up the resulting 2-bits vector into a single bit. In Algorithm 1, we can see that by multiplying the resulting bits with the state and input encoding (lines 7, 9), we ensure that only the fitting transition is chosen as the rest become 0. Blindly summing up all results of all next states and outputs (line 10) results in the desired (secret shared) next state and output.

Algorithm 1: Blindly Matching a Transition Tuple

input : transition table T, state *current* with length L and input i
output: next state and output

1   $x \leftarrow$ encode(*current*); $y \leftarrow$ encode(i);   // encode in the redundant form
2   *result* $\leftarrow 0$
3   **foreach** *line in T* **do**
4     $xT \leftarrow line[0]$; $yT \leftarrow line[1]$;   // unpack each tuple
5     $sum \leftarrow 1$;
6   **for** $i \leftarrow 0$ to $2L$ **do**
       // perform multiplication with previous and current sum (i += 2)
7       $sum \leftarrow sum \cdot (x[i] \cdot xT[i] + x[i+1] \cdot xT[i+1])$;
8   **end**
9     $sum \leftarrow sum \cdot (y[0] \cdot yT[0] + y[1] \cdot yT[1])$;
10    $result \leftarrow result + sum \cdot T[line]$;   // accumulate conditioned next state
11 **end**
12 **return** decode(*result*)

Utilization of an FHE Mechanism. Nowadays, the concept of Fully Homomorphic Encryption (FHE) has become highly popular in the field of modern cryptography. In a nutshell, FHE scheme is an encryption scheme that allows the evaluation of arbitrary functions on encrypted data. The problem was first suggested by Rivest, Adleman, and Dertouzos [22], and thirty years later, implemented in the breakthrough work of Gentry [17]. A major application of FHE is in cloud computing. This is because nowadays a user can store data on a remote server that has more storage capabilities and computing power than theirs. However, the user might not trust the remote server, as the data might be sensitive, so they send the encrypted data to the remote server and expect it to perform some arithmetic operations on it, without learning anything about the original raw data. In our case, an FHE scheme is employed to preserve the privacy among the participants, each being a remote server, blindly following the computation.

Algorithm 2: Dealer Extended FHE Procedure

input : initial value x, an operation **op**, and a stream of inputs stm
output: result of **op** applied on x with all the the inputs in stm

```
 1  context ← initFHE() ;                    // context allows encryption+decryption
 2  primes ← genPrimes(K);
 3  q ← queue();
 4  for i ← 1 to K do
 5  │   m ← primes[i];
 6  │   xEncrypted ← encrypt(mod(x), context) ;          // encrypt x (mod m)
 7  │   workers[i] ← startWorker(m, op, xEncrypted, q);
 8  end
 9  while hasNext(stm) do
10  │   y ← next(stm);
11  │   yEncrypted ← encrypt(y, context) ;               // encrypt incoming input
12  │   q.push(yEncrypted);
13  end
14  for i ← 1 to K do
15  │   rEncrypted ← stopWorker(workers[i]);
16  │   results[i] ← decrypt(rEncrypted, context) ;       // decrypt result
17  end
18  return recover(primes, results)
```

The dealer's procedure described in Algorithm 2 is an extension of the original distributed computation algorithm depicted in [9] that supports FHE behavior. The dealer now initializes an FHE context with which they encrypt both the initial value and the incoming inputs (lines 6, 11). From this point, they continue in the same way as before (line 7, 12), except for a decryption step at the end (line 16) and scheduled bootstrapping steps during the computation. For the sake of generality, the bootstrapping step is omitted but can be regarded as the assignment of the first share of the input to be the share of the initial state. After completing all of the decryptions, the results are reassembled by the CRT into a single solution as shown before.

Algorithm 3: Worker Extended FHE Procedure

---

input : modulus m, operation op, encrypted initial value x, and encrypted
            inputs queue q
output: encrypted result of op applied on x and all the encrypted inputs

1 **while** notSignaled() **do**
2     $y \leftarrow$ tryPop(q);
3     $x \leftarrow$ op(x, y);
4     $x \leftarrow$ blindMod(x, m) ;   // can be implemented in several ways
5 **end**
6 **return** x

Equally, the participants (workers) are dealt with a plaintext modulus in which they operate. By keeping the modulus in the clear, we do not leak any meaningful information and aid the participant in carrying out the computation with respect to their finite field. As before, after a worker is initialized, they start receiving encrypted inputs and apply the operator to them (line 3). As opposed to the operator application in a general field, these blind applications are expected to be done in a finite field that is typically different from the binary field in computers (e.g., 8 bits for BYTE or 32/64 for a computer WORD). Therefore, the worker performs a dedicated balancing step after each iteration (line 4). Namely, they perform a *blind* modulo reduction to the result, thus keeping it inside the field. This step is possible due to a unique feature of FHE bitwise calculations that allows a blind conditioned output. One popular library that supports this feature is IBM's HELib [24]. The idea behind this implementation is based on an aggregation of the condition results. A suggested implementation is outlined in Algorithm 4 where line 3 creates an unknown bit and line 5 reflects a conditioned output based on that bit. The subtraction is aggregated by using the differences computed in line 4.

Algorithm 4: Blind Modulo Reduction

---

input : encrypted integer x, modulus m
output: result of encrypted $x \pmod{m}$

1 $levels \leftarrow$ maxLevels(m) ;   // max possible value i.e $\lfloor \frac{(m-1)^2}{m} \rfloor \approx m$
2 **for** $j \leftarrow 0$ **to** $levels$ **do**
3     $i \leftarrow$ compare(x, m);
4     $d \leftarrow x - i$;
5     $x \leftarrow xi \cdot d + (1 - i) \cdot x$;
6 **end**

Utilizing this feature is essential during the procedure of a worker in our CRT based approach as the worker should be oblivious to the fact they carry out the same procedure only on encrypted data. As long as they know how to perform homomorphic operations such as additions and multiplications, while staying within the boundaries of the computer's binary representation, the homomorphism of the operations over the CRT secret shares is preserved.

3 Polynomial Based CRT DUFSM

We present an alternative to further improve the secrecy of the transition function of the FSM that is based on polynomial representation. In case we use the Lagrange interpolation, it is essential to choose the parameter $M > 0$ of the ring $\mathbb{Z}/M\mathbb{Z}$ wisely. Otherwise, the interpolation fails. Since is not guaranteed that every number $x \in \mathbb{Z}/M\mathbb{Z}$ is invertible (e.g., zero), and the denominators in the basis polynomials are comprised of differences between two numbers, the different divisions might not be possible. Therefore, for a set of points $\{(x_i, y_i)|i = 0, \ldots, n\}$, it is crucial to choose such ring $\mathbb{Z}/M\mathbb{Z}$, where all the differences $x_i - x_j$ are invertible. Consider a set of points in the finite ring $\mathbb{Z}/K\mathbb{Z}$, such that $K = \prod_i^n p_i$ for relatively primes p_i. To successfully interpolate this set of points using Lagrange's method, we need to verify that neither of the differences has a common factor in $\{p_1, \ldots, p_n\}$.

Consider a given FSM that is represented by a truth table. Namely, we are interested in the relations between the different states and the possible inputs or outputs. We suggest a (non-perfect) encoding scheme that allows us to represent this FSM completely by polynomials. First, we encode the different states and transitions in some grid-compatible representation, where a transition in that context, is a 2-tuple $e = (u, v)$ such that the state u has a valid input that leads to v. One simple encoding is through positive integers representation. Given a set of states V, and a set of transitions E, the 2-D point *unique* encoding of them is calculated as follows in Algorithm 5.

Algorithm 5: FSM Encoding Procedure

  input : V, E
  output: A list of points $P_1 = (x_1, y_1), \ldots, P_n = (x_n, y_n)$ where $n = |E|$

1 $rangeV \leftarrow \texttt{randRange}(1, |V|)$;   // generate numbers for each state
2 $rangeE \leftarrow \texttt{randRange}(1, |E|)$;   // generate numbers for each transition
3 $points = [\,]$;
4 **for** $i \leftarrow 1$ **to** $|E|$ **do**
5 | $u, v \leftarrow \texttt{unpack}(E[i])$;   // unpack the states in transition
6 | $x \leftarrow rangeV[\texttt{indexOf}(u, V)] + rangeE[i]$;
7 | $y \leftarrow rangeV[\texttt{indexOf}(v, V)]$;
8 | $points.append((x, y))$;
   | /* each point P is calculated such that $P = (r_u + r_e, r_v)$ where
   | r_u, r_v are the random numbers chosen for states u, v and r_e is
   | the random number chosen for transition e */
9 **end**
10 **return** $points$

Since the y value of a point is comprised only of a state encoding, the decoding process is simple. It is however not guaranteed for the x value, as it is comprised of an encoded summation that might overlap other encoded values. One possible way to deal with this, is to simply work on different scales, more specifically, we use a factor $f = 10^t$ where $t > 0$ to choose the integers in line 1 from the range $\{f+1\ldots|V|\cdot f\}$. Also, considering that there might be many transitions to cause an overflow between the scales, the parameter t needs to be bounded such that $t > \log|E|$ and $f = 10^t > |E|$ holds.

Evaluating Polynomial within FHE. Since the polynomials are both encrypted and already evaluated in a specific field, the only information a participant can learn stems from the encryption parameters and the finite field modulus assigned to them beforehand. By keeping the modulus clear, we simplify the assignment process while not revealing any meaningful data to the participants, as all the other data they receive is encrypted. The encryption parameters, however, including the public key, might hint at the computational security of the scheme, in case the participant is interested in breaking it. The Homomorphic Encryption Standard [1] may assist in choosing recommended parameters for implementation. In practice, the suggested process provides the participants with a reduced polynomial in some finite field, but the actual application of different operations does not consider that fact. Fortunately, we can maintain the result in the respected finite field by applying a *blind* modulo operation on each polynomial evaluation. This can be done by the previous method described in Algorithm 4. Moreover, to successively evaluate the polynomial without consuming all the noise budget of the FHE scheme, one can utilize a bootstrapping method, thus allowing the computation to carry on endlessly.

4   Concluding Remarks

Communication-less secure multi-party computation, where the servers that perform the computation are not aware of the other servers' identity and location, introduces a new facet of security, where colluding is much harder to be coordinated. Efficiency is an obvious additional benefit as in many cases the (typically quadratic) communication overhead is significantly more expensive than the local computation. One more important aspect to note is that we no longer need to synchronize the actions of the servers, as they may process their own (secret shared) inputs whenever convenient before the eventual output collection. Our various implementations demonstrate the practicality of our scheme and for the sake of brevity can be found online.

Lastly, it is possible to integrate an error-correction encoding into our scheme that copes with Byzantine participants. This includes increasing the size of the mutual primes $p_1 < p_2 < \ldots < p_k$ to avoid overflow of the computation with respect to $p_1 \cdot p_2, \ldots \cdot p_k$, and adding more mutual primes $q_1 < q_2 < \ldots < q_l$ that are larger than p_k, and where l is a function of the maximal number of errors, and in a way, may introduce an error correcting code.

References

1. Albrecht, M., et al.: (2018). https://eprint.iacr.org/2019/939.pdf
2. Asmuth, C., Bloom, J.: A modular approach to key safeguarding. IEEE Trans. Inf. Theory **29**(2), 208–210 (1983)
3. Avni, H., Dolev, S., Gilboa, N., Li, X.: SSSDB: database with private information search. In: Karydis, I., Sioutas, S., Triantafillou, P., Tsoumakos, D. (eds.) ALGO-CLOUD 2015. LNCS, vol. 9511, pp. 49–61. Springer, Cham (2016). https://doi.org/10.1007/978-3-319-29919-8_4
4. Bitan, D., Dolev, S.: Optimal-round preprocessing-MPC via polynomial representation and distributed random matrix (extended abstract). IACR Cryptology ePrint Arch. **2019**, 1024 (2019)
5. Blakley, G.R.: Safeguarding cryptographic keys. In: Proceedings of the 1979 AFIPS National Computer Conference (1979)
6. Boyle, E., Gilboa, N., Ishai, Y.: Secure computation with preprocessing via function secret sharing. In: Hofheinz, D., Rosen, A. (eds.) TCC 2019. LNCS, vol. 11891, pp. 341–371. Springer, Cham (2019). https://doi.org/10.1007/978-3-030-36030-6_14
7. Derbeko, P., Dolev, S.: Polydnn polynomial representation of NN for communication-less SMPC inference. In: Cyber Security Cryptography and Machine Learning - Fifth International Symposium, CSCML 2021, Be'er Sheva, Israel, 8–9 July , 2021, Proceedings, volume 12716 of Lecture Notes in Computer Science. Springer (2021)
8. Dolev, H., Dolev, S.: Toward provable one way functions (2020)
9. Dolev, S., Doolman, S.: Blindly follow: Sits CRT and FHE for DCLSMPC of DUFSM. Cryptology ePrint Archive, Report 2021/410 (2021)
10. Dolev, S., et al.: Secure self-stabilizing computation, Brief announcement (2017)
11. Dolev, S., Garay, J., Gilboa, N., Kolesnikov, V.: Secret sharing krohn-rhodes: private and perennial distributed computation. In: ITCS, pp. 32–44 (2011)
12. Dolev, S., Garay, J.A., Gilboa, N., Kolesnikov, V., Kumaramangalam, M.V.: Perennial secure multi-party computation of universal turing machine. Theor. Comput. Sci. **769**, 43–62 (2019)
13. Dolev, S., Garay, J.A., Gilboa, N., Kolesnikov, V., Yuditsky, Y.: Towards efficient private distributed computation on unbounded input streams. J. Math. Cryptology **9**(2), 79–94 (2015)
14. Dolev, S., Gilboa, N., Li, X.: Accumulating automata and cascaded equations automata for communicationless information theoretically secure multi-party computation. Theor. Comput. Sci. **795**, 81–99 (2019)
15. Dolev, S., Lahiani, L., Yung, M.: Secret swarm unit: reactive k-secret sharing. Ad Hoc Netw. **10**(7), 1291–1305 (2012)
16. Dolev, S., Li, Y.: Secret shared random access machine. In: Karydis, I., Sioutas, S., Triantafillou, P., Tsoumakos, D. (eds.) ALGOCLOUD 2015. LNCS, vol. 9511, pp. 19–34. Springer, Cham (2016). https://doi.org/10.1007/978-3-319-29919-8_2
17. Gentry, C.: Fully homomorphic encryption using ideal lattices (2009)
18. Goldreich, O., Ron, D., Sudan, M.: Chinese remaindering with errors. IEEE Trans. Inf. Theory **46**(4), 1330–1338 (2000)
19. Jaiswal, R.: Chinese remainder codes : using lattices to decode error correcting codes based on Chinese remaindering theorem (2007)
20. Lamport, L.: Fast paxos. Distrib. Comput. (2006)
21. Lamport, L.: Time, clocks, and the ordering of events in a distributed system Communication. ACM, July 1978

22. Rivest, R.L., Adleman, L., Dertouzos, M.L.: On data banks and privacy homomorphisms. In: FOCS, pp. 169–179 (1978)
23. Shamir, A.: How to share a secret. Commun. ACM **22**(11), 612–613 (1979)
24. Wang, H., Feng, Y., Ding, Y., Tang, S.: A homomorphic arithmetic model via Helib. J. Comput. Theor. Nanosci. **14**, 5166–5173 (2017)

Implementing GDPR in Social Networks Using Trust and Context

Nadav Voloch[1]([⊠]), Ehud Gudes[1], and Nurit Gal-Oz[2]

[1] Ben-Gurion University of the Negev, P.O.B. 653, 8410501 Beer-Sheva, Israel
voloch@post.bgu.ac.il
[2] Sapir Academic College, 79165 Sderot, Israel

Abstract. The GDPR (General Data Protection Regulation) is a regulation for data protection and privacy for citizens of the EU. It also addresses the export of personal data outside the EU, thus creating a regulation the affects most, as all, of the commercial companies, government institutions, and other sectors that maintain personal information of their customers or audiences. Social Networks are, of course, major interested parties both for the GDPR since their core definitions involve both private user's information, and data ownership issues. Thus, there is an urgent need for a sustainable and reliable privacy model for these networks, that does not currently exist. In our previous research we have devised a comprehensive Trust-based model for security in Social Networks, that uses Trust, Access Control and Flow Control. In this paper we use this model, and add an element of context to it, for creating an implementation in Social Networks, that will better enforce the GDPR and rights management regulations.

Keywords: GDPR · Social networks security · Flow control · Access control · Trust

1 Introduction, Background, and Related Work

The rapid growth of Online Social Networks (OSN) and their increasing popularity in the past decade as major communication channels, have raised some new shapes of security and privacy concerns. In our previous work, we have created a privacy model that is composed of three main phases addressing three of its major aspects: trust, role-based access control in [1] and in [2], and information flow, by creating an Information Flow-Control model for adversary detection [3], or a trustworthy network [4]. We represent a social network as an undirected graph, where nodes are the OSN users, and edges represent relations between them such as friendship relations. An Ego node (or Ego user) is an individual focal node, representing a user whose information flow we aim to control. An Ego node along with its adjacent nodes are denoted Ego network. Our comprehensive Trust-based model uses Access Control for the direct friends of the Ego-user, and Information Flow Control for the users that are in a further distance.

We use OSN parameters, such as total number of friends, age of user account, and friendship duration to characterize the quality of the network connections as will be

© Springer Nature Switzerland AG 2021
S. Dolev et al. (Eds.): CSCML 2021, LNCS 12716, pp. 497–503, 2021.
https://doi.org/10.1007/978-3-030-78086-9_36

explained in this paper. The GDPR [5] is a regulation for data protection and privacy for citizens of the EU. It refers also to the use of personal data outside the EU, thus creating a regulation the affects most, as all, sectors that involve personal data. Social Networks are a vast source of personal information just by their core definition, and this exposes them to the liability of these regulations. The most important aspect of GDPR, which is "the right to be forgotten" can be applied by the monitoring of data instances flowing to users by our model in the OSN.

Handling the effects of GDPR on Social Networks is crucially important since the regulations have been enforceable since May 2018. A strong reliable and viable method of action has not still been introduced, and a lot of resources are put in beginning to find suitable infrastructures that can satisfy these demands. This is especially hard in Social Networks, where endless amounts of data are spread constantly. [6] examine the principles outlined in the GDPR in the context of social network data and analyze the consequences of their implementation in OSN. The main ideas of this analysis are that the problems need to be adhered are first, the initial data processing consent by the data owners (OSN users) vs. the public nature of the Social Network. Second, the primary and secondary data collections issue and their lack of transparency. Third, the depth and spread of OSN data (and for that, the flow part of our model is a good solution). Fourth, the data profiling and analysis problem- that is a serious breach of data ownership and privacy. Last is the issue of data storage, that may breach the important GDPR principal of "the right to be forgotten". The efficacy of GDPR in OSN is presented in [7], where the challenges of implementing the regulations on OSN are shown, and the association of their causes to the nature of the communication are presented in general, with the indication of the problematic aspects of data spreading in the network. This paper specifically addresses the "right to be forgotten" issue in Facebook.

2 The Trust-Based Model and GDPR Implementation

The model we have presented in previous work [1–4] is composed of three main phases addressing three of its major aspects: trust, role-based access control and information flow. In the First phase, the Trust phase, we assign trust values on the edges connecting direct friends to the Ego node in their different roles, e.g., Family, Colleagues etc. In the second phase, the Role Based Access Control phase, we remove direct friends that do not have the minimal trust values required to grant a specific permission to their roles. A cascade removal is carried out in their Ego networks as well. After this removal, the remaining user nodes and their edges are also assigned with trust values.

In the third and last phase, the Information Flow phase, we remove from the graph edges and nodes that are not directly connected to the Ego-user, and have low trust values, to construct a privacy preserving trusted network.

A data instance can be characterized by its context (e.g., politics, sports, etc.), and the trust measure must be refined by this context. For context evaluation, we categorize different users in the Ego network by their Trust per context. We calculate this Trust for the friends in the Ego network: different trust values for every category, meaning that they have a User Trust Value per category denoted here as UTV_κ for each category κ. The calculation is presented in [8]. We can see an example for such a set of UTV_κ's and access granting for certain data instances in Fig. 1, where the Minimum Trust Value of a certain category of a data instance is presented as $MTV\kappa$. Three out of four users hold the necessary trust value ($UTV\kappa$) for $\kappa = Politics$, thus have access to it, while only one user hold the necessary $UTV\kappa$ for $\kappa = Sales$ and has access to it. A problem arises when we take a closer look in the Social Network's data instances. We can divide all OSN activities to atomic ones and non-atomic ones. Non-atomic actions are ones that can create linked actions, for example, writing a post can create comments and likes from friends in the network. Writing a comment is also non-atomic since it can create likes and sub-comments. Atomic actions, such as likes, accordingly, are ones that cannot create linked actions. The problematic aspect of non-atomic actions is the question of data ownership. If the Ego user writes a post, and then Alice comments on this post, who does the comment belong to? It might seem negligible if the comment is of simple nature, but comments are a platform that sometimes go well beyond a simple data instance and can be elaborated and data sensitive as the post itself, and even more. Comments themselves are non-atomic actions that can create linked actions, e.g. Bob replies to Alice's comment, or likes it. In terms of OSN, this ownership problem is quite important, especially considering the GDPR. Comments, for example, can be deleted either by the Ego node (who writes the post) or by the commenter himself. The challenges in this problem are finding the proper ownership outline, handling the data distribution without privacy or ownership conflicts, and wisely devising the implementation algorithms in a comprehensive but efficient manner. Here we divide the GDPR issues in Social Network into two different parts: Data dispersion in the network, and erasing data from the network ("right-to-be-forgotten"). There are three main types of data instances in OSN: **Private-shared data** – this type is a data instance that can shared, commented on, etc., but will not be copied fully and separately to another user, meaning the original data will remain as the data owner's instance, and no other instances (objects) will be created. For example – Alice posts a picture, her friends comment and share it, but none of them copies and uploads it as a separate picture in his feed. **Private-shared data with leakage** – this type is a data instance that also can shared, commented on, etc., but is copied fully and separately to another user, meaning that another different instance (object) is created.

For example – Alice posts a picture, and one of her friends copies and uploads it as a separate picture in his feed. **Private-controlled data** – this type is a data instance cannot be shared, but only viewed or liked or any other atomic action.

This type of data is very relevant to video or audio files that need to be restricted in their dispersion. This type of data can be shared only with followers or subscribers and will not be freely shared to other parts of the network. For example – Alice is a singer, that shares a new song only with her followers in their private group and disables the sharing option for this song. For the problem of data dispersion in the network, which is relevant to both types of private-shared data, but not to the private-controlled data, subject to GDPR, we suggest a three-stage process for non-atomic OSN actions: **In the first stage**, we look at the data instance origin as it is generated. This origin can be consisted of multiple ownerships, e.g.- a photo uploaded with several tagged users in it, a song uploaded by an artist, that involves the record company, tagged in the post. For this preliminary stage we need the consent of all the original data owners.

In the second stage, we begin monitoring the spread of the data, and decide whether a certain user, that is connected to the data owner, is even allowed to access the data. This stage is done by our Trust-based model described in the previous section. This stage is especially important since our model can detect problematic and low-trusted users, and those might have the potential to use this data unlawfully and with copyright infringement. So, this stage is used for determining which user can gain access to the data instance. An important part of this stage is the contextual validation phase that was described in the previously. **In the third stage**, that regards non-atomic actions, and is done after the completion of the second stage, when we know the granted accesses for users, we need to create an access and usage agreement, even before a user creates the sub-data instance itself, (comment on the original post, share of the post, etc.) and by doing that he or she are spreading this data instance to their network. The user that takes this action is the one that needs this agreement, since he is the one creating data that is connected to the original data of the other user, and his data can be erased or controlled by the other user. For example, Alice writes a post, then Bob comments lengthily on this post. His comment can vanish if Alice deletes the post, or even just his comment. For this- they must have a usage agreement on the comment itself. An implementation example for it is a pop-up window that contains the agreement when a user tries to begin commenting on a post. The friends of the commenter also need to access this comment, and if they wish to act on this comment, the same usage agreement must apply.

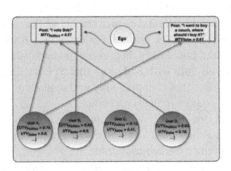

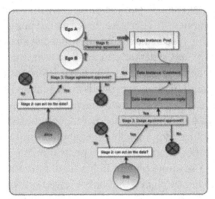

Fig. 1. Access decisions in different categories   **Fig. 2.** Monitoring non-atomic OSN actions

The meaning of usage agreement is as follows: The new user agrees that his comment is part of the data instances, including the posts and the comments connected to it. This creates a chain of data instances, and this implies that if someone that is upper in the chain removes his data, the new user's data is removes. For example, if Alice writes a post, and then Bob comments on it, and then Charlie replies on Bob's comment, Charlie's reply could be erased in three cases: If he deletes it himself, if Bob deletes his comment- and then the reply is erased, and if Alice deletes her post, thus erasing all the data chain. The difference between the ownership agreement and the usage agreement is that the ownership is done only on the original data – if it involves more than one user- and this is an agreement of mutual and equal ownership, and the usage agreement is hierarchical by nature – in which the users that act on the data have lesser privileges and their derivative data on the origin can be erased by the data origin's owners. The manifestation of this process is portrayed in Fig. 2. We can see that in Stage 1 there is an ownership agreement between Ego A and Ego B, that are the owners of the original data instance. Stage 2 includes the screening of the user named Alice- she has to gain the necessary contextual trust to act on the data (in this case, commenting on the post). In stage 3 we can see that the final approvement of acting on the data (thus, spreading it) is dependent on the usage agreement for Alice. We can see that Bob, that is a friend of Alice, wishes to reply on her comment, thus creating another branching in the data tree. The usage agreement is between him and Alice, and by that it is also derived from the usage agreement of Alice and the Ego. If Bob wished only to see the comment, and not act upon it, then he would just need to have the sufficient context-trust level. This approach is a viable solution to the problematic aspects of GDPR in Social Networks and can create a much more sustainable solution to the dispersion and ownership problem of data instances in the Social Network. For the problem of erasing data from the network we suggest a two-stage process for non-atomic OSN actions:

In the first stage, we look at the data instance origin. As mentioned in the previously, this origin can consist of multiple ownerships. For this preliminary stage we need the consent of all the original data owners – that the data instance is going to be erased. We use the same ownership agreement mentioned in the first stage of the dispersion solution, that involves the implementation of a Consent Management Solution. In case we do not delete the original post, but a comment in the chain of comments, the second stage starts from this comment only. **The second stage** of this process is erasing all the data instances that were spread in the network along the chain. This task is specifically hard due to the OSN sizes of users and data, but our obvious advantage is the context and trust screening we did in the dispersion of data. The amount of data to be checked is considerably reduced, and it is only the subset of the active users (ones that created data or acted upon data) from the subset of the trustworthy (above a certain $MTV\kappa$) users in a certain category.

3   Experimental Evaluation

The basic Trust-based model's experimental results and evaluations can be seen in our previous work: [1–4]. For this research we did two experiments to validate the two approaches mentioned in the previous section: one for the dispersion problem, and one for the erasure problem. For the dispersion part, we took three different Ego networks and requested the Ego users to each take 50 actions from their Facebook activity log, that involve another person (a friend from the network). We then asked for every action to first be categorized (like share, comment on a post, etc.), and then requested the Ego user to state the level of closeness to the friend involved in this action on a scale of 0 to 10. The last part the Ego user needed to do per each action is to answer the question: "If you needed to fill out a consent form before performing this action, that states that you have joint ownership on this action with the friend involved, thus never being able to erase it by yourself, would you still perform this action?". The answer should be between 0, meaning wouldn't do this action, and 10, meaning will do this action. We can see the results in Table 1, all the datasets are for non-atomic actions. We can see that there is a correlation between the level of closeness to the friend and the level of consent on performing an action in the OSN. We can see that the lowest average score for closeness is given in Dataset No. 2 (4.97) and accordingly, the average level of consent is the lowest (6.52). As for the erasure part: in the context part results, that were mentioned earlier, we wanted to find out how efficient would it be to reduce the amount of data needed to be checked, by using only the relevant part of the Ego network, meaning we check only the subset of the active users (ones that created data or acted upon data) from the subset of the trustworthy (above a certain $MTV\kappa$) users in a certain category.

Table 1. Results of consent form option on Facebook activities

Dataset	Number of actions	Avg. connection closeness level with the friend	Avg. consent on performing the action with a consent form
No. 1	36	8.05	8.42
No. 2	33	4.97	6.52
No. 3	50	8.5	8.22

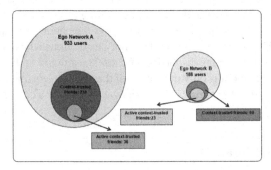

Fig. 3. Results of the context phase experiment in sizes of the active sub-networks

For that purpose, we took two different Ego networks, both in the context topic of "politics" (in these networks this topic was very relevant and had significant traffic. We checked the Ego- networks for trustworthy friends in the category of politics ($MTVpolitics > 0.8$). After this screening we examined this sub-network, and looked for only active users, that posted or acted on data relating to politics. The results are shown in Fig. 3, and we can see the substantial differences in the number of users that are relevant (trustworthy and active) in relation to the entire network. This choice is very efficient: the difference in efficiency of searching 238 users instead of 933 users, and then erasing data from only 36 users, for example, in Network A is huge. These results demonstrate the importance of the context phase of the model and show the effectiveness of our approach for implementing the GDPR "right-to-be-forgotten".

4   Conclusion

In this research we presented an implementation of a Trust-based for Social Networks that will better enforce the unresolved the GDPR. The control over the user's data, and its monitoring gives us the ability to adhere to the GDPR in Social Networks. The results of the experimental part of this paper give us the perspective of real OSN users on how to implement this process.

References

1. Voloch, N., Nissim, P., Elmakies, M., Gudes, E.: A role and trust access control model for preserving privacy and image anonymization in social networks. In: Meng, W., Cofta, P., Jensen, C.D., Grandison, T. (eds.) IFIPTM 2019. IAICT, vol. 563, pp. 19–27. Springer, Cham (2019). https://doi.org/10.1007/978-3-030-33716-2_2
2. Voloch, N., Levy, P., Elmakies, M., Gudes, E.: An access control model for data security in online social networks based on role and user credibility. In: International Symposium on Cyber Security Cryptography and Machine Learning (CSCML 2019). Springer, Cham (2019). https://doi.org/10.1007/978-3-030-20951-3_14
3. Gudes, E., Voloch, N.: An information-flow control model for online social networks based on user-attribute credibility and connection-strength factors. In: Dinur, I., Dolev, S., Lodha, S. (eds.) CSCML 2018. LNCS, vol. 10879, pp. 55–67. Springer, Cham (2018). https://doi.org/10.1007/978-3-319-94147-9_5
4. Voloch, N., Gudes, E.: An MST-based information flow model for security in online social networks. In: The 11th IEEE International Conference on Ubiquitous and Future Networks (ICUFN 19) (2019)
5. Regulation (EU) 2016/679 of the European Parliament and of the Council of 27 April 2016 on the protection of natural persons with regard to the processing of personal data and on the free movement of such data, and repealing Directive 95/46/EC (General Data Protection Regulation) OJ L 119, 4.5.2016, pp. 1–88 (2016)
6. Kotsios, A., Magnani, M., Vega, D., Rossi, L., Shklovski, I.: An analysis of the consequences of the general data protection regulation on social network research. ACM Trans. Soc. Comput. 2(3), 1–22 (2019)
7. Patil, V.T., Shyamasundar, R.K.: Efficacy of GDPR's right-to-be-forgotten on Facebook. In: Ganapathy, V., Jaeger, T., Shyamasundar, R.K. (eds.) ICISS 2018. LNCS, vol. 11281, pp. 364–385. Springer, Cham (2018). https://doi.org/10.1007/978-3-030-05171-6_19
8. Voloch, N.: Using sentiment analysis and context evaluation for preserving trust-based privacy in social networks (2020)